COMPUTER VISION SYSTEMS

ACADEMIC PRESS RAPID MANUSCRIPT REPRODUCTION

Papers from the Workshop on Computer Vision Systems, held at the University of Massachusetts, Amherst, Massachusetts, June 1–3, 1977.

COMPUTER VISION SYSTEMS

Edited by

ALLEN R. HANSON

School of Language and Communication
Hampshire College
Amherst, Massachusetts

EDWARD M. RISEMAN

Computer and Information Science Department
University of Massachusetts
Amherst, Massachusetts

ACADEMIC PRESS, INC.

(Harcourt Brace Jovanovich, Publishers)

Orlando   San Diego   San Francisco   New York   London
Toronto   Montreal   Sydney   Tokyo   São Paulo

ACADEMIC PRESS, INC.
Orlando, Florida 32887

United Kingdom Edition published by
ACADEMIC PRESS, INC. (LONDON) LTD.
24/28 Oval Road, London NW1 7DX

Library of Congress Cataloging in Publication Data

Workshop on Computer Vision Systems, University
of Massachusetts, Amherst, 1977.
Computer vision systems.

1. Image processing—Congresses.   I. Hanson,
Allen R.,   II.   Riseman, Edward M.
III.   Title.
TA1632.W67   1977   001.6'443   78-13210
ISBN 0-12-323550-2

PRINTED IN THE UNITED STATES OF AMERICA

83 84 85   9 8 7 6 5 4 3 2

Contents

v

THEORY AND PSYCHOLOGY

SYSTEMS

List of Contributors

Numbers in parentheses indicate the pages on which authors' contributions begin.

R. BAJCSY (263), Moore School of Electrical Engineering, University of Pennsylvania, Philadelphia, Pennsylvania 19104

D. H. BALLARD (271), Computer Science Department, University of Rochester, Rochester, New York 14627

H. G. BARROW (3), Artificial Intelligence Center, Stanford Research Institute, Menlo Park, California 94025

J. M. BRADY (283), Department of Computer Science, University of Essex, Essex, United Kingdom

C. M. BROWN (271), Computer Science Department, University of Rochester, Rochester, New York 14627

B. L. BULLOCK (27), Hughes Research Laboratories, Malibu, California 90265

L. S. DAVIS (101), Department of Computer Science, University of Maryland, College Park, Maryland 20742

R. W. EHRICH (111), Electrical and Computer Engineering Department, University of Massachusetts, Amherst, Massachusetts 01003 and Virginia Polytechnic Institute, Blacksburg, Virginia 24061

L. D. ERMAN (37), Department of Computer Science, Carnegie-Mellon University, Pittsburgh, Pennsylvania 15213

J. A. FELDMAN (271), Computer Science Department, University of Rochester, Rochester, New York 14627

M. A. FISCHLER (47), Artificial Intelligence Center, Stanford Research Institute, Menlo Park, California 94025

J. P. FOITH (111), Institut für Informationsverarbeitung, Karlsruhe, Germany

A. R. HANSON (129, 303), School of Language and Communication, Hampshire College, Amherst, Massachusetts 01002

R. M. HARALICK (199), Electrical Engineering and Computer Science Departments, University of Kansas, Lawrence, Kansas

D. A. HUFFMAN (213), Department of Information Sciences, University of California, Santa Cruz, California

A. K. JOSHI (263), Moore School of Electrical Engineering, University of Pennsylvania, Philadelphia, Pennsylvania 19104

S. M. KOSSLYN (223), Department of Psychology, Harvard University, Cambridge, Massachusetts

V. R. LESSER (37), Computer and Information Science Department, University of Massachusetts, Amherst, Massachusetts 01003

M. D. LEVINE (335), Department of Electrical Engineering, McGill University, Montreal, Canada

A. K. MACKWORTH (53), Department of Computer Science, University of British Columbia, Vancouver, B.C., Canada

W. MAGUIRE (243), Department of Psychology, State University of New York, Buffalo, New York 14226

D. MARR (61), Artificial Intelligence Laboratory, Massachusetts Institute of Technology, Cambridge, Massachusetts 02139

R. NEVATIA (81), Image Processing Institute and Computer Science Department, University of Southern California, Los Angeles, California 90007

R. REDDY (89), Department of Computer Science, Carnegie-Mellon University, Pittsburgh, Pennsylvania 15213

E. M. RISEMAN (129, 303), Computer and Information Science Department, University of Massachusetts, Amherst, Massachusetts 01003

A. ROSENFELD (101), Computer Science Center, University of Maryland, College Park, Maryland 20742

Y. SHIRAI (353), Electrotechnical Laboratory, Nagatacho, Chiyodaku, Tokyo

S. P. SHWARTZ (223), Department of Psychology, The Johns Hopkins University, Baltimore, Maryland 21218

S. L. TANIMOTO (165), Department of Computer Science, University of Washington, Seattle, Washington

J. M. TENENBAUM (3), Artificial Intelligence Center, Stanford Research Institute, Menlo Park, California 94025

L. UHR (363), Computer Sciences Department, University of Wisconsin, Madison, Wisconsin

D. L. WALTZ (175), Coordinated Science Laboratory, University of Illinois, Urbana, Illinois 61801

N. WEISSTEIN (243), Department of Psychology, State University of New York, Buffalo, New York 14226

B. J. WIELINGA (283), Department of Computer Science, University of Essex, Essex, United Kingdom

W. A. WOODS (379), Bolt Beranek and Newman Inc., 50 Moulton Street, Cambridge, Massachusetts 02138

S. W. ZUCKER (187), Department of Electrical Engineering, McGill University, Montreal, Canada

Preface

The papers contained in this volume are the result of the three-day Workshop on Computer Vision Systems, held at the University of Massachusetts, Amherst, Massachusetts, June 1–3, 1977. The workshop was made possible by funds provided under the sponsorship of the Information Systems Program of the Office of Naval Research. Preparation for the workshop was initiated in January 1976, and the participants were involved in two rounds of written communication during the 18 months before the meeting was actually held. This collection represents the second round of papers, which in some cases were extensively revised following the meeting in Amherst.

After the workshop, each paper was reviewed very carefully and the editors provided each author with detailed (sometimes quite lengthy) criticisms of his paper. This was an effort on our part to complete some of the discussions that did not take place at the workshop itself. The reviews documented errors, challenged the individuals to support loose statements, asked for major revisions on portions that were unclear or not completely developed, asked authors to relate their work to others, and strongly urged inclusion of experimental results wherever possible. Several of the papers included here were written for the first time after the workshop. It is to the credit of the individual participants, their dedication, and responsibility, that most responded by rewriting their papers in a rather short time span. The papers were not carefully reviewed again; we have placed our faith in the experience and capabilities of the fine group of individuals who have participated in this lengthy and demanding process. All of those involved have made an effort to keep the cost of this book as low as possible by forsaking royalties and by preparing camera-ready copy of their papers for Academic Press.

The order of presentation of papers in this volume does not follow the organization of the workshop. Many of the papers address a range of issues and as a result they can be divided according to several criteria. The decision as to how to best present them was a difficult one; the organization we selected divides the papers into four sections: Issues and Research Strategies, Segmentation, Theory and Psychology, and Systems. This stratification should provide the reader with a sense of the important issues and their place in vision research. Within each section, papers are arranged alphabetically by first author.

The workshop ended on a note of optimism. There was a general feeling of progress and some sense of convergence on important issues in computer vision. The personal goals and motivations of those present were as varied as the problems addressed: some want to understand and model human vision, some want to develop comprehensive theories of perception, some want to solve fundamental problems in artificial intelligence, and others want to solve practical problems in vision applications. The field is philosophy-driven and, in a domain as complex as vision, one can expect continuing controversy. But the field is healthy and the research continues to be challenging and exciting. We hope that this volume of papers, augmenting the available literature, will provide some structure to the bewildering, and yet fascinating, research on computer vision systems.

Acknowledgments

We wish to thank the many individuals who aided us in this venture. This includes our secretary Janet Turnbull, who persevered through all the stages of written communication, from the first invitations to the mailing of the final manuscript, Michael Arbib for his original suggestions in developing the unusual format of these activities and his support of our efforts, Marvin Denicoff of the Office of Naval Research for providing the financial sponsorship of the workshop and a belief in the importance of these research efforts, the Advisory Committee consisting of Thomas Binford, Jerry Feldman, D. Raj Reddy, Azriel Rosenfeld, and Jay M. Tenenbaum for their helpful advice at many points over the year and a half of planning, Victor Lesser for his advice in the latter stages of planning the workshop as well as the fine selection of wine at the reception in our laboratory, Roger Ehrich for his aid in the early stages of planning, our own group of graduate students, Ralf Kohler, Kurt Konolige, John Lowrance, Paul Nagin, John Prager, Tom Williams, and Bryant York, who aided in numerous ways during the long development of the workshop and whose assistance was invaluable in making the three days in Amherst comfortable and successful, and finally both the participants in the workshop itself and the contributors to this book.

Introduction

I. DEFINING THE FIELD OF COMPUTER VISION

During the past decade, the field of computer vision, often referred to as scene analysis or image understanding, has developed from the seminal work performed by a small number of researchers at the few existing centers for Artificial Intelligence (AI) into a major subfield of AI with widespread involvement. The construction of effective general-purpose computer vision systems has proven to be exceedingly difficult. It is now over a decade since interest was first focussed upon this problem domain. Now the field contacts such diverse disciplines and areas as cognitive psychology, pattern recognition, image processing, computer systems hardware and software, computer graphics, electrical engineering, neurophysiology, and mathematics, and shares common problems from areas closer to home in artificial intelligence, including speech recognition, representation of knowledge, and robotics. The boundaries of this research area are rather amorphous, particularly if the important application domains are included, e.g., biomedical image processing, industrial automation, military applications, and ERTS (Earth Resource Technology Satellite) image processing.

Broadly stated, the goal of research in computer vision is the understanding of complex visual processes and the construction of effective computer-based visual systems. These systems usually receive a scene in terms of large arrays of digitized sensory information and are expected to provide as output either a symbolic description of the scene or the specification of information/actions relevant to specific goals of the system. The most popular paradigm which has guided these efforts consists of segmentation followed by interpretation; first the image is partitioned into components, various descriptive attributes are then extracted, and finally knowledge-directed or goal-oriented analysis is applied. There are, however, competing paradigms in this rapidly evolving field. For example, there have been efforts to integrate semantic processing into the first stages of segmentation. Another view seriously questions any notion of segmentation which does not take into account the characteristics of physical surfaces and lighting conditions which gave rise to the sensed data.

It is not our purpose here to discuss in depth the paradigms and research issues facing the field; we leave that to the many papers and points of view contained in this volume. Rather we wish to provide the reader with an introductory overview of the breadth of problems which must be considered in the development of general computer vision systems. We will briefly discuss low-level, intermediate-level, and high-level vision although the dichotomization into these categories is not particularly clean. Low-level vision refers roughly to the study of those processes that operate close to the numeric arrays of sensory data which represent an image. High-level vision refers to the study of those systems necessary for interpreting the relevant components of an image in the context of the goals and a priori knowledge of the domain from which it was obtained. Also, in many task domains intermediate levels of processing can be used to take advantage of the cues provided by physical surfaces.

Low-level vision primarily has been focussed upon the segmentation, or partitioning, of large two-dimensional arrays of numeric values, usually representing color and intensity distributions over the visual field, although additional information such as range data is sometimes available. These arrays typically vary in size from 128 × 128 to over 2000 × 2000 picture elements (referred to as pixels), depending upon the image resolution that is needed and/or is available. This information must be transformed into a more descriptive form, one which captures the important visual characteristics of the data and helps to achieve the system's goals. Basic techniques include the segmentation of the image into line boundaries and regions, on the basis of properties such as color, intensity, texture, etc. While the statement of this goal is straightforward, the development of effective segmentation algorithms is beset by many bewildering difficulties. Important subproblems which bear upon the efficient extraction of meaningful boundaries and regions include those relating to the transduction (digitization) process, the physics of light and surfaces in the real world, texture, color, shadows and highlights, stereopsis and other ranging mechanisms, motion, machine architectures including parallel array machines, etc. Many of these problems carry over to later stages of processing and can be rather formidable, even in highly constrained domains. The field of character recognition, for example, has had difficulty in overcoming the problems caused by dirty, smudged, and incomplete characters.

There also exist a number of interesting problems in the transition from the two-dimensional representation of the image to the inferred three-dimensional description of the real world. These involve the definition of three-dimensional space in terms of surfaces and volumes. These intermediate levels are useful because they provide means for inferring a description of the physical world which does not involve the recognition and naming of objects. Topics of interest here include analysis of vertex types, two-dimensional shape, highlights and shadows, texture gradients, perspective, and occlusion. Pursuing some of these problems leads to subtopics in mathematics (e.g., projective geometry, functional approximation), computer graphics, psychology, art, etc.

The meaning conveyed by an image usually is not derivable solely from the sensory data being processed. It is dependent upon the goals of the analysis and prior knowledge of various aspects of the image domain (or natural world). Image interpretation, then, can be viewed as a transformation of the sensory data into an internal structure of symbols that represent the relevant concepts and relationships of the world depicted in the image. This task involves the processing of incomplete, unreliable, and sometimes conflicting information from the many paths by which hypotheses can be formed on the basis of visual cues and stored world knowledge. Consequently, the interpretation task of computer vision significantly overlaps the subfield of AI called "representation of knowledge." Here, we are concerned with techniques for defining, storing, and retrieving knowledge of the world, as well as the ways of utilizing this knowledge given a particular task. Additional important problems in high-level vision include the representation and use of three-dimensional shape descriptions, perspective, occlusion, distributed computation, control structures, search, data base management, AI languages, and more.

In many vision applications, it is not necessary to consider the totality of problems since the goals of the specific system may be achieved using a subset of the available techniques and approaches. It may not be necessary to build an interpretation system if goals are achieved directly from the output of the segmentation processes. The penalty is that the resulting system may not generalize easily to other applications. For some domains the intermediate descriptions of surfaces and volumes are not crucial because the world is basically two-dimensional, e.g., in the analysis of blood cells or aerial imagery. However, even in these cases intermediate descriptions cannot be entirely ignored; for example occlusion can still occur in the former domain, and surface topology can be an important factor in the latter domain.

Some of the motivation for these efforts is provided by the tantalizing mystery of the human visual system. The understanding of these processes is of interest not only to psychologists, neurophysiologists, and philosophers, but to some researchers in machine vision as well. When we interact with our physical world, many very complex visual tasks are accomplished without apparent burden. Objects in our immediate vicinity are identified and recognized quickly, usually without any conscious effort on our part. We see things, and yet we are not aware how. Unravelling this mystery by constructing systems which in some way model the human system is one of the challenges facing research in machine vision systems. Others in the field look at biological systems only as an existence proof that such a system is possible.

In the human system, information enters through a variety of transducers and undergoes a series of transformations. Neurophysiologists have determined that there are massive amounts of processing which take place at all levels in biological systems and they have carefully analyzed the first stages of the transformation of data. Structure is present not only at the most local levels of feature extraction (e.g., at the retinal level) but also well beyond into the major processing centers of the cortex. Our field can provide a powerful test-bed for models of these processes, while at the same time building generally useful visual processing systems for domains more constrained than all of our natural world.

It is difficult to imagine any new simple approach arising out of research efforts on isolated problems which will result in a major breakthrough in machine perception. While these efforts are extremely valuable in developing an understanding of important subareas, it appears that additional insight can be gained from system approaches to computer vision. The redundancy of information derivable from an image, and the constraints imposed on the manner in which this information fits together, implies that a system of coordinated processes could perform more effectively than any single process applied in isolation. Thus, where two components of a system both produce a meaningful analysis of the same or related parts of an image, the combined results should be more reliable than either alone. For example, a first cue for the presence of a surface might be a region which is homogeneous in its brightness, color and/or textural properties. In addition, the variations in the reflection of light off a surface can be an important cue to the presence and orientation of that surface. The shape of the 2D region that is projected by the surface, say a window of a house, also allows shape and perspective analysis (projective geometry) to infer a surface. Certainly motion of the observer, as well as stereopsis or distance information from laser ranging devices, provide cues which ultimately may lead to increasing evidence for a surface. Finally stored knowledge about the surfaces of known objects may also be usable. This is just a single example among many.

The degree to which our current understanding of the individual components of vision provides a sufficient basis for constructing effective and general image understanding systems remains an open question. It was the intent of the workshop to examine this question.

II. THE STRUCTURE OF THE WORKSHOP

On June 1-3, 1977, a small group of researchers in computer vision met at the University of Massachusetts (Amherst) to assess the state-of-the-art in image understanding systems. The planning which led up to the workshop, the discussion which took place, and the subsequent events are the subject of this section.

The workshop was made possible by support from the Information Systems Program of the Office of Naval Research, under the direction of Marvin Denicoff. During the Fall of 1975, discussions with ONR led to a proposal by a group at UMass to hold a workshop focussing on the current status of computer vision systems. From its initial formulation, a decision was made to keep the group of participants small in order to facilitate an active informal interchange of ideas. The specific goals that were delineated in the invitation to participants included:

1) sharing and evaluating techniques which have proven to be successful and reliable in various complex image domains,

2) dissemination of negative results so that others can benefit from the experience,

3) delineation of the critical problem areas which must be overcome before general vision systems will be feasible,

4) evaluation of short term and long term prospects for working systems, and

5) establishment of research priorities for use by funding agencies.

The workshop was organized by an executive committee composed of Michael Arbib, Roger Ehrich, Allen Hanson, and Edward Riseman. In order to gain advice and support from the vision community, an Advisory Committee was formed consisting of Thomas Binford, Jerry Feldman, Raj Reddy, Azriel Rosenfeld, and Jay Tenenbaum. Their participation was instrumental in getting the workshop off the ground.

There were several factors that led to the unusual structure of our workshop. While large conferences with concurrent sessions, invited papers, and panel discussions play an important role in disseminating ideas from a few to many, this format often does not lead to a deep exchange and interaction of ideas by those delivering papers. We decided that it would be desirable to bring this group together with an emphasis on informal dialogue and little formal structure while together.

In order to operate in the manner described, a decision was made to invite in most cases only a single representative from a particular research group or institution. This led to the most difficult decisions concerning whom to invite. Here we consulted the advisory committee individually, but made the final decisions ourselves. There was a desire to include all of those who were most active in the evolving field of computer vision systems at that time. While the field has been well represented by those invited, it should be understood that this group represents some of those who have contributed to the subject in the past and does not include many who are active now.

In order to allow informed and in-depth discussions to develop in as short a period as possible, we held two structured rounds of written communication and feedback prior to the actual three-day workshop. The process was similar to a Delphi study in that at the end of each round of dialogue, the entire set of responses was collected and circulated to all participants. This structure for the workshop was derived from suggestions by Michael Arbib. Table I is an outline of the plan for the workshop as it was envisaged in January, 1976.

The first round involved a rather limited amount of work for each participant: developing an initial summary position paper (4 or 5 pages). As an aid in focussing these papers on the critical issues facing the field, we developed a set of questions with the cooperation of the workshop advisory committee. The position papers were to address one or many of these issues depending upon whether a focussed or broad stance was developed. These short statements were to form lines of constructive debate. The position questions are listed in Table II.

In the second round each participant was to write a 10-25 page pre-workshop paper of their current work and/or a critique of the approaches suggested in the position papers of the other participants. These were to be circulated prior to the workshop and form the basis for structuring the actual sessions at the workshop.

Note that although the short position papers were written almost a year before the meeting, the workshop papers were to be written fairly late in the process and represent up-to-date research results, problems, positions, and plans for future systems. The point of the elaborate format prior to the workshop was an attempt to have all understand the basic methodology used by the other participants, and to gain some measure of agreement upon the leading problems that we should address during the actual meeting.

The position questions that were posed to the participants were divided into four major areas: Segmentation, Representation, Systems, and Research Directions/Evaluation. These topics also formed the content of the four half-day sessions held at the meeting. None of the questions could be easily addressed, particularly in a several page position paper. Nevertheless, interesting points of view did begin to form.[1] The position papers were collected and mailed back to the

---

[1] Some of the papers in this volume reference the position papers. Since most of the position papers were very informal and contained preliminary ideas, they have not been included in this volume and there are no plans to publish them as a collection. Specific position papers may be available from individual authors.

```
┌─────────────────────────────────────────────────────────────┐
│ ROUND I                                                       │
│                                                               │
│     1.  March, 1976 - Invitations will be extended to about 25│
│         participants, at least one full year prior to the     │
│         conference. The invitation will include the set of    │
│         questions which are to be addressed in the position   │
│         papers.                                               │
│                                                               │
│     2.  June 1, 1976 - Each participant supplies a reprint    │
│         (or preprint) of a paper as well as a 4 or 5 page     │
│         position paper which will be circulated to all other  │
│         participants.                                         │
│                                                               │
│            The reprint or preprint will provide others with   │
│         already-developed ideas in relation to the general    │
│         theme of the workshop.                                │
│                                                               │
│            The position paper will provide a broader view of  │
│         work, particularly the directions and methodology     │
│         believed to be most important for the development of  │
│         computer vision systems. If one's work establishes a  │
│         position with respect to one or more of these         │
│         questions, the position paper can be used to          │
│         elucidate and summarize the approach.                 │
│                                                               │
│     3.  July 1, 1976 - The position papers will be circulated │
│         to all participants. A list of the reprints will be   │
│         provided so that each person can select those         │
│         reprints which he is not already familiar with.       │
│                                                               │
│ ROUND II                                                      │
│                                                               │
│     4.  November 1, 1976 - Each participant supplies a final  │
│         workshop paper (10-25 pages) of their own work        │
│         including a critique of the approaches suggested in   │
│         the position papers of the other participants. This   │
│         will allow us to more clearly structure the lines of  │
│         discussion at the workshop, avoiding a considerable   │
│         loss of time selecting issues and in defining         │
│         terminology.                                          │
│                                                               │
│     5.  January 1, 1977 - The workshop papers will be         │
│         distributed to all participants.                      │
│                                                               │
│ ROUND III                                                     │
│                                                               │
│     6.  Spring, 1977 - Three day workshop.                    │
│                                                               │
│     7.  Summer, 1977 - Papers edited and collected into a     │
│         Proceedings. The authors will have an opportunity to  │
│         modify their papers during this period.               │
└─────────────────────────────────────────────────────────────┘
```

TABLE I. ORIGINAL PLAN OF WORKSHOP STRUCTURE (January, 1976)

Segmentation

1. What should be the primary basis of segmentation: regions, edges, clusters in feature space? Are these equivalent? (How) should they be combined?

2. How can multiple features and sensory modalities, including color, texture, depth, motion, be used to simplify segmentation? What are the current limitations in reliably processing each of those features? Given these difficulties, what is the relative utility of each to the segmentation process.

3. Which techniques will be powerful enough to deal with the textural variations of natural scenes? What techniques (e.g., histograms) are necessary (or desirable) to extract global feature activity? How can different levels of texture (micro-macro) be detected and utilized?

4. Do parallel vs. sequential approaches lead to different methodologies? To what extent should we be concerned with the development of parallelism at this point?

5. How does the resolution of the sensory data affect the segmentation process and ultimate performance of the system? Can crude segmentation be obtained from coarsely sampled data? Should we be considering the equivalent of eye movements and/or foveation? Is the processing of a hierarchy of resolution levels helpful? How can a scene be 'glanced at' to quickly determine and locate one or two objects or relationships of immediate interest?

6. How can (or should) semantic knowledge be used to guide low level segmentation? What level(s) of knowledge is needed e.g., domain independent interpretation of grey levels as surfaces; domain specific interpretation of regions as objects?

7. How well can (must) segmentation be performed at the retinal level without explicit knowledge? With only domain independent knowledge?

Representation

8. As logical 'units' for higher processing, what primitive visual features are necessary (or sufficient) to adequately characterize the nature of a region? A line? A surface? An object? What are the deficiencies of our current representations of these features?

9. Given that there is a transformation from the sensory data to the symbols representing the 'meaning' of the sensory data, where is the point in the process that the numbers and symbols meet? Are there any well-defined intermediate levels between sensory data and symbols? If so, what form do these intermediate representations take?

Systems

10. How should the overall systems be organized? How should semantic knowledge be represented and applied? Should there be a hierarchically structured knowledge base? Frame-like structures? Relaxation or constraint satisfaction methods?

11. How can multiple sources of knowledge be integrated?

12. How should goal-oriented vision systems be developed? Can general systems be provided goals after their design is fixed? Or should task-specific systems be developed out of standardized components? How can the goals be integrated into the control strategy to affect the focus of its processing and the depth of its analysis?

13. Does vision have anything to learn from speech understanding systems? Is there any 'visual linguistics'? Are syntactic methods viable?

Research Directions

14. Are our current techniques representative of the full range of possibilities? What are their fundamental and practical limitations? Can they be extended to much larger domains (to handle a much larger number of objects using less domain specific knowledge)? Are distinctly different approaches (e.g., from brain studies) required or potentially useful?

15. What are important and promising directions for further research and what problems can be expected?

16. What are the potential applications of these systems, special purpose (near-term) or general? Is a general vision system a viable goal for research or should research be applications driven?

Evaluation

17. What is the criteria for judging the performance of vision systems, both applications and general systems?

18. What are reasonable expectations for computer vision systems? All agree that vision is hard, but how hard is it? What is the level of complexity, amount of knowledge, computational capacity needed? Can we expect general vision systems in five years? Ten years? Fifty years?

TABLE II. POSITION QUESTIONS (January, 1976)

Representatives from Research Groups

Michael A. Arbib, Computer and Information Science Department, University of Massachusetts
Ruzena Bajcsy, Moore School of Electrical Engineering, University of Pennsylvania
Harry G. Barrow, Artificial Intelligence Center, Stanford Research Institute
Thomas O. Binford, Computer Science Department, Stanford University
J. Michael Brady, Department of Computer Science, University of Essex
Bruce Bullock, Hughes Research Laboratories
Roger W. Ehrich, Electrical and Computer Engineering Department, University of Massachusetts
Jerome A. Feldman, Computer Science Department, University of Rochester
Martin A. Fischler, Lockheed Research Laboratory
Joergen Foith, Institute für Informationsverarbeitung, Karlsruhe, Germany
Allen R. Hanson, School of Language and Communication, Hampshire College
Robert M. Haralick, Electrical Engineering and Computer Science Department, University of Kansas
David Huffman, Department of Information Sciences, University of California
Stephen M. Kosslyn, Department of Psychology, The Johns Hopkins University
Victor R. Lesser, Computer and Information Science Department, University of Massachusetts
Martin D. Levine, Department of Electrical Engineering, McGill University
Lawrence Lieberman, Automation Research Group, IBM Thomas J. Watson Research Center
Alan Mackworth, Department of Computer Science, University of British Columbia
David Marr, Artificial Intelligence Laboratory, Massachusetts Institute of Technology
Ramakant Nevatia, Image Processing Institute and Computer Science Department, University of S. California
D. Raj Reddy, Computer Science Department, Carnegie-Mellon University
Edward M. Riseman, Computer and Information Science Department, University of Massachusetts
Azriel Rosenfeld, Computer Science Department, University of Maryland
Yoshiaki Shirai, Electrotechnical Laboratory, Nagatacho, Chiyodaku, Tokyo
Steven L. Tanimoto, Electrical Engineering and Computer Science Department, University of Connecticut
Jay M. Tenenbaum, Artificial Intelligence Center, Stanford Research Institute
Leonard Uhr, Computer Sciences Department, University of Wisconsin
David Waltz, Coordinated Science Laboratory, University of Illinois
Naomi Weisstein, Psychology Department, State University of New York
Patrick Winston, Artificial Intelligence Laboratory, Massachusetts Institute of Technology
William Woods, Bolt Beranek and Newman Inc.
Steven W. Zucker, Department of Electrical Engineering, McGill University

Representatives from Funding Agencies

David Carlstrom, Advanced Research Projects Agency
Kent Curtis, National Science Foundation
Gordon Goldstein, Office of Naval Research
Robert Grafton, Office of Naval Research
Henry Halff, Office of Naval Research
William Sander, U.S. Army Research Office

TABLE III. WORKSHOP PARTICIPANTS

1, Morning - Systems
            Moderator, D. Raj Reddy
   Afternoon - Representation
            Moderator, Martin A. Fischler
     Evening - Informal wine and cheese reception
            and demonstration at University
            of Massachusetts vision laboratory.
            Hosted by UMass vision group.

2, Morning - Segmentation
            Moderator, Jay M. Tenenbaum
   Afternoon - Research Directions and Evaluation
            Moderator, Robert M. Haralick

3, Morning - Open Session

TABLE IV. WORKSHOP SCHEDULE

research on vision. Although each of the subsystems may not be fully understood, the complex interactions and control of the processes cannot be tested in isolation. Consequently, these topics will remain important even when each module is developed. The empirical question, given our current understanding, is whether modules can be developed to a minimally sufficient degree in each area so that a whole system can reach some lower bound of acceptability. Each process can only be evaluated in the context of the goals and quality of performance of the other modules. Experience in speech understanding, for example, seems to indicate that development of systems leads to an elucidation of gaps in our understanding and indicates profitable directions for further research.

Representation

The focus of the discussion in this session was on human performance and the representations underlying this performance. Surface information was stressed by some to be crucial in the generation of adequate visual descriptions. The bulk of the discussion was stimulated by evidence that mental representations of images are maintained in a non-propositional (non-symbolic) form with spatial relationships directly encoded in the representation. This led to a protracted discussion of iconic vs. symbolic imagery. If objects are stored in terms of primitives that are close to the sensory data, such that spatial properties are maintained directly, then it is iconic, whereas the symbolic storage of primitives and relationships between them (particularly spatial) leads to very different kinds of processes. There seemed to be no real agreement on the definition of terms nor on the representation(s) used in human vision. This discussion fragmented and ended with a multitude of views.

Segmentation

The discussion which took place here did not lead to any conclusive positions. Most agreed that visual information is very noisy and that the partitioning of an image alone does not, and cannot, provide sufficient information for the interpretation of the scene. The discussion was primarily concerned with the mechanisms for extracting relevant information and the level at which this information should be extracted, ranging from edges and regions defined on the original representation of pixels through extraction of three-dimensional surfaces directly. Much of the ensuing discussion focussed on the inadequacies of current techniques, the perceived need to make more explicit the phenomena which give rise to an image (e.g., luminance, reflectance, surface geometry, and view-point), and the representational mechanisms required.

There was quite a bit of discussion on relaxation techniques as a control mechanism for low-level processes and there was some disagreement as to how relaxation techniques should be viewed: as a fundamental process underlying certain aspects of vision or as a programming language in which to define distributed computation of data. At one point it was whimsically suggested that relaxation is a process that allows two different things to be considered before each other. Several argued that it is an effective embodiment of distributed computation which, if properly utilized, can lead to an increased understanding of local analysis and interactions in producing global results. However, there was some uneasiness expressed over the use of these techniques since they are not fully understood; for example, it is not clear under what circumstances they converge, what results are produced under convergence, how difficult it is for a human to debug processes with parallel interactions, etc.

Although there was not a critical evaluation of the range of segmentation techniques that are available, there did seem to be a consensus that more powerful methods for dealing with visual texture are needed.

Research Directions/Evaluation

In this, the final session, a wide range of general views were expressed and some warnings offered. Many of the discussions of the previous sessions were concerned with the difference between an engineering approach to vision and a scientific study of vision. In the name of science, a fundamentalist point of view had been urged upon the field.

The clear response was that there were many directions worth pursuing, including the building of systems. Although a substantial increase in our understanding of particular problems is required, there are many problems which can be dealt with given our current understanding.

It was emphasized that throughout the workshop we had been concerned with systems approaching the level of human performance, but that much could be done given our current techniques. More could be done given modest advances in hardware technology, particularly the development of micro-computer array processors (to improve response time), which should spur the development of parallel processing in vision systems.

It was generally agreed that there are numerous profitable avenues of research which should be actively pursued and which, in the long run, will add to our understanding of visual information processing and the knowledge necessary to construct effective computer vision systems. Finally, Azriel Rosenfeld reminded us of the seven deadly sins of research in computer vision:

1) Anger: Let us not be impatient with each other! The field needs critical standards, but let us draw a line between constructive criticism and prejudice.

2) Envy: Let us not reject others' ideas because we did not think of them first.

3) Gluttony: Let us not be hungry to capture all the funding: there's room for new blood in the field.

4) Greed: Let us not be miserly with our knowledge, but give it good dissemination, so others can benefit from it (and so the new blood will not repeat our mistakes).

5) Lust: Let us not be obsessed solely with "solving the vision problem"; there are many useful contributions that we can make as byproducts.

6) Pride: Let us not refuse to abandon our pet ideas when they do not stand the test of time.

7) Sloth: Let us not indulge in too much relaxation! Or, more seriously: Vision is hard; let us not keep hoping for easy solutions.

Open Session

The last session included a stimulating presentation of the theory of paper-folding based upon a mathematical analysis of surfaces and curvature by David Huffman. The presentation was supplemented with a delightful demonstration of the formation of intricate geometric structures from simple folds in sheets of paper, all specified by his theory of curvature. The remainder of this session was devoted to informal small group discussions which concluded the workshop.

IV. THE FUTURE OF THE FIELD

At one point during the workshop, it was estimated that our current state of understanding is only a small fraction of that needed to construct a general computer vision system which is comparable in performance to human vision. This implies that a considerable amount of research, in all areas, is necessary before such systems can become truly sophisticated. There are, however, two major problems which most active researchers in vision face, but rarely acknowledge. The first is the range of expertise that must be developed within a single research group which hopes to build a more powerful vision system. The second major problem is the limitation of hardware available to some researchers and the degree of systems development that must accompany the actual research.

Let us consider the first of these difficulties. As we outlined earlier, the range of subproblems in which it might be meaningful for a

researcher to exclusively embed himself without paying careful attention
to other related areas of vision include the physics of light and surfaces and their role in image formation, segmentation algorithms, texture, color, two-dimensional shape, surface cues, three-dimensional
shape, perspective, occlusion, stereopsis, motion, distributed computation, representation of knowledge, among many others. There is now
widespread research activity on many of these topics. From another
viewpoint, the solution to a meaningful application of a vision system
often involves a selection of a subset of useful techniques from a subset of the areas discussed above. While this latter approach can lead
to solutions to particular problems, the resulting design may not
generalize easily to other, even very similar, applications.

Let us now consider the systems problems. Many of those who have
focussed primarily on segmentation have enough interesting problems to
keep them preoccupied in this subarea. Besides the actual segmentation
algorithms that are at the heart of their research, very large amounts
of information must be manipulated. In order to work with images which
exhibit a reasonable degree of resolution, scenes are usually digitized
to at least 256×256 pixels, and sometimes much higher as in the
resolution of ERTS imagery. This requires a minimum of 64,000 data
points and if it is carried out in color, there is at least three times
as much data. Such massive amounts of data can place a severe strain on
available computer resources. This often leads to requirements for
image data base and filing systems, as well as attention to efficient
programming techniques. In general, the researcher must develop a
special-purpose operating system. Similarly, the efforts required to
deal with representing shape, manipulating and matching 2D and 3D
descriptions, as well as all of the graphics support that is necessary
for effective display of information, also leads to substantial system
support development. These activities may consume as much as 75% of the
research effort over protracted periods of time. Clearly, the severity
of the problems cited depend upon the subproblems which are chosen to be
explored.

These problems are mitigated somewhat by developments in hardware
technology and the large investment already made in system software.
The cost of hardware has continued to plummet and now it is easier for
many groups to have access to very powerful machines. The new generation of minicomputers that are being produced are very fast and support
large memories. It appears that adequate computational facilities will
be available to many in the near future. In addition, software for
image processing systems has been developed at many different installa-
tions. The potential for shared software increases, and whether or not
this actually does take place, the required design and development
effort has already been invested by active groups in the field.

The effort invested in the support mechanisms for the VISIONS image
understanding system currently being developed by our group is not an
atypical example of the impact of these problems on a research effort.
In our effort we chose to structure our segmentation algorithms by
simulating hierarchical parallel hardware and computation. We had to
construct an efficient image file management system, build data
structures to interface various intermediate segmentation results,
develop several different forms for displaying segmentation results on
our color monitor, black and white vector display, and line printers,
construct a graph processing language and a relational data base in
LISP, and over all of this construct a special-purpose operating system.
This latter system (which we call our model buiding system) manages the
application of the many modular processes which are being implemented and
is responsible for integration of the results produced by these processes. At least half of our total research effort (which has been quite
large) over the past four years has been on systems support for the
research and not on the research itself.

Where does this leave the field at the current moment in time.
There are several research efforts that are exploring major theoretical
design paradigms for various aspects of computer vision. Relaxation
processes, production systems, and other forms of distributed parallel
processing are being developed; highly structured systems are potentially
important ways to approach complex system development. There also is an
increasing number of successful results in constrained domains. These

should continue to bear fruit and as they do, the constraints on the problems to which they are applicable will be decreased. Research on important theoretical questions continues and, in concert with efforts to develop systems, should add important new insights into the extremely complex problem of visual information processing.

How effective will general systems perform in the next several years? It is difficult to answer this question without indulging in speculation. We now have a better sense of why the problem is so complex, but no one knows how effectively a vision system will perform if the state-of-the-art approaches in each subarea are brought together. Such a system certainly would not reach human levels of performance, but it might be highly effective in domains that are only slightly con- strained and extend far beyond our current machine capabilities.

Issues and Research Strategies

During the past decade of research in computer vision, numerous avenues have been explored; theories and paradigms have been developed, tested, accepted, or more often, rejected; successes and failures have been critically evaluated (although sometimes incompletely); and a multitude of application domains have been analyzed. From these explorations have emerged a collection of observations which address a number of common issues relevant to the development of computer vision systems. The papers in this section cover a wide range of these issues and the breadth of the considerations reflects the breadth of the field. While the issues raised here share concerns which are the primary focus of other sections of the book, the common theme here is the selection of research strategies employed and the paradigms underlying vision research. Several of these papers also present system designs and results; the reader should note that these papers should be compared with related papers in other sections.

Barrow and Tenenbaum argue that an appropriate role for early visual processing is the direct recovery of scene descriptions on the basis of surfaces. They outline an analysis, based on the physics of light and surfaces, by which intrinsic surface properties may be recovered from intensity images. Bullock argues for the development of special-purpose low-level vision systems which can be flexibly reconfigured as the need arises, rather than pay the price incurred through the use of inefficient universal operations. A system organization is described which can be tailored into a problem-specific system using a flexible modification strategy. Fischler raises interesting questions concerning the currently accepted paradigm of a symbolic representation of the structure of a scene and the need for complete segmentation prior to interpretation. He argues that a representation which directly preserves spatial properties might be essential for natural scenes.

Lesser and Erman are concerned with the design, development, and implementation of large systems from the human engineering point of view. They argue that careful attention must be paid to system engineering considerations at all levels of system development, including interfaces, maintenance, reconfiguration and efficiency. Mackworth suggests that the vision researcher choose a limited domain in which a range of problems relevant to a general theory can be examined. Using a system designed to interpret free-hand sketches of maps, he defends the choice of a system with conservative partial segmentation, and a uniform control structure which propagates local consistency constraints.

Marr addresses issues relating to the representation of visual information and argues that in the early stages of processing the representations depend on the information that it is possible to extract from an image rather than on what is ultimately desired. Drawing upon

1

psychophysical evidence, he outlines a system which moves from analysis of intensity changes in a two-dimensional image, through the representation of properties of surfaces, to object-centered descriptions of three-dimensional structures. Although the views of Marr and of Barrow and Tenenbaum are philosophically similar, they differ in the way in which three-dimensional constraints on the two-dimensional image are employed.

Nevatia presents a classification of vision tasks, from constrained domains in which there is a priori information about the spatial relationships of a small number of known objects, to unconstrained domains in which a large number of possible objects may appear with few constraints on the relationships between them. He concludes that a general purpose vision system must be capable of generating rich descriptions without a priori knowledge of specific objects in a scene. Finally, Reddy defines a broad set of system design choices concerning machine vision, including those affecting low-level analysis, high-level representations, acquisition of knowledge, and system architectures. Drawing on recent work in vision and previous work in speech understanding, the implications of these choices are examined.

The reader who carefully examines the issues raised in this set of papers will be prepared to critically evaluate the system designs and approaches that appear in the remainder of the book.

RECOVERING INTRINSIC SCENE CHARACTERISTICS FROM IMAGES

H.G. Barrow and J.M. Tenenbaum,
SRI International,
Menlo Park, CA 94025.

ABSTRACT

We suggest that an appropriate role of early visual processing is to describe a scene in terms of intrinsic (veridical) characteristics -- such as range, orientation, reflectance, and incident illumination -- of the surface element visible at each point in the image. Support for this idea comes from three sources: the obvious utility of intrinsic characteristics for higher-level scene analysis; the apparent ability of humans to determine these characteristics, regardless of viewing conditions or familiarity with the scene; and a theoretical argument that such a description is obtainable, by a noncognitive and nonpurposive process, at least, for simple scene domains. The central problem in recovering intrinsic scene characteristics is that the information is confounded in the original light-intensity image: a single intensity value encodes all the characteristics of the corresponding scene point. Recovery depends on exploiting constraints, derived from assumptions about the nature of the scene and the physics of the imaging process.

I INTRODUCTION

Despite considerable progress in recent years, our understanding of the principles underlying visual perception remains primitive. Attempts to construct computer models for the interpretation of arbitrary scenes have resulted in such poor performance, limited range of abilities, and inflexibility that, were it not for the human existence proof, we might have been tempted long ago to conclude that high-performance, general-purpose vision is impossible. On the other hand, attempts to unravel the mystery of human vision, have resulted in a limited understanding of the elementary neurophysiology, and a wealth of phenomenological observations of the total system, but not, as yet, in a cohesive model of how the system functions. The time is right for those in both fields to take a broader view: those in computer vision might do well to look harder at the phenomenology of human vision for clues that might indicate fundamental inadequacies of current approaches; those concerned with human vision might gain insights by thinking more about what information is sought, and how it might be obtained, from a computational point of view. This position has been strongly advocated for some time by Horn [18-20] and Marr [26-29] at MIT.

Current scene analysis systems often use pictorial features, such as regions of uniform intensity, or step changes in intensity, as an initial level of description and then jump directly to descriptions at the level of complete objects. The limitations of this approach are well known [4]: first, region-growing and edge-finding programs are unreliable in extracting the features that correspond to object surfaces because they have no basis for evaluating which intensity differences correspond to scene events significant at the level of objects (e.g., surface boundaries) and which do not (e.g., shadows). Second, matching pictorial features to a large number of object models is difficult and potentially combinatorially explosive because the feature descriptions are impoverished and lack invariance to viewing conditions. Finally, such systems cannot cope with objects for which they have no explicit model.

Some basic deficiencies in current approaches to machine vision are suggested when one examines the known behavior and competence of the human visual system. The literature abounds with examples of the ability of people to estimate characteristics intrinsic to the scene, such as color, orientation, distance, size, shape, or illumination, throughout a wide range of viewing conditions. Many experiments have been performed to determine the scope of so-called "shape constancy," "size constancy," and "color constancy" [13 and 14]. What is particularly remarkable is that consistent judgements can be made despite the fact that these characteristics interact strongly in determining intensities in the image. For example, reflectance can be estimated over an extraordinarily wide range of incident illumination: a black piece of paper in bright sunlight may reflect more light than a white piece in shadow, but they are still perceived as black and white respectively. Color also appears to remain constant throughout wide variation in the spectral composition of incident illumination. Variations in incident illumination are independently perceived: shadows are usually easily distinguished from changes in reflectance. Surface shape, too, is easily discerned regardless of illumination or surface markings: Yonas has experimentally determined that human accuracy in estimating local surface orientation is about eight degrees [37]. It is a worthwhile exercise at this point to pause and see how easily you can infer intrinsic characteristics, like color or surface orientation, in the world around you.

The ability of humans to estimate intrinsic characteristics does not seem to require familiarity with the scene, or with objects contained therein. One can form descriptions of the surfaces in scenes unlike any previously seen, even when the presentation is as unnatural as a photograph. People can look at photomicrographs, abstract art, or satellite imagery, and make consistent judgements about relative distance, orientation, transparency, reflectance, and so forth. See, for example, Figure 1, from a thesis by Macleod [25].

Looking beyond the phenomenological aspects, one might ask what is the value of being able to estimate such intrinsic characteristics. Clearly, some information is valuable in its own right: for example, knowing the three-dimensional structure of the scene is fundamental to many activities, particularly to moving around and manipulating objects in the world. Since intrinsic characteristics give a more invariant and more distinguishing description of surfaces than raw light intensities, they greatly simplify many basic perceptual operations. Scenes can be partitioned into regions that correspond to smooth surfaces of uniform reflectance, and viewpoint-independent descriptions of the surfaces may then be formed [29]. Objects may be described and recognized in terms of collections of these elementary surfaces, with attributes that are characteristic of their composition or function, and relationships that convey structure, and not merely appearance. A chair, for example, can be described generically as a horizontal surface, at an appropriate height for sitting, and a vertical surface situated to provide back support. Previously unknown objects can be described in terms of invariant surface characteristics, and subsequently recognized from other viewpoints.

A concrete example of the usefulness of intrinsic scene information in computer vision can be obtained from experiments by Nitzan, Brain and Duda [30] with a laser rangefinder that directly measures distance and apparent reflectance. Figure 2a shows a test scene taken with a normal camera. Note the variation in intensity of the wall and chart due to variations in incident illumination, even though the light sources are extended and diffuse. The distance and reflectance for this scene as obtained by the rangefinder are shown in Figure 2b. The distance information is shown in a pictorial representation in which closer points appear brighter. Note that, except for a slight amount of crosstalk on the top of the cart, the distance image is insensitive to reflectance variations. The laser images are also entirely free from shadows.

Using the distance information, it is relatively straightforward to extract regions corresponding to flat or smooth surfaces, as in Figure 2c, or edges corresponding to occlusion boundaries, as in Figure 2d, for example. Using reflectance information, conventional region- or edge-finding programs show considerable improvement in extracting uniformly painted surfaces. Even simple thresholding extracts acceptable surface approximations, as in Figure 2e.

Since we have three-dimensional information, matching is now facilitated. For example, given the intensity data of a planar surface that is not parallel to the image plane, we can eliminate the projective distortion in these data to obtain a normal view of this surface, Figure 2f. Recognition of the characters is thereby simplified. More generally, it is now possible to describe objects generically, as in the chair example above. Garvey [10] actually used generic descriptions at this level to locate objects in rangefinder images of office scenes.

The lesson to be learned from this example is that the use of intrinsic characteristics, rather than intensity values, alleviates many of the difficulties that plague current machine vision systems, and to which the human visual system is apparently largely immune.

The apparent ability of people to estimate intrinsic characteristics in unfamiliar scenes and the substantial advantages that such characteristics would provide strongly suggest that a visual system, whether for an animal or a machine, should be organized around an initial level of domain-independent processing, the purpose of which is the recovery of intrinsic scene characteristics from image intensities. The next step in pursuing this idea is to examine in detail the computational nature of the recovery process to determine whether such a design is really feasible.

In this paper, we will first establish the true nature of the recovery problem, and demonstrate that recovery is indeed possible, up to a point, in a simple world. We will then argue that the approach can be extended, in a straightforward way, to more realistic scene domains. Finally, we will discuss this paradigm and its implications in the context of current understanding of machine and human vision. For important related work see [29].

II THE NATURE OF THE PROBLEM

The first thing we must do is specify precisely the objectives of the recovery process in terms of input and desired output.

The input is one or more images representing light intensity values, for different viewpoints and spectral bands. The output we desire is a family of images for each viewpoint. In each family there is one image for each intrinsic characteristic, all in registration with the corresponding input images. We call these images "Intrinsic Images." We want each intrinsic image to contain, in addition to the value of the characteristic at each point, explicit indications of boundaries due to discontinuities in value or gradient. The intrinsic images in which we are primarily interested are of surface reflectance, distance or surface orientation, and incident illumination. Other characteristics, such as transparency, specularity, luminosity, and so forth, might also be useful as intrinsic images, either in their own right or as intermediate results.

Figure 3 gives an example of one possible set of intrinsic images corresponding to a single, monochrome image of a simple scene. The intrinsic images are here represented as line drawings, but in fact would contain numerical values at every

H. G. Barrow and J. M. Tenenbaum

(a) CASTANOPSIS (X 3500)

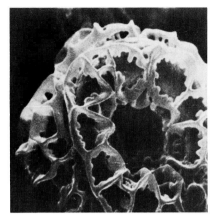

(b) DRIMYS (X 3200)

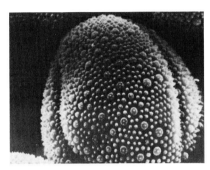

(c) FLAX (X 1000)

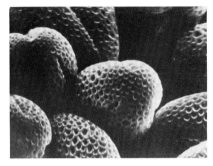

(d) WALLFLOWER (X 1800)

Figure 1   Photomicrographs of pollen grains (Macleod [20])

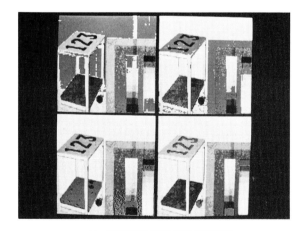

(e)   THRESHOLDING REFLECTANCE

(f)   CORRECTED VIEW OF CART TOP

Figure 2   Experiments with a laser rangefinder

H. G. Barrow and J. M. Tenenbaum

(a) ORIGINAL SCENE

Figure 3   A set of intrinsic images derived from a
single monochrome intensity image

The images are depicted as line drawings,
but, in fact, would contain values at
every point.   The solid lines in the
intrinsic images represent discontinuities
in the scene characteristic; the dashed
lines represent discontinuities in its
derivative.

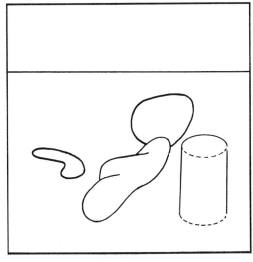

(b) DISTANCE

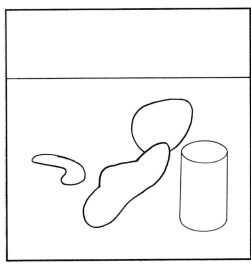

(c) REFLECTANCE

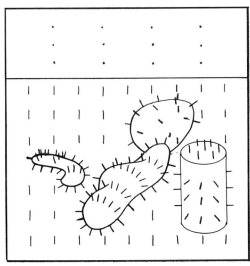

(d) ORIENTATION (VECTOR)

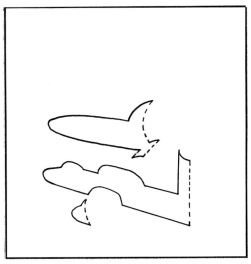

(e) ILLUMINATION

Characteristics from Images

7

point. The solid lines show discontinuities in the represented characteristic, and the dashed lines show discontinuities in its gradient. In the input image, intensities correspond to the reflected flux received from the visible points in the scene. The distance image gives the range along the line of sight from the center of projection to each visible point in the scene. The orientation image gives a vector representing the direction of the surface normal at each point. It is essentially the gradient of the distance image. The short lines in this image are intended to convey to the reader the surface orientation at a few sample points. (The distance and orientation images correspond to Marr's notion of a 2.5D sketch [29].) It is convenient to represent both distance and orientation explicitly, despite the redundancy, since some visual cues provide evidence concerning distance and others evidence concerning orientation. Moreover, each form of information may be required by some higher-level process in interpretation or action. The reflectance image gives the albedo (the ratio of total reflected to total incident illumination) at each point. Albedo completely describes the reflectance characteristics for lambertian (perfectly diffusing) surfaces, in a particular spectral band. Many surfaces are approximately lambertian over a range of viewing conditions. For other types of surface, reflectance depends on relative directions of incident rays, surface normal and reflected rays. The illumination image gives the total light flux incident at each point. In general, to completely describe the incident light it is necessary to give the incident flux as a function of direction. For point light sources, one image per source is sufficient, if we ignore secondary illumination by light scattered from nearby surfaces.

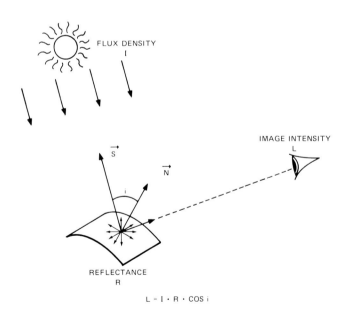

Figure 4 An ideally diffusing surface

When an image is formed, by a camera or by an eye, the light intensity at a point in the image is determined mainly by three factors at the corresponding point in the scene: the incident illumination, the local surface reflectance, and the local surface orientation. In the simple case of an ideally diffusing surface illuminated by a point source, as in Figure 4, for example, the image light intensity, L, is given by

$$L = I * R * \cos i \qquad (1)$$

where I is intensity of incident illumination, R is reflectivity of the surface, and i is the angle of incidence of the illumination [20].

The central problem in recovering intrinsic scene characteristics is that information is confounded in the light-intensity image: a single intensity value encodes all the intrinsic attributes of the corresponding scene point. While the encoding is deterministic and founded upon the physics of imaging, it is not unique: the measured light intensity at a single point could result from any of an infinitude of combinations of illumination, reflectance, and orientation.

We know that information in the intrinsic images completely determines the input image. The crucial question is whether the information in the input image is sufficient to recover the intrinsic images.

III   THE NATURE OF THE SOLUTION

The only hope of decoding the confounded information is, apparently, to make assumptions about the world and to exploit the constraints they imply. In images of three-dimensional scenes, the intensity values are not independent but are constrained by various physical phenomena. Surfaces are continuous in space, and often have approximately uniform reflectance. Thus, distance and orientation are continuous, and reflectance is constant everywhere in the image, except at edges corresponding to surface boundaries. Incident illumination, also, usually varies smoothly. Step changes in intensity usually occur at shadow boundaries, or surface boundaries. Intrinsic surface characteristics are continuous through shadows. In man-made environments, straight edges frequently correspond to boundaries of planar surfaces, and ellipses to circles viewed obliquely. Many clues of this sort are well known to psychologists and artists. There are also higher-level constraints based on knowledge of specific objects, or classes of object, but we shall not concern ourselves with them here, since our aim is to determine how well images can be interpreted without object-level knowledge.

We contend that the constraints provided by such phenomena, in conjunction with the physics of imaging, should allow recovery of the intrinsic images from the input image. As an example, look carefully at a nearby painted wall. Observe that its intensity is not uniform, but varies smoothly. The variation could be due, in principle, to variations in reflectance, illumination, orientation, or any combination of them. Assumptions of continuity immediately rule out the situation of a smooth intensity variation arising from cancelling random variations in illumination, reflectance, and orientation. Since surfaces are assumed to be uniform in reflectance, the intensity variation must thus be due to a smooth variation in illumination or surface shape. The straight edge of the wall suggests, however, that the wall is planar, and that the variation is in illumination only. To appreciate the value of this constraint, view a small central portion of the wall through a tube. With no evidence from the edge, it is difficult to distinguish whether the observed shading is due to an illumination gradient on a planar surface, or to a smooth surface curving away from the light source.

The tube experiment shows that while isolated fragments of an image have inherent ambiguity, interactions among fragments resulting from assumed constraints can lead to a unique interpretation of the whole image. Of course, it is possible to construct (or occasionally to encounter) scenes in which the obvious assumptions are incorrect -- for example, an Ames room (see [13] for an illustration). In such cases, the image will be misinterpreted, resulting in an illusion. The Ames illusion is particularly interesting because it shows the lower-level interpretation, of distance and orientation, dominating the higher-level knowledge regarding relative sizes of familiar objects, and even dominating size constancy. Fortunately, in natural scenes, as commonly encountered, the evidence is usually overwhelmingly in favor of the correct interpretation.

We have now given the flavor of the solution, but with many of the details lacking. Our current research is aimed at making the underlying ideas sufficiently precise to implement a computational model. While we are far from ready to attack the full complexity of the real world, we can give a fairly precise description of such a model for recovering intrinsic characteristics in a limited world. Moreover, we can argue that this model may be extended incrementally to handle more realistic scenes.

IV   SOLUTION FOR A SIMPLE WORLD

A.   Methodology

To approach the problem systematically, we select an idealized domain in which a simplified physics holds exactly, and in which there are explicit constraints on the nature of surfaces and illuminants. From these assumptions, it is possible to enumerate various types of scene fragments and determine the appearance of their corresponding image fragments. A catalog of fragment appearances and alternative interpretations can thus be compiled (in the style of Huffman [21] and Waltz [34]).

We proceed by constructing specific scenes that satisfy the domain assumptions, synthesizing corresponding images of them, and then attempting to recover intrinsic characteristics from the images, using the catalog and the domain knowledge. (By displaying synthetic images, we could check that people can interpret them adequately. If they cannot, we can discover oversimplifications by comparing the synthetic images to real images of similar scenes.)

B.   Selection of a Domain

Specifications for an experimental domain must include explicit assumptions regarding the scene, the illumination, the viewpoint, the sensor, and the image-encoding process. The initial domain should be sufficiently simple to allow exhaustive enumeration of its constraints, and complete cataloging of appearances. It must, however, be sufficiently complex so that the recovery process is non-trivial and generalizable. A domain satisfying these requirements is defined as follows:

* Objects are relatively smooth, having surfaces over which distance and orientation are continuous. That is, there are no sharp edges or creases.

* Surfaces are lambertian reflectors, with constant albedo over them. That is, there are no surface markings and no visible texture.

* Illumination is from a distant point source, of known magnitude and direction, plus uniformly diffuse background light of known magnitude (an approximation to sun, sky, and scattered light). Local secondary illumination (light reflected from nearby objects) is assumed to be negligible. (See Figure 5.)

* The image is formed by central projection onto a planar surface. Only a single view is available (no stereo or motion parallax). The scene is viewed from a general position (incremental changes in viewpoint do not change the topology of the image).

* The sensor measures reflected flux density. Spatial and intensity resolution are sufficiently high that quantization effects may be ignored. Sensor noise is also negligible.

Such a domain might be viewed as an approximation of a world of colored Play-Doh objects in which surfaces are smooth, reflectance is uniform for each object, there is outdoor illumination, and the scene is imaged by a tv camera. The grossest approximations, perhaps, are the assumptions about illumination, but they are substantially more realistic than the usual single-point-source model, which renders all shadowed regions perfectly black.

For this domain, our objective is to recover intrinsic images of distance, orientation, reflectance, and illumination.

C.   Describing the Image

Elementary physical considerations show that a portion of a surface that is continuous in visibility, distance, orientation, and incident illumination, and has uniform reflectance, maps to a connected region of continuous intensity in the image. Images thus consist of regions of smoothly varying intensity, bounded by step discontinuities. In our domain, reflectance is constant over each surface, and there are two states of illumination, corresponding to sun and shadow. Image regions therefore correspond to areas of surface with a particular state of illumination, and the

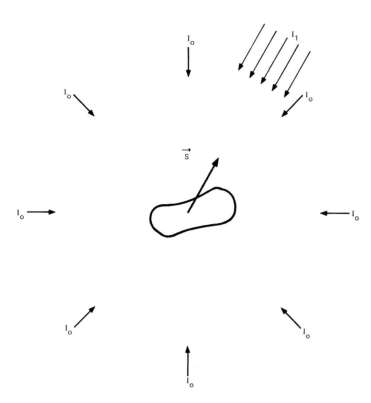

Figure 5   Sun and sky illumination model

boundaries correspond to occluding (extremal) boundaries of surfaces, or to the edges of shadows. There are also junctions where boundaries meet. Figure 6b shows the regions and edges for the simple scene of Figure 3.

To be quantitative, we assume image intensity is calibrated to give reflected flux density at the corresponding scene point. Reflected flux density is the product of integrated incident illumination, I, and reflectance (albedo), R, at a surface element. Thus,

$$L = I * R \qquad (2)$$

The reflected light is distributed uniformly over a hemisphere for a lambertian surface. Hence, image intensity is independent of viewing direction. It is also independent of viewing distance, because although the flux density received from a unit area of surface decreases as the inverse square of distance, the surface area corresponding to a unit area in the image increases as the square of distance.

In shadowed areas of our domain, where surface elements are illuminated by uniform diffuse illumination of total incident flux density I0, the image intensity is given by

$$L = I0 * R \qquad (3)$$

When a surface element is illuminated by a point source, such that the flux density is I1,

from a direction specified by the unit vector, S, the incident flux density at the surface is I1 * N.S , where N is the unit normal to the surface, and . is the vector dot product. Thus,

$$L = I1 * N.S * R \qquad (4)$$

In directly illuminated areas of the scene, image intensity, L, is given by the sum of the diffuse and point-source components:

$$L = (I0 + I1 * N.S) * R \qquad (5)$$

From the preceding sections, we are now in a position to describe the appearance of image fragments in our domain, and then to derive a catalog.

1. Regions

For a region corresponding to a directly illuminated portion of a surface, since R, I0, and I1 are constant, any variation in image intensity is due solely to variation in surface orientation. For a region corresponding to a shadowed area of surface, intensity is simply proportional to reflectance, and hence is constant over the surface.

We now catalog regions by their appearance. Regions can be classified initially according to whether their intensities are smoothly varying, or constant. In the former case, the region must correspond to a nonshadowed, curved surface with constant reflectance and continuous depth and orientation. In the latter case, it must correspond to a shadowed surface. (An illuminated planar surface also has constant intensity, but such surfaces are excluded from our domain.) The shadowing may be due either to a shadow cast upon it, or to its facing away from the point source. The shape of a shadowed region is indeterminable from photometric evidence. The surface may contain bumps or dents and may even contain discontinuities in orientation and depth across a self-occlusion, with no corresponding intensity variations in the image.

2. Edges

In the same fashion as for regions, we can describe and catalog region boundaries (edges). An edge should not be considered merely as a step change in image intensity, but rather as an indication of one of several distinct scene events. In our simple world, edges correspond to either the extremal boundary of a surface (the solid lines in Figure 3b), or to the boundary of a cast shadow (the solid lines in Figure 3e). The "terminator" line on a surface, where there is a smooth transition from full illumination to self-shadowing (the dashed lines in Figure 3e), does not produce a step change in intensity.

The boundary of a shadow cast on a surface indicates only a difference in incident illumination: the intrinsic characteristics of the surface are continuous across it. As we observed earlier, the shadowed region is constant in intensity, and the illuminated region has an intensity gradient that is a function of the surface orientation. The shadowed region is necessarily darker than the illuminated one.

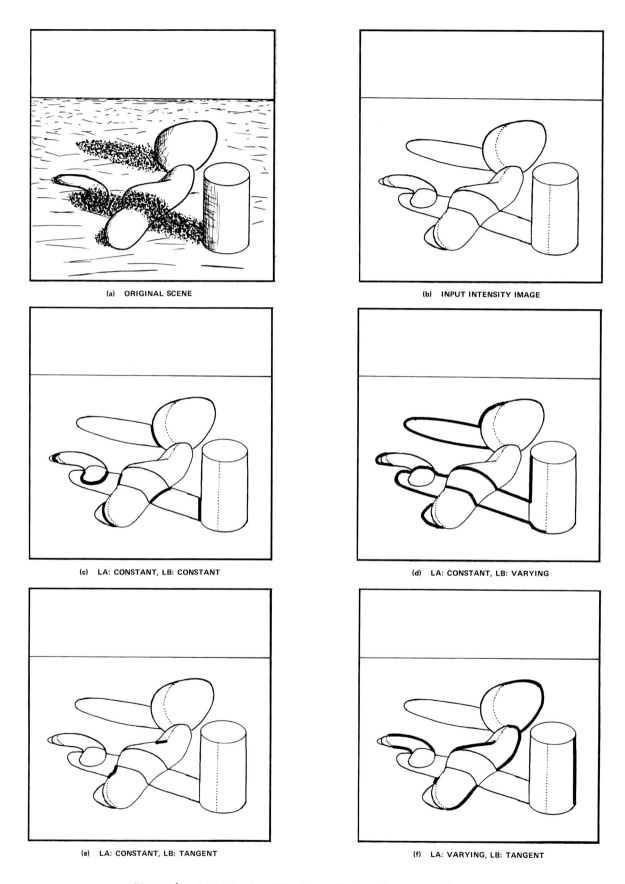

(a) ORIGINAL SCENE

(b) INPUT INTENSITY IMAGE

(c) LA: CONSTANT, LB: CONSTANT

(d) LA: CONSTANT, LB: VARYING

(e) LA: CONSTANT, LB: TANGENT

(f) LA: VARYING, LB: TANGENT

Figure 6   Initial classification of edges in an example scene

An extremal boundary is a local extremum of the surface from the observer's point of view, where the surface turns away from him. Here one surface occludes another, and all intrinsic characteristics may be discontinuous. In our world, it is assumed that depth and orientation are always discontinuous. Reflectance is constant on each side of the edge, and will only be continuous across it if the two surfaces concerned have identical reflectance, or when a single surface occludes itself.

A very important condition results from the fact that an extremal boundary indicates where a smooth surface turns away from the viewer: the orientation is normal to the line of sight, and to the tangent to the boundary in the image. Hence the absolute orientation of the occluding surface can be determined along an extremal boundary. The boundary must first be identified as extremal, however.

The regions on either side of an extremal boundary are independently illuminated. When both are in shadow, they both have constant intensity, and the ratio of intensities is equal to the ratio of the reflectances: it is not possible to determine from local intensity information which region corresponds to the occluding surface.

When a region is illuminated, intensity varies continuously along its side of the boundary. We noted that the image of an extremal boundary tells us precisely the orientation of the occluding surface at points along it. The orientation, together with the illumination flux densities, I0 and I1, and the image intensity, L, can be used in Equation (5) to determine reflectance at any point on the boundary. For a true extremal boundary, our assumption of uniform reflectance means that estimates of reflectance at all points along it must agree. This provides a basis for recognizing an occluding surface by testing whether reflectances derived at several boundary points are consistent. We call this test the tangency test, because it depends upon the surface being tangential to the line of sight at the boundary. This test is derived by differentiating the logarithm of Equation (5):

$$dL/L = dR/R + (I1*dN.S)/(I0 + I1*N.S) \qquad (6)$$

The vector dN is the derivative of surface orientation along the edge, and may be determined from the derivative of edge direction. The derivatives dL and dR are taken along the edge. Equation (6) may be rewritten to give dR/R explicitly in terms of L, dL, N, dN and the constants I0, I1, and S. The tangency condition is met when dR/R is zero. The tangency condition is a powerful constraint that can be exploited in further ways, which we will discuss later.

Strictly speaking, where we have referred to derivatives here, we should have said "the limit of the derivative as the edge is approached from the side of the region being tested." Clearly, the tests are not applicable at gaps, and the tangency test is not applicable where the edge is discontinuous in direction.

We can now catalog edges by their appearances, as we did for regions. Edges are classified according to the appearance of the regions on either side in the vicinity of the edge. This is done by testing intensity values on each side for constancy, as before, and for satisfaction of the tangency test, and by testing relative intensities across the edge. Table 1 catalogs the possible appearances and interpretations of an edge between two regions, A and B.

In this table, "Constant" means constant intensity along the edge, "Tangency" means that the

Table 1   The Nature of Edges

Region Intensities LA	LB	Edge Type	Region Types	Intrinsic Edges Intrinsic Values D	N	R	I
Constant	Constant	Occluding sense unknown	A B shadowed	EDGE	EDGE	EDGE RA RB	IA IB
Constant	Varying	1 Shadow	A shadowed B illuminated		NB.S	RA RB	EDGE IA IB
		2 A occludes B	A shadowed B illuminated	EDGE DA DB	EDGE NA	EDGE RA	EDGE IA
Varying	Varying	Inconsistent with domain					
Constant	Tangency	B occludes A	A shadowed B illuminated	EDGE DA DB	EDGE NB	EDGE RA RB	EDGE IA IB
Varying	Tangency	B occludes A	A B illuminated	EDGE DA DB	EDGE NB	EDGE RB	EDGE IB IA
Tangency	Tangency	Not seen from general position					

tangency condition is met, and "Varying" means that neither of these tests succeeds. The entry "EDGE" denotes a discontinuity in the corresponding intrinsic attribute, with the same location and direction as the corresponding image intensity edge. The magnitude and sense of the discontinuity are unknown, unless otherwise shown. Where the value of an intrinsic attribute can be determined from the image (see Section IV.D), it is indicated by a term of the form RA, RB, DA, etc. (These terms denote values for reflectance, R; orientation, vector N; distance, D; and incident flux density, I; for the regions A and B, in the obvious way.) Where only a constraint on values is known, it is indicated by an inequality. There is a special situation, concerning case 1 of the second type of edge, in which a value can be determined for NB.S, but not for NB itself.

Note that, from the types of intensity variations, edges can be interpreted unambiguously, except for two cases: namely, the sense of the occluding edge between two shadowed regions, and the interpretation of an edge between illuminated and shadowed regions when the tangency test fails. Figure 6 illustrates the classification of edges according to the catalog for our example scene.

3. Junctions

Since the objects in our domain are smooth, there are no distinguished points on surfaces. Junctions in the image, therefore, are viewpoint dependent. There are just two classes of junction, both resulting from an extremal boundary, and both appearing as a T-shape in the image (see Figure 7).

The first type of junction arises when one object partially occludes a more distant boundary, which may be either a shadow edge or an extremal edge. The crossbar of the junction is thus an extremal edge of an object that is either illuminated or shadowed. The boundary forming the stem lies on the occluded object and its edge type is unconstrained.

The second type of junction arises when a shadow cast on a surface continues around behind an extremal boundary. In this case, the crossbar is again an extremal edge, half in shadow, while the stem is a shadow edge lying on the occluding object.

Note that in both cases the crossbar of the T corresponds to a continuous extremal boundary. Hence the two edges forming the crossbar are continuous, occluding, and have the same sense.

The T junctions provide constraints that can sometimes resolve the ambiguities in the edge table above. Consider the cases as follows: if all the regions surrounding the T are shadowed, the edge table tells us that all the edges are occluding, but their senses are ambiguous. The region above the crossbar, however, must be occluding the other two, otherwise the continuity of the crossbar would be due to an accident of viewpoint. If one or more of the regions is illuminated, the occlusion sense of the crossbar is immediately determined from the tangency test. Thus we can always determine the nature of the two edges forming the crossbar of the T, even when they may have been ambiguous according to the edge table.

If the region above the crossbar is the occluder, we have the first type of T junction, and can say no more about the stem than the edge tests give us. Otherwise, we have the second type (a shadow edge cast over an extremal boundary), and any ambiguity of the stem is now resolved.

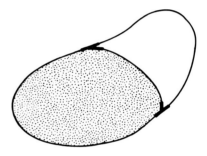

Figure 7   Two types of T-junction

D. Recovery Using the Catalog

The ideal goal is to recover all intrinsic scene characteristics, exactly, everywhere in an image that is consistent with our domain. In this section, we outline the principles of recovery using the catalog and address the issue of how nearly our goal can be attained. The following section will describe a detailed computational model of the recovery process.

The recovery process has four main steps:

(1)   Find the step edges in the input intensity image.

(2)   Interpret the intrinsic nature of the regions and edge elements, according to the catalog. Interpretation is based on the results of constancy and tangency tests.

(3)   Assign initial values for intrinsic characteristics along the edges, based on the interpretations.

(4)   Propagate these "boundary" values into the interiors of regions,

using continuity assumptions. This step is analogous to the use of relaxation methods in physics for determining distributions of temperature or potential over a region based on boundary values.

For pedagogical purposes, in this section only, we assume that it is possible to extract a perfect line drawing from the intensity image. The recovery process described later does not depend on this assumption, because it perfects the line drawing as an integral part of its interpretation. Let us now consider the ultimate limitations of the recovery paradigm in our simple domain.

Shadowed and directly illuminated areas of the image are distinguished immediately, using the constancy test. Reflectance everywhere in shadowed areas is then given by Equation (3).

The orientation of a region corresponding to an illuminated surface can be determined along extremal boundaries identified by the tangency test. Reflectance of this region can then be determined at the boundary by Equation (5), and thus throughout the region based on the assumption that reflectance is constant over a surface.

So far, recovery has been exact; the intrinsic values and edges that can be exactly inferred from intensity edges are shown in Table 1. Surface orientation within illuminated regions bounded, at least in part, by extremal edges can be reasonably estimated, as follows: Equation (5) can be solved, knowing L, R, I0, and I1, for N.S, the cosine of the angle of incidence of the direct component of illumination, at each point. This does not uniquely determine the orientation, which has two degrees of freedom, but it does allow reasonable estimates to be obtained using the assumption of smoothness of surfaces and the known orientation at extremal boundaries to constrain the other degree of freedom. Two examples of how this reconstruction can be done are given by the work of Horn [19] and Woodham [35] on "shape from shading."

Orientation can be integrated to obtain relative distance within the regions, and the tangency test gives distance-ordering across the boundary.

Since a shadowed region of surface appears uniform in the intensity image, its shape cannot be determined from shading information. A plausible guess can be made, however, by interpolating in from points of known orientation, using the smoothness assumption. This can be done only if at least part of the boundary of the shadowed region can be interpreted as extremal boundary (e.g., using T-junctions), or as a shadow edge with the shape on the illuminated side known.

Not surprisingly, little can be said about regions, shadowed or illuminated, with no visible portions of boundary identifiable as extremal (e.g. a region seen through a hole, or shadowed, with no T-junctions). It is still reasonable to attempt to interpret such inherently ambiguous situations, but it is then necessary to introduce further, and perhaps less general, assumptions. For example: an object is predominantly convex, so the sense of an occlusion can be guessed locally from the shape of the boundary; the brightest point on an illuminated surface is probably oriented with its normal

pointing at the light source, providing a boundary condition for determining the surface reflectance and its shape from shading. Of course, such assumptions must be subordinate to harder evidence, when it is available.

We conclude that, in this limited domain, unambiguous recovery of intrinsic characteristics at every point in an image is not generally possible, primarily because of the lack of information in some regions of the intensity image. Thus, in some cases, we must be content with plausible estimates derived from assumptions about likely scene characteristics. When these assumptions are incorrect, the estimates will be wrong, in the sense that they will not correspond exactly to the scene; they will, however, provide an interpretation that is consistent with the evidence available in the intensity image, and most of the time this interpretation will be largely correct.

Though perfect recovery is unattainable, it is remarkable how much can be done considering the weakness (and hence generality) of the assumptions, and the limited number of cues available in this domain. We used no shape prototypes, nor object models, and made no use of any primary depth cues, such as stereopsis, motion parallax, or texture gradient. Any of these sources, if available, could be incorporated to improve performance by providing information where previously it could only be guessed (for example, texture gradient could eliminate shape ambiguity in shadows).

V   A COMPUTATIONAL MODEL

We now propose a detailed computational model of the recovery process. The model operates directly on the data in a set of intrinsic images and uses parallel local operations that modify values in the images to make them consistent with the input image and constraints representing the physical assumptions about imaging and the world.

A.   Establishing Constraints

Recovery begins with the detection of edges in the intensity image. If quantization and noise are assumed negligible in the domain, we can easily distinguish all step discontinuities, and hence generate a binary image of intensity edges, each with an associated direction. This image will resemble a perfect line drawing, but despite the ideal conditions, there can still be gaps where intensities on two sides of a boundary happen to be identical. Usually this will occur only at a single isolated point -- for example, at a point where the varying intensities on the two sides of an occlusion boundary simultaneously pass through the same value. Complete sections of a boundary may also occasionally be invisible -- for example, when a shadowed body occludes itself. Our recovery process is intended to cope with these imperfections, as will be seen later.

Given the edge image, the next step is to interpret the intrinsic nature of the edge elements according to the edge table. Interpretation is based on the results of two tests, constancy and tangency, applied to the intensities of the regions immediately adjacent to an edge element. The constancy test is applied by simply checking whether the gradient of intensity is zero. The tangency test is applied in its differential form by checking whether the derivative of estimated reflectance, taken along the edge, is zero.

The resulting edge interpretations are used to initialize values and edges in the intrinsic images in accordance with the edge table. The table specifies, for each type of intensity edge, the intrinsic images in which corresponding edge elements should be inserted. Values are assigned to intrinsic image points adjacent to edges, as indicated in the table. For example, if an intensity edge is interpreted as an occlusion, we can generate an edge in the distance and orientation images, and initialize orientation and reflectance images at points on the occluding side of the boundary.

When the edge interpretation is ambiguous, we make conservative initializations, and wait for subsequent processing to resolve the issue. In the case of an extremal boundary separating two shadowed regions, this means assuming a discontinuity in distance, orientation and reflectance, but not assuming anything else about orientation or relative distance. In the case of ambiguity between a shadow edge and a shadowed occluding surface, we assume discontinuities in all characteristics, and that the illumination and reflectance of the shadowed region are known. It is better to assume the possible existence of an edge, when unsure, because it merely decouples the two regions locally; they may still be related through a chain of constraints along some other route.

For points at which intrinsic values have not been uniquely specified, initial values are assigned that are reasonable on statistical and psychological grounds. In the orientation image, the initial orientation is assigned as N0, the orientation pointing directly at the viewer. In the illumination image, areas of shadow, indicated by the constancy test, are assigned value I0. The remaining directly illuminated points are assigned value I1 * N0.S . In shadowed areas, reflectance values are assigned as L/I0 , and in illuminated areas, they are assigned L/(I0 + I1 * N0.S) . Distance values are more arbitrary, and we assign a uniform distance, D0 everywhere. The choice of default values is not critical, they simply serve as estimates to be improved by the constraint satisfaction processes.

Following initialization, the next step is to establish consistency of intrinsic values and edges in the images. Consistency within an individual image is governed by simple continuity and limit constraints. In the reflectance image, the constraint is that reflectance is constant -- that is, its gradient must be defined and be zero everywhere, except at a reflectance edge. Reflectance is additionally constrained to take values between 0 and 1. Orientation values are also constrained to be continuous, except at occlusion edges. The vectors must be unit vectors, with a positive component in the direction of the viewpoint. Illumination is positive and continuous, except across shadow boundaries. In shadowed regions, it must be constant, and equal to I0. Distance values must be continuous everywhere

-- that is, their gradient must be defined and finite, except across occlusion edges. Where the sense of the occlusion is known, the sense of the discontinuity is constrained appropriately. Distance values must always be positive.

All these constraints involve local neighborhoods, and can thus be implemented via asynchronous parallel processes. The continuity constraints, in particular, might be implemented by processes that simply ensure that the value of a characteristic at a point is the average of neighboring values. Such processes are essentially solving Laplace's equation by relaxation.

The value at a point in an intrinsic image is related not only to neighboring values in the same image, but also to values at the corresponding point in the other images. The primary constraint of this sort is that image intensity is everywhere the product of illumination and reflectance, as in Equation (2). Incident illumination is itself a sum of terms, one for each source. This may conveniently be represented by introducing secondary intrinsic images for the individual sources. The image representing diffuse illumination is constant, with value I0, while that for the point source is I1 * N.S, where N.S is positive and the surface receives direct illumination, and zero elsewhere. These constraints tie together values at corresponding points in the input intensity, reflectance, primary and secondary illumination, and orientation images. The orientation and distance images are constrained together by the operation of differentiation.

B.   Achieving Consistency

Consistency is attained when the intra- and inter-image constraints are simultaneously satisfied. That occurs when values and gradients everywhere are consistent with continuity assumptions and constraints appropriate to the type of image, and the presence or absence of edges. The intraimage constraints ensure that intrinsic characteristics vary smoothly, in the appropriate ways. Such constraints are implicit in the domain description, and are not usually made so explicit in machine vision systems. The interimage constraints ensure that the characteristics are also consistent with the physics of imaging and the input intensity image. It is these constraints that permit an estimate of surface shape from the shading within regions of smoothly varying intensity [19].

Consistency is achieved by allowing the local constraint processes, operating in parallel, to adjust intrinsic values. The explicitly determined values listed in the initialization table, however, are treated as boundary conditions and are not allowed to change. As a result, information propagates into the interior of regions from the known boundaries.

The initial assignment of intrinsic edges is, as we have already noted, imperfect: edges found in th intensity image may contain gaps, introducing corresponding gaps in the intrinsic edges; certain intrinsic edges are not visible in the intensity image -- for example, self-occlusion in shadow; some intrinsic edges were assumed in the interests of conservatism, but they may be incorrect. From the recovered intrinsic values, it may be clear where further edges should be inserted in (or deleted from) the corresponding intrinsic image. For example, when the gradient in an image becomes very high, insertion of an edge element is indicated, and, conversely, when the difference in values across an edge becomes very small, deletion is indicated. Insertion and deletion must operate within existing constraints. In particular, edge elements cannot be manipulated within a single image in isolation, because a legal interpretation must always be maintained. For example, in our world, occlusion implies edges in distance and orientation simultaneously. Within an intrinsic image, continuity of surfaces implies continuity of boundaries. Hence, the decision to insert must take neighboring edge elements into consideration.

Constraints and boundary conditions are dependent upon the presence or absence of edges. For example, if a new extremal edge is inserted, continuity of distance is no longer required at that point, and the orientation on one side is absolutely determined. Consequently, when edge elements are inserted or deleted, the constraint satisfaction problem is altered. The constraint and edge modification processes run continuously, interacting to perfect the original interpretation and recover the intrinsic characteristics. Figures 8 and 9 summarize the overall organization of images and constraints.

So far we have not mentioned the role of junctions in the recovery process. At this point, it is unclear whether junctions need to be treated explicitly since the edge constraints near a confluence of edges will restrict relative values and interpretations. Junctions could also be used in an explicit fashion. When a T-configuration is detected, either during initialization or subsequently, the component edges could be interpreted via a junction catalog, which would provide more specific interpretations than the edge table. Detection of junctions could be performed in parallel by local processes, consistent with the general organization of the system. The combinatorics of junction detection are much worse than those of edge detection, and have the consequence that reliability of detection is also worse. For these reasons, it is to be hoped that explicit reliance upon junctions will not be necessary.

The general structure of the system is clear, but a number of details remain to be worked out. These include: how to correctly represent and integrate inter- and intra-image constraints; how to insert and delete edge points; how to correctly exploit junction constraints; how to ensure rapid convergence and stability. Although we do not yet have a computer implementation of the complete model, we have been encouraged by experiments with some of the key components.

We have implemented a simple scheme that uses a smoothness constraint to estimate surface orientation in region interiors from boundary values. The constraint is applied by local parallel processes that replace each orientation vector by the average of its neighbors. The surface reconstructed is a quadratic function of the image coordinates. It is smooth, but not uniformly curved, with its boundary lying in a plane. It appears possible to derive more complex continuity constraints that result in more

uniformly curved surfaces, interpolating, for example, spherical and cylindrical surfaces from their silhouettes.

The above smoothing process was augmented with another process that simultaneously adjusts the component of orientation in the direction of steepest intensity gradient to be consistent with observed intensity. The result is a cooperative "shape from shading" algorithm, somewhat different from Woodham's [35]. The combined algorithm has the potential for reconstructing plausible surface shape in both shadowed and directly illuminated regions.

VI EXTENDING THE THEORY

Our initial domain was deliberately oversimplified, partly for pedagogic purposes and partly to permit a reasonably exhaustive analysis. The approach of thoroughly describing each type of scene event and its appearance in the image, and then inverting to form a catalog of interpretations for each type of image event, is more generally applicable. Results so far appear to indicate that while ambiguities increase with increasing domain complexity, available constraints also increase proportionately. Information needed to effect recovery of scene characteristics seems to be available; it is mainly a matter of thinking and looking hard enough for it.

In this section, we will briefly describe some of the ways in which the restrictive assumptions of our initial domain can be relaxed, and the recovery process correspondingly augmented, to bring us closer to the real world.

The assumption of continuous, noise-free encoding is important for avoiding preoccupation with details of implementation, but it is essential for a realistic theory to avoid reliance upon it. With these assumptions, problems of edge detection are minimized, but, as we noted earlier, perfect line drawings are not produced. Line drawings conventionally correspond to surface outlines, which may not be visible everywhere in the image. The recovery process we described, therefore, incorporated machinery for inserting and deleting edges to achieve surface integrity. Relaxing the assumption of ideal encoding will result in failure to detect some weak intensity edges and possibly the introduction of spurious edge points in areas of high intensity gradient. Insofar as these degradations are moderate, the edge-refinement process should ensure that the solution is not significantly affected.

The assumption of constant reflectance on a surface can be relaxed by introducing a new edge type -- the reflectance edge -- where orientation, distance, and illumination are still continuous, but reflectance undergoes a step discontinuity. Reflectance edges bound markings on a surface, such as painted letters or stripes. The features distinguishing the appearance of an illuminated reflectance edge are that the ratio of image intensities across the edge is constant along it and equal to the ratio of the reflectances and the magnitude of intensity gradient across the edge is also equal to the ratio of the reflectances, and

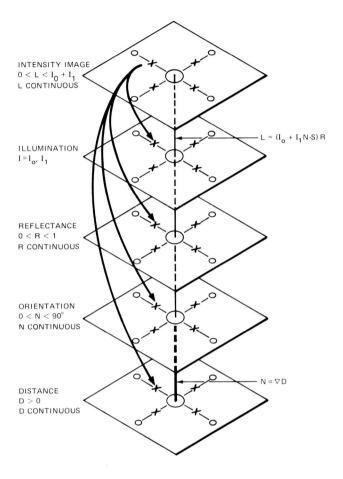

INTENSITY IMAGE
$0 < L < I_0 + I_1$
L CONTINUOUS

ILLUMINATION
$I = I_0, I_1$

$L = (I_0 + I_1 N \cdot S) R$

REFLECTANCE
$0 < R < 1$
R CONTINUOUS

ORIENTATION
$0 < N < 90°$
N CONTINUOUS

DISTANCE
$D > 0$
D CONTINUOUS

$N \propto \nabla D$

Figure 8   A parallel computational model for recovering intrinsic images

The basic model consists of a stack of registered arrays, representing the original intensity image (top) and the primary intrinsic arrays. Processing is initialized by detecting intensity edges in the original image, interpreting them according to the catalog, and then creating the appropriate edges in the intrinsic images (as implied by the downward sweeping arrows).

Parallel local operations (shown as circles) modify the values in each intrinsic image to make them consistent with the intraimage continuity and limit constraints. Simultaneously, a second set of processes (shown as vertical lines) operates to make the values consistent with interimage photometric constraints. A third set of processes (shown as Xs) operates to insert and delete edge elements, which locally inhibit continuity constraints. The constraint and edge modification processes operate continuously and interact to recover accurate intrinsic scene characteristics and to perfect the initial edge interpretation.

Characteristics from Images   **17**

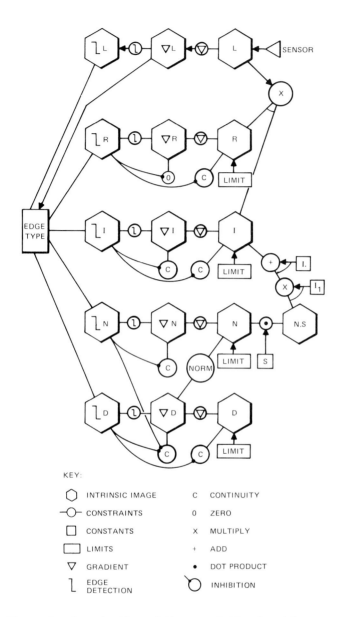

KEY:

⬡ INTRINSIC IMAGE		C	CONTINUITY
─○─ CONSTRAINTS		0	ZERO
☐ CONSTANTS		X	MULTIPLY
▭ LIMITS		+	ADD
▽ GRADIENT		•	DOT PRODUCT
⌐ EDGE DETECTION		↻	INHIBITION

Figure 9   Organization of the computational model

The input intensity image and primary intrinsic images each have an associated gradient image and an edge image. Additional images represent intermediate results of computation, such as N.S . (All images are shown as hexagons.) The constraints, shown here as circles, are of three varieties: physical limits (e.g., 0 =< R =< 1), local continuity, and interimage consistency of values and edges. Continuity constraints are inhibited across edges. For example, values of illumination gradient are constrained to be continuous, except at illumination edges.

its direction is the same on both sides. These characteristics uniquely identify illuminated reflectance edges, and provide constraints relating intrinsic characteristics on the two sides.

In shadow, it is not possible to locally distinguish a pure reflectance edge from an extremal edge between surfaces of different reflectance, for which the ratio of intensities is also equal to the ratio of reflectances.

The existence of reflectance edges introduces a new type of X-shaped junction, where a shadow edge is cast across a reflectance edge. The detection of an X-junction in the image unambiguously identifies a shadow edge, since the reflectance edge may be easily identified by the ratio test.

An interesting case of surface markings is that of reflectance texture. Texture has certain regular or statistical properties that can be exploited to estimate relative distance and surface orientation. If we can assume statistically uniform density of particular textural features, the apparent density in the image relates distance and inclination of the surface normal to the viewing direction. A second cue is provided by orientation of textural features (for example, reflectance edge elements). As the surface is viewed more obliquely, the orientation distribution of image features tends to cluster about the orientation of the extremal boundary, or of the horizon. These cues are important, since they provide independent information about surface shape, perhaps less precisely and of lower resolution than photometric information, but in areas where photometric information is unavailable (e.g., shadowed regions) or ambiguous (e.g., an illuminated region seen through a hole).

The assumption of smoothness of surfaces can be relaxed by introducing a further edge type, the intersection edge, which represents a discontinuity in surface orientation, such as occurs at a crease or between the faces of a polyhedron. There are two distinct ways an intersection edge can appear in an image, corresponding to whether one or both of the intersecting surfaces are visible. We shall call these subcases "occluding" and "connecting," respectively.

At a connecting intersection edge, only distance is necessarily continuous, since faces can be differently painted, and illuminated by different sources. The strong assumption of continuity of orientation is replaced by the weaker one that the local direction of the surface edge in three dimensions is normal to the orientations of both surfaces forming it. The effect of this constraint is that if one surface orientation is known, the surface edge direction can be inferred from the image, and the other surface orientation is then hinged about that edge, leaving it one degree of freedom. Even when neither orientation is known absolutely, the existence of a connecting edge serves to inhibit application of continuity constraints, and thereby permit more accurate reconstruction of surface shape.

At an occluding intersection edge, nothing is known to be continuous, and the only constraint is on relative distance.

H. G. Barrow and J. M. Tenenbaum

In the image, an illuminated intersecting edge can be distinguished from an extremal edge since the intensity on both sides is varying, but the tangency test fails, and it can be distinguished from a reflectance edge since the ratio of intensities across the edge is not constant. The constraint between surface orientations forming the edge makes it appear likely that a test can also be devised for distinguishing between connecting and occluding intersection edges.

In shadowed regions, intersection edges are only visible when they coincide with reflectance edges, from which they are therefore locally indistinguishable. Creases in a surface are thus invisible in shadows.

When one surface is illuminated and the other shadowed, an intersection edge cannot be locally distinguished from the case of a shadowed object occluding an illuminated one.

Extremal and intersection boundaries together give a great deal of information about surface shape, even in the absence of other evidence, such as shading, or familiarity with the object. Consider, for example, the ability of an artist to convey abstract shape with line drawings. The local inclination of an extremal or intersection boundary to the line of sight is, however, unknown; a given silhouette can be produced in many ways [27]. In the absence of other constraints, the distance continuity constraint will ensure smooth variation of distance at points along the boundary. An additional constraint that could be invoked is to assume that the torsion (and possibly also the curvature) of the boundary space curve is minimal. This will tend to produce planar space curves for boundaries, interpreting a straight line in the image as a straight line in space, or an ellipse in the image as a circle in space. The assumption of planarity is often very reasonable: it is the condition used by Marr to interpret silhouettes as generalized cylinders [27].

The assumption of known illumination can be relaxed in various ways. Suppose we have the same "sun and sky" model of light sources, but do not have prior knowledge of I0, I1 and S . In general, we cannot determine the flux densities absolutely, since they trade off against reflectance. We may, however, assign an arbitrary reflectance to one surface (for example, assume the brightest region is white, $R = 1.0$), and then determine other reflectances and the flux densities relative to it. The initial assignment may need to be changed if it forces the reflectance of any region to exceed the limits, $0.0 < R < 1.0$.

The parameters of illumination, flux densities I0 and I1, and unit vector S, can be determined by assuming reflectance and exploiting a variation of the tangency test. If we have an illuminated extremal boundary, Equation (5) gives a linear equation in the parameters for each point on the edge. The equations for any four points can be solved simultaneously to yield all the parameters. The remaining points on the boundary can be used with the now-known illumination to verify the assumption of an extremal boundary. An independent check on the ratio of I0 to I1 can be made at any shadow edge where surface orientation is known. This method of solving for illumination parameters can be extended to multiple point sources by merely

increasing the number of points on the boundary used to provide equations. Care is required with multiple sources because it is necessary to know which points are illuminated by which sources. The method works for a centrally projected image, but not for an orthogonally projected one, since, in the latter case, all the known surface normals are coplanar.

Even modelling illumination as a set of point sources does not capture all the subtleties of real-world lighting, which include extended sources, possibly not distant, and secondary illumination. Extended sources cause shadows to have fuzzy edges, and close sources cause significant gradients in flux density and direction. Secondary illumination causes local perturbations of illumination that can even dominate primary illumination, under some circumstances (e.g., light scattered into shadow regions). All these effects make exact modelling of illumination difficult, and hence cast suspicion on a recovery method that requires such models.

In the absence of precise illumination models that specify magnitude and direction distributions of flux density everywhere, accurate point-wise estimation of reflectance and surface orientation from photometric equations alone is not possible. It should still be possible, however, to exploit basic photometric constraints, such as local continuity of illumination, along with other imaging constraints and domain assumptions, to effect recovery within our general paradigm. As an example, we might still be able to find and classify edges in the intensity image: reflectance edges still have constant intensity ratios (less than 30:1) across them, shadow edges may be fuzzy with high intensity ratios, occlusion and intersection edges are generally sharp without constant ratios. The occlusion and intersection edges, together with reflectance texture gradient and continuity assumptions, should still provide a reasonable initial shape estimate. The resulting knowledge of surface continuity, the identified reflectance edges, and the assumption of reflectance constancy enable recovery of relative reflectance, and hence relative total incident flux density. The ability to determine continuity of illumination and to discriminate reflectance edges from other types thus allows us to generalize Horn's lightness determination process [18] to scenes with relief, occlusion, and shadows.

Having now made initial estimates of intrinsic characteristics, it may be possible to refine them using local illumination models and photometric knowledge. It may be possible, using assumptions of local monotonicity of illumination, to decide within regions whether the surface is planar, curved in some direction, or whether it inflects.

Even with all the extensions that we have so far discussed, our scene domain is still much less complex than the real world, in which one finds specularity, transparency, luster, visible light sources, three-dimensional texture, and sundry other complications. Although, at first sight, these phenomena make recovery seem much harder, they also represent additional intrinsic characteristics for more completely describing the scene, and potentially rich sources of information for forming the description. There are also many well-known sources of information about the scene, that make use of multiple images, including stereo, motion parallax, and color. We believe that the framework we have put forward can be extended to accommodate these additional sources.

At this point, it is not clear whether adding complexity to our domain will lead to fewer ambiguities, or more. So far, however, we have seen no reason to rule out the feasibility of recovering intrinsic scene descriptions in real-world situations.

VII DISCUSSION

The concept of intrinsic images clarifies a number of issues in vision, and generalizes and unifies many previously disjoint computational techniques. In this section, we will discuss some implications of our work, in the contexts of system organization, image analysis, scene analysis, and human vision.

A. System Organization

The proper organization of a visual system has been the subject of considerable debate. Issues raised include the controversy over whether processing should be data-driven or goal-driven, serial or parallel, the level at which the transition from iconic to symbolic representation should occur, and whether knowledge should be primarily domain-independent or domain-specific [4]. These issues have a natural resolution in the context of a system organized around the recovery of intrinsic images, as in Figure 10.

The recovery process we have outlined is primarily data-driven and dependent only on general domain assumptions. Subsequent goal-oriented or domain-specific processes (ranging from segmentation to object recognition) may then operate on information in the intrinsic images.

Intrinsic images appear to be a natural interface between iconic and symbolic representations. The recovery process seems inherently iconic, and suited to implementation as an array of parallel processes attempting to satisfy local constraints. The resulting information is iconic, invariant, and at an appropriate level for extracting symbolic scene descriptions. Conversely, symbolic information from higher levels (e.g., the size or color of known objects) can be converted to iconic form (e.g., estimates of distance or reflectivity) and used to refine or influence the recovery process. Symbolic information clearly plays an important role in the perception of the three-dimensional world.

Multilevel, parallel constraint satisfaction is an appealing way to organize a visual system because it facilitates incremental addition of knowledge and avoids many arbitrary problems of control and sequencing. Parallel implementations have been used previously, but only at a single level, for recovering lightness [18], depth [28], and shape [35]. Each of these processes is concerned with recovering one of our intrinsic images, under specialized assumptions equivalent to assuming values for the other images. In this

paper, we have suggested how they might be coherently integrated.

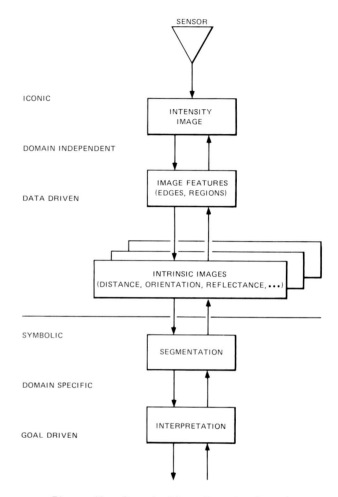

Figure 10   Organization of a visual system

Issues of stability and speed of convergence always arise in iterative approaches to constraint satisfaction. Heuristic "relaxation" schemes (e.g., [32]), in which "probabilities" are adjusted, often use ad hoc updating rules for which convergence is difficult to obtain and prove. By contrast, the system we have described uses iterative relaxation methods to solve a set of equations and inequalities. The mathematical principles of iterative equation solving are well understood [2] and should apply to our system, at least, for a fixed set of edges. Insofar as local edge modifications have only local consequences, operations such as gap filling should affect convergence to only a minor extent.

Speed of convergence is sometimes raised as an objection to the use of cooperative processes in practical visual systems; it is argued that such processes would be too slow in converging to explain the apparent ability of humans to interpret an image in a fraction of a second. This objection can be countered in several ways: first, full convergence may not be necessary to achieve acceptable accuracy; second, information propagation may be predominantly local, influenced primarily by nearby edges; third, there are ways of speeding up long-range propagation -- for example, using hierarchies of resolution [15].

B. Image Analysis

Image analysis is usually considered to be the generation of a two-dimensional description of the image, such as a line drawing, which may subsequently be interpreted. We believe it is important to take a more liberal view, and include some consideration of the three-dimensional meaning of image features in the earliest descriptions.

A topic often debated is segmentation -- the process of partitioning an image into semantically interpretable regions. Fischler [9] and others have raised a number of critical questions: is segmentation meaningful in a domain-independent sense, is it possible, and how should it be done?

Partitioning of an arbitrary intensity image into regions denoting objects is an illusory goal, unless the notion of what constitutes an object is precisely defined. Since objects are often collections of pieces whose association must be learned, general object segmentation seems impossible in principle. It seems more reasonable, on the other hand, to partition an image into regions corresponding to smooth surfaces of uniform reflectance. This is often the implicit goal of programs that attempt to partition an image into regions of uniform intensity. Unfortunately, intensity does not correspond directly to surface characteristics. There is no way of determining whether merging two regions is meaningful, and consequently there is no reliable criterion for terminating the merging process. Segmentation based on intrinsic images avoids these difficulties.

Another elusive goal, the extraction of a perfect line drawing from an intensity image, is also impossible in principle, for similar reasons: the physical significance of boundaries does not correlate well with the magnitude of intensity changes. Surface boundaries can be hard, and, in some places, impossible, to detect; shadows and texture contribute edge points in abundance, which, in this context, are noise. To attain a line drawing depicting surface boundaries, we must take into account the physical significance of intensity discontinuities. It is quite clear from depth and orientation intrinsic images where edges are necessary for consistency and surface integrity. A perfect line drawing could be regarded as one of the products of the process of recovering intrinsic characteristics.

From this point of view, all attempts to develop more sophisticated techniques for extracting line drawings from intensity images appear inherently limited. Recently, relaxation enhancement techniques for refining the imperfect results of an edge detector have attracted considerable interest [32 and 15]. These techniques manipulate edge confidences according to the confidences of nearby points, iterating until equilibrium is achieved. This approach is really

attempting to introduce and exploit the concept of edge continuity, and does lead to modest improvements. It does not, however, exploit the continuity of surfaces, nor ideas of edge type, and consequently produces curious results on occasion. Moreover, as we noted earlier, convergence for ad hoc updating rules is difficult to prove.

The major problem with all the image analysis techniques we have mentioned is that they are based on characteristics of the image, without regard to how the image was formed. Horn at MIT for some time has urged the importance of understanding the physical basis of image intensity variations [20]. His techniques for determining surface lightness [18] and shape from shading [19] have had an obvious influence on our own thinking. To achieve a precise understanding of these phenomena, Horn considered each in isolation, in an appropriately simplified domain: a planar surface bearing regions of different reflectance lit by smoothly varying illumination for lightness, and a simple smoothly curved surface with uniform reflectance and illumination for shading. These domains are, however, incompatible, and the techniques are not directly applicable in domains where variations in reflectance, illumination, and shape may be discontinuous and confounded. We have attempted to make explicit the constraints and assumptions underlying such recovery techniques, so that they may be integrated and used in more general scenes.

The work most closely related to our own is that of Marr [29], who has described a layered organization for a general vision system. The first layer extracts a symbolic description of the edges and shading in an intensity image, known as the "Primal Sketch." These features are intended to be used by a variety of processes at the next layer (e.g., stereo correlation, texture gradient) to derive the three-dimensional surface structure of the image. The resulting level of description is analogous to our orientation and distance images, and is called the "2.5D sketch." Our general philosophy is similar to Marr's, but differs in emphasis, being somewhat complementary. We are all interested in understanding the organization of visual systems, in terms of levels of representation and information flow. Marr, however, has concentrated primarily on understanding the nature of individual cues, such as stereopsis and texture, while we have concentrated primarily on understanding the integration of multiple cues. We strongly believe that interaction of different kinds of constraints plays a vital role in unscrambling information about intrinsic scene characteristics.

A particular point of departure is Marr's reliance on two-dimensional image description and grouping techniques to perfect the primal sketch before undertaking any higher-level processing. By contrast, we attempt to immediately assign three-dimensional interpretations to intensity edges to initialize processing at the level of intrinsic images, and we maintain the relationship between intensities and interpretations as tightly as possible. In our view, perfecting the intrinsic images should be the objective of early visual processing; edges at the level of the primal sketch are the consequence of achieving a consistent three-dimensional interpretation. We shall discuss consequences of these differing organizations with reference to human vision shortly.

C. Scene Analysis

Scene analysis is concerned with interpreting images in three dimensions, in terms of surfaces, volumes, objects, and their interrelationships. The earliest work, on polyhedral scenes, involved extracting line drawings and then interpreting them using geometric object prototypes [31, 8]. A complementary approach analyzed scenes of simple curved objects by partitioning the image into regions of homogeneous intensity and then interpreting them using relational models of object appearances [5, 3]. Both these early approaches were limited by the unreliability of extracting image descriptions, as discussed in the preceding section, and by the lack of generality of the object prototypes used. It was soon discovered that to extract image descriptions reliably required exploiting knowledge of the scene and image formation process. Accordingly, attempts were made to integrate segmentation and interpretation. The general approach was to assign sets of alternative interpretations to regions of uniform intensity (or color), and then alternately merge regions with compatible interpretations and refine the interpretation sets. The process terminates with a small number of regions with disjoint (and hopefully unique) interpretations. Yakimovsky and Feldman [36] used Bayesian statistics for assigning interpretations and guiding a search for the set of regions and interpretations with the highest joint likelihood. Tenenbaum and Barrow (IGS [33]) used an inference procedure, similar to Waltz's filtering [34], for eliminating inconsistent interpretations. These systems performed creditably upon complex images and have been applied in a variety of scene domains. They are not, however, suitable as models of general-purpose vision because they are applicable only when all objects are known and can be distinguished on the basis of local evidence or region attributes. Unknown objects not only cannot be recognized; they cannot even be described.

What seems needed in a general-purpose vision system are more concise and more general descriptions of the scene, at a lower level than objects [4 and 38]. For example, once the scene has been described at the level of intrinsic surface characteristics, surfaces and volumes can be found and objects can then readily be identified. There is still the need to guide formation of lower level descriptions by the context of higher level ones, but now the gaps between levels are much smaller and easier to bridge.

Huffman [21], Clowes [6], and Waltz [34] demonstrated the possibility of interpreting line drawings of polyhedral scenes without the need for specific object prototypes. Their level of description involved a small set of linear scene features (convex edge, concave edge, shadow edge, crack) and a set of corner features, where such edges meet. These scene features were studied systematically to derive a catalog of corresponding image features and their alternative interpretations. Interpretation of the line drawing involved a combinatorial search for a compatible set of junction labels. Waltz, in particular, identified eleven types of linear feature, and three cases of illumination for the surfaces on each side. The resulting catalog of junction interpretations contained many thousands of entries. To avoid combinatorial explosion in determining the correct interpretations, Waltz used a pseudo-parallel local filtering paradigm that eliminated junction interpretations incompatible with any possible interpretation of a neighboring junction.

While we also create and use a catalog, the whole emphasis of our work is different. We have attempted to catalog the appearances of edges in grey-scale images, for a much wider class of objects, and have described them in a way that results in a much more parsimonious catalog. Instead of interpreting an ideal line drawing, we, in a sense, are attempting simultaneously to derive the drawing and to interpret it, using the interpretation to guide the derivation. In contrast to the junctions in line drawings, many grey-scale image features can be uniquely interpreted using intensity information and physical constraints. We are thus able to avoid combinatorial search and "solve" directly for consistent interpretations of remaining features. Our solution has a definite iconic flavor, whereas Waltz's has largely a symbolic one.

Mackworth's approach to interpreting line drawings [24] is somewhat closer to our point of view. He attempts to interpret edges, rather than junctions, with only two basic interpretations (Connect and Occluding); he models surfaces by representing their plane orientations explicitly; and he tries to solve constraints to find orientations that are consistent with the edge interpretations. The use of explicit surface orientation enables Mackworth to reject certain interpretations with impossible geometry, which are accepted by Waltz. Since he does not, however, make explicit use of distance information, there are still some geometrically impossible interpretations that Mackworth will accept. Moreover, since he does not use photometry, his solutions are necessarily ambiguous: Horn has demonstrated [20] that when photometric information is combined with geometry, the orientations of surfaces forming a trihedral corner may be uniquely determined. The fundamental point to be noted is that intrinsic characteristics provide a concise description of the scene that enables rejection of physically impossible interpretations.

Intermediate levels of representation have played an increasingly important role in recent scene analysis research. Agin and Binford [1] proposed a specific representation of three-dimensional surfaces, as generalized cylinders, and described a system for extracting such representations using a laser rangefinder. Marr and Nishihara [29] have described techniques for inferring a generalized cylinder representation from line drawings, and for matching geometrically to object prototypes in recognition. Cylindrical volume representations are being used in the VISIONS system, under development by Riseman et al. [16]. This system also includes explicit representation of surfaces, which are inferred from a two-dimensional image description using higher-level cues, such as linear perspective and the shape of known objects. Symbolic representations at the level of surfaces and volumes should be easier to derive from intrinsic images than from intensity images, line drawings, or even from noisy rangefinder data.

H. G. Barrow and J. M. Tenenbaum

D. <u>Human</u> <u>Vision</u>

In this paper, we have been concerned with the computational nature of vision tasks, largely independent of implementation in biological or artificial systems. This orientation addresses questions of competence: what information is needed to accomplish a task, is it recoverable from the sensed image, what additional constraints, in the form of assumptions about the world, are needed to effect the recovery?

Psychologists have been asking similar questions from their own viewpoint for many years. For example, there has been a long-standing debate, dating back at least to Helmholtz, concerning how, and under what circumstances, it is possible to independently estimate illumination and reflectance. Recent participants include Land, with his Retinex theory of color perception [23], and Gilchrist, who has identified a number of ways in which intensity edges may be classified (e.g., the 30:1 ratio, intersecting reflectance and illumination edges) [12].

From such work, a number of theories have been proposed to explain human abilities to estimate various scene characteristics. No one, however, has yet proposed a comprehensive model integrating all known abilities. While we have no intention of putting forward our model as a complete explanation of human vision, we think that the recovery of intrinsic characteristics is a plausible role for early stages of visual processing in humans.

Figure 11   A subjective contour

This hypothesis would appear to explain, at least at a superficial level, many well-known psychological phenomena. The constancy phenomena are the obvious examples, but there are others. Consider, for example, the phenomenon of subjective contours, such as appear in Figure 11. Marr suggests [26] that such contours result from grouping place tokens corresponding to line endings in the primal sketch, and further suggests a "least-commitment" clustering algorithm to control the combinatorics of grouping. We suggest, as an alternative explanation, that the abrupt line

endings are locally interpreted three dimensionally as evidence of occlusion, causing discontinuity edges to be established in the distance image. The subjective contours then result from making the distance image consistent with these boundary conditions and assumptions of continuity of surfaces and surface boundaries: they are primarily contours of distance, rather than intensity. The net result is the interpretation of the image as a disk occluding a set of radiating lines on a more distant surface.

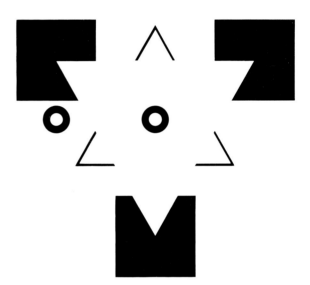

Figure 12   Subjective depth (Coren [7])

There is considerable evidence to support the hypothesis that subjective contours are closely correlated with judgements of apparent depth. Coren [7] reports a very interesting demonstration. In Figure 12, the two circles subtend the same visual angle; however, the apparent elevation of the subjective triangle causes the circle within it to be perceived as smaller, consistent with the hypothesis that it is nearer. Surfaces perceived when viewing Julesz stereograms [22] have edges that are purely subjective. There are no distinguishing cues in the originating intensity images: the edges result solely from the discontinuity in disparity observed in a stereo presentation. Hochberg [17] has investigated the subjective contours produced by shadow cues to depth, seen in figures like Figure 13. Most observers report that Figure 13a is perceived as a single entity in relief, while Figure 13b is not. The figures are essentially equivalent as two-dimensional configurations of lines. The difference between the figures is that in b, the lines are not consistent with the shadows of a single solid entity cast by a directional light source.

We can generalize our argument that subjective contours arise as a consequence of three-dimensional organization to other phenomena of perceptual organization, such as the Gestalt laws. For example, the law of continuity follows directly from assumptions of continuity of surfaces and boundaries, and the law of closure follows from integrity of surfaces.

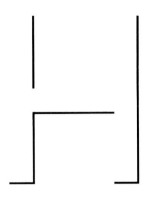

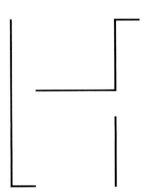

Figure 13   Subjective figures (Hochberg [17])

A system that is attempting to form a consistent interpretation of an image as a three-dimensional scene will, in principle, do better than one that is attempting to describe it as a two-dimensional pattern. The organization of a chaotic collection of image features may become clear when they are considered as projections of three-dimensional features, and the corresponding constraints are brought into play.

Gregory has emphasized the importance of three-dimensional interpretations and has suggested that many illusions result from attempting to form inappropriate three-dimensional interpretations of two-dimensional patterns [13 and 14]. He also suggests that certain other illusions, such as those involving the Ames room, result from applying incorrect assumptions about the nature of the scene. The distress associated with viewing ambiguous figures, such as the well-known "impossible triangle" and "devil's pitchfork," arises because of the impossibility of making local evidence consistent with assumptions of surface continuity and integrity.

Recent experiments by Gilchrist [11] demonstrate that judgements of the primary

intrinsic characteristics are tightly integrated in the human visual system. In one experiment, the apparent position of a surface is manipulated using interposition cues, so that it is perceived as being either in an area of strong illumination or in one of dim illumination. Since the absolute reflected flux from the surface remains constant, the observer perceives a dramatic change in apparent reflectance, virtually from black to white. In a second experiment, the apparent orientation of a surface is changed by means of perspective cues. The apparent reflectance again changes dramatically, depending upon whether the surface is perceived as facing towards or away from the light source.

We do not present our model of the recovery of intrinsic scene characteristics as a comprehensive explanation of these psychological phenomena. We feel, however, that it may provide a useful viewpoint for considering at least some of them.

VIII   CONCLUSION

The key ideas we have attempted to convey in this paper are:

* A robust visual system should be organized around a noncognitive, nonpurposive level of processing that attempts to recover an intrinsic description of the scene.

* The output of this process is a set of registered "intrinsic images" that give values for such characteristics as reflectance, orientation, distance, and incident illumination, for every visible point in the scene.

* The information provided by intrinsic images greatly facilitates many higher-level perceptual operations, ranging from segmentation to object recognition, that have so far proved difficult to implement reliably.

* The recovery of intrinsic scene characteristics is a plausible role for the early stages of human visual processing.

* Investigation of low-level processing should focus on what type of information is sought, and how it might be obtained from the image. For example, the design of edge detectors should be based on the physical meaning of the type of edge sought, rather than on some abstract model of an intensity discontinuity.

We have outlined a possible model of the recovery process, demonstrated its feasibility for a simple domain, and argued that it can be extended in a straightforward way towards real-world scenes. Key ideas in the recovery process are:

* Information about the intrinsic characteristics is confounded in the intensities of the input image. Therefore, recovery depends on exploiting assumptions and constraints from the physical nature of imaging and the world.

* Interactions and ambiguities prohibit independent recovery of the intrinsic

H. G. Barrow and J. M. Tenenbaum

characteristics; the recovery process must determine their values simultaneously in achieving consistency with the constraints.

* Interpretation of boundaries plays a key role in recovery; they provide information about which characteristics are continuous and which discontinuous at each point in the image, and they provide explicit boundary conditions for the solution.

* The nature of the solution, involving a large number of interacting local constraints, suggests implementation of the recovery process by an array of local parallel processes that achieve consistency by a sequence of successive approximations.

Our model for recovering intrinsic characteristics is at a formative stage. Important details still to be finalized include the appropriate intrinsic images, constraints, constraint representations, and the paths of information flow relating them. Nevertheless, the ideas we have put forth in this paper have already clarified many issues for us and suggested many exciting new prospects. They also raise many questions to be answered by future research, the most important of which are "Can it work in the real world?" and "Do people see that way?" To the extent that our model corresponds to the human visual system, valuable insights may be gained through collaboration between computer and vision scientists.

IX   ACKNOWLEDGEMENTS

This work was supported by a grant from the National Science Foundation.

Edward Riseman's persistent exhortations provided the necessary motivation to commit our ideas to paper, and his valuable editorial comments improved their presentation.

Bill Park's artistic hand penned the drawings of intrinsic images.

REFERENCES

1. Agin, G. J. and Binford, T.O. Computer description of curved objects. Proc. 3rd. International Joint Conference on Artificial Intelligence, Stanford University, Stanford, 1973.

2. Allen, D. N. de G. Relaxation Methods in Engineering and Science. McGraw-Hill, New York, 1954.

3. Barrow, H. G., and Popplestone, R.,J. Relational descriptions in picture processing. in Machine Intelligence, Vol. 6, B. Meltzer and D. Michie (Eds.), Edinburgh University Press, Edinburgh, Scotland, 1971, pp 377-396.

4. Barrow, H. G., and Tenenbaum, J. M. Representation and use of knowledge in vision. Tech. Note 108, Artificial Intelligence Center, SRI International, Menlo Park, CA, 1975.

5. Brice, C., and Fennema, C. Scene analysis using regions. Artificial Intelligence, 1, No. 3, 1970, 205-226.

6. Clowes, M. B. On seeing things. Artificial Intelligence, 2, No. 1, 1971, 79-112.

7. Coren, S. Subjective contour and apparent depth. Psychological Review, 79, 1972, 359.

8. Falk, G. Interpretation of imperfect line data as a three-dimensional scene. Artificial Intelligence, 4, No. 2, 1972, 101-144.

9. Fischler, M. A. On the representation of natural scenes, in Computer Vision Systems, A. Hanson and E. Riseman (Eds.), Academic Press, New York, 1978.

10. Garvey, T. D. Perceptual strategies for purposive vision. Tech. Note 117, Artificial Intelligence Center, SRI International, Menlo Park, CA, 1976.

11. Gilchrist, A. L. Perceived lightness depends on perceived spatial arrangement. Science, 195, 1977, 185-187.

12. Gilchrist, A. L. Private communication.

13. Gregory, R. L., Eye and Brain. Weidenfeld and Nicholson, London, 1966.

14. Gregory, R. L. The Intelligent Eye. McGraw-Hill, New York, 1970.

15. Hanson, A., and Riseman, E. Segmentation of natural scenes, in Computer Vision Systems, A. Hanson and E. Riseman (Eds.), Academic Press, New York, 1978.

16. Hanson, A., and Riseman, E. VISIONS: A computer system for interpreting scenes, in Computer Vision Systems, A. Hanson and E. Riseman (Eds.), Academic Press, New York, 1978.

17. Hochberg, J. In the mind's eye, in Contemporary Theory and Research in Visual Perception, R. N. Haber (Ed.), Holt, Rinehart and Winston, New York, 1968.

18. Horn, B. K. P. Determining lightness from an image. Computer Graphics and Image Processing, 3, 1974, 277-299.

19. Horn, B. K. P. Obtaining shape from shading information. in The Psychology of Computer Vision, P. H. Winston (Ed.), McGraw-Hill, New York, 1975.

20. Horn, B. K. P. Understanding image intensities. Artificial Intelligence, 8, No. 2, 1977, 201-231.

21. Huffman, D. A. Impossible objects as nonsense sentences. in Machine Intelligence, Vol. 6, B. Meltzer and D. Michie (Eds.), Edinburgh University Press, Edinburgh, 1971, pp 295-323.

22. Julesz, B. Foundations of Cyclopean Perception. University of Chicago Press, Chicago, 1971.

23. Land, E. H. The Retinex theory of color vision. *Scientific American*, 237, No. 6, Dec. 1977, 108-128.

24. Mackworth, A. K. Interpreting pictures of polyhedral scenes. *Artificial Intelligence*, 4, 1973, 121-138.

25. Macleod, I. D. G. A study in automatic photo-interpretation. Ph. D. thesis, Department of Engineering Physics, Australian National University, Canberra, 1970.

26. Marr, D. Early processing of visual information. AI Memo-340, Artificial Intelligence Lab., MIT, Cambridge, Mass., 1976.

27. Marr, D. Analysis of occluding contour. *Proc. Roy. Soc.* Lond. B, 197, 1977, 441-475.

28. Marr, D., and Poggio, T. Cooperative computation of stereo disparity. *Science*, 194, 1977, 283-287.

29. Marr, D. Representing visual information. in *Computer Vision Systems*, A. Hanson and E. Riseman (Eds.), Academic Press, New York, 1978.

30. Nitzan, D., Brain, A. E., and Duda, R. O. The measurement and use of registered reflectance and range data in scene analysis. *Proc. IEEE*, 65, No. 2, 1977, 206-220.

31. Roberts, L. G. Machine perception of three-dimensional solids. in *Optical and Electro-Optical Information Processing*, J. T. Tippett et al. (Eds.), MIT press, Cambridge, Mass., 1965.

32. Rosenfeld, A., Hummel, R. A., and Zucker, S. W. Scene labelling by relaxation operations", *IEEE Transactions on Systems, Man and Cybernetics*, *SMC-6*, 1976, 420-433.

33. Tenenbaum, J. M., and Barrow, H. G. Experiments in interpretation-guided segmentation. *Artificial Intelligence*, 8, No. 3, 1977, 241-274.

34. Waltz, D. L. Generating semantic descriptions from drawings of scenes with shadows. Tech. Rept. AI-TR-271, Artificial Intelligence Lab., MIT, Cambridge, Mass., Nov. 1972.

35. Woodham, R. J. A cooperative algorithm for determining surface orientation from a single view. *Proc. 5th. International Joint Conference on Artificial Intelligence*, MIT, Cambridge, Mass., 1977.

36. Yakimovsky, Y. Y., and Feldman, J. A semantics-based decision theoretic region analyzer. *Proc. 3rd. International Joint Conference on Artificial Intelligence*, Stanford Univ., Stanford, 1973.

37. Yonas, A. Private communication, Institute of Child Development, University of Minnesota, 1977.

38. Zucker, S., Rosenfeld, A., and Davis, L. General purpose models: Expectations about the unexpected. *Proc. 4th. International Joint Conference on Artificial Intelligence*, Tbilisi, Georgia, USSR, 1975.

H. G. Barrow and J. M. Tenenbaum

THE NECESSITY FOR A THEORY
OF SPECIALIZED VISION

Bruce L. Bullock
Hughes Research Laboratories

Introduction

One motivation for developing computer vision is to provide a practical, application-oriented tool vital to the solution of a wide range of important contemporary problems. Many of the successful scene analysis systems constructed in the past to provide such a tool are frequently criticized for their ad hoc working principles.[1,2,3] Experience has shown that these ad hoc systems have a limited domain of specialized application and a fragile range of operating characteristics and lack well-understood principles that can be easily extended or re-used.

Recently, several proposals have been made, particularly about segmentation, to remedy these limitations, for example Refs. 4,5, and 6. These proposals usually favor one or more of the following: general-purpose vision systems, universal low-level operations, or human-based vision theories. In essence, these suggestions are aimed at developing competent, but re-usable, vision systems by concentrating on two notions: generality at the system level and extensibility at the internal working principle level. These proposals imply that it is natural and desirable to progress, as the field matures, from the existing special-purpose systems to "general-purpose" vision systems. The development of such general-purpose systems must, by definition, address the problem of system re-usability. Further, these proposals imply that progress toward such generality at the system level can be aided by concentrating on the development of extensible working principles. By basing the fundamental building blocks on such principles or methods, rather than on a clumsy set of ad hoc processes, the development never has to be repeated for another application.[2]

This paper examines the goals of generality and extensibility. It will be argued that, although a vision system with generality and extensibility may not have the limitations of ad hoc systems mentioned above, it will actually be sub-optimal in many respects. It will be argued that, for any specific application, a system with a wide range of general performance may not be as desirable as a system that is highly specialized and

optimized. The goal of re-usability could then be achieved, not through generality, but through flexible reconfiguration. The discussion will proceed by examining, in turn, the initial assumption about the desirability of general-purpose vision systems, the merits of several sources of extensible vision principles, and an alternative for the development of specialized application-based vision systems using flexible reconfiguration of both extensible and special-purpose knowledge.

General Versus Specialized Vision Design Goals

Many of the recent discussions about improved methodology for the development of computer vision assume that a move towards systems with a generalized capability is both natural and desirable. Although concern for generality would appear natural in the context of biological vision or abstract vision theory, it is not necessarily a desirable characteristic of a methodology directed towards application-oriented vision systems. This is not surprising since uniform, general mechanisms are almost always less desirable than a special mechanism, which uses domain-specific knowledge. The realization of this has resulted in the gradual transition in artificial intelligence from general-purpose problem solvers to knowledge-specific systems.[3]

A general vision system can be roughly characterized as a system with capabilities as broad as human vision.[7] This usually implies that the range of familiar objects and backgrounds is enormous and that system performance is invariant to large changes in viewing angle, illumination angle, contexts, and obscured areas. Finally, a vital but seldom-mentioned characteristic is the ability of general vision systems to tolerate many rapid context changes. An example of such a context change is the one that occurs in going from an indoor to an outdoor environment.

Current vision systems have not achieved any real generality since they have not even one of the characteristics listed above for complex scenes. Experience has shown that it is very difficult to realize these aspects. This implies that they are technically very complex and are also a potential

This work was partially supported by the U.S. Air Force Office of Scientific Research under Contract F44620-74-C-0054.

source of high computational burden in any useful system. An important practical question is, then, just how much generality is necessary or desirable in the development of functional, application-based computer vision systems? To answer this question, it is instructive to briefly look at the necessary system characteristics in terms of a range of real problems from several application domains. To do this, computer vision tasks will be divided into three categories: matching, cueing, and interpretation. These span the range of image understanding difficulty from simple to complex and provide mechanisms with which many practical problems can be solved. They also correspond to application-based systems that are currently under development.

Matching

Although there are many variations of the basic scene-matching problem, it characteristically deals with a single scene or object about which there is a great deal of a priori knowledge. Typical examples of matching vision are the industrial tasks of assembly or inspection of a single repetitive part or product.[8] Other variations include image comparison and change detection[9,10,11] and image navigation.[12] In all cases, although the scene can be very complex, an exact model of the expected scene shapes, relations, and even expected context variation is available. The primary task is to compare the scene with a model, which can be a procedure, a data structure, or both.[13] The purpose is to first verify the expected object's existence or nonexistence and then to specify its exact position.[13]

Matching, as just described, does not require sophisticated image understanding beyond that variation built into the single-object model representation. It can be mechanized by the basic functional system organization shown in Figure 1. The adequacy and reliability of this basic matching scheme can be increased by a great deal of variation in model organization and feedback paths.

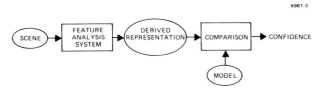

Figure 1. Basic Model Matching System

Cueing

The cueing problem is an extension of matching vision but is considerably more complex. Typically, cueing deals with a prespecified collection of objects or scenes rather than a single object, as in matching. Often, little is known about the expected number or position of the objects. Examples of cueing problems include biological screening tasks, target cueing,[14,15] and product quality control. Although systems built in the past for these purposes have been limited to object class sizes of about 10, even the most advanced applications would probably not require knowledge about more than 1000 objects.

Because the application is specialized, like the matching problem, exact models of all the objects of interest are available. Although the context is not always established, as is usually possible in matching problems, it is often limited to a small collection of expected context classes (e.g., ground terrain objects in a rural area) with limited and predictable changes (as in a change from terrain to sky). The cueing task is certainly more difficult than simple matching vision, but it is still far from a general vision problem. The organization of a basic cueing system is shown in Figure 2.

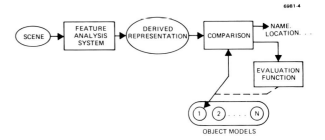

Figure 2. Basic Cueing System

Interpretation

Examples of image interpretation tasks include analysis of reconnaissance imagery, analysis of environmental and resource monitoring imagery, automatic production of maps from imagery, and question/answering tasks (such as consultation and diagnosis, dealing with image data). These interpretation tasks are by far the most sophisticated tasks in the taxonomy. Interpretation systems are similar to the previous cueing systems in that there are multiple objects of interest in possibly unknown positions, quantity, and context. The most important difference is in the detail or actual understanding of an object or scene beyond basic naming or counting. For example, it may actually be necessary to query the system about components of an object or its context. This question-answering capability greatly complicates the representation and analysis of scene information. It often requires using generic models of context information, rather than a small set of fixed, exact models.[16] Again, however, the number of general object and context classes is quite small in a given application domain (e.g., bridges, terrain features) and static, making even this difficult problem orders of magnitude less difficult than general vision.

Comparison

To quantify this discussion, many of the pertinent characteristics of the above systems are estimated in Table 1. This table clearly shows several distinctions between general (human) and application-driven computer vision.

The discussion of the first four distinctions really deals with the limitations of the human implementation of a general-purpose vision system and would not necessarily relate to general-purpose hardware, were it available. These differences are important, however, and will be referred to later in relation to extensible principles based on biological models.

Bruce L. Bullock

Table 1. System Characteristic Comparison

Characteristic	Human	Vision System		
		Interpretation	Cueing	Matching
Object set size	$\gg 10^6$	10^2–10^3	10^2–10^3	1
Object set variance	High	Low	Low	Low
Context set size	$\gg 10^6$	$<10^3$	$<10^3$	1
Understand context	Yes	Yes	No	No
Context variation	High	Low	Low	Low
Frame size, pixels/frame	10^7	10^{10}	10^4	10^4
Frame rate, frames/sec	10	10^{-2}	10^2	10
Maximum data rate, pixels/sec	10^8	10^8	10^6	10^5
Reliability	35–50%	60–80%	60–80%	60–80%

There are two obvious practical distinctions between general (human) vision and specialized vision. These are the need for systems with faster response and greater single frame size in many specialized vision applications. Another important distinction is in long-term reliability. The human vision system cannot maintain high performance on tasks where interesting information occurs only infrequently, the data rates are high and endurance long.[17,18,19] Although human performance starts high, it quickly degrades to a level below even the performance of current crude computer vision systems for some applications. The limitations of human performance for long-endurance tasks means that a special-purpose vision system need not perform perfectly to be useful in these applications.

Among the important distinctions between general-purpose and special-purpose vision systems is the combined effect of small object and context class sizes and low variance within these classes for specialized tasks. These two factors alone justify a strong distinction between general and specialized vision systems and their associated theories and representation mechanisms. A specialized system must only embed enough knowledge to deal with subtle variations within the application object class (e.g., all vehicles). But a general system must have all of this first-order knowledge and also be able to deal with unexpected second-order differences and goals involving the full set of understandable objects. This is because a general vision system spends most of its effort on widely different objects and, unlike specialized vision systems, only seldom has the opportunity to view large quantities of similar objects.

An additional justification for specialization is the lack of dynamic context changes in computer vision. This can be viewed as a lack of unpredictable variance in the context set. A specialized vision system will usually have knowledge about expected contexts (e.g., types of ground terrain). Although the problem of dealing with all possible terrain types, as in cartography, is certainly not trivial, it is at least bounded. The expected changes in the context of a specialized task are also usually quite predictable, as in continuous, gradual variations in range or resolution. General vision, on the other hand, must have all this specialized knowledge plus mechanisms for efficiently dealing with rapid context switches, as in going from an outdoor to an indoor environment. Because of environmental constraints, such radical context switches and wide class variations are very limited and are certainly not the dominant problem in specialized vision applications.

Another aspect of vision-system dynamics is the frequency of overall goal changing. A general (human) vision system may be required to drastically change primary goals quite frequently. A human, for example, may be required to drive to work, perform a work task, select food, and go shopping, all in less than a day. On the other hand, once a specialized vision system is developed for an application, it will probably be dedicated to the problem for a long period, or may never be asked to deal with another problem domain. Such singular dedication diminishes the utility of achieving both competency and re-usability through a single uniform (and difficult to accomplish) mechanism: general purposeness. Instead, competency can be achieved through special-purpose optimization, and the problem of re-usability can be treated separately as a combination of extensible working principles and flexible system reconfiguration mechanisms. Such a design approach overcomes the limitations of ad hoc systems and is easier to achieve.

The preceding informal discussion illustrated some of the major distinctions between "general" and "specialized" vision. The characteristics of specialized vision can be summarized as follows:

- Goal-directed
- Small object set size
- Small object set variance
- Small context set size

- Predictable context changes

- Fast response or large frame size

- Uniform long-term reliability

- Dedicated special-purpose application.

Application-driven systems that can be characterized in these terms will be called specialized vision systems. In comparison to the current state of the art, the "desired" systems with these characteristics are still very advanced, but the important fact is that the application requirements can be met by a system with capabilities far less than general.

Extensibility in General Purpose Versus Special Purpose Systems

The proposals described earlier were directed towards developing competent, re-usable vision systems by concentrating on the goals of generality and extensibility. Arguments have been presented above to question the generality goal, at least for application-based development. Extensibility, on the other hand, is a goal that seems consistent with any proposal to overcome the limitations of ad hoc systems. It is important, however, to note the effect that a shift from a general to a specialized orientation would have on the utility of various approaches toward extensibility. Currently there are three potential sources of extensible vision system working principles. These follow from biological analogs,[4] physical theory,[20] and task/prototype free models.[4,5]

Biologically Based Computer Vision Principles

Much of the earlier work in scene analysis and pattern recognition was inspired by biological and neurophysiological concepts. Awareness of important biologically motivated features (including the detection of edges, lines, and junctions) had a strong impact on early developments in computer vision.[21] Studies of the computational basis limitations and parameters in human visual perception have also provided valuable insight into the scope of the general problem.[22,23] Because biological vision systems are the only general scene analyzers known, it has seemed natural to attempt a transfer of such biological design clues to computer vision systems.

The biological approach towards extensibility currently receiving the most attention is called the "primal sketch" and deals with low-level vision.[4] It involves using domain-independent early processing to develop a symbolic image rich enough to enable all further processing to be derived from the sketch without having to undo past computations. This idea is based on the "principle of least commitment," which says that one should avoid commitments to decisions at low levels that may turn out to be incorrect.[24] The origin of this idea is based on the widespread belief among psychologists that the early stages of processing do not depend on one's knowledge or expectations about the situation.[25]

It is hard to dispute many of the arguments for applying the principle of least commitment to domain-independent low-level processing. Low-level vision certainly is in need of a great deal of development to deal with the difficulties of outdoor scenes.[26] It would also be desirable to be able to derive enough low-level information about a scene in one pass, using operations that are as simple as possible, so that no higher-level intervention or backtracking would be necessary. Finally, it is also true that ignoring these low-level issues while developing elaborate high-level mechanisms will not solve the problems at the bottom levels.[7]

On the other hand, several objections have been raised against the use of primal sketch.[27,28] The objections raised here are to the commitment to a specific primal sketch and to the claim that it is a "universal" and "complete" vocabulary or set of operations.[4]

Although humans probably can do almost any vision task with primal sketch operations, such operations may not allow the visual system to accomplish the task optimally. The search for biological vision vocabulary and theory may be the job of the physiologist, but in computer vision, driven by specialized vision tasks, such an orientation ignores the benefits available from using a specialized knowledge base. The currently defined primal sketch is only one implementation of the principle of least commitment. It is not necessarily true that it should be hard-wired for this vocabulary simply because it is based on a "theory" or because of a feeling that (for general-purpose vision) representations based on human visual clues are most likely to succeed.[4]

When efficiency and reliability are important, as in a methodology for specialized vision, it would seem more appropriate to apply the principle of least commitment based on theory or methods available from the specific application domain.

A simple example of such specialized low-level feature extraction is in the analysis of forward-looking infrared (FLIR) imagery. In such imagery, an important cue is the location of hotspots. These usually appear as isolated bright areas against a much lower contrast background. Certainly these areas could be extracted by running primal sketch bar masks over the scene to detect edges, but the problem would remain of aggregating the bar edge points into connected areas. In reality, for many applications, trivial schemes have been developed that rely on thresholding. Computationally, the savings over a complete primal sketch can be substantial, and the data can be of equal or better quality.

Additional examples of specialized domains that are more complex are presented briefly in the next section. Because these examples are based on physical phenomena, rather than analogy to a biological model, they are truly extensible. In a computer vision system designed to incorporate specialized domain features, system re-usability is obtained by allowing the low-level system to be easily re-specialized, not by claiming universality (as with the primal sketch). A method for achieving such re-specialization, using flexible system reconfiguration at a vision primitive microcode level, is described later.

The primal sketch is one example of a scheme with biological origins that is not as appropriate for specialized vision as it is for general purpose vision. It is not the only one, however. Another example is the increasingly popular group of "glancing" operators.[29] Although glancing is supposedly used by humans in a pre-attentive phase, such mechanisms may be inappropriate in some specialized tasks. Its applicability is a matter of precision. Some tasks (some types of cueing) might need to take a quick, cheap glance to determine the mode and location of more complex analysis. The use of such economy may be inappropriate in other tasks (some types of interpretation), however, and may actually cause the system to miss an object less apparent to the glance, but perhaps very important.

Although it would be naive not to consider biological clues,[30,22,21] the examples described briefly above show that it is dangerous to assume that the general-purpose biological origin of a method is enough to guarantee its universal applicability in specialized vision tasks. Similar caution was voiced much earlier in the pattern recognition era by Harmon.[31]

Extensible Principles from Physical Theory

The second type of extensible computer vision principles receiving current attention are based on actual physical theory. Increased interest in such principles is based on the realization that the physical laws of how images are formed must be understood.[32] Surprisingly, the current state of optical and photogrammetric knowledge has often been insufficient. A few significant contributions have been made recently[33,34] are now under development.[20] Basing extensible computer vision principles on physical theory is the most rational approach in the long run. Depending solely on such technology, however, can lead to two problems. First, it will probably require many years before an adequate theory is sufficiently developed for visual wavelengths.[6] Second, even after such a theory is developed, there are many important non-visual sensors (e.g., FLIR, synthetic-aperture radar (SAR), x-ray) that will require nontrivial extensions or new theory.

In some cases, such as SAR and x-ray, substantial theory already exists (for an informal introduction see Ref. 35) to explain how images are formed. In SAR imagery, for example, there are five well known "cues," actually based on physical theory. These are forward scatter, glint, layover, multipath, and scintillation. Forward scatter is the lack of a return due to energy being reflected away from the radar; it appears as "black" image regions. Forward scattering can be caused by large terrain features and smooth surfaces such as concrete or water. Because forward scatter is so much darker than the surroundings, it can be isolated by simple schemes similar to the FLIR hotspot case mentioned earlier. Glint is caused by strong returns from reflections from one or more flat surfaces and is characteristic of man-made objects. It appears as very bright spots or areas and is often highly directional. Again, specialized feature extraction is relatively easy since these are very bright spots. Layover (or elevation displacement) is the apparent displacement in the image

(of an elevated object) caused by radar ranging. Layover is distinguished by very bright, highly extended lines. These features are easily detected by schemes tailored to straight, high-contrast, connected lines. Multipath is caused by more than one propagation path and appears as multiple images. These images can be detected by a straight parallel line detector. Finally, scintillation is caused by spatial variation in return strength due to complex scatters causing interference. Scintillation produces a texturing that is often characteristic of "cultural" areas, but usually provides little basic and quantifiable information.

From this discussion, it can be seen that ideal extensible computer vision principles can be based on physical theory. The theory provides both an indication of what is important in a scene and information about how to specifically interpret what is found. Unfortunately, the state of the art is very crude and has proven slow to develop. Therefore, practical near term computer vision schemes must compromise and combine existing physical theory with other extensible feature-organizing principles. One such scheme is outlined next.

Extensible Principles Based on Task or Prototype Free Models

The third type of extensible computer vision principle currently receiving attention are called task, prototype, or knowledge-free models.[4,5] These models are a blend of common sense, physical theory when available, and frame-like[1,32] data structures. Although there are many forms of task-free models, the specific one developed here is the notion of a general-purpose model (GPM).[5] These models suggest reasonable descriptions for a scene in terms of features, regions, or groups of these, in the absence of specific context. They include models for edges, lines, angles, and depth cues. Such a scheme has the advantages of not being restricted to a fixed or so-called universal set of primitives at the feature level, as with the primal sketch, and of no strict dependence on physical theory.

GPMs have been cleverly described as models in which the semantics become "fossilized" and turned into syntax.[5] This view of fossilization makes it easier to understand the limits of the primal sketch. It is simply a model in which the fossilization halted in a state adapted to the teleological constraints of human behavior. It would have, therefore, been more appropriate to attack the ad hoc nature of previous low-level schemes (fossilized in another mode) not with a fixed set of primal sketch primitives, but with a systematic set of microcode primitives for low-level operators, as mentioned earlier. Such low-level microcode vocabularies are actually GPMs. Such a path of development would resemble the use of a microcode in providing a systematic alternative to ad hoc, hard-wired control in contemporary computers.[36] A low-level processor organized in this way could then "emulate" the low-level operations most appropriate to a specific application domain.

Recent work on the problem of outdoor motion vision for man-made objects provides an example of a higher level GPM using specialized features. Although there have been models for viewing angle changes, there has been little work dealing with range changes. This dynamic model builds on the idea of a rich isolated feature model, consisting of texture prominence features and strong isolated line segments for capturing information about the specialized domain of man-made objects (e.g., buildings, roads, vehicles) in outdoor scenes.[12] The concept of a "footprint" was proposed as a GPM to capture important information about objects in such scenes at different distances.[37] Several footprints at different distances can then be linked to represent the effect of continuous range motion changes on a given object. An example of linked footprints to represent range changes is shown in Figure 3. Such a linked data structure can be elaborated by procedural attachment to form a frame-like representation that captures specific meta-knowledge about the expected changes between footprints. An example of this elaboration is shown in Figure 4. The use of this specialized linked footprint structure for goal-directed analysis is shown in Figure 5. This example shows how a given goal can be used to retrieve the several relevant linked footprint structures needed for a given analysis goal. These stored footprints are then merged to form a composite footprint with the necessary information for various ranges. This composite model can then be used to establish a match at a distant range, and this match used to

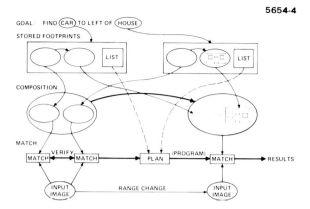

Figure 5. Goal driven analysis and plan composition

force a composition of the associated meta-information to form a plan for finding the goal objects at a closer range. A set of sequential range footprints for a specific object is shown in Figure 6. This shows the texture prominences as boxes and predominant lines are darkened. The actual footprints at these four ranges would represent the type and orientation of the texture and line features by graphs, as shown in Figure 4. These could be used as special-purpose models to establish a match with the actual object over a very wide span of range.

Although the notion of GPMs appear attractive for the development of extensible fundamental principles for specialized computer vision, there is a complaint concerning their organization. Because of the previous concentration on general-purpose (rather than special-purpose) systems, the system organizations using GPMs (as also for FRAMES[1] and in VISIONS[16] imply the use of large numbers of GPMs to cover a wide range of "unexpected" situations. In a reorientation to special-purpose computer vision, the indiscriminate use of such a range would ignore both a priori knowledge about the application domain and further restriction due to the sole dedication to that domain.

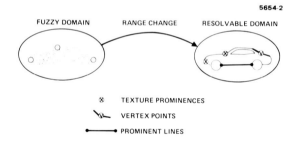

Figure 3. Range change (linked footprints)

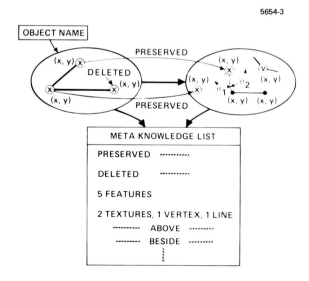

Figure 4. Data structure

Figure 6. Range change footprints

Re-Usability through System Reconfiguration

There are two ways to construct a competent, re-usable, application-oriented computer vision system. One is in terms of a truly general purpose system that is capable of being re-used for many applications simply because of the breadth of its capabilities. A second, more practical, approach involves concentrating on specialized systems using GPMs that blend both physical theory and special-purpose knowledge. Although such a system would be competent, it would not necessarily be re-usable. A mechanism will be outlined here for achieving re-usability in such a specialized system by allowing flexible reconfiguration controlled by the GPM of the current analysis goal. The motivation for such a mechanism is based heavily on the idea of a knowledge-based system.[38,39,40]

Knowledge-based systems are application-based systems that utilize large stores of domain-specific knowledge as a basis for high performance. The domain-specific knowledge is built through a process of knowledge acquisition. The system achieves re-usability by also allowing its organization to be restructured by the knowledge base.[39] Extensibility is achieved by adding more information to the knowledge base. In the case of specialized scene analysis, this information is in the form of GPMs.

The knowledge-acquisition process for a specialized scene-analysis task involves several steps. First, a collection of feature-analysis operators are constructed. Because these are based on GPMs, there is no restriction on the use of physical or special-purpose analysis principles. Simple operators have been constructed interactively in a similar manner in MSYS.[41] The second part of the knowledge-acquisition process involves attacking feature interpretation rules to the operators.

These two sets of basic feature rules can now be used to form a specialized feature-extraction system, as shown in Figure 7. In present analysis schemes, there is very little flexibility in the construction of such feature-extraction processors beyond the tuning of a collection of "canned" procedures.

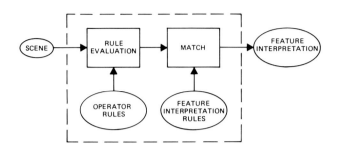

Figure 7. Specialized feature extraction system

The feature-extraction system, once constructed, can be used to bootstrap to the next higher level model, representing spatial information. This is done by passing a prototype scene through the specialized feature extractor to produce a feature model for the given scene. A set of interpretation rules can then be formed for the spatial relations. The complete specialized matching system is shown in Figure 8.

The capabilities of the specialized, knowledge-based scene-analysis system just described obviously are very crude. Many of the details, such as rule format and integration of knowledge through meta-rules,[39] have been ignored here. But this simple description is felt to show that a specialized vision system capable at least of the matching task mentioned earlier could be built in this manner. Further, such a system incorporating specialized competent behavior that can be re-used overcomes many of the limitations mentioned earlier for ad hoc vision systems.

The development of such a specialized vision system is now underway. It is hoped that once the problems at the level of specialized matching are met, that the system can be re-used as a basic building block to build more complex cueing and interpretation systems, organized as shown earlier.

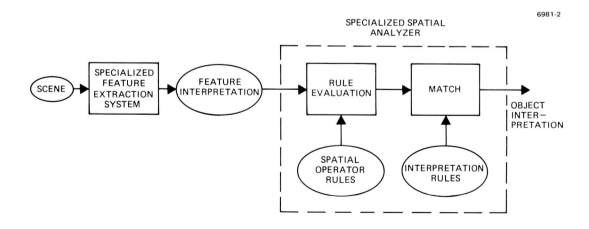

Figure 8. Complete specialized system

Conclusion

There are two paths to the construction of a competent, re-usable vision system. The system can be general purpose enough to deal with all tasks or, more practically, it can be specialized with optimal characteristics that can be easily reconfigured. It was argued that, for application-based computer vision, the specialized system is probably more desirable. It was shown that a specialized system can be made extensible through the use of GPMs and re-usable through the use of knowledge-based reconfiguration. The resulting system, with these characteristics, suffers few of the limitations of ad hoc vision systems and is more practical to construct than a truly general-purpose system.

References

1. M. Minsky, "A Framework for Representing Knowledge," in The Psychology of Computer Vision, P. Winston, Ed. (McGraw-Hill, 1975).

2. D. Marr, "Artificial Intelligence — A Personal View," Artificial Intelligence, September 1977.

3. P. Winston, The Psychology of Computer Vision (McGraw-Hill, 1975).

4. D. Marr, "Analyzing Natural Images," A.I. Memo 334, A.I. Lab., M.I.T., June 1975.

5. S. Zucker, A. Rosenfeld, and L. Davis, "General-Purpose Models: Expectations About the Unexpected," ACM-SIGART Newsletter, No. 54, Oct. 1975. Also TR-347, Computer Science Center, U. of Maryland, June 1975.

6. P. Winston, "Proposal to the ARPA," A.I. Memo 366, A.I. Lab., M.I.T., May 1976.

7. R. Nevatia, paper appearing in this book.

8. T. Binford, et al., "Exploratory Study of Computer Integrated Assembly Systems," AIM-285, A.I. Lab., Stanford University, August 1976.

9. K. Price and R. Reddy, "Symbolic Image Registration and Change Detection," Proc. IJCAI (1977).

10. T. Truit, "A Change Detection and Classification System for Side-Look Radar Images," Proc. NAECON Record (1976).

11. R. Lillestrand, "Techniques of Change Detection," IEEE Trans. Computers C-21, No. 7, July 1972.

12. B. Bullock, "Finding Structure in Outdoor Scenes," Pattern Recognition and Artificial Intelligence (Academic Press, 1976).

13. S. Dudani, et al., "Model-Based Scene Matching," Research Report 509, Hughes Research Laboratories, July 1977.

14. G. Klein, "Locating Man-Made Objects in Low-Resolution Outdoor

14. G. Klein, "Locating Man-Made Objects in Low-Resolution Outdoor Scenes," Proc. Int. Optical Computing Conf., San Diego, Aug. 1977.

15. M. Geokezas, "A Real-Time Imagery Screener," Proc. EIA Symp. on Automatic Imagery Pattern Recognition, Washington, D.C. (1975).

16. T. Williams et al., "Model Building in the Visions System," Proc. International Joint Conf. on Artificial Intelligence, Aug. 1977.

17. Shelton Mac Leod, Photointerpretation Performance Studies, RADC-TDR-64-326, September 1964.

18. I.L. Goldstein, W.A. Johnston, and W.C. Howell, "Complex Vigilance: Relevant and Irrelevant Signals," Journal of Applied Psychology 53 (1), 45-48 (1969).

19. C.H. Harris, "The Nature of Industrial Inspection," Human Factors 11 (2) 139-148 (1969).

20. B. Horn, "Understanding Image Intensities," Artificial Intelligence 8, No. 2, April 1977.

21. H. Barlow, R. Narasimhan, and A. Rosenfeld, "Visual Pattern Analysis in Machines and Animals," Science 177 No. 4049, Aug. 18, 1972.

22. T. Binford and A.J. Thomas, "Information Processing Analysis of Visual Perception: A Review," AIM-227, A.I. Lab., Stanford, 1974.

23. B. Horn, P. Winston, and J. Arkcorn, "Review of Human Vision Facts," Vision Flash 40, M.I.T., A.I. Lab., March 1973.

24. D. Marr, "Early Process of Visual Information," A.I. Memo, MIT A.I. Lab., Dec. 1975. Also, Proc. Ray. Soc. B 275, 483-524, Oct. 1976.

25. U. Neisser, Cognitive Psychology (Appelton-Century-Croft, 1967).

26. B. Bullock, "Real World Scene Analysis in Perspective," Proc. ACM 75, Minneapolis (1975).

27. R. Ehrich, "Detection of Global Linear Features in Remote Sensing Data," Tech. Report, U. of Mass (1976).

28. A. Hanson et al., "A Progress Report on Visions," COINS TR-76-9, U. Of Mass., July 1976.

29. M. Kelly, "Edge Detection Using Planning," Machine Intelligence VI (Edinburgh University Press, 1971).

30. A.J. Thomas, "Discussions: Puccetti on Machine Pattern Recognition," British Journal of Philosophy of Science 26, 227-239 (1975).

31. L. Harmon, "Natural and Artificial Synopses," in Self-Organizing Systems (Spartan Books, 1962).

Bruce L. Bullock

32. P. Winston, <u>Artificial Intelligence</u> (Addison-Wesley, 1977).

33. T. Binford and A. Herskovits, On Boundary Detection, MIT Project MAC, A.I. Memo 183, 1970.

34. B. Horn, "Obtaining Shape from Shading Information," in <u>The Psychology of Computer Vision</u>, P. Winston, Ed. (McGraw-Hill, 1975).

35. Synthetic Aperture Radar, <u>Scientific American</u>, October 1977.

36. A. Agrawala and T. Rauscher, "Microprogramming: Perspective and Status," IEEE Trans. on Computers <u>C-23</u>, No. 8, August 1974.

37. B. Bullock, "Footprints: A Representation for Restricted Motion in Outdoor Scenes," Third International Joint Conf. on Pattern Recognition, San Diego, Nov. 1976.

38. E. Shortliffe, "MYCIN: <u>A Computer-Based Medical Consultant</u> (American Elsevier, 1976).

39. R. Davis, "Applications of Meta Level Knowledge to the Construction, Maintenance, and Use of Large Knowledge Bases," AIM-283, A.I. Lab., Stanford, July 1976.

40. D. Lenat, "BEINGS: Knowledge as Interacting Experts," Proc. 4th International Joint Conference on Artificial Intelligence (1975).

41. J. Tenenbaum, et al. "MSYS," Tech. Note 187, A.I. Center, SRI International, 1976.

SYSTEM ENGINEERING TECHNIQUES FOR ARTIFICIAL INTELLIGENCE SYSTEMS

Lee D. Erman and Victor R. Lesser[1]

Department of Computer Science[2]
Carnegie-Mellon University, Pittsburgh, Pa. 15213

ABSTRACT

It is impossible to develop a large knowledge-based artificial intelligence system successfully without careful attention to issues of system engineering. A set of principles is presented for organizing the design and implementation of such a system. Problems of maintainability and configuration control, human engineering, performance analysis, and efficiency must be faced. Tools used to solve these problems are described, along with examples of their use in the Hearsay-II speech understanding system.

INTRODUCTION

In the last several years, there has been a trend in Artificial Intelligence (AI) research to develop high-performance systems specialized for particular problem domains (e.g., medical diagnosis, chemical analysis, image understanding, and speech understanding). In order to attain the high performance desired, these systems need to use a large amount of problem-specific knowledge and, often, large numbers of heuristics. These systems are commonly called "knowledge-based" systems, which differentiates them from the earlier AI systems that used a small number of general heuristics and little problem-oriented knowledge.

Several of the characteristics common to high-performance knowledge-based systems have significant implications for their development:

- The systems are large, because of the large amount of knowledge; they are often structurally complex, because of the diversity of their knowledge and the complexity of the heuristics required for applying this knowledge.

- The development of such systems is marked by much experimentation and redesign. This occurs because the problem is not well enough understood to enable the knowledge needed or the methods of its application to be pre-specified. In addition, because the knowledge and heuristics interact in a complex way, models cannot be built to predict the system's performance -- instead, the system itself must be run.

- The systems are computationally expensive (in time and/or space). Part of the expense is inherent in the problem domain and in the demands of high-performance. The expense is increased because the

knowledge is imperfect and the strategies for applying it are not optimal. Much of the cost often manifests itself as search for a problem solution within a large space.

- Many researchers may be needed to develop such a system and they may have diverse expertise. The system must provide a structure for coordinating their individual efforts.

Thesis:
We believe that it is impossible to develop a high-performance, knowledge-based system successfully without careful attention to system engineering considerations derived from the characteristics listed above. These considerations dictate the tools needed for the system. Many of these tools are missing in even the most sophisticated general-purpose computing environments and must be built. Many of the tools that already exist must be modified to make them suitable for the special demands of these systems. Thus, there must be a flexibility and a willingness to experiment with all levels of the computing facility -- hardware, firmware, operating system, programming system, terminal system, etc.

In expanding this thesis, which is based primarily on our experience in a long-term effort in building speech understanding systems, we will address the following four problems that we have found to be crucial[3]:

The Maintainability and Configurability Problem:
The system is constantly evolving in an asynchronous manner, with various components in different states of development. No component is ever "finally" stabilized, but is subject to further modification and reimplementation. In the face of this flux, the system must be usable by each researcher when he wants it, independent of the ongoing modifications being made by others to components not directly of interest to him. Modification of a component should require minimal if any modifications to other components.

While developing one component of the system, it is often desirable to be able to experiment with that component in relative isolation, i.e., with just enough of the other components present to provide the necessary context. Thus, it should be easy to configure a subsystem consisting of that necessary subset of components.

---

1 V. R. Lesser's current address: Department of Computer and Information Science, University of Mass., Amherst, Mass. 01003.

2 This work was supported at Carnegie-Mellon University by the Defense Advanced Research Projects Agency (F44620-73-C-0074) and is monitored by the Air Force Office of Scientific Research.

3 These problems are faced in the design and implementation of any large programming system. Research in software engineering particularly relevant to the techniques discussed in this paper include Parnas [72] on modular decomposition; Dijkstra [68], Liskov [72], and Habermann et al [76] on hierarchical structuring; Liskov and Zilles [74], Flon [75], Guttag [76], and Wulf et al [76] on abstract data types; and Habermann [78] and Cooprider [78] on configuration management techniques.

In addition, the software system should allow the user to configure a system with the most up-to-date tested versions of components produced by the other researchers, as long as they are consistent with the version of his component that he would like to test. Thus, the system should automatically check that the configuration being assembled is constructed from compatible versions of the various components.

The Human Engineering Problem:

Unless the system is relatively easy to use, it will be a confusing morass for the researcher. When we speak of "the" researcher experimenting with and modifying the system, we really mean many researchers with diverse interests and often significantly different levels of expertise with computers and programming. Thus the system design must be sensitive to these varying interests and skills. For example, a researcher will in general not be intimate with more than some fraction of the system. Thus, the system must allow him to interact effectively without having a detailed knowledge of the components he has not considered.

The Performance Analysis Problem:

The major part of the experimentation is the refinement and augmentation of the various pieces of knowledge and their interactions. To accomplish this, the researcher must be able to determine the effects of each piece of knowledge. The complex interactions between the large amounts of knowledge makes this analysis difficult. Thus, the system must provide tools which make it easier for the researcher to isolate and trace the effects of particular knowledge.

The Efficiency Problem:

The overall computational efficiency is important for producing a usable performance system, as well as for experimenting with the system during its development. In a large and changing system, it is difficult and inappropriate to optimize across the whole system. Rather, an evolutionary approach is called for, in which those aspects of the system that become bottlenecks are selectively optimized.

Efficiency is a relative issue, based on the ways that the system is being stressed at each stage of development. The critical bottlenecks change as use of the system evolves, as the system is changed in response to the changing use, and as bottlenecks are removed through optimization. In order to support selective optimization, the system must make it convenient to measure costs and re-implement the components responsible for bottlenecks at the appropriate level (e.g., in micro-code, in machine language, within the operating system, at some level within the programming language, or at some level within the implementation of the system). Such modifications should require minimal modifications to other system components.

The next section presents a brief overview of the Hearsay-II speech understanding system, to provide a context for what follows. Although Hearsay-II is used as the motivating example for this paper, we believe that the problems and solutions presented are relevant to other AI system efforts, and, in fact, to many other large system efforts as well. Following the Hearsay-II overview is a description of several principles for organizing the system implementation. Finally, there is a listing of many of the key tools used in the Hearsay-II system.

OVERVIEW OF HEARSAY-II

In 1971-72, the Hearsay-I speech understanding system was developed at Carnegie-Mellon University -- the first of a series of such systems. Hearsay-I [Reddy et al 73 and Erman 74] was a successful attempt to solve the problem of machine understanding of speech in specialized task domains. In this early system, the size of the vocabulary (fewer than 100 words) and complexity of the grammar were very limited. Experiences with Hearsay-I led to the more generalized Hearsay-II architecture [Lesser et al 75, and Erman and Lesser 75] in order to handle more difficult problems (e.g., larger vocabularies and less-constrained grammars). The Hearsay-II system has been successful: it came close to the original ARPA performance goals set out in 1971 to be met by the end of 1976 [Newell et al 73]. Its performance in September, 1976, was 90% correct semantic interpretation of sentences over a 1011-word vocabulary and constrained syntax [CMU 77].

The Hearsay-II Architecture[4]

At the beginning of the Hearsay-II effort in 1973, based on our experiences with Hearsay-I, we expected to need types of knowledge and interaction patterns whose details could not be anticipated. (As mentioned above, this uncertainty is characteristic of the development of knowledge-based systems.) Instead of designing a specific speech understanding system, we considered Hearsay-II as a model for a class of systems and a framework within which specific configurations of that general model could be constructed and studied. One can think of Hearsay-II as a high-level system for programming speech understanding systems of a certain type -- i.e., those that conform to the Hearsay-II model.

In the Hearsay-II model of knowledged-based systems, each of the diverse types of knowledge needed to solve a problem is encapsulated in a knowledge source (KS). For speech understanding, typical KSs incorporate information about syntax, semantics, acoustic-phonetics, prosodics, syllabification, coarticulation, etc. The current Hearsay-II system configuration has about ten KS modules. KSs are kept separate, anonymous, and as independent as possible, in order to make the creation, modification, and testing of KS modules as easy as possible.

The KSs interact to solve the problem (i.e., interpret a spoken utterance) by communicating via a shared global data-base called the blackboard. The blackboard is partitioned into distinct information levels (e.g., "phrase", "word", "syllable", and "phone"); each level holds a different representation of the problem space. The current state of problem solution is represented in terms of hypotheses on the blackboard. An hypothesis is an interpretation of a portion of the spoken utterance at a particular level (e.g., an hypothesis might be that the word 'today' occurred from millisecond 100 to millisecond 600 in the utterance). All hypotheses, no matter what their level, have a uniform attribute-value structure. For example, each hypothesis has attributes containing its level, begin- and end-time within the utterance, and plausibility ratings. Hypotheses are connected through a directed graph structure, usually across levels.

---

4 Little attempt is made here to motivate this architecture from an AI viewpoint. For more information on Hearsay-II, see Lesser et al [75], Erman and Lesser [75], and Lesser and Erman [77].

Lee D. Erman and Victor R. Lesser

Each knowledge source is activated in an asynchronous manner, based on the occurrence on the blackboard of patterns of hypotheses specific to its interests. Once activated, a KS may examine the blackboard, typically in the vicinity of the hypotheses that activated it. Based on its knowledge, the KS may then modify those hypotheses or other hypotheses, or create new hypotheses. Such actions establish new patterns on the blackboard; these potentially cause other KSs to be activated. This mechanism for KS activation implements a data-directed form of the hypothesize-and-test paradigm.

The Hearsay-II Implementation

Based on the model just described, a high-level programming system was constructed to provide an environment for programming KSs, configuring groups of them into systems, and executing them. All interactions of KSs are via the blackboard -- triggering on patterns, accessing hypotheses, and making modifications. Because the blackboard has a uniform structure, KS interactions are also uniform. Thus, one set of facilities can serve all KSs. Facilities are provided for:

- defining the levels on the blackboard,
- configuring groups of KSs into runnable systems,
- accessing and modifying hypotheses on the blackboard,
- activating and scheduling KSs.

These facilities, along with other utilities to be described below, are called the Hearsay-II 'kernel'. The kernel is the high-level environment for creating and testing KSs and configurations of them.

Hearsay-II is implemented in the SAIL programming system [Reiser 76], an Algol60 dialect which has a sophisticated compile-time macro facility and a large number of data structures (including lists and sets) and control modes which are implemented fairly efficiently. The Hearsay-II kernel provides a high-level environment to KSs at compile-time by extending SAIL's data types and syntax through declarations of procedure calls, global variables, and complex macros. This extended SAIL provides an explicit structure for the specification of a KS and its interaction with other KSs (through the blackboard). The high-level environment also provides mechanisms that enable KSs to specify to the kernel (usually in non-procedural ways) a variety of information which the kernel uses when configuring a system, scheduling KS activity, and controlling user interaction.

The knowledge in a KS is represented in SAIL data structures and code, in whatever form the KS developer finds appropriate. The kernel environment provides the facilities for structuring the interface between this knowledge and the other KSs, via the blackboard. For example, the syntax KS contains a grammar for the specialized task language that is to be recognized; this grammar is in a compact, network form. The KS also contains procedures for searching this network, for example, to parse a sequence of words. The kernel provides facilities (1) for triggering this KS whenever new word hypotheses appear on the blackboard, (2) for the KS to read those word hypotheses (in order to find the sequence of words to be parsed), and (3) for the KS to create new hypotheses on the blackboard, indicating the structure of the parse.

There are two aspects of KS specification in the Hearsay model which appear to drive an implementation in opposite directions -- one for _diversity_ and the other for _uniformity_:

- Because the KSs are diverse, the kinds of data and control structures that are natural and efficient for their implementation are also diverse. No single pair of structures (e.g., lists as data structures and a production system as a control structure) is optimal. Thus, this first aspect pushes the implementation in the direction of diversity (i.e., to provide a diverse set of KS-specific data and control structures).

- Because the KSs are to cooperate, they must interface with the rest of the system. Given that one needs to be able to add new KSs easily and construct a set of utilities applicable to all KSs, it is desirable to have this interface be uniform. In addition, if the interface declarations are designed properly, it should be possible to make extensive modifications to the implementation of these facilities without having to modify the KSs. Thus, this second aspect pushes the implementation in the direction of a uniform set of data and control structures.

By having a uniform high-level framework for KS interaction while still permitting KS developers to code the knowledge in whatever form is found to be most convenient, an appropriate balance has been struck between diversity and uniformity.

Development of Hearsay-II

The active development of Hearsay-II extended for three years. About twenty KS modules were developed during that time, each a one- or two-person effort lasting from two months to three years. The modules range from about 10 to 200 pages of source-code (with 60 pages typical); additionally, each KS has up to about 100K bytes of information in its local data base.

The kernel is about 300 pages of code. About one-third of that is made up of the declarations and macros that create the extended environment for KSs. The remainder is made up of the code for implementing the architecture -- primarily activation and scheduling of KSs, maintenance of the blackboard, and a variety of other standard utilities (to be described below). During the three years of active development, an average of about two full-time research programmers were responsible for the implementation, modification, and maintenance of the kernel. Included during this period were a half dozen major reimplementations and scores of minor ones; these changes usually were specializations or selective optimizations, designed as experience with the system led to a better understanding of the usage of the various constructs.

Implementation of the first version of the kernel began in the autumn of 1973, and was completed by two people in four months. The first major KS configuration, though incomplete, was running in early 1975. The first complete configuration, called "C1", was running in January, 1976. This configuration had very poor performance -- less than 10% sentence accuracy over a 250-word vocabulary. Experience with this configuration led to a substantially different KS configuration, "C2", that performed much better (90% accuracy over a 1011-word vocabulary), coming very close, in September, 1976, to the original goals of the project.

ORGANIZING PRINCIPLES

Four design principles were used in organizing the Hearsay-II kernel and surrounding facilities:

- The design should start with a general framework which is then tailored as needed.

Two of the principles are derived from the observation that a system is naturally implemented as a series of levels, which form a loose hierarchy:

- In order to implement a complex system, all the supporting levels (hardware through programming language) must be subject to change.
- The application to be implemented on top of the programming system level should be implemented as a series of levels, rather than as a single level.

The fourth principle deals directly with the problem of experimentation:

- Facilities for analysis and debugging must be an integral part of the system design from the beginning.

Tailoring a General Framework

The approach taken in the project was one of starting with a general model for a class of speech systems and then specializing this general model based on experience. Three ways of tailoring can occur:

o The elimination of excess generality, based on the ways the system is actually used. For example, Hearsay-II began with a set of complex primitives for interconnecting hypotheses across levels; as experience was gained with real KSs, it was discovered that these facilities could be simplified.

o The addition of new features, as needed. For example, the invocation of KSs was expanded to include, for scheduling purposes, an abstract description of the potential action of the KS.

o The reimplementation of existing features, for efficiency. For example, the internal representation of hypotheses went through several reimplementations, based on changing usage patterns of the blackboard primitives.

The notion of a general framework provides a context for tailoring so that the overall system retains a coherence, rather than evolving in a haphazard manner with one change piling on the next.

Such an approach has a potential disadvantage: the start-up cost is relatively high; the danger is that the model may be inadequate for keeping the high-level system usable long enough to amortize those costs. However, if the framework is suitable, it can be used to explore different configurations within the model more easily than if each configuration were built in an ad hoc manner. Additionally, a natural result of the continued use of any high-level system is its improvement in terms of enhanced facilities, increased stability and efficiency, and more familiarity on the part of the researchers using it.

Hearsay-II has been successful in this respect; we believe that the total cost of creating the high-level system and using it to develop KS configurations C1 and C2 was less than it would have been to generate C1 and C2 in an ad hoc manner. It should be stressed that the construction of even one configuration is itself an experimental and evolving

process. The high-level programming system provides a framework, both conceptual and physical, for developing a configuration in an incremental fashion. The speed with which C2 was developed is some indication of the advantage of the system-design approach used in Hearsay-II. And, we are still far from exhausting the possibilities of the existing Hearsay-II framework.

Levels

The usual approach to building an application system is to take as given a language system and its supporting levels (e.g., hardware, firmware, and operating system) and construct the application directly on top of the language system. However, for the efficient implementation of a complex application, it is often necessary to modify these lower levels. For example, the Hearsay efforts led to these modifications:

- At the hardware level:[5] Special-purpose audio devices were constructed. A hardware device-poller was constructed because the existing software polling on the PDP-10 was not fast enough to support the real-time audio devices. Graphics terminals and printers were added to the system.
- At the operating system level: Highly optimized service routines were needed to handle the audio and graphics devices. The scheduler was modified to handle real-time jobs and very large jobs in special ways. Changes were made in I/O handling to support overlaying efficiently.
- At the language system level: The compile-time macro facility was greatly expanded, the memory allocator was modified to handle the demands of large, long-running jobs, and an overlaying facility was added. In addition, the compiler was modified so that it could be pre-initialized with the kernel-provided declarations, significantly decreasing the time to compile each KS.
- At the utilities level: The loader was modified to handle overlaying. A cross-referencing program was implemented which could dynamically search through the many source-code files which make up the kernel and the KSs.

In order to make such modifications, it is necessary to have both the expertise and appropriate control over the computing facilities.

The second principle concerning levels deals with the highest levels, those usually lumped together and called the application level.[6] As this level becomes more complex, the implementation distance between it and the underlying language system increases. Rather than trying to bridge this distance in a single jump, one or more intermediate levels should be built. These layers should reflect the components and structure of the application. Such a layered

---

5 The system used has no microstore; this level, however, is becoming increasingly attractive for application-dependent modification.

6 The fact that the highest level is conventionally called the "application" level is indicative that the principle of modifying any necessary level is not usually adopted. That is, most people consider only the level above the language-system as application-dependent; all the lower levels are taken as immutable.

implementation is easier to understand, debug, and modify because the complexity of interactions between components is reduced.

For example, a KS in Hearsay-II modifies an attribute of an hypothesis on the blackboard through four layers of procedures and macros: (1) At the highest level, each attribute has its own modification macro, part of whose function is to append the name of the modifying KS. (2) These macros call one of the modification procedures; these routines are generalized over a set of the hypothesis attributes and do parameter checking (e.g., to insure that the thing pointed to is really an hypothesis and that the new value is appropriate for the attribute). (3) These procedures in turn call a lower level procedure which is attribute-independent; this procedure is also called directly by other kernel routines in places where the parameter checking is not required. (4) Finally, this procedure calls a macro which actually modifies the attribute.

By hiding, through such layers of macros and procedure calls, the details of how an hypothesis on the blackboard is stored and accessed, it has been possible to re-implement these aspects of the blackboard with only minimal changes required elsewhere; it has also allowed the addition of specialized options to the standard retrieval commands for the needs of specific KSs without affecting other KSs. For instance, during the lifetime of the project, the hypothesis storage and accessing functions went through four major implementations:

- Initially, all attribute/value pairs of an hypothesis were stored as an attribute/value list structure.[7]

- This storage scheme was then modified so that integer-valued attributes of an hypothesis (e.g., its rating and begin- and end-times) were stored as compacted bit-fields in a linear block of memory, thus permitting these fields to be accessed by a simple index and byte extraction operation.

- Next, the storage of standard list attributes of an hypothesis (e.g., the list of connected hypotheses) was changed into a compacted list structure with each list directly accessible through an index operation.

- Finally, optional attributes of an hypothesis were stored in a compacted attribute/value list structure.

The net result of these optimization steps was an improvement of about an order of magnitude in both storage space and accessing time. Similarly, other aspects of the system, such as retrieval functions and their associated data bases, the scheduler, and the activation records of KS processes were successively reimplemented as we gained a better understanding of how these system functions were actually used, both in terms of time and space. Each of these changes resulted in significant increase of system-wide efficiency, in some places orders of magnitude, without requiring any changes to the KS source-code, and only localized changes within the kernel.

Integrated Analysis and Debugging Facilities

The principle of having analysis and debugging facilities as an integral part of the system design at all levels follows from several observations:

- The size and complexity of the system require automatic analysis facilities within the system; one cannot understand the internal functioning of the system just by observing its external behavior.

- The experimental nature of a knowledge-based system results in modification of the system throughout its lifetime. No part of the system is ever "final"; any part is subject to modification at any time and hence may need analysis and debugging facilities at any time.

- Debugging and analysis facilities are needed at all levels within the system. In particular, facilities appropriate to the application levels built on top of the language system are crucial. Facilities provided within the language system may be helpful but are not sufficient for debugging and analyzing the higher levels. Data and control structures at higher levels should be displayed in terms of concepts appropriate to the level rather than in terms of their implementation in the base language (which might be several levels removed). For example, the "rating-state" attribute of an hypothesis in Hearsay-II can take on values from the set "unrated", "accepted", "rejected", etc. Internally, these values are small integers; the KS developer, however, usually does not want to see the integers, but rather their names.[8]

It is important to consider analysis and debugging facilities as an integral part of the system design. Pragmatically, they are especially important when the system is young, but must also endure as the system evolves. If their design is ad hoc and not well-integrated, they will be difficult to modify to keep pace with the system modification.

Good debugging and analysis facilities need not be computationally costly if implemented with selective enabling. In particular, compile-time disabling of such a facility permits it to be retained in the system at no run-time cost; when needed again, it can be re-enabled without code modification.

SYSTEM-BUILDING TOOLS

The organizing principles outlined in the preceding section provided a context for developing many of the tools in the Hearsay-II system. Following is a description of these tools, classified roughly in three groups: configuration management, user interaction, and performance analysis. We feel that similar tools are required in any large, knowledge-based system. Obviously, many other tools are possible; those presented here were found useful for Hearsay-II and indicate the broad range of facilities required.

---

[7] The values of attributes can be integers of varying numbers of bits or variable-length lists or sets, each element being the name of some hypothesis or a small (12-bit) integer.

[8] Notice that the external representation (i.e., the name) is independent of the internal representation; one can optimize the internal representation without sacrificing the natural representation used for interaction if appropriate facilities are included at each implementation level.

Configuration Management Tools

As described earlier, the configuration control problem is one of selecting pieces to comprise a system. An important aspect of this problem is ensuring the consistency of those selections. In a complex system, there are a large number of selections that need to be made in order to create and execute a configuration. For Hearsay-II, some of these include selecting:

- A version of the kernel.
- A set of KSs and a version of each.
- The local knowledge base(s) for each selected KS.
- Settings for the many local parameters which fine-tune the knowledge in the KSs.
- The set of optional facilities (tracing, timing measurement, graphical display, special-purpose analysis, etc.).
- The vocabulary and grammar of the spoken language to be recognized. (Languages of several different sizes and grammatical complexities were developed).
- The set of test data (utterances, either live or "canned") to be run through.

A simplified diagram of the sequence of events necessary to create a Hearsay-II configuration is given in Figure 1. The processors, represented in the figure by nodes, include the SAIL compiler, the system linking loader, special-purpose compilers for data-structures to be used during system execution, and a runnable Hearsay-II system. For each process, a set of input objects must be specified, represented in the figure by labeled arrows. The result of the execution of the process with the inputs is one or more output objects.

In order to make the system usable, configuration management tools must be provided which make it easy to select the input objects for each process. Mechanisms must also be provided for automatic consistency checks across the specified input objects. For example, referring to the figure, such checking should make sure that all the KS modules that are loaded together with the kernel module were originally compiled with kernel declarations that match that version of the kernel load module. Similarly, each data object module should be consistent with the accessing procedures contained in the corresponding KS object module that is loaded with it. There are a variety of other types of consistency checks that need to go on. These occur during all phases: compile-time, load-time, and execution-time.

In order to accomplish this consistency checking, each output object of a processor is labeled with a header indicating the type of processing that occurred, the version number of the program performing the processing, and a condensed form of the header information of all the input objects and key parameter settings of the processing. Before processing, the header information of the input objects is checked in order to determine if those objects are consistent with each other and appropriate for the processor and mode of processing selected.

Sometimes information in the headers of one or more of the input objects can be used by the processor to calculate the names and versions of the other input objects that are needed. This mechanism reduces the amount of information that the user needs to specify explicitly (because it is redundant in the header information in these cases), simplifying the task and reducing the likelihood of error in the specification.

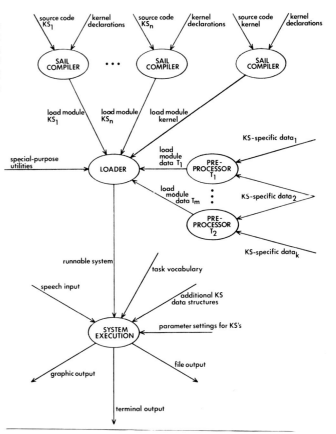

Figure 1. Creating and executing a Hearsay-II system (simplified).

Another way to reduce the amount of external specification needed is by building into the processors default values for selecting their input objects and parameter settings. Thus, only exceptions to the defaults need be specified. This allows the researcher to build added flexibility into a processor without complicating its control for those users not needing that flexibility.

Although these techniques for automatic selection do reduce the total number of parameters to be set and options to be selected, there are still many left to be specified explicitly by the user. In general, command files for processors greatly simplify this task by clustering the specifications for "standard" configurations and allowing them to be named. In addition to standard types of command files for the compiler and loader, a tailored "job control language" has been constructed in Hearsay-II for configuration control and user interaction at execution time. This language permits a user to construct files, called cliche files, which contain sequences of parameter settings and selection control for the various "processes" within an executable Hearsay-II system. Cliche files can contain commands to execute other cliche files and to override parameter settings accomplished in previously executed cliches. Nesting and resetting together provide a simple mechanism for constructing specialized configuration control files from a set of standard sub-configuration cliche files.

Lee D. Erman and Victor R. Lesser

The need for consistency checking at all phases of the system cannot be emphasized strongly enough. Errors resulting from inconsistent configurations are the most difficult to detect and trace to their sources. Early versions of the Hearsay-II system did very little such checking, resulting in many hours and days lost.

User Interaction Tools

Since this research is based on the philosophy of the experimental paradigm (build a system to try out ideas), the ease with which the researcher interacts with the system is crucial.

When we speak of the "researcher" experimenting with and modifying the system, we really mean several researchers with diverse interests and, perhaps, significantly different levels of expertise with computers and programming. A user has different goals at different times, thus providing the need for different interaction modes for even a single researcher. The system design must be sensitive to these varying interests and skills. In particular, the interaction facility must permit the user to interact with the system at a high level, i.e., in terms of the information units most natural to the way he is thinking about the problem.

In Hearsay-II, the primary mode of user interaction is via a facility that permits the user at the terminal to display and modify in a high-level manner both kernel-implemented data structures (e.g., the blackboard) and those specific to each KS. Since the meanings and structures of KS-specific data bases are highly individualized, a mechanism that allows for the display of data structures only in terms of their implementation is inadequate. Rather, a debugging interface tailored for each KS is necessary.

This interface should be integrated into the terminal interaction facility in a coherent manner so that the researcher does not suffer from major changes in context as he moves from one interface to another; similar actions by the user in different interface packages should cause similar reactions by the system.

Each KS module in the Hearsay II system has its own package of routines for interfacing with the researcher at his terminal. Each interface package is tailored to the module, but they all share a common syntax. While "talking" with a module's interface, the researcher may display and alter data, set break-points in the module, and execute actions of the module. In addition, he may set switches that enable data dumping at prescribed points during the module's processing; this data may be dumped at the terminal and/or to a file for later processing.

Multiple special-purpose interfaces might seem to require much more programming than a single interface. In fact, this is not true. The kernel provides macros and associated procedures which enable a user to build this interface easily. For example, a macro, called MakeVariable, is provided which permits a user to declare a SAIL variable in his KS while also specifying routines to be used to display and update the value of the variable at the terminal. In addition, the user has the choice of building his own display and update routines or choosing from a predefined set in the kernel. An example of a declaration using built-in display routines is the following:

```
MakeVariable( VwlAThrsh, CvS,
        GetInteger( 20, 40, 33,
                "Vowel amplitude threshold" ))
```

This declares a variable with the name "VwlAThrsh". Whenever the user asks to display its value, the CvS ("convert an integer to string") procedure will be used; this is a standard SAIL run-time procedure. Whenever the user asks to change the value, the kernel-supplied GetInteger procedure will be used. This procedure will prompt the user for a new value for VwlAThrsh; if the user asks for the default, it will be 33. If the user specifies a new value, GetInteger will guarantee that it will be not less than 20 nor greater than 40. Also, if the user responds with a "?", he will be further prompted with the comment string.

The terminal interaction facility has a number of additional features which make it convenient to use without remembering a vast amount of detail: cliche files, default values, a spelling corrector and automatic abbreviation recognizer for variable and command names, user-defined prompts (comments on the meaning and range of variables and commands), range checking on parameter values, and menu display capabilities for determining the variables and commands available within a specific KS and at the system level. These features make it possible for the system to be somewhat self-documenting. This is important because it is difficult to keep manuals up-to-date in a complex, evolving system.

Another requirement for the use of the system is that the user be able to regain control from an executing system when certain types of events occur. There are three kinds of interrupts that can stop the system and place the researcher in communication with the terminal interaction facility: The user can cause an asynchronous interrupt from his terminal any time the system is executing; this causes the system to halt and allows him to access the interface routines. Breakpoints may be set which will cause the system to halt at predetermined points in its execution. Internal error conditions also cause interrupts. After processing an interrupt, the user can cause the system to continue or can abort execution.

Analysis Facilities

As described in the introduction, understanding and improving the system comes largely from analyzing experiments made with the system. The kinds of data that need to be analyzed include both the final results of running the system (i.e., its "outputs") and the intermediate results (i.e., the internal processing that causes the final results). For example, the final output of an execution of the Hearsay-II system on a spoken utterance is the system's interpretation of that utterance; an analysis of this could mean determining to what degree the result is correct (e.g., matched the intention of the speaker). Intermediate results of Hearsay-II most often of interest are hypotheses on the blackboard; analyses of these might include a determination of how correct the hypotheses are, as well as assignment of credit or blame for their existence to individual KSs. Analyses often need to be aggregated over multiple runs, either to compare the performance of different versions of the system or to provide a statistical validity of performance measurement.

In order to understand the internal processing of the system, a tracing facility has been developed. This facility dumps, at selectable levels of detail, snapshots of the state of processing. Because of the large amount of internal activity in the system, system behavior is difficult and time-consuming to understand from just the trace output, even though that output is carefully formatted and at a high level of abstraction. In a typical run of one utterance in Hearsay-II, 300 to 600 KSs activations occur. Each activation creates on the average two to three new hypotheses. A typical data set contains about twenty-five such utterances.

In order to make the trace information more comprehendible, a mode has been added which allows the trace facility to distinguish correct hypotheses from incorrect ones and to mark the hypotheses on the trace output accordingly. This correct mode requires that the system be supplied with a file specifying, for each utterance being processed, the characteristics of the correct hypotheses at one or more levels of representation on the blackboard. As new hypotheses are created, they are marked "correct" if they match those pre-specified characteristics or are correctly derived from correct hypotheses. Hypotheses labeled "correct" can be highlighted in the trace output, as can descriptions of KS activations that are working on correct hypotheses. Thus it becomes easy to distinguish in the trace output between areas of correct and incorrect processing. The ability to distinguish between correct and incorrect hypotheses also permits the automatic computation of analyses such as the average rank order of the correct hypotheses.

Some KS problems can also be detected by using the automatic labeling of correct hypotheses in another way, called automatic pruning. In this mode, any incorrect hypotheses that a KS attempts to create are discarded: this guarantees that only correct hypotheses will be on the blackboard and, thus, that all KS activations will have only correct hypotheses to work on. In a system in which the knowledge is incomplete and errorful, there is no guarantee that a KS will produce correct output given correct input. Automatic pruning identifies such problems very quickly by eliminating all consideration of incorrect inputs on all KS activations.

The ability to create and execute partial configurations of KSs is also useful for making analysis more efficient. With this ability, a system which is smaller and requires less computation can be used if only a small number of KSs are to be tested. One can also save the results of a run of a (partial) configuration by dumping the blackboard; the saved state can be loaded subsequently into a system with a different configuration of KSs, saving the cost of regenerating the state. The Hearsay-II system is often run in two non-overlapping configurations of KSs: the first partial configuration does preprocessing of the speech signal and the second uses those results. With some simple changes to the command files only, a complete system (i.e., containing the KSs in both partial configurations) can be created and executed.

Facilities are also required to make it convenient to run and analyze a large number of test cases. Often it is possible to do these analyses in an automatic manner by post-processing the system trace output. Thus, it is important to format the output so that it is machine-readable. Appropriate header information must also be included in the output in order to identify it; this is important because many different trace files are produced and need to be distinguished. For Hearsay-II, typical header information includes the name and creation date of the KS configuration, settings of key parameters, the task vocabulary and grammar, and the name of the utterance being recognized.

It is often convenient to have several concurrent destinations for trace output, e.g., an interactive terminal, a comprehensive log file, and a file with trace information about a particular KS. Hearsay-II provides a mechanism so that a user is able to select those output channels to which each kind of trace information should be routed.

Much effort goes into making the system work well interactively. However, it is often desirable to run in batch-mode, in order to analyze large numbers of test cases. A special-purpose facility has been implemented within the Hearsay-II kernel to facilitate batch processing. Traditional batch facilities are not adequate for handling the errors that occur often while running large, experimental systems. Typical errors are running excessively long, exhausting some resource (e.g., memory space), and the execution of an illegal operation (e.g., array subscript out of bounds or parameter mismatch on a procedure call). Normal batch systems react to such errors by aborting execution, perhaps with some low-level dump of the system state. In order to produce meaningful dumps, the experimental system itself needs to regain control; it can then use its high-level display and trace facilities to provide information for subsequent analyses. Often, the system can recover from such errors, either continuing to process the same test case, or, at worst, going on to the next. In order to retain this control, the experimental system must be able to detect such errors before the controlling batch-system detects them; it must also be able to interpret the errors and take appropriate action.

In order to help analyze and improve the efficiency of system execution, a timing facility has been integrated into the kernel for use of KS and system developers. This timing facility is a compile-time option and thus (like debugging statements) incurs no overhead when not used. This facility allows the programmer to name blocks of code that are to be timed. For each such timed block, statistics are accumulated on the number of block entries, time spent in the block, and time spent in the block but excluding time spent in any timed block (dynamically) nested within it. The timing package is very economical to use: typical costs for extensive use are 4% overhead in computation time (which the package also keeps statistics on) and 6% increase in job size. The package has seen considerable use in selectively optimizing the Hearsay-II system.

CONCLUSION

The sections on tools for configuration management, user interaction, and analysis have indicated the large amount of thought and effort involved in system engineering aspects of Hearsay-II. This effort was well spent -- without it the project would not have been successful. We feel such an effort is necessary for the success of any large, complex knowledge-based system.

A set of organizing principles found helpful in accomplishing this system engineering has been described:

- The design should start with a general framework which is then tailored as needed.
- In order to implement a complex system, all the supporting levels (hardware through programming language) must be subject to change.
- The application to be implemented on top of the programming system level should be implemented as a series of levels, rather than as a single level.
- Facilities for analysis and debugging must be an integral part of the system design from the beginning.

By following these principles, we have found that a complex system can be constructed and can evolve without becoming an unmanageable kludge.

Lee D. Erman and Victor R. Lesser

ACKNOWLEDGMENTS

Rick Fennell, Greg Gill, Gary Goodman, Richard Neely and others have contributed to the tools developed in the course of the Hearsay efforts. Bill Broadley, George Robertson, Jim Teter, Howard Wactlar, and many others have expertly made the hardware and operating system changes changes described here. The developers and maintainers of SAIL at Stanford University have been very responsive over the years -- Jim Low, John Reiser, Hanan Samet, Bob Sproull, and Dan Swinehart. This paper has benefited greatly from readings by Lee Cooprider, Mark Fox, Don McCracken, John McDermott, and Jack Mostow.

REFERENCES

CMU Computer Science Speech Group (1977) Summary of the CMU Five-year ARPA effort in speech understanding research. Tech. Report, Comp. Sci. Dept., Carnegie-Mellon Univ.

Cooprider, L. W. (1978, to appear) Representation of families of systems. Ph.D. thesis, Comp. Sci. Dept., Carnegie-Mellon Univ.

Dijkstra, E. W. (1968) The structure of the "THE"-multiprogramming system. *Comm. ACM, 11,* (5), 341-346.

Erman, L. D. (1974) An environment and system for machine understanding of connected speech. Tech. Report, Carnegie-Mellon Univ. (Ph.D. Dissertation, Comp. Sci. Dept., Stanford Univ.).

Erman, L. D. and Lesser, V. R. (1975) A multi-level organization for problem solving using many diverse cooperating sources of knowledge. *Proc. 4th Inter. Joint Conf. on Artificial Intelligence,* Tbilisi, USSR, 483-490.

Flon, L. (1975) Program design with abstract data types. Tech. Report, Comp. Sci. Dept., Carnegie-Mellon Univ.

Guttag, J. V. (1976) Abstract data types and the development of data structures. *Comm. ACM, 20,* (6).

Habermann, A. N., Flon, L., and Cooprider, L. W. (1976) Modularization and hierarchy in a family of operating systems. *Comm. ACM, 19,* (5), 266-272.

Habermann, A. N. (1978, to appear) On system development control.

Lesser, V. R., Fennell, R. D., Erman, L. D. and Reddy, D. R. (1975) Organization of the Hearsay-II speech understanding system. *IEEE Trans. on ASSP 23,* 11-23.

Lesser, V. R. and Erman, L. D. (1977) A retrospective view of the Hearsay-II architecture. *Proc. Inter. Joint Conf. on Artificial Intelligence,* Cambridge, MA, 790-800.

Liskov, B. (1972) The design of the VENUS operating system. *Comm. ACM, 15,* (3), 144-149.

Liskov, B. and Zilles, S. (1974) Programming with abstract data types. *SIGPLAN Notices, 9* (4), 50-59.

Newell, A., Barnett, J., Forgie, J., Green, C., Klatt, D., Licklider, J. C. R., Munson, J., Reddy, R. and Woods, W. (1973) *Speech Understanding Systems: Final Report of a Study Group.* North-Holland.

Parnas, D. L. (1972) On the criteria to be used in decomposing systems into modules. *Comm. ACM, 15,* (12), 1053-1058.

Reddy, D. R., Erman, L. D., Fennell, R. D. and Neely, R. B. (1973) The Hearsay speech understanding system: an example of the recognition process. *Proc. 3rd IJCAI,* Stanford, CA, 185-193.

Reiser, J. F. (1976) SAIL. Stanford Artificial Intel. Lab., Memo AIM-289.

Wulf, W. A., London, R. A., and Shaw, M. (1976) An introduction to the construction and verification of Alphard programs. *IEEE Trans. Software Eng., 2,* (4), 253-265.

Techniques for Artificial Intelligence Systems

ON THE REPRESENTATION OF NATURAL SCENES

Martin A. Fischler *
Artificial Intelligence Center
SRI International

ABSTRACT

This paper questions the efficacy of two central elements in the currently accepted paradigm for machine vision: The primarily symbolic/linguistic approach to scene representation and analysis; and the use of relatively complete scene segmentation as an initial step in the analysis process. It is suggested that for natural scenes, some form of isomorphic/iconic representation is essential. Such a representation, together with a global optimization paradigm for imposing a meaningful structure on a scene, can avoid many of the problems of the symbolic/linguistic paradigm.

I ISOMORPHIC vs NON-ISOMORPHIC REPRESENTATION

Visual Perception and the Computer Paradigm

Visual perception is currently viewed as the partitioning** of a scene into "regions" or "primitive objects"; these objects are then characterized by some fixed set of attributes, and the scene itself is characterized by linking the objects to each other in terms of a fixed set of predicates or relations (e.g. above, larger than, next to, etc.).

The paradigm thus involves (but typically in an iterative manner).
  a) Decomposition or segmentation

  b) Naming (labeling) or classification

  c) Synthesis or description

The above paradigm is not unique to vision research; it exactly mirrors the general sequential/analytic/logical/digital-computer paradigm, and is based on the practical requirements of formulating a problem for digital computer solution. In particular, the digital computer is a symbol processor (symbol in the sense of arbitrary relationship between the real world object and its coded representation in the machine), and thus requires that its inputs be distinct quantities (variables) with names or labels. The computational complexity of symbolic problems with more than a few variables is such that most practical procedures require the partitioning or decomposition of complex problems into essentially independent subproblems of a few variables each. Similarly, any final description must be expressed in terms of a sequence or network of relations/predicates of a few variables each.

Limitations of the Existing Computer Paradigm

Let us now consider those attributes of the existing computer paradigm which lead to its inadequacy in achieving Real World perception:

(1) The requirement (imposed by the existing paradigm) to describe a scene as a network of relationships among a small number of discrete named entities cannot be satisfied in a practical manner because of the complexity of most Real World scenes. If we decide to use bigger "chunks" of the scene as our "primitives" in an attempt to reduce descriptive complexity, we can indeed decrease the total number of primitives required to partition a given scene. However, we now must deal with an exponentially larger set of primitive types, which are correspondingly more difficult to identify or classify, and which present a more complex set of inter-relationships which must be deduced in order to describe the scene.

The argument here does not imply that it is completely impossible to describe a natural scene using linguistic constructs; but rather that it is unreasonable to expect to be able to adequately (for at least some tasks) describe a perceptually continuous scene with a compact description based on a limited vocabulary. For example, consider the problem of verbally describing a forest or meadow scene well enough so that the listener could view the scene and determine if anything has changed or moved, even a leaf or a blade of grass. Can you verbally describe your face well enough to a stranger so that he could recognize you if he should ever accidentally and unexpectedly encounter you in person?

----
* An initial version of this paper (May, 1976) was produced while the author was a member of the Lockheed Palo Alto Research Laboratories.

** Such partitioning is usually based on the attributes of points in the image which are assumed to correspond to the point attributes of surfaces in the scene, such as reflectance, orientation, range from the image receptor, etc.

(2) Because of the non-isomorphic character of the conventional digital computer representation of information, all Real World constraints and idiosyncrasies must be explicitly determined, described, stored, and checked in analyzing or manipulating visual data. Thus, if we have stored the information that object A is to the left of object B, it is also necessary to explicitly store the information that object B is to the right of A; should we store the general rule:

(X, Left, Y)<->(Y, Right, X) rather than the complete set of explicit statements for the relative positions of A and B, then we must continually check to see if the above (and similar) rules should be invoked.

Isomorphic Representation

We have identified some of the problems with the current paradigm for visual perception, now let us see what we can offer in the way of a possible solution.

The heart of the problem was shown to be the need to translate from a continuous domain characterized by many variables with complex interrelations, to a completely symbolic representation, based on a sometimes unnatural partitioning of the scene into a small set of discrete named entities. This representation must explicitly describe all of the resulting relationships and their constraints.

The problems involved in performing the translation, and the computational inefficiencies of explicitly manipulating the relational constraints could be greatly reduced if an isomorphic (analogic) representation could be used in place of, or at least in addition to, the current symbolic one.

An isomorphic representation is one in which the laws and relationships governing the real world objects are inherent in the data structures and operations of the representation. In particular, selected physical properties of the medium in which the representation is embedded, are incorporated into the representation. Since these selected physical properties (such as space or time) are identical to those in the situation being represented, explicit description of the nature of these properties and their relationships is not required. For example, assume I use a conventional (symbolic) computer representation to store the order in which cities occur on a particular highway; and that I later want to know the distances between these cities, and also if any three of the cities lie on a straight line. This additional information is not available in the symbolic representation unless it was specifically inserted into the data base. On the other hand, if the representation I employed was a road map (a representation involving a spatial isomorphism), the answers to my additional questions could be obtained by making physical measurements on the representing medium (i.e., the map), even though I did not anticipate the need to answer the particular questions at the time the representation was created.

The only type of isomorphic representation currently available for modeling the visual world in the digital computer is the "pictorial template" and some of its generalizations. A classical pictorial template (e.g., as the term is used in "template matching") is a representation in which an image is stored as an array of numbers, each such number typically representing a point or local attribute of a scene (e.g., hue, brightness, brightness gradient, edge "operator" score, etc.). The physical location of any attribute in the (possibly 3-dimensional) array is spatially isomorphic, under some known transformation, to the location in the scene to which the attribute corresponds. Thus, for example, implicit information about the shapes, relative positions, and proximity of objects is inherent in the representation, it does not have to be explicitly extracted and stored as auxiliary data unless it is needed as such; often, such information can be used in implicit form. Because the scene is directly modeled there is no need for artificial partitioning or naming, and a small change in the Real World scene requires only a small change in the representation. Finally, certain Real World constraints are built into the representation; e.g., only one object can occupy one location at one time.

The most obvious generalization of the pictorial template is the "Map", which can be considered to be a set of registered overlays. Each overlay of the map is a template indicating the (likelihood of the) presence of a particular attribute of the scene, with the option of pointers to more general symbolic information (a conventional road or contour map would be an example of this type of representation).

The Map itself can be generalized to permit the specification of arbitrary displacements or relations between the overlays; and futher, an iterated hierarchy of such structures can be employed; i.e., each element of an overlay in the Generalized Map can itself be a Generalized Map describing some lower level, or more detailed type of information. A Generalized Map type of representation was used in Fischler [1].

The pictorial template, and its currently known generalizations falls considerably short of what will probably be required for a general solution to the problem of modeling Real World vision. This is partly due to our lack of knowledge about how certain visual functions are performed, and partly due to the limitations of current computer architectures. In particular, we are presently limited to a static spatial isomorphism, largely because of computer architecture constraints (see next section), and we are still uncertain as to where the dividing line falls between operations which are generic to almost all scene processing, and those that require domain specific knowledge. In spite of these limitations, isomorphic representations form the basis for the few existing practical applications involving Real World picture processing (e.g., for navigation and guidance of airborne vehicles via "Map" matching).

There is also a growing volume of experimental evidence to indicate that humans use an isomorphic representation in at least some of their visual tasks. For example, Roger Shepard [2,3] has shown that when subjects are asked to mentally transform the spatial orientation of solid figures, they perform mental operations that are highly analogous to the transformations used to reorient the corresponding real (physical) objects in space.

Martin A. Fischler

Kolers [4] has shown that when two solid or outline shapes are illuminated briefly at a rate of 3 or 4 Hertz, the brain interpolates a sequence of images so that they appear to change into each other in a smooth and continuous fashion.

Julesz [5] has shown that the brain can internally manipulate random dot sterograms to obtain fusion (e.g., up to 6 minutes of angular displacement and 10% of scale can be handled for retinally stabilized images).

Kosslyn [6,7] has shown that the stored mental images used by human subjects appear to preserve distance, in that such operations as "scanning" took longer when the objects searched for were "further" apart. More to the point, Kosslyn's work has provided an additional demonstration that the experienced mental pictorial image is indeed functional.

Given the advantages of the isomorphic representation, the problem is how to implement this representation when the symbolic language is the language of the digital computer. It is possible that as currently implemented and employed, the sequential digital computer is not a suitable mechanism for achieving Real World perception!

Implications for Computer Architecture

It appears to be the case that problems requiring an "intelligent" response are of two rather distinct types; a major distinguishing characteristic being the number of interacting variables needed to represent a given problem.

The digital computer, as we now know it, was evolved mainly to deal with symbolic problems, which, as noted earlier, are characterized by reasonably few variables with limited interaction. Designers strove for generality by, as completely as possible, isolating the algorithmic languages in which the problems are described from the physical characteristics of the machinery which implements the algorithms. For most symbolic problems, the gain in generality appears to be well worth the loss, if any, in representational and algorithmic efficiency.

Is it reasonable to believe that all natural problems are describable in terms of a few key variables with limited interaction? The problem of weather forecasting is one of many currently intractable problems which does not appear to satisfy this requirement. In the preceding section, we argued that problems concerned with natural scene representation and analysis offered additional examples in which a purely symbolic approach was often inadequate. If this thesis is accepted, then we must also accept the fact that a computing device suitable for dealing with such problems cannot be completely general purpose, but must have at least some of its hardware specially tailored to the properties of the particular problem domain of interest.

The nature of the requirements for a computing device tailored to deal with vision problems can best be appreciated by reference to Table 1 which lists the basic problems in visual understanding and reasoning. An operation necessary for the solution of many of the listed problems is the evaluation of "similarity". Except in the simplest cases, a direct measurement of the individual attributes of two images will not provide a suitable means for evaluating their similarity. What is required is something akin to the experimental procedure of superimposing the images and distorting one to match the other. While it can be shown that this matching process can be formulated as an optimization problem and solved symbolically (Fischler [1]), the conceptual simplicity of the experimental approach is very attractive in comparison to the computational problems presented by formal optimization (especially in a problem with many interacting variables).

As an aside, there are many pretty examples in which a simple experiment can be used to solve a complicated optimization problem. Consider the problem of finding the shortest route from city A to city B over some given network of roads. Construct a "map" made out of pieces of string to represent the roads connecting the cities. Let the length of each piece of string be proportional to the length of the road segment it represents, and knot together the strings at places where roads intersect. Now with both hands, grasp the points in the string map corresponding to cities A and B and pull these points in opposite directions. The shortest path will correspond to the road segments represented by the strings supporting the rest of the dangling road network.

The performance of something similar to a physical experiment, in place of symbolic description and formal algorithmic solution, appears to be especially important in "rearrangement" problems. Consider the problems of determining whether an irregularly shaped object could be guided through an obstacle course of rigid structures without striking any of the obstacles. For example, could a car successfully navigate through a section of forested terrain without colliding with any of the vegetation. To attempt to formulate and solve this problem on a computer would be an almost impossible undertaking; and yet, a person working with a scale model of the car and the terrain could probably arrive at a correct answer without an excessive amount of time or effort.

The preceding discussion showed the utility of "physical experiment" in solving vision problems. An additional advantage is related to the fact that a physical experiment can proceed without complete specification or understanding of the problem domain. Symbolic procedures, at the least, require complete specification. A machine capable of performing a physical experiment requires some type of isomorphic representation and/or must directly interact with the external world (eyes and hands).

Thus, the challenge* for computer architects is two fold:

(1) We require a computing device capable of the equivalent of performing physical experiments, with normal physical

----
* Brian Funt [9] has addressed some of these problems, and shares many of the views presented in this paper. Other investigations concerned with the use of analogic or iconic/isomorphic type representations include references [10-16]. I recently became aware of Sloman [10], and consider his paper to be especially relevant to the material presented here.

constraints, on a model (isomorphic representation) of some given segment of the visual world. This should include the movement or rearrangement of objects in the scene; and the comparison of objects by determining the amount of distortion necessary to make one object "look like" the other.

(2) We require some effective way of extending the "experimental space" of the machine to include segments of the outside world, since it is not clear that there is any reasonable way to capture, and store in some computer memory, a suitably complete model which reflects all the complexity and detail of a real world scene. (For example, a person would probably move his head to experimentally determine how a viewed scene changes with a change in viewing position, rather than attempting to deduce this information by computation on a stored internal model of the scene).

II   SCENE SEGMENTATION

The Role of Segmentation in Scene Analysis

Scene partitioning or segmentation is generally accepted to be one of the basic problems in current vision research. This acceptance has permitted a number of key questions to remain unasked. In particular: what role does segmentation play in scene analysis; is it really necessary; and at what stage in the analysis process should it be accomplished.

In the current symbolically oriented scene analysis paradigm, the answers to the above questions are obvious: segmentation is necessary to control computational complexity by reducing the input intensity array to some manageable number of named entities; it is thus an essential task which occurs as one of the first steps in the analysis sequence. The named segments also play a role in any final scene description.

From a theoretical standpoint, we note that whenever decisions are made in sequence (rather than simultaneously), unless they are truly independent, the result is a loss in performance. Thus, performing the segmentation step before a "gestalt" for the complete scene has been achieved is a matter of practical necessity rather than an optimal choice.

While the point may not be fully appreciated, some of the recent approaches to scene analysis (e.g., Fischler [1]) which employ a global optimization paradigm*, rather than the sequential linguistic/symbolic paradigm, do not require a segmentation step in the conventional sense. If a linguistic description is desired, this can be accomplished after the "gestalt" has been achieved. Rather than making disjoint partitioning decisions, the global optimization paradigm allows multiple

----
* The "Optimization Paradigm" is essentially the concept that interpreting a scene in terms of prestored models can be viewed as an optimization problem. In this context, we must define an objective function (i.e., a global criterion) which allows us to compare alternative interpretations.

(probabilistically weighted) interpretations at every location (or node) in the image representation. These multiple interpretations are then resolved "simultaneously" on the basis of global criteria. Only in those parts of the scene where the interpretation is locally unambiguous, does the global optimization paradigm produce something resembling a partial segmentation at an initial stage in the processing. When such a partial segmentation does occur, it leads to a reduction of computational complexity even for the global optimization paradigm.

Thus, we see that segmentation, as it is currently interpreted, is not an essential step in scene analysis, but rather an adjunct to a particular paradigm.

Complete vs Partial Segmentation

Complete segmentation** for natural scenes probably requires high level knowledge beyond that reasonable for current systems, and is not normally performed by man/animal visual systems, nor is it necessary for most practical applications. The problem is that objects in natural scenes frequently do not have well defined complete outlines. For example, tree outlines typically merge into neighboring tree outlines; lake boundaries often shade into marsh, rather than being sharply defined; rock formations or open terrain, with patches of plants, dirt, and shadows, offer no simple partitioning; etc.

As noted earlier, the attempt to completely segment a scene is largely an outgrowth of the parsing operation which is necessary for the "linguistic" representation of a scene. Since I question the practicality of the linguistic approach to natural scene description, I claim that efforts towards complete segmentation are misdirected as a technique for general purpose vision, and do not lead to appropriate methods for accomplishing partial scene segmentation*** which can play a critical role in scene perception.

Considerations in Achieving Segmentation

The technical details of how scene segmentation (at any level) should be accomplished are still to be resolved. However, as is almost universally true, the more information/modalities/context involved, the better the final result. Since the human visual system invokes a rather complex decision procedure for accomplishing the equivalent of scene segmentation,

----
** The term "complete" segmentation indicates an operation on a scene in which the scene is decomposed into disjoint regions; each such region typically being associated with a single (named) object.

*** "Partial" segmentation involves the locating of possibly incomplete (non-closed) boundary lines in the scene which are not necessarily associated with the true boundaries of physical objects. For example, such a boundary line might be located between two regions of differing texture. An interesting implication of partial segmentation is that boundary finding techniques and region growing techniques give distinct and complementary results, in contrast to the situation in complete segmentation in which these two approaches are expected to provide identical information.

Martin A. Fischler

as can be observed in studies of retinal rivalry, and the perception of retinally stabilized images (Vernon [8]), we can expect that any effective procedure for segmentation will require an equally sophisticated mechanism.

III   CONCLUDING COMMENTS

A major theme of this paper is the assertion that building machines with a general vision capability will be difficult, if not impossible, if we continue to pursue a purely symbolic approach to scene representation and analysis. Further, the unaugmented modern digital computer, because it is a general purpose symbol processor, does not offer the appropriate machinery for solving a significant subset of vision problems.

What is required is a device which can support a representation which is isomorphic to the spatial (and possibly visual) properties of the Real World. Such a device should permit the equivalent of physical experiments, and further, the experimental space of the machine should extend into the Real World (i.e., it may have to perform experiments on the Real World objects themselves in order to prove conjectures or draw conclusions).

The key points offered in this paper are briefly summarized below:

(1)   Many vision problems are not describable in symbolic terms.

(2)   We cannot practically make explicit all of the knowledge needed to create a device capable of general purpose vision.

(3)   Because of limited understanding of the visual world, as well as the impracticality of formal symbolic solution techniques for many vision problems, many such vision problems will have to be solved by a process resembling physical experimentation.

(4)   Where the complexity of the problem environment prevents us from modeling it at a suitable level of detail, the "experimental space" of a device capable of general purpose vision may have to extend out into the Real World.

(5)   Items (1-4) imply the need for employing some form of isomorphic representation, as well as a computing device capable of supporting such a representation, if we are to successfully deal with the problem of general purpose vision.

(6)   Psychological experiments indicate that the mental images humans experience serve a purpose in visual processing. (Do the two hemispheres of the human brain support the two distinct types of representations: isomorphic and symbolic?)

(7)   The currently accepted symbolic paradigm for general purpose vision, requiring relatively complete scene segmentation as an early step in the processing sequence, has distorted the role that scene segmentation should play in image analysis and created an artificial problem that may not have a reasonable solution.

REFERENCES

1.   M. A. Fischler and R. A. Elschlager, "The representation and matching of pictorial structures". IEEE Trans on Computers, Vol. 22 (1), 1973, pp 67-92.

2.   Roger N. Shepard, "Studies of the Form, Formation, and Transformation of Internal Representations", (Stanford University Report).

3.   R. N. Shepard and S. Chipman, "Second order isomorphism of internal representations: shapes of states". Cognitive Psychology, Vol. 1 (1), . Jan. 1970.

4.   Paul Kolers and Michael von Grunau, "Visual construction of color is digital". Science, Vol. 187, 28 Feb. 1975, pp 757-758.

5.   Bela Julesz, "Cooperative phenomena in binocular depth perception". American Scientist, Jan-Feb. 1974, pp 32-43.

6.   S. M. Kosslyn and S. P. Schwartz, "Visual Images as Spatial Representations in Active Memory," Advanced Papers for the Workshop on Computer Vision Systems, June 1977.

7.   S. M. Kosslyn and J. R. Pomerantz, "Imagery, Propositions, and the Form of Internal Representations," Cognitive Psychology, 9, 1977, pp. 52-76.

8.   M. D. Vernon, "The psychology of perception". Pelican Books, 1963, pp 175-177.

9.   B. V. Funt, "WHISPER: A Computer Implementation Using Analogues in Reasoning," Technical Report 76-09, Department of Computer Science, University of British Columbia, December 1976.

10.   A. Sloman, "Interactions Between Philosophy and Artificial Intelligence: the role of intuition and non-logical reasoning in intelligence," Second International Joint Conference on Artificial Intelligence (Advance Papers), September 1971.

11.   S. L. Tanimoto, "An Iconic/Symbolic Data Structuring Scheme," Pattern Recognition and Artificial Intelligence, (C.H. Chen, editor), Academic Press, 1976.

12.   B. L. Bullock, A Very High-Level Programming Environment for Pictorial Problem Solving, (unpublished paper, May, 1977).

13.   M. A. Fischler, "On Communicating About Pictures," Workshop on Standards for Image Pattern Recognition, June 1976 (NBS Special Publication 500-8, Issued May 1977).

14.   H. Gelernter, "Realization of a Geometry Theorem Proving Machine," Computers and Thought, (Ed. E. A. Feigenbaum and J. Feldman), McGraw Hill, 1963, pp. 134-152.

On the Representation of Natural Scenes

15. R. A. Baker, "A Spatially-Oriented Information Processor which Simulates the Motions of Rigid Objects," <u>Artificial</u> <u>Intelligence</u>, Vol. 4(1), 1973, pp. 29-40.

16. C. M. Eastman, "Automated Space Planning," <u>Artificial</u> <u>Intelligence</u>, Vol. 4(1), 1973, pp. 41-64.

Table 1. BASIC PROBLEMS IN VISUAL UNDERSTANDING AND REASONING

a) Location/Correspondence Determination: where am I in respect to the scene I am viewing; what is the location of the scene I am viewing with respect to other locations known to me? What is the correspondence between points in two different images of the same scene.

b) Scene/Object Recognition: have I ever seen this particular scene before? Have I ever seen the individual parts (or objects) of this scene before?

c) Generic Classification: are parts of the scene I am viewing instances of known classes of objects I am familiar with (the classes can be defined by function, shape, or any observable characteristic)?

d) Scene Rearrangement: is it possible to rearrange (by the equivalent of physical movement) designated parts of the scene I am viewing to achieve a specified goal? E.G., is there a "navigable" path observable in the scene which will permit a car to move from location A to location B.

e) Anomaly Detection: where are there "discontinuities" in the scene I am viewing; where are there (small) pieces of the scene which are distinct from their surroundings?

f) Primal Description: how can I disambiguate the interaction of illumination, distance, and surface reflectance and orientation so that I can accurately label each point in the scene I am viewing with the proper values of these variables?

g) Scene Segmentation: how can I decompose the scene I am viewing into pieces that correspond to objects, surfaces, or regions, having some internal coherence?

h) Linguistic/Symbolic Description: how can I describe the scene I am viewing in terms of the vocabulary and syntax of some given language, so that for a given purpose the description will be an adequate replacement for the scene itself?

Martin A. Fischler

VISION RESEARCH STRATEGY:
BLACK MAGIC, METAPHORS, MECHANISMS, MINIWORLDS AND MAPS*

Alan K. Mackworth

Department of Computer Science
University of British Columbia
Vancouver, B.C., Canada

Abstract

Machine vision will advance substantially only if it continues to develop a coherent theory. As with all fledgling sciences, the framework for such a paradigm has emerged as a result of restricting the scope of attention to limited but non-sterile domains that serve the current needs of the theory. An example of such a domain is the class of freehand sketches. These occupy a position in vision analogous to that of speech in that they are designed for person-to-person communication and thereby have a rich, conventional semantics which can be exploited. The goals of a project to understand sketches are given. A very brief description of a program, MAPSEE, that interprets sketch maps illustrates the argument. A conservative partial segmentation yields a variety of cues which invoke models that interact according to a uniform control structure: a network consistency algorithm. The necessary deficiences of the segmentation, their effect on the interpretation and using the interpretation to refine the segmentation are all mentioned. This example is used to focus discussion of a variety of vision issues such as the chicken-and-egg problem, the power of descriptive models and their corresponding weaknesses, the incremental nature of constraint methods, cue/model hierarchies, the modularity and generality problems and procedural adequacy. Finally a cyclic theory of perception is used to characterize a variety of vision programs.

1. Strategies for Vision

If we intend to continue developing a science of perception--for that is what I believe we are doing--our research must become self-conscious. We must be aware of our strategies and scholarly in the development of the field. Our efforts must be informed by what has been done, why it has been done and what has been learned. It should be clear that we <u>have</u> a developing paradigm [25,26,2,11,12] and that research goals should be based not on fashion but on the needs of that paradigm. It should also be clear that <u>any</u> science at this early stage must, perforce, close its eyes to almost all the allures and mysteries

of nature and choose a highly circumscribed fragment of reality to examine. Indeed, glancing back at the history of science, the fragment chosen is usually not even part of nature as she is but merely an abstracted, stylized slice which can illuminate the murky recesses of current theory. Galileo chose, as his blocks world, bodies sliding down a friction-free inclined plane in a vacuum; Newton considered point masses of infinite density; Chomsky the ideal speaker-hearer's competence. In vision, Roberts [20] realized that the enormous effort being made to solve the problems of pattern classification was contributing little to the theory of machine perception. He then retreated from the "real-world" problems of character recognition to understand his blocks world: black velvet background, matte surfaces carefully lit and all. The decade of research inspired by his decision proved its correctness. The cumulative, puzzle-solving activity of viewing the world through polyhedral spectacles provided a theoretical base and practical support for the seeds of a new vision paradigm.

Perhaps the most important blocks world lesson is that only by patiently teasing out the semantics of a domain (that is, the relationship of representation [6]: the relationship between objects in the world and their pictorial traces) will we be able to write programs which interpret pictures in that domain. So we start by looking at the semantics of pictures.

2. Clean and Dirty Semantics: The Laws of Convention or the Laws of Physics?

It is still instructive to look for parallels between vision and natural language understanding without making a commitment to, say, a linguistic approach to vision or, even further, to the primacy of syntax in both domains or, on the other hand, to an imagery-based approach to language. One can establish an analogy between successions of task areas in the visual and aural domains ranging from perfect line diagrams through free-hand sketches to "real" images of natural scenes in the former and from perfect presegmented text through speech to arbitrary natural sounds in the latter. This admittedly crude analogy depends upon a variety of underlying factors. These include the nature of the representational medium and the presumption of

---

* The work reported here is supported in part by the National Research Council of Canada's Operating Grant A9281.

perfect segmentation but, primarily, the analogy depends upon the extent to which the laws of convention rather than the laws of physics dictate the relationship of representation.

The analogy demonstrates that vision researchers have largely ignored an area which has been the primary focus for our aural counterparts. We have ignored man-made images designed for person-to-person communication, images whose semantics are fixed by convention, and concentrated on images of natural scenes, images whose semantics are dictated by the laws of optics. Man-made images have, by their very nature and purpose, a rich, clean and useful semantics which can be codified and sensibly exploited. Again, this is not to say that we should discontinue work on recovering the relationship between incident and reflected light, the nature of surfaces, edges, textures, and shadows and so on; as in speech understanding, progress will require a judicious admixture of both approaches.

3. Freehand Sketches and Maps

A common class of image designed for communication is the free-hand sketch diagram. For several years we have had the ability to draw such diagrams directly on graphical data tablets but this ability has not been heavily exploited. Most uses have been very mechanical and ad hoc. Only rarely [1,18] can a program be truly said to be interpreting the sketch.

In studying images sketched free-hand on a data tablet, this project has many goals. They include:

I) To see if we can broaden the scope of our vision programs by applying the theory developed in the blocks world decade to other domains. At the same time, reworking and extending the theory.

II) To explore the relationship between natural and conventional representations.

III) To determine the extent to which highly domain-specific knowledge can be factored out of

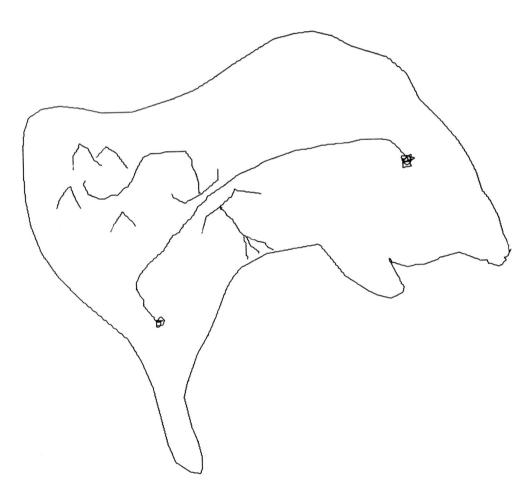

Figure 1. A Sketch Map of an Island

Alan K. Mackworth

the image interpretation program, to be supplied by the user.

IV) To make available a useful interpretation program for some restricted but important classes of sketches.

V) To provide an experimental vehicle for studying the control structures required to implement schema-based theories of perception.

The initial domain chosen was a set of sketch maps drawn on a data tablet typified by the map shown in Fig. 1.

This is, deliberately, so badly sketched that many people have to be told, before they can <u>see</u> it, that it represents an island on which there is a road that connects two towns and crosses a bridge over a river that rises in a mountain range and ends in a delta.

This domain allows us to explore ways of satisfying the goals listed above. In particular, besides having a satisfying mixture of conventional and direct representations, such maps are related to the work we are doing on understanding LANDSAT (ERTS) images [22] which have primarily optical semantics. In the long run, such understanding would proceed more successfully if programs were able to accept advice, in the form of sketch maps, about the geography underlying the image.

4. How to Interpret Sketch Maps

In describing how to interpret sketch maps, I cannot here do justice to the current program, MAPSEE, an implementation in LISP recently completed. Without giving the details of its operation--these are presented elsewhere [13,14]--I will place the ideas behind MAPSEE in context. Furthermore, the short-range and long-range goals of the project will be distinguished as they are, at times, in apparent opposition. (But then, the tension between them establishes a productive dialectic.)

4.1 Cues and Models

In any world it is crucial to ask: what can various picture fragments depict? Here, it is clear that a line element can, in total isolation represent part of a road, a river, a bridge, a mountainside or a shoreline (of lake or the sea, with water on one side, land on the other or <u>vice versa</u>). An areal element could be land, lake or sea. The design of an interpretation scheme starts with the fact that, as in the blocks world, the enormous ambiguity of interpretation can be progressively reduced by considering picture fragments in wider and wider context. Individual picture fragments, or cues, invoke local models which serve to explain or interpret the immediate locale of the cue that invoked them. These models must talk to each other and agree on the interpretation of picture fragments that they mutually interpret. To discover the first level of model information the following experiment is recommended: cut a small hole in a sheet of paper and move it

about Figure 1. Being familiar with the class of maps represented, you would discover a wide variety of informative local picture parts. The point clusters, the chain links (where a chain of line segments joins back on itself), the free ends, the sharp kinks in the chains and the various junctions all contain much interesting but totally ambiguous information. Alternatively, one can say that each part invokes a set of models for its environment. A catalogue of picture parts, known as "primary cues," and their possible models is not given here. Simply, note that each of the many possible interpretations of a primary cue places an interpretation on each of the line and region fragments that comprise the part. As shown in [14] the primary cue interpretation catalogue captures a wide variety of geographic and cartographic inferences.

4.2 Control Structure

If we suppose, for the sake of exposition, that our images were perfectly presegmented line drawings of maps then finding such cues in the picture and searching for a mutually compatible interpretation would be analogous to that process in the blocks world with some important exceptions and extensions. Mackworth [10] presents a series of algorithms designed to instantiate, in given domains, each of a set of variables that must satisfy a set of binary relations. Those algorithms, called there <u>network</u> <u>consistency</u> <u>algorithms</u> as exemplified by Waltz's arc consistency algorithm [24] and Montanari's path consistency algorithm [17], are often better than backtracking for such a task. In Waltz's case the variables or nodes are the junctions, the binary relations or arcs are the lines between the junctions, that is, the network of relations is isomorphic to the line drawing being interpreted. In MAPSEE the variables or nodes are the chains and the regions (which also must be interpreted--everything need not be packed into the chain labels). The relations, no longer just binary, are generalized to n-ary relations that consist of the primary cue models. The control structure for the interpretation phase of MAPSEE is a new network consistency algorithm, NC. See [10] and [23] among others for other uses of the constraint satisfaction approach.

4.3 Representations

Pictures must have a variety of representations according to the needs of the various components of the task. In MAPSEE there are three: a procedural representation as, for example, originally created by the stylus tracking routines, a network representation of objects, relations between objects and local function definitions [7] and an array representation indexed by x-y coordinates.

Pictorial representations should encourage the use of a level of detail appropriate to the task at hand. Each of the three representations allows that. The primary cues, for example, are found by searching the most appropriate picture structure, exploiting the levels of detail to make the search effort as efficient as possible.

4.4 Conservative Segmentation

The earlier supposition that we have perfectly presegmented maps is totally wrong. The segmentation into chains, regions and the variety of primary cues is not given and cannot be done perfectly by any means. For example, as there can be substantial gaps between lines that were "intended" to meet, the region segmentation is difficult. Indeed, in a real sense, it cannot be done at all until the map has been interpreted! This is one of the many chicken and egg problems of scene analysis: segmentation is interpretation and vice versa[11]. However, an initial partial region segmentation is possible. A quick segmentation, using a Warnock-type algorithm in the tree of space occupation arrays followed by a merge of all adjacent regions can be done. The top-down tree search is stopped well before it could get into trouble, at a level whose resolution size is much greater than any unintentional gaps in the drawing. This guarantees no region leakage. No region so found corresponds to more than one "intended" region. But, of course, an intended region can be segmented into more than one found region. In Fig. 1, the large connected land region is split into three regions: one between the upper mountains and the river, one in the peninsula in the south-west and one consisting of the rest of the island except for the river delta. On the other hand, other intended regions are not represented by any found regions. In Fig. 1, the two small land regions in the river delta are not found.

The essential character of this approach to partial segmentation is its conservatism (or, if you prefer, it follows Marr's principle of least commitment [15]). Two other major aspects of the segmentation process are similarly conservative. In the search for primary cues there are many border-line cases of cue instances. These are all rejected: the criteria are always very tight. We must guarantee that no false cues are found. The obvious price is that many real cues are ignored. Finally, given a cue, it must be fleshed out with the picture fragments corresponding to its various subparts. The search for these in the picture is conservative. In looking for a region associated, in a certain direction, with a primary cue, for example, MAPSEE crawls carefully from a starting point in the given direction. If it finds a region within a very short distance, well and good, but if it doesn't it gives up even though the region may be found by continuing, because if it continued it could pick up the wrong one. If it gives up it creates a region ghost [4] which stands for the region that should be there but hasn't yet been found.

Thus, there are four classes of discrepancy between the partial segmentation and the segmentation intended by the user: the missing cues, the region ghosts, the missing regions and the extra regions. The effect of each of these discrepancies on the interpretation process is unique, but they have in common the vital property that they can not cause the elimination of interpretations that would remain if the segmentation were perfect. This is the true sense of the word "conservative" that has been used to characterize all aspects of this segmentation.

The missing cues have no serious effect on the consistency process, provided, of course, that sufficient remain. A missing cue simply fails to supply its extra constraints on the possible interpretations of the chains and regions. In this domain, however, there is such a welter of cues invoking consistent models that there is a multitude of partially independent but mutually confirming inference paths. Breaking a few of those inference paths causes no degredation in the interpretation. It is tempting to postulate that most perceptual tasks, in the real world as opposed to the psychological laboratory, have the rich semantics which give rise to this robustness property if we can but discover the appropriate language for the inferences and appropriate mechanisms for carrying them out.

The region ghosts are, if you like, region intensions while the found regions are (imperfect) region extensions [27]. A ghost is an intension in that it may be specified as, for example, "the region on the reflex angle side of this acute L." The intension/extension distinction forms a spectrum rather than a strict dichotomy here. Recall that a ghost arises when a cue fails to find an associated region. It may fail either because it stopped looking too soon even though there is a found region there or because there is no found region. The ghosts participate in the consistency process just as do the found regions. The single cue that created a region ghost constrains it and it is quite possible for interpretations of the ghost to be progressively ruled out. After the consistency process we still do not know the extension of a ghost but we may know more about it than before; for example, it may now be forced to have the interpretation "land".

The missing regions, as in the river delta, for example, also do not seriously affect the consistency process. The cues in the neighbourhood of a missing region will have used ghosts in its stead. But, standing in for a single missing region there will be several ghosts so the constraining effect will be weakened somewhat.

Similarly, the extra regions created by the splitting of a single intended region participate independently in the consistency process thereby exerting a weaker constraining effect than if the region had not been split. However, the semantic richness overcomes that weakening and forces the three found regions corresponding to the single intended land region to have that single interpretation. Again, as in the other cases, if the region splitting is so severe as to cut too many inference paths then the process will degrade gracefully. In that case the various found regions would not have the intended interpretation uniquely --it would simply be in the intersection of the possible interpretations of the found regions.

We can go further and use the results of the consistency process to refine the initial partial segmentation. There are four ways, currently being implemented, in which this can be done: a) establishing distinct ghosts with the same interpretation and location as co-extensive b) considering the merge of found regions with the same interpretation c) establishing a found region as the extension of a ghost with the same interpretation and d) discovering a new found region as the extension of one or more ghosts. These all involve revisiting the picture and segmenting more purposefully, more carefully and at a finer level of detail in the particular areas concerned.

Alan K. Mackworth

The above description of MAPSEE is only a superficial sketch. For full details on the program, the cue-model structure, the n-ary network consistency algorithm and a trace of its interpretation of the sketch map of Figure 1 see [14]. The description given here, though, should suffice to indicate the power of this approach to vision.

One of the fundamental advantages of a cautious segmentation combined with cue-invoked descriptive models that are made to interpret the picture consistently is that the constraining effect of the picture objects discovered is additive and incremental not all-or-none. As additional information is discovered in the picture it contributes its own specialized constraints to the interpretation in a uniform way. As a result, picture objects missed in the segmentation, objects split in two, undiscovered relations between objects and picture objects hallucinated to stand in for ones that cannot be found all can cause, at best, a slower convergence to the same interpretation or, at worst, a graceful degradation [15] to a more ambiguous interpretation rather than a catastrophic failure.

5. The Search for Generality: Model Descriptions

One of the legitimate criticisms of the miniworld approach to vision or artificial intelligence advocated here is that it can degenerate into a series of implementations for a series of worlds with little transfer of theory (or code) from one to the next. This can be avoided if the worlds are chosen with regard to the needs of the theory, not vice versa. Moreover, in the search for generality, one should consider families of worlds which allow a high degree of theory-sharing. Here, for example, the family of sketch worlds and the organization of MAPSEE allow us to contemplate a PLANSEE, for sketch plans of a building, a FLOWCHARTSEE, . . . even a BLOCKSEE for sketches of blocks! To change to such a new world minimally requires a new primary cue interpretation table and, perhaps, extending the vocabulary of primary cues. The modularity of this paradigm is one of its encouraging aspects: the domain dependence is highly localized within the code.

Note that the primary cue interpretation table is implicitly compiled from a set of models of cartographic objects. To further explore the problem of generality that process of compilation must be made explicit and then automated. This would require a source language in which to specify the structure of the scene objects which could exist (here the cartographic objects: mountains, bridges, roads, towns, river systems, shorelines, lakes, seas, . . .) and their possible interaction in terms of a specified repertoire of primary cues. The compilation would essentially invert those descriptions to construct the primary cue interpretation table. Note that we would not then throw away the model description. The primary cue interpretation table only captures local knowledge. The primary cues serve as indices into the set of models: their complete interpretations could then impose more global constraints on the consistency process.

As a short range strategy, this would lead even further in the direction of satisfying goal III—factoring out the highly domain-specific knowledge. But, although network consistency algorithms

are probably the best uniform procedure for satisfying descriptive models, we are, in the long run, going to be forced to abandon them if we want to explore goal V: exploring control strategies for schema-based theories of perception. This conflict will lead to a divergence in the project. One path will continue to explore descriptive models, network consistency and modular vision programs while the other will explore the concept of models as procedural schemata.

6. A Ptolemaic Theory of Perception

This paper started with an appeal to the history of science so it is appropriate, given that perception is a snake swallowing its tail, for it to end with such an appeal. I have always preferred the Ptolemaic description of the motion of the heavenly bodies to the Keplerian-Copernican view so, although Ptolemy's model is currently in disfavour for the material universe, I shall offer it, semi-seriously, as a metaphor for the universe of perception.

This approach to perception assumes that Helmholtz, Bartlett, Minsky, Clowes and Gregory are right! Although such knowledge-based theories of perception are riddled with large holes, hand-waving, errors and mystifications, there is enough evidence from both machines and humans to know that they are, in essence, correct. One view of Roberts' achievement in creating a machine vision paradigm is the realization that he established a working model of perception as an alternation of segmentation and interpretation or, in more detail, as a cycle of four processes: discovering cues, activating a hypothesis, testing the hypothesis and inferring the consequences of an established hypothesis.

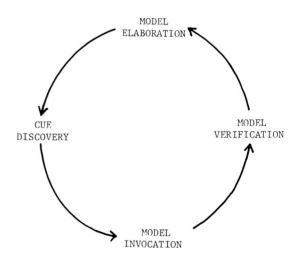

Figure 2. The cycle of perception

In Figure 2 these four processes are called cue discovery, model invocation, model verification and model elaboration. Everyday human perception is an ongoing equilibrium of similar processes. Although we can so do, we are rarely called upon to start up the cycle context-free in either bottom-up or top-down mode. But we place our programs in that situation all the time and then argue about whether bottom-up or top-down methods are more appropriate. In this metaphor, the chicken-and-egg problem simply reflects the fact that the circle is indeed unbroken.

It is possible to characterize almost all vision programs by the way they treat the cycle of perception while ignoring many other issues of descriptive and procedural adequacy. Roberts' program starts with the cues and goes through the cycle several times--each time in a different area of the picture:

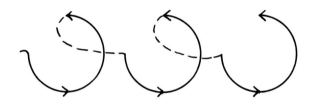

The Huffman-Clowes-Waltz approach starts with context-free cue discovery and does not complete the cycle:

Among other things, MAPSEE has closed that gap. The several programs that use a planning approach such as Kelly's [8] and Shirai's [21] are bi-cycle theories or, as the English might say, penny-farthing theories:

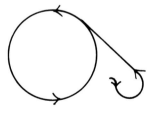

in that the first cycle, on a reduced picture, provides the context for the second.

The semantics-driven region segmentation schemes invented by Yakimovsky and Feldman [28], generalized by Tenenbaum and Barrow [23] and modified by Starr and Mackworth [22] start with context-free segmentation of the "strongest" regions as cues. These regions are interpreted and their interpretations then provide the context for further segmentation and interpretation. This process continues until the entire picture is segmented/interpreted. This "island-driving" approach (which is

strongly analogous to similar approaches in speech understanding [19] can be diagrammed as:

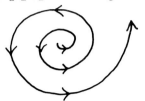

We showed [22] that a version of this technique is much more effective than traditional pattern recognition techniques in the interpretation of LANDSAT image data in that it allows 2D spatial and meaning contexts to guide the segmentation process.

Finally, in this metaphor, we need to discuss the use of hierarchies of cues and models. Mackworth [12] presents a variety of intelligent uses of composition (part-of) and generalization (is-a) hierarchies in the blocks world. In Minsky's [16] seductive vision of frame systems such hierarchies produce epicycles on the cyclic structure! (The image of this is left to your imagination.) From the metaphor it should be clear that the top-down control strategy with shared terminals transferred on failure suggested by Minsky and elaborated by Kuipers [9] is an attractive but inadequate control structure. Havens [7], in a contribution to the solution of the chicken-and-egg problem, has provided mechanisms in a programming language, MAYA, which allow the user to specify how bottom-up and top-down techniques are to intermingle in a perceptual task. Havens is pursuing the possibilities of this approach in a frame system for the blocks world. The procedural fork of our project will continue to explore the adequacy of control structures for schema-based theories of perception.

7. Conclusion

The thesis that vision research benefits most from choosing to understand limited but non-sterile domains that stretch the current theory has been supported by the example given from the sketch world. In that context, some light has been thrown on a wide variety of vision issues, such as a conservative partial segmentation, its effect on the interpretation, the possibility of a uniform control structure, network consistency with descriptive models, using the interpretation to refine the segmentation, the incremental nature of constraint methods, cue/model hierarchies, conventional versus optical semantics, and the modularity and generality problems that conflict with the procedural adequacy requirement placed on any theory of perception.

Alan K. Mackworth

8. References

1. Anderson, R.H. Syntax-directed recognition of hand-printed two-dimensional mathematics. Ph.D. thesis, Div. Eng. and Appl. Phys., Harvard, 1968.

2. Barrow, H.G. and Tenenbaum, J.M. Representation and use of knowledge in vision. SIGART Newsletter, 52, June, 1975, 2-8.

3. Bobrow, D.G. and Collins, A.M. (Eds.) Representation and Understanding, Academic Press, N.Y., 1975.

4. Bobrow, D.G. and Winograd, T. An overview of KRL, a knowledge representation language. Journal of Cognitive Science, December, 1976.

5. Canadian Soc. Comp. Studies of Int. Proc. First National CSCSI/SCEIO Conf. Dept. of Comp. Sci., Univ. of B.C. Vancouver, B.C., August, 1976.

6. Clowes, M.B. On seeing things. Artificial Intelligence, 2, 1, 1971, 79-112.

7. Havens, W.S. Can frames solve the chicken-and-egg problem? in [5], pp. 232-242.

8. Kelly, M. Visual identification of people by computer. Memo AI-130, Comp. Sci. Dept., Stanford Univ., July, 1970.

9. Kuipers, B.J. A frame for frames: representing knowledge for recognition. in [3].

10. Mackworth, A.K. Consistency in networks of relations. TR 75-3, Dept. of Comp. Sci., Univ. of B.C., Vancouver, 1975, and Artificial Intelligence 8, 99-118, 1977.

11. Mackworth, A.K. How to see a simple world. in Machine Intelligence 8, E.W. Elcock and D. Michie (eds.), Wiley, 1977, pp. 510-537.

12. Mackworth,A.K. Model-driven interpretation in intelligent vision systems. Perception 5, 1976, 349-370.

13. Mackworth, A.K. Making maps make sense. in [5], pp. 42-51.

14. Mackworth, A.K. On reading sketch maps. Proc. Fifth Int. Joint Conf. on Artificial Intelligence, M.I.T., Cambridge, Mass., August 1977, pp. 598-606.

15. Marr, D. Early processing of visual information. A.I. Memo 340, M.I.T., Cambridge, Mass., 1975.

16. Minsky, M.L. A framework for representing knowledge. in [25], pp. 211-277.

17. Montanari, U. Networks of constraints: fundamental properties and applications to picture processing. Information Sciences, 7, 1974, 95-132.

18. Negroponte, N. Recent advances in sketch recognition. AFIPS NCC Proc., 42, pp. 663-675.

19. Paxton, W.H. Experiments in speech understanding system control. in [5] pp. 1-21.

20. Roberts, L.G. Machine Perception of three-dimensional objects. in Optical and Electro-optical Information Processing, Tippett. et al. (eds.), M.I.T. Press, Cambridge, Mass., 1965, pp. 159-197.

21. Shirai, Y. A context sensitive line finder for recognition of polyhedra. Artificial Intelligence, 4, 2, 1973, 95-119.

22. Starr, D.W. and Mackworth, A.K. Interpretation-directed segmentation of ERTS images. Proc. ACM/CIPS Pacific Regional Symp. 1976, pp. 69-75.

23. Tenenbaum, M. and Barrow, H.G. IGS: a Paradigm for integrating image segmentation and interpretation. in Pattern Recognition and Artificial Intelligence, 1976, Academic Press.

24. Waltz, D.L. Generating Semantic Descriptions from Drawings of Scenes with Shadows. MAC AI-TR-271, M.I.T., Cambridge, Mass.

25. Winston, P.H. The MIT robot. in Machine Intelligence 7, Meltzer, B. and Michie, D. (eds.), Edin. Univ. Press, 1973, pp. 431-463.

26. Winston, P.H. The Psychology of Computer Vision. McGraw-Hill, N.Y., 1975.

27. Woods, W.A. What's in a link. in Representation and Understanding, D.G. Bobrow and A. Collins (eds.), Academic Press, 1975.

28. Yakimovsky, Y. and Feldman, J. A semantics-based decision-theoretic region analyzer. Proc. 3IJCAI, Stanford, Calif., 1973, pp. 580-588.

REPRESENTING VISUAL INFORMATION
- a computational approach

D. Marr

M.I.T. Artificial Intelligence Laboratory,
545 Technology Square, Cambridge, Mass. 02139.

ABSTRACT: Vision is the construction of efficient symbolic descriptions from images of the world. An important aspect of vision is the choice of representations for the different kinds of information in a visual scene. In the early stages of the analysis of an image, the representations used depend more on what it is possible to compute from an image than on what is ultimately desirable, but later representations can be more sensitive to the specific needs of recognition. This essay surveys recent work in vision at M.I.T. from a perspective in which the representational problems assume a primary importance. An overall framework is suggested for visual information processing, which consists of three major levels of representation; (1) the primal sketch, which makes explicit the intensity changes and local two-dimensional geometry of an image, (2) the $2\frac{1}{2}$-D sketch, which is a viewer-centered representation of the depth, orientation and discontinuities of the visible surfaces, and (3) the 3-D model representation, which allows an object-centered description of the three-dimensional structure and organization of a viewed shape. The analysis of processes for obtaining these representations rests on discovering constraints that are obeyed by the physical world, and which provide valid assumptions of sufficient power to allow a computation to be defined. Several computational theories of this kind have recently been formulated, including those for stereopsis, visual motion, shape from contour and shape from shading. Finally, the adequacy of these formulations are judged by comparing them with the behavior of the human visual processor.

Contents

0: Introduction

0.1: Understanding information processing tasks

    Vision is an information processing task, and like any other, it needs understanding at two levels. The first, which I call the computational theory of an information processing task, is concerned with what is being computed and why; and the second level, that at which particular algorithms are designed, with how the computation is to be carried out (Marr & Poggio 1977a). For example, the theory of the Fourier transform is a level 1 theory, and is expressed independently of ways of obtaining it (algorithms like the Fast Fourier

This work was conducted at the Artificial Intelligence Laboratory, a Massachusetts Institute of Technology research program supported in part by the Advanced Research Projects Agency of the Department of Defense, and monitored by the Office of Naval Research under contract number N00014-75-C-0643.

"Representing Visual Systems"

Lectures on Mathematics in the Life Sciences, Volume 10
by permission of the American Mathematical Society

Transform, or the parallel algorithms of coherent optics) that lie at level 2. Chomsky calls level 1 theories competence theories, and level 2 theories performance theories. The theory of a computation must precede the design of algorithms for carrying it out, because one cannot seriously contemplate designing an algorithm or a program until one knows precisely what it is meant to be doing.

I believe this point is worth emphasizing, because it is important to be clear about the level at which one is pursuing one's studies. For example, there has recently been much interest in so-called cooperative algorithms (Marr & Poggio 1976) or relaxation labelling (Rosenfeld, Hummel & Zucker 1976). The attraction of this technique is that it allows one to write plausible constraints directly into an algorithm, but one must remember that such techniques amount to no more than a style of programming, and they lie at the second of the two levels. They have nothing to do with the theory of vision, whose business it is to derive the constraints and characterize the solutions that are consistent with them.

0.2: Understanding vision

If one accepts in broad terms this statement of what it means to understand an information processing task, one can go on to ask about the particular theories that one needs to understand vision. Vision can be thought of as a *process*, that produces from images of the external world a description that is useful to the viewer and not cluttered by irrelevant information. These descriptions, in turn, are built or assembled from many different but fixed representations, each capturing some aspect of the visual scene. In this article, I shall try to present a summary of our work on vision at M.I.T. seen from a perspective in which the representational problems assume a primary importance. I shall include summaries of our present ideas as well as of completed work.

The important point about a representation is that it makes certain information *explicit* (cf the principle of explicit naming, Marr 1976). For example, at some point in the analysis of an image, the intensity changes present there need to be made explicit, so does the geometry -- of the image and of the viewed shape -- and so do other parameters like color, motion, position and binocular disparity. To understand vision thus requires that we first have some idea of which representations to use, and then we can proceed to analyze the computational problems that arise in obtaining and manipulating each representation. Clearly the choice of representation is crucial in any given instance, for an inappropriate choice can lead to unwieldy and inefficient computations. Fortunately, the human visual system offers a good example of an efficient vision processor, and therefore provides important clues to the representations that are most appropriate and likely to yield successful solutions.

This point of view places the nature of the representations at the center of attention, but it is important to remember that the limitations on the processes that create and use these representations are an important factor in determining their structure, because one of the constraints on vision is that the description ultimately produced be derivable from images. In general, the structure of a representation is determined at the lower levels mostly by what it is possible to compute, whereas later on they can afford to be influenced by what is desirable to compute for the purposes of recognition.

1: Early processing problems

1.0: The primal sketch

There are two important kinds of information contained in an intensity array, the intensity changes present there, and the local geometry of the image. The primal sketch (Marr 1976) is a primitive representation that allows this information to be made explicit. Following the clues available from neurophysiology (Hubel & Wiesel 1962), intensity changes are represented by blobs and by oriented elements that specify a position, a contrast, a spatial extent associated with the intensity change, a weak characterization of the type of intensity change involved, and a specification of points at which intensity changes cease (so-called termination points). The representation of local geometry makes explicit two-dimensional geometrical relations between significant items in an image. These include parallel relationships between nearby edges, and the relative positions and orientations of significant places in the image. These significant places are marked by "place-tokens", and they are defined in a variety of ways, by blobs or local patches of different intensity, by small lines, and by the ends of lines or bars. The local geometrical relations between place-tokens are represented by inserting virtual lines that join nearby place-tokens, thus making explicit the existence of a relation between the two tokens, their relative orientation, and the distance between them (Marr 1976 figure 12a).

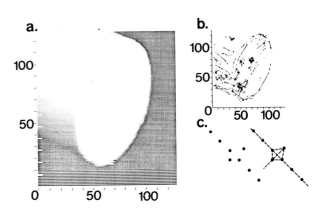

1. The primal sketch makes explicit information held in an intensity array (1a). There are two kinds, one concerns the changes in intensity, and this is represented by oriented edge, line and bar elements, associated with which is a measure of the contrast and spatial extent of the intensity change. The other kind of information is the local two-dimensional geometry of significant places in the image. Such places are marked by "place-tokens", which can be defined in a variety of ways, and the geometric relations between them are represented by inserting "virtual lines" between nearby tokens. (Marr 1976 figures 7 and 12a).

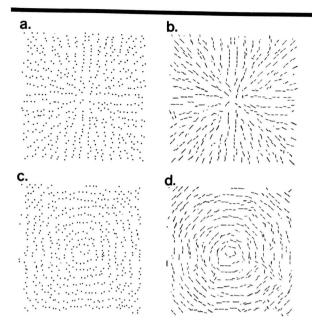

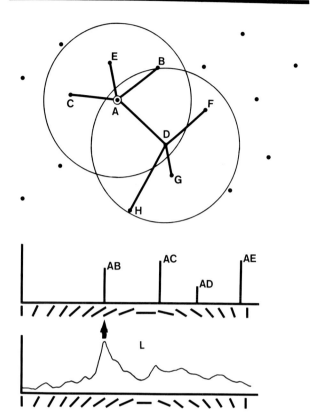

2. 2a and 2c are random-dot interference patterns of the kind described by Glass (1969). 2b and 2d exhibit the results of running the algorithm described in the text and figure 3. The neighborhood radius was such that roughly 8 neighbors were included. (Stevens 1977 figure 5).

1.1: Random-dot interference patterns

The idea of place-tokens and of this way of representing geometrical relations arose from considering the computational problems that are posed by early visual processing, and one of the questions we have been asking is, can one find any psychophysical evidence that the human visual system makes use of a similar representation? We have recently obtained two results related to this point. Stevens (1977) has examined the perception of random-dot interference patterns (figure 2), constructed by superimposing two copies of a random dot pattern where one copy has undergone some composition of expansion, translation, or rotation transformations (Glass 1969). He found that a simple algorithm suffices to account quantitatively for human performance on these patterns. The algorithm consists of three steps:

(1) Each dot defines a place-token. For example some dots can be replaced by small lines or larger blobs without disrupting the subjective impression of flow.

(2) Virtual lines are inserted between nearby place-tokens, and the neighborhood in which the virtual lines are inserted depends in a predictable way on the density of the dots.

(3) The orientations of the virtual lines attached to all the points in each neighborhood are histogrammed, and locally parallel organization is found by searching for a peak in this histogram. The bucket width that best matches human performance is about 10 degrees.

The details of these steps are set out in figure 3. The interesting features of the algorithm are; (a) It is not iterative. Stevens could find no evidence that human

3. The algorithm for computing locally parallel structure has three fundamental steps. Place tokens that are defined in the image are the input to the algorithm, which is applied in parallel to each one. Since, in the case of the Moiré dot patterns, each dot contibutes a place token, the first step is to construct a virtual line from that dot to each neighboring dot (within some neighborhood centered on the dot). A virtual line represents the position, separation, and orientation between a pair of neighboring dots. To favor relatively nearer neighbors, relatively short virtual lines are emphasized. The second step is to histogram the orientations of the virtual lines that were constructed for each of the neighbors. For example, the neighbor D would contribute orientations AD, DF, DG, and DH to the histogram. The final step (after smoothing the histogram) is to determine the orientation at which the histogram peaks, and to select that virtual line (AB) closest to that orientation as the solution. (Stevens 1977 figure 4).

performance rests on a cooperative algorithm, although this type of problem is ideal for that approach. (b) The algorithm is purely local. No global-to-local or top-down interactions are necessary to explain human performance. (c) What the algorithm finds is locally parallel organization. In this case, the organization lies in the virtual lines constructed between nearby dots, but locally parallel organization among the real edges and lines in an image also forms an important part of the structure of an image (Marr 1976).

1.2: Texture discrimination

The second study is one by Schatz (1977) on texture vision discrimination. Marr (1976) suggested that such discriminations could be carried out by first-order discriminations acting on the description in the primal sketch (p.501). Marr supposed that certain grouping processes were needed before the discriminations are made in order to account for the full range of human texture discrimination, but in a careful examination of the problem, Schatz found that many of the examples he constructed could be explained by assuming that the discriminations are made only on real edges or on virtual lines inserted between neighboring place-tokens. If this were generally true, it would stand in elegant relation to Julesz's (1975) conjecture, that a necessary condition for the discriminability of two textures is that their dipole statistics differ. This condition is known not to be sufficient, a state of affairs that one can view as implying that we have access to only a proper subset of all dipole statistics. It is possible that this proper subset consists only of real edges and of the virtual lines that join nearby place-tokens.

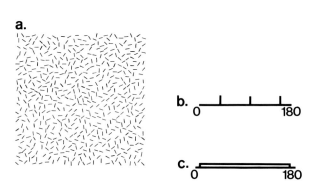

a.

b. 0 ⊢⊣⊢ 180

c. 0 ═══ 180

4. The pattern 4a contains two regions, one of whose line segments has the orientation distribution shown in 4b, and the other has the distribution 4c. Surprisingly, three orientations cannot be distinguished from a random orientation distribution. If human texture discrimination is based on first-order discriminations acting on the description held in the primal sketch, the discriminants that can be brought to bear on this information are weak.

1.3: Discrimination ability

If one accepts that texture discrimination relies upon first-order discriminations of this type, it is natural to ask how sensitive are the particular discrimination functions that we can bring to bear on an image. Riley (1977) has found evidence that the available functions are extremely coarse. For example, figure 4 consists of a background in which the line segments have a random orientation, surrounding a square containing lines of only three orientations. Surprisingly, the square cannot be discerned without scrutiny. One interpretation of this and related findings is, that discriminations on orientations other than horizontal and vertical are made on the output of 5 channels, each nearly binary, and with an angular width of

about 35 degrees -- in other words, only very little information is available about the distribution of orientations in an image. It appears that our discrimination ability is as poor or poorer for the other stimulus dimensions, for example intensity distribution (Riley 1977).

1.4: Light source effects

In another study concerned with what can be extracted from an image, Ullman (1976a) enquired about the possible physical basis for the subjective quality of fluorescence, which is normally associated with the presence of a light source. He noted that at a light source boundary, the ratio of intensity to intensity gradient changes sharply, whereas this is not true at reflectance boundaries unless the surface orientation changes sharply. He showed that, in the mini-world of Mondrians, the discriminant to which this leads predicts human performance satisfactorily.

Forbus (1977) has extended this work to the detection of surface luster. Since glossiness is due to the specular component of a surface reflectivity function, one can treat the detection of gloss as essentially the detection of light sources that appear reflected in a surface (see Beck 1974), and this depends ultimately on the ability to detect light sources. Forbus divided the problem into three categories; (a) in which the specularity is too small to allow gradient measurements, (b) in which both intensity and gradient measurements are available, but the specularity is local (as it is for a curved surface or a point source), and (c) in which the surface is planar and the source is extended. He derived diagnostic criteria for each case.

1.5: Regions from a discriminant

Whenever a region is defined in an image by a predicate, for example by a difference in texture or brightness, one faces the problem of delimiting the region accurately. There are two approaches to designing algorithms for this problem; one is to use the predicate directly, deciding whether a given location lies within or without the region by testing some function of the predicate there. The second approach is to differentiate the predicate, defining the region by its boundaries rather than by properties of its interior.

The difficulties with the problem arise because one is usually ignorant beforehand of the scale at which significant predicate signals may be gathered. For example, suppose one wished to find the boundary between two regions that are distinguished by different densities of dots. Dot density has to be measured by selecting a neighborhood size and counting the number of dots that lie within it. If the neighborhood size is too large, one may not be able to resolve the regions. If it is so small as to contain zero, one or two dots, natural fluctuations may obscure any changes in density.

One solution to this problem is to make the measurements simultaneously at several neighborhood sizes, looking for agreement between the results obtained in those neighborhood sizes that lie just above the size at which random fluctuations appear. This technique can be applied to region finding or to boundary finding, and an example of the results is given in figure 5. The dot density here is not known *a priori*.

This issue is of considerable techical interest, but it is important not to lose sight of the underlying computational problem, which is what kind of boundary is to be found, and why? The techniques of O'Callaghan (1974) for example are designed to find boundaries in dot patterns so accurately that

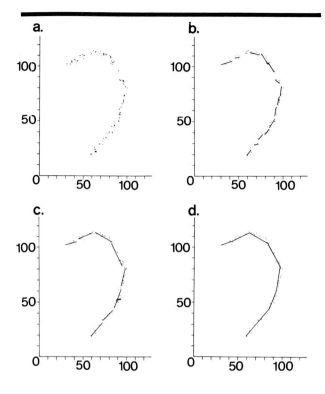

5. Finding a boundary from dot (or place-token) density changes. Once a rough assignment of boundary points has been made (5a), local line-fitting (5b) and grouping (5c & d) techniques can recover a rough specification of the boundary quite easily.

6. An example of a region whose rough boundary is clear, but whose exact boundary is not. (Drawing by K. Prendergast, 1977).

their positions are determined up to the decision about which dots it passes through. The justification for this type of study is that humans can assign boundaries this accurately, but the difficulty lies in formulating a reasonable definition of what the boundary is.

This problem is a deep one, touching the heart of the question of what early vision is *for*. I shall return to it later in this essay, but it is perhaps worth remarking here that there seems to be a clear need for being able to do early visual processing roughly and fast as well as more slowly and accurately, which means having ways of handling rough descriptions of regions -- ways of characterizing their approximate extent and shape -- *before* characterizing their precise boundaries. Figure 6 contains one example of a region whose rough extent is clear, but whose exact boundary is not.

The motivation for wanting this is that rough descriptions are very useful during the early stages of building a shape description for recognition (Marr & Nishihara 1977). For example a man often appears as a roughly vertical rectangle in an image, and this information is useful because it eliminates many other shapes from consideration quite early. Campbell (1977) has suggested that the extraction of rough descriptions from an image may depend on the ability to examine its lower

spatial frequencies. Even if this is one of the available mechanisms it is unlikely to be the only one, because sparse line drawings can raise the same problems while having almost no power in their low frequencies. It may be that some notion of rough grouping applied to low resolution place-tokens set up by pieces of contour in the image provides a useful approach to this problem.

1.6: Lightness

Ever since Ernst Mach noticed the bands named after him, there has been considerable interest in the problem of computing perceived brightness. Of especial interest is the recent work of Land & McCann (1971) on the retinex theory (see also Horn 1974), which is concerned with the quantity they call lightness; and that of Colas-Baudelaire (1973) on the computation of perceived brightness. Lightness is an approximation to reflectance that is obtained by filtering out slow intensity changes, the underlying idea being that these are usually due to the illuminant, not to changes in reflectance. The problem with this idea is of course that some slow changes in intensity are perceptually important (see Horn 1977 for an analysis of shape from shading). The linear filter model of Colas-Baudelaire performs well on images in which there are no sharp changes in intensity, but the author found it difficult to extend his model to the more general case. The recent finding of Gilchrist (1977), that perceived depth influences perceived brightness, suggests that some aspects of the problem occur quite late -- in our terms, at the level of the $2\frac{1}{2}$-D sketch (see below).

Our own work on the brightness problem is probably not relevant to the perception of brightness, but it is interesting as a demonstration that the primal sketch loses very little information. Woodham & Marr (unpublished program) have written a program that inverts the primal sketch, so that its output is an intensity array. The basic idea is to scan outwards from edges, assigning a constant brightness to points along the scan lines, and arresting the scan when it encounters another edge. Figure 7 exhibits the results of running this program, showing the original image (7a), the primal sketch (7b), and the reconstructed intensity array (7c).

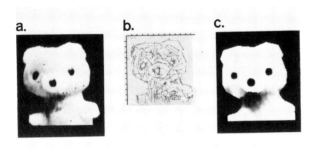

7. An image (7a), the spatial components of its primal sketch (7b), and a reconstruction of the image from the primal sketch (7c). This shows that the our current primal sketch programs lose little of the information in an image.

2: Process-oriented theories

2.0: Introduction

I said earlier that, especially at the earlier stages of visual information processing, the representations and processes are determined more by what it is possible to compute from an image than by what is desirable. Examples are the problems associated with structure from motion, stereopsis, texture gradients, and shading.

2.1: Structure from motion

Given a sequence of views of objects in motion, the human visual system is capable of interpreting the changing views in terms of the shapes of the viewed objects, and their motion in three-dimensional space. Even if each successive view is unrecognizable, the human observer easily perceives these views in terms of moving objects (Wallach & O'Donnell 1953). To answer the question of how a succession of images yields an interpretation in terms of three-dimensional structure in motion, Ullman (1977) divided the problem into two parts: (1) finding a correspondence between elements in successive views; and (2) determining the three-dimensional structures and their motion

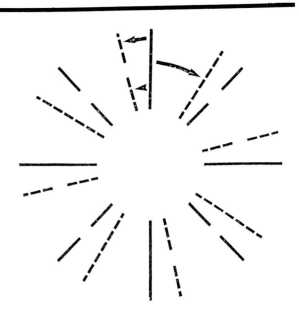

8. Evidence that the correspondence problem for apparent motion involves matching operations that act at a low-level. Frame 1 is shown with full lines and frame 2 with dotted lines. Instead of seeing a single wheel rotating, when appropriately timed the wheel splits, the outer and inner rings rotating one way, and the center rotating the other, as indicated by the arrows. This suggests that matching is carried out on elemental line segments, and is governed primarily by proximity. (Adapted from Ullman 1977).

from the way corresponding elements move between views.

An important preliminary question about the correspondence problem concerns the level at which it takes place. Is it primarily a low-level relation, established between small and simple parts of the scenes and largely independent of higher-level knowledge and three-dimensional interpretation? Or do higher level influences, like the interpretation of the whole of a shape from one frame, play an important part in determining the correspondence?

Ullman has assembled a considerable amount of evidence that the former view is correct. For example, figure 8 shows two successive frames, one denoted with full lines and the other with dotted lines. If the whole pattern were being analyzed from one frame, the shape of the wheel extracted, and used to match the elements in the next frame, the observer presented with these frames in rapid succession should perceive them as a whole wheel rotating. Notice however that the inner and outer parts of the wheel have their closest neighbors in one direction, whereas the center parts have theirs in the other; because of this, if the matching were done early and locally, the observer should see the center part rotating one way, and the inner and outer rings rotating the other (as shown with arrows in figure 8). When appropriately timed, this is in fact what happens.

Another line of evidence is the following. The most important factor in finding a correspondence between elements is the distance the element moves from one view to the next. But is this distance an objective two-dimensional measurement or an interpreted movement in three-dimensional space? There is some confusion in the literature about this point, since many studies have assumed that correspondence strength is linked to the smoothness of apparent motion (Kolers 1972), and this is apparently more closely related to three- than to two-dimensional distances. Ullman (1977) has however shown that this assumption is false, and that it is the two-dimensional distance alone that determines the correspondence.

The second part of the problem is to determine the three-dimensional structure once the correspondence between successive views has been established. Unless this problem is constrained in some way, it cannot be solved, so one has to search for reasonable assumptions on which to base the design of one's algorithms. (This state of affairs is a common one in the theory of visual processes, as we shall see when we discuss the problems of stereopsis, and shape from contour). Ullman suggested basing the interpretation on the following assumptions; (1) any two-dimensional transformation that has a unique interpretation as a rigid body moving in space should be interpreted as such an object in motion, and (2) that the imaging process is locally an orthogonal projection. He then showed that under orthogonal projection, three-dimensional shape and motion may be recovered from as little as three views each showing the image of the same five points, no four of which are coplanar. This result leads to algorithms capable of

recovering shape and motion from scenes containing arbitrary objects in motion. The final question is whether the algorithms that humans employ to recover shape and motion rely on these same two assumptions, and this question is currently under investigation. The important point here is that for more human-like algorithms, the number of views can be traded off against the accuracy of the computation, decreasing the emphasis on the particular number "three".

2.2: Stereopsis

Ever since Julesz's (1971) studies on random-dot stereograms, it has been clear that at least to a first approximation stereo vision can be regarded as a modular component of the human visual system. Marr (1974) and Marr & Poggio (1976) formulated the computational theory of the stereo matching problem in the following way:

(R1) *Uniqueness.* Each item from each image may be assigned at most one disparity value. This condition rests on the premise that the items to be matched correspond to physical marks on a surface, and so can be in only one place at a time.

(R2) *Continuity.* Disparity varies smoothly almost everywhere. This condition is a consequence of the cohesiveness of matter, and it states that only a relatively small fraction of the area of an image is composed of boundaries.

By representing these constraints geometrically, Marr & Poggio (1976) embodied them in a cooperative algorithm. In figure 9, Lx and Rx represent the positions of descriptive elements from the left and right views, and the horizontal and vertical lines indicate the range of disparity values that can be assigned to left-eye and right-eye elements. The uniqueness condition then corresponds to the assertion that only one disparity value may be "on" along each horizontal or vertical line. The continuity condition states that we seek solutions that tend to spread along the dotted diagonals, which

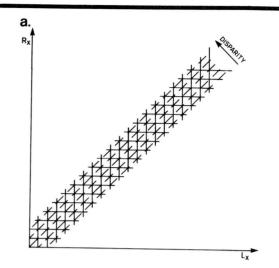

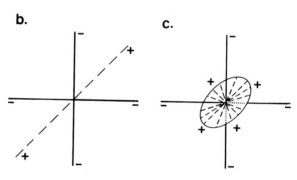

9. Figure 9a shows the explicit structure of the two rules *R1* and *R2* for the case of a one-dimensional image, and it also represents the structure of a network for implementing the algorithm described by equation 1. Solid lines represent "inhibitory" interactions, and dotted lines represent "excitatory" ones. 9b gives the local structure at each node of the network 9a. This algorithm may be extended to two-dimensional images, in which case each node in the corresponding network has the local structure shown in 9c. Such a network was used to solve the stereograms exhibited in figures 10 and 11. (Marr & Poggio 1976 figure 2).

are lines of constant disparity, and between adjacent diagonals. Figure 9b shows how this geometry appears at each intersection point. Figure 9c gives the corresponding local geometry when the images are two-dimensional rather than one.

It can be shown (Marr, Poggio & Palm 1977) that, if a network is created with the positive and negative connections shown in figure 9c, states of such a network that satisfy the constraints on the computation are stable, and that given suitable inputs, the network will converge to these stable states for a wide variety of the control parameters. Thus one can think of the network as defining an algorithm that operates on many input elements to produce a global organization *via*

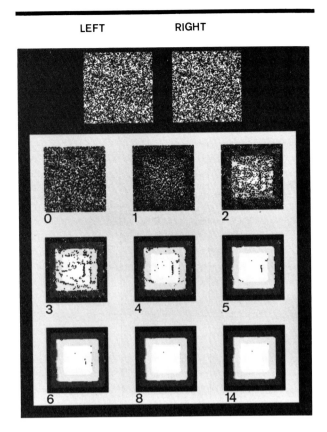

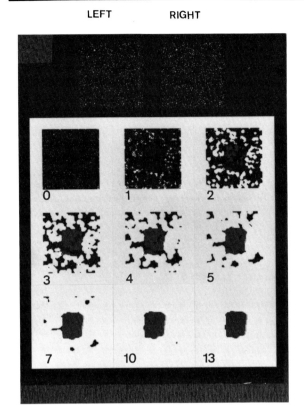

10. This and the following figure show the results of applying the algorithm defined by equation (1) to two random-dot stereograms. The initial state of the network C_{xyd} is defined by the input such that a node takes the value 1 if it occurs at the intersection of a 1 in the left and right eyes (see figure 9), and it has value 0 otherwise. The network iterates on this initial state, and the parameters used here, as suggested by the combinatorial analysis, were $\theta = 3.0$, $\epsilon = 2.0$ and $M = 5$, where θ is the threshold and M is the diameter of the "excitatory" neighborhood illustrated in figure 9c. The stereograms themselves are labelled LEFT and RIGHT, the initial state of the network as 0, and the state after n iterations is marked as such. To understand how the figures represent states of the network, imagine looking at it from above. The different disparity layers in the network lie in parallel planes spread out horizontally, so that the viewer is looking down through them. In each plane, some nodes are on and some are off. Each of the seven layers in the network has been assigned a different gray level, so that a node that is switched on in the top layer (corresponding to a disparity of +3 pixels) contributes a dark point to the image, and one that is switched on in the lowest layer (disparity = -3) contributes a lighter point. Initially (iteration 0) the network is disorganized, but in the final state, stable order has been achieved (iteration 14), and the inverted wedding-cake structure has been found. The density of this stereogram is 50%. (Marr & Poggio 1976 figure 3).

11. The algorithm of equation 1, with parameter values given in the legend to figure 10, is capable of solving random-dot stereograms with densities from 50% down to less than 10%. For this and smaller densities, the algorithm converges increasingly slowly. If a simple homeostatic mechanism is allowed to control the threshold θ as a function of the average activity (number of "on" cells) at each iteration, the algorithm can solve stereograms whose density is very low. In this example, the density is 5% and the central square has a disparity of +2 relative to the background. The algorithm "fills in" those areas where no dots are present, but it takes several more iterations to arrive near the solution than in cases where the density is 50%. When we look at a sparse stereogram, we perceive the shapes in it as cleaner than those found by the algorithm. This seems to be due to subjective contours that arise between dots that lie on shape boundaries. (Marr and Poggio 1976 figure 4).

local but highly interactive constraints. Formally, the algorithm reads:

$$C_{xyd}^{(n+1)} = u\left\{ \sum_{x'y'd' \in S(xyd)} C_{x'y'd'}^{(n)} - \epsilon \sum_{x'y'd' \in O(xyd)} C_{x'y'd'}^{(n)} + C_{xyd}^{(o)} \right\} \quad (1)$$

where $u(z) = 0$ if $z < \theta$, and $u(z) = 1$ otherwise; S and O are the circular and thick line neighborhoods of the cell C_{xyd} in figure

D. Marr

9c. This is an example of a "cooperative" algorithm (Marr & Poggio 1977a), and it exhibits typical non-linear cooperative phenomena like hysteresis, filling-in, and disorder-order transitions. Figures 10 and 11 illustrate two applications of the algorithm to random-dot stereograms.

There are a number of findings that cast doubt on the relevance of this algorithm to the question of how human stereo vision works. The most important of these findings are (a) the apparently crucial role played by eye-movements in human stereo vision (see especially Richards 1977); (b) our ability to tolerate up to 15% expansion of one image (Julesz 1971 figure 2.8.8); (c) our ability to tolerate the severe defocussing of one image (Julesz 1971 figure 3.10.3); (d) evidence that stereo detectors are organized into "three pools" (convergent, zero disparity, and divergent) and that this organization is important for stereo vision (Richards 1971); and (e) our ability to perceive depth in rivalrous stereograms (Mayhew & Frisby 1976). These difficulties led Marr & Poggio (1977b) to formulate a second stereo algorithm, designed specifically as a model for human stereopsis.

Our first stereo theory was inspired by Julesz's belief that stereoscopic fusion is a cooperative process -- a belief based primarily on the observation that it exhibits hysteresis. The main problem with the cooperative algorithm is that it apparently works too well in some ways (it performs better that humans do when eye-movements are eliminated), and not well enough in others (humans see depth in rivalrous stereograms). Our ability to fuse two images when one is blurred, the rivalrous stereogram results of Mayhew & Frisby (1976), and the recent results of Julesz & Miller (1975) on the existence of independent spatial-frequency-tuned channels in binocular fusion, suggest that several copies of the image, obtained by successively coarser filtering, are used during fusion, perhaps helping one another in a way similar to that in which local regions help each other in our cooperative algorithm.

The second idea was a notion that originated with Marr & Nishihara (1977) and about which I shall have more to say later, which is that one of the things early visual processing does is to construct a "depth map" of the surfaces round a viewer. In this map, each direction away from the viewer is associated with a distance (or some function of distance) and a surface orientation. We have christened the resulting datastructure the $2\frac{1}{2}$-D sketch.

The important point here is that the $2\frac{1}{2}$-D sketch is in some sense a memory. This provided the key idea: Suppose that the hysteresis Julesz observed is not due to a cooperative process at all, but is in fact the result of using a memory buffer in which to store the depth map of the image as it is discovered. Then, the fusion process itself need not be cooperative, and in fact it would not even be necessary for the whole image ever to be fused everywhere provided that a depth map of the viewed surface were built and maintained in this intermediate memory. This idea leads to the following theory. (1) Each image is convolved with bar-shaped masks of various sizes, and matching takes place between peak mask values for disparities up to about twice the panel-width of the mask (see Felton, Richards & Smith 1972), for pairs of masks of the same size and polarity. (2) Wide masks can control vergence movements, thus causing small masks to come into correspondence. (3) When a correspondence is achieved, it is held and written down somewhere (e.g. in the $2\frac{1}{2}$-D sketch). (4) There is a backwards relation between the memory and the masks, perhaps simply through the control of eye-movements, that allows one to fuse any piece of a surface easily once its depth map has been established in the memory.

This theory leads to many experimental predictions, which are currently being tested.

3: Intermediate processing problems

3.0 Introduction
We have discussed the types of information that need to be represented early in the processing of visual information, and we have examined the computational structure of some of the processes that can derive and maintain this information. We turn now to the question of what all this information is to be used for.

3.1 Difficulties with the idea of image segmentation
The current approach to machine vision assumes that the next step in visual processing consists of a process called *segmentation*, whose purpose is to divide the image into regions that are meaningful either in terms of physical objects or for the purpose at hand. Despite considerable efforts over a long period, the theory and practise of segmentation remain primitive, and once again I believe that the main reason lies in the failure to formulate precisely the goals of this stage of the processing. What for example is an object? Is a head one? Is it still one if it is attached to a body? What about a man on horseback?

These questions point to some of the difficulties one has when trying to formulate what should be recovered as a region from early visual processing. Furthermore, however one chooses to answer them, it is usually still impossible to recover the desired regions using only local grouping techniques acting on a representation like the primal sketch. Most images are too complex, and even the simplest images cannot often be segmented entirely at that level (e.g. Marr 1976 figure 13).

Something additional is clearly needed, and one approach to the dilemma has been to invoke specialized knowledge about the nature of the scenes being viewed to aid segmentation of the image into regions that correspond roughly to the objects expected in the scene. Tenenbaum & Barrow (1976), for example, applied knowledge about several different types of scene to the segmentation of images of landscapes, an office, a room, and a compressor. Freuder (1974) used a similar approach to identify a hammer in a simple scene. If this approach were correct, it would mean that a central problem for vision is arranging for the right piece of specialized knowledge to be made available at the appropriate time during segmentation. Freuder's work, for example, was almost entirely devoted to the design of a heterarchical control system that made this possible. More recently, the constraint relaxation technique of Rosenfeld, Hummel & Zucker (1976) has attracted considerable attention for just this reason, that it appears to offer a technique whereby constraints drawn from disparate sources may be applied to the segmentation problem whilst incurring only minimal penalties in control. It is however difficult to analyze such algorithms rigorously even in very clearly defined situations (see e.g. Marr, Poggio & Palm 1977), and in the naturally more diffuse circumstances that surround the segmentation problem, it may often be impossible.

3.2: Reformulating the problem
The basic problem seems to be how to formulate

precisely the next stage of visual processing. Given a representation like the primal sketch, and the many possible boundary-defining processes that are naturally associated with it, which boundaries should one attend to and why? The segmentation approach fails because objects and desirable regions are not visually primitive constructions, and hence cannot be recovered reliably from the primal sketch or similar representation without additional specialized knowledge. If we are to succeed, we must discover precisely what information it is that needs to be made explicit at this stage, what, if any, additional knowledge it is appropriate to apply, and we must design a representation that matches these requirements.

In order to search for clues to a suitable representation, let us return to the physics of the situation. The primal sketch represents intensity changes and the local two-dimensional geometry of an image. The principle factors that determine these are (1) the illuminant, (2) surface reflectance, (3) the shape of the visible surface, and (4) the vantage point. The first two factors raise the difficult problems of color and brightness, and I shall not discuss them further. The third and fourth factors are independent of the first two (whether two shapes are the same does not depend upon their colors or on the lighting), and so may be treated separately.

I shall argue that, since most early visual processes extract information about the visible surface, it is these surfaces, their shape and disposition relative to the viewer, that need to be made explicit at this point in the processing. Furthermore, because surfaces exist in three-dimensional space, this imposes constraints on them that are general, and not confined to particular objects. It is these constraints that constitute the *a priori* knowledge that it is appropriate to bring to bear next.

One example of the exploitation of fairly general constraints was the work of Waltz (1975), who formulated the constraints that apply to images of polyhedra. The representation on which that work was based was line drawings, but these are not suitable for our needs here, because part of the task we wish to carry out is the discovery of physical edges that are only weakly present or even absent in the primal sketch. The approach of Mackworth (1973) was closer to what we want, since it involved a primitive way of representing surfaces.

3.3: General classification of shape representations

Part of our task in formulating the problem of intermediate vision is therefore the examination of ways of representing and reasoning about surfaces. We therefore start our enquiry by discussing the general nature of shape representations. What kinds are there, and how may one decide among them? Although it is difficult to formulate a completely general classification of shape representations, Marr & Nishihara (1977) attempted to set out the basic design choices that have to be made when a representation is formulated. They concluded that there are three characteristics of a shape representation that are largely responsible for determining the information that it makes explicit. The first is the type of *coordinate system* it uses, whether it is defined relative to the viewer or to the object being viewed; the second characteristic concerns the nature of the *shape primitives* used by the representation, that is, the elements whose positions the coordinate system is used to define. Are they two- or three-dimensional, in what sizes do they come, and how detailed are they? And the third is concerned with the organization a representation imposes on the information in a description, for example is the description modular or does it have little internal structure? We have two sources of information that can help us to formulate the important issues in intermediate visual information processing, firstly the computational problems that arise, and secondly, psychophysics.

3.4: Some observations from psychophysics

Vision provides several sources of information about shape. The most direct are stereo and motion, but texture gradients in a single image are nearly as effective, and the theatrical techniques of facial make-up rely on the sensitivity of perceived shape to shading. It often happens that some parts of a scene are open to inspection by some of these techniques, and other parts by others. Yet different as the techniques are, they have two important characteristics in common. They rely on information from the image rather than on *a priori* knowledge about the shapes of the viewed objects; and the information they specify concerns the depth or surface orientation at arbitrary points in an image, rather than the depth or orientation associated with particular objects.

If one views a stereo pair of a complex surface, like a crumpled newspaper or the "leaves" cube of Ittelson (1960), one can easily state the surface orientation of any piece of the surface, and whether one piece is nearer to or further from the viewer than its neighbors. Nevertheless one's memory for the shape of the surface is poor, despite the vividness of its surface orientation during perception. Furthermore, if the surface contains elements nearly parallel to the line of sight, their apparent surface orientation when viewed monocularly can differ from the apparent surface orientation when viewed binocularly.

From these observations, one can perhaps draw some simple inferences.

(a) There is at least one internal representation of the depth, or surface orientation, or both, associated with each surface point in a scene.

(b) Because surface orientation can be associated with unfamiliar shapes, its representation probably precedes the decomposition of the scene into objects. (This point is particularly relevant to our discussion of intermediate visual information processing.)

(c) Because the apparent orientation of a surface element can change, depending on whether it is viewed binocularly or monocularly, the representation of surface orientation is probably driven almost entirely by perceptual processes, and is influenced only slightly by specific knowledge of what the surface orientation actually is. Our ability to "perceive" the surface much better than we can "memorize" it may also be connected with this point.

In addition, it seems likely that the different sources of information can influence the *same* representation of surface orientation.

3.5: The computational problem

In order to make the most efficient use of these different and often complementary sources of information, they need to be combined in some way. The computational question is, how best to do this? The natural answer is to seek some representation of the visual scene that makes explicit just the information these processes can deliver.

Fortunately, the physical interpretation of the representation we seek is clear. All these processes deliver information about the depth or surface orientation associated

Table 1

The form in which various early visual processes deliver information about the changes in a scene.

r = depth
δr = small, local changes in depth
Δr = large changes in depth
$\underline{s}$ = local surface orientation

Information source	Natural parameter
Stereo	Disparity, hence especially δr and Δr
Motion	r, hence δr, Δr
Shading	$\underline{s}$
Texture gradients	$\underline{s}$
Perspective cues	$\underline{s}$
Occlusion	Δr

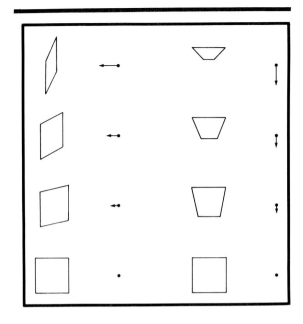

with surfaces in an image, and these are well-defined physical quantities. We therefore seek a way of making this information explicit, of maintaining it in a consistent state, and perhaps also of incorporating into the representation any physical constraints that hold for the values that depth and surface orientation take over the kinds of surface that occur in the real world. Table 1 lists the type of information that the different early processes can extract from images. The interesting point here is that although processes like stereo and motion are in principle capable of delivering depth information directly, they are in practise more likely to deliver information about local *changes* in depth, for example by measuring local changes in disparity. Texture gradients and shading provide more direct information about surface orientation. In addition, occlusion and brightness and size clues can deliver information about discontinuities in depth. (It is for example amazing how clear an impression of depth can be obtained from a monocular image containing bright or dim rectangles of different sizes against a dark background). The main function of the representation we seek is therefore not only to make explicit information about depth, local surface orientation, and discontinuities in these quantities, but also to create and maintain a global representation of depth that is consistent with the local cues that these sources provide. We call such a representation the $2\frac{1}{2}$-D sketch, and the next section describes a particular candidate for it.

3.6: A possible form for the $2\frac{1}{2}$-D sketch

The example I give for the $2\frac{1}{2}$-D sketch is a viewer-centered representation, which uses surface primitives of one (small) size. It includes a representation of contours of surface discontinuity, and it has enough internal computational structure to maintain its descriptions of depth, surface orientation and surface discontinuity in a consistent state. The representation itself has no additional internal structure.

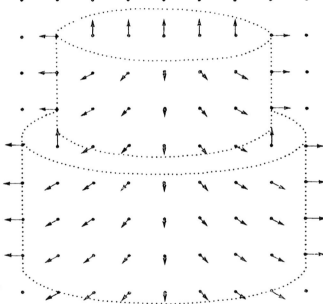

12. The $2\frac{1}{2}$-D sketch represents depth, contours of surface discontinuity, and the orientation of visible surfaces. A convenient representation of surface orientation is described in the text and illustrated here. The orientation of the needles is determined by the projection of the surface normal on the image plane, and the length of the needles represents the dip out of that plane (12a). A typical $2\frac{1}{2}$-D sketch appears in 12b, although depth information is not represented in the figure. (Marr & Nishihara 1977 figure 2).

Depth may be represented by a scalar quantity r, the distance from the viewer of a point on a surface. Surface discontinuities may be represented by oriented line elements. Surface orientation may be represented by a unit vector (x, y, z) in three-dimensional space. Following those who have used gradient space (Huffman 1971, Horn 1977) we can rewrite this as $(p, q, 1)$, which can be represented as a vector (p, q) in two-dimensional space. In other words, surface orientation may be represented by covering an image with needles. The length of each needle defines the dip of the surface at that point, so that zero length corresponds to a surface that is perpendicular to the vector from the viewer to that point, and the length increases as the surface tilts away from the viewer. The orientation of the needle defines the direction of the surface's dip. Figure 12 illustrates this representation.

In principle, the relation between depth and surface orientation is straightforward -- one is simply the integral of the other, taken over regions bounded by surface discontinuities. It is therefore possible to devise a representation with intrinsic computational facilities that can maintain the two variables, of depth and surface orientation, in a consistent state. But note that, in any such scheme, *surface discontinuities* acquire a special status (as curves across which integration stops). Furthermore, if the representation is an active one, maintaining consistency through largely local operations, curves that mark surface discontinuities (e.g. contours that arise from occluding contours in the image) must be "filled in" completely, so that at no point along an object boundary can the integration leak across it. It is interesting that subjective contours have this property, and that they are closely related to subjective changes in brightness (cf section 1.6) that are often associated with changes in perceived depth. If the human visual processor contains a representation that resembles the $2\frac{1}{2}$-D sketch, it would therefore be interesting to ask whether subjective contours occur within it. (See Ullman (1976) for an analysis of the shape of curved subjective contours).

In summary, my argument is that the $2\frac{1}{2}$-D sketch is useful because it makes explicit information about the image in a form that is closely matched to what early visual processes can deliver. We can formulate the goals of intermediate visual processing as being primarily the construction of this representation, discovering for example what are the surface orientations in a scene, which of the contours in the primal sketch correspond to surface discontinuities and should therefore be represented in the $2\frac{1}{2}$-D sketch, and which contours are missing in the primal sketch and need to be inserted into the $2\frac{1}{2}$-D sketch in order to bring it into a state that is consistent with the structure of three-dimensional space. This formulation avoids the difficulties associated with the terms "region" and "object", and allows one to ask precise questions about the computational structure of the $2\frac{1}{2}$-D sketch and of processes to create and maintain it. We are currently much occupied with these problems.

4: Later processing problems

4.0: Introduction

The $2\frac{1}{2}$-D sketch is a poor representation for the purposes of recognition because it is unstable (in the sense of Marr & Nishihara 1977), it depends on the vantage point, and it fails to make explicit pieces of a shape (like an arm) that are larger than the primitive size. Except for the simplest of purposes, it is an inadequate vehicle for a visual system to

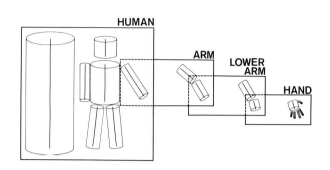

13. This diagram illustrates the organization of shape information in a 3-D model description. Each box corresponds to a 3-D model; with its model axis on the left side of the box and the arrangement of its component axes are shown on the right side. In addition some component axes have 3-D models associated with them and this is indicated by the way the boxes overlap. The relative arrangement of each model's component axes, however, is shown improperly since it should be in an object-centred system rather than the viewer-centred projection used here. This example shows a coarse overall description of a human shape along with an elaboration of one of its components (the arm). The important characteristics of this type of organization are: (i) each 3-D model is a self-contained unit of shape information and has a limited complexity, (ii) information appears in shape contexts appropriate for recognition (the disposition of a finger is most stable when specified relative to the hand that contains it), and (iii) the representation can be used flexibly (components can be elaborated according to the needs of the moment or the time available, and a 3-D model description of a component is easily added to a description of the whole shape). The major limitation imposed on the representation by this form of oraganization is on its scope, since it will only be useful for shapes for which the decomposition into 3-D models is well defined. (Marr & Nishihara 1977 figure 3).

convey information about shape to other processes, and so I turn now to representations that are more suitable for recognition tasks.

If one were to design a shape representation to suit the problems of recognition, one would naturally base it on an object-centered coordinate system. In addition, one would have to include shape primitives of many different sizes, so as to be able to make explicit shape characteristics that can range from a wart to an elephant. Marr & Nishihara (1977) discuss these questions in detail, and I shall not repeat their observations here. The deepest issues are those raised by having to define an object-based coordinate system. Since they are central to the problem of defining representations for use in later processing of visual information, I shall spend the remainder of the essay discussing this topic.

4.1: Nature of an object-centered coordinate system

Marr & Nishihara (1977) pointed out that there are two types of object-centered coordinate system that one might attempt to define precisely. One refers all locations on an object to a single coordinate frame that embraces the entire object, and the other distributes the coordinate system, making it local to each articulated component or individual shape characteristic. Marr & Nishihara concluded that the second of these schemes is the more desirable, and they gave as an example the representation illustrated in figure 13. But with a representation of this kind, the most difficult questions begin after its internal structure has been defined. How can one define canonically the coordinate scheme for an arbitrary shape, and even more difficult, how can such a thing be found from an image *before* a description of the viewed shape has been computed? Some kind of answers to these questions must be found if the representation is to be used for recognition.

4.2: Shapes having natural coordinate systems

If the coordinate system used for a given shape is to be canonical, its definition must take advantage of any salient geometrical characteristics that the shape possesses. For example, if a shape has natural axes, distinguished by length or by symmetry, then they should be used. The coordinate system for a sausage should take advantage of its major axis, and for a face, of its axis of symmetry.

Highly symmetrical objects, like a sphere, square, or circular disc, will inevitably lead to ambiguities in the choice of coordinate systems. For a shape as regular as a sphere this poses no great problem, because its description in all reasonable systems is the same. One can even allow other factors, like the direction of motion or of spin, to influence the choice of coordinate frame. For other shapes, the existence of more than one possible choice probably means that one has to represent the object in several ways. This is acceptable provided that the number of ways is small. For example, there are four possible axes on which one might wish to base the coordinate system for representing a door, the midlines along its length, its width, its thickness, and to represent how the door opens, the axis of its hinges. For a typewriter, there are two choices at the top level; an axis parallel to its width, because that is usually its largest dimension, and the axis about which a typewriter is roughly symmetrical.

In general, if an axis can be distinguished in a shape, it can be used as the basis for a local coordinate system. One approach to the problem of defining object-centered coordinate systems is therefore to examine the class of shapes having an axis as an integral part of their structure. One such is the class of *generalized cones*. (A generalized cone is the surface swept out by moving a cross section of constant shape but smoothly varying size along an axis, as in figure 14). Binford (1971) drew attention to this class of surfaces, suggesting that it might provide a convenient way of describing three-dimensional surfaces for the purposes of computer vision. I regard it as an important class not because the shapes themselves are easily decribable, but because the presence of an axis allows one to define a canonical local coordinate system. Fortunately many objects, especially those whose shape was achieved by growth, are described quite naturally in terms of one or more generalized cones. The animal shapes in figure 15 provide some examples -- the individual sticks are simply axes of generalized cones that approximate the shapes of parts of

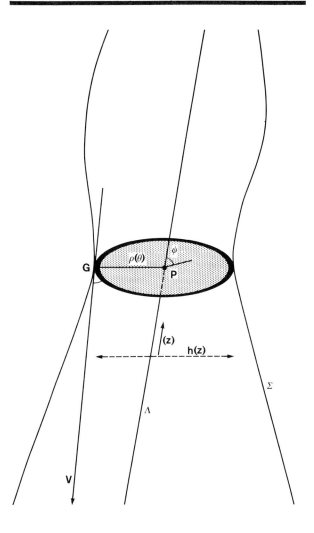

14. The definition of a generalized cone. In this article, a generalized cone is the surface generated by moving a smooth cross-section ρ along a straight axis Λ. The cross-section may vary smoothly in size (as prescribed by the function $h(z)$), but its shape remains constant. The eccentricity of the cone is the angle ψ between its axis and a plane containing a cross-section.

(Figure 5 of Marr 1977).

these animals. Many artifacts can also be described in this way, like a car (a small box sitting atop and in the middle of a longer one), and a building (a box with a vertical axis).

It is important to remember that there exist surfaces that cannot conveniently be approximated by generalized cones, for example a cake that has been cut at its intersection with some arbitrary plane, or the surface formed by a crumpled newspaper. Cases like the cake can be dealt with by introducing suitable surface primitives that describe the plane of the cut, but the crumpled newspaper poses apparently intractable problems.

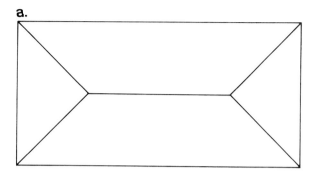

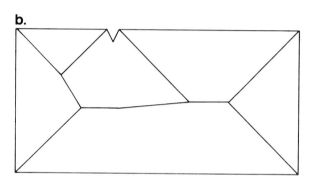

15. These pipecleaner figures illustrate the point that a shape representation does not have to reproduce a shape's surface in order to describe it adequately for recognition; as we see here, animal shapes can be portrayed quite effectively by the arrangement and relative sizes of a small number of sticks. The simplicity of these descriptions is due to the correspondence between the sticks shown here and natural or canonical axes of the shapes described. To be useful for recognition, a shape representation must be based on characteristics that are uniquely defined by the shape and which can be derived reliably from images of it. (Marr & Nishihara 1977 figure 1).

16. Blum's (1973) grassfire technique for recovering an axis from a silhouette is undesirably sensitive to small perturbations in the contour. 16a shows the Blum transform of a rectangle, and 16b, of a rectangle with a notch. (Redrawn from Agin 1972).

4.3: Finding the natural coordinate system from an image

Even if a shape possesses a canonical coordinate system, one is still faced with the problem of finding it from an image. Blum (1973), Agin (1972) and Nevatia (1974) have addressed problems that are related to this question. Blum's sym-axis theory is an interesting one, because he specifies precisely what it is that is computed from a two-dimensional outline. Unfortunately, it is not clear that what this theory computes is in fact useful for shape recognition (see e.g. figure 16), and when applied to a three-dimensional shape, the sym-axis is in general a two-dimensional sheet, so it cannot easily be used to define an object-centered coordinate system. Agin's and Nevatia's work, on the other hand, concerns the analysis of a depth map. This is an important problem, and it would be

interesting to see a careful analysis of the conditions under which their techniques will succeed.

My own interest in the problem grew from the 3-D representation theory of Marr & Nishihara (1977), in particular from the question of how to interpret the outlines of objects as seen in a two-dimensional image. The rest of this essay summarizes a recent article by Marr (1977). The starting point for this work was the observation that when one looks at the silhouettes in Picasso's work "Rites of Spring" (figure 17), one perceives them in terms of very particular three-dimensional shapes, some familiar, some less so. This is quite remarkable, because the silhouettes could in theory have been generated by an infinite variety of shapes which, from other viewpoints, have no discernable similarities to the shapes we perceive. One can perhaps attribute part of the phenomenon to a familiarity with the depicted shapes; but not all of it, because one can use the medium of a silhouette to convey a new shape, and because even with considerable effort it is difficult to imagine the more bizarre three-dimensional surfaces that could have given rise to the same silhouettes. The paradox is, that the bounding contours in figure 17 apparently tell us more than they should about the shape of the dark figures. For example, neighboring

17. "Rites of spring" by P. Picasso. We immediately interpret the silhouettes in terms of particular 3-D surfaces, despite the paucity of information in the image. In order to do this, we must be bringing additional assumptions and constraints to bear on the analysis of these contours' shapes. Marr (1977) enquired about the nature of this *a priori* information.

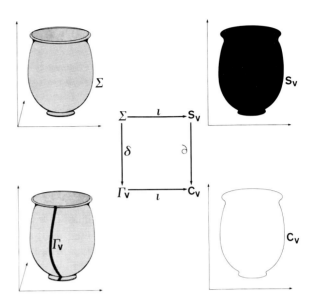

18. From viewpoint V, the three-dimensional surface Σ forms the silhouette S_V in the image *via* the imaging process ι. The boundary of S_V, obtained by the boundary operator ∂ is denoted by C_V and we call it the contour of Σ. The set of points on Σ that ι maps onto C_V we call the contour generator of C_V, and it is denoted by Γ_V. The map from Σ to Γ_V induced by ∂ is denoted by δ. (Figure 2 of Marr 1977).

points on such a contour could in general arise from widely separated points on the original surface, but our perceptual interpretation usually ignores this possibility.

The first observation to be made here is that the occluding contours that bound these silhouettes are contours of surface discontinuity, that is precisely the contours with which the $2\frac{1}{2}$-D sketch is concerned. Secondly, because we can interpret them as three-dimensional shapes, then implicit in the way we interpret them must lie some *a priori* assumptions that allow us to infer a shape from an outline. If a surface violates these assumptions, our analysis will be wrong, in the sense that the shape we assign to the contours will differ from the shape that actually caused them. An everyday example of this phenomenon is the shadowgraph, where the appropriate arrangement of one's hands can, to the surprise and delight of a child, produce the shadow of an apparently quite different shape, like a duck or a rabbit.

What assumptions is it reasonable to suppose that we make? In order to explain them, I need to define the

four structures that appear in figure 18. These are (1) some three dimensional surface Σ; (2) its image or silhouette S_V as seen from a viewpoint V; (3) the bounding contour C_V of S_V; and (4) the set of points on the surface Σ, that project onto the contour C_V. We shall call this last set the *contour generator* of C_V, and we shall denote it by Γ_V.

If one is presented with a contour in an image, without any knowledge of the surface or perspective that caused it, there is very little information on which one can base one's analysis. The only obvious feature available is the distinction between convex and concave pieces of contour -- that is, the presence of inflection points. In order that inflection points be "reliable", one needs to make some assumptions about the way the contour was generated, and I chose the following restrictions:

R1: The surface Σ is smooth.

R2: Each point on the contour generator Γ_V projects to a different point on the contour C_V.

R3: Nearby points on the contour C_V arise from nearby points on the contour generator Γ_V.

R4: The contour generator Γ_V of C_V is planar.

The first restriction is only a technical one. The second and third say that each point on the contour in the image comes from one point on the surface (which is an assumption that facilitates the analysis but is not of fundamental importance), and that where the surface looks continuous in the image, it really is continuous in three dimensions. The fourth condition, together with the constraint that the imaging process be an orthogonal projection, is simply a necessary and sufficient condition that the difference between convex and concave contour segments reflects properties of the surface, rather than characteristics of the imaging process.

It turns out that the following theorem is true, and it is a result that I found very surprising.

Theorem. If *R1* is true, and *R2 - R4* hold for all distant viewing directions that lie in some plane, then the viewed surface is a generalized cone.

This means that if, for distant viewpoints whose viewing directions lie parallel to some plane, a surface's shape can successfully be inferred using only the convexities and concavities of its bounding contours in an image, then that surface is a generalized cone or is composed of several such cones. The interesting thing about this result is that it implicates generalized cones. We have already seen that the important thing about these cones is that an axis forms an integral part of their structure. But this is a feature of their three-dimensional organization, and ought in some sense to be independent of the issues raised by vision. What the theorem says is that there is a natural link between generalized cones and the imaging process itself. The combination of these two must mean, I think, that generalized cones will play an intimate role in the development of vision theory.

4.4: Interpreting the image of a single generalized cone

If we take this result at face value, we can now ask an obvious question. Let us assume that our data consist of contours of surface discontinuity in the image of a generalized cone, since without this assumption we can deduce nothing. How may such contours be interpreted? To specify a generalized cone, we have to specify its axis Λ, cross-section $\rho(\theta)$, and axial scaling function $h(z)$ (figure 14); how can we discover them from an image?

The answer to this question is based on the notion of the *skeleton* of a generalized cone. The skeleton is not a difficult idea, since it is very like the set of lines a cartoonist draws to convey the shape of a curved object. It consists of three classes of contour: (a) the contours that occur in a generalized cone's silhouette; (b) the contours that arise from maxima and minima in a cone's axial scaling function (called the cone's *radial extremities*); and (c) contours that arise from maxima and minima in the cone's cross-section (its *fluting*). These categories are illustrated in figure 19.

The reason why the skeleton is a useful construct for recognition is that one can detect its presence in an image by the many relationships that exist among its parts. For example, radial extremities are all parallel to each other, and the silhouette and fluting have a kind of symmetry about the image of the cone's axis. It turns out that one can use these relationships to set up constraints on a set of contours such that, if those constraints are all satisfied by a unique interpretation of the contours in the image, one can be reasonably certain that a skeleton has been found, and hence that the contours can be interpreted as arising from a generalized cone whose axis is then determined. The practical importance of this result is

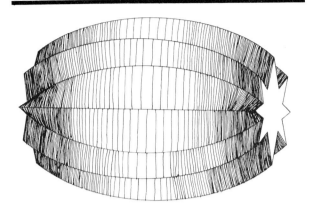

19. A sketch of a generalized cone showing its silhouette (the circumscribing contour), and its fluting (the contours spanning its length). The radial extremeties of a generalized cone are illustrated in figure 20.

20. Methods based on the theory described in the text suffice to solve this image of a bucket. An axial symmetry is established by its sides about the bucket's axis (shown thickened), and a parallel relationship holds between components of its radial extremity. (Figure 14 of Marr 1977).

illustrated in figure 20, where one can see that the image of the "sides" is symmetrical about the bucket's axis, and there is a clear parallel relationship between the image of the bucket's top, the corrugations in its side, and the visible part of its base (the bucket's radial extremities). These relations, of symmetries and parallelism, are preserved by an orthogonal projection. Hence

D. Marr

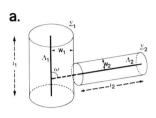

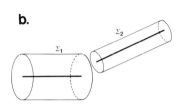

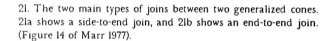

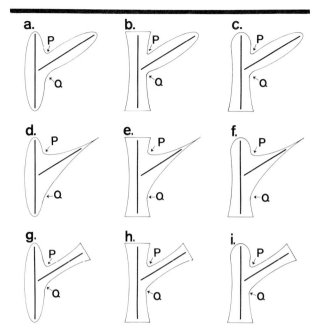

21. The two main types of joins between two generalized cones. 2la shows a side-to-end join, and 2lb shows an end-to-end join. (Figure 14 of Marr 1977).

22. This figure illustrates the types of side-to-end join that can occur between two short generalized cones. In the first column, the left-hand cone is convex; in the center column it is concave, and in the third column, it is convex on one side of the join, and concave on the other. The other cone is convex in the top row, and concave in the other two. Segmentation depends upon finding the points P and Q, which are defined by theorem 7 of Marr (1977) and illustrated here for each case. (Figure 18 of

Marr 1977).

provided that the contours are formed along a viewing direction that is not too close to the axis of the cone, these relations will still be present in the image. If the viewing direction lies so close to the cone's axis that its image is substantially foreshortened, these relationships will no longer be present, but it is part of the overall theory that such views have to be handled differently (Marr & Nishihara 1977).

4.5: Surfaces composed of two or more generalized cones

Real-life objects are often approximately composed of several different cones, joined together in various ways (see figure 13), and we therefore have to study ways of decomposing a multiple cone into its components -- for example, a human body into arms, legs, torso and head. Marr (1977) analyzed the two types of join shown in figure 21, giving criteria that define segmentation points on the contour produced by two joined cones (theorems 7 and 8). Figure 22 exhibits the segmentation points P and Q for the case in which two short cones are joined side-to-end. P. Vatan has written a computer program that can carry out this segmentation, and an example of its operation is illustrated in figure 23. The legend to the figure describes the particular algorithm used.

4.6: Some comments on the limitations of this theory

The results of this theory are limited in their scope to a particular class of views and surfaces, but on the other hand, they use only a limited kind of visual information, little more than occluding contours that are formed in an image by rays that graze a smooth surface. Interestingly, these particular contours are unsuitable for use in stereopsis or

structure-from-motion computations, because they are not formed from markings that define precise locations on the viewed surface. Creases and folds on a surface also give rise to contours in an image, and these have yet to be studied in detail. Information about shape from shading, texture, stereo or motion information has not yet been considered. By adding these other sources of information, I hope that a set of methods can eventually be assembled that together approach a comprehensive treatment of possible image configurations.

5: Summary

I have tried to make three main points in this article. The first is methodological, namely that it is important to be very clear about the nature of the understanding we seek (Marr & Poggio 1977a, Marr 1977b). The results we try to achieve should be precise, at the level of what I called a computational theory, and should deal with problems that can confidently be attributed to a real aspect of vision, and not (for example) to an artifact of the limitations of one's current vision program.

The second main point is that the critical issues for vision seem to me to revolve around the nature of the representations used - that is, the particular characteristics of the world that are made explicit - and the nature of the processes

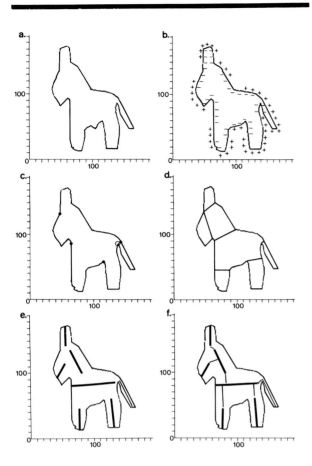

Table 2

A framework for the derivation of shape information from images.

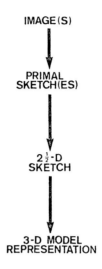

IMAGE(S)

PRIMAL SKETCH(ES)

Describes the intensity changes present in an image, labels distinguished locations like termination points, and makes explicit local two-dimensional geometrical relations.

$2\frac{1}{2}$-D SKETCH

Represents contours of surface discontinuity, and depth and orientation of visible surface elements, in a coordinate frame that is centered on the viewer.

3-D MODEL REPRESENTATION

Shape descriptions that include volumetric shape primitives of a variety of sizes, whose positions are defined using an object-centered coordinate system. This representation imposes considerable modular organization on its descriptions.

23. The occluding contours in an image can be used to locate the images of the natural axes of a shape composed of generalized cones (Marr 1977). The initial outline in (a) was obtained by applying local grouping processes to the *primal sketch* of the image of a toy donkey (Marr 1976). This outline was then smoothed and divided into convex and concave sections to get (b). Next, strong segmentation points, like the deep concavity circled in (c), are identified and a set of heuristic rules are used to connect them with other points on the contour to get the segmentation shown in (d). The component axes shown in (e) are then derived from these. The resulting segments are checked to see that they obey the rules for images of generalized cones. The boundaries must for example be symmetric about the axes, and in the case of side-to-end joins, the axis of the cone that is attached by its end must intersect the segmentation points that separate the two cones' contours. In this example, most of the symmetry relations have degenerated into parallelism. The thin lines in (f) indicate the position of the head, leg, and tail components along the torso axis, and the snout and ear components along the head axis. (This algorithm is due to P. Vatan).

that recover these characteristics, create and maintain the representations, and eventually read them. By analyzing the spatial aspects of the problem of vision (Marr & Nishihara 1977), an overall framework for visual information processing is suggested, that consists of three principal representations: (1) the primal sketch, which makes explicit the intensity changes and local two-dimensional geometry of an image; (2) the $2\frac{1}{2}$-D sketch, which is a viewer-centered representation of the depth and orientation of the visible surfaces and includes contours of discontinuities in these quantities; and (3) the 3-D model representation, whose important features are (a) that its coordinate system is object-centered, (b) that it includes volumetric primitives, that make explicit the space occupied by an object and not just its visible surfaces, and (c) that primitives of various sizes are included, arranged in a modular, hierarchical organization.

The third main point concerns the study of processes for recovering the various aspects of the physical characteristics of a scene from images of it. The critical act in formulating computational theories for such processes is the discovery of valid constraints on the way the world behaves, that provide sufficient additional information to allow recovery of the desired characteristic. Several examples are already available, including Land & McCann (1971), which rests on the distinction between sharp and shallow intensity changes; stereopsis (Marr 1974, Marr & Poggio 1976, 1977b) which uses continuity and uniqueness; structure from visual motion (Ullman 1977), which uses rigidity; fluorescence (Ullman 1976a), and shape from contour (Marr 1977a). The discovery of

D. Marr

constraints that are valid and sufficiently universal leads to results about vision that have the same quality of permanence as results in other branches of science (Marr 1977b).

Finally, once a computational theory for a process has been formulated, algorithms for implementing it may be designed, and their performance compared with that of the human visual processor. This allows two kinds of result. Firstly, if performance is essentially identical, one has good evidence that the constraints of the underlying computational theory are valid and may be implicit in the human processor; and secondly, if a process matches human performance, it is probably sufficiently powerful to form part of a general purpose vision machine.

Acknowledgements: I thank the members of the M.I.T. Artificial Intelligence Laboratory vision group for making this survey possible, especially Keith Nishihara with whom much of the overall framework was developed, Dr. Tomaso Poggio, Prof. Whitman Richards and Dr. Shimon Ullman for many stimulating discussions, and Karen Prendergast for preparing the illustrations. *Science* kindly gave permission for the reproduction of figures 9, 10 and 11, end the Royal Society for figures 1, 12, 13, 14, 15, 17, 18, 20, 21 and 22. This work was conducted at the Artificial Intelligence Laboratory, a Massachusetts Institute of Technology research program supported in part by the Advanced Research Projects Agency of the Department of Defense, and monitored by the Office of Naval Research under contract number N00014-75-C-0643.

6: References

Agin, G. J. (1972) Representation and description of curved objects. *Stanford A.I. Memo 173.*

Beck, J. (1974). *Surface color perception.* Ithaca, N. Y.: Cornell University Press.

Binford, T. O. (1971) Visual perception by computer. Presented to the IEEE Conference on Systems and Control, Miami, December.

Blum, H. (1973) Biological shape and visual science, (part 1). *J. theor. Biol.* , *38*, 205-287.

Campbell, F. W. C. (1977) Sometimes a biologist has to make a noise like a mathematician. *NRP Bulletin on Neurophysiology and Psychophysics* (in the press).

Colas-Baudelaire, P. (1973) Digital picture processing and psychophysics: a study of brightness perception. *Report No. UTEC-CSC-74-025 from the Department of Computer Science, University of Utah.*

Forbus, K. (1977) Light source effects. *M.I.T. A.I. Lab. Memo 422.*

Freuder, E. C. (1974) A computer vision system for visual recognition using active knowledge. *M.I.T. A.I. Lab. Technical Report 345.*

Glass, L. (1969) Moire effect from random dots. *Nature, 243,* 578-580.

Gilchrist, A. L. (1977) Perceived lightness depends on perceived spatial arrangement. *Science, 195,* 185-187.

Horn, B. K. P. (1974) Determining lightness from an image. *Computer Graphics and Image Processing, 3,* 277-299.

Horn, B. K. P. (1977) Image intensity understanding. *Artificial Intelligence,* in the press.

Hubel, D. H. & Wiesel, T. N. (1962) Receptive fields, binocular interaction and functional architecture in the cat's visual cortex. *J. Physiol., Lond. 160* 106-154.

Huffman, D. A. (1971) Impossible objects as nonsense sentences. In *Machine Intelligence 6,* Eds. R. Meltzer & D. Michie, pp 295-323. Edinburgh: The Edinburgh University Press.

Ittelson, W. H. (1960) *Visual space perception,* pp145-147. New York: Springer.

Julesz, B. (1971) *Foundations of Cyclopean perception.* Chicago: The University of Chicago Press.

Julesz, B. (1975) Experiments in the visual perception of texture. *Scientific American 232,* 34-43, April.

Julesz, B. & Miller, J. E. (1976) Independent spatial-frequency-tuned channels in binocular fusion and rivalry. *Perception 4,* 125-143.

Kolers, P. A. (1972) *Aspects of motion perception.* New York: Pergamon Press.

Land, E. H. & McCann, J. J. (1971) Lightness and retinex theory. *J. opt. Soc. Am. 61,* 1-11.

Mackworth, A. K. (1973) Interpreting pictures of polyhedral scenes. *Artificial Intelligence 4,* 121-138.

Marr, D. (1974) A note on the computation of binocular disparity in a symbolic, low-level visual processor. *M.I.T. A.I. Lab. Memo 327.*

Marr, D. (1976) Early processing of visual information. *Phil. Trans. Roy. Soc. B. 275,* 483-524.

Marr, D. (1977) Analysis of occluding contour. *Proc. Roy. Soc. B. 197,* 441-475.

Marr, D. (1977b) Artificial Intelligence - a personal view. *Artificial Intelligence 9,* 37-48.

Marr, D. & Nishihara, H. K. (1977) Representation and recognition of the spatial organization of three-dimensional shapes. *Proc. Roy. Soc. B. 200,* 269-294.

Marr, D. & Poggio, T. (1976) Cooperative computation of stereo disparity. *Science 194,* 283-287.

Marr, D. & Poggio, T. (1977a) From understanding computation to understanding neural circuitry. *Neurosciences Res. Prog. Bull. 15,* 470-488.

Marr, D. & Poggio, T. (1977b) A theory of human stereo vision. *M.I.T. A.I. Lab. Memo 451.*

Marr, D. , Poggio, T. & Palm, G. (1977c) Analysis of a cooperative stereo algorithm. *Biol. Cybernetics 28*, 223-239.

Mayhew, J. E. W. & Frisby, J. P. (1976) Rivalrous texture stereograms. *Nature 264*, 53-56.

Nevatia, R. (1974) Structured descriptions of complex curved objects for recognition and visual memory. *Stanford A.I. Memo 250.*

O'Callaghan, J. F. (1974) Computing the perceptual boundaries of dot patterns. *Computer Graphics and Image Processing 3*, 141-162.

Richards, W. A. (1971) Anomalous stereoscopic depth perception. *J. Opt. Soc Amer. 61*, 410-414.

Richards, W. A. (1977) Stereopsis with and without monocular cues. *Vision Res.* (in the press).

Riley, M. (1977) Discriminant functions in early visual processing. (In preparation).

Rosenfeld, A. , Hummel, R. A. & Zucker, S. W. Scene labelling by relaxation operations. *IEEE Transactions on Systems, Man and Cybernetics, SMC-6*, 420-433.

Schatz, B. R. (1977) On the computation of texture discrimination. *To be given at the Fifth International Joint Conference on Artificial Intelligence, August 1977.*

Stevens, K. A. (1977) Computation of locally parallel structure. *M.I.T. A.I. Lab Memo 392.*

Tenenbaum, J. M. & Barrow, H. G. (1976) Experiments in interpretation-guided segmentation. *Stanford Research Institute Technical Note 123.*

Ullman, S. (1976a) On visual detection of light sources. *Biol. Cybernetics 21*, 205-212.

Ullman, S. (1976b) Filling-in the gaps: The shape of subjective contours and a model for their generation. *Biol. Cybernetics 25*, 1-6.

Ullman, S. (1977) The interpretation of visual motion. *M.I.T. Ph. D. Thesis, June.*

Wallach, H. & O'Connell, D. N. (1953) The kinetic depth effect. *J. exp. Psychol. 45*, 205-217.

Waltz, D. (1975) Understanding line drawings of scenes with shadows. In: *The psychology of computer vision*, Ed. P. H. Winston, pp19-91. New York: McGraw-Hill.

Characterization and Requirements of
Computer Vision Systems*

by

Ramakant Nevatia
Image Processing Institute
and
Computer Science Department
University of Southern California
Los Angeles, California 90007

ABSTRACT

The environments in which the vision systems operate, and their goals, need to be specified for an analysis of the visual strategies and processes appropriate for them. Three broad classes of increasing generality are defined and other parameters affecting system design are included. The difficulties of some general processes such as edge detection, segmentation and shape description, and the resulting simplifications for special purpose systems are discussed. An expressed view is that a general purpose vision system must be capable of generating rich descriptions without knowledge of specific objects in a scene, as such information is not always available.

1. INTRODUCTION

Discussions about the strategies for building machine vision systems usually center on issues such as the control strategies, viz top-down versus bottom-up, the type, the amount of, and the level at which the world knowledge is used, the techniques of image analysis such as edge and region analysis and many more (summarized by Riseman and Hanson[1]). However, before these questions can be debated meaningfully, the goals of the system and the environments in which it must perform need to be specified. Proponents of two conflicting strategies may well be attempting to build systems with differing goals and capabilities.

The problem of specifying such capabilities is complex and difficult. This paper aims at defining a structure for broad characterization of vision systems. The requirements and design considerations for building different classes of systems and difficulties of realizing some generally useful processes such as segmentation and shape description are also discussed.

2. DESCRIPTIONS OF VISION SYSTEMS

Describing the capabilities of a vision system requires, at the least, a description of its operating environment and the tasks it is able to perform in that environment. In general, these characteristics may be described along many dimensions. Only in extremely limited situations, e.g. for a fixed font, printed character recognition machine, have the specifications been made precise.

Task Environments:

An important dimension in the description of systems is the specification of the number and the types of the objects, the constraints placed on their size, location and orientation, and the amount of a priori knowledge, if any, about the operating environment. Three qualitative and broad classes are specified below.

I. The objects in the scene are completely known and their approximate locations and orientations are also known (the location may be specified by relations, such as the only object on the left half of a table). A goal for the machine may be to determine exact location and orientation of the objects. Many industrial automation tasks belong to this class, for example determining the exact orientation of a silicon chip for automated lead bonding [2]. Automatic vehicle guidance systems with sufficiently accurate map information would also belong to this class.

II The world of objects is small and known. However, the specific objects in the scene, and their locations and orientations are unknown. The goals of the system may be to identify the objects, determine their location or to validate the presence of certain specified objects (with or without specified spatial relations). This environment has been typical of the laboratory systems studied in the past, such as the earlier "block's world" analysis systems (e.g. see [3]), and also many of the recent attempts to work with more complex objects.

* This research was supported by the Advanced Research Projects Agency of the Department of Defense and was monitored by the Wright-Patterson Air Force Base under Contract No. F-33615-76-C-1203. The views and conclusions in this paper are those of the author and should not be interpreted as necessarily representing the official policies, either expressed or implied of the ARPA or the U.S. Government.

III. The number of objects is large, not explicitly known, and the objects may occur in any physically permissible spatial relationships (with possible preferences for certain relationships). This class of systems is clearly broad, depending on the number of objects in their world. Our normal perception of the everyday world is towards the most complex end of this spectrum. Systems of class I and II may be special cases of class III systems in particular situations where known context delimits the task environment.

Useful sub-classes of increasing difficulty could be defined for the above three classes. The processing capabilities necessary for the three types of systems that operate in different environments are likely to be different. Top-down, goal directed approaches using only very simple pictorial analysis may be the most effective and economical for class I systems, but completely inadequate for class III systems. Requirements and difficulties for realization of the different classes of systems are discussed later.

The following additional factors need to be considered in specifying the environments of vision systems:

(a) Sensor type: Different sensors such as visible spectrum achromatic, color or multiple spectral bands, forward looking infrared (FLIR), or synthetic aperture radar (SAR) sensors have different characteristics, which may either help the analysis or create complications to be reckoned with. Some characteristics of the latter two are described in [4].

(b) Resolution of data: High resolution data is necessary for describing small, fine details in a scene. However, processing of a complete image at its maximum photographic resolution is usually prohibitive because of the computation time and storage requirements. The available resolution also affects the higher levels of processing, as certain features may be hard to detect in low resolution data, and the fine detail and texture of high resolution data may create difficulties for the description processes.

(c) Type of objects: In much of past work, the type of objects present in the scene were assumed to be solid and opaque. Only the surfaces oriented towards the viewer are visible for such objects. Organization of surfaces into objects is much more difficult for transparent and translucent objects. Easily deformed objects, for example wearing apparel, present difficulties in shape analysis as the shape changes are not easily characterized or predicted.

(d) Complexity of the scene: The term complexity is used here to relate to the difficulty of analyzing a particular scene. Even within the constraints of a class as defined above, some scenes are much more complex than others. Factors contributing to such complexity are not well understood but probably include the following: dynamic range and contrast of a scene, the number of objects, the range of object sizes and the presence of fine texture, shadows or reflections in a scene, and the necessity of three-dimensional analysis.

The above characterization of system goals and environments is obviously incomplete. These parameters can be described along many more dimensions with several gradations along each dimension. Even the dimensionality of this description space is unknown. However, it is hoped that even such a sketchy characterization of visual systems will hlep focus the debate on optimal or appropriate strategies and processes.

3. CONSIDERATIONS FOR A "GENERAL PURPOSE" VISION SYSTEM

In the absence of a specific definition, a "general" vision system may be presumed to have capabilities as broad as that of humans in a range of similarly complex environments. In terms of the above classifications, a general system will be taken to be one belonging to class III.

A highly schematic view of the author's concept of such a system is shown in figure 1. The division in different levels is somewhat arbitrary and the functions of the levels overlap. A brief description of the processing at various levels is followed by a discussion of some of the difficulties in their implementation.

(a) Preprocessing: Preprocessing is to transform the input image into a form more suitable for subsequent processing. Some examples are: processing of the input signal to compensate for known sensor defects or sensor dependent attributes, and transformation of color picture data into a desirable coordinate system.

(b) Feature extraction (primitive descriptions): Refers to the processing that can be performed directly on an image using only local neighborhoods with little or no interaction from other parts of the image. Some examples are: single pixel attributes, such as spectral distributions, local edge detection, formation of regions having a uniform attribute, and computation of statistical texture features in a given window.

(c) Symbolic descriptions: This level covers a broad range of operations that generate higher level descriptions from the primitive descriptions that are useful in forming hypotheses for the presence of specific objects in a scene. Typical operations are those of organizing local edge elements into larger boundary segments (or merging of local regions into larger regions), generating shape descriptions of parts of a scene and describing relationships of different structures in a scene. The relationships between parts may be spatial, e.g. adjacency and containment, or semantic such as support, shadow casting hypotheses and texture gradient descriptions.

An important characteristic of this system is that the descriptions at this level need not be unique. Multiple descriptions are passed onto the higher levels where more context and model specific knowledge is available to choose between alternate hypotheses. Ability to construct useful symbolic descriptions is of central importance. Development of these processes has been slow and difficult problems encountered remain unsolved.

Ramakant Nevatia

(d) Interpretation: At this level, hypotheses for the objects or structures in the image based on the symbolic descriptions are generated. The interpretation process draws on the repertory of objects known to it. It is crucial that only a small number of reasonable hypotheses be generated even when the number of objects known is large. The performance of this level is highly dependent on the quality of the available symbolic descriptions. This level also directs further processing to explain the differences between observed descriptions and expected descriptions. Such verification may require new feature extraction, such as location of a low contrast edge with the added context available now, or a restructuring of the existing primitives into different symbolic descriptions. Clearly, the previous stages must be designed to accept such feedback and use the context supplied from this level. Also, the paradigm permits acquisition of a "Visual Memory," i.e. the models can be acquired by storing machine generated descriptions of observed scenes.

The major premise of the proposed system is that class III systems must be capable of "bottom-up" processing to the point of generating rich and useful descriptions without the knowledge of specific objects in a scene. Knowledge is often prescribed as a remedy for correcting mistakes or inadequacies of low level description processes. However, prototype specific knowledge is readily available only for class I systems. For class III systems, as the number of objects grows, it becomes increasingly more expensive to match each model in the memory with the computed descriptions. The difficulty is compounded if all viewing angles and possible occlusions must be considered.

It is clear that for prototype specific knowledge to be useful here, an indexing procedure to retrieve a small number of relevant prototypes is essential. Further, it is the author's view that effective indexing procedures cannot, in general, be based on local descriptions such as intensity, color (if available), local texture or local shape. These local attributes have a limited discriminating ability and are not necessarily the essential attributes of all objects. For example, many solid objects may be painted in various colors and textured patterns and remain easily identifiable.

Two simple examples are given to support the above views. Consider the perception of a familiar office scene, with known pieces of furniture in likely configurations. While such a priori information is clearly useful, a human would have little difficulty in perceiving the same office with furniture drastically rearranged or even with the room filled with objects not normally found in an office (ignoring delays on the order of hundreds of milliseconds). In these circumstances, the system must build descriptions without any a priori, prototype specific knowledge, and use the descriptions to index previously unexpected models. The alternative of verifying or rejecting each known model seems unlikely, even if a highly parallel computational structure is

assumed to be available.

The importance of descriptions is even more evident in the perception of unfamiliar objects. No recognition is posssible here, by definition, but a description of similarities and differences with known objects is of importance. E.g. consider the situation of observing a purple, five-legged "cow". Ability to generate uguided and structured shape descriptions seems essential for such an observation.

The problem of generating descriptions without model specific knowledge is difficult. Ability to generate largely correct segmentations is essential, as is the ability to work from incomplete and imperfect segmentations. Many of the required processes are unknown. Some of the essential processes and difficulties associated with them are discussed below.

4. SOME GENERAL PROCESSES AND ASSOCIATED PROBLEMS

Consider the example in figure 2 which shows an image digitized at 256 x 256 pixels resolution, each pixel intensity being in the range of 0 - 255. The picture is simple in that only one man-made object is present, the image is of high quality (high signal to noise ratio and good contrast), and the resolution is adequate to distinguish many fine details of the object. The complexity of the picture is in the presence of a textured background and shadows, and the intricacy of the detailed shape of the object and its many small components.

If this image were an input to a class III system, little a priori information about the likely objects in it would be available, as is presumably the case for a first-time reader of this paper. The system goal might be to recognize the object or to generate a description of it. In a class II system the problem may be to identify the object as being one of a known, small set of vehicles. In a class I system the object is known and a goal could be to determine the exact location and orientation of the truck.

In the following, using the above image as an example, difficulties of implementing some general processes, and the simplifications occurring for class I and II systems are examined. (It is assumed that the environment is complex enough that classification based on single pixel attributes is not adequate.)

(a) Primitive operations: These are defined to be the operations that are performed directly and locally on images, e.g. edge detection and formation of regions with a uniform, local property. Edge detection algorithms abound in the literature, for a survey see [5]. The different techniques use different concepts of what constitutes an edge. One class of edge detectors looks for areas of rapid intensity changes. Others find particular intensity profiles that are assumed to correspond to an ideal edge, as in [6].

Most edge detection algorithms can provide a number indicating the strength or a confidence value for an edge. These values are usually thresholded to give a binary decision to simplify further processing. However, little work has been reported on automatic selection of an appropriate threshold value.

Another important parameter is the size of the neighborhood over which the edge properties are computed. A larger neighborhood allows for detection of lower contrast edges but the detection of two nearby edges is poorer. Rosenfeld and Thurston [7], and Marr [8] have described approaches toward choice of an optimal neighborhood size.

Normally, the edge detection algorithms assume that the edges sought are between surfaces (or parts of surfaces) that are homogeneous in some picture property such as color or brightness. These algorithms may perform well in the presence of random noise, but not necessarily so in the presence of fine texture, as is often the case in natural scenes. When such edge detectors are applied to scenes containing texture, the performance is erratic as expected.

Figure 3 shows the edges obtained by applying the Hueckel edge detector, [6], to the image in figure 2. Some of the edges along the truck boundary, particularly along the segment between the top of the truck and a background bush, are not detected. This is attributed to the presence of texture in these areas. Also some of the final detail is lost in the areas around the truck cab, probably because of the large neighborhood size of the edge operator (approximately eight pixels in diameter) compared to these features.

The missing edges could perhaps be filled in by higher level processes such as by extrapolation of extracted line segments or hypothesizing parallel lines. Depth information would be helpful, but extraction of depth from a monocular view is a difficult problem in itself. However, many of the missing edges may be perceivable without any additional context. For example, a close examination of the truck-bush boundary in figure 2, by obscuring the remainder of the picture, indicates that a subtle edge is visible.

The tradeoffs between the use of higher level processing to compensate for the deficiencies of lower level processes and the development of better low level operators, such as texture edge detectors are unclear. However, for a general purpose system, the ability to discriminate textures seems essential, as evidenced by human's ability to distinguish between random dot texture patterns having no semantic or three-dimensional information. The edge detector described by Rosenfeld and Thurston [7] is applicable to detection of texture edges, but the difficult problems of choosing suitable texture measures remain.

The texture edge detection problem may be simpler for special purpose systems. Simple, statistical texture measures may suffice here and the particular measures to use may be known in advance.

(b) Segmentation: The primitive descriptions generated by an edge detection or atomic region formation process need to be organized into larger structures for segmentation and other higher level processing. The number of such Gestalt-like processes is believed to be large and only a few of them are explicitly known (e.g. see [8]). Further, these processes are expected to be quite complex.

One operation believed to be of basic importance is that of linking local edge elements into long, straight or slowly curving, line segments. Such segments often correspond to man-made objects in an image. A technique for constructing such segments has been described by the author in [9] (a similar technique has also been used by Marr [8]) and the resulting linked segments from the edges in figure 3 are shown in figure 4 (the wide spots are present because no thinning of edges was performed before linking them).

The boundary segments have been constructed fairly well around the carrier part of the truck. However, many gaps exist and the details around the cab are lost almost completely. Segmentation of the truck from the background, without a priori prototype knowledge, starting from this data seems to be a difficult task. Some of the deficiencies are caused by the edge detection operator and others by the linking process. Both of these processes can undoubtedly be improved to yield better results.

The important issue is whether improved lower level processes can be expected to give fundamentally different results. Judging by the local nature of the edge detection process and the difficulties experienced in the line extraction for simple polyhedral scenes in the past, it seems reasonable to contend that such processes cannot, in general, be expected to yield closed boundaries or preserve details of all sizes without feedback from the higher level processes. In this case, a general purpose system will need the ability to generate useful higher level descriptions from such imperfect, but largely correct, data.

A complementary approach to boundary construction for segmentation is that of region construction. The region based methods aim at finding areas of an image over which certain properties are constant, rather than find points of discontinuity (e.g. see [10]). While the region methods always give closed boundaries, by construction, the difficulties caused by texture and the problems of grouping regions into solid objects are analogous to those for edge based methods. For specific applications, one or the other method may have distinct advantages. A comparison of the two segmentation techniques may be found in [11].

The segmentation problems may be considerably simpler for special purpose systems. Complete boundaries or figure-ground separation may not be necessary, and only extraction of few prominent features such as some vertices or large uniform regions may suffice. Also, information aiding segmentation may be available a priori, such as in the form of approximate location of a vertex and orientations of its lines, or the color and brightness range of a desired region. These features may be sufficient to establish model specific context to guide further feature extraction. Region growing segmentation techniques described in [12, 13] are examples of results achievable when the domain of application is limited, and its properties known a priori.

(b) Shape description: Another generally needed, major process is that of shape description. A generalized cone representation for the shape of complex objects has been suggested by Binford [14] and appears to have gained wide acceptability (see the papers of Brady, Marr and Waltz in this volume). The advantages of this representation are discussed elsewhere (e.g. see [15]). However, the computation of the generalized cones from image data is complex and relatively few implementations have been described [15-18].

All of these methods assume availability of complete data. Nevatia and Binford [17], and Marr and Nishihara [18] require complete object boundaries, whereas Agin and Binford [15] require complete three-dimensional range of the visible surfaces. These techniques also assume, implicitly or explicitly, that the cone cross-sections contain no slope discontinuities. Therefore, they do not apply to describing some simple objects, such as rectangular polyhedra. These shape description processes are inadequate, if only incomplete boundaries, as shown in figure 4, can be expected to be generated by the lower level processes.

It is unclear if these shape description problems are simpler for special purpose systems. The main simplification may be that complex volume shape descriptions are not always necessary, and the simpler descriptions, such as lines and regions can be matched directly with the stored models.

(d) Indexing: Indexing refers to the retrieval of similar models from memory based on a description of the scene. If the descriptions are complete and error free, indexing of one or more models with the same attributes is straightforward (the attributes used for indexing need not be sufficient to give a unique match). Little attention has been paid to the indexing problem in the presence of expected variability and errors in the descriptions [17].

The indexing difficulty may be viewed as the main source of different strategies being appropriate for the different types of systems. For class I systems indexing is unnecessary, the specific objects being known in advance. For class II systems, simple and incomplete descriptions, aided by known context may suffice.

5. CONCLUSIONS

The main view expressed here is that a general purpose vision system must possess the ability to generate complex descriptions, utilizing a

segmentation that is correct to the extent that useful indexing into a store of models can be achieved. The problems of unguided segmentation and scene description are difficult and not expected to have short term solutions. Fortunately, many applications of practical interest do not require the full capabilities of a general purpose system, and complex high level descriptions may not be necessary. However, even for restricted applications, improved low level processing such as for the extraction of lines and uniform regions, is likely to be necessary and useful. The need for developing specialized, application oriented systems is well expressed by Bullock in [4].

ACKNOWLEDGEMENTS

Comments of Drs. E. Riseman and A. Hanson on earlier versions have been extremely helpful in the preparation of this paper.

REFERENCES

1. Riseman, E., and Hanson, A. Position questions . Preface , this volume.

2. Baird, M.L. An application of computer vision to automated IC chip manufacture. Proceedings of the Third International Joint Conference on Pattern Recognition, November 1976, Coronado, California , pp. 3-7.

3. Winston, P.H. (Ed.). The Psychology of Computer Vision. McGraw-Hill, New York, 1975.

4. Bullock, B. The necessity for a theory of specialized vision. Workshop on Computer Vision Systems, June 1977, University of Massachusetts, Amherst, Massachusetts (in this volume).

5. Davis, L.S. A survey of edge detection techniques. Computer Graphics and Image Processing Vol. 4, No. 3, September 1975, pp. 248-270.

6. Hueckel, M. An operator which locates edges in digitized pictures. Journal of the ACM, Vol. 18, No. 1, January 1971, pp. 113-125.

7. Rosenfeld, A., and Thurston, M. Edge and curve detection for visual scene analysis. IEEE Transactions on Computers, Vol. 20, May 1971, pp. 562-569.

8. Marr, D. Early processing of visual information. Massachusetts Institute of Technology Artificial Intelligence Laboratory, AIM-340, December 1975.

9. Nevatia, R. Locating object boundaries in textured environments. IEEE Transactions on Computers, Vol. 25, No. 11, November 1976, pp. 1170-1175.

10. Ohlander, R. Analysis of natural scenes. Ph.D. Thesis, Carnegie-Mellon University, Pittsburgh, Pennsylvania, August 1975.

11. Nevatia, R., and Price, K. A comparison of some segmentation techniques. Proceedings of Image Understanding Workshop, April 1977, pp. 55-57.

12. Feldman, J.A., and Yakimovsky, Y. Decision Theory and Artificial Intelligence: A semantics based region analyzer. Artificial Intelligence, Vol. 5. 1974, pp 349-371.

13. Tenenbaum, J.M., and Barrow, H.G. IGS: A paradigm for integrating image segmentation and interpretation. In *Pattern Recognition and Artificial Intelligence* (C.H. Chen, Editor), Academic Press, New York, 1976, pp. 472-507.

14. Binford, T.O. Visual perception by a computer. IEEE Conference on Systems and Controls, Miami, Florida, December 1971.

15. Agin, G.J., and Binford, T.O. Computer description of curved objects. *IEEE Transactions on Computers*, April 1976, pp.439-449.

16. Nevatia, R. *Computer Analysis of Scenes of 3-Dimensional Curved Objects*. Birkhauser-Verlag, Basel, Switzerland, 1976.

17. Nevatia, R., and Binford, T.O. Description and recognition of curved objects. *Artificial Intelligence*, Vol. 8, 1977. pp. 77-98.

18. Marr, D., and Nishihara, H.K. Representation and recognition of the spatial organization of three-dimensional shapes. Massachusetts Institute of Technology, AI Memo 377, August, 1976.

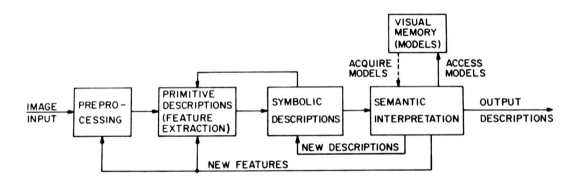

Figure 1. Block Diagram of an Image Understanding System

Figure 2. An Outdoor Scene.

Figure 3. Edges Detected in Figure 2.

Figure 4. Linked Segments Constructed
From Edges in Figure 3.

Characterization and Requirements of Systems

PRAGMATIC ASPECTS OF MACHINE VISION

Raj Reddy
Department of Computer Science
Carnegie-Mellon University
Pittsburgh, Pa. 15213

ABSTRACT

Over the last decade some aspects of machine vision such as edge detection, segmentation, and shape representation have received relatively more attention than other aspects of the machine vision problem. In this paper we examine some of the many different choices available to the designer of a machine vision system and discuss how lack of attention to any of these could seriously affect the research progress. We provide specific examples by drawing on current research in the CMU environment.

INTRODUCTION

Aspects of representation, matching, and search continue to be, and rightfully so, the central issues of vision research. However the slow progress over the last decade is directly attributable to non-visual computational issues such as limitations of architectures, file structures, image databases, and so on. Before we can prove or disprove a conjecture regarding a representation or control structure, we must have a system providing rapid response, within which one can design experiments to understand the contributions of competing hypotheses. In this paper we consider the large number of design choices that affect the long term success and viability of a vision research effort.

Figure 1 lists the design choices in a machine vision system. The design choices are grouped together to form general topics. The designer of a total system is faced with about 10 to 15 design choices each of which have 3 to 10 reasonable alternative choices. Thus the solution space of vision systems seems to contain 10^6 to 10^8 possible system designs! In the following sections, we consider many of these design decisions and discuss how they affected our own research effort.

TASK CHARACTERISTICS

Choice of the task is probably the most important design decision in a vision system. Selection of a sterile and/or overly contrived task might lead to techniques and systems which are not extendable. On the other hand, aiming for a general purpose vision system which can interpret any and all types of images can at best lead to some untested theories and unfulfilled expectations.

We have chosen to look at two or three different tasks which together exhibit a wide range of image source variability, sensor characteristics, and noise characteristics. The three tasks currently under exploration are: interpretation of uncontrived arbitrary images representing different views of downtown Pittsburgh (3-D world); location of a landmark or identification of an image from satellite and aerial images of the Washington D.C. area (2-D World);

detection of changes in an image using symbolic techniques. The downtown Pittsburgh task involves several interesting subtasks: scene-type identification (indoor, outdoor, office, ...), camera position identification (scale, location and orientation aspects of the image); image structure understanding (relative positions of buildings); and image detail understanding (detect cars, bushes, people walking after the larger context of a "road" is established). Each of these seem to need different knowledge bases, different primitive picture elements, different feature spaces, and different matching strategies.

SIGNAL-TO-SYMBOL TRANSFORMATION

As we see from Figure 1, there are many system design issues besides segmentation that require careful consideration in generating a symbolic representation from the signal. Besides segmentation, one must define feature descriptors (shape descriptors being one of many) of the label classes and their distinguishing features, choice of metrics for label matching, etc.

The choice of the symbolic description depends to a large extent on the intended use by the total system. Thus, the type of information required when one is attempting to determine the scene-type (indoor vs. outdoor scene) would be very different to the one needed for scene structure understanding. This suggests that the low level processing would have to be goal directed at least to some extent. That is, it should be capable of generating different types of symbolic and feature descriptions of the unknown image, for use at different levels of a general purpose vision system.

Segmentation

To segment or not to segment.... Since there is no such thing as error-free segmentation, our approach is designed to work on a pixel-by-pixel basis, if necessary. However, any aggregation of pixels into segments with uniform properties not only improves accuracy (Landgrebe, 1977) but also leads to substantial speedup in matching and search.

Our approach to segmentation is typified by the work of Ohlander (Ohlander, 1975) and Price (Price, 1976) and is similar in some respects to the work of Tomita et. al. (1973) and Horowitz and Pavlidis (1974). The method is a top-down technique but is basically non-goal-directed. It has the flexibility to either permit "glances" at dominant features of the scene or to provide a complete and detailed segmentation as needed by the task situation. It is non-goal-directed in that only the inherent properties of images, rather than the task-specific information, control the segmentation process. However, the system can utilize knowledge such as thresholds obtained from a "previous

```
┌─────────────────────────────────────────┐
│  TASK CHARACTERISTICS                     │
│      Image Source Variability             │
│         3-D or 2-D                        │
│         Number of objects                 │
│         Size, shape, color, texture       │
│         Possibilities for task simplification │
│            Selectability                  │
│            Adaptability                   │
│      Sensor characteristics               │
│         Optical, radar, FLIR              │
│         Spatial resolution                │
│         Dynamic range                     │
│         Adaptation and accommodation      │
│      Noise characteristics                │
│                                           │
│  SIGNAL-TO-SYMBOL TRANSFORMATION          │
│      Type of segmentations, if any        │
│         Edges                             │
│         Regions                           │
│      Feature spaces                       │
│      Label class selection                │
│      Metrics for template matching        │
│                                           │
│  KNOWLEDGE SOURCE REPRESENTATION          │
│      Networks                             │
│      Procedural                           │
│      Frames                               │
│      Productions                          │
│                                           │
│  MATCHING AND SEARCH                      │
│      Relaxation  / breadth-first          │
│      Blackboard  / best-first, island driven │
│      Productions / best-first             │
│      Locus       / beam search            │
│                                           │
│  KNOWLEDGE ACQUISITION                    │
│      Manual                               │
│         Protocol analysis                 │
│      Expert guided                        │
│      Automatic symbolic learning          │
│                                           │
│  SYSTEM ARCHITECTURE                      │
│      Real time                            │
│      File structure                       │
│      Graceful interaction                 │
│                                           │
│  IMAGE DATABASE                           │
│                                           │
│  PERFORMANCE EVALUATION                   │
└─────────────────────────────────────────┘
```

FIGURE 1. Design Choices in a Machine Vision System.

look" as a guide to segmentation.

Although top-down region-splitting based on histogram thresholding is a main component, it by no means describes our entire segmentation strategy which has evolved over several years. Figure 2 outlines the structure of the segmentation process. The main features of this process are the detection and extraction of bright and dark areas, noisy and non-noisy areas prior to the region-splitting operation. This permits selective feature extraction and data-directed segmentation strategies. We believe multi-dimensional histograms should be used only when uni-dimensional histograms lead to non-distinct peak structure.

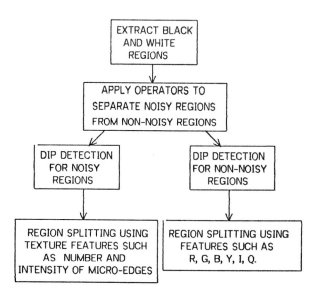

Figure 2. Structure of the CMU segmentation process permits selective feature extraction and data-directed segmentation.

Price (1976) extended the work of Ohlander by speeding up the segmentation process by a factor of 20 using Planning (Kelly, 1970) and other optimization techniques. New features such as number and intensity of micro-edges in a window were introduced for use with monochromatic images. Figure 3 gives an example of the segmentation of a cityscape scene. More complete descriptions of the segmentation procedure with typical segmentations achieved is given in Ohlander, Price and Reddy (1978).

Feature Extraction

Several researchers have suggested sets of features to be extracted from regions after segmentation (Duda, 1973; Tenenbaum and Barrow, 1976a; Price, 1976). Price used features such as shape, size, location, compactness, orientation, length to width and fractional fill in his work. In addition, structural features such as region neighbors and relative position were useful in order to perform symbolic matching.

Label classes and Metrics

Given a picture segment and a list of features associated with the segments, one sometimes wishes to match the features with a predefined set of label classes. This involves the use of a conventional pattern classification paradigm and also raises all the associated problems: how does one arrive at the set of label classes that adequately describe all pictures of interest for a given class; how does one establish symbol-to-signal correspondence; how does one match an unknown segment with the label classes to determine the nearest neighbor, and so on. We are exploring the use of clustering over a large set of training data to determine the label classes, and averaging over many exemplars to specify the feature templates for a label. A variance-weighted Euclidean metric is used to generate a vector of probabilities associated with each label class.

Raj Reddy

Figure 3. An example of the segmentation of a typical cityscape
scene. Each separate region is shown a different intensity.
The brightest regions are the areas of the image left unsegmented.

KNOWLEDGE SOURCE REPRESENTATION

The central problem in machine vision is the representation and use of all the available sources of knowledge in the interpretation and description of an image. The problem of representation is complicated by the diversity of the sources of knowledge. Some knowledge sources are task dependent while others are task independent. Specifying the task to be performed involves defining the object set, structure and relationships among objects, and task-related contextual and pragmatic knowledge. Task independent knowledge includes iconic and feature specification of label classes, theory of shadows, highlights and occlusions, binocular vision, and so on.

The subject of knowledge representations has been a popular subject and there are many reasonable alternative representations such as networks, frames, productions, and procedural embedding. It is also assumed that any one of the above representations can support hierarchically structured knowledge bases.

At CMU, we are at present investigating the strengths and limitations of PPE graph structures. PPEs (primitive picture elements) are a predefined set of label classes that are assumed to be adequate to describe all pictures of interest in a given task domain. A PPE is a small atomic patch, all pixels of which share the same properties. A PPE might represent a whole object, a surface, a patch (part of a surface), or even a pixel. The actual choice of PPEs for a given domain would depend on the structure and complexity of various objects. If the whole object can be described in terms of a set of invariant machine extractable features, then it could be used directly as a PPE e.g. sky, grass, etc. However if an object exhibits different structural and spectral features in different views one has to express it in terms of component parts which exhibit invariant properties.

A PPE graph structure is one in which all the images that are admissible by the world model are represented in terms of a graph structure whose nodes are PPEs. Such a

representation is derived from a conventional semantic network model containing whole-part, structural, and probabilistic relations by iteratively redefining higher level structures in terms of simpler objects until it is no longer possible to redefine a node, i.e. when a node in the network represents a PPE, the smallest atomic picture element in terms of which all images are describable.

MATCHING AND SEARCH

Attempts to match the bottom-up symbolic representation of the image with a world model so as to obtain an optimal and consistent image interpretation leads to combinatorial search. Many different control structures have been proposed to contain the combinatorial explosion: relaxation, blackboard model, production systems, beam search and so on. Implicit within each of these models is the search paradigm: breadth-first, best-first, island driven search, beam search, and so on.

At CMU we are exploring a specific framework for matching and search which appears to be both sufficient and efficient for a wide variety of image interpretation tasks (Rubin and Reddy, 1977). The framework for image interpretation is based on the Locus model successfully used in speech understanding research (Lowerre and Reddy, 1977). The Locus model is a non-backtracking, non-iterative, beam search technique in which a beam of near-miss alternatives around the best path are extended to determine the near-optimal description of an image.

The representation and matching techniques used in the Locus model is a natural outgrowth of work in <u>languages</u> (Aho and Ullman, 1972), <u>syntax directed pattern recognition</u> (Narasimhan, 1966; Clowes, 1969; and Fu, 1976), <u>constraint satisfying search</u> (Waltz, 1975; Feldman and Yakimovsky, 1975; Tenenbaum and Barrow, 1976b; Rosenfeld, Hummel and Zucker, 1976), <u>graph search and dynamic programming</u> (Nilsson, 1971; Bellman and Dreyfus, 1962; Fischler and Elschlager, 1973), and <u>representation and search in the presence of uncertainty</u> (especially in the area of speech understanding - Reddy et al, 1973; Lesser et al, 1975; Erman et al, 1977; Woods et al, 1977; Baker, 1975; and Lowerre, 1976). More detailed discussion of similaries and differences with these earlier approaches is given in Rubin and Reddy (1977).

The basic premise underlying the Locus model is that the problem of image interpretation can be viewed as a problem of search in the presence of uncertainty. Given a specific knowledge representation paradigm and a signal-to-symbol transformation paradigm, a highly efficient search can be used to obtain, except in rare cases, a globally optimal solution satisfying all the constraints of the world model.

In the absence of any constraints, the optimal assignment of labels to pixels can be obtained by selecting the best label in each pixel neighborhood. However, given the semantic, syntactic, structural, and segmental properties of scenes that are acceptable within a micro-world model, one wishes to choose that assignment of labels to pixels that is both globally optimal and consistent with the world model.

Given a PPE graph structure representation of the world model and a signal-to-symbol transformation technique, the problem of interpreting an unknown image can be viewed as finding the optimal path through the graph, i.e., finding a sequence of labels which best describes each of the pixel neighborhoods of the unknown image, subject to constraints defined by the knowledge sources represented by the graph.

Research in progress at CMU (Rubin, 1978) uses the Locus model in the interpretation of uncontrived high resolution color images of downtown Pittsburgh. Knowledge of the maps, shape and heights of buildings, and features of surfaces are encoded into graph structure representation using 3-D perspective projections such as the one given in Figure 4. This knowledge is used to constrain the labeling alternatives. Figure 5 is one of the views of downtown Pittsburgh and Figure 6 is the labeling resulting from the interpretation process. Preliminary results indicate that 80 to 85 percent labeling accuracy can be achieved even without the use of all available constraints.

KNOWLEDGE ACQUISITION

Once we have acceptable paradigms for knowledge representation and search, the main focus has to be towards paradigms for automatic learning of knowledge sources. This would include learning features of label classes, structure learning at all levels from single and/or multiple exemplars, and near-miss analysis for disambiguating between similar structures.

There are three types of knowledge acquisition strategies currently employed in AI research. In situations where little or no systematic knowledge is available one uses some form of protocol analysis (Newell, 1968; Woods and Makhoul, 1974; Akin and Reddy, 1977) to discover and systematize relevant knowledge. This knowledge is mainly to help the researcher who then has to manually encode this knowledge into the system. In task situations such as the development of Dendral and Mycin where there is a great deal of accumulated knowledge, interactive knowledge acquisition and verification systems have been used to acquire and assimilate new knowledge based on expert advice (Feigenbaum et al., 1968; Shortliffe, 1976). Automatic structure learning and grammatical inference techniques have been a subject of study for many years (Feldman et al., 1969; Winston, 1975; Fu and Booth, 1975; Hayes-Roth and Mostow, 1975). Progress has been slow, not so much because the basic ideas are of limited generality, but because of the lack of total systems within which the concepts could be explored, validated and improved using non-toy problems.

The choice of a data structure for knowledge representation must not only be based on its utility for image matching and search but also on how one can assimilate new knowledge without leading to inefficiencies and contradictions. The rest of this section describes some related work at CMU.

Picture-Puzzle. (Akin and Reddy, 1977) The "picture-puzzle" paradigm was designed to simulate a visual understanding system using human subjects. Subjects are required to find the contents of color photographs of natural scenes. The experimenter, trained to simulate a "primitive" scene analyzer, answers these questions using

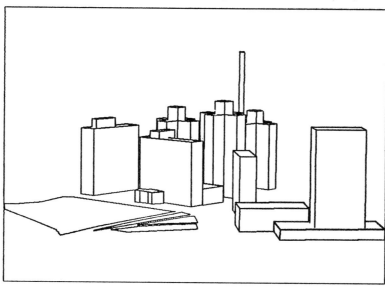

Figure 4. A typical machine generated 3-D perspective drawing detailing a portion of the downtown Pittsburgh skyline. This knowledge is used to generate a network representation used in the Locus search.

Raj Reddy

Figure 5. One of the views of downtown Pittsburgh currently being studied. Note the variety of objects in the scene: roads, park area, city buildings, background hillside and a portion of the Allegheny river.

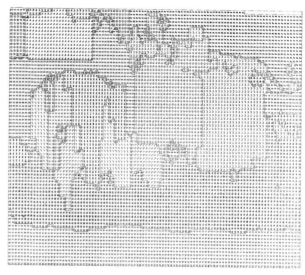

Figure 6. This is a pixel by pixel labeling produced by the ARGOS system (Rubin, 1978) for the downtown Pittsburgh scene given in Figure 5. Note that much of the image is correctly segmented into symbolically meaningful regions.

information about the color, shape, location, texture, etc. of lines and regions found in the scenes. Subjects are required to report about the inferences they make using these low level properties while generating higher level concepts, i.e., car, person tree, house, buildings, sky, etc.

The reports of subjects were used to infer the use of three kinds of knowledge: a) Primitive Feature Extraction Operators, b) Rewriting Rules, and c) Rules of Control Flow. The Operators repeatedly used by all subjects are categorized into several classes; location, size, shape, quantity, color, texture, patterns and scene components. Six kinds of Rewriting Rules are identified based on their role in the problem environment; assertions, negative assertions, context-free, conditional, generative and analytical rules. Control Flow resembled the hypothesize-and-test paradigm. Many Rewriting Rules with inadequate generality were used in cooperation to generate correct interpretations of specific aspects of the scenes. The knowledge sources identified provide a reasonable subset of those necessary for computer implementations.

Perception of Visual Detail. (Akin, McBride and Reddy, 1977). A major dimension used in processing information selectively is stimulus resolution. The overall structure and the fine detail found in the visual environment can be used separately or together to understand its different aspects. In order to understand the use of detail in visual perception an experimental paradigm has been devised. The subjects are required to examine the different size projections of slides of natural scenes. They verbally report what they see during the experiments. The projected images are looked at from 55 feet with six image sizes ranging from 3-1/2" by 5" to 19" by 27".

Lack of detailed information in the smaller sizes distorted the scenes beyond recognition. The minimum size at which each scene was correctly perceived correlated with the "commonplace"-ness of the overall structure of each scene. Scenes with the sky-buildings-river, person-with-objects-in-the-background structure fit well the image structures ordinarily expected by the subjects. On the

other hand, scenes where the camera was positioned overhead the structure of the scenes were not recognized in any of the lower three levels. At the lowest levels scene properties, such as edges, textures, color, that were below threshold values of resolution with respect to the size of the receptors in the retina, were perceived erroneously.

Perception in the presence of conflict. One of the issues least understood in the perception of natural scenes is the use of shade-shadow, occlusions, perspective, gravitational support, etc. Some studies in psychology indicate that processing time is increased considerably when such scene features are manually distorted to conflict with the rest of a natural scene (Loftus, 1974). It is of interest for image understanding research to discover the underlying processes that account for these increased processing times. Future investigation of this paradigm is being planned. The success of such an investigation relies largely on an a priori theory of vision that can predict the variance in information processing as a function of conflict in object properties such as shadows, occlusions, perspective, etc.

Tunnel Vision. (Akin and McBride, 1977). Farley (1974) examined perception of single line drawings by allowing subjects to observe a small portion of the drawing at a time. The mechanism used was a small peep-hole allowing subjects to move it around on the drawing. This mechanism is roughly analogous to a series of eye-fixations which would have been ordinarily made by the subject. We carried the analogy further by building a peep-hole with a translucent periphery to simulate the peripheral vision capabilities of the human eye. Preliminary results indicate that although the peripheral vision aided search, the use of natural scenes as stimuli presented difficulties. It seems that natural scenes are too complex to reconstruct from the limited information provided in the peep-hole. The experimental paradigm has to be refined further to resolve this difficulty. The advantage of this paradigm is that it allows the subjects to infer a scene from fine detail. In this sense the paradigm is seen as a complementary tool to the visual detail perception experiment where the reconstruction seems to originate from the overall structure of the scene.

Knowledge guided structure learning. (Fox and Reddy, 1977) Fox and Reddy propose that structure learning is yet another combinatorial search problem in AI and therefore can benefit from any and all available knowledge that can be used to constrain search. They discuss three aspects of structure learning: generating a minimal-state symbolic (graph-like) description from an example, combining evidence from several exemplars, and determining potential sources of ambiguity with structures of other classes (near-miss analysis) and modifying the structure.

ARCHITECTURES FOR VISION RESEARCH

To segment a 600x800x3 color image our current programs takes about 25 minutes of processing time on a PDP-10 (KA) computer (it used to take 10 hours!). This is equivalent to about 1100 operations per pixel. Even if we assume further optimizations, special functional units, tailored firmware and so on, it appears that a machine vision system will require at least a 1000 operations per pixel. Figure 7 gives the processor speed required for an image understanding system for different size pictures and response times assuming 1000 operations per pixel.

Desired response time	Picture 1024×1024×3 high resolution TV	Size 2500×3300×4 ERTS
1 Sec	1000 mips	10000 mips
10 Sec	100 mips	1000 mips
100 Sec	10 mips	100 mips

(mips = millions of instructions per second)

Figure 7. Processor speed required for an image understanding system for different size pictures assuming 1000 operations per picture element.

Figure 7 shows that a general purpose vision system with a reasonable response time would require 1 to 10 BIPS (billion instructions per second) of computational power. Although a uni-processor capable of operating at these speeds would simplify the problems of algorithm decomposition and systems software, currently only parallel organizations offer the promise of reaching the desired instruction rates. Special programmable architectures such as CLIP-4 (Duff, 1976) and cellular arrays such as GLOPR (Preston, 1977) appear to be useful only in specific low-level applications. Whether these architectures can be extended for use in symbolic processing in vision systems is questionable at present. A more flexible approach appears to be to develop asynchronous multi-processor systems such as C.mmp (Wulf et al, 1972) and CM* (Swan, Fuller et al, 1976) containing fewer but more powerful processors than programmable arrays. Such systems can be dynamically restructured to be parallel, pipe-line or parallel-pipeline architectures depending on the sub-task of the moment.

Figure 8 illustrates the structure of MIPS (Multi-sensor Image Processor System), a low-cost system based on C.mmp architecture but specialized for image processing applications. It uses a 4 by 4 switch with total potential memory bandwidth of 120 megabits per second. The two PDP-11/40E processors (Fuller et al, 1976) equipped with writable control store, provide 3 to 6 mips processing power. We are currently developing a special instruction set for image processing applications using the writable microstore. MIPS has a primary memory capacity of one megabyte, secondary memory capacity of 500 megabytes, and disk-to-memory bandwidth of two megabytes per second. Displays, and other components were chosen so as to produce a balanced system for large image processing applications at a cost under $200K. At a later date, we expect to augment the system with 15-20 ns cycle time high-speed processor elements specially designed for image processing.

Though asynchronous parallel processors such as C.mmp are more flexible than arrays, they also raise many issues of algorithm decomposition and optimization (Hon and Reddy, 1977). These systems degrade in interesting ways as one relaxes various architectural design choices such as bandwidth, memory capacity, memory access-time and processing power.

IMAGE DATABASE

In addition to the raw signal representations, it often becomes desirable to have symbolic descriptions of the content of the image. Such a description, if properly associated with the corresponding portion of the image signal, would be invaluable in performance analysis, error analysis, and automatic learning from exemplars. Unified acquisition, representation, and retrieval procedures for

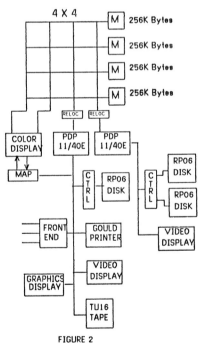

Figure 8. The Multi-sensor Image Processing System architecture. This system is currently operational and runs the UNIX timesharing operating system (Richie and Thompson, 1974). This organization has a large file storage, high bandwidth, a wide variety of input/output devices, and facilities for microprogramming achieved at a low cost.

Raj Reddy

symbolic and signal data from the image database greatly simplifies the design of systems and permits rapid experimentation. Many interesting problems are often not identified or explored until we process many images capturing much of the variability.

We have developed a database system which satisfies many of these goals. MIDAS, a Multi-sensor Image DAtabase System (McKeown and Reddy, 1977a), is currently running on a PDP-10 and we have begun to move the system over to MIPS which runs the UNIX timesharing system (Richie and Thompson, 1974). Our database is organized as a collection of hierarchical descriptions where each level in the hierarchy represents a different conceptual abstraction of the image. Both the symbolic and signal descriptions are organized into the database which allows efficient and accurate generation, representation and retrieval of images. While the number and type of representations may vary from task to task MIDAS provides mechanisms to add or modify representations as necessary.

PERFORMANCE ANALYSIS

Given the many reasonable alternatives to each of the design choices in Figure 1, it is clear that we must begin to develop methodologies and algorithms for systematic comparative evaluation of segmentation, labeling, knowledge representation, search strategies and so on. Two basic requirements of any performance analysis subsystem are the availability of a modular total system that is operational and a representation of the "truth".

An operational vision system, with well specified interfaces, will permit systematic replacement of component subsystems. The main question, of course, is whether there is enough agreement among the researchers in the field about the component subsystem modules and interface conventions between producers and consumers. There is enough commonality of structure within various systems that such an agreement might be feasible.

The requirement of representation of "truth" about an image is essential for quantitative analysis and comparison of machine performance with human performance. Description of an image in terms of symbolic descriptions at various levels of abstraction is a tedious and time-consuming process and requires a great deal of human interaction. The process is also error-prone in that it involves subjective judgements of humans. The human effort can be reduced somewhat as scene analysis systems begin to produce acceptable first approximations of symbolic descriptions. These descriptions can be then modified by humans to correct for any residual errors.

At CMU, we have begun to develop tools for interactive generation of accurate symbolic descriptions of the images in our data base. These descriptions capture the important objects or regions as identified by human subjects. They represent an arbitrary description of information contained in the image and are a model against which the performance of automatic procedures may be measured. Given that human segmentations may be arbitrary and errorful, facilities must be provided to gracefully modify representations.

We have been exploring techniques for performance evaluation of component subsystems such as segmentation, labeling, and semantic descriptions (McKeown and Reddy, 1977b). We wish to identify those region boundaries which are missing or added in machine segmentation. Given that a boundary position is not always unique, one cannot use simple evaluation techniques for detecting missing and added boundaries. Thus, in the symbolic description, we permit an interval within which the presence of a boundary would be considered acceptable. Further, certain types of shifts in position may be anticipated and permitted for particular classes. Figure 9 shows how a machine detected (realized) edge may differ from an actual (idealized) edge and still be acceptable.

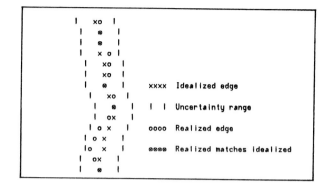

Figure 9. A machine detected (realized) edge may differ from an actual (idealized) edge and still be acceptable.

The evaluation of labels and label accuracy can be performed by the generation of a confusion matrix of expected labels and the actual label assigned. Figure 10 shows a confusion matrix of expected labels and actual labels of an image using pixel by pixel comparison. This help to identify which label classes are confusable and require further attention. Many problems arise when entire segments are treated as aggregates because of missing and extra bounderies. Regions representing multiple label classes may be grouped together as a result of segmentation. In such cases the confusion matrix is not an appropriate medium for evaluation.

The evaluation of high level symbolic descriptions is highly task dependant. While the system may be errorful in both segmentation and labeling, we are primarily interested in whether or not the description is semantically correct independent of whether components are individually correct. Thus we may accept the identification of an office scene even though a chair is incorrectly labeled or various objects omitted. Performance analysis at this level of abstraction is easily performed given high level semantic descriptions.

DISCUSSION

Many of our views on machine vision have already been discussed in the preceeding sections. The following comments answer some of the questions for the workshop.

We prefer region-based description of scenes. Edges would yield equivalent descriptions, provided they were connected and all edges associated (including holes) with a region were easily retrieved as part of the representation.

Since there will be no such thing as error-free segmentation, systems must permit association of several contiguous segments to a single symbol. An implication of such a choice is that such a system can also work on unsegmented images by considering each pixel as a segment. Another implication is that region features such as shape, size, location and orientation would have to be treated as supra-segmented features rather than segmented features.

We use as logical units PPEs, primitive picture elements, the largest symbolic image unit which can be matched with the signal purely in terms of features and/or parameters yielding a probability representing the likelihood of the presence of that PPE. The set of PPEs are not restricted to a single level or type of description, i.e., some PPEs can be surfaces while others are objects.

CONFUSION MATRIX   (FREQUENCY)

PPE -	1	2	3	4	5	6	7	8	9	10	11	12	13	14	15	16	LABELING
-	366	255	157	38	-	-	45	323	105	-	-	51	324	319	796	77	2856
1	410	2	-	10	-	-	-	5	23	-	-	-	-	-	1	-	451
2	-	114	-	-	-	-	4	-	70	-	-	-	-	-	8	-	196
3	-	304	212	-	-	-	-	-	2	-	-	-	-	-	14	-	532
4	6	57	9	69	-	-	-	-	-	-	-	-	-	-	8	-	149
5	-	-	-	-	-	-	-	-	-	-	-	-	-	-	-	-	-
6	-	-	-	-	-	-	2	15	-	-	-	-	-	-	-	-	17
7	-	16	-	-	-	-	52	-	35	-	-	-	-	-	-	-	103
8	2	-	-	-	-	-	1	385	-	-	-	-	-	-	-	-	388
9	-	16	-	-	-	-	-	6	126	-	-	-	-	-	-	-	149
10	-	-	11	-	-	-	-	-	-	12	-	1	48	-	-	-	72
11	-	-	-	-	-	-	-	-	-	-	-	-	-	-	-	-	-
12	6	101	71	-	-	-	-	-	-	-	-	365	-	-	16	-	559
13	-	-	-	-	-	-	-	55	-	-	-	-	5	-	-	-	60
14	14	-	-	-	-	-	-	3	-	-	-	-	2	215	-	-	234
15	-	2	-	-	-	-	-	-	-	-	-	-	-	-	687	8	697
16	-	-	-	-	-	-	-	-	-	-	-	-	-	-	-	1037	1037
TRAINING TOTALS	804	867	461	117	-	2	117	777	361	12	-	417	379	534	1530	1122	

1 HILTON
2 GATEWAY 1
3 GATEWAY 2
4 GATEWAY 3
5 GATEWAY 4
6 JENKINS ARCADE
7 HORNES
8 PITTSBURGH PRESS
9 STATE OFFICE
10 RIVER
11 ONE GATEWAY
12 GATEWAY TOWERS
13 ROAD
14 PARK
15 MOUNTAINS
16 SKY
- Not Assigned

Figure 10.   Is a confusion matrix which details the frequency with which a pixel of one PPE class is incorrectly labeled as another PPE class. This type of simple performance evaluation indicates those PPEs for which a near-miss analysis should be performed.

Our views are consonant with non-cylindrical space occupancy models (Brady, 1977), problem-specific feature extraction (Bullock, 1977), iconic representation (Fischler, 1977), symbolic and knowledge source pyramids as well as signal pyramids (Hanson and Riseman, 1977; Uhr, 1977), and goal-directed vision which is not blind to the image content (Ballard et al., 1977; Barrow and Tenenbaum, 1977; Haralick, 1977; Rosenfeld and Davis, 1977).

Given the large number of design choices for a machine vision system one might reasonably ask whether the human research strategy in solving this and other similar problems can benefit from search reduction heuristics that are commonly used in AI programs. Indeed, as we look around, it is not uncommon to find research paradigms analogous to depth-first exploration, breadth-first with shallow cut-off, backtracking, "jumping-to-conclusions", thrashing and so on.

Our own research has been dominated by two such paradigms. First is a variant of the best-first search: find the weakest link (and thus the potential for most improvement) in the system and attempt to improve it. Second is a variant of the beam search: when several alternative approaches look promising, we use limited parallel search with feed-forward. Faced with prospects of developing systems with a large number of unknowns, we believe it is appropriate to develop several intermediate "throw-away" systems rather than work towards a single carefully designed ultimate system.

Many system design decisions require an operational total systems framework to conduct experiments. However, it is not necessary to have a single system that permits all possible variations of system design. Given enough working components, with well designed interfaces, one can construct new systems variants without excessive effort.

CONCLUSION

Over the last decade some aspects of machine vision such as segmentation, shape representation, knowledge representation and matching have received relatively more attention while many other aspects have received little or no attention at all. This may have been an appropriate research strategy in the early stages but no longer appears to be justified. Indeed much of the slow progress in this area can be attributed directly to:

1. Lack of adequate computational, display and digitization facilities.
2. Lack of an image data base containing both signal and (manually generated) symbolic representations of a large number of rich and diverse sets of images.
3. Lack of sharing of data and programs among researchers.
4. Lack of total system environments within which competing strategies could be evaluated.
5. Lack of methodologies, techniques, and algorithms for performance evaluation of various strategies within a system.
6. Inadequate attention to some components of vision systems: theory of shadows, occlusions, and highlights; universal set of label classes, metrics for matching signals and symbols, and so on.

In the end success and progress toward machine vision will depend as much on non-visual computational aspects as on the central issues of Vision and AI.

ACKNOWLEDGEMENTS

The author would like to thank David McKeown and Omer Akin for their help in the preparation of this paper, and Allen Hanson, Alan Mackworth, Ed Riseman, Azriel Rosenfeld and Steve Rubin for their helpful comments about the paper. This work was supported by the Advanced Research Projects Agency of the Office of the Secretary of Defense under contract number F44620-73-C-0074 and is monitored by the Air Force Office of Scientific Research.

Raj Reddy

REFERENCES

Aho, A. V. and Ullman, J. D. (1972). The Theory of Parsing, Transtation, and Compiling, Prentice-Hall, Englewood Cliffs, N. J.

Akin, O., McBride, S. and Reddy, R. (1977). "Perception of Visual Detail," Technical Report (in preparation), Dept. of Comp Sci, Carnegie-Mellon University, Pittsburgh, PA.

Akin, O. and Reddy, D. R. (1977). "Knowledge Acquisition for Image Understanding," Journal of Computer Graphics and Image Processing, 6, pp. 307-34.

Arbib, M. A. (1977). Paper in this volume.

Baker, J. K. (1975). "The DRAGON system--An overview", IEEE Trans. ASSP 23, pp. 24-29.

Ballard, C. et. al. (1977). Paper in this volume.

Barrow, H. and Tenenbaum, J. (1977). Paper in this volume.

Bellman, R. and Dreyfus, S. (1962). Applied Dynamic Programming, Princeton Univ. Press, Princeton, N.J.

Bisiani, R. and Reddy, D. R. (1977). "Problem Oriented Computer Architecture" Tech Report (to appear), Dept. of Comp Sci, Carnegie-Mellon University, Pittsburgh, PA.

Brady, J. R. (1977). Paper in this volume.

Bullock, B. L. (1977). Paper in this volume.

Clowes, M. C. (1969). "Pictorial relationships - A Syntactic Approach", Machine Intelligence IV (Meltzer and Michie, eds.), American Elsevier, New York.

Duda, R. O. and Hart, P. E. (1973) Pattern Classification and Scene Analysis, Wiley, New York.

Duff, M. J. B. (1976). "CLIP-4: an LSI Array Parallel Processor", Proc. of IJCPR-4, pp. 728-733.

Erman, L. D., et al. (1977). The Hearsay-II System, (in preparation).

Erman, L. and Lesser, V. (1975). "A Multi-Level Organization for Problem Solving using Many Diverse, Cooperating Sources of Knowledge," Proc. of IJCAI-75, pp. 483-490.

Farley, A. M. (1974). "VIPS: a Visual Imagery Perception System", Ph.D. Thesis, Dept. of Comp. Sci., Carnegie-Mellon University.

Feigenbaum, E., Lederberg, J. and Buchanan, B. (1968). "Heuristic Dendral" Proc. of Hawaii International Conference on System Sciences, Univ. of Hawaii and IEEE (Univ. of Hawaii Press 1968).

Feldman, J. A. et al (1969). "Grammatical Complexity and Inference," Stanford AI Memo 89.

Feldman, J. A. and Yakimovsky, Y. (1975). "Decision Theory and Artificial Intelligence: I. A Semantics Based Region Analyzer," Artificial Intelligence, 5, pp. 349-371.

Fischler, M. A. and Eschlager, R. A. (1973). "The Representation and Matching of Pictorial Structures," IEEE Transactions on Computers, C-22, pp. 67-92.

Fischler, M. A. (1977). Paper in this volume.

Fox, M. S. and Reddy, R. (1977). "Knowledge guided learning of structural descriptions," in Proc. of IJCAI-77 (Short note) pg 318.

Fu, K. S. and Booth, T. L. (1975). "Grammatical Inference - Introduction and Survey - Part I and II," in IEEE Trans. Syst., Man., Cybern., SMC-5, Jan, July.

Fu, K. S. (1976). "Syntactic (Linguistic) Pattern Recognition," in Digital Pattern Recognition (Fu, ed.), Springer Verlag, New York.

Fuller, S. H., et al. (1976). "PDP-11E Microprogramming Reference Manual," Technical Report, Dept. of Comp Sci, Carnegie-Mellon University, Pittsburgh, PA.

Hanson, A. R. and Riseman, E. M. (1977). Paper in this volume.

Haralick, R. M. (1977). Paper in this volume.

Hayes-Roth, F. and Mostow, D. J. (1975). "An Automatically Compilable Recognition Network For Structured Patterns," Proc. of IJCAI-75 pp. 246-52.

Hon, R. W. and Reddy, D. R. (1977). "The Effect of Computer Architecture on Algorithm Decomposition and Performance," Proc. of Symposium on High Speed Computers and Algorithm Organization, Univ. of Illinois, Urbana.

Horowitz, S. L. and Pavlides, T. (1974). "Picture Segmentation by a directed split-merge procedure," Proc. of IJCPR-2, pp. 424-433.

Kelly, M. D. (1970). "Visual Identification of People by Computer" Ph. D. Thesis, AIM-130, Stanford University.

Landgrebe, D. A. (1977). Personal communication.

Lesser, V. R., Fennell, R. D., Erman, L. D., and Reddy, D. R. (1975). "Organization of the Hearsay-II Speech Understanding System," IEEE Trans. ASSP Vol. 23, pp. 11-23.

Loftus, G. R. (1974). "A Framework for a Theory of Picture Recognition," presented at National Academy of Sciences Specialist's Meeting on Eye Movements and Psychological Processes, Princeton, N.J. April, 1974.

Lowerre, B. T. (1976). "The HARPY Speech Recognition System," Ph.D. Thesis, Dept. of Comp. Sci. Carnegie-Mellon University, Pittsburgh, PA.

Lowerre, B. T., and Reddy, D. R. (1977). "Representation and Search in the Harpy Connected Speech Recognition System," Paper in preparation.

Mackworth, A. K. (1977). Paper in this volume.

McKeown, D. M., Jr. and Reddy, D. R. (1977a). "A Hierarchical Symbolic Representation for an Image Database," Proc. of IEEE Workshop on Picture Data Description and Management, Chicago, Illinois.

McKeown, D. M., Jr. and Reddy, D. R. (1977b). "The MIDAS sensor database and its use in performance evaluation", Proc of Image Understanding Workshop, Palo Alto, CA. Oct.

Narasimhan, R. (1966). "Syntax-Directed Interpretation of Classes of Pictures," CACM, 9,3 pp. 166-172.

Newell, A. (1968). "On the analysis of human problem solving protocols," Calcul et Formalisortion dans les Sciences de L'Homme, ed. by J. C. Cordin and B. Jaulin, pp. 146-185, Center National de la Recherche Scientifique, Paris.

Nilsson, N. (1971). Problem Solving Methods in Artificial Intelligence, McGraw Hill.

Ohlander, R. (1975). "Analysis of Natural Images," Ph.D Thesis, Dept. of Comp. Sci., Carnegie-Mellon University, Pittsburgh, PA.

Ohlander, R., Price, K., and Reddy, R, (1978). "Picture Segmentation using a recursive region splitting method," to appear in Computer Graphics and Image Processing.

Preston, K. (1977). "Application of the Golay Transform to Image Analysis in Cytology and Cytogenetics," in Digital Image Processing and Analysis, Nordhoff International.

Price, K. (1976). "Change Detection and Analysis of Multi-Spectral Images," Ph.D Thesis, Dept. of Comp Sci, Carnegie-Mellon University, Pittsburgh, PA.

Reddy, D. R. et. al (1973). "A model and a system for machine recognition of speech" IEEE Trans. Audio Electroacoust., vol. AU-21, pp. 229-38.

Richie, D. M. and Thompson, K. (1974). "The UNIX Time-Sharing System", CACM, 17,7 pp. 365-75.

Rosenfeld, A., Hummel, R. A. and Zucker, S. W. (1976). "Scene labelling by relaxation operations," IEEE Trans. Syst., Man, Cybern., SMC-6, pp. 420-33.

Pragmatic Aspects of Machine Vision

Rosenfeld, A. and Davis, L. (1977). Paper in this volume.

Rubin, S. M. and Reddy, R. (1977). "The Locus Model of Search and its Use in Image Interpretation," Proc of IJCAI-77 pp. 590-95.

Rubin, S. M. (1978). "The ARGOS Image Understanding System" (thesis in preparation) Department of Computer Science, Carnegie-Mellon University, Pittsburgh, Pa.

Shortliffe, E. H. (1976). MYCIN: Computer-Based Medical Consultations American Elsevier.

Sloan, K. P. and Bajcsy, R. (1977). "World Model Driven Recognition of Natural Scenes," Proc. of IEEE Workshop on Picture Data Description and Management, Chicago, Illinois.

Swan, R. J., Fuller, S. H. and Siewiorek, D. P. (1976), "The Structure and Architecture of Cm*: a Modular, Multi-Microprocessor", Computer Science Research Review 1975-1976, Dept. of Comp. Sci., Carnegie-Mellon Univ., Pittsburgh, PA.

Tenenbaum, J. M. and Barrow, H. G. (1976a). "MSYS: A System for Reasoning about Scenes," AI Technical Note 121. SRI International, Menlo Park, CA.

Tenenbaum, J. M. and Barrow, H. G. (1976b). "Experiments in Interpretation-Guided Segmentation," Technical Note 123, SRI International, Menlo Park, CA.

Tomita, F., Yachida, M., Tsuji, S. (1973). "Detection of Homogenous Regions by Structural Analysis," Proc of IJCAI-73 pp. 564-71.

Uhr, L. (1977). Paper in this volume.

Waltz, D. (1975). "Understanding Line Drawings with Shadows," The Psychology of Computer Vision, (P. Winston, Ed.), McGraw-Hill N.Y.

Winston, P. (1975). The Psychology of Computer Vision McGraw-Hill, N.Y. 1975.

Woods, W. and Makhoul, J. (1974). "Mechanical Inference Problems in Continuous Speech Understanding," Artificial Intelligence 5.

Woods, W. W., et al. (1977). "Final Report on Speech Understanding Systems," Bolt, Beranek and Newman Inc., Cambridge, MA.

Wulf, W. A. and Bell, C. G. (1972). "C.mmp - a Multi-Mini-Processor", Proc. of Fall Joint Computer Conference pg. 765-777.

Raj Reddy

SEGMENTATION

One generally accepted paradigm treats vision as a process for inferring more and more information about a scene as the data undergoes a
series of transformations from one representation to another. In this
paradigm, segmentation of an image into relevant components and the
extraction of features from these components form the first stage of
analysis. Note, however, that there are divergent views on the adequacy
of this view (for a discussion see the papers by Barrow and Tenenbaum,
Fischler, Mackworth, and Marr in the previous section). There seems to
be wide agreement that "perfect" or "correct" segmentations are not
achievable, or in fact meaningful, since the utility of a given segmentation depends upon the ultimate use to which it will be put. Consequently,
a reasonable goal for low-level analyses is a partial segmentation, which
may be refined as processing continues.

The major problem facing segmentation processes is the presence of
ambiguity and noise in textured images. The papers in this section
address the problem of how to integrate local context-sensitive decisions
to produce a global organization of that information. Other dominant
themes include parallel processing methods for handling the vast amount
of information which must be processed, the representation of visual
information, the organization of cooperative local processes each of
which produces partial results, and hierarchical structures in representing and processing data.

Davis and Rosenfeld, Zucker, and Hanson and Riseman all employ
relaxation labelling algorithms as a means by which local evidence can
be organized in a parallel, iterative manner. An important feature of
these algorithms is the propagation of local contextual effects in a
paradigm of competition and cooperation. Waltz outlines a different
parallel processing scheme involving the extraction of interesting
features from the image and the transmission of messages between processes
about these local events of interest. These messages are aggregated into
collections in a transform space and used to provide a segmentation of
the image.

Ehrich and Foith examine assumptions usually hidden in edge detection
processes, and describe a hierarchical representation for image data which
facilitates region growing, edge detection, and texture analysis. They
argue for processes which utilize increasingly more global views of the
topology of the sensory data in order to improve local decisions. The
papers by Davis and Rosenfeld and by Zucker address this same problem of
local-global relationships by extending the relaxation labelling process
into hierarchical algorithms which permits context-sensitive local decisions. Davis and Rosenfeld provide results from a waveform processing
application, in which the processing is guided by a grammar which captures
waveform events of interest, while Zucker presents results obtained from
analyzing dot patterns.

Tanimoto provides a survey of parallel hierarchical structures which utilize increasingly coarser levels of image resolution. These representations, also known as "pyramid" or "cone" structures, have been employed in a range of image analysis tasks. Their utility and limitations in vision systems is outlined. Hanson and Riseman describe their effort towards integrating a segmentation subsystem into a general computer system for visual interpretation of scenes. Both the segmentation algorithms and the communication paths to and from the semantic processes are considered. Results of applying segmentation processes to images of natural (e.g., outdoor) scenes are presented by Ehrich and Foith, and Hanson and Riseman.

HIERARCHICAL RELAXATION

FOR WAVEFORM PARSING

L. S. Davis*
A. Rosenfeld

Computer Science Center
University of Maryland
College Park, MD 20742

ABSTRACT

Waveform parsing can be regarded as a hierarchical process of constraint satisfaction, in which a label is applicable to a segment of the waveform provided it is consistent with neighboring segments and forms part of a higher-level label. An iterative, parallel ("relaxation") scheme is described that applies such constraints to an noisy input waveform and determines a set of globally consistent hierarchical labellings.

1. Introduction

Images and waveforms can often be described hierarchically as consisting of parts that are in turn made up of subparts, and so on, down to a level of "primitive" parts; where at each level, the parts are in approximately specified positions relative to one another. Such a hierarchical structure is essentially a layered system of "spring-loaded" templates [1]. The process of recognizing that a description of this type applies to a given image or waveform is essentially a process of parsing with respect to a stratified context-free grammar (see below), with the primitive parts as terminal symbols. Combinations of these parts are recognized (by virtue of matching with particular spring-loaded templates), and labeled with nonterminal symbols; combinations of these symbols are recognized using higher-level templates; and so on until the entire input is accounted for.

In [2], a parallel, iterative method (called a "relaxation" method) of detecting spring-loaded template matches was proposed. In this method, matches to the subtemplates are detected, and for each such match, supporting evidence is sought -- i.e., do other matches occur in the expected relative positions. Subtemplate matches for which sufficient evidence is lacking are discarded, and the process is iterated (since discarding one subtemplate may weaken the evidence for another one). This process can be carried out in parallel for all the subtemplate matches, so as to rapidly eliminate all but those that belong to matches of the entire spring-loaded template.

The present paper generalizes the relaxation method of [2] to hierarchical spring-loaded templates. Here the interactions among the parts are more complicated; when a part is discarded at one level, this can cause other parts to be discarded at other levels, and further iteration may be needed at all of these levels. For simplicity, we treat a waveform example, but the approach should also be applicable to images.

Section 2 of the paper describes the hierarchical relaxation system, Section 3 illustrates its application to a noisy waveform, and Section 4 discusses possible extensions of the system, including the use of planning [3], of fuzzy or probabilistic constraints [4], and of semantic information.

A stratified grammar is a grammar in which each symbol has associated with it a "level number" in the range 0 to n, where the terminal symbols are at level 0 and the starting symbol S is at level n, and where in any rule $A \rightarrow \alpha$, if A is at level k ($1 \leq k \leq n$), then the symbols in the string α are all at level k-1. Note that there cannot be recursive rules in such a grammar, and that its language is finite (but possibly very large).

2. Hierarchical relaxation

Given a stratified grammar that

The support of the National Science Foundation under Grant MCS-76-23763 is gratefully acknowledged, as is the help of Mrs. Shelly Rowe in preparing this paper. The authors also wish to thank Narendra Ahuja for programming assistance.

*Present address: Dept. of Computer Science, University of Texas, Austin, TX 78712

implicitly defines a class of waveforms, our hierarchical relaxation procedure (HRP) for waveform analysis consists of the following steps:

0) Primitive detection: The primitive subpatterns are detected in the waveform, and labelled with the appropriate terminal symbols. It is assumed that this detection process can be carried out with a very low false dismissal rate (see further comments on this at the end of the section). Of course, this generally implies a high false alarm rate, but HRP is expected to weed out the false alarms by applying the constraints defined by the grammar.

1) Layer creation (procedure BUILD): The primitive detection process creates level 0 of the layered network, containing the terminal symbols of the grammar. More generally, given layer M of the network, one can create level M+1 by using those rules of the grammar that are applicable to level M. For each match of such a rule to layer M, an (M+1)st-level symbol is created, linked to the Mth-level symbols that gave rise to it.

2) Layer reduction (procedure REDUCE): If an Mth-level symbol does not contribute to any (M+1)st-level symbol, it is deleted. Conversely, if an Mth-level symbol is deleted, any (M-1)st-level symbol that contributed only to it is deleted.

3) Within-layer relaxation (procedure RELAX): The BUILD procedure requires us to examine many combinations of symbols on the given (Mth) level. We can reduce the cost of this process by eliminating symbols from level M based on a simple context-checking process. (A more elaborate version of this process, applied to shape matching, is described in [5].) To give only one very simple example, suppose that the Mth-level symbols are A, B, C, D and that the applicable rules are X → BAB, Y → CAD. Then we can eliminate any A unless it is preceded by a B or a C, and followed by a B or a D. [In general, we can use any set of intersymbol relations that are derivable from the grammar as contextual constraints. For waveforms, the easiest relations to apply are "precedes" and "follows", but for images a much richer set of relations would be available.] This process can be repeated, since whenever a symbol is eliminated, it may become possible

to eliminate other symbols that needed the first one as context.

After the initial primitive detection step, HRP proceeds as follows:

a) Apply RELAX to weed out symbols from level 0.

b) When repeated applications of RELAX yield no further change to level 0, apply BUILD to create leve 1.

c) Apply REDUCE to eliminate from level 0 all symbols that do not contribute to any symbol on level 1.

d) This may make it possible to apply RELAX once again to level 0. If this eliminates any symbols, the symbols at level 1 that depend on these can also be eliminated; REDUCE can then be used again to eliminate additional symbols at level 0; RELAX can then be applied again; and so on. This goes on until no further change takes place on levels 0 and 1.

e) We now apply RELAX to level 1. This may yield further changes on level 0 (via REDUCE), and so on, as in steps (c-d).

f) When there is no further change to levels 0 and 1, apply BUILD to create level 2.

g) Repeat stepts (c-e) until there is no further change to levels 2, 1, and 0; then apply BUILD to create level 3; and so on.

It should be evident that even after the weeding out done by RELAX on level M, symbols may still remain that do not contribute to any symbol on level M+1. This is becuase RELAX uses only local constraints derived from the grammar, rather than applying the rules of the grammar itself, which would be more costly. Thus even after RELAX has stabilized, and BUILD is used to construct level n+1, there may well be symbols on level n that can be eliminated by REDUCE.

The RELAX and REDUCE processes could, in principle, be performed in parallel, but in practice the nodes on which they are to operate must be examined sequentially. We can thus lower their computational cost by applying them only to those nodes on which they could possibly have any effect. For example, when a node is eliminated by REDUCE, we need only examine its neighbors (at its own and the adjacent levels) to determine whether they can now be eliminated by RELAX or REDUCE; no other nodes need be examined.

The above description of HRP considered only the one-dimensional waveform case, but an analogous procedure could evidently be applied to higher-dimensional languages. For example, consider a language of labelled graphs generated by a stratified, context-free graph grammar. At the lowest (zero) level, we create a terminally labelled graph by detecting primitives (say in a scene) and relationships among them; the primitives would be represented by node labels in the terminal graph, and the relationships by arc labels. We then use RELAX to eliminate nodes that failed to have the proper local context, as defined by the set of rules at level 1. When this results in no further change, we use BUILD to create nodes at level 1 corresponding to specified subgraphs (= right-hand-sides of graph grammar rules) in the level-0 graph, and we use REDUCE to eliminate any level-0 nodes that do not contribute to this process. RELAX can then be applied again to level 0, and so on, exactly as in the waveform case. In this general case, we can regard the grammatical rules at level m as defining k-ary relations on the level-m nodes. The contextual conditions used by RELAX might be, e.g., the binary relations derived (by projection) from these k-ary relations; there are many other possibilities.

It should be pointed out that the repeated use of RELAX, BUILD, and REDUCE provides both bottom-up and top-down flow of control in HRP, as constraints propagate to both higher and lower levels in the network.

As defined here, HRP has no control over the extraction of the primitives; it can eliminate them, but it cannot reconsider their extraction under the guidance of predictions made by higher levels. If such a capability were added, the system could recover from cases in which crucial primitives failed to be detected.

More generally, one could allow HRP to create (M+1)st-level symbols whenever partial matches to the level-M rules are found. These symbols could then predict the presence of the missing parts, which would in turn lead to a search for constituents of these parts on lower levels. Such an extension to HRP would provide greatly increased top-down analysis capability.

3. An example

In this section we describe the application of HRP to synthetic waveforms created by a specified grammar. The terminal symbols of this grammar are straight line segments having given slopes and lengths; thus the ideal waveforms are piecewise linear.

Input data for HRP is created by using the grammar to generate an ideal waveform, and then distorting it by perturbing the ordinate of each point of the waveform by a randomly chosen amount. [A second noise process, in which the slope and length of

each line segment are perturbed by randomly chosen amounts, was also provided in the HRP program, but was not used in the example described in this section. We can think of this second process as representing variability in the waveform model, while the second process represents noise in our measurements.]

The grammar used in our experiments involved terminal symbols having the slopes and lengths given in Table 1. (Mnemonics: u, U = upslope; d, D = downslope; h = horizontal; P = peak; V = valley.) The rules of the grammar are given in Table 2.

The waveform that will be used in our example is $u_2 \, h_2 \, u_1 \, h_1 \, d_1 \, h_2 \, u_2 \, d_1 \, h_1 \, d_1 \, h_2$. Its derivation is displayed in Figure 1. This waveform is shown in Figure 2a, and its noisy version, in which the primitives were detected, is shown in Figure 2b. The noisy waveform was obtained by adding white noise with standard deviation .75 to the ordinate of each point in the ideal waveform.

The primitives were detected in the noisy waveform by applying a piecewise linear approximation procedure that was very similar to the split-and-merge technique introduced by Pavlidis and Horowitz [6]. This technique is an iterative procedure for decomposing a waveform into linearly approximated segments, such that the approximation satisfies some error criterion. During each iteration, we first examine each segment from the previous iteration (at iteration 0 the entire waveform is one segment) and split any segment that is not well approximated by a line segment. The second part of each iteration involves examining pairs of adjacent segments. If combining the pair into a single segment would result in a segment whose fit to a line is either:

1) at least as good as either of the small segments, or

2) better than some predefined threshold,

then the pair is merged. The procedure terminates when the piecewise linear approximation satisfies some uniformity criterion. Ordinarily, the procedure requires an endpoint adjustment step after each iteration. However, our experience with the synthetic waveforms indicates that if segments are broken at points of locally maximal and high curvature (instead of at points which are maximally far from the approximating line), then we can dispense with the endpoint adjustment step.

The uniformity criterion used in our split-and-merge procedure was that the MSE error on each segment not exceed some threshold t. We used several values of t (1.75, 2.5, 5, 7.5, and 10); the low values yield many short segments, while the high values yield longer ones.

Each detected segment was given the most similar terminal symbol as a label. Table 3 lists the 25 segments found in this way on the Figure 2b waveform; these formed the input to HRP. For several segments it was not obvious which terminal symbol they should be assigned to; we assigned them to all the reasonably similar terminal symbols (see, e.g., segments 17 and 18).

The underlying level-0 relaxation network was constructed by introducing labeled arcs between nodes corresponding to segments that were adjacent to one another, where we defined "adjacent" as being within distance 2.

The first step in applying HRP to this network is to run RELAX at level 0. RELAX demands that each level-0 node be preceded and followed by allowable symbols (see the discussion in the preceding section). As a result of applying RELAX to level 0, nine nodes are deleted from the level-0 network. The level-0 nodes that survive RELAX are listed in Table 4.

Since level 0 is now stable under RE-LAX, we next apply BUILD to level 0 to obtain level 1, which is shown in Table 5. As a result of applying BUILD, one node (#7) was deleted from level 0 by REDUCE. RELAX is next applied to level 1, and two nodes (#s 31 and 32) are deleted from the level 1 network. Since some nodes have been deleted from level 1, REDUCE can be applied at level 0, and two more level 0 nodes (#s 16 and 17) are deleted.

The network is now stable under RELAX at both levels 0 and 1, so we can BUILD level 2. Table 6 shows the level 2 nodes constructed by BUILD. BUILD causes one node (#33) to be deleted from level 1 and then REDUCE can delete one more node (#20) from level 0. Both levels 0 and 1 are now stable under RELAX, and after the application of RELAX to level 2, the entire network is stable and is described in Table 7.

Finally, level 3 is constructed. This causes two nodes at level 2 (#s 37 and 38) to be deleted from the level 2 network. This in turn causes node #28 to be deleted from level 2, which in turn causes node #9 to be deleted from level 1. Level 3 contains a single node S, and the network is now stable at all levels. The final set of nodes is represented by the parse tree shown in Figure 3. The noisy segmentation represented by the initial level-0 network (Table 3) has been successfully parsed; 14 of the 25 initial primitives have been eliminated.

The example clearly indicates the value of multiple levels of representation and constraints. Applying the constraints at level 0 only did not entirely eliminate the ambiguity of the initial segmentation.

In fact, level 0 did not stabilize until after level 2 had been constructed and the effects of applying the constraints at level 2 had been fed back to the lower levels of the network.

Although HRP was able to analyze the waveform in the example, we feel that it needs substantial extensions before it can serve as a viable tool for waveform analysis. Some of these extensions are discussed in the next section.

4. Extensions

HRP provides the nucleus of a waveform analysis system. In this section we discuss some extensions to HRP that would be necessary to make it a useful tool for waveform analysis.

4.1 Planning

The general notion of planning [3] involves attempting to first solve a simple version of one's original problem in the hope that such a solution would provide both a framework and guidance for solving the larger problem. This concept can be incorporated in HRP in the following way.

Instead of assuming that only the lowest-level symbols of the grammar are directly discoverable from the data, we will assume that there are several such levels for which direct discovery procedures are available. HRP would now begin by detecting primitives at some suitably high level in the grammar, and applying RELAX, BUILD and REDUCE to the resulting layered network. Once HRP has stabilized (i.e., all higher levels built and all constraints satisfied), the resulting set of lowest-level hypothesis in the network can serve to guide the search for still lower-level, and probably less reliably detected, primitives in the original waveform.

As a simple illustration of the type of situation in which such a strategy would be particularly effective, consider the ideal piece of waveform shown in Figure 4a. Inasmuch as an observable waveform is much more likely to appear as in Figure 4b, it would probably be effective to provide a symbol 'ABCD' in the grammar at a level above the symbols A, B, C and D. If HRP should preserve a node corresponding to the hypothesis 'ABCD', then the search for the small segments B and C can be much more directed and successful than it would have been in the absence of a planning mechanism.

4.2 Fuzzy or probabilistic constraints

We have so far essentially ignored the fact that the lowest-level symbols are detected in the waveform with varying degrees of certainty, and have regarded the layered network as consisting of equally likely hypotheses. HRP can then eliminate all hypotheses that are not part of some parse, but cannot distinguish between a likely and an unlikely parse in order to choose some best description of the waveform.

One could use a fuzzy or probabilistic relaxation process (see [4]), rather than the discrete process used in HRP, to assign symbol probabilities to segments of the waveform, and iteratively adjust these probabilities until (hopefully) a nearly unambiguous parse is obtained. Such processes have been used successfully for a variety of low-level image segmentation tasks. It remains to be seen how successful they would be when used in a hierarchical framework.

Alternatively, given some criterion function for measuring the merit of a parse, conventional search procedures can be used to determine the maximal-merit parse contained in the layered network. However, as Barrow and Tenenbaum [7] have shown, the efficiency of such a search can be greatly increased by the incorporation of a fuzzy relaxation procedure into the search. This suggests that a very valuable extension to HRP would be to embed it into a version of [7] that can deal with hierarchical structures and constraints.

4.3 Semantic models

It is unreasonable to expect that we can easily embed all of our knowledge about the class of waveforms under consideration into constraints that are implicit in the grammar. Events occurring at one part of the waveform can, conceivably, affect our expectations and subsequent interpretation of events at some other remote part of the waveform. Trying to capture such dependencies in the grammar is, of course, possible, but leads to an explosion in the size of the grammar, thus making it a considerably less useful model.

One possible way to overcome the shortcomings of a grammatical representation is to augment the grammar by including a "semantic" model. A particularly promising approach would be to use a property grammar, where the properties are assigned to the nodes in a parse by procedures that are generalizations of Knuth's notions of synthesized and inherited attributes [8].

The procedures described by Knuth define attributes of the symbols in the derivation tree through the association of functions with each production in the grammar. A synthesized attribute is one defined in terms of the immediate descendents of a node in a derivation tree, while an inherited attribute is defined in terms of the ancestor of a node. The attributes of terminal symbols can be regarded as the "constants" which the symbols represent and are neither synthe-

sized nor inherited.

One possible generalization to the above approach is that, instead of regarding an attribute of a node as being either synthesized or inherited, we can associate a higher-order relation with every production of the grammar and perform assignments through various projections of this relation*.

The appealing aspect of this approach is that it provides a very homogeneous technique for dealing with both the syntactic and semantic knowledge that is available; both forms of knowledge are eventually treated as constraint expressions. Furthermore, just as the notion of syntactic well-formedness can be extended to encompass evaluations of competing parses in fuzzy situations, so can the notion of semantic well-formedness be extended to include evaluations of competing global interpretations.

5. Concluding remarks

We have presented a simplified design of a waveform analysis system which is based on the notion of a hierarchical relaxation network. Our current plans include extending the system along the lines of the suggestions made in Section 4, and then applying it to several real-world problems, such as arterial pulse waveforms (Stockman [9]). Ultimately, we hope that what we learn from dealing with waveforms will help us in designing a similar system for analyzing images.

References

1. M. A. Fischler and R. A. Elschlager, The representation and matching of pictorial structures, IEEE Trans. Computers C-22, 1973, 67-92.

2. L. S. Davis and A. Rosenfeld, An application of relaxation labeling to spring-loaded template matching, Proc. 3IJCPR, 1976, 591-597.

3. M. D. Kelly, Edge detection in pictures by computer using planning, Machine Intelligence 6, 1971, 379-409.

4. A. Rosenfeld, R. A. Hummel, and S. W. Zucker, Scene labeling by relaxation operations, IEEE Trans. Systems, Man, Cybernetics SMC-6, 1976, 420-433.

5. L. S. Davis, Shape matching using relaxation techniques, Technical Report 480, Computer Science Center, University of Maryland, College Park, MD, September 1976.

6. T. Pavlidis and S. L. Horowitz, Segmentation of plane curves, IEEE Trans. Computers C-23, 1974, 860-870.

7. H. Barrow and J. M. Tenenbaum, MSYS:

---

*We are indebted to Shmuel Peleg for this suggestion.

A system for reasoning about scenes, Technical Note 121, Artificial Intelligence Center, Stanford Research Institute, Menlo Park, CA, April 1976.

8. D. E. Knuth, Semantics of context-free languages, Mathematical Systems Theory 2, 1968, 127-145.

9. G. C. Stockman, A problem-reduction approach to the linguistic analysis of waveforms, Technical Report 538, Computer Science Center, University of Maryland, College Park, MD, May 1977.

Symbol	Slope	Length	Example
u_1	1	5	/
u_2	1	10	/
h_1	0	5	—
h_2	0	10	——
d_1	-1	5	\
d_2	-1	10	\

Table 1. Terminal symbol definitions.

Level	Symbols	Rules
3	S	
		$S \rightarrow PP \mid VVP$
2	P,V	
		$P \rightarrow UD \mid UUD; \quad V \rightarrow DU$
1	U,D	
		$U \rightarrow u_1h_1 \mid u_2h_2 \mid u_2d_1h_1; \quad D \rightarrow d_1h_2 \mid d_2u_1h_1$
0	$u_1, u_2, h_1, h_2,$ d_1, d_2	

Table 2. The waveform grammar.

Segment	Terminal Symbol	Starting Position	Ending Position
1	u_2	1	11
2	h_1	12	16
3	h_2	12	21
4	h_1	17	21
5	u_1	22	27
6	h_2	22	30
7	u_2	22	30
8	h_1	28	31
9	d_1	28	35
10	d_1	32	35
11	h_2	36	43
12	u_1	44	47
13	u_2	44	55
14	u_1	48	55
15	d_1	56	60
16	d_1	56	62
17	h_2	57	67
18	d_2	57	67
19	h_1	61	66
20	d_1	64	71
21	d_1	67	70
22	h_1	67	74
23	h_1	71	74
24	h_2	71	80
25	h_1	75	80

Table 3. Segments founds by the split-and-merge procedure.

Node #	Terminal Symbol	Starting Position	Ending Position
1	u_2	1	11
3	h_2	12	21
5	u_1	22	27
7	u_2	22	30
8	h_1	28	31
9	d_1	28	35
10	d_1	32	35
11	h_2	36	43
13	u_2	44	55
15	d_1	56	60
16	d_1	56	62
17	h_2	57	67
19	h_1	61	66
20	d_1	64	71
21	d_1	67	70
24	h_2	71	80

Table 4. Level 0 after the application of RELAX.

Node #	Symbol	Rule	Underlying level 0 nodes	Start-End
26	U	u_2h_2	1,3	1-21
27	U	u_1h_1	5,8	22-31
28	D	d_1h_2	9,11	28-43
29	D	d_1h_2	10,11	32-43
30	U	$u_2d_1h_1$	13,15,19	44-66
31	D	d_1h_2	15,17	56-67
32	D	d_1h_2	16,17	56-67
33	D	d_1h_2	20,24	64-80
34	D	d_1h_2	21,24	64-80

Table 5. Level 1 constructed by BUILD, using the rules

$$U \rightarrow u_1h_1 \mid u_2h_2 \mid u_2d_1h_1$$

$$D \rightarrow d_1h_2 \mid d_2u_1h_1$$

Node #	Symbol	Rule	Underlying level 1 nodes	Start-End
35	P	UUD	26,27,29	1-43
36	P	UD	27,29	22-43
37	V	DU	28,30	28-66
38	V	DU	29,30	32-66
39	P	UD	30,34	44-80

Table 6. Level 2 nodes constructed by BUILD, using the rules

$$P \rightarrow UD \mid UUD$$

$$V \rightarrow DU$$

Hierarchical Relaxation for Waveform Parsing

Node #	Symbol	Level
1	u_2	0
3	h_2	0
5	u_1	0
8	h_1	0
9	d_1	0
10	d_1	0
11	h_2	0
13	u_2	0
15	d_1	0
19	h_2	0
21	d_1	0
24	h_2	0
26	U	1
27	U	1
28	D	1
29	D	1
30	U	1
34	D	1
35	P	2
37	P	2
38	P	2
39	P	2

Table 7. Stable network at levels 0, 1, 2.

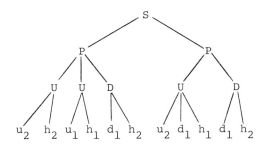

Figure 1. Derivation of test waveform.

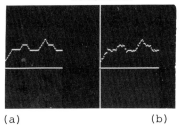

(a)   (b)

Figure 2. The test waveform: a) Ideal. b) Noisy.

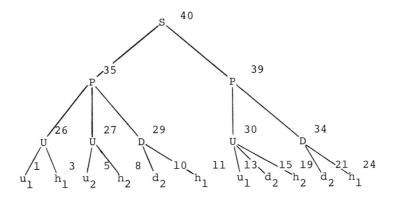

Figure 3. Parse tree constructed by
HRP. The number above and
to the right of each symbol
is its node number.

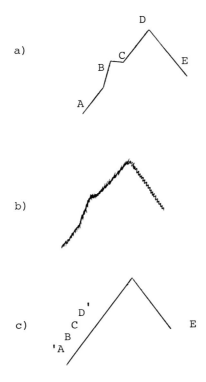

a)

b)

c)

Figure 4. Example illustrating the usefulness
of planning. a) Ideal waveform.
b) Nosiy version of (a). c) Higher-
level representation of (a).

TOPOLOGY AND SEMANTICS OF INTENSITY ARRAYS

R.W. Ehrich[1]   J.P. Foith[2]

VPI&SU   IITB
Blacksburg   Karlsruhe
Virginia, USA   W-Germany

ABSTRACT

One lesson that has been learned from previous approaches to scene analysis is that local methods are insufficient for extracting reliable information about the contents of a scene. Two different procedures that have been tried in order to remedy this deficiency are (1) the use of knowledge via a priori information and internal models and (2) multilevel analysis based upon hierarchies of representations such as cone systems. Even the meaning of small local events, such as intensity changes, is always embedded into some larger context and cannot be fully understood without explicit knowledge of that context. Therefore, before performing any analysis at all - even a crude one - a collection of contextual information and a representation thereof must precede the first processing steps. This paper is therefore concerned with the nature of the first processing steps. Since these first steps must be data driven, the second procedure is adopted, although the techniques differ from those used in cone systems.

In this paper we posit a comprehensive hierarchical data structure that requires no parameters for its construction. The technique is not based upon preselected windows, but rather uses context-dependent criterea. The data structure is versatile, easily computed, and invertible in the sense that the original image is completely recoverable. The data structure represents contextual information that facilitates region growing, texture analysis, and edge detection.

REPRESENTING AND PROCESSING INTENSITY ARRAYS

In the past, a multitude of approaches to many of the important tasks in scene analysis has given insight into some of the underlying problems of computer vision. Despite that multitude of approaches, the really hard and important problems have not been solved. An analysis of the reasons for the insufficiency of previous techniques must go all the way back and identify the issues of low level representation. These deal with the transition from the raw intensity data to the basic representation within the framework of which the basic processing techniques are applied.

In many systems the first processing steps provide a transition from the intensity array to some kind of 'edge image'. The transition is usually based upon implicit models of what an edge should be, and these models generally provide a scheme for local analysis of the data. However, any analysis that is based solely on local evidence is prone to errors, misinterpretations, and failure. This has long been recognized, and two different procedures have been tried in order to remedy these deficiencies.

(1) In the first, a priori information and internal models provided expectations about the kinds of local structures that could be located in an image and what instances of such structures would look like. It is inappropriate to drive the very first levels of analysis by a priori knowledge and models. Not only is it too difficult to use global knowledge in a way that is general enough to direct low level processing, but there is a need for powerful data driven mechanisms that might, at a later stage, evoke internal models. If internal models are evoked with too little evidence, too many models apply and the search space explodes.

(2) The second approach toward the use of global information has been the use of hierarchical representations where a crude analysis makes available global, scene-dependent information that can then be used to drive the low level processing.

Experience has shown that analysis of a scene cannot be performed in one single step or with a few drastic transformations. Rather, there must be a number of intermediate results that reflect a slowly increasing state of knowledge about the scene. This leads to the "paradigm of multiple representations," a system in which many representations with various characteristics and functions are used. Hanson and Riseman have concluded that a number of intermediate data structures are necessary for storing the information required for semantic processing. For early processing they use a cone system [1] that provides scene information at varying resolution levels. Then they propose an RSE data structure [2] that contains hypotheses

[1] R.W. Ehrich is with the Virginia Polytechnic Institute and State University, Department of Computer Science. He is on leave from the ECE Department, University of Massachusetts.

[2] J.P. Foith is with the Institut für Informationsverarbeitung in Technik und Biologie der Fraunhofer Gesellschaft e.V., Karlsruhe, Germany.

This work was supported in part by the National Science Foundation under grant GK43319 and in part by the Bundesministerium für Forschung und Technologie.

about regions and boundaries that have been obtained from the cone system by various operators. Marr [3] forms from the intensity array a representation called the primal sketch that contains a record of early statistical interpretations of directional intensity events. The next steps of analysis construct from the primal sketch a viewer-oriented representation, the 2-1/2 D sketch, and then the final result, the 3D model representation [4].

The paradigm of multiple representations involves a number of completely different representations whose merits must be discussed separately. For the issues of early processing it is necessary to discuss the use of hierarchical low level representations. Intensity arrays are frequently transformed into low level representations such as gradient images, numerical approximations, cooccurrence matrices, frequency images, cones, or symbolic arrays. Unfortunately, the problem of selecting a representation has not been thoughtfully discussed in the literature. Instead of investigating the underlying issues of the use of such representations, much effort has been put into the evaluation of the results that one achieves with them. The issue of selecting the representations to be used at various stages in computer vision is still very much open.

The purpose of a viable low level scene representation is to provide a data structure that describes in a useful way the intensity distribution in a scene and facilitates determining the meaning of intensity events and their interrelationships. There are at least five criteria by which such a low level representation is selected.
(1) SELECTION OF PRIMITIVES: What should be the primitives of the representation? One must decide what kinds of intensity events will be essential for the analysis tasks later on and what information will facilitate those tasks.
(2) EXTRACTION OF PRIMITIVES: By which techniques should the primitives be extracted? There appear to be two major classes of techniques here -- those that are statistical (interpretational) in nature and those that are structural (representational). The latter techniques reflect the topology of the intensity arrays without committments to preliminary, and therefore error-prone, interpretations. In other words, interpretational techniques try to match the intensity events with some predefined models while representational techniques describe the structures that are there. In the latter case interpretations are made only at a later stage when more information is available.
(3) DATA STRUCTURES: What kind of data structures are required? A data structure stores the primitives and expresses their interrelationships; thus it provides essential contextual information. The data structure determines the ease and the efficiency with which semantic processing can be performed.
(4) AGGREGATION STRUCTURES: How do the primitives aggregate into larger and more global units, and how should these aggregates be represented? The contextual information necessary to build these aggregates must be provided by the data structures. If, for example, the formation of a line drawing of region boundaries is to be fundamental to the analysis, then the representation ought to facilitate the formation of the boundaries. If, on the other hand, region growing is to be the primary

goal, one has to consider the representation of information that is essential for deciding the grouping of intensity events into regions.
(5) AGGREGATION RULES: How are the aggregation modules going to function? This has been one of the most difficult problems associated with low level processing. We simply don't know the best way to form boundaries or the best way to bound regions of heavy textures, and many investigators believe that aggregation modules will consist of a set of submodules that produce a rich collage of alternative groupings. Again, one must remember that the types of submodules that can be implemented depend a great deal upon the representation.

The importance of a good low level representation can hardly be overemphasized; misinterpretations at the transition from the intensity data to the basic representation will influence all the subsequent stages of analysis. Therefore the first steps must be taken with the greatest care possible. It is here that one must strictly obey Marr's "Principle of Least Committment" (PLC) [3], and this is best done by using representational techniques that don't require premature interpretations. In order to make scene analysis less of an art and more of a science, the representation should be general enough for diverse applications. It should not be necessary to use a different representation for each different application, as seems to be the case at the present time. While computational expediency may dictate the use of a less general representation for tracking bubble chamber events than for analyzing a LANDSAT frame, the theory, at least, should be the same.

PROBLEMS WITH EARLY INTERPRETATIONS

In our work we have long been dissatisfied with the performance of edge and bar shaped filter masks in edge and line detection applications. Filters with discontinuous receptive fields have Fourier transforms that contain many zeros in the finite frequence plane. Consequently, if one wished to reconstruct a scene that has been filtered by such a mask, one would find that the inverse reconstruction filter has many singularities because information has been lost in certain spectral bands.

There seem to be a number of reasons why such filter masks have found considerable following. For one, such detectors seem to model the detectors that are believed to exist in the neural layers behind the retina of the human visual system. For another, such detectors are reminiscent of some powerful theorems about matched filters that at first glance would appear to be applicable. Regarding the first point, it is clear that the human visual system must contain differencing circuitry with which to detect intensity changes. However, little is known about the actual neural implementations, and equally little is known about how luminance information is encoded in the transmissions from the retina. The second point requires somewhat more elaboration. The theorems about matched filters are derived about known signals in isolation under conditions of disturbances with known statistics. In Figure 1a is shown a scan line across an image that contains white lines normal to the scan direction. One possible method for detecting these lines is to apply to the scan line bar filters such as those shown in Figures 1c and 1e. The positive

R. W. Ehrich and J. P. Foith

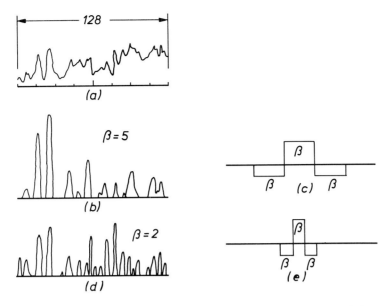

Figure 1 - Scan line (a), filter output (b) for filter mask (c),
and filter output (d) for filter mask (e).

outputs of these filters are given in Figure 1b and
1d for the two different filter parameters; these
outputs represent two different interpretations of
Figure 1a. The problem with the use of these
filters is that they are context dependent in a
very complicated way; the close proximity of two
lines substantially affects the filter outputs for
both. Since the smaller filter makes use of less
context, its output is a more explicit representation of the scan line structure. In any case,
such filters must be used with great care, and
their use probably should not be regarded to be an
application of matched filtering. A more detailed
discussion of this issue can be found in [5].

It is the purpose of this paper to propose a
technique that produces a highly informative scene
representation; it is a structural technique in the
sense that it analyzes the topology of the intensity array without generating interpretations. It
finds and represents the structures that are
actually there as opposed to computing a statistical measure of how closely the picture function
resembles the shapes of some preselected masks.

Those of us who have designed a complex system with hierarchical decision making are aware of
the way in which an insignificant decision at the
bottom of the hierarchy can topple the entire system if made irrevocably but incorrectly. The PLC
states that one should never make a decision based
upon thin evidence that will later have to be
changed because of the consequences of that decision farther up the hierarchy. In other words, to
the maximum extent possible, decision making elements should be placed in a feedback loop so that
firm decisions are deferred until the evidence
becomes compelling. The PLC provides for the
inclusion of the correct interpretation among the
alternatives produced at each decision stage. To
minimize the number of alternatives that must be
explicitly retained, it is essential to transform
the information at the earliest stages in such a
way that the difficulty of making decisions is
minimized while at the same time no viable alternatives are removed from consideration. For this

reason the early representation of scene information is a most critical issue in the conceptual
design of an automatic scene analysis system.

Marr forms his primal sketch by applying edge
and bar filters to the raw image and including in
the sketch a summary of the significant information
in the outputs of these filters. While Marr's
illumination of the issues of low level vision
represents an important contribution to the field,
we question the wisdom of using from the outset a
representation that appears to violate his own PLC.
By using different techniques it is possible to
form a much more accurate and sophisticated representation of the original scene deterministically
so that the PLC is not violated at the representation level. By collecting contextual evidence
before attempting to make any interpretations at
all, it is possible to make more informed decisions
about the meaning of intensity events. For these
reasons, structural processing of intensity arrays
is an important tool for the first steps in
computer vision.

STRUCTURAL REPRESENTATION OF INTENSITY ARRAYS

There has been considerable interest in the
decomposition of scenes and the description of
those decompositions. Often the resulting data
structures are tree structures, and the decompositions are regular in the sense that the image is
divided into quadratic windows according to various
criteria. Klinger and Dyer [6], for example, used
a tree representation for compact storage of images
as well as for rapid search for image features.
Their criterion required that each subwindow have
constant intensity. A more flexible criterion is
Freuder's concept of affinity [7] which results in
an "affinity tree" where nodes correspond to adjacent regions whose features share some affinity.
Yet another criterion, used by Pavlidis and
Horowitz, results in a piecewise approximation of
the picture function by polynomial surfaces [8].
These approximations are computed for a tentative
partitioning which is then refined by a split-and-

merge procedure. For each region one computes the best polynomial surface and the corresponding figure of merit. Regions with poor merit are split into smaller regions, and adjacent regions with similar coefficients are merged until a satisfactory decomposition has been achieved. The technique, however, fails to represent any relationships among the regions of the decomposition and is primarily a means of establishing a simpler description of the surface topology. The principal drawback of such a technique in scene analysis is that the coefficient labels attached to the segments may not have much meaning in the image domain, although the original image will be recoverable to any desired accuracy.

Another regular decomposition, this time along the intensity axis, was used by Krakauer [9]. By thresholding an image at each discrete intensity and delineating the contours of the regions, one obtains a tree, each branch of which corresponds to regions that are contained one within the other. Although a few region shape descriptors were computed, not much use was made of the description. Other investigators have sensed that significant information can be obtained directly from the topology of the picture function, though no particular theories have evolved. For example, Enomoto and Katayama [10] use differential geometry to establish rigorous definitions for topological features such as ridges and edges. While all these techniques are 2-dimensional, inherently 1-dimensional techniques may also be used to obtain quasi-2-dimensional results. Lozano-Perez [11] developed a method for detecting objects in a scene by using a syntactic description of intensity profiles along scan lines. The syntax is stored in the form of an ATN (Augmented Transition Network) grammar for which a scan line parser was constructed. The deficiency of such a technique is that it is object-specific and does not represent the topology of the image.

Since 1975, Ehrich and Foith [12-15] have been investigating picture processing algorithms using a scene description based upon a data structure for representing intensity profiles that is called a relational tree or simply, R-tree. An R-tree is a tree that is used to store a comprehensive description of the 1-dimensional contextual relationships defined by the peaks and valleys of an intensity profile. Pointers from the tree vertices link the structural elements to attribute lists from which the original scene can be completely reconstructed. Since this data structure is the key concept for this entire paper, a brief review of relational trees is given next.

In Figure 2 is shown a simple intensity profile containing a few peaks and valleys. Notice that peaks appear to be recursively nested within larger and larger peaks that might be concatenated with and nested within even even larger peaks. The peaks themselves are delineated by the highest of the valleys on either slope. For example, the small peak p_7 is concatenated with the small peak p_9, and both together form a larger peak that is delineated by the valley at data point 4 and whose width extends from point 4 to point 10. Since p_7 is the higher (or dominant) peak, this larger peak is labeled p_7. This recursive nesting of waveform peaks is conveniently reflected in a tree, called a relational tree, that is given for this example in Figure 3. In this tree, several vertices are labeled 19:21 due to the fact that the dominant

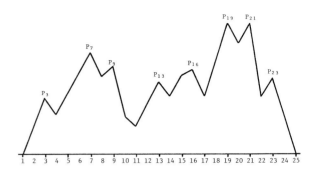

Figure 2 - Sample intensity profile.

peaks in part of the waveform are p_{19} and p_{21} since both have the same height. The vertex with four descendants is due to the fact that the valleys at data points 14, 17, and 22 are all at the same height. Each non-frontier vertex of the R-tree is

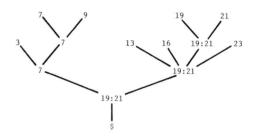

Figure 3 - Relational tree for Figure 2.

physically due to a unique valley of the intensity profile, and it is labeled with that peak among those induced by the valley that is dominant. The vertices in the frontier of the tree form a left to right ordering of all the local intensity maxima of the profile.

The R-tree is computed using a fast 3-stack algorithm that processes an intensity profile from left to right. The algorithm produces a great deal of information about the peaks and valleys of the profile, and this is stored in attribute lists that are attached to the vertices of the R-tree. In our implementation the widths, heights, and locations of peaks are stored together with valley locations and pointers that permit quick traversal of the tree.

Let τ_t be the transformation, called the tree transformation, that produces the list of R-trees that forms the representation. The first concern is with the invertibility of τ_t, since if the original image cannot be recovered, τ_t is interpretive rather than representational. In Figure 4a is an image of a pile of capacitors, and in Figure 4b is the reconstruction of the image from the data structure. Notice the legibility of the code on the capacitor at left center and the crisp object boundaries. To give some feeling for the algorithm itself, Figure 5 shows scan line 136 in Figure 4a in addition to the R-tree for that line.

While the original concept was developed

R. W. Ehrich and J. P. Foith

A

B

Figure 4 - Raw image (a) and reconstruction from the data structure (b).

mainly for intensity modulated textures, it was clear that for the representation of uniform regions an extension of the concept would be necessary. The reconstruction in Figure 4b was generated by drawing straight line segments between adjacent peaks and valleys. Due to digitization noise and small intensity variations, even the virtually uniform regions consist of many micropeaks whose reconstruction by straight line segments will always be close to perfect. Without those micropeaks uniform regions would be of constant intensity, and such regions cannot be represented accurately by peaks. To illustrate this, the scan lines of the image in Figure 4a were smoothed by a special hysteresis algorithm [16] that eliminates small peaks and valleys while preserving exactly the shape and locations of all the major intensity maxima and minima. The smoothed scan line 136 is

shown at the top of Figure 6, and the visual effect of the smoothing on the image is almost imperceptible. The problem of representing homogeneous regions was solved by detecting regions of zero slope, called plateaus, and storing them in the data structure. If one considers the plateaus to be peaks of zero relative height, the basic algorithm is not changed. In fact, one might also consider the possibility of quantizing slope and storing in the data structure regions of constant slope. A further extension might be to store the shape of the intensity function by describing peaks by chain codes or polynomial approximations. The R-tree and the reconstruction for scan line 136 are also shown in Figure 6. No effort has been made to aggregate adjacent plateaus at different heights, since such simple interpretive processes should occur farther along in the processing

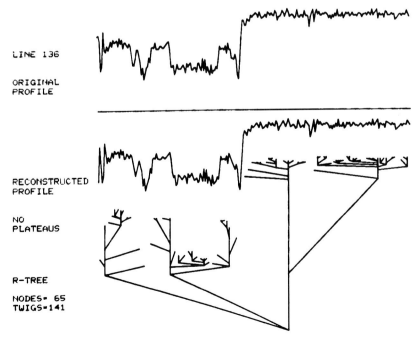

LINE 136

ORIGINAL PROFILE

RECONSTRUCTED PROFILE

NO PLATEAUS

R-TREE

NODES= 65
TWIGS=141

Figure 5 - Scan line 136 of Figure 4a and R-tree.

Topology and Semantics of Intensity Arrays

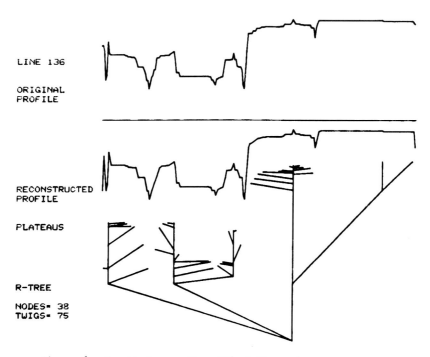

LINE 136

ORIGINAL
PROFILE

RECONSTRUCTED
PROFILE

PLATEAUS

R-TREE

NODES= 38
TWIGS= 75

Figure 6 - Smoothed scan line 136 of Figure 4a and R-tree.

sequence. Instead, every effort has been made to ensure that there are absolutely no parameters at this stage of visual processing.

One of the useful properties of R-trees is that large intensity peaks that correspond to large 1-dimensional regions are located near the root of the R-tree while their substructures are located closer to the frontier. Therefore one can choose to ignore image substructures that are judged too insignificant to be of importance in the problem at hand. On the other hand, the presence of these substructures in the data structure permits very precise description of large image structures without the loss of resolution that is characteristic of systems employing windows.

We would like to include here a few remarks on our choice of peaks as the primitives for the representation. Since a peak is basically a 2-dimensional region, the use of such a representation leads to a region-oriented as opposed to a boundary-oriented theory. However, as will be demonstrated, boundaries are part of the concept of a peak, and they can be determined explicitly from the data structure. When one looks at a gradient image the brain deceives us into believing that we have found the object boundaries by aggregating edge assertions for us. In boundary formation, the really hard job is the linking of the edge elements into lines. Here, a region-oriented approach can improve the performance of a line finder by providing information about the regions on either side of the line. The R-trees not only provide such information, but they also provide contextual information in a hierarchical way that facilitates the implementation of autonomous low level processes.

It is almost certainly possible to achieve better knowledge-independent results than have been achieved in the past, and it is important to do so to provide the semantic processing routines with the best possible input. The primitives of the basic scene representation should organize picture elements of the intensity array into gestalts such as segments of constant slope, curvature, intensity, or whatever attributes are considered to be important. Marr has made a strong case for directional microedges and slope segment boundaries; these, however, are linear primitives whose only relationships are concatenation, and they do not account for luminance information in any useful way. We have selected the next most feasible primitive called a _peak_ because the gestalt it represents is a self-contained intensity region in the picture function. Peaks have the advantage of representing luminance information directly, and since they are self-embedding, their relationships are much richer and more descriptive. Once a primitive has been selected, the remaining issue involves the way in which it is computed. Here again we differ with Marr because the actual instances of the primitives should be recorded instead of correlations with a set of ideal primitives.

There are a few other considerations that have not yet been discussed. For example, while directional intensity changes can be tracked in the trees, it is not at all clear that this would be the best approach. The reason that R-trees do not record directional information is that they are computed from 1-dimensional data. Additional information can be obtained by blurring the image directionally first and then computing the R-trees in the direction normal to the blurring. Since in a blurred image the R-trees are not independent, not all of them need to be stored. Directional blurring is identical to the concept of _directional averaging functions_ [17] that were used for detecting very subtle lines and edges in remote reconnaissance. The R-trees for the blurred images will provide a very sharp and precise description of long lines or edges whose gradients are normal to the blurring direction. The number of orientations required for the blurring process is related to the degree of blurring, and that relationship is

R. W. Ehrich and J. P. Foith

defined more precisely in [17].

After the computation of the tree representation, an interpretive phase is initiated whose result will be a number of competing and cooperating results that will be stored in a layered data structure. Here the sorting of information and the resolution of conflicts begins. The interpretations stored here are the result of analysis of the trees for edges, lines, and atomic regions, tracking for extension to two dimensions, aggregation by mechanisms based upon contextual criteria, and aggregation of heavy textures. There is much work to be done in developing effective mechanisms for edge detection, region growing, and texture analysis, and the selection of proper representations will be a solid advance toward these goals. Before showing techniques for using the R-trees it is necessary to take a close look at the image elements that one wants to extract from an image and some of the associated semantics.

SEMANTICS OF BOUNDARIES AND REGIONS

Today it is well understood that there are many levels of description of a scene and, therefore, many levels of analysis. Boundary and region formation are among the first levels. In order to construct well-behaved algorithms for these tasks one must first determine substructures that are meaningful parts of boundaries, lines, or regions. Of course, these substructures are local edge elements, line elements, and texture elements. The semantics of these elements are determined by the physical structure of the scene, the topology of the intensity array, and the way in which these structures are perceived.

A full semantic model of boundaries and regions must take into consideration the issues of illumination, reflectance functions, physical and geometrical constraints within the scene, and the visual mechanisms that analyze and aggregate elements in the intensity array into meaningful parts. Limited yet useful work has been done on these issues, especially for images from the blocks world [18]. An excellent example is Horn's analysis of intensity distributions and techniques for recovering from them the shape of objects [19, 20]. In a study of profiles that are typical for edges in the blocks world, Hershkowitz and Binford [21] find three typical instances of edges - the step, the roof, and the peak shaped edge, and they correlate these to the physical structures that cause them. Unfortunately, in the world of real scenes the problems are not equally well defined, and much more must be done to find even the particular instances of image elements such as edges, lines, or texture elements. In particular, the correspondence between the picture function and the visual effects with which it is associated is frequently very deceptive. In a case study we wish to discuss some of the relations between the visual effects and their underlying structures in the intensity array.

The most frequently used model of an edge is that of a step function. Figure 7a shows a scene where the objects appear to have visually clear, high contrast edges. A look at Figures 7b and 7c reveals the surface structures of the corresponding intensity array. In these drawings the intensities have been complemented so that large values correspond to black objects. Although the edge is visually crisp and smooth, its topology is highly irregular. Figure 7b shows a shoulder on the top of the edge that would cause a bar type detector to report an edge strength that underestimates the visual effect of the edge. Another disturbing event is the small bump sticking out of the edge scarp in Figure 7c which cannot be seen visually. All of these irregularities make it difficult to define the exect location of the edge. Decisions about the location of the pixel that is to represent a particular edge element must often be postponed until more global information is available. Since simple filter masks output many representatives for each edge element, thresholding or non-maximum suppression is required. It is quite clear that many conventional edge detectors are quite sloppy about the way in which they analyze microevents. Instead, actual structures must be stored which preserve the information about the particular instance of the edge so that more informed processes at a later stage can decide exactly where to place the edge.

Closely related to edge elements are line elements. Figures 8a through 8c show a line taken from Figure 7a which is the upper horizontal wire. The line has a relatively smooth skeleton with fuzzy boundaries and almost constant intensity. The shape near the bottom, however, varies drastically, and the cross section of the line changes considerably along its length. Thus the local context as well as the width change in an unpredic-

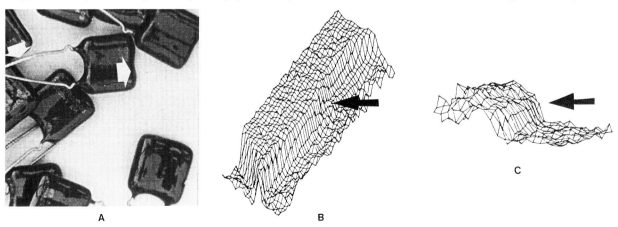

A   B   C

Figure 7 - Capacitor scene (a) and high contrast edge (b,c).

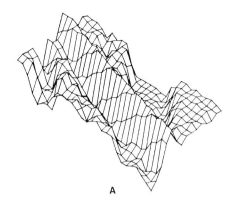

A

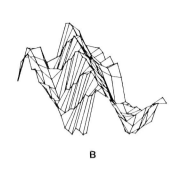

B

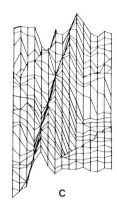

C

D

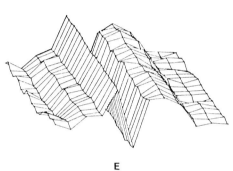

E

Figure 8 - Wire from capacitor
scene of Figure 7a (a-c), house
scene (d), parallel lines (e).

table way.

One more problem becomes apparent from Figure 8e which is a plot of the bottom line of the roof above the door in the house scene in Figure 8d. Visually there appear to be two distinct white lines separated by a black band. The 3D plot, however, shows that the two white lines are immediately adjacent. Since the two lines have different widths, no single bar type filter would be optimal for both, and the adjacency of the two lines would cause mutual interference as was discussed in the section on early processing.

Many of the really hard problems in computer vision are due to texture. Because of the variability of textures it is hard to design models and exhibit prototypes of texture elements. In Figure 9a one sees a heavy texture where the texture elements are like small fuzzy blobs, an example of which (circle) is shown from various viewpoints in Figures 9b through 9f. The problem of texture description is one of describing in three dimensions the shape, orientation, and relationships among such elements. Traditional texture measures such as those obtained from cooccurrence matrices [22], edge density measurements [23], run length statistics [24], or spot detectors [25] only grasp local aspects of such texture elements.

Cooccurrence matrices are 1-dimensional, and statistics about texture elements such as the one in Figure 9b are obtained by analyzing slices through that element. The relative success of cooccurrence matrices indicates that the analysis of 1-dimensional profiles is a useful means for extraction of texture features. Ehrich and Foith

[12,13] have used a texture model based upon maxima and minima of 1-dimensional profiles. There, structural parameters of the peak gestalts such as height, contrast, and width prove to be effective in discriminating among textures. Mitchell et al. [26,27] show through careful experiments that densities of 1-dimensional extrema tallied at various local contrast levels can be used for texture discrimination and segmentation. These results indicate that peaks are good texture elements to measure for a large class of textures, especially natural textures.

The last point that we wish to make concerns the aggregation of these elements into complicated regions. As an example, consider the large region in Figure 10 that corresponds to the capacitor in the lower right corner of Figure 7a. This region has, in turn, many smaller substructures that correspond to specular reflections from the capacitor surface. Although these subregions appear visually uniform, structurally this is not the case, and the regions appear as coherent ridges. Here one must remember that an analysis of these compound structures will not be tractable if drastic distortions have been made at the lowest processing levels.

Therefore, the semantic issues concerning boundaries and regions include the following: visual elements such as edges, lines, or texture elements are rich in variety and subject to distortions and changes in particular instances. The meanings of these elements cannot be fully understood without explicit knowledge of their context. Therefore any low level vocabulary that is to

R. W. Ehrich and J. P. Foith

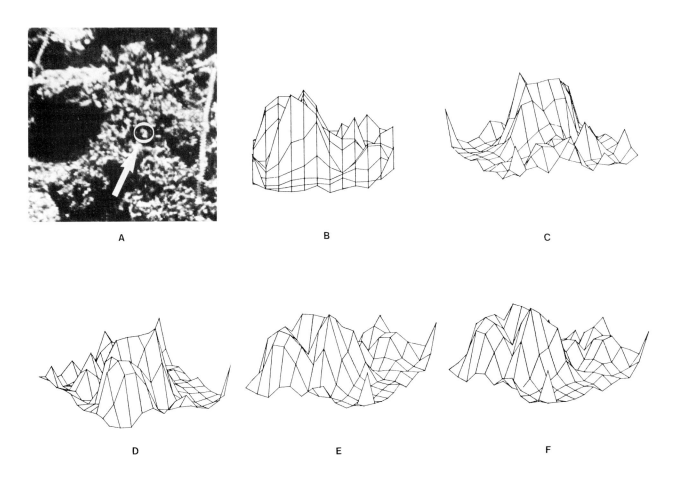

A   B   C

D   E   F

Figure 9 - Heavy texture (a) and views of a single element (b-f).

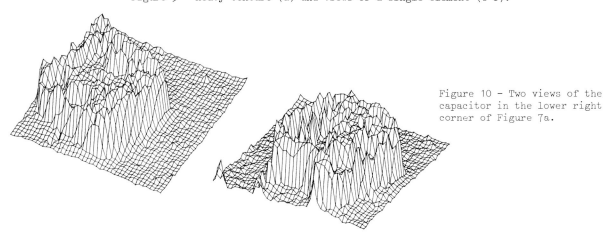

Figure 10 - Two views of the capacitor in the lower right corner of Figure 7a.

describe the image elements and their relationships must preserve information about specific instances and not just correlations with ideal models.

BOUNDARY FORMATION

Since in a general system one cannot make assumptions about the nature of the low level data, the need for preselecting a set of models is distressing. A better approach would be to provide a representation in which any particular model can be tested directly, and our representation is especial-ly suited for that. From our point of view, edges are derived structures and are a consequence of the ordering of picture elements intensities on the sides of the basic regions which are the peaks and valleys. A great deal of contextual information is available that facilitates determining the nature of the regions that an edge separates.

Let us consider one of the simplest possible structural edge detection algorithms. In Figure 11a is shown a house scene that contains both sharp boundaries and heavy texture. For comparison, the output of the Sobel operator is given in Figure 11b

Figure 11 - House scene (a), Sobel operator with threshold 40 (b),
structural edge detector with threshold 40 (c), and structural edge detector
with 3 pixel blurring normal to the profiles and with threshold 40 (d).

thresholded at intensity 40 which is close to the
level at which the roof-sky boundary begins to dis-
integrate. Figure 11c shows the result of applying
a simple structural edge detection algorithm independently to row and column profiles of the image
and then merging the results into a new pseudo-
image. The edge detector functions in the following
way. From the R-tree of each profile the slope
segments between each pair of adjacent plateaus,
peaks, and valleys are located. Suppose that $p_1=(x_1,y_1)$ and $p_2=(x_2,y_2)$ are the endpoints of such a
slope segment on a given intensity profile as shown
in Figure 12. A file is generated that contains
the value $|y_2-y_1|$ at an arbitrarily selected coor-
dinate $x=(x_1+x_2)/2$, and in Figure 11c are shown
those edge points that exceeded a threshold of 40.

One might argue against the advisability of
making decisions about the presence of edge points
using context only in the profile direction because
one is ignoring the usual semantic requirement of
edge continuity. There are several possibilities
here. One would be to check adjacent profiles
before making the edge assertion. Another way of
introducing context normal to the profile has some
of the spirit of the Sobel operator itself. The
image is blurred vertically before detecting horizontal edges and horizontally before detecting
vertical edges so that when a slope segment is
located in the R-tree for a given profile it already
implies that the slope segment is continued in the
adjacent profiles. The result of edge detection
after directional blurring is shown in Figure 11d

R. W. Ehrich and J. P. Foith

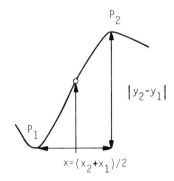

Figure 12 – Structural edge detector.

for blurring with a sliding average of 3 picture elements out of a total scan line length of 256 elements. Once again, a threshold of 40 has been selected.

This structural edge detector produces edges that are thin because each edge element is represented by a single pixel. Unlike most edge detectors the structural edge detector requires no post-processing steps to remove redundant edge elements. By storing the coordinates and intensities of the neighboring valley and peak one preserves the information about the range of that edge element; no shape descriptors are required.

A greater responsibility is given to the system designer to specify what he means by an edge – in fact, all options are left open. For example, in this implementation, a long slope that is interrupted by a short plateau will be interpreted as two smaller edges. Sufficient information is present in the R-trees to facilitate much more complex interpretations, and adjacency of multiple edges does not confuse the edge detector in the least. Notice how the Sobel operator glues the window boundaries and porch supports into ambiguous aggregates, while the structural detector produces rather clear separation of the significant slopes. The roof line above the door that was viewed as a 3D plot in Figure 8e is an excellent example for comparing the accuracy of the two edge detectors. The Sobel operator produces a misinterpretation of the underlying structure because it finds three high contrast edges where there are actually four. The output of the structural edge detector exactly reflects the strengths of the edges according to the topology that is revealed in Figure 8e. Notice that the contextual algorithm produces fewer noise points than the line by line algorithm.

In another experiment we have analyzed the magnitudes of the slopes of the slope segments detected by the structural edge detector and have not found the information to be valuable. Slope information will be helpful for identifying shadings produced by curved surfaces, but apparently the edges occurring in the house scene are all quite sharp. In such images it is purely edge contrast that is critical to interpretation.

While most edge detectors in the literature only estimate gradient strength in a small fixed local neighborhood, structural edge detectors can be very flexibly designed to make use of contextual information in determining the shape of the edge elements. This information can be used to generate symbolic descriptions for edge or line elements. These, in turn, can be used to compute symbolic

descriptions for more global edges and lines. Therefore it is possible to define a vocabulary for low level events, and in Figure 13 is shown part of such a vocabulary.

As can be seen from Figure 13, statistics about the parameters of the elements that constitute a particular edge or line are computed in order to provide information about that instance of that edge or line. An even more elaborate version of such a vocabulary would consist of a simplification of generalized cylinders where an edge or line would be given as a skeleton which at intervals would be linked with explicit descriptions of the edge or line cross-section at that point. Such a vocabulary may seem to be too rich and therefore require too much computation and storage, but one must remember that the task at hand is so complex that one must not hope to succeed in general applications without immense efforts.

REGION ANALYSIS

One of the most difficult and important problems is to determine how picture elements should be aggregated into regions. Aggregation processes may be entirely data driven or entirely directed by prior knowledge; typically they are directed by both. Although hardly anything is known about how the visual system uses prior knowledge, it is a reasonable guess that the lowest level processing algorithms are not modified by prior expectations. Attempts to construct a hierarchical vision system would be greatly complicated if no knowledge-independent low level processing was permitted. The basic scene representation is used precisely to organize the results of knowledge-independent processing. Later a number of more complex grouping processes are activated simultaneously. Their outputs compete and cooperate to produce regions at higher and higher levels of structural complexity.

In the work that we have done to date we have concentrated much more on region growing than on edge detection. If it were possible to achieve proper aggregation of peaks into regions, edge boundaries could be determined easily after aggregation rather than before. The first step is to consider 1-dimensional regions within an intensity profile. An R-tree segments an intensity profile into recursively nested regions according to the relationships among the intensity maxima and minima within the profile. These are tentative region components whose identity will depend in large part upon the presence or absence of corresponding structures in adjacent profiles. In [12] we investigated the possibility that there were fundamental structural transformations that map R-trees into simpler R-trees by grouping peak substructures. Two examples of such transformations are known as the splinter and trunk transformations. Omitting the theoretical discussion of these transformations, the effect these transformations have on the surface structures of intensity profiles can be rather easily described.

Algorithm 1 – Splinter Rule

Locate in the intensity profile all maximal sets of consecutive peaks whose valleys strictly ascend in height from left to right and then strictly descend. The peaks in each such peak group are merged into a new peak whose height and location is that of the dominant (highest) peak in that group.

EDGE (1 , 2 , 3 , 4 , 5 , 6 , 7)

CONTEXT = [global gradient, neighboring regions]

SHAPE = [shape of the skeleton line]

ORIENTATION = [ϑ]

CONTRAST = [relative height $\overline{rh}$, rh_{min}, rh_{max}]

WIDTH = [$\overline{w}$, w_{min}, w_{max}]

ENDPOINTS = [(x_1,y_1), (x_2,y_2)]

TYPE = [structure of edge elements, shading edge, convex edge, ...]

LINE (1 , 2 , 3 , 4 , 5 , 6 , 7 , 8)

CONTEXT = [neighboring regions]

SHAPE = [shape of the skeleton line]

ORIENTATION = [ϑ]

CONTRAST = [relative height $\overline{rh}$, rh_{min}, rh_{max}]

WIDTH = [$\overline{w}$, w_{min}, w_{max}]

ENDPOINTS = [(x_1,y_1), (x_2,y_2)]

RIGHT FLANK = [shape of right slope elements]

LEFT FLANK = [shape of left slope elements]

Figure 13 - Low level vocabulary for edges and lines.

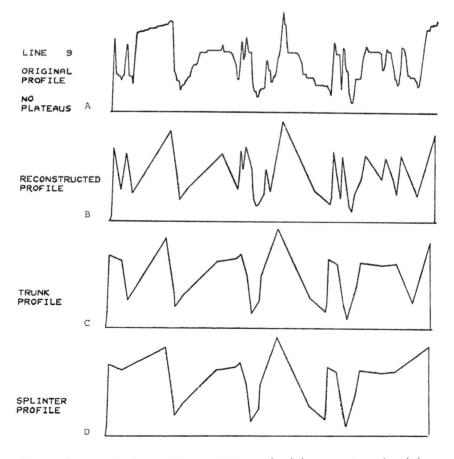

LINE 9
ORIGINAL PROFILE
NO PLATEAUS   A

RECONSTRUCTED PROFILE   B

TRUNK PROFILE   C

SPLINTER PROFILE   D

Figure 14 - Smoothed scan line 9 of Figure 4a (a), reconstruction (b),
trunk rule (c), and splinter rule (d).

Algorithm 2 - Trunk Rule

As in the splinter rule, locate all maximal sets of consecutive peaks whose valleys strictly ascend in height from left to right and then strictly descend. For each such group, mark the peak, p_0, between the ascending and descending valleys. Move one by one from the highest valley to the lowest, marking the peaks for each new valley until either all peaks in the group are marked or dominance changes from p_0 to another peak. When dominance changes, only the peaks due to the higher valleys are retained in the peak group.

After the grouping, for each of the peak groups one must generate a new intensity profile that describes how the peaks merge. In the example of Figure 14, the reconstruction of the aggregated intensity profile follows the tops of the peaks within a group of peaks that are merged. Notice in Figure 14 that the trunk rule results in less aggressive aggregation because the groups of peaks to be merged are split by dominance changes. Notice also that these grouping rules act on peaks and remove the valleys within a peak group. Thus these rules act to aggregate white figures on a black background, and if one wished to aggregate black figures on a white background, one would first form the complement of the image.

In Figures 15 and 16 are shown the results of recursively applying the splinter rule for a total of 7 cycles. In Figure 15 the image was first complemented so that merging of black elements would occur. In the case of Figure 16, each iteration consisted of applying the splinter rule to rows and columns independently and then averaging the result.

In Figure 15b one sees that intermediate gray values tend to shift toward the black because of the nature of the grouping rules. Notice how the black regions grow outward and claim the adjacent regions. As previously mentioned, the new intensity profile is generated by following the peak tops of merged peaks; this is a conservative strategy that only gradually moves the gray regions toward the black. Major boundaries are essentially preserved. The stripes in Figure 15b result from

A   B

Figure 15 - Original capacitor scene (a) and splinter image after 7 iterations (b).

 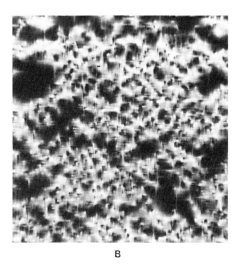

A   B

Figure 16 - Original texture scene (a) and splinter image after 7 iterations (b).

small local variations that cause valleys and peaks near major boundaries to merge with the wrong peak groups. This is to be expected for several reasons. First, no edge semantics are embedded in the grouping mechanism which may therefore override boundaries. Second, the grouping algorithm is, in this case, strictly 1-dimensional.

In Figure 16b some degree of 2-dimensional processing was provided using both scan lines and columns. In this case, white peaks were merged, and one sees how gray peaks tend to cluster around the bright centers of the texture elements to form fairly distinct regions. Due to the pseudo-2D processing the striping of Figure 15b is not so predominant. With additional processing steps such as thresholding or contour following one would obtain clearly defined macro-regions that are

most difficult to obtain by other methods.

While these simple aggregation mechanisms are inadequate in themselves for region growing, they demonstrate that simple hypotheses about regions can be formed according to criteria that are entirely structural in nature. Planning will be helpful for determining how many peaks should be grouped at each merge step, and as the regions grow more complex, semantics will surely have to be applied to the process. Most important, grouping must also make use of context in the direction normal to the intensity profiles, and later methods will be given for accomplishing this. For the moment, however, let us explore some of the other properties of peaks and valleys.

In an earlier investigation of a set of texture samples [12] we discovered that the histograms

A   T = 200 to 255

B   T = 0 to 123

C   T = 25 to 255

D   T = 25 to 255

Figure 17 - 1D peaks(a), 1D valleys (b),
1D relative peak heights (c), and 1D relative valley depths (d).

R. W. Ehrich and J. P. Foith

of one-dimensional extrema (peaks and valleys of row and column profiles) tended to be nearly identical to the histograms for all picture elements, almost as though the picture elements had been inserted for cosmetic effect. However, the histograms for peaks alone or for valleys alone tended to differ considerably both from each other and from the histogram for all picture elements. It occurred to us that it might be possible to segment regions of heavy texture on the basis of peak and valley attributes. In Figure 17 are slices from four pseudo-images generated from the house scene in Figure 11a. Figures 17a and 17b contain all 1-dimensional peaks and all 1-dimensional valleys, respectively, whose intensities fall within the specified thresholds. To obtain a simple measure of texture contrast the relative heights of peaks on the frontier of the R-trees were computed, and in Figure 16c those peaks having relative heights between the specified thresholds were marked. Relative peak height is the vertical distance between the top of a peak and the valley that induces it, and this information is part of the R-tree data structure. Figure 17d is a plot of the relative peak heights (i.e., valley depths) in the negative image whose intensities are between the given thresholds.

The textures in the house scene in Figure 11a are typical of natural textures, and a great deal of information about those textures is contained in Figure 17. Most of the important regions such as the clouds, tree foliage, house, lawn, shadows, and shrubs form isolated point clusters in one or another of the four pseudo-image slices. Regions such as clouds have low variance so that peaks and valleys cluster tightly within a small intensity range. Other regions such as the trees have high variance so that intensity extrema are widely separated. Notice how in Figures 17c and 17d the tree is separated from the front of the house by relative peak height measurements. This result cannot be obtained by thresholding the raw intensities because the house has the same intensity as many of the tree texture elements. Thus the densities, variances, and locations of intensity extrema are important features for texture analysis, and all regions, whether textured or not can be treated in the same way. A feature such as the relative height of extrema also has considerable importance because it gives the contrast of texture elements without regard to brightness. In Figure 17 many of the important boundaries such as window, porch, and roof boundaries are ridges of colinear intensity extrema and may be detected directly. What is needed are good algorithms for bounding point clusters in multidimensional spaces and for determining which of those are linear clusters. Unlike lines and edges, the vocabulary for describing textures is potentially extremely large, and not enough is known yet to form a good one.

Let us now turn briefly to one final topic. The theory that has been discussed is fundamentally a 2-dimensional theory, whereas the implementation is strictly one-dimensional. While 2-dimensional information is not lost in the data structure, it is not there explicitly; one reason for not using a data structure that describes 2-dimensional regions directly is the potential complexity of such a data structure. It is possible, however, to link the vertices of the R-trees of adjacent scan lines to generate 2-dimensional regions.

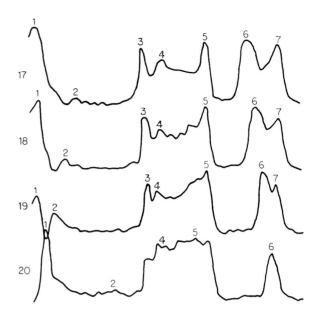

Figure 18 - Scan lines from Figure 4a.

In Figure 18, four sequential scan lines have been plotted from an inverted, low resolution (64 x 64 element) copy of the capacitor scene in Figure 4a. Lines 17 to 20 in that scene fall across the capacitor in the upper center of the photo, and the three major peaks correspond to capacitor bodies. The R-trees for scan lines 17-20 have been plotted in Figure 19. In each of these four scan lines, the

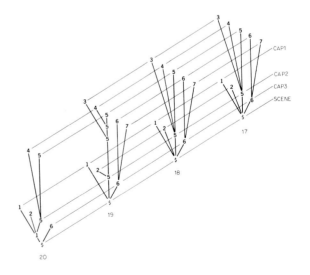

Figure 19 - Coupled relational trees for scan lines 17-20.

largest region that covers the entire scene is represented at the root of each corresponding tree. Moving up each tree one now finds vertices that correspond to smaller regions labeled 1, 5, and 6. These correspond with the outlines of the three capacitors crossed by the scan lines. Moving still higher in the trees one finds the vertices of still smaller subregions that correspond with specular reflections from the capacitor surfaces. The process of region growing in the direction normal to the scan lines involves linking the vertices of corresponding structures.

Clearly not all vertices in all trees will link to adjacent scan lines, and it is necessary to decide not only how a vertex links but whether or not it links at all. The procedure is to match scan line surface structures by a discrete relaxation process as shown in the example in Figure 20. Establishing a link between peaks establishes a link between the frontiers of the corresponding R-trees. On the other hand, establishing a link between valleys induces a link between vertices in the deep structure of the R-trees. The information in the R-tree data structure provides all the neccessary feature measurements on peaks and valleys on which the relaxation can be based. Furthermore, the tree structure facilitates the design of hierarchical relaxation procedures that act simultaneously on large image regions and on the small subregions from which they are constructed [28,29].

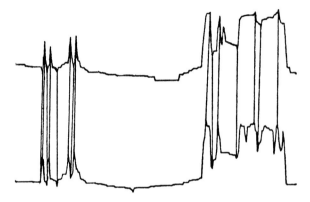

Figure 20 - Linked surface structures.

DISCUSSION

Most problems of low level computer vision are related to or caused by the underlying representations that are used during the first steps of processing. Distortions, misinterpretations, or loss of information due to the basic representations are likely to affect all subsequent processing modules and make the following analysis more difficult, if not impossible. It is important that the low level representation facilitate the extraction and description of visual primitives and their interrelationships. As was discussed, problems arise from the use of windows, locally constrained analysis, and interpretations that are based on preselected ideal models of primitives. Instead, we have argued for the use of representational techniques that preserve the structure of the intensity array, allow faithful description of the instances of primitives, and provide contextual information about the interrelationships among primitives.
The proposed techniques are based upon the concept of relational trees, and we have suggested several ways in which boundary formation, region and texture analysis can be achieved. These techniques are 1-dimensional, and it has to be explained why 1-dimensional techniques can be applied. First,

there are a number of directly evident advantages such as ease of computation or convenience within image scan systems that are inherently sequential. More important, the structures that one has to describe are far less complex (see figure 8-10 for the complexity of true 3-dimensional structures). Experience shows that 1-dimensional techniques can indeed provide satisfying results. There is one more point about 1-dimensional processing that concerns the philosophy of processing that is reflected in the "Principle of Least Committment." A technique that first processes along scan lines (or columns) leads to the formation of weak hypotheses about the nature of the primitives such as, "these points might be part of an edge." By linking these hypotheses across scan lines they are strengthened or weakened according to the context of neighboring scan lines. This is a conservative strategy that facilitates careful analysis of the intensity array data.

REFERENCES

1. Hanson, A.R. and Riseman, E.M. Processing cones: a parallel computational structure for scene analysis. COINS Technical Report 74C-7, University of Massachusetts, Amherst, 1974.

2. Hanson, A.R. and Riseman, E.M. Representation and control in the construction of visual models. COINS Technical Report 76-9, University of Massachusetts, Amherst, July 1976.

3. Marr, D. Early processing of visual information. AI Memo 340, MIT AI Laboratory, Cambridge, December 1975.

4. Marr, D. Representing visual information. Proc. Workshop on Computer Vision, Amherst, 1977.

5. Ehrich, R.W. Detection of global linear features in remote sensing data. Proc. Joint Workshop on Pat. Rec. and AI, Hyannis, Mass., June 1976, pp. 51-57.

6. Klinger, A. and Dyer, C.R. Experiments on picture representation using a regular decomposition, CGIP 4, 1975, pp. 68-105.

7. Freuder, E.C. A computer system for visual recognition using active knowledge. MIT AI Laboratory Tech. Report, TR-345, June 1976.

8. Pavlidis, T. and Horowitz, S. Segmentation of plane curves. IEEE Trans. Comp. vol. C-23, August 1974, pp. 860-870.

9. Krakauer, L.J. Computer analysis of visual properties of curved objects. MIT Technical Report TR-82, Project MAC, May 1971.

10. Enomoto, H. and Katayama, T. Structural lines of images. Proc. 2nd USA-Japan Computer Conf., 1975, pp. 470-474.

11. Lozano-Perez, T. Parsing intensity profiles. AI Memo 329, MIT AI Laboratory, Cambridge, May 1975.

12. Ehrich, R.W. and Foith, J.P. A view of texture topology and texture description. ECE Department Technical Report, University of Massachusetts, July 1975.

13. Ehrich, R.W. and Foith, J.P. Representation of random waveforms by relational trees. IEEE Trans. Comp., vol. C-25, July 1976, pp. 725-736.

14. Foith, J.P. and Ehrich, R.W. Relational Bäume: eine Datenstruktur zur Beschreibung von Bildzeilen in Grauwertbildern. Digitale Bildverarbeitung; Informatik Fachbericht 8, H.H. Nagel, Ed., Springer, 1977, pp. 80-100.

15. Foith, J.P. Symbolische Repräsentationen von Grauwertbildern für Szenenanalysen. Dissertation, University of Erlangen, 1977.

16. Ehrich, R.W. A symmetric hysteresis smoothing algorithm that preserves principal features. Computer Science Technical Report, Virginia Poly. Inst. and State University, Blacksburg, May 1977.

17. Ehrich, R.W. Detection of global edges in textured images. IEEE Trans. Comp., vol. C-25, June 1977.

18. Shirai, Y. Analyzing intensity arrays using knowledge about scenes. The Psychology of Computer Vision, P. Winston, Ed., McGraw Hill, 1975, pp. 93-113.

19. Horn, B.K.P. Obtaining shape from shading information, ibid. pp. 115-155.

20. Horn, B.K.P. Understanding image intensities. Artificial Intelligence 8, 1977, pp. 203-231.

21. Herskowitz, A. and Binford, T.O. On boundary detection. MIT AI Memo 183, MIT AI Laboratory, Cambridge, July 1970.

22. Haralick, R.M., Shanmugam, K., and Dinstein, I. Textural features for image classification. IEEE Trans. Syst., Man, and Cybernetics, vol. 3, November 1973, pp. 610-621.

23. Rosenfeld, A. and Troy, E.B. Visual texture analysis. Conf. Rec. on the Symp. on Feat. Extraction and Selection in Pat. Rec., 1970, pp. 115-124.

24. Galloway, M. Texture analysis using gray level run lengths. CGIP 4, 1975, pp. 172-179.

25. Zucker, S.W., Rosenfeld, A., and Davis, L.S. Picture segmentation by texture discrimination. Computer Science Center Tech. Report TR-356, University of Maryland, February 1975.

26. Mitchell, O.R., Myers, C.R. and Boyne, W. A max-min measure for image texture analysis. IEEE Trans. Comp., April 1977, pp. 408-414.

27. Carlton, S.G. and Mitchell, O.R. Image segmentation using texture and gray level. Proc. Conf. on Pattern Rec. and Image Proc., Troy, 1977, pp. 387-391.

28. Rosenfeld, A. and Davis, L. Hierarchical relaxation. Proc. Workshop on Computer Vision, Amherst, 1977.

29. Zucker, S.W. Vertical and horizontal processes in low level vision. Proc. Workshop on Computer Vision, Amherst, 1977.

Segmentation of Natural Scenes[1]

Allen R. Hanson
School of Language and Communication
Hampshire College
Amherst, Massachusetts 01002

Edward M. Riseman
Computer and Information Science
University of Massachusetts
Amherst, Massachusetts 01003

Abstract

The extraction of information from a two-dimensional image which is sufficient for constructing a description of the image is a complex task. The VISIONS system employs two distinct parallel iterative segmentation algorithms. The first utilizes local views of the image to aggregate edges into boundaries, while the second utilizes global histograms and a local spatial analysis to form regions with much of the textural detail suppressed. After merging these results into a single representation, features are extracted to produce a description of each region and boundary segment, including two-dimensional shape attributes. This information is symbolically labelled and passed to interpretation processes.

Table of Contents

I. Introduction

The structure of a developing system, known as VISIONS (Visual Integration by Semantic Interpretation Of Natural Scenes), for understanding relatively unconstrained images of natural scenes is outlined in this paper and in a companion paper elsewhere in this volume. The focus of this paper is on segmentation processes, often referred to as "low-level" vision, which partition large amounts of visual sensory data (derived from a static color image) into organized syntactic units which form the basis for further processing. The second paper describes the interpretation processes, often referred to as "high-level" vision, which receive the segmented data and attempt to construct an interpretation in the form of a description of the physical world portrayed in the scene.

The general goal of the low-level system is the transformation of a large spatial array of pixels (i.e., picture elements) into a more compact description of the image in terms of visually distinct syntactic units and their characteristics, including location. By a variety of means, the visual information in the image must be aggregated, labelled with symbolic names and attributes, and then interfaced to higher level knowledge structures. The syntactic units considered here are boundary segments (connected sets of edges between pixels) and regions (connected sets of pixels) whose attributes include relevant properties of color, texture, size, shape, location, etc.

[1]This research has been supported by the Office of Naval Research under Grant N00014-75-C-0459.

The low-level system of VISIONS is outlined in Figure 1. The two processes for extracting regions and boundaries both employ parallel, iterative "relaxation" procedures. The boundary formation process produces initial edges from local spatial views of the data, followed by interactions in local contexts which aggregate these edges into more global segments. The region analysis initially forms a set of possible labels for each pixel based upon clusters in global histograms (feature space), and then uses local spatial relationships to aggregate these pixels into regions with minor textural variations suppressed.

After merging the results from these two segmentation processes into a single representation, features are extracted to produce a description of each region and boundary. These features include those obtained by fitting two-dimensional shapes to regions and segments of boundaries, as well as other visual attributes.

To a certain extent it may seem artificial to select any particular dividing line in the sequence of transformations leading to an interpretation of an image. However, the task of developing a system for general visual perception is extremely complex and there is a compelling need to decompose the overall problem into more manageable portions, particularly during exploration and development [HAN76]. The grossest natural decomposition of such a system seems to lie between the processing of two-dimensional image information -- the low-level segmentation processes -- and the inference of three-dimensional hypotheses about the physical world -- the high-level interpretation processes.

This decomposition is also consistent with our belief that segmentation processes should, in many instances, be effective without recourse to semantics. The partitioning of an image (even a nonsense scene) can be based on differences in visual patterns of color, brightness, and texture. It should be noted, however, that there have been successful efforts in effectively integrating

semantics into segmentation processes [YAK73, TEN76], and that there are divergent views on the necessity and desirability of the dichotomy between low- and high-level processes [ZUC75,RIS77,FIS78]. Whatever the limitations imposed by the structure of our system decomposition, they should be ameliorated by the inclusion of feedback paths to lock the interpretation and segmentation processes into a closed loop. These paths may be used to provide semantic guidance in the refinement of the image segmentation and to direct further extraction of features. Thus, segmentation which is initially semantic free is followed by a phase of semantically directed segmentation, and then the systems would be intertwined in further cooperative analysis.

The complexity of the data which is to be examined by the segmentation processes has had a significant effect upon the design of those processes. With relatively complex, unconstrained images, any approach to segmentation will be quite prone to error. Highly textured objects (such as trees), shadows and highlights on regular and irregular surfaces, varied and uncontrolled lighting conditions, etc., all contribute to the difficulty of analysis. Few objects/surfaces can be expected to exhibit uniform visual features, and methods for dealing with this variability must be incorporated.

These problems are exemplified by the sequence of photographs of a tree (Figure 2) taken at varying distances. These images also make clear the problem of separating figure and ground as resolution is varied; the point at which the texture elements of the bark should be extracted as regions in themselves instead of contributing to the descriptors of the tree trunk as a whole, is ambiguous. Goal orientation and focus of attention will be quite important in the formation of useful image segmentations. This leaves ambiguous the level of detail which should be pursued in the first stages of non-semantic segmentation. We do not have definitive answers

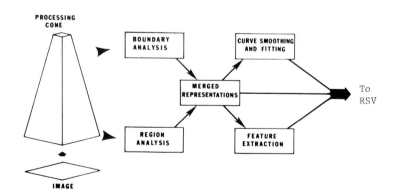

Figure 1. The Segmentation System of VISIONS. Segmentation algorithms and feature extraction processes are applied in a simulated hierarchical parallel array processor. Two distinct parallel iterative algorithms are employed, one to aggregate edges into boundaries, the other to aggregate pixels into regions. The resultant segmentations of the image are merged, regions and boundary segments are smoothed and fitted with simple primitive shapes where possible, and additional features are extracted and associated with each element. The result of this processing is a layered directed graph of regions, segments, and vertices (RSV) which is passed to interpretation processes. These processes involve the construction of a description of the physical world depicted in the image.

Allen R. Hanson and Edward M. Riseman

Figure 2. Images of a tree at different distances. The resolution of the objects in the image influences the expected segmentation. From our point of view the initial segmentation processes should not be semantically directed, but rather should be based solely upon the relative visual characteristics of the image.

concerning these issues, but our approaches to segmentation have incorporated the representations and flexibility required to move across varying levels of description. The procedure for aggregating edges is structured to easily increase or decrease its sensitivity in the formation of boundaries; in this way the boundary analysis may be set to extract boundaries of any given degree of contrast and/or confidence. The region analysis incorporates a different, but complementary, form of flexibility by producing a hierarchical segmentation down to a varying level of detail. This strategy provides a structure for results which vary according to the needs of the overall system.

II. A Parallel Computational Structure for Processing Images

II.1 Parallel Computation

One characteristic of image analysis which is difficult to ignore is the massive amount of visual data which must be processed. For a full-color image of reasonable spatial (512^2) and color resolution (3 colors, 6 bits/color), close to 5 million bits of information must be processed, often repeatedly. Faced with this data overload, we made a commitment to parallel processing at the very beginning of our research effort [HAN74, RIS74]. If such large amounts of sensory data are eventually to be processed by a machine in close to real time, then the use of large parallel array computers appears to be necessary. It is relevant to note that developments in technology imply that such devices could be economically feasible in the near future.

Given a choice of developing either serial or parallel algorithms (or both), we have developed parallel algorithms wherever possible. A commitment to the discipline of developing algorithms as local parallel operations pays off in providing a way of thinking about transformations of visual data. Many algorithms can be implemented in both sequential and parallel versions. However, in much the same way that language appears to affect thought, thinking in terms of parallel computation leads to the development of algorithms which are often not at all obvious in sequential terms. In addition successful demonstration of segmentation algorithms for simple parallel hardware makes future implementation on real machines far more clear.

Finally, there is a distinct need to reduce the large amounts of visual information, while at the same time extracting features from local areas of the image. Many interesting features (including textural properties) are not a function of individual pixels, but rather a function across the set of points in a local "window" of the image, where the size of this window will vary. Extracting such features would be facilitated by a hierarchical organization of layers of decreasing image (and processing) resolution.

II.2 The Processing Cone: A Hierarchical Parallel Array Computer

We have chosen to simulate a general parallel computational structure for analyzing large arrays of visual data. It is a parallel array computer, called the "processing cone", which is hierarchically organized into layers of decreasing spatial resolution in which information extracted from increasing sizes of receptive fields can be stored and processed further. This structure, which is described in detail in [HAN74] and applied in [HAN75,NAG77], is also related to the recognition cones of Uhr [UHR72], the hierarchical data structures of Klinger [KLI 76], the pyramids of Tanimoto and Pavlidis, and Levine [TAN75,LEV78], the computational structure of algorithms developed by Rosenfeld et. al [ROS71,HAY74], the planning algorithms of Kelly [KEL71] and Price [PRI77], and the knowledge-directed analysis of Ballard, Brown, and Feldman [BAL78]. A survey of some of these uses appears in this volume [TAN78].

The function of our processing cone is the transformation and reduction of the massive amount of image data, while at the same time providing a structure in which information at higher levels can direct more detailed processing at lower levels of the cone. The processing cone can be thought of as a simulation of hierarchically organized parallel arrays of microcomputers (Figure 3), where each microcomputer, at a given level, has access to a window of data in a set of planes at the level below it. Note that each level could have an

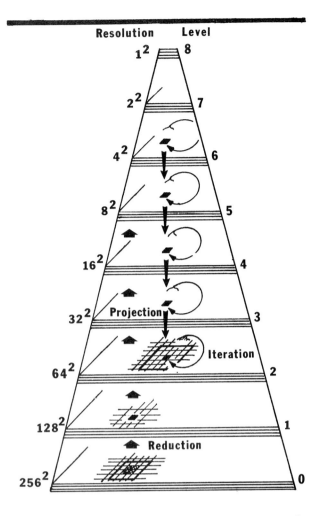

and/or transformed at a single level of the cone; the size of the array remains constant due to overlapping of windows. A _projection_ process allows information in upper layers to influence computation in lower layers. Thus, information flows up, down, and laterally within the cone. These three modes may be intermixed, providing a rich logical structure in which to implement parallel segmentation algorithms. We will assume that at any moment of time, computation will be taking place at only one level, and therefore the algorithms are defined by a sequence of operations over time, each at a particular level.

While the processing cone has provided a framework in which to think in parallel hierarchical terms, the primary computation of the two segmentation algorithms described in the following sections takes place at only a single level of resolution. There exist a number of possibilities for utilizing the hierarchical structure of the cone. For example, if hierarchical relaxation procedures can be defined [DAV78], then computation at many levels might take place simultaneously. It is also possible to develop planning algorithms which use upper levels of the cone to efficiently direct finer resolution algorithms lower in the cone [KEL71, HAN74,NAG77,PRI77]. It may also be feasible to develop methods for hierarchically refining segmentations in parallel, but several problems, including those caused by non-overlapping windows, remain to be resolved. However, the hierarchy definitely enhances the parallel extraction of textural features over increasingly larger receptive fields. Thus, while we believe that algorithms utilizing multiple levels of resolution are possible, further research in this direction has been put aside until a more complete development of our system has taken place.

III. Boundary Analysis

III.1 Introduction

One approach to the description of a scene is as a collection of boundaries hopefully delineating many of the objects (or parts of objects) in the scene. The boundaries themselves are usually composed of a collection of edges obtained by the application of a spatial differentiation operator to local neighborhoods in the digitized representation of the scene.[1] The edges represent local points of discontinuity in a particular feature, usually intensity, but possibly color or less often some textural feature. A variety of differentiation operators have been defined in the literature (for a review, see Davis [DAV75], and Rosenfeld and Kak [ROS76a].

The problems encountered with these operators are intrinsically related to the data upon which they operate as well as artifacts introduced by the operators themselves [RIS77]. The class of scenes being examined here produces edge data which is

Figure 3. The Processing Cone. This structure is a parallel array of microcomputers hierarchically organized into layers of decreasing spatial resolution. The function of the cone is the transformation and reduction of the massive amounts of image data. Three modes of processing are defined within the cone: reduction of information upward, iteration where information is transformed at a single level, and projection of information at upper layers downward. The actual functions of the data computed during these modes are programmable; each is defined for a local window of data and at some moment in time applied in parallel across all the local windows at a specified level.

arbitrary number of planes in which to store input data, partial results, and final results.

The function computed by each microcomputer is applied in parallel to local windows across the entire array at the specified level. The result obtained from each local window is stored either at the same level or at the next higher level. There are three major modes of operations in the processing cone. During a _reduction_ process upward through the layers in the cone, the data is reduced because portions of each window are nonoverlapping. An _iteration_ process allows the data to be analyzed

---

[1]Edge detection based on sequential tracking techniques will not be discussed here. It should be obvious that they are not well-suited to the class of images under consideration due to difficulties encountered in tracking through texture.

Allen R. Hanson and Edward M. Riseman

quite noisy. Boundaries very often are not described by step functions, but rather are formed by sometimes slow, and often irregular, changes in intensity. As a result, edge strengths are often distributed over an area as a function of lighting conditions, shadowing, surface properties, and shape. Variation in the form of texture produces high edge activity which is locally indistinguishable from "object" edges - indeed, in some cases an object boundary is not composed of well-defined edges at all [MAR75]. Thus, it should be evident that many decisions regarding boundaries cannot and should not be made purely at the local level, but instead should be delayed until contextual information can be brought to bear on the decision. Thus, the initial edge data should be as faithful to the original image data as possible, and implicit decisions based solely on local edge masks should be avoided [EHR78].

In this section, we first discuss the problems introduced by the choice of edge representation and operator, then the desirability of an interpixel representation of only horizontal and vertical

edges, next an edge extraction analysis which allows the full horizontal and vertical components of a gradient boundary to be examined, and finally a relaxation process for updating edge probabilities based on their context. This process organizes the intensity data into locally consistent global boundaries.

III.2 Considerations in the Development of an Edge Representation

The minimal amount of useful information obtainable from any spatial differentiation operator is an estimate of the magnitude of the intensity (or some other feature) change detectable over a local neighborhood, say the 3×3 window shown in Figure 4a. The resulting edge strength is often associated with the central pixel in the local window (assuming an odd window size). However, the magnitude of the gradient change provides no indication of the orientation of the edge, which might be crucial later when aggregating collections of edges into boundaries. Assuming that orientation is quantized to 45° intervals, any of the four

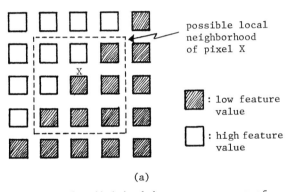

(a)

A portion of a digitized image as an array of pixels. For purposes of this discussion a 3×3 local neighborhood around a pixel is the local view assumed.

: low feature value

: high feature value

possible local neighborhood of pixel X

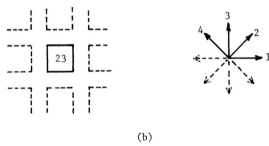

(b)

The magnitude of an edge in the vicinity of a pixel is assumed to be 23, but without orientation information there is ambiguity among the four orientations shown.

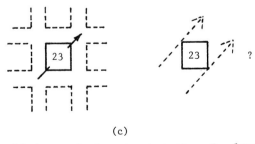

(c)

Even if the magnitude and orientation of a local edge is extracted, the placement of the edge relative to the pixel is still ambiguous.

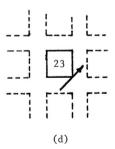

(d)

An edge in a local neighborhood is unambiguously represented by a magnitude, orientation, and placement.

Figure 4. Considerations in the Development of an Edge Representation. Accurate placement of edges on an array of pixels demands that the magnitude, orientation, and placement of edges relative to the pixels be extracted and maintained.

directions shown in Figure 4b is possible. Therefore, let us assume our local operator determines
the orientation of edges.

Even though the magnitude and orientation of
the local edge is determined, there remains
ambiguity in the placement of the edge (Figure 4c).
We make the assumption that edges at a local level
do not pass through a pixel, but rather partition
the array of pixels into regions. It is usually
the case that boundaries of surfaces in the physical
world do not project onto a discrete array of
digitized data exactly between pixels. However,
local views of the data do not provide sufficient
information to place the position and orientation
of edges reliably on a continuous scale of image
coordinates. We prefer to perform this placement
after a more global boundary of many edges has been
extracted. Therefore, an edge must be placed either
to one side or the other of the pixel (Figure 4d).
We conclude that an unambiguous placement and
orientation of the gradient magnitude of a local
edge is desirable.

Since the Kirsch spatial differentiation operator [KIR71,RIS77] is simple to compute and provides
an estimate of both magnitude and direction, it
appeared to be a good choice and we initially used

it as our standard operator. It is defined on a
3×3 window, and for each pixel X it provides a
local estimate of the edge contrast S(X), as well
as edge orientation and placement D(X) (refer to
Figure 5). This operator utilizes a fixed mask
geometry at all orientations around a pixel; the
best fit is associated with the submask whose output is maximum. Application of the operator at
all pixel locations defines a transformation of
the original feature data into an edge image. This
implies an edge representation with eight <u>possible</u>
orientation/placements of an edge with respect to
each pixel as shown in Figure 5d. Examination of
this figure yields several rather interesting
observations which led us to abandon it entirely.

First, note that multiple, but logically
equivalent, indications of each edge are possible.
In Figure 6a diagonal edges d and e are associated
with pixels X and Y, respectively, but a <u>single</u>
edge through the window caused <u>both</u>. Clearly, it
is desirable to have a unique indication of a
single edge. This problem is resolved by adopting
a canonical representation for the orientation/
placement of edges, as shown in Figure 6b. Edges
not in these standard positions can be shifted in a
unique way to the pixel which has a logically
equivalent edge in the canonical representation.

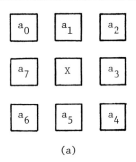

(a)

Local window for the Kirsch spatial differentiation
operator.

$$M_i = \left| 5(a_i + a_{i+1} + a_{i+2}) - 3(a_{i+3} + a_{i+4} + a_{i+5} + a_{i+6} + a_{i+7}) \right| ; \quad i = 0,1,\ldots,7$$

$$S(X) = \max_i M_i$$

$$D(X) = \{i \mid M_i \text{ is max}\}$$

(b)

Definition of the Kirsch operator where
indices are computed modulo 8. S(X) is the
magnitude and D(X) is the orientation of the
best edge associated with X.

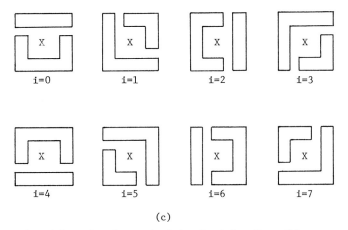

(c)

The eight submasks used; i is the index from (b).

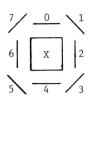

(d)

Alternative orientation/placements of an
edge around X.

Figure 5. The Kirsch Operator. This operator provides the information required from an edge detector. It
selects the strongest response from the set of eight alternative orientation/placements as the best edge.

Allen R. Hanson and Edward M. Riseman

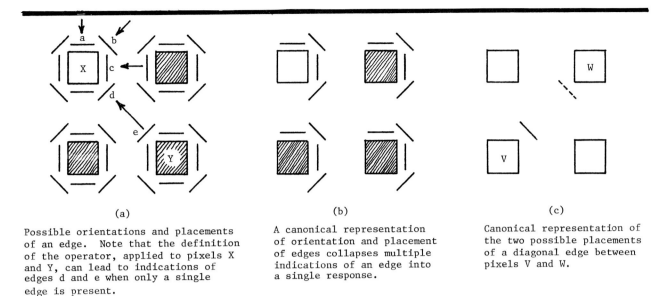

(a)

Possible orientations and placements
of an edge. Note that the definition
of the operator, applied to pixels X
and Y, can lead to indications of
edges d and e when only a single
edge is present.

(b)

A canonical representation
of orientation and placement
of edges collapses multiple
indications of an edge into
a single response.

(c)

Canonical representation of
the two possible placements
of a diagonal edge between
pixels V and W.

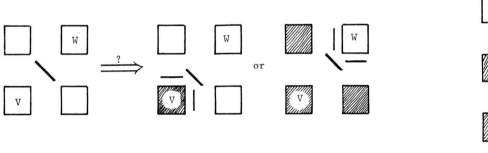

(d)

The presence of a diagonal between V and W is still ambiguous; the
diagonal could be due to either corner of the type shown on the
right.

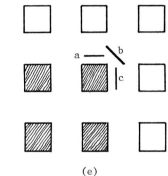

(e)

There are eight edges competing for survival at each
pixel. The existence of
strong edges (a and c) is
lost if only the single best
edge associated with X is
saved; the operator would
represent the corner with the
ambiguous diagonal edge b.

Figure 6. Further Development of an Edge Representation. Multiple indications of edges may be removed by
a definition of a canonical orientation/placement, but diagonals remain ambiguous.

However, there are still 8 edges competing around
a single pixel (or 4 edges if masks are associated
only with their canonical positions).

Second, note that even with a canonical representation for diagonal edges, there is still inherent ambiguity in the partitioning of pixels.
Figure 6c-d shows that if a diagonal edge between
the pixels X and Y is not allowed to pass through
the other pixels, then the representation of a
diagonal, assuming no further information is extracted, is not sufficient to disambiguate between
the two paths for this edge on the array of pixels
(Figure 6d). If the diagonal edge is represented
as a horizontal-vertical pair, then the local

representation is disambiguated. This is an
argument for delaying the decision about the exact
orientation of a local edge until a later point
when a more global view of a boundary is available.

Finally, the third problem with this representation compounds the previous problem. Note that
only one of the 8 possible edges may be associated
with the central pixel if a unique choice for the
orientation/placement of the best edge is desired.
Selection of the single best edge implies
that potentially crucial information is being discarded; with eight edges competing for survival,
the selection of the maximum contrast edge causes
7/8 of the edge information to be thrown away. In

Figure 6e edges a and c would be two of eight competing edges, and it is possible that only diagonal edge b at this orientation would survive; no indication of edges a and c would survive. Thus, this selection criterion allows events of potential interest to be discarded in favor of other events in the immediate vicinity.

The net result is a misrepresentation of the structure of the underlying information in that spurious orientations, odd gaps, and ambiguities appear in the edge data. One solution is to store more than one edge with a pixel. However, we have shown the redundancy that exists between diagonals and horizontal-vertical pairs. Maintaining multiple edges could lead to undue complexity in the organizational processes that are responsible for aggregating local edges into boundaries, because the interaction between adjacent edges is confused by the placement and orientation of redundant edges. The representation is not a clean one; we will not attempt to modify it any further and will discard it in favor of a simpler, more natural one.

The characteristics which edge operators and a good local representation of edges must exhibit in order to avoid the problems just described may be summarized as:
   a) an edge should not pass through a pixel;
   b) an edge should have an unambiguous location and orientation on the array of pixels;
   c) there should not be multiple indications of a single local edge;
   d) competition between edges should not cause a potentially interesting edge to be suppressed by another edge in the immediate vicinity;
   e) the representation should lead to simplicity and clarity in the organizational processes for extracting global boundaries.

These constraints are satisfied by the choice of the interpixel representation of horizontal and vertical edges depicted in Figure 7 combined with the edge operator selected in the next section. In this representation the possible locations of edges are clearly defined and each edge has a unique position and orientation with respect to the pixels from which they were obtained. Thus, during application of the edge operator, edges of differing orientations do not have to compete for survival. This is a return to the representation in early work on region growing [BRI70] and used more recently in [YAK76,PRA77]. The final requirement, that it lead to clarity in organizing boundaries, will be the subject of the remainder of this section of the paper.

III.3 Problems with Large Edge Masks

There are still the problems arising from multiple edge indications from a single boundary. These effects can be traced directly to:
   1) the size of the mask (or "window") over which the edge operator is defined; and
   2) the spatial extent of the contrast change which forms the boundary (i.e., the gradient width).
If a boundary is defined by a step function, only a very small view is sufficient to see the entire change in contrast. On the other hand, small mask

sizes will only have a partial view of boundaries defined by a gradient distributed over several (or many) pixels. This has led to approaches in which a hierarchical set of increasingly larger mask sizes are employed [ROS71,HAN74,MAR75,RIS77].

Let us examine the effect of using various mask sizes. One of the penalties incurred by using masks defined over large local neighborhoods is that responses will be obtained from masks placed at relatively large distances from the actual boundary. Given the interpixel representation, masks need to be applied at only two orientations: horizontal and vertical. Let us consider ideal boundaries which are represented by a step function between adjacent pixels. Figure 8 graphically illustrates the results obtained from several reasonable operators -- masks of size 1×2, 3×2, and 3×4 -- applied to an ideal image of a corner. It is easy to generalize these responses to conclude that all masks of size larger than 1×2 give rise to multiple indications of a single edge, thereby introducing a sometimes bewildering array of spurious edges at positions where none are actually present; in addition, edges at some of the correct positions have reduced responses for the larger masks. In these cases, the 1×2 edge mask is the only operator that will produce responses that are faithful to the underlying data. Given our concern about minimizing the distortion of data, we will only use the 1×2 mask, although the effect of this choice given boundaries defined by a wider gradient is not yet clear. We will show that use of the 1×2 mask is not a severe constraint and actually leads to an edge process which effectively is not limited to a fixed mask size.

III.4 Collecting the Gradient of Boundaries

As we have noted, any boundary which is not a step function across a pair of adjacent pixels will not have its total contrast detected by the 1×2

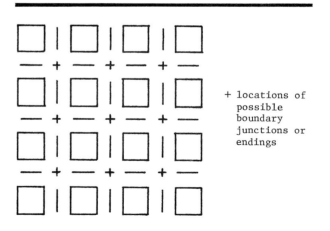

+ locations of possible boundary junctions or endings

Figure 7. The Representation of Edges in VISIONS. The ambiguous diagonals have been removed leaving an interpixel representation of horizontal and vertical edges. This representation makes the placement and orientation of edges precise, as well as the location of possible boundary vertices (both junctions and terminations).

Allen R. Hanson and Edward M. Riseman

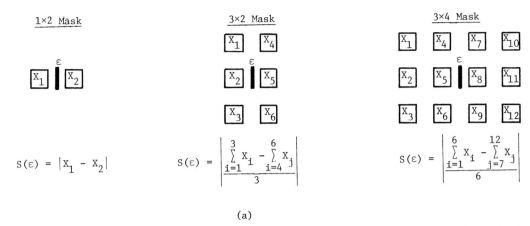

$$S(\varepsilon) = |X_1 - X_2|$$

$$S(\varepsilon) = \left| \frac{\sum\limits_{i=1}^{3} X_i - \sum\limits_{i=4}^{6} X_j}{3} \right|$$

$$S(\varepsilon) = \left| \frac{\sum\limits_{i=1}^{6} X_i - \sum\limits_{j=7}^{12} X_j}{6} \right|$$

(a)

Definitions of edge masks of size 1×2, 3×2, and 3×4. The horizontal edge mask is obtained by a simple rotation of the vertical edge mask. S(ε) is the magnitude of the edge, orientation of the edge is implicit in the position of the edge, and the direction of the gradient change may be maintained by removing the absolute value (assuming appropriate care in the interpretation of the sign).

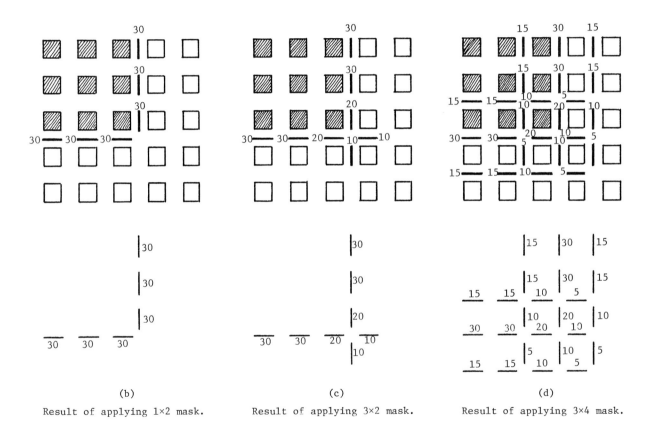

(b)

Result of applying 1×2 mask.

(c)

Result of applying 3×2 mask.

(d)

Result of applying 3×4 mask.

Figure 8. Comparison of Edge Operators. Examination of the results obtained after applying edge masks of varying size illustrates the difficulties encountered when larger masks are used. Note that in this figure cross-hatched pixels are assumed to have a brightness value of 10 and the others 40.

operator. Our solution to this problem is to extract the total contrast of a boundary by collecting the horizontal and vertical components of the gradient and to place the resultant value at a representative edge location.

For sake of discussion, let us consider only vertical edges, recognizing the symmetry involved. If the signed difference from the 1×2 operator is maintained, as depicted in Figure 9a, then the horizontal component of a gradient across several pixels is represented by a contiguous collection of vertical edges with the same sign; note that small local deviations of opposite sign or small

plateaus (where there are no edges), could also be bridged. Therefore, it is straightforward to collect the total contrast into a single edge difference. Thus, the use of the 1×2 mask is actually a commitment to avoid the use of masks entirely; since the 1×2 operator preserves the topology of the intensity scan line [EHR78] (up to a constant), the effective mask size is easily determined dynamically by the actual structure of the data. The magnitude, width, and position of the undistorted gradient is available in the local edge data.

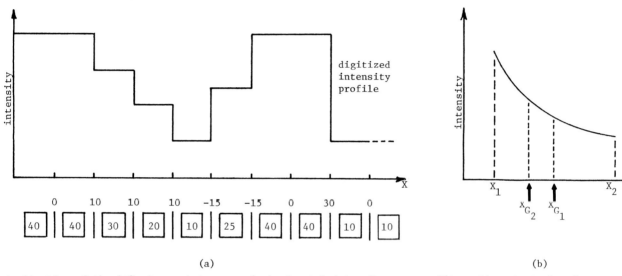

(a)

Application of the 1×2 edge mask to a sample horizontal intensity scan line. The topology of the scan line is preserved by the 1×2 mask and may be reconstructed from the signed edge values up to a constant. In effect the 1×2 mask is not really a mask in the usual sense; it is a measure of the local horizontal (or vertical) component of the gradient.

(b)

Alternative strategies for placement of the collected magnitude of the gradient include the midpoint X_{G1} of the gradient, and the position X_{G2} where the first moment about that point is zero.

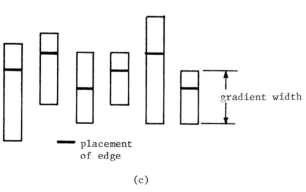

(c)

No matter what method of edge placement is used, misalignment of edges from one scan line to the next, due to local changes in the width and topology of the gradient, must be expected.

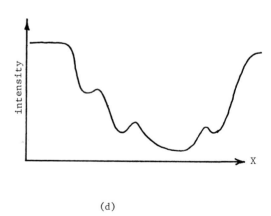

(d)

A gradient may not be strictly monotonic; a more global context-sensitive decision concerning the extent of the gradient should be made before the edge defined by the gradient can be determined.

Figure 9. The Gradient Collection Process. The 1×2 mask has only a local view of wider gradients. More global contrast across gradients must be extracted.

Allen R. Hanson and Edward M. Riseman

There are a variety of strategies for placing the collected magnitude as a (set of) positions(s) as shown in Figure 9b. It could be placed at the geometric center of the gradient width. The one used in this paper is to place the value at the interpixel location closest to the center of gravity of the gradient (i.e., where the first moment is zero). Due to local variations in adjacent scan lines, this can lead to placement of adjacent edges which are misaligned as shown in Figure 9c. Recall that these initial local analyses are to form the input to an edge aggregation process which will be responsible for globally organizing the set of edges. Therefore, in order to avoid errors, a function of the total constrast of a boundary will be placed at several potentially "good" positions around the center of gravity. The final value assigned to an edge location in a gradient is the total contrast detected over the gradient scaled down by its distance from the center of gravity of the gradient. All other edges in the boundary are suppressed to some small non-zero value. Thus, the potential for positioning errors is explicitly recognized, and final decisions regarding edge placement and boundary organization is left to the context-sensitive relaxation processes to be described shortly.

There are additional problems in that the one-dimensional gradient of a boundary is not always monotonic (Figure 9d), and might require a more complex context-sensitive examination of the scan line in the gradient collection process [EHR78]. Ultimately, it ought to be possible to utilize a gradient collection process which varies the particular model of gradient activity under the direction of semantic processing. This model could be obtained from a higher level shape processor, for example, which may predict a particular gradient model based on shape attributes (e.g., expected shading given a light source and 3D surface properties). Such a system would initially utilize a simple gradient model and then use the predicted model to further refine edge placement.

III.5 Organizing Edges into Boundaries Via Relaxation Processes

The information contained in the edge representation is still unorganized in that the edges have been obtained from local processes and have not yet utilized contextual information to organize them into boundary segments (sometimes referred to as lines) and vertices. A powerful method for accomplishing this is based on a paradigm of local cooperation and competition between edges; that is, a local edge should be viewed in the context of surrounding edges, and decisions regarding edge properties (including existence) should be delayed until the context is clear. By suitably defining a local neighborhood of an edge, the edge activity in that neighborhood may either support the central edge or deny its existence. By overlapping the neighborhood and iterating the decision process, local effects can propagate and affect surrounding neighborhoods. For each iteration, the totality of effects in the local context will be used to update the probability of the existence of each edge. Thus, the approach taken here is the definition of a local neighborhood, the definition of a set of contextual "events" in the neighborhood of the

edge, and the embedding of these definitions in a uniform iterative procedure, called a relaxation process [ROS76b], for performing the updating of the edge probabilities.

The smallest meaningful neighborhood for an edge in our representation (Figure 10) must include the three edges to either side where continuation of that edge could occur as a line; it must also include the two parallel edges which are possible alternative placements for the collected gradients. Note that the (signed) probability of an edge may be obtained by normalizing the absolute value of the signed edge strengths with the maximum absolute value after gradient collection.[1] The sign will be maintained with this probability as an encoding of the direction of contrast change.

Now let us provide a brief review of the key ideas of relaxation processes; for a more complete discussion see [ROS76b,ZUC76,RIS77]. The general idea is to compute some probability updating contribution Δ for the central edge as a function of the probability of the neighboring edges. It is assumed that each edge location has a set of N possible labels $\{\lambda_1,...,\lambda_n\}$ which can be associated with it (e.g., in other applications n labels have been the n-1 alternative orientations for the edge and a label for the absence of an edge). We will use $P_i(\lambda_k)$ to denote the probability of label k at the ith edge location, LOC_i. Furthermore, it is assumed that there is some means for computing a reasonable initial probability for each label at each edge location. Then each label at each LOC_j contained in the neighborhood N_i of LOC_i will be used to update $P_i(\lambda_k)$, k = 1,...,n. $P_i(\lambda_k)$ will be increased (decreased) by label λ_m at LOC_j if the labels are compatible (incompatible) where the effect of this change is weighted by $P_j(\lambda_m)$.

---

[1] A more effective procedure is to normalize the strength of an edge by the maximum strength edge over a large, but local, neighborhood. Otherwise a single very strong edge anywhere in the image could reduce the probability of edges to a small value everywhere in the image.

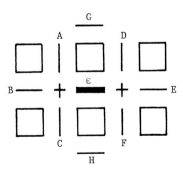

Figure 10. The Local Neighborhood of an Edge. ε is the central edge to be updated as a function of the edges in the neighborhood. The set of edges {A,B,C} and {D,E,F} represent possible continuations of ε to each of its sides; parallel edges G and H are potential competitors for ε; + represents possible vertex locations.

Compatibility is defined in terms of a function r_{ij}:

$$r_{ij}(\lambda_k, \lambda_m) > 0 \quad \text{if } \lambda_k \text{ and } \lambda_m \text{ are compatible,}$$
$$< 0 \quad \text{if } \lambda_k \text{ and } \lambda_m \text{ are incompatible,}$$
$$= 0 \quad \text{if } \lambda_k \text{ and } \lambda_m \text{ are independent.}$$

Then, $\Delta P_i(\lambda_k) = \sum_{j \in N_i} d_{ij} \sum_{m=1}^{n} r_{ij}(\lambda_k, \lambda_m) P_j(\lambda_m)$, where

d_{ij} is a weighting of the influence of LOC_j upon LOC_i and keeps ΔP_i in the interval from -1 to $+1$. Denoting the probability of label λ_k after the tth iteration as $P_i^{(t)}(\lambda_k)$, it will be updated as follows:

$$P_i^{t+1}(\lambda_k) = \frac{P_i^t(\lambda_k)[1+\Delta P_i^t(\lambda_k)]}{\sum_{k=1}^{n} [P_i^t(\lambda_k)(1+\Delta P_i^t(\lambda_k))]}.$$

Note that the denominator is a normalizing factor computed across the new probabilities of the n labels, so that the new values for P_i^{t+1} will sum to one.

The interpixel edge representation we have chosen again provides simplification. There are only two labels at each location, EDGE and NOEDGE. Only a single probability, $P_i(\text{EDGE})$, is necessary for determining the probability of both labels since $P_i(\text{NOEDGE}) = 1-P_i(\text{EDGE})$. In effect the updating process is only a function of the probabilities of EDGEs in the neighborhood. Now we will make one more simplifying assumption, that it will only be necessary to compute $\Delta P_i^t(\text{EDGE})$, and that $\Delta P_i^t(\text{NOEDGE}) = 0$. The effect of this assumption is that it is sufficient to allow the likelihood of NOEDGE to vary inversely with the likelihood of EDGE. Now we can use P_i^t to represent $P_i^t(\text{EDGE})$. The computation of P_i^{t+1} follows the general equation

$$P_i^{t+1} = \frac{P_i^t[1+\Delta P_i^t]}{P_i^t[1+\Delta P_i^t]+(1-P_i^t)}$$

and simplifies to

$$P_i^{t+1} = P_i^t \left[\frac{1+\Delta P_i^t}{1+P_i^t \Delta P_i^t} \right]$$

III.6 Labels in a Local Context are not Independent

Now we must specify the mechanisms for computing the updating factor Δ. One might try to specify meaningful compatability coefficients [ZUC76] for each edge in the defined neighborhood (Figure 10). For example there ought to be positive compatability coefficients on edges at the six locations representing possible continuations of ε (three to each side), whereas there ought to be negative coefficients for edges at locations of parallel edges G and H with the same gradient sign. Note that we cannot use a negative coefficient for the absence of an edge at locations A, B, or C, for example, because the absence of one of these should not inhibit ε -- one of the other two might be present forming a path of good line continuation. As we shall show next, this is a distinct limitation of the relaxation process as it is formulated in the previous section.

As the updating process has been specified, the two labels at each edge location in the neighborhood of ε would be used independently to contribute to Δ. The following notation for edges and the categorization of the junctions to either side is very useful for further analysis and we follow [PRA77] in this regard. Figure 11a describes the notation used for

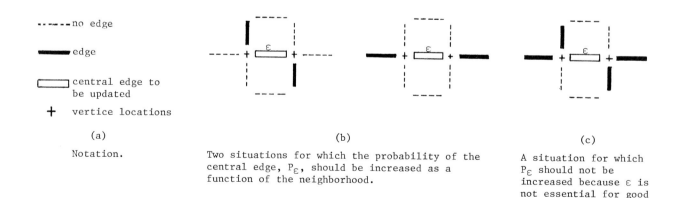

......no edge

━━━edge

▭ central edge to be updated

✛ vertice locations

(a)

Notation.

(b)

Two situations for which the probability of the central edge, P_ε, should be increased as a function of the neighborhood.

(c)

A situation for which P_ε should not be increased because ε is not essential for good line continuation to the left or right (refer to Figure 13).

Figure 11. The relaxation updating process is often restricted to a linear function of the labels on the edges in the local neighborhood, where compatability coefficients act as variable weights. There is no set of compatability coefficients for a linear function which leads to the desired updating in all the contexts which can occur.

the presence and absence of edges in the figures
that follow. Figure 11b portrays two cases where
ε should be increased, whereas Figure 11c portrays
a case where ε should not be increased because it
is not necessary for good line continuation (the
basis for these decisions will be discussed further
in the next section). Since the last situation is
a linear combination of the other two, there is no
linear combination of weights to satisfy these
requirements. The independent use of labels prevents many events of interest (which are entirely
observable within the neighborhood of ε) from
influencing ε. Since the events cannot be expressed
as a linear combination of the labels, they cannot
be specified as separate events; n-ary relations
on the labels are required.

This limitation may be overcome by generalizing
the notion of a label to that of a pattern defined
over the neighborhood. The probability of a pattern
is expressed as a (potentially) non-linear function
of the probabilities of the 8 edges in the neighborhood. The compatability coefficient is now between
the ith pattern of neighborhood labels and the
labels of ε, not between labels of the jth neighboring edge and the labels of ε. Thus, r_{ij} is replaced
by a weight (positive or negative) which determines
the effect that the pattern should have on ε. (Of
course this approach could be generalized to larger
neighborhoods.) The total contribution Δ is then
defined as a linearly weighted sum of the probability of the n patterns:

$$\Delta^t = \sum_{i=1}^{n} \Delta_i^t = \sum_{i=1}^{n} W_i P_i^t$$

This generalization of relaxation bears some
relationship to production systems in which each
production rule is specified as a pattern for
triggering the rule, and a response form to be
executed once the rule has been triggered. Each
of our patterns can be thought of as a rule with
some probability of being present -- in other
words, all patterns are simultaneously true to
some degree. As the effect of some patterns propagate and begin to organize local contexts, other
patterns become true to a different degree. Each
edge responds to changes in its context, but in
places where there is ambiguity, the updating
often has competing influences causing organization in the local context to be delayed. In this
way influence will spread from islands of unambiguous contexts within the image. If this dynamic
process is to have a meaningful result, it is
incumbent upon the designer of the patterns to
capture the syntax/semantics of line boundaries
(e.g., laws of good gestalt) in the local contextual patterns.

It is worth noting that initially an edge with
probability P on the array of pixels must have some
non-zero continuation on both of its ends. In fact
among its three possible continuations, the minimum

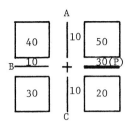

Figure 12. Constraints on the Edges in the Neighborhood of an Edge. An edge of some strength P on
a square array of pixels must have evidence of continuation no less than P/3 on at least one of the
three edges to each of its sides.

possible value of MAX$\{P_A, P_B, P_C\}$ is P/3 because the
pixels which produced the evidence of this edge are
related to the other three edges.[1] As the edges
around a vertex are crossed in a clockwise or
counter-clockwise direction, the signed differences
must sum to zero. A simple illustrative example
appears in Figure 12.

III.7 Contextual Patterns for Updating Edge Probabilities

It only remains now to define the patterns
over the local neighborhood of an edge. Since the
goal of the analysis is to extract continuous
boundary segments, the patterns should focus on
those conditions which support or deny the hypotheses that the central edge is part of a more global
boundary.

The central edge ε has junctions at both of its
ends. If edge ε is ignored for the moment[2], each
junction can be viewed as a vertex of some degree
between 0 and 3; the classification of vertex types
is summarized in Figure 13a. Let us use the notation i-j to denote the case where the pair of
vertices has degree i and j respectively. Subject
to symmetry i-j≡j-i, and only i-j vertices where
i≤j will be referred to. Also, for this treatment,
a configuration of n edges will be considered an
equivalence class regardless of their particular
location in the three possible locations. Then,
only cases 0-0 through 3-3 shown in Figure 13
[PRA77] and parallel edges G and H need be considered.

Before discussing these cases in detail, let
us first briefly summarize the edge semantics
associated with equivalence classes of these cases:

---

[1]Note that if the edges are represented on a discrete scale that this condition is true up to the integer
error at the lowest levels of numeric resolution. Also note that the effects of gradient collection can
cause this condition to be violated by inconsistent placement of collected edges.

[2]Note that when ε is also considered (as will be true after the edge updating process is complete), a vertex
can have degree between 0 and 4. A vertex of degree 1 represents a line termination, of degree 2 a line
continuation, and of degrees 3 and 4 a line intersection.

1) {0-0} is an "isolated edge" and ε should
   have negative support;
2) {0-2,0-3} is a "spur" and ε should have
   negative support;
3) boundary continuation
   3.1) {0-1} is an "uncertain boundary con-
        tinuation" or "boundary termination"
        and ε will have weak positive support;
   3.2) {1-1} is "certain boundary continua-
        tion" and ε will have strong positive
        support;
   3.3) {1-2,1-3} is "continuation to a
        boundary junction" and ε will have
        medium positive support;

4) {2-2,2-3,3-3} is an ambiguous "bridge
   between boundaries" which is potentially
   unnecessary, and will have no effect upon
   ε;
5) {edges G,H│sgn(G)=sgn(ε),sgn(H)=sgn(ε)} are
   "competing parallel edges" and will have a
   negative effect upon ε.

Figure 13b is the 0-0 case where ε is an
isolated edge and should be inhibited (i.e., in
the absence of any additional information, P_ε
should be reduced). Figure 13c,d, cases 0-2 and
0-3, are both "spurs," where ε has no continuation
to one side while there is a line continuation or

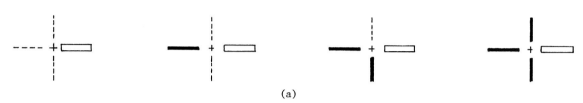

(a)

Classification of vertex types. The degree of a vertex is defined to be the number of edges at one end of
the central edge (but not including the central edge). From left to right they are Type 0, 1, 2, and 3
vertices, respectively.

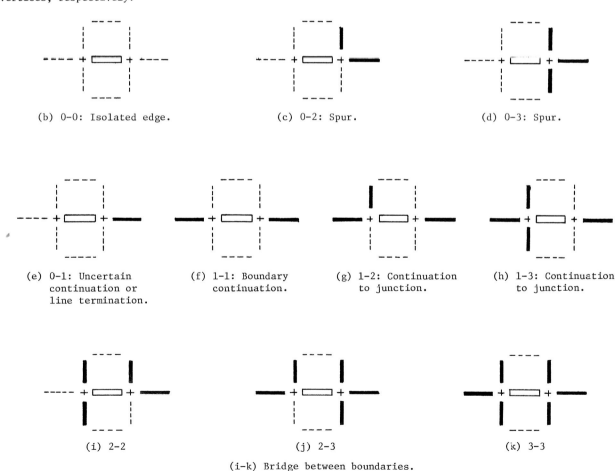

(b) 0-0: Isolated edge.   (c) 0-2: Spur.   (d) 0-3: Spur.

(e) 0-1: Uncertain   (f) 1-1: Boundary   (g) 1-2: Continuation   (h) 1-3: Continuation
    continuation or   continuation.   to junction.   to junction.
    line termination.

(i) 2-2   (j) 2-3   (k) 3-3

(i-k) Bridge between boundaries.

Figure 13. Equivalence Classes of Vertex Pairs. i-j≡j-i represents a vertex pair of degree i and j,
respectively. Ignoring parallel edges G and H in Figure 10, there are only 10 cases, which form 4 major
contextual events (one of which is divided into 3 subevents).

Allen R. Hanson and Edward M. Riseman

line intersection on the other side; here we also inhibit ε so that unnecessary spurious lines do not grow out from many places on a continuing boundary, or at a junction of lines.

Figure 13e represents the 0-1 case where a line terminates and its continuation is uncertain. It has been argued [PRA77] that no updating should take place here because it is not dependent upon the local neighborhood, but a wider context instead; for example if there is a similar line termination close by, it is probably desirable to grow the boundaries together. If the size of the local neighborhood is increased, the number of patterns to be examined increases sharply, with an associated sharp increase in computation. Therefore, the analysis will be kept simplified by constraining it to the small neighborhood defined in Figure 10. We allow the edge ε in the 0-1 case to be weakly supported, providing slow growth of the boundary. Note that with a line termination, all three edges which are absent will receive this support, and the line will grow in all directions seeking another boundary to which it can anchor. This problem can be alleviated by allowing the original data to guide this growth so that the entire process is anchored to "reality." This will be examined in more detail elsewhere [KOH78].

The desirability of supporting ε is clearer in the 1-1, 1-2, and 1-3 cases shown in Figure 13f-h. The clearest case is for the 1-1 case, where ε is necessary for good line continuation. Its absence would form a discontinuity in the boundary and the two edges nearby each other would become boundary terminations. In the 1-2 and 1-3 contexts, the central edge ε is necessary only for continuation of the single edge associated with the degree 1 vertex. Thus, the presence of edge ε is only necessary for good continuation of one edge in the 1-2 and 1-3 contexts, while it is necessary for two edges in the 1-1 context. Consequently, support of ε from the 1-1 context can be weighted more heavily. Also note the difference between the negative effect of the 0-2 (0-3) case and the positive effect of the 1-2 (1-3) case. An edge hanging off a line continuation is a "spur" if it has no other edge with which to link -- if there is no local evidence of a boundary to one of the sides of ε. On the other hand, the one edge in the 1-2 case could represent a left boundary which is to link to the right boundary for which there is already evidence (i.e., the degree 2 vertex).

The last three local vertex pairs, 2-2, 2-3, and 3-3, (Figure 13i-k) represent cases where there is evidence of two lines passing nearby each other. The central edge ε is not a function of these lines because its presence or absence does not affect good line continuation for the edges which are present, and therefore the central edge ε will not be inhibited or supported, but instead left alone. To the extent that the patterns of one of these last cases is actually present (in terms of probability), all of the other patterns we have discussed are not present, allowing the updating process to decouple. In other words, the probability that cases b to h are present is equal to the complement of the probability that cases i to k are present. The effect is that ε will have some

initial probability based upon the image data, and then it will be updated (the probability increased or decreased) by the patterns described until the degree 2 vertices have probability one to either side. Thus, $P_ε$ will be updated via the context, and if the context clearly forms itself into a 2-2, 2-3, or 3-3 vertex pair, edge ε will no longer change. Its value will remain stable at the last value it had before the neighboring edges reached probability 1. This will happen over a number of iterations and further analysis of the situation will be left for post-processing.

Now we must specify the computation of the probability of each of the patterns in Figure 13 in terms of the probabilities of the edges in the local neighborhood. We emphasize again that each of the cases shown can simultaneously have some non-zero probability. If the probability of a vertex of degree i, i=0,...,3, is defined, then the probability of an i-j vertex pair will be the product of the probability of each of the two vertices. Since the semantics of a vertex of degree 3 is identical to those of a vertex of degree 2 in all the cases described, then only a vertex of degree at least 2 will be computed to represent both. For a reduction in computation, the probabilities of vertices of degree i will be approximated as a function of the three edges A, B, and C as follows:

$$P(\text{vertex of degree } 0) = 1 - MAX(P_A, P_B, P_C)$$
$$P(\text{vertex of degree } 1) = MAX(P_A, P_B, P_C) * [1 - MAX2(P_A, P_B, P_C)]$$
$$P(\text{vertex of degree at least } 2) = MAX(P_A, P_B, P_C) * MAX2(P_A, P_B, P_C)$$

where MAX is the largest of the values and MAX2 is the second largest of these values. Due to the approximation of the probabilities of vertices, instead of exact computation, they will not sum to one; this is not important because they are only used to compute relative changes in the label probabilities which are then renormalized. Finally, note that the probability of both an i-j vertex and a j-i vertex must be used to update ε.

There is one more condition that must be considered: parallel edge suppression for edges with the same gradient sign. At the beginning of the process such edges will be present throughout the image because of the multiple placement of edges during gradient collection. These then compete for the honor of representing the boundary. The probability of this condition will be defined to be the maximum of the edges G and H which have the same gradient sign as ε; if neither do, the probability of this pattern will be set to zero.

III.8 Results

The results of this process are shown in the following series of figures. Figure 14a shows a black and white intensity image produced by averaging over the three color components. The image, differentiated using the 1×2 operator, is shown in Figure 14b, where the brightness of edges encodes the strength of the edge. Figure 14c shows the gradient collected image which has been normalized to a zero-one range by the maximum strength edge, brightness now encoding the edge probability. The results after iterations, 1, 2, 5, 10, and 20 are shown in Figure 14d-h. The results are quite effective and capture most of the local variations

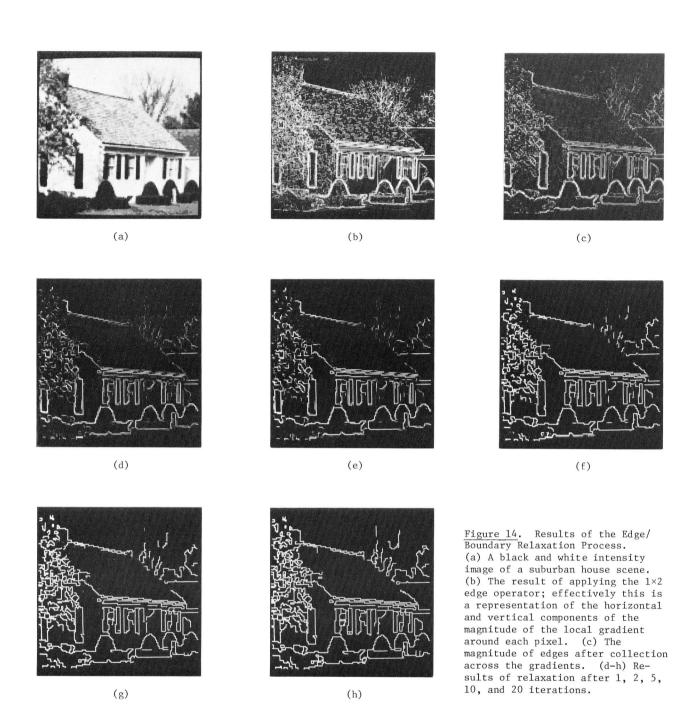

(a)

(b)

(c)

(d)

(e)

(f)

(g)

(h)

Figure 14. Results of the Edge/ Boundary Relaxation Process. (a) A black and white intensity image of a suburban house scene. (b) The result of applying the 1×2 edge operator; effectively this is a representation of the horizontal and vertical components of the magnitude of the local gradient around each pixel. (c) The magnitude of edges after collection across the gradients. (d-h) Results of relaxation after 1, 2, 5, 10, and 20 iterations.

within the image.

The weight associated with the isolated edge case (0-0) can be used as a boundary sensitivity control. As this negative weight is increased, the edges which organize into boundaries and then support each other must be stronger in order to grow in the face of this increased suppression. This weight acts as a negative umbrella across all edges. Thus, stronger or weaker boundaries can be extracted by varying this value. The boundaries extracted for an increased value of this weight are shown in Figure 15. Note that only the stronger edges of Figure 14 survive to organize into boundaries. Figure 16 shows the results of the analysis on a different image.

We believe that the approach described here represents a significant improvement over earlier approaches to boundary/edge analysis. The decoupling of effects of representation, differentiation operators, gradient analyses, and aggregation processes leads to a clear delineation of the requirements of each process. The representation allows an extremely clear analysis of edges in relation to pixels and could potentially lead to a comprehensive theory of edges and pixels.

IV. Region Formation

The boundary formation algorithm described in the previous section involved the aggregation of edge information based on *local* spatial views of

Allen R. Hanson and Edward M. Riseman

Figure 15. Varying the sensitivity to edge/boundary strength. Increasing the weight associated with isolated edges results in only (relatively) stronger boundary segments surviving. Similarly, decreasing this weight allows weaker segments to survive. The results shown are after 10 iterations, using the same parameters as for Figure 14 except for decreased sensitivity via the weight on isolated edges; weaker boundary segments do not survive.

the data. In this representation of the image data, all local variations are potentially important. Therefore, in textured areas, the boundaries produced by this algorithm tend to delineate reasonably small homogeneous regions in the image, such as the patchwork of boundaries in the tree region on the left side of Figure 14.

Our goal in the formation of regions is to organize the image on the basis of a more global view of the data. We wish to suppress the local textural variations in an attempt to produce a representation of the image in terms of a relatively small number of major regions with associated attribute descriptors. One of the standard techniques in the literature involves the analysis of cluster activity in global histograms. However, there are serious difficulties with these approaches in general scenes having a significant degree of textural complexity [RIS77].

In this section we will first outline the transformation of color data to produce effective color features. Then we will examine the fundamental problems in the standard use of histograms: they do not provide an effective linkage between image space and feature space. This linkage may be provided by defining a mapping from extracted clusters in histogram space to probabilities in image space, where the probabilities reflect the degree to which an image point belongs to each of the clusters. This permits a straightforward relaxation process to be defined for the spatial organization of regions. Results are presented to support the effectiveness of this process. Finally, we describe a hierarchical representation for segmentation results.

IV.1 Color Feature Space

The histogram analysis techniques depend on the measurement of some feature(s) of the image points, possibly including those originally used to represent the actual scene. For color images, the usual features initially measured are the red, green, and blue components (RGB) of the light level at each point in the scene. From this information, a variety of other representations, such as normalized RGB, or hue, saturation, and intensity (HSI), may be derived [TEN74,RIS77]; because many of these transformations are nonlinear, they give rise to distributions with unavoidable singularities [KEN76]. The presence of these singularities may severely complicate analysis of the resulting histogram. In order to avoid these difficulties, it has been suggested that analysis be restricted to linear transformations of RGB, such as the YIQ representation used in the television industry.

(a)   (b)   (c)

Figure 16. Results of the Edge/Boundary Relaxation Process. (a) 1×2 differentiation operator applied to an intensity image of a farmhouse scene (Figure 24a). (b-c) Results of relaxation process after 2 and 20 iterations.

More recently, Sloan and Bajcsy [SLO75] have argued for the use of an opponent-color representation which has been proposed as underlying the color mechanisms in human vision [COR70]. Simply stated, the effect of this transformation is to parameterize the RGB color data into an equivalent set of features which have particular complementary colors at the extremes of their scales; for example, a feature whose opponents are blue and yellow would provide information on the relative amounts of blue and yellow present. The "zero" point in the scale, where equal amounts of each hue are present, is white.

Figure 17 illustrates a very simple linear computation of opponent color features. Figure 17a is a standard way of depicting color information on a triangle, where the most saturated possible values of R, G, and B are associated with the vertices. A point interior to the triangle represents a color which can be obtained by combining specific amounts of the R, G, and B primaries; points on the perimeter are totally saturated while interior points are less saturated (i.e., diluted by white light). The interior point W, equidistant from the vertices, represents white light composed of equal amounts of R, G, and B. It forms a neutral gray, including black and white.

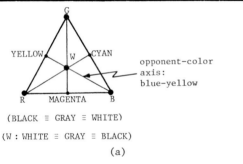

(a)

The color triangle. The axes passing through the neutral gray point represent the opponent-color features.

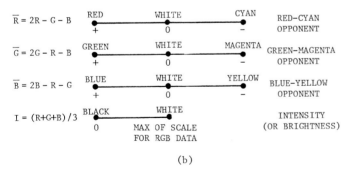

(b)

Opponent color features are approximated as a linear function of the RGB data. They provide a way for assessing actual color as a scalar feature in a more meaningful way.

Figure 17. Computation of Opponent-Color Features

Each of the three axes shown in Figure 17a represents an opponent-color feature and is uniquely determined by the line from each vertex passing through W. These opponent-color features will be approximated by the linear functions shown in Figure 17b, with a constant added to each feature in order to obtain a range of positive values. The features will be referred to as $\bar{R}$, $\bar{G}$, and $\bar{B}$, but the reader should remember that the letter used represents only one end of the feature. These features are an approximation to the opponent features. As the computation of $\bar{R}$ = 2R - G - B illustrates there are many values of G and B which produce the same value for $\bar{R}$, although the feature is an accurate measure of cyan only when G and B have equal values. The reader should also note that $-\bar{R} - \bar{G} + \bar{B}$, and therefore only two of the three features are independent. By adding an intensity feature, computed as the average of the R, G, and B components, all the information in the original RGB data is preserved. Also note that the axes are not orthogonal to each other; $\bar{R}$, for example, can be expressed as $\bar{R} = \frac{1}{2}[3(R - B) - \bar{G}]$. This dependency leads to the orderly spacing of $\bar{R}$ and $\bar{G}$ components (for example) when two-dimensional histograms are computed (refer to Figure 23).

If the axes are not constrained to go through W, there are an infinite number of possible opponent-color features. It should be possible to tailor the features actually used, via feedback from semantic processes, to provide the greatest discrimination between particular objects of interest.

While only three of the four features described are independent, in a particular circumstance any may be useful. Consequently, all four features plus the three RGB features will be utilized as point properties (as opposed to textural features) of the data.

IV.2 Image Space, Feature Space and the Failure of Histogram Analysis

A number of the techniques in scene analysis commonly used for organizing global visual information are based on histogram analysis. Here, the values of some feature (e.g., intensity) across the image are counted and the resulting distribution is examined. A classic technique has been to make use of "clusters" in the distribution to set a threshold on the feature values [OHL75,NAG77,ROS77a,b]. Each image point is then labelled according to the histogram cluster of which it is a member. A light object can be separated from a dark background (or vice-versa) by a proper setting of this threshold. However, in images with some degree of textural complexity, such a result cannot be expected. The distributions of the individual goal regions can overlap and clusters from regions can be obscured.

A more recent development in histogram analysis [OHL75] is the recursive iterative examination of one-dimensional histograms associated with a set of features. The clearest cluster in the set of histograms is extracted and used to "turn on" associated points in the image. The hope is that a large subset of the points contributing to the cluster will come from a spatially connected set of image points; this would allow the region to be extracted using simple techniques. By recursively histogramming the subregions which are formed (as well as the areas of the image which remain), the analysis attempts to isolate and remove the largest

Allen R. Hanson and Edward M. Riseman

regions so that the presence of less noticeable peaks will become obvious. Textured areas are extracted by a "busyness" measure based on the density of edges. The recursive analysis can be quite effective, because each resegmentation potentially enhances the effectiveness of other features.

A variation of this technique employing 2D histograms for a pair of features has been employed [HAN75] with the histogram itself analyzed in the processing cone [HAN74]. More recently this has led to techniques for gross histogram clustering in order to develop region plans [NAG77] (more on this in Section IV.8).

These approaches have had dramatic success for some images. However, there are very serious difficulties. Although histograms provide a global view of the feature data, they do not reflect the spatial information in the image from which they were derived. Figure 18 illustrates the type of problems that arise. Assuming the core of clusters C_1 and C_2 are obvious and easy to find, there is ambiguity concerning the proper cluster affiliation of point x in feature space. Now suppose that the clusters map back primarily to two distinct areas of the image, forming regions R_{C_1} and R_{C_2}. Each of the image points contributing to histogram point x can lie anywhere in the image. Ambiguity could be resolved if it was entirely surrounded in the image by points from either C_1 or C_2. Actually, this ambiguity exists for all histogram points, even those in the middle of a cluster.

The weakness of histogram clustering followed by a mapping of cluster labels back to the image is three-fold:

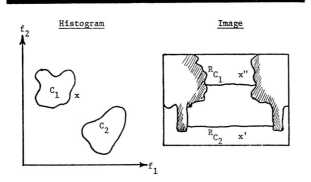

Figure 18. Histograms, Feature Space, and Image Space. The projection of histogram cluster labels back to the image provides only a weak mapping of information between feature space and image space. Consider some point x in the histogram of two features, f_1 and f_2, where its affiliation to cluster C_1 or C_2 is ambiguous. Now assume that R_{C_1} and R_{C_2} are regions produced by the clusters C_1 and C_2, respectively. A pixel contributing to histogram point x may have an image location x' or x", or in fact lie anywhere else in the image. The problem is more complex since this uncertainty exists even if x is in the cluster core of C_1 or C_2. Decisions regarding the region association of x should be a function of the information in both feature space and image space.

a) formation of clusters in feature space does not take into consideration the spatial distribution of points in the image which formed the clusters;
b) the extent of a cluster in feature space is often ambiguous (e.g., the valley between clusters might be a plateau), and decisions concerning cluster definition are prone to error; and
c) the mapping of a single symbolic cluster label back to the image is only a gross representation of feature space information, which loses the relationship of each point to the cluster as a whole in feature space.

The result is that only a <u>small</u> portion of the information relating image space (spatial relationships of pixels) and feature space(distribution of feature values in the histogram) have been correlated in these algorithms.

IV.3 Relaxation in Image Space Using Feature Clusters

The general idea of the approach we employ [NAG78] is mentioned in [SCH77]. It will take into account <u>both</u> the global information in feature space and the spatial organization of this data in the image space. Instead of mapping a single cluster label back to each image point, the probability that an image point belongs to each of the clusters will be mapped back to the image. This will be accomplished by extracting a representative center point for each cluster and using the relative distance of the feature values of the pixel to these clusters in feature space to determine the probability for each cluster label. The effect is to map most of the information in feature space back into the image where spatial information can be employed. A relaxation labelling process is now rather natural since the probability that an image point belongs to each of N clusters is available. Similar labels will support each other, while different labels will compete over local neighborhoods in the image. As we shall show, the relative cluster distances will be used to determine the compatibility coefficients.

Note that each of the three weaknesses in the process of mapping histogram clustering labels back to the image have either been entirely circumvented or else reduced. The extent of the cluster does not have to be determined, and much of the information in feature space is mapped to the image. Cluster centers still have to be determined and we will say more about this shortly.

IV.4 Assigning Initial Probabilities of Cluster Labels to Image Points

The relaxation labelling process described earlier assumes that given a set of N possible labels, $\lambda_1,...,\lambda_N$, each point in the image has associated probabilities $p(\lambda_1),...,p(\lambda_N)$ that the labels are correct. In the current formulation, the labels will be the cluster identifications and the probabilities reflect the confidence that the image point is a member of that cluster. Thus, the probabilities of the labels for some image point should be a function of the distance of its position X from each cluster center in feature space. Figure 19 illustrates the situation in the two-dimensional case. Our choice among several possibilities for computing the initial probabilities is

$$P_X(\lambda_i) = \frac{1/d_i}{\sum\limits_{i=1}^{N} 1/d_i} \; .$$

This choice has the property that the probability is a monotonically decreasing function of the Euclidean distance of the point X from the ith cluster center. The denominator represents a normalization to a true probability.

It will be useful to keep the probabilities of all labels non-zero. Once a label has probability zero it will remain there during relaxation because the updating of probabilities involves a multiplicative function (refer to Section III.5). Therefore, points with $d_i = 0$ (i.e., which are zero distance from the ith cluster center) are treated as a special case; for these points, the ith label will have probability approaching one while other labels are assigned small (but non-zero) values so that they sum to one; thus, all labels will have non-zero probabilities. This will allow the probabilities of other labels to grow if the context so demands, even for image points associated with a cluster center.

An alternative choice for the initial probability computation is

$$P_X(\lambda_i) = \frac{1 - d_i/D}{\sum (1 - \frac{d_i}{D})} = \frac{D - d_i}{\sum (D - d_i)} \quad \text{where } D = \sum d_i$$

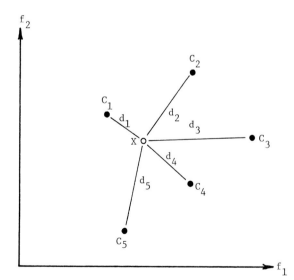

Figure 19. Initial Probabilities of Cluster Labels. The initial probability that histogram point X belongs to cluster C_i will be a function of distance d_i relative to the set of d_j, $j \neq i$.

which de-emphasizes the strength of close clusters whose contribution grew nonlinearly ($\frac{1}{d_i}$) in the first case. The results cited below were obtained using the first probability function.

IV.5 Identification of Cluster Centers in Feature Space

The initial labelling process depends only upon the identification of a single representative prototype point for the center of each cluster in the histogram. It will not be sensitive to relatively small misplacements of the center unless cluster centers are very close. The limits of each cluster no longer have to be determined -- the probability of belonging to a cluster will automatically decrease with distance from the cluster center. A number of techniques can be used to find these centers, but several potential problems must be kept in mind. Since the goal is to eventually obtain regions which are in close correspondence to the objects (or parts of objects) appearing in the scene, the algorithm should minimize the chances of arbitrarily splitting regions due to misidentification of cluster centers. This can occur in two ways: if a cluster is missed or if a cluster is mistaken to be two clusters.

If the clustering algorithm misses an obvious cluster in feature space (and consequently no label for this cluster is defined), the image points comprising this cluster will gravitate towards the clusters which are nearest in feature space. If there is only one, then the net effect will be to absorb the missing cluster into one which has been labelled. This type of error is not serious since recursive application of the region formation process will eventually recover it. On the other hand, if the cluster which is missed happens to lie between two or more clusters, then some of the feature points of the missing cluster may lie closer to one of the identified clusters, while others may be near a different cluster. This is a more difficult error from which to recover. Regions in image space corresponding to the missing cluster could be split and absorbed into different regions, if the regions happen to be associated with the clusters competing for the affiliation of the points in the missing cluster. It is much more difficult to recover from this kind of splitting since local evidence of similarity no longer exists -- the characteristics of the split region can be swamped by each of the regions which absorbed the pieces.

Arbitrary splitting also occurs if a single cluster is identified as two distinct clusters. The result is split regions which also could lead to the problems described above. However, in some cases two adjacent regions could be merged afterwards based upon similarity of their region characteristics.

Let us briefly review several alternatives for the extraction of cluster center representatives. We wish to point out that a variety of clustering algorithms appear in the pattern recognition literature. In pattern recognition applications, clustering algorithms are often applied only once to produce a characterization of the underlying data; in the application discussed here, clustering

Allen R. Hanson and Edward M. Riseman

is one of many steps in region formation and must be repeated many times during the course of segmenting an image. In this case computational cost is an important factor in the selection of a clustering method.

We will examine this problem from a different viewpoint. The problem of extracting these prototype points is not nearly as difficult for one-dimensional histograms as it is in higher dimensional spaces. In the following discussion, we will consider only one- and two-dimensional histograms; some of the approaches generalize to the n-dimensional case and others do not.

Ohlander [OHL75] has defined a set of rules for cluster detection based on analysis of local peaks and valleys, and their relative distances in one-dimensional histograms. In two dimensions the problem is more difficult because it appears to involve a search in two-space for the worst-case valley between two clusters. If the minimum value on each possible path between clusters represents the degree to which that path is considered to be a valley, then the limiting valley is that path which maximizes across all paths the minimum value on the path. This implies that an examination of all connected paths between the clusters is necessary -- a computationally expensive process which is even worse in higher dimensions.

Another approach is to use a conservative clustering algorithm in an attempt to define cluster cores [HAN75,NAG77]. The two-dimensional histogram is treated as a pseudo-image in the processing cone; it is two-dimensionally averaged by reducing spatial resolution (reduction), and then weak values are thresholded. The effect is to spatially collapse relatively high values of the histogram which are in close spatial proximity into a connected cluster region, while deleting the valleys. A region growing process is then used to label the cluster cores in this reduced resolution histogram. This process is reasonably effective, although the criteria by which the threshold is determined as a function of the reduced values must be carefully studied for reliability. One mechanism that has been used to compute the threshold involves an examination of a histogram of the histogram (i.e., the distribution of histogram values).

An iterative peak enhancement process has been described by Rosenfeld [ROS77b]. On every iteration, each histogram bucket is compared pairwise to each bucket over a predefined neighborhood. The central bucket is increased or decreased as a function of the values in the neighborhood; the amount is directly proportional to the difference in bucket values and inversely proportional to their distance apart. This algorithm can be applied in parallel to all buckets, causing clusters to dynamically organize themselves. It appears quite appealing in that thresholds are not necessary, but it is sensitive (hopefully weakly) to the choice of neighborhood size.

In the following discussion, we assume that a set of N prototype points $X_1,...,X_N$, representing cluster centers in feature space, have been extracted. For the sample results that follow,

they have been <u>set by hand</u>, but it should be possible to extract most clusters automatically. This problem is under continuing examination.

IV.6 The Compatibility Coefficients and Updating Probabilities

The compatibility coefficient between each pair of labels defines whether labels of neighboring pixels support each other or compete with each other. The coefficient is positive for identical labels and negative for differing labels. The simplest choice is to have

$$r_{ij}(\lambda,\lambda') = 1 \quad \text{if} \quad \lambda = \lambda'$$
$$r_{ij}(\lambda,\lambda') = -1 \quad \text{if} \quad \lambda \neq \lambda'$$

Notice that the linear summation across labels (refer to Section III.5) implies that the updating contribution from pixel j to $\Delta p_i(\lambda_K)$ will be zero if the probability of λ_K at location j is equal to .5 and will be negative if the probability is less than .5. However, even if all labels have total contributions which are negative, the probability of that label whose Δp_i is least negative will increase, relative to the other labels.

This simple specification of compatibility coefficients works reasonably well, but it can be improved by introducing relative weights on the coefficients which reflect the confidence that the two clusters really are distinct in feature space. This effect is incorporated for labels λ and λ' simply by scaling its negative contribution by the ratio of the distance between clusters λ and λ' to the maximum distance between any pair of clusters. Let $d_{MAX} = \underset{\lambda,\lambda'}{MAX}[d_{\lambda\lambda'}]$; then

$$r_{ij}(\lambda,\lambda') = -\frac{d_{\lambda\lambda'}}{d_{MAX}} \quad \text{for } \lambda \neq \lambda'.$$

This slows down the changes in label probabilities induced by the relaxation process in ambiguous cases·where clusters are close together, and speeds up the change (relatively) in clear cases where clusters are far apart. Note that the most distant pair of clusters will have an $r_{ij} = -1$.

There is one additional problem in the definition of the neighborhood of a region. If an

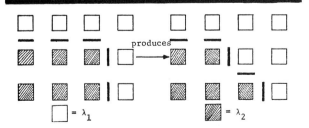

Figure 20. An 8-adjacency Neighborhood Causes Problems at Corners. As the label probabilities converge, the label λ_2 of the corner pixel will have competition from the high probability labels λ_1 at five neighboring pixels, and support from high probability labels λ_2 at only three neighboring pixels. As the neighborhood of labels converge, the corner pixel will switch affiliation from λ_2 to λ_1. The use of a 4-adjacency neighborhood removes this difficulty.

8-neighborhood is employed, right angle corners often cannot survive as probabilities converge to one. Figure 20 shows a pixel with label λ_2 at the corner of a region. In its 8-neighborhood there are only three similar labels of λ_2 and five dissimilar labels. This causes the central pixel at the corner to change affiliation from λ_2 to λ_1 which then produces a stable situation. Use of a 4-neighborhood removes this difficulty, and any particular diagonal element still will have an influence upon the central pixel indirectly via two intermediate neighbors.

It should also be pointed out that this relaxation algorithm forces all pixels to eventually become associated with a cluster, since no null label was defined. It might be argued that those pixels equidistant from two or more clusters, or far removed from any cluster, are ambiguous. It might be advantageous to include a null label in those cases to "catch" the ambiguous pixels, and examine null label regions after convergence on a more global basis. This has not been explored yet. Finally note that patterns of labels could be used in the region relaxation process, just as in the edge relaxation process, if patterns of labels (e.g., corners) have meaning.

IV.7 Results of Relaxation on Cluster Labels

The intensity (I) of the suburban house scene shown in Figure 21a is used to demonstrate this algorithm. The RGB color data is transformed to produce the red-cyan ($\overline{R}$) feature which is shown in Figure 21b. The one-dimensional histograms of I and $\overline{R}$ are shown in Figure 21c and d. These two features produce the two-dimensional histogram shown in Figure 21e; the six cluster centers that were selected are circled, of which all but two are quite obvious; the remaining two should be extractable by improved clustering algorithms.

Figure 22 shows the results obtained by projecting this information back to the image. The images in the first six columns display the probability of each of the six cluster labels at each pixel, where brightness is proportional to the label probability -- black representing a probability of zero and white a probability of one. The last column is an image formed by selecting the maximum probability cluster label for each pixel; each label is then encoded as a distinct gray level and the image displayed. The row organization is by number of iterations -- the first row being iteration zero (i.e., initial probabilities), followed by results after 1, 3, and 5 iterations.

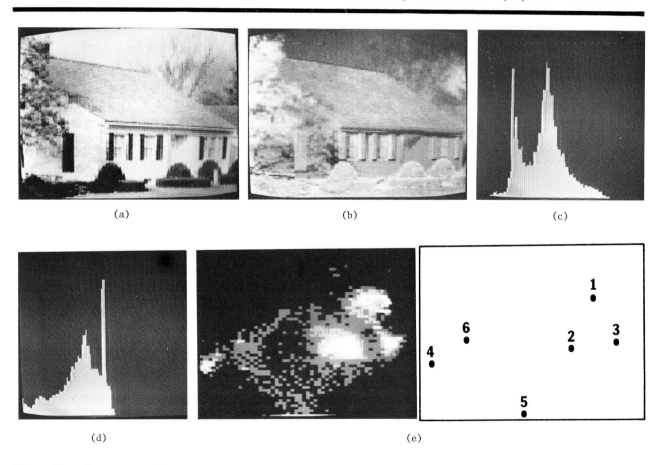

Figure 21. Features used in Region Formation. (a) Intensity image of suburban house scene. (b) The scene in terms of $\overline{R}$, the red-cyan opponent. (c) One-dimensional histogram of I (intensity). (d) One-dimensional histogram of $\overline{R}$ (red-cyan). (e) Two-dimensional histogram of intensity (x-axis) versus $\overline{R}$ (y-axis; cyan is at the top and red is at the bottom); the six cluster centers that were selected are shown in the sketch on the right.

Allen R. Hanson and Edward M. Riseman

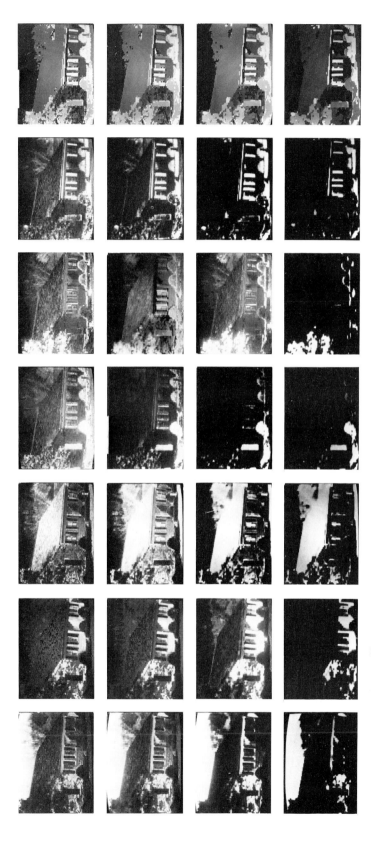

Figure 22. Results of Region Formation. Images in each of the first six columns represent the spatial distribution of the probabilities of labels of a particular cluster. Brightness is proportional to probability with black being 0. Images in the last column are formed by selecting the cluster label with maximum probability for each pixel; six distinct gray levels are used to denote the clusters. The rows represent iterations of the relaxation process.

The relaxation process, making use of both spatial proximity and feature value proximity, effectively extracts many of the globally interesting regions in the image. In the next section, we discuss techniques for further segmenting the image based on these results.

IV.8 Hierarchical Decomposition of the Image

In order to obtain a useful decomposition of the image in terms of regions, there remain two problems to be overcome:
1) the "correct" level of decomposition is still not known; and
2) histogram clusters can still be "hidden" by larger or stronger clusters due to histogram overlap.

However, we have pointed out that any given scene depicted in an image admits to various levels of description; for example as an outdoor scene; or house, trees, sky, and grass; or windows, doors, roof, leaves, blue sky, clouds, blades of grass, etc. Clearly, each of these descriptions is appropriate given particular goals. In addition the physical distance to objects affects the resolution and thereby the information in the image,

as portrayed in Figure 2. It is certainly not the responsibility of a general (non-semantically directed) region analysis to favor one interpretation over the other. Therefore, we are examining a multi-level description of the scene based on region properties.[1] A region at any stage can be related to the parent region derived from a coarser degree of segmentation and to descendant subregions using finer degrees of segmentation. These results could be stored hierarchically [FRE76], where relationships between ancestors and descendants represent descriptive properties of the structure of the visual elements.

Unrestricted recursive decomposition of regions and subregions could lead to serious computational problems when the number of regions in scenes with texture increase exponentially as finer and finer detail is extracted. This is clearly not a desirable effect of the algorithm. When a region breaks up into many smaller regions, possibly representing textural elements, the parent region ought to be given appropriate

---

[1]This research, currently in progress, is being conducted by Paul Nagin of the COINS Department at the University of Massachusetts.

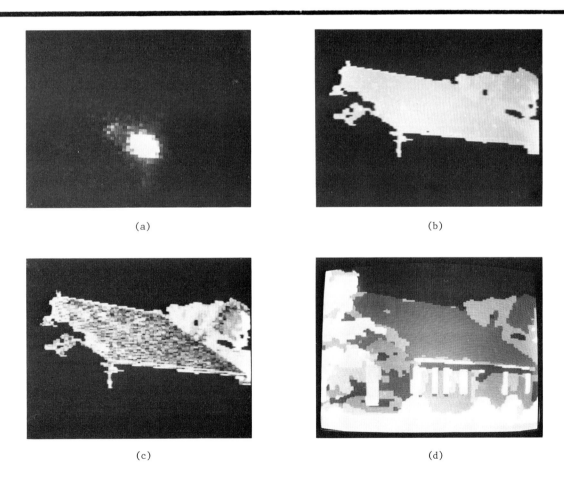

(a)   (b)

(c)   (d)

Figure 23. Recursive Segmentation of the Roof Area. (a) 2D histogram of overmerged roof region in Figure 22 forms a major and a minor cluster. (b) Initial probabilities for major cluster. (c) Initial probabilities for minor cluster. (d) Final segmentation with recursive analysis of roof area incorporated into results of Figure 22.

Allen R. Hanson and Edward M. Riseman

descriptors of the decomposition without saving each specific subregion; only information on the spatial distribution of the distinct types of sub-regions (e.g., red and yellow polka dots on clothing) need be saved. On the other hand a textured tree region might have descendant arcs to large subregions representing macro-texture elements, such as large dark shadow areas or large leafy branch clumps; here each large subregion would be explicitly represented.

The process by which the hierarchical decomposition would be obtained also alleviates (but does not remove) the hidden cluster problem if we base this process on a multi-stage recursive histogram analysis [OHL75]. The purpose of the first stages of this analysis can be thought of as "planning" [KEL71,HAN74,PRI77], where only gross structure is extracted by reducing the amount of detail in a scene to a bare minimum. Then, each of the grossly overmerged regions can be carefully refined [NAG77]. Thus, refined regions at one level become plans at the next level, with the histogram overlap confined to the plan regions instead of the whole image.

The idea of refinement is demonstrated in Figure 23 where the roof was partitioned by a recursive pass on that portion of the image. The house roof, garage roof, and the tree with bare branches all have very similar features. When the 2D histogram is confined to only the overmerged roof region, the subtle visual differences in these areas appear as a major cluster with a nearby minor cluster. An image of a farmhouse and histograms of two features are shown in Figure 24. It is partitioned in Figure 25 using three clusters, and produces an effective plan for further decomposition in the manner described.

IV.9 Guidance from High-Level Interpretation

This region formation approach delegates to the high-level system the responsibility for sorting out the correct level of description in the hierarchical segmentation by fitting interpretations to different levels, or by extracting useful levels depending on size and properties of regions. The final output of the low-level region analysis system is a hierarchical segmentation providing increasing levels of detail in the scene. In

(a)   (b)

(c)   (d)

Figure 24. Features used in Region Formation. (a) Intensity image of farmhouse scene. (b) The scene in terms of $\overline{R}$, the red-cyan opponent (shown on left) and $\overline{G}$, the green-magenta opponent. (c) The one-dimensional histograms of features used, $\overline{R}$ (left) and $\overline{G}$ (right). (d) Two-dimensional histogram of $\overline{R}$ (x-axis; cyan is to the left and red towards the right) and $\overline{G}$ (y-axis; green is at the bottom and magenta at the top); the three clusters that were selected are shown. Note that the orderly appearance of the histogram entries is due to the feature dependencies noted in Section IV.1

Segmentation of Natural Scenes   153

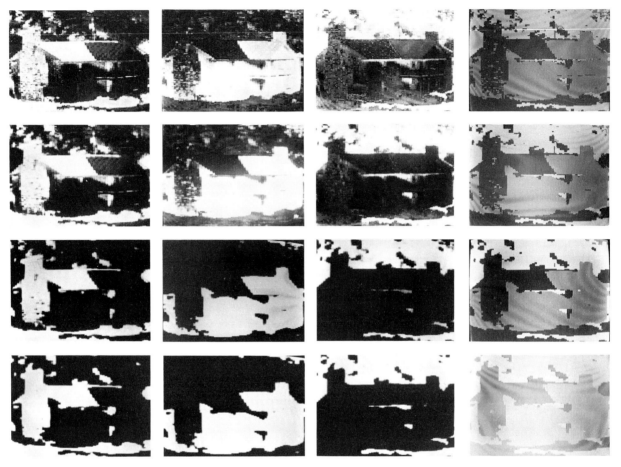

Figure 25. Results of Region Formation. Images in each of the first three columns represent the spatial distribution of the probabilties of labels of a particular cluster. Brightness is proportional to probability with black being 0. Images in the last column are formed by selecting the cluster label with maximum probability for each pixel; three distinct gray levels are used to denote the clusters. The rows represent iterations of the relaxation process.

addition, the refinement process could be guided by feedback from object verification strategies so that some portions of the hierarchical plan representation would be refined to a greater level of detail, using features carefully selected for recognition and discrimination. Here, a comparison of region attributes at any level of the hierarchy with stored object attributes can determine good hypotheses for region identities. Ambiguity in hypotheses can direct feature extraction for discrimination between hypotheses, while lack of a good match could lead to further decomposition and matching. The linkage between the region segmentation process and the interpretation system is still in the design stage.[1]

V. Merging Multiple Representations

Since regions and closed boundaries implicitly define each other, we have selected the edge/boundary representation as the common form in which to compare results from the two algorithms. The set of regions that have been produced imply boundary segments in terms of interpixel edges. The goal is to integrate the edge and region information to produce a segmentation of the image which is more reliable than either.[2]

It is not surprising that the results obtained from the two analyses do not agree in some portions of the image. Consider the set of tree trunk images

[1]This work is currently under development by Paul Nagin and Tom Williams of the COINS Department, University of Massachusetts.

[2]This research, currently in progress (and continuation of that reported in Section III) is being conducted by Ralf Kohler of the COINS Department at the University of Massachusetts.

Allen R. Hanson and Edward M. Riseman

in Figure 2, and the disparate micro/macro views of the data which would be afforded the two analyses. In addition the results we have presented in this paper have been obtained using different features, monochromatic intensity for the boundaries and color features for the region analysis.

The simplest correlation of the two segmentations is to perform a direct intersection of the results. The edges which survive are those which have been produced in exactly the same location by both the region and edge analyses. However, it is to be expected that the placement of a boundary will often be ambiguous, particularly where there are wide gradients. In such places the edge analysis forms a decision of good line continuation as a function of the gradient model used to determine edge placement during gradient collection and the interaction of local contexts during relaxation. In region analysis, wide gradients can be viewed as a slow transition from one region to another, appearing in the histogram as a trail of points connecting one cluster to another. Where the regions terminate (i.e., where the boundary between two regions is located) depends upon the spatial relationships and feature cluster relationships of the pixels in this area to the regions they lie between.

To allow for small differences in the results, a "k-intersection" is defined, in which the edges within k pixels of each other appear in the intersection. The results in Figure 26 show the intersections for k = 0,1, and 2. In this figure, exact (i.e., 0-intersection) matches are shown by the brightest boundaries, matches within one pixel (1-intersection) are medium bright, while the lowest intensity boundaries are 2-intersection matches.

Rather than using such an arbitrary intersection of the results, the spatial extent of the gradient (used to collect edges) can provide a local view of the alternative placements of the boundary. For large gradient widths, the acceptable disparity between region-induced boundaries and those from the edge analysis can be increased. Investigation of this dynamic intersection process, and the problem of where to place the resultant edge, is currently under way. A sophisticated method of integrating segmentation results ought to use the width of the gradient in the boundary analysis, the confidences associated with elements in each segmentation, an understanding of the weakness of the algorithms in areas of texture, and the incorporation of gestalt laws of line continuation and completion. A variety of strategies are being examined here, but are still in an early stage of development.

In the remainder of this section we outline a measure of confidence for boundary segments that has two purposes. First, it will be used in resolving conflicts between the representations. Second, the merged results, symbolically labelled and with associated descriptors, form the input to the interpretation processes (see Section VII and the companion paper) and it will be quite useful to have a measure of reliability of the various portions of the segmentation. These confidences could then be used to determine the confidence of less primitive constructs (for example, primitive two-dimensional shapes; see next section).

The confidence in the segment S will be based on information in the neighborhoods T_1 and T_2 to either side of the segment. These neighborhoods will be defined differently in order to reflect the data used by each algorithm. An interesting measure of confidence involves a test of the hypothesis H_1 that the points in T_1 and T_2 belong to different regions, against hypothesis H_0 that points in T_1 and T_2 belong to the same region; this measure was originally developed to guide the boundary formation process itself [YAK76].

This statistical test is defined as follows. Let $T_0 = T_1 \cup T_2$. Under the hypothesis H_0, the set of pixels T_0 is a single region modelled by the normal distribution $N(\mu_0, \sigma_0)$; under the hypothesis H_1 the two sets of pixels T_1 and T_2 are modelled by distributions $N(\mu_1, \sigma_1)$ and $N(\mu_2, \sigma_2)$, respectively. A maximum-likelihood analysis leads to the measure of confidence in H_1 as

Figure 26. Results of Merging Boundary and Region Data. Exact boundary matches (k=0 intersection) are shown by the brightest boundaries. Matches within one pixel (k=1 intersection) are medium bright, while matches within two pixels (k=2 intersection) are of lowest intensity (note that these latter matches may not be visible in the figure as reproduced here).

$$\frac{(\sigma_0^2)^{n_0}}{(\sigma_1^2)^{n_1}(\sigma_2^2)^{n_2}}$$

where n_i is the number of pixels in T_i, and $n_0 = n_1 + n_2$. The actual test we utilize is an extension of this formula to account for (linear) spatial gradients in the data as opposed to the assumption that the normal distributions are independent of their location in the image; more details will appear in [PRA78].

The only difference in the computation of confidences for the edge/boundary-produced segments and the region-produced segments is the definition of the neighborhoods of T_1 and T_2. In the case of the edge analysis, the data that produced the segment was relatively local; consequently T_i will be defined to include pixels within a distance k (for our application k = 2) to one side of the segment. In the region analysis the data was more global and therefore T_i will be defined to include all the pixels in a region to one side of the boundary. Thus, the confidence of a segment reflects the local or global data which was involved in the computation of that segment.

VI. Curve Fitting and 2D Shape

The results obtained from the segmentation processes and the merging operation will be symbolically labelled regions and boundaries (to be discussed in Section VII), but the representation of the boundaries (either regions or edges) is still in a form very close to the original data (e.g., x-y coordinates). One of the justifications for the horizontal/vertical inter-pixel edge representation was that decisions concerning global attributes of boundaries (for example slope) should be delayed until information over larger areas of the image has been organized. It is at this point that we wish to attach to each region and boundary segment some of the appropriate symbolic attributes of shape which will eventually allow access to objects stored in the knowledge base [YOR78a]. These attributes are related to the 2D properties of the boundaries; extraction of other properties, for example, those relating to the transition from 2D to 3D space, are delayed until even more information is examined and utilized ([HAN78], this volume).

Each boundary segment must be fit with a smooth curve, the type of curve then becoming one of the attributes of that segment. In addition, each region (described in terms of the segments forming the full perimeter of the region) will be examined for good fits by conics [AGI72,SHI78], triangles, rectangles, and polygons in general [FEN75,PAV75].

Prior to performing the fitting analyses, however, there are several difficulties to be overcome. The first is shown in Figure 27a. Let us suppose that the smooth curve shown there has been broken into three segments S_1, S_2, and S_3. The best third degree fit for each segment will not necessarily join smoothly at their endpoints. As a

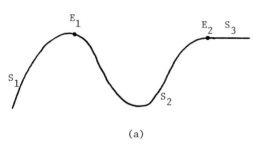

(a)

Segments individually fit with smooth curves must be joined together smoothly. This can be achieved by using splines.

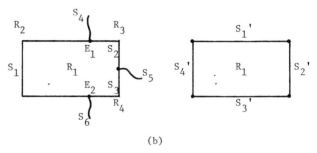

(b)

The segments bounding a region must be restructured by choosing new vertices for further processing of shape.

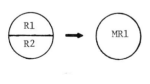

(c)

Regions sometimes must be merged before a primitive shape can be associated with regions. This problem can be produced by shadows (which may also provide cues for directing this merging.

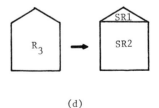

(d)

A region may have to be split in order to fit simple primitive shapes.

Figure 27. Additional Considerations in Shape Fitting.

Region	RMS Errors of fits for segments	Average RMS error of boundary
20	1.53, .93, .48	.98
45	0, 0, 0	0
47	0, 0, 7.59, .43	2.01
76	0, .48, 0, 1.15	.41
91	.723, 1.50, 0	.74
94	0, 4.59, 1.49, 0	1.52

Table I. Straight line fits to selected segments of Figure 28b.

Similarly, second order curves that have low mean square error will be preferred to marginally better third order fits. Of course the use of such precedence leads to ambiguity when the RMS errors of the fits do not provide a clear decision; in such cases both fits should be carried forward.

VII. The RSV Graph: A Symbolic Representation for Segmented Images

We have already motivated the reasons for a transformation of the spatial array of numeric data into a symbolic representation. This representation can be organized via some of the natural spatial relationships which exist between the segmentation elements which are extracted; regions can be defined by the boundary segments which delineate them, and segments can be terminated by vertices (which also have visual properties).

The representation chosen for a segmented 2D image is a layered graph, known as the RSV[1] graph, containing three planes in which the symbolic labels for regions, boundary segments, and vertices appear as nodes; relevant attributes are attached to each node. The RSV graph captures the visual spatial syntax of the image in the arcs between entities, allowing these relationships to be easily accessed and manipulated. Interpretation processes will need access to, for example, the segments which bound a region and the regions which are adjacent to each other. At least these properties should be directly accessible in the RSV graph.

The directed layered graph provides a convenient and flexible representation for the image data -- it provides a repository for features extracted from collections of image points, since each node on a plane (R, S, or V) represents specific instances of that class of entities in the image. The arcs between the nodes (both inter- and intra-planar) capture important two-dimensional, spatial relationships. These relationships (between nodes at one level) appear as a node at other levels in the representation. For example, the fundamental

relationship of region adjacency is implicitly available as a segment node; it is represented by an arc from each region node to their common line segment node. Thus, a region is defined by the set of line segments which form its boundary.

Regions which are adjacent to each other in the segmentation are a function of the original scene and the way three-dimensional surfaces project onto the two-dimensional image. The visual properties (e.g., contrast) of the boundary of a region can be expected to vary in arbitrary ways as the boundary is traversed. However, the properties of segments which lie between a pair of regions can be expected to remain far more invariant. In RSV, a line segment is defined by a pair of adjacent regions, unless it is a nonbounding segment contained in a single region; this is a highly desirable property of the representation.

A line segment is anchored in two space by the position of its terminating vertices.[2] A vertex of degree 0 is an isolated point, a vertex of degree 1 is an endpoint of a single segment (no continuation), and a vertex of degree 2 is a junction of two distinct segments. In general, a vertex of degree n is the junction of n distinct line segments. Vertices of degree 1 or degree $\geq$ 3, by definition, cause termination of a segment. The meeting of line segments is represented by arcs to their common vertex node. If regions must later be split or joined as object recognition proceeds, this representation affords the flexibility for redirecting a few pointers to update the low-level visual data.

Figure 30 is a simple illustrative example. The R plane projects down upon the S plane which in turn projects down upon the V plane. In particular, regions are enclosed by segments (and can, in turn, enclose non-bounding line segments, such as S9). Note that R* is a special region which includes everything outside the picture and therefore points to the line segment(s) on the boundary of the image. In this example we have further subdivided a boundary segment into segments which are straight when this property is applicable (except in the case of the picture boundary where they are artificial). Obviously other properties, such as points of high curvature (see Section V), also could be used to subdivide segments. Also note that segments such as S5 and S9 which are entirely contained in a region will be called "isolated" segments and are immediately apparent because only a single region node points to them.

Only a limited subset of the possible two-dimensional spatial relationships between regions and lines are being used to form the logical structure of this layered network, namely the adjacency of regions mapping onto segments and connectedness of segments mapping onto vertices. There are many other relationships that can be represented and extracted as explicitly labelled directed arcs between nodes on a plane. For example, containment of region R_2 by region R_1 can

---

[1] In previous papers RSV was called RSE since the term "endpoints" was used instead of "vertices." Originally only the termination points of boundary segments were employed, but we have generalized this definition as described later in this section.

[2] A line segment which is closed has no vertices; in this case an arbitrary vertex of degree 2 is selected so that the location of the line can be fixed in the image.

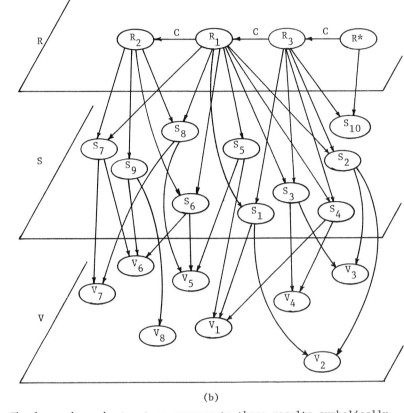

(a)

The segmented image with regions
(R_I), segments (S_I), and vertices
(V_I) labelled. Vertices have also
been inserted to mark the ends of
straight line segments.

(b)

The layered graph structure represents these results symbolically.
Regions are linked by arcs to their boundary segments, which are
linked by arcs to the vertices at their ends. Arcs representing
other relationships such as region containment (C) can be added. R*
is a special region representing everything outside the image; it
points to segments on the boundary of the image.

Figure 30.   Illustrative Example of RSV Structure.

be. represented by a "C" arc from R_1 to R_2. In
this way the syntactic graph representation can
be enriched by the addition of any further relationships that may be necessary, such as arcs
between parallel line segments or endpoints near
each other.

The descriptive properties associated with
nodes include:

regions --   location, color, satura-
                          tion, brightness, tex-
                          ture, size, shape, orien-
                          tation, centroid, hori-
                          zontal and vertical
                          extent, etc.
boundary segments -- location, length, con-
                          trast, width of gradient,
                          orientation, shape, etc.;
                          and
vertices --   location, orientation,
                          type (such as the poly-
                          hedral fork, arrow, T),
                          etc.

Given the symbolic RSV graph it is straightforward to define routines to determine:

1) the common boundary segments of two regions,
2) the set of regions adjacent to a given
   region,
3) the connected boundary around a region,
4) line dominance cues on segments emanating
   from a vertex ([HAN78a], this volume).

The operation of determining region containment is
not at all straightforward in the RSV graph once the
spatial array representation is discarded. It is
locally unclear whether R_2 contains R_1 which contains R_3, or whether R_3 contains R_1 which contains
R_2. One must recursively trace out to the picture
boundary and R* to determine the correct case.
Consequently, we assume that containment relationships are computed directly from the image and C
arcs placed in the R plane. Once C arcs are available, it is easy to extend operation (3) above to
determine inner and outer boundaries for regions
which contain other regions. More details on these
operations appear in [HAN76].

The RSV structure thus provides a transitional
representation between the spatially organized image
data and the symbolic description of the image in
terms of the high-level visual entities of surfaces,

Allen R. Hanson and Edward M. Riseman

volumes, and objects. It also provides a decomposition between the development of segmentation and feature extraction processes and the development of the high-level interpretation processes. It is a well-defined interface between these two systems, providing a repository and organization for the output of the segmentation system, and the source of input data for the interpretation system.

VIII. Conclusion

The data structures, processes, and algorithms that have been discussed here are a step toward the construction of a general low-level segmentation system which confronts a broad range of problems in vision. They have reached a point where they appear to provide usable results for interpretation processes. While we do not consider these results as preliminary, neither should they be considered, in any sense, final. There are further extensions and improvement to each of the algorithms currently under study, and feedback from semantic processes seems to have great potential.

The two avenues to initial image segmentation are based on complementary approaches to the extraction of visual information from the image. The boundary formation process responds to local changes in the data while the region formation process is sensitive to global similarities in the data. The edge/boundary analysis provides a representation of local feature discontinuities as a collection of horizontal and vertical edges. The iterative edge aggregation processes then allow semi-global contextual interactions to organize collections of edges into boundary segments through a paradigm of local cooperation and competition. Our approach to region analysis makes use of a gross global analysis of similarity over one or more selected features. Information derived from cluster analysis in feature space is mapped back to the image, followed by spatial adjacency interactions which organize the pixels into regions. Utilizing multiple features and processes based on histogram clustering and relaxation methods, recursive refinement of the decomposition provides a hierarchical description of the scene in terms of regions, each with properties that are invariant (where invariance is computed relative to the particular image).

Both the boundary and region formation algorithms can be extended and work continues in this direction. The relaxation processes which aggregate the edge data ought to be anchored to the original data in terms of the gradient widths which have been extracted and the region characteristics to each side of the gradient; this characteristic has already been explored and appears promising, but requires further investigation. Also, the local neighborhood around an edge can be enlarged so that the patterns for neighborhood edge support have a wider view of the context in which the edge resides. The global region analysis might be improved by the addition of a null label for image points which are ambiguous in feature space, rather than forcing affiliation to a particular cluster. The problems of cluster identification, and the effects of both mistakenly splitting a cluster or missing a cluster must be better understood. Finally, the utility of hierarchical region descriptions must be assessed.

The techniques for merging multiple representations is still at an early stage of development. The topology of the raw information in terms of the gradient widths and expected effects of textural variation on each of the algorithms are being considered. Confidences of boundaries between regions are being supplied by each of the algorithms to direct the merging.

The integration of the relaxation processes for regions and boundaries into a single relaxation process is possible [ZUC77], and this might also be extended to hierarchical relaxation [DAV78] in our processing cone. Segmentations from other sources could be merged to provide information that neither of our current segmentation algorithms have access to. In particular we and some of our colleagues are studying motion cues across a temporal sequence of images, and researchers at other institutions have extracted range data via stereopsis or laser-range devices.

The evaluation of the effectiveness of segmentation processes cannot be divorced from the goals of the semantic processes employing the segmentation results. Thus, the manner and degree of refinement of our low-level system must take into account the quality and effectiveness of the interpretation. With feedback from high-level processing, many problems which are unsolvable during "start-up" of segmentation algorithms yield rich alternative solutions. The evaluation of the segmentation processes in VISIONS must await the evaluation of the VISIONS system as a whole.

Acknowledgements

This research was supported in part by the Office of Naval Research under Contract N00014-75-C-0459. We would like to express our gratitude to the Computer and Information Science Department at the University of Massachusetts for providing a congenial atmosphere in which to conduct this research. The support, constructive criticism, and advice offered by many of colleagues is greatly appreciated. We thank Azriel Rosenfeld for constructive suggestions at various points in the long development of these ideas. The research reported here was made possible by the untiring efforts of Ralf Kohler, Paul Nagin, John Prager, Tom Williams, and Bryant York upon whose research this paper is based. These individuals and those who have contributed to the interpretation system of VISIONS have formed a rare cooperative research group whose dedication, and sometimes personal sacrifice, will always be appreciated. Finally, we wish to thank Ms. Janet Turnbull for her help and patience in producing the various drafts of this manuscript and many others during the past three years.

References

[AGI72] G.J. Agin, "Representation and Description of Curved Objects," Stanford AI Memo 73, 1972.

[AHL67] Ahlberg, Nilson, Walsh, Theory of Splines and Their Application, Academic Press, New York, 1967.

[BAL78] D.H. Ballard, C.M. Brown, and J.A. Feldman, "An Approach to Knowledge-Directed Image

Analysis," in Computer Vision Systems (A. Hanson and E. Riseman, Eds.), Academic Press, New York, 1978.

[BAR78] H.G. Barrow and J.M. Tenenbaum, "Recovering Intrinsic Scene Characteristics from Images," in Computer Vision Systems (A. Hanson and E. Riseman, Eds.), Academic Press, New York, 1978.

[BRI70] C.R. Brice and C.L. Fennema, "Scene Analysis Using Regions," Artificial Intelligence, 1, 205-226, 1970.

[COR70] T.N. Cornsweet, Visual Perception, Academic Press, New York, 1970.

[DAV75] L.S. Davis, "A Survey of Edge Detection Techniques," Computer Graphics and Image Processing, 4, 248-270, 1975.

[DAV78] L.S. Davis and A. Rosenfeld, "Hierarchical Relaxation for Waveform Parsing," in Computer Vision Systems (A. Hanson and E. Riseman, Eds.), Academic Press, New York, 1978.

[EHR78] R.W. Ehrich and J.P. Foith, "Topology and Semantics of Intensity Arrays," in Computer Vision Systems (A. Hanson and E. Riseman, Eds.), Academic Press, New York, 1978.

[FIS78] M.A. Fischler, "On the Representation of Natural Scenes," in Computer Vision Systems (A. Hanson and E. Riseman, Eds.), Academic Press, New York, 1978.

[FEN75] H.Y. Feng and T. Pavlidis, "Decomposition of Polygons into Simpler Components: Feature Extraction for Syntactic Pattern Recognition," IEEE Trans. on Computers, C-24, 636-650, 1975.

[FRE76] E.C. Freuder, "Affinity: A Relative Approach to Region Finding," Computer Graphics and Image Processing, 5, 254-264, 1976.

[GOR74] W.J. Gordon and R.F. Riesenfeld, "B-Spline Curves and Surfaces," in Computer Aided Geometric Design (Barnhill and Riesenfeld, Eds.), Academic Press, New York, 1974.

[HAN74] A. Hanson and E. Riseman, "Preprocessing Cones: A Computational Structure for Scene Analysis," COINS Technical Report 74C-7, University of Massachusetts, September 1974.

[HAN75] A.R. Hanson, E.M. Riseman, and P. Nagin, "Region Growing in Textured Outdoor Scenes," Proc. of 3rd Milwaukee Symposium on Automated Computation and Control, 407-417, 1975.

[HAN76] A.R. Hanson and E.M. Riseman, "A Progress Report on VISIONS: Representation and Control in the Construction of Visual Models," COINS Technical Report 76-9, University of Massachusetts, 1976.

[HAN78] A.R. Hanson and E.M. Riseman, "VISIONS: A Computer System for Interpreting Scenes," in Computer Vision Systems (A. Hanson and E. Riseman, Eds.), Academic Press, New York, 1978.

[HAY74] K.C. Hayes, Jr., A.N. Shah, and A. Rosenfeld, "Texture Coarseness: Further Experiments," IEEE Trans. Systems, Man, and Cybernetics, 4, 467-472, 1974.

[HOR75] B.K.P. Horn, "Shape from Shading: A Method for Obtaining the Shape of a Smooth Opaque Object from One View," in The Psychology of Computer Vision (P. Winston, Ed.), McGraw-Hill, New York, 1975.

[KEL71] M.D. Kelly, "Edge Detection in Pictures by Computer Using Planning," Machine Intelligence, 6, 379-409, 1971.

[KEN76] J.R. Kender, "Saturation, Hue and Normalized Color: Calculation, Digitization Effects, and Use," Technical Report, Department of Computer Science, Carnegie-Mellon University, November, 1976.

[KIR71] R.A. Kirsch, "Computer Determination of the Constituent Structure of Biological Images," Computers and Biomedical Research, 4, 315-328, 1971.

[KLI76] A. Klinger and C.R. Dyer, "Experiments on Picture Processing Using Regular Decomposition," Computer Graphics and Image Processing, 5, 68-105, March 1976.

[KOH78] R. Kohler, COINS Technical Report, University of Massachusetts, in preparation.

[LEV78] M.D. Levine, "A Knowledge Based Computer Vision System," in Computer Vision Systems (A. Hanson and E. Riseman, Eds.), Academic Press, New York, 1978.

[MAR75] D. Marr, "Early Processing of Visual Information," AI Memo 340, Massachusetts Institute of Technology, 1975.

[NAG77] P.A. Nagin, A.R. Hanson and E.M. Riseman, "Region Extraction and Description Through Planning," COINS Technical Report 77-8, University of Massachusetts, May 1977.

[NAG78] P.A. Nagin, COINS Technical Report, University of Massachusetts, in preparation.

[OHL75] R. Ohlander, "Analysis of Natural Scenes," Ph.D. Thesis, Carnegie-Mellon University, April 1975.

[PAV75] T. Pavlidis, "Polygonal Approximations by Newton's Methods," Technical Report No. 194, Computer Science Laboratory, Princeton University, October 1975.

[PRA77] J.M. Prager, A.R. Hanson and E.M. Riseman, "Extracting and Labelling Boundary Segments in Natural Scenes," COINS Technical Report 77-7, University of Massachusetts, May 1977.

[PRA78] J.M. Prager, COINS Technical Report, University of Massachusetts, in preparation.

[PRI77] K. Price and R. Reddy, "Change Detection and Analysis in Multispectral Images," Proc. of 5th International Joint Conference on Artificial Intelligence, Cambridge, 619-625, 1977.

[RIS74] E.M. Riseman and A.R. Hanson, "The Design of a Semantically Directed Vision Processor," COINS Technical Report 74C-1, University of Massachusetts, January 1974.

Allen R. Hanson and Edward M. Riseman

[RIS77]   E.M. Riseman and M.A. Arbib," Computational
           Techniques in the Visual Segmentation of
           Static Scenes," Computer Graphics and Image
           Processing, 6, 221-276, 1977.

[ROS71]   A. Rosenfeld and M. Thurston, "Edge and
           Curve Detection for Visual Scene Analysis,"
           IEEE Trans. Computers, 562-569, 1971.

[ROS76a]   A. Rosenfeld and A.C. Kak, Digital Picture
           Processing, Academic Press, New York, 1976.

[ROS76b]   A. Rosenfeld, R.A. Hummel and S.W. Zucker,
           "Scene Labelling by Relaxation Operations,"
           IEEE Trans. Systems, Man, and Cybernetics,
           6, 420-433, 1976.

[ROS77a]   A. Rosenfeld, "Iterative Methods in Image
           Analysis," TR-517, Computer Science Center,
           University of Maryland, April 1977.

[ROS77b]   A. Rosenfeld and L.S. Davis, "Iterative
           Histogram Modification," TR-519, Computer
           Science Center, University of Maryland,
           April 1977.

[SCH77]   B.J. Schachter, L.S. Davis and A.
           Rosenfeld, "Some Experiments in Image
           Segmentation by Clustering of Local Feature
           Values," TR-510, Computer Science Center,
           University of Maryland, March 1977.

[SHI78]   Y. Shirai, "Recognition of Real-World
           Objects Using Edge Cue," in Computer
           Vision Systems (A. Hanson and E. Riseman,
           Eds.), Academic Press, New York, 1978.

[SLO75]   K.R. Sloan and R. Bajcsy, "A Computational
           Structure for Color Perception," Proc. of
           ACM75, Minneapolis, Minnesota, 1975.

[TAN75]   S.L. Tanimoto and T. Pavlidis, "A Hier-
           archical Data Structure for Picture Pro-
           cessing," Computer Graphics and Image
           Processing, 2, 104-119, June 1975.

[TAN78]   S.L. Tanimoto, "Regular Hierarchial Image
           and Processing Structures in Machine
           Vision," in Computer Vision Systems (A.
           Hanson and E. Riseman, Eds.), Academic
           Press, New York, 1978.

[TEN74]   J.M. Tenenbaum, T.D. Garvey, S. Weyl, and
           H.D. Wolf, "An Interactive Facility for
           Scene Analysis Research," SRI Technical
           Note 87, Artificial Intelligence Center,
           Stanford Research Institute, 1974.

[TEN76]   J.M. Tenenbaum and H.G. Barrow, "IGS: A
           Paradigm for Integrating Image Segmentation
           and Interpretation," Pattern Recognition
           and Artificial Intelligence (C.H. Chen,
           Ed.), Academic Press, 472-507, 1976.

[UHR72]   L. Uhr, "Layered 'Recognition Cone' Net-
           works That Preprocess, Classify, and
           Describe," IEEE Trans. Computers, 758-768,
           1972.

[YAK73]   Y. Yakimovsky and J.A. Feldman, "A
           Semantics-Based Decision Theory Region
           Analyzer," Proc. of 3rd International
           Joint Conference on Artificial Intel-
           ligence, Stanford University, 580-588,
           1973.

[YAK76]   Y. Yakimovsky, "Boundary and Object Detec-
           tion in Real World Images," Journal of the
           ACM, 23, 599-618, 1976.

[YOR78a]   B. York, "Shape Representation in the
           VISIONS System," COINS Technical Report,
           University of Massachusetts, in prepara-
           tion.

[YOR78b]   B. York, "Symbolic Classification of
           Primitive Two-Dimensional Shapes," COINS
           Technical Report, University of
           Massachusetts, in preparation.

[ZUC75]   S. Zucker, A. Rosenfeld and L. Davis,
           "General Purpose Models: Expectations
           About the Unexpected," Proc. 4th Inter-
           national Joint Conference on Artificial
           Intelligence, 716-721, September 1975.

[ZUC76]   S.W. Zucker, "Relaxation Labelling and
           the Reduction of Local Ambiguities," Proc.
           of 3rd International Joint Conference on
           Pattern Recognition, San Diego, 1976.

[ZUC77]   S.W. Zucker, "Computing the Shape of Dot
           Clusters, I: Labelling Edge, Interior, and
           Noise Points," TR-543, Computer Science
           Center, University of Maryland, May 1977.

REGULAR HIERARCHICAL IMAGE AND PROCESSING STRUCTURES IN MACHINE VISION*

Steven L. Tanimoto

Department of Computer Science
University of Washington
Seattle, Washington

ABSTRACT

A collection of image processing techniques is
examined whose underlying commonality is the use
of regular hierarchical structures. In general
such a structure is a processing network which
actively performs computations on image data.
These processing networks, known as recognition
cones or processing cones, are organized teams of
microprocessors which transform image data in a
sequential-parallel manner. First these processing cones are described. Then, in order to
simplify the design and analysis of an image
processing system one may choose to omit or
ignore the processing aspect of these networks
and treat the data structure independently. Two
data structures are examined here. In one, the
regular decomposition, an image is represented
by a quaternary (four-way branching) tree whose
depth varies locally with the amount of detail in
the image. In the other, the pyramid, an image
is represented as a sequence of arrays of increasing dimension. Both the processing cones and
data structures are designed to benefit from and
preserve the spatial nature of image data. A
basic limitation of these regular hierarchical
structures is their inappropriateness for non-
spatial symbolic computation. Thus a complete
system for machine vision requires in addition
such modules as a semantic data base and an
executive control processor. However, the techniques described here offer substantial utility
in the development of machine vision systems and
insight into the possible nature of human
vision.

Introduction

Since the late 1950's computer programmers
and theorists have taken up the challenge of
designing a machine that can see to the extent
of making human-like decisions about the contents of an image or scene. The challenge
still remains. Thousands of research articles
have been written about many facets of processing
pictorial information, and yet an adequate
system has neither been demonstrated in theory
nor in practice, even if we take the vision of a
one-year old child as a standard.

* Supported in part by NSF Grant ENG76-09924
at the University of Connecticut.

Most of the efforts to design machines that
see have been predominantly guided by existing
mathematical techniques for data processing. One
example of this kind of technique is the use of
linear transformations on image matrices as a
means for the extraction of features to be used in
classifying the contents of the image [Tou and
Gonzalez 1974, ch.7]. Such methods have been used
successfully to solve very constrained image analysis tasks, but have not been generalizable to
other vision problems.

Some other approaches have been motivated by
structures of animal visual systems. An early one
of these was the perceptron neural network approach
[Rosenblatt 1957]. More recent efforts have produced computational models of high-level phenomena
such as Gestalt clustering [Zahn 1971]. What had
been lacking until the last five years or so was
an integrated scheme for combining simple and sound
image processing techniques with the overall structure of natural vision systems to produce natural-
ly-structured machine vision systems.

There is now new hope for success. Improvements in computer technology and in understanding
natural perception promise new tools for solving
the machine vision problem. Some of the important
advancements currently being made are in the areas
of control structures for parallel processes, new
inexpensive microprocessors, and a study of the
relationship between an animal's (or machine's)
knowledge about the world and the operation of its
perceptual processes.

A number of researchers are investigating data
structures and processors based on natural hierarchical structure in order to provide a framework
for the embodiment of these new advancements.
Each of the structures contains image data at
multiple levels of abstraction and the data is
spatially organized within each level. The experimenters include L. Uhr, A. Klinger, A. Hanson,
E. Riseman, S. Tanimoto, T. Pavlidis, M. Levine,
C. Dyer, A. Rosenfeld, and others.

Some of the researchers have been developing
structures which actively process the image data
[Uhr 1977, Hanson and Riseman 1976b]. These structures may be described as regular layered networks
of microcomputers which accept image data at their
bottom levels. The networks process the information by performing local transformations and

passing output (from each microcomputer) to a neighboring microcomputer in the network. These networks are referred to alternately as "recognition cones" and "processing cones" by their developers. They are described in more detail in the second section of this paper.

Other researchers have studied hierarchical data structures apart from processor networks for machine vision. While any recognition cone includes a regular hierarchical data structure implicitly, there are some strategic advantages to studying the (passive) data structures apart from the processing parts of a recognition cone. One advantage is that the simplicity gained by treating only the data permits in-depth study of data relationships among the levels of abstraction [Tanimoto 1976a]. A second advantage is that data-structural tools may be developed which have applicability in a wider variety of image processing environments than those tied to specific processor configurations. A possible third advantage is that postponing consideration for controlling a network of microcomputers, each having only (spatially) local access to image data, design may be easier; with a general purpose processor having random access to the entire data structure, one may be more likely to build a machine which computes what it should compute rather than what it can compute. Eventually, of course, the processors and data structures must be studied together.

The data structures have been studied along two similar approaches which differ in the properties of the structures that they emphasize. One approach is to describe an image as a hierarchy of square regions [Klinger 1971, Horowitz and Pavlidis 1976]. In this way a tree is used to represent an image such that each node represents a square region and the four sons of a node represent four square subregions (that form a 2 x 2 partition of the father region). The depth of the tree varies across the image depending on the amount of detail present in each part of the image. This representation technique is referred to as "regular decomposition" and is described in more detail later.

The second approach while similar to the first, emphasizes the sequence of resolution levels more than the partitioning of the image. In the second approach, the hierarchical data structure is a sequence of digitizations of an image at successively higher spatial sampling rates. This sequence of arrays is referred to as a "pyramid" [Tanimoto and Pavlidis 1975]. Normally the sampling rate increases by a factor of four from one level to the next so that a regular decomposition is implicit in a pyramid. Similarly when each node of a regular decomposition contains the average image brightness for its region and the regular decomposition is a balanced tree, it contains an implicit pyramid. The pyramid is a structure which readily avails itself to picture processing using planning [Kelly 1971, Hanson, Riseman and Nagin 1975, Tanimoto 1975]. Pyramids are described in more detail later.

All of the structures share the attributes of being regular and hierarchical. They all provide the capability for handling picture processing tasks at all levels in a global-to-local stratostructure.

Here we will examine some of the actual and apparent limitations of these structures and discuss their proper role in complete machine vision systems.

Regularly-structured microprocessor networks

It is apparent that in animal visual systems, a high degree of parallelism occurs in processing the data from the retina. Neurophysiologists have given us enough of a description of the structure of neural interconnections in the visual pathway to excite our imaginations for designing artificial perception systems. The perceptrons of Rosenblatt and others were an outgrowth of this enthusiasm. The downfall of this research effort was that too much was expected of these structures. There was a demonstration which showed that any layered perceptron composed of linear threshold elements connected in an acyclic network would be incapable of computing region connectivity in an image [Minsky and Papert 1969]. This proof, coupled with the general lack of success, served to discourage subsequent research using perceptrons. However the recent research described here suggests that aspects of perceptrons, such as their parallel-serial interconnection patterns, have yet to make their full impact.

In 1971 L. Uhr proposed that processor networks called "recognition cones" be used in machine perception. These cones are more general than perceptrons in that they permit transformations composed of primitives other than summing and thresholding, and in that they permit sequential operations to be performed as well as parallel operations. Like perceptrons, cones may be composed of processing elements connected together in a network. The interconnections would form a regular pattern in each of a series of layers. The initial layer consists of an array of processors that are fed the light intensity (possibly multispectral) data. Each processor sees one local region of the image so that the entire image is covered. Successive layers of the cone contain arrays of processors that "see" the output of the layer directly below (typically). The arrays get smaller as the layers get higher, so that eventually there is an apex of a single processor at which the entire cone converges. Uhr suggested that each processor be capable of performing not only preprocessing operations, but also "characterizing" operations such as assigning a symbol to a location in the image, to represent a local interpretation. A detailed description of recognition cones is given elsewhere in this volume [Uhr 1977].

Some primitive operations to take place in cones have been suggested by E. Riseman and A. Hanson. In addition to Uhr's averaging and differencing (referred to by Riseman and Hanson as "reduction" operations), there are "data projection" operations in which the microprocessors pass image data down to a lower layer. Also there are operations in a category called "iterative" or "lateral" in which a processor performs an operation based solely on data from neighboring processors in the same layer.

Steven L. Tanimoto

Riseman and Hanson use the term "processing cone" rather than "recognition cone" for their structure because the computations performed there are pre-recognition (before identification of the major objects in a scene). One example of a computation which can be performed in a processing cone has been described by them [Hanson and Riseman 1976a,1977] and is outlined here in a somewhat modified form. The purpose of this sequence of operations is to determine the important (not noise) edges in an image.

Processing cone program for edge determination:

Step 1. (lateral) Apply a weighted-average filter over 5 x 5 neighborhoods to smooth minor variations in the image, results being returned to the central element of each neighborhood.

Step 2. (lateral) Apply a 3 x 3 spatial differentiation operator to detect the presence of edges.

Step 3. (lateral) Suppress any parallel "secondary" edges ("ghosts") to eliminate redundant information.

Step 4. (reduction) Pass the maximum edge values from each 2 x 2 element block (of a partition) in the finest level up to the next (coarser) level of processing elements.

Step 5. (reduction) Continue to pass the maximum values up the cone until a preset termination level is reached, say the $2^{32} \times 2^{32}$ level.

Step 6. (lateral) In this termination level, grow the "max edges" into a plan by applying a rule such as "if an element has two neighbors with max edges above a threshold t, make this element part of the plan, and also make any element whose max edge exceeds t part of the plan."

Step 7. (projection) In the level immediately below (finer than) the termination level, "turn on" those elements whose max edge value matches that of the element above (and only if it is in the plan).

Step 8. (lateral) In this level fill in edges by turning on elements that are adjacent to elements already on (see [Prager, Hanson and Riseman 1976, 1977]).

Step 9. (projection and lateral) Repeat the sequence of steps 7 and 8 down until the original finest level is reached.

In this example, the basic flow of information in the cone may be described as "up then down". Bottom-up computation is used to form a plan (steps 1-6), which is in turn used in a second phase in top-down manner (steps 7-9). This scheme for image processing was also employed by Levine for region analysis and will be discussed in the section "Pyramids of increasingly resolved images."

Cones have a great potential. Currently there are several difficulties that are challenging researchers in this area. For one thing since the best means of interconnection of the processors themselves are unknown, cones are being simulated in software rather than built in hardware. The models are invariably tested on a sequential machine at very slow emulation rates. This problem will probably go away within two or three years, since it likely that at least one of two solutions will become practical. One solution is that the emulation can be done faster. This would require that the emulator be written in a language which permits parallelism, and that the computer system actually provide some parallelism. The second possible solution is that the cost of assembling arrays of microprocessors will become so low that some cones can be implemented in hardware. Other parallel processors for vision have already been developed with large-scale integrated circuits [Duff 1976, Uhr 1977].

A second point of difficulty in using cones is making the decision as to exactly what processing should be performed in the cone and what processing should be performed outside it by a high-level module. If the cone is to be used only for pre-recognition processing, where should the line be drawn? Are edge-detection and region-finding operations considered to be recognition? It has been made clear in recent years that successful segmentation cannot be performed on natural scenes without semantic (world) information. However, this difficulty is one of the fundamental problems of machine vision re-embodied: "How can a low-level system and a high-level system be designed and integrated to successfully perform vision?" Therefore this difficulty is not specific to the use of cones and should not stand in the way of their use.

A third challenge with cones is that their design demands that their designers "think parallel". Programmers have been trained for the most part according to serial modes of computing. Few of us have any real experience programming a task for a large parallel collection of processors. This problem should not be viewed as a limitation of cones, but rather as a general problem of programming parallel processes. Programmers are and will continue to develop the necessary abstractions for thinking about parallel algorithms and designing integrated and efficient parallel systems.

Regular decompositions

One of the difficulties in designing recognition cones is that one must confront both an abstract image processing problem and a processor network design problem. In order to simplify things, one can consider hierarchical data structures apart from processor networks. Regular decompositions are one kind of hierarchical picture data structure.

The problem of computing hidden surfaces for two-dimensional views of three-dimensional polyhedra was solved in one novel way [Warnock 1969] which had an important lesson for the image analysis field. In Warnock's algorithm the two dimensional picture space (or a square subspace of it) was recursively subdivided into four squares whenever the picture space (or the square subspace of it) contained a boundary between two faces of polyhedra or between a face and the background. Any square subspace not containing any boundaries of objects was not subdivided, but just displayed on a graphics screen. If subdivision reached the limit of the screen's resolution, the square would be displayed with the color of the most prominent object within the square. The algorithm even gives good results when the color of an arbitrary object within the square is displayed. It has been shown [Klinger 1973] that the recursive subdivision technique could be applied to tasks of searching and describing digitized natural images. Using regular decomposition, an image is stored as a tree whose nodes have either four or zero immediate descendants. In the most recent scheme [Klinger et al 1977], a separate image array is associated with each node. If only arrays corresponding to the leaves (tip nodes) are stored, the image data is non-redundant. However the data for interior nodes only requires roughly 33% more storage and it enables more rapid access to desired data than would be possible without it. Each node's image array corresponds to some square region of the original picture, with the root of course corresponding to the whole picture.

In addition to aiding the implementation of logarithmic search processes, regular decompositions can achieve significant data compaction ratios. By storing (e.g.) color information only for the portions of the image where there is change and activity, and thereby eliminating most of the redundancy in the descriptions of uniform areas, storage savings are achieved.

Within the context of regular decompositions, a useful notation for subpictures of an image has been devised that allows convenient protocol for accessing refinements of picture data [Klinger et al 1977]. This system, like the Dewey decimal cataloging system, indicates successive refinement by appending symbols following a decimal point. For a picture P, the portion denoted by P.c.b is shown in figure 1.

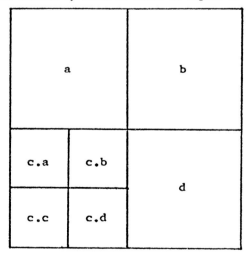

Figure 1. The subpicture notation of Klinger et al.

If we assume that each subpicture of the regular decomposition is represented as a (say) 2^{128} by 2^{128} array, then while array P.c has the same size array as P.c.b, the latter is a refinement of a portion of the former.

These researchers have devised efficient methods for storing and accessing images as collections of subimages on magnetic tapes, disks and drums. Their methods become more and more useful as machine vision experimenters work on higher-resolution images or with smaller laboratory computers short on main memory.

In addition to speeding up search operations, regular decompositions speed up region segmentation. It has been shown [Horowitz and Pavlidis 1976] that bottom-up merging of pixels into regions can be improved upon by first performing "splits" from a coarse level of a regular decomposition. In this way, the number of merges and the maximum number of region descriptors needed can be substantially reduced, and computing time saved.

In the split-and-merge procedure, segmentation proceeds as follows. A starting level in the regular decomposition tree is selected (based on a priori knowledge about the picture class). The partition of the image imposed by the regular decomposition at this starting level is taken as the starting segmentation (figure 2a). If any of these blocks satisfy a brightness uniformity condition (maximum deviation from the mean within a tolerance) and can be merged with adjacent blocks to still satisfy the condition and form a new regular decomposition block, the merge is performed in each case (figure 2b). Most of the remaining blocks do not satisfy the condition and must be split into pieces that do (figure 2c). The splitting operations are kept simple by conforming to the divisions specified by regular decomposition (quadrant divisions). A final bottom-up "grouping" operation completes the segmentation into regions by merging appropriate fragments that remain after the splitting operation (figure 2d).

Image representation by regular decomposition must be regarded as a fundamental technique of image processing. It differs from the straight matrix representation in that resolution of the grids partitioning the image varies. However the form of the partitioning is fixed. Only square regions may be subdivided and then only into blocks of four subsquares. Regular decompositions store the image in a fashion readily amenable to top-down searching, and they often achieve substantial data compaction.

Pyramids of increasingly resolved images

Aside from the fact that recursive refinements of image partitions are useful in representation and segmentation, another aspect of regular hierarchical image data structures is highly significant. That is the provision of image data at many levels of resolution. While multiple levels of resolution are achieved in both the microcomputer cone networks and the regular decomposition data structures, the structure which brings out the resolution sequence most clearly is the pyramid. This is because in the pyramid the processors of the cones have been removed, and the grids imposed

Steven L. Tanimoto

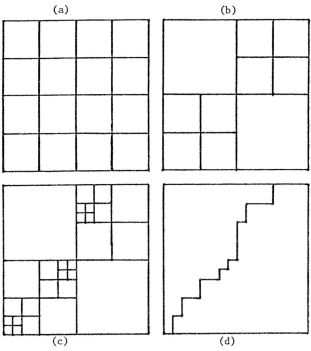

(a)   (b)

(c)   (d)

Figure 2. Stages in segmentation according to the split-and-merge algorithm [Horowitz and Pavlidis 1975].

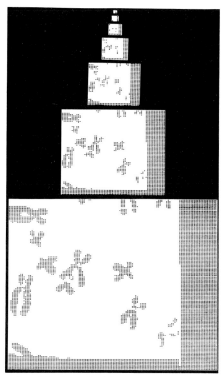

Figure 3. Black and white pyramid constructed from a 128 x 128 picture of human chromosomes [Tanimoto and Pavlidis 1975].

by regular decomposition have been made implicit rather than explicit. A pyramid is a sequence of digitizations of the same image at increasingly higher degrees of spatial resolution. In a pyramid for which the linear resolution doubles with each successive layer, the pyramid has a structure isomorphic to that of a balanced regular-decomposition tree where each node is associated with only a single pixel (a 1 x 1 array ... to be consistent). The standard relationship between a level and the level directly beneath it in this kind of pyramid is that the color (or other local picture property) of a cell is an <u>average</u> of the colors (etc.) of its four immediate descendant cells. Color averages are easily computed in a red-blue-green additive color mixing system. In fact, this pyramid of data could be computed by a processing cone whose design is quite simple.

An example of a black and white pyramid is shown in figure 3.

The interlevel resolution-change factor need not be two. In fact it is conceivable that pyramid data accesses should be performed by an optical system capable of providing enlargements (to the digitizer) of a continuous image at any magnification in a continuous range on command. The resolution or magnification of data to be used varies with the image, the application, and during the execution of each vision task. Clear demonstrations of the incredible differences possible between local and global views of the same "scene" have been made: The Charles and Rae Eames movie "The Powers of Ten" based on the book "The Universe in 40 Jumps" is one. We often need microscopes, telescopes, fish-eye lenses, or suitable

removal and perspective to see ultralocal or ultraglobal patterns in a scene.

The use of more than one resolution level in image processing is most often attributed to M. Kelly for his development of "planning" to speed up edge detection [Kelly 1971]. With planning, a picture processing operator is applied to a coarse-resolution digitization with results that indicate the gross structure of the transform. These gross results are called a plan. In many cases it is apparent from the plan where processing can be applied in a fine-resolution digitization to refine the crude transform with a minimum of wasted effort. A pyramid provides a wide range of resolutions and thus facilitates judicious employment of planning.

In addition to using pyramids for streamlining edge-detection, they are also used for region analysis and template-matching. A scheme for region-growing using planning has been devised which uses bottom-up followed by top-down processing [Levine and Leemet 1976]. In this scheme, pixels are clustered or grouped at a coarse level of the pyramid first. Then these groupings are refined by gradually descending to the finer levels of the pyramid. Another group of researchers has devised a scheme to perform correlation matching of aerial imagery using hierarchical search [Hall et al 1976]. What normally is a very slow and costly process has been made remarkably economical. Another convincing demonstration of planning applied to template-matching uses a two-level method [Rosenfeld and Vanderbrug 1977].

There are some difficulties in the implementation of systems that use planning in pyramids. One of these is the problem of handling textures. The averaging relationship between levels of a standard pyramid leads to the obscuring of fine textures. When texture is to be the primary basis of picture analysis, other transforms than averaging should be used. A study of the use of Fourier descriptors in regular decomposition segmentation was begun, but more work needs to be done [Tanimoto 1975, Pavlidis and Tanimoto 1975].

Another problem in the use of planning and pyramids is the fact that time/accuracy trade-offs must be administered [Tanimoto and Pavlidis 1975]. With planning, the greatest computational savings are made by starting at a very coarse pyramid level and developing a very crude plan, on which the remaining computation is based. The cruder the plan, the more chance for error in judgment regarding the importance of processing various localities of the fine image. Thus there are the added complexities of choosing the starting levels and the refining tolerances. A system that doesn't use planning has no need for these parameters. On the other hand, reasonable values for these parameters are usually easy to choose. Also it has been shown that in spite of added overhead in maintaining and accessing data in the pyramid, in many practical situations, planning-based methods still gain large savings [ibid].

Fundamental limitations of regular hierarchical structures

Apart from the various design challenges facing the vision community that plans to advance regular hierarchical structures, there is one fundamental limitation of such structures. This is that they are appropriate only for that part of vision in which spatial predication of symbols (representing pictorial features) is essential. It is well known by now that the interpretation of visual stimuli often depends on non-visual knowledge as well as visual [Toussaint 1977]. For example, the 13 in figure is reasonably interpreted as a B because English linguistic semantics make this consistent.

THROW THE 13ALL

Figure 4. Influence of the non-visual in perceptual interpretation.

Regular hierarchical structures are symmetric, invariant under 90° rotation. Without an external executive processor having random access to the data cells, there are no neat data paths between parts of the regular hierarchical structure and any semantic store such as a relational database or a concept network. Our structures are ill-suited to symbolic computations of a linguistic sort. While it is reasonable that the structures be directed by high-level processes having access to all kinds of general and specific information about the contents of pictures (scenes) and how to measure and identify their contents, these

spatial structures should not be the computing places for global deductive inferencing. If a regular hierarchical structure were designed to do this, the spatial arrangement of the storage and/ or processing elements would be wasted, and the processors in the structure wastefully powerful. One should not build a vision processing network out of 349525 DEC-SYSTEM 10's (the number required for a 512 x 512 based cone with inter-layer reduction factor 4)!

Complete vision systems

As a consequence of the judgments that non-spatial symbolic processing is required in vision and that regular hierarchical structures are inappropriate for such processing, we have the conclusion that a complete vision system ought to contain more than a regular hierarchical structure alone. Most researchers who are implementing complete systems for scene analysis using cones or pyramids have followed this design criterion. In one case, a processing cone is the front end of a system that builds structural descriptions of scenes [Hanson and Riseman 1975, Hanson, Riseman and Williams 1976]. In another, pyramids are operated upon by the low-level processing procedures in order to obtain segmentations which are then represented in a symbolic way for subsequent high level processing [Levine and Leemet 1976, Levine 1977]. In neither case are the spatial structures used in the high-level, symbolic parts of vision.

The relationships of the regular hierarchical structures to the entire systems can be seen in a rough way by looking at system diagrams for the implementations mentioned above.

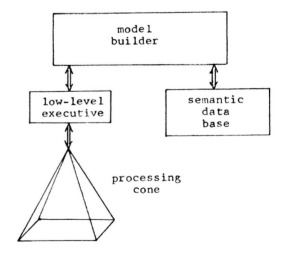

Figure 5. Essential processing modules of the UMass VISIONS system.

Figure 5 roughly represents the VISIONS system [Hanson and Riseman 1975, 1976b]. There a processing cone is one of several modules comprising the system. The other modules include a "model builder" which constructs a symbolic description of the scene being analyzed, a "low-level executive"

Steven L. Tanimoto

which coordinates the microcomputers in the processing cone to perform segmentation, and a "semantic data base" which manages (accesses and organizes) the system's knowledge, necessary for successful segmentation and interpretation. In this project, the modules are being developed separately as subprojects, with the aim of combining them into an integral automated system. The cone is only a single component of the system.

The other system implementation described above is that at McGill University under the direction of M. Levine. A detailed description of that system can be found elsewhere in this volume [Levine 1977]. This system divides the processing for vision into three stages: low-level, intermediate-level, and high-level. The low-level processing procedures construct five pyramids from the original image, one based on each of intensity, hue, saturation, texture and edge. After region outlines have been computed by the low-level section, the intermediate and high-level sections match known objects' descriptions with computed region outlines to identify objects. Again, the spatial structure, in this case the pyramid, is used only in low-level processing.

However it is conceivable that if the processors in a recognition cone are powerful enough, the entire vision function could be performed within a regular hierarchical structure, regardless of whether the structure is appropriate (cost effective) for the non-spatial aspects of vision. This approach has the appeal that all of vision would be done within a single processing structure as a bottom-up sequence of abstraction operations. It may also be easier to comprehend human vision as working this way (based on what we know about neural connections in the retina and the visual cortex) than as working through a primarily sequential series of feature tests [Uhr 1974]. An initial implementation demonstrates the nature of this "cone-only" approach [Uhr 1977]. Semantic knowledge is "known" to many of the microprocessors in the cone in the form of characterizing transforms. These transforms are condition-dependent operators which act on spatial, spatial-symbolic, and pure symbolic data yielding spatial-symbolic and pure symbolic results. Two major challenges facing the "cone-only" or "all-in-the-cone" approach will be the efficient storage of and access to semantic knowledge and development of general transform sequences for complex recognition tasks.

A proposed alternative system

To conclude this survey, another diagram will be given to suggest an approach alternative to the systems heretofore described. While the UMass, McGill and Wisconsin vision systems are all primarily bottom-up systems as they are currently implemented (although each design has provisions for feedback of some sort). The proposed system would operate in a primarily top-down manner. Making use of the fact that search operations are logarithmically efficient using hierarchical data structures [Tanimoto 1975, Klinger and Dyer 1976, Hall et al 1976, Dyer and Rosenfeld 1977], the system is based around hierarchical search. Figure 6 illustrates the overall design of the search-based system.

Accessing pictorial data from a pyramid, each of a collection of parallel independent search processors seeks out a specific pictorial phenomenon (e.g. sharp corners, bright red regions, leafy textures, generally dark areas, vertical boundaries, a specific object, etc.) on command of a control unit, returning the information gained. The search processors have random access to both the pyramid and a database of world knowledge. The database, not restricted to storing knowledge of immediate utility in vision, straddles the vision sub-system boundary. The larger system, of which the vision subsystem is a part, may be considered a general problem solving, learning and intelligent system which processes other forms of input as well as visual. Hence the control module of the visual subsystem is subservient to a problem-solving control module in the larger system (not shown).

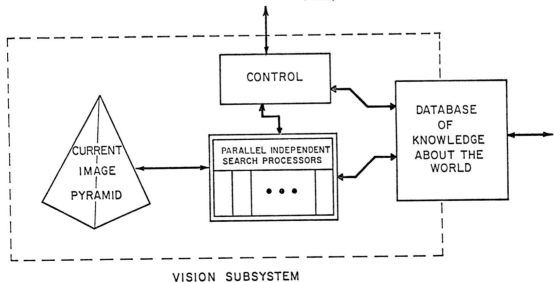

VISION SUBSYSTEM

Figure 6. Diagram for a proposed vision (sub)system based on hierarchical search in a pyramid.

The hardware required for implementing the proposed vision subsystem (ignoring the larger system for simplicity) consists of first a large and fast random access memory (e.g. core) for storing the pyramid, a library of reentrant search routines and miscellaneous data to be shared by the search processors. Second there are private memories for the search processors, where temporary data can be accessed without contending for common memory and with implicit protection against trespasses by other processors. Thirdly a reasonable number of general purpose processors are required, at least one and better many more. If many are available a hierarchical control system should be incorporated to permit maximum utilization of processing resources.

The addressing scheme used to access the cells of the pyramid should distribute cells across interleaved memory modules so as to minimize memory contention among "competing" searches. The database may be on high-speed disk, ready to supply the private memory of any process with desired background information relevant to the search at hand. Similarly, a process (perhaps the control module) charged with a visual search task such as finding out the time of day (e.g. day or night based on sky color, presence of stars, clocks, etc.), may send the results of that search to the database for possible subsequent use by other processes.

A possible advantage of this proposed system is that no segmentation of the entire scene is needed. Obstacles to general region-formation and edge determination algorithms are avoided by sidestepping the problem. When dictated by the control module, specialized boundary-tracing processes may be carried out, but only in the context of specific goals and decision criteria.

Another advantage of the system is that parallelism is achieved without sacrificing flexibility of the processes they carry out. There are no hardwired commitments to a specific cone configuration. By separating the geometrically restricted data structure (pyramid) from the processors, processing power can be added incrementally to the system in any amounts without incurring assymmetry and without any need for redesign of the system. The addition of a new processor simply means that the control unit now assigns n + 1 concurrent search tasks instead of n.

Another advantage to this separation of processors from the regular hierarchical structure is that it leads to a less expensive system. Even at the cheapest current microprocessor prices, the 349525 processors needed to build the 512 x 512 based processing cone would cost much more than a search-based system using 50 LSI-11's as search processors [Foster 1976].

Summary

A class of structures which includes some processor networks and some data structures has been examined. Its members have been referred to as regular hierarchical structures. The class

includes the recognition cones, processing cones, regular decompositions and pyramids in use by machine vision investigators. The commonalities and distinctions between these structures have been discussed. Some of the image processing techniques associated with this class of structures have been mentioned. The techniques include planning, split-and-merge analysis, efficient representation and access, and hierarchical search. Current implementations of machine vision systems employing regular hierarchical structures emphasize the appropriateness of regular hierarchical structures in low-level processing, and not for high-level semantic processing. Finally a proposed system was sketched which is intended to capitalize on the efficiency of top-down searching in regular hierarchical data structures.

Acknowledgement

The author would like to thank A. Hanson, E. Riseman and L. Uhr for constructive comments regarding this paper.

References

1. Arnheim, R., Visual Thinking, Univ. of Calif. Press, Berkeley, 1969.

2. Bobrow, D. G. and Winograd, T. An overview of KRL, a knowledge representation language. Cognitive Science 1, Jan. 1977, pp. 3-46.

3. Duff, M.J.B., CLIP 4: a large scale integrated circuit array parallel processor. Proc. Third Int. Joint Conf. on Pattern Recognition, Coronado, Calif. Nov. 1976, pp. 728-733.

4. Dyer, C. R. and Rosenfeld, A. Cellular pyramids for image analysis. (submitted for publication), Computer Science Center, Univ. of Maryland, 1977.

5. Foster, C. C. Computer Architecture, 2nd ed. NY: Van Nostrand, 1976.

6. Ginsburg, H. and Opper, S. Piaget's theory of intellectual development, and introduction. Prentice-Hall, Englewood Cliffs, NY, 1969.

7. Goldstein, I., and Papert, S. Artificial intelligence, language, and the study of knowledge. Cognitive Science 1, Jan. 1977, pp. 84-123.

8. Hall, E. L., Rouge, Lt. J., and Wong, R. Y. Hierarchical search for image matching. Proc. 1976 IEEE Conf. on Decision and Control. Clearwater Beach, Fla., Dec. 1976, pp. 791-796.

9. Hanson, A. R. and Riseman, E. M. The design of a semantically directed vision processor (revised and updated). COINS Tech. Report. 75C-1, Univ. of Mass., Amherst, February 1975.

10. Hanson, A. R. and Riseman, E. M. A progress report on VISIONS: representation and control in the construction of visual models. COINS Tech. Rept. 76-9, Univ. of Mass., Amherst, July 1976.

Steven L. Tanimoto

11. Hanson, A. R. and Riseman, E. M. Processing cones: a parallel computational structure for scene analysis. COINS working paper, Univ. of Mass., Amherst, 1976.

12. Hanson, A. R., Riseman, E. M., and Williams, T. Constructing semantic models in the visual analysis of scenes. Proc. Milw. Symp. Auto. Comp. & Contr. 4, 1976, pp. 97-102.

13. Hanson, A. R. and Riseman, E. M. Personal communication, 1977.

14. Horowitz, S. L. and Pavlidis. Picture processing by graph analysis. Proceedings of the Conference on Computer Graphics, Pattern Recognition and Data Structure, Beverly Hills, California, May 1975, pp. 125-129.

15. Horowitz, S. L. and Pavlidis, T. Picture Segmentation by a Tree Traversal Algorithm. Journal of the ACM 23, 1976, pp. 368-388.

16. Kelly, M. D. Visual identification of people by computer. Report No. CS168, Dept. of Comp. Sci.,Stanford Univ., August 1970.

17. Kelly, M. D. Edge detection in pictures by computer using planning. Machine Intelligence 6, Michie, D. (ed). 1971. pp. 379-409.

18. Klinger, A. Patterns and search statistics. In Optimizing Methods in Statistics (J.S. Rustagi, ed.) Academic Press, NY 1971.

19. Klinger, A. Data structures and pattern recognition. Proc. First Int. Joint Conf. on Pattern Recognition, Wash., D.C., Oct. 30-Nov. 1, 1973, pp. 497-498.

20. Klinger, A. and Dyer, C. R. Experiments on picture representations using regular decomposition. Computer Graphics and Image Processing 5, No. 1, Mar. 1976, pp. 68-105.

21. Klinger, A., Rhodes, M. L., and To, V. T. Accessing image data. Proc. IEEE Comp. Soc. Conf. on Pattern Recog. and Image Processing, Rensselaer Polytech. Institute, Troy, NY, June 6-8, 1977, pp. 29-37.

22. Levine, M. D. and Leemet, J. A method for non-purposive picture segmentation. Proc. Third Intl. Joint Conf. on Pattern Recog., Coronado, Calif., Nov. 1976, pp. 494-498.

23. Levine, M. D. A knowledge-based computer vision system. In this volume. 1977.

24. Marr, D. Early processing of visual information. A. I. Memo 340, M.I.T., Cambridge, Mass. 1975.

25. Minsky, M. and Papert, S. Perceptrons. M.I.T. Press, Cambridge, Mass. 1969.

26. Nagin, P. A., Hanson, A. R., and Riseman, E.M. Region extraction and description through planning. COINS Tech. Rept. 77-8, Univ. of Mass., Amherst, May 1977.

27. Pavlidis, T. and Tanimoto, S. L. Texture identification by a directed split-and-merge procedure. Proceedings of the Conference on Computer Graphics, Pattern Recognition and Data Structure, Beverly Hills, California, May 1975, pp. 201-203.

28. Piaget, J. The Psychology of Intelligence, (Trans. by M. Piercy 1950) London: Lowe and Brydone (First publ. in France 1947).

29. Prager, J. M., Hanson, A. R., and Riseman, E. M. Extracting and labelling boundary segments in natural scenes. COINS Tech. Rept. 77-7, Univ. of Mass., Amherst, May 1977.

30. Rosenblatt, F. The perceptron - a perceiving and recognizing automaton. Report 85-460-1, Cornell Aeronautical Laboratory, Ithaca, NY, Jan. 1957.

31. Rosenblatt, F. Principles of Neurodynamics: Perceptrons and the theory of brain mechanisms. Spartan Books, Washington, D.C., 1962.

32. Rosenfeld, A. and VanderBrug, G. J. Coarse-fine template matching. IEEE Trans. Systems, Man, and Cybernetics SMC-7, No. 2, Feb. 1977, pp. 104-107.

33. Rosenfeld, A. and Davis, L. S. Hierarchical relaxation. In this volume. 1977.

34. Tanimoto, S. L. and Pavlidis, T. A hierarchical data structure for picture processing. Computer Graphics and Image Processing No. 2, June 1975, pp. 104-119.

35. Tanimoto, S. L. Hierarchical approaches to picture processing, Ph.D. dissertation, Dept. Elect. Engrg. Princeton Univ. Aug. 1975. (avail. from Univ. Microfilms, Ann Arbor, MI.)

36. Tanimoto, S. L. Pictorial feature distortion in a pyramid. Computer Graphics and Image Processing 5, No. 3, Sept. 1976, pp. 333-352.

37. Tanimoto, S. L. An iconic/symbolic data structuring scheme. Pattern Recognition and Artificial Intelligence, C. H. Chen (ed.) Academic Press, NY, 1976, pp. 452-471.

38. Tanimoto, S. L. Analysis of biomedical images using maximal matching. Proceedings of the 1976 IEEE Conference on Decision and Control Adaptive Processes, Clearwater Beach, FL. December 1-3, 1976, pp. 171-176.

39. Tou, J. T. and Gonzalez, R. C. Pattern Recognition Principles. Addison-Wesley, Reading, MA. 1974.

40. Toussaint, G. T. The use of context in pattern recognition. Proc. IEEE Comp. Soc. Conf. on Pattern Recog. and Image Processing, Troy, NY, June 8-11, 1977, pp. 1-10.

41. Uhr, L. Layered "recognition cone" networks that preprocess, classify and describe. Proc

Image and Processing Structures in Machine Vision

<u>Conf</u>. <u>on</u> <u>Two</u>-<u>Dimensional</u> <u>Image</u> <u>Processing</u>,
1971. (also in <u>IEEE</u> <u>Trans</u>. <u>Comput</u>. <u>C-21</u>,
1972, pp. 758-768).

42. Uhr, L. A model of form perception and scene
    description. Computer Sciences Technical
    Report #231, Univ. of Wisconsin-Madison,
    Nov. 1974.

43. Uhr, L. 'Recognition cones' and some test
    results; the imminent arrival of well-
    structured parallel-serial computers;
    positions.   In this volume, 1977.

44. Warnock, J. E. A hidden-surface algorithm
    for computer-generated half-tone pictures.
    TR 4-15, Computer Science Department,
    Univ. of Utah, 1969.

45. Zahn, C. T. Graph-theoretical methods for
    detecting and describing Gestalt clusters.
    <u>IEEE</u> <u>Trans</u>. <u>Comput</u>. <u>C-20</u>, No. 1, Jan. 1971,
    pp. 68-86.

Steven L. Tanimoto

A PARALLEL MODEL FOR LOW-LEVEL VISION[1]

David L. Waltz
Coordinated Science Laboratory
University of Illinois
Urbana, Illinois 61801

ABSTRACT

A parallel model for a general low-level, task-free vision system is presented. The scheme of the model involves (1) finding local features (e.g. line or edge segments); (2) propagating information describing each local feature outward with decreasing strength from the location of the feature; (3) looking for and noting significant intersecting messages in a "transform space"; (4) retransforming from the points in transform space to allow selection of "important" features and suppression of "unimportant" ones, and to allow grouping of features into lines, edges, regions, etc. The scheme can be layered to aid in handling regions and textures. Examples are worked out to show how the model can be used to:

(1) find axes of reflectional symmetry;

(2) find and fill in regions in a scene with high line curvature (such as corners), a perennially difficult problem for line/edge finders (and an operation apparently important in human vision);

(3) find plausible line/edge completions, dashed line completions, subjective contours, and in general implement Gestalt laws of "good completion";

(4) find and "color" similarly textured regions, so that such regions can be segmented, and features within them can be handled appropriately.

(5) combine two views of a scene to obtain binocular range data for points in the scene.

1. Background and Credits

This work has its origin in several sources.

First, it was suggested by comments made by Max Clowes and Azriel Rosenfeld in talks at MIT 7 or 8 years ago. Clowes had been arguing

that human visual processing was "controlled hallucination." He began to show slides, the first of which was out of focus. The slide was apparently a cube on a surface with its shadow, but when focused, it turned out to be a photo of two pieces of cut-out construction paper glued to a background (see figure 1). The point

Figure 1.

This appears to be a cube and shadow when defocussed.

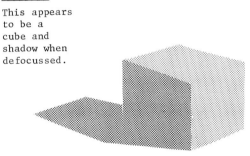

was that we prefer three-dimensional interpretations and fill in information to substantiate such an interpretation, unless cues in the scene preclude it (as when the slide was focused).

Rosenfeld argued that a large fraction of visual processing proceeds independent of the task domain (e.g. looking for a lost object, enjoying a painting, etc.). At the time, we (at MIT) were much influenced by top-down processing and "heterarchy"; we were using high-level heuristics to patch up imperfect line drawings (filling in missing edges, creating covers by extending partial lines, etc.). I think Rosenfeld was right; this paper is a step toward realizing the kind of "task-free" low-level visual processing he suggested.

Another main influence was my thesis work on what are now called "relaxation methods" [5,13,16-18]. Variations on these methods of interaction between local scene features have

---

1. The work reported in this paper was supported in part by the Joint Services Electronics Program (U.S. Army, U.S. Navy, U.S. Air Force) under Contract No. ONR-N00014-75-C-0612.

resurfaced here, as should become clear below. Also related to my thesis work is the use of potentially parallel procedures.

A fourth main influence was the so-called "prairie fire" work of Blum [3] and Calabi [4]. Briefly, this work suggested finding "skeletons" of figures by imagining them to be fields of dry grass, starting fires along their boundaries, and marking places where the fire "quenched itself." Some figures and "skeletons" are shown in figure 2. Note that there are

Figure 2.

"Skeletons" found by "prairie fire" techniques.

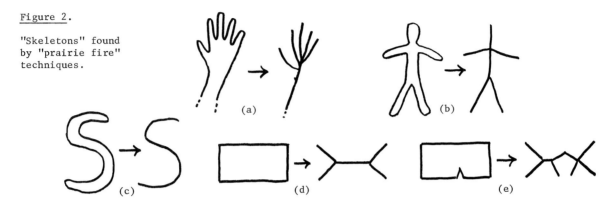

some problems with the prairie fire technique: (1) figure-ground relationships are necessary to decide where to start fires; in a "real" scene, it may not be at all obvious where to start fires; (2) skeletons can vary wildly for relatively similar figures (e.g. figures 2d and 2e); this is not desirable if skeletons are to have value for describing objects; (3) while for some figures (e.g. 2a-c) skeletons seem to be appropriate, for other figures (e.g. rectangles or squares as in figures 2d-e) the skeletons do not seem appropriate. Most of these problems of "prairie fires" are solved by the scheme described in this paper.

I have also followed with great interest the work of Marr and his collaborators at MIT [8-11]. Many ideas here are influenced by, supported by, or suggested by Marr's work. Ullman's recent work on subjective contours [15], which I read during the preparation of this paper, also has interesting relations to this model.

2. Guiding Principles

I feel it is important to begin exploring algorithms which could be used on arrays of processors (potential parallel algorithms) for the following reasons:

(1) Such arrays offer the possibility of dramatically increased computer power, _if_ we have ways to program them; in particular real time vision may not be forever an elusive goal.

(2) It will soon be economically feasible to produce hardware arrays;

(3) If we know what types of processing and what memory requirements are necessary for each processor in the array, then each array element may be much simpler and less expensive than a full microcomputer.

(4) Such arrays can provide a much more natural environment for modeling human vision, and for posing interesting neurophysiological questions.

There are also some simple neurophysiological/computational assumptions which I have made in constructing this model:

(1) I have assumed that the structure of the visual cortex is like a layered map of the retina.

(2) I have further assumed that the visual cortex is rather like a crystal structure, so that layers are identical, i.e., there are not many different types of layers as one moves upward from the "retina". An exception is the bottom layer which interfaces gray level pixels in a rectangular grid with the rest of the layers, which operate with "features" in an hexagonal array.

(3) Within each layer, only relatively local portions of the layer may communicate.

(4) The stacked layers form a cone [12,14], i.e. at each level larger portions of the retina are represented by one point.

3. The Model

I will describe each step of the processing, and give as concrete examples the actual implementation I am working on. I would like to emphasize that this implementation is not the ultimate way I feel that this model should be realized, but merely a first test, using the simplest possible assumptions.

David L. Waltz

The scheme has four main steps:

(1) Extract descriptive information for scene windows;

(2) Propagate this information in all directions from its origins;

(3) Note and save interesting information intersections

(4) Use the intersection information to construct higher level descriptive information, and repeat steps 2, 3, and 4 on successive layers with coarser resolution.

These steps are described in some detail in the following sections.

3.1 Extracting descriptive information

Descriptive information is obtained from local windows in a 236 x 256 64 gray level pixel array. The descriptive information ("features") consist of the following items:
$$\{t, d, m\}$$
t stands for "type," where type may be edge, line, gradient or homogeneous; d stands for "direction of the brightness gradient" (dark to bright). Direction values are quantized: $d \in \{D_1, D_2, \ldots, D_{11}, D_{12}\}$ where D_i corresponds to the set of all vectors lying in a 30° (one hour) sector centered at i o'clock. (See figure 3)

Figure 3

"Dodecants" correspond to hours on a clock.

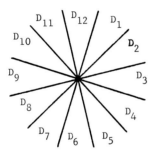

m stands for "magnitude." m = ⌊log of brightness difference in local region⌋ (see footnote 2).

Features are extracted only for local windows surrounding "cells;" cells correspond to certain pixels, and form an (approximately) hexagonal array, as shown in figure 4.[3] A given cell, x, located at (j,k) has as neighbors the set of cells: {(j-1,k+2), (j+1,k+2), (j+2,k), (j+1,k-2), (j-1,k-2), (j-2,k)}

I am experimenting with several schemes and window sizes for finding features at cell sites; the particular methods are not novel, and are not of particular interest here.

Figure 4.

"Approximately Hexagonal" array superimposed on grid of pixels. 0 or · is a cell

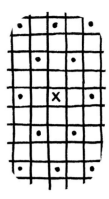

3.2 Propagating information

Once features have been extracted for all cell sites, the next processing step is to look for correlations between individual cells. This is facilitated by propagating "messages," (feature descriptions) in all directions from each cell site, like ripples spreading outward from a stone dropped into water. Messages move in discrete steps between cells. Message "strength" decreases as messages propagate outward. Each message has a direction of propagation which is part of the message, and which controls its spread. I am considering two main types of propagation:

(1) Messages can be started from cell sites which are not homogeneous, and a new level of features can be generated whenever "interesting" message intersections occur. (See discussion of "interesting" below). Messages need not die when they intersect.

(2) Messages can be started from every cell site, and a new level of features can be generated for "homogeneous regions," where homogeniety in this case means that cells have similar features, not necessarily similar gray levels.

The distance a message has propagated is available as a global variable, t; a decaying global variable f(t) = ⌊k/t⌋ is also available for weighting message strengths. The maximum distance messages can travel, if message strengths are multiplied by f(t), is thus controlled by k. In particular, the maximum distance a message can travel is the smallest integer value of t for which ⌈k/t⌉ = 1 (≈ k). For the lowest processing levels, this distance is assumed to be ≪ overall retinal diameter. (Interactions between relatively distant parts of the retina can still be found by later processing layers.)

Each message is retained in each cell for two time units; otherwise messages can "skip over" each other, as shown for a one-dimensional case in figure 5.

---

2. ⌊x⌋ means "largest integer less than x;" ⌈x⌉ means "smallest integer greater than x."

3. I suspect that too much resolution may be lost at this point; eventually I may add an intermediate layer of special processing to go from a complete (236 x 256) array of descriptive information to the array of cells.

Figure 5.

Messages must
be retained in
cells for two
time units
to avoid
"skipping over"
each other.

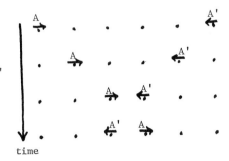

time

and the process begins again. For the most part,
this is the variation considered in this paper.

(2) "Continuous transmission mode"[4]

In this mode feature information is "continuously" transmitted from each cell. In snapshot mode, the distance a message has propagated
can be determined by consulting a single global
"clock"; in continuous transmission mode, it is
not possible to judge whether intersecting
messages have come equal distances, unless each
message also contains a "counter" to keep track
of the distance it has travelled.

3.3 Looking for "interesting" message inter-
       sections

At each cell site, after each time increment, "interesting" message intersections are
found and noted. As an example, if a cell x
lies on a line between two features and is
equidistant from both, and if the features are
reflections of each other with respect to the
line joining them, then there is an increment of
evidence that cell x lies on a symmetry axis
which is perpendicular to the line between the
two features (see extended discussion below of
interesting intersections).

Each time an interesting intersection occurs,
a new feature is created at that cell. The
feature has a type, magnitude and direction,
(although these have different meanings from the
type, magnitude and direction of line and edge
features discussed earlier) and a distance as
well. For example, type can be axis of reflectional symmetry, line completion, corner, subjective contour, texture fragment, etc.
Magnitude is relatively straightforward; it is
computed using message strengths. Direction is
coded by noting the directions from which the
intersecting messages arrived. Distance is the
distance from the origins of the intersecting
messages.

Most of the example which follow in section
4 demonstrate different types of message intersections, and how each can be computed.

3.4 Using message intersection information

Once new features have been found, they
may be used in several ways. In all cases,
features of similar type will be kept separate,
e.g. symmetry axis and corner features are not
mixed.

(1) For each type of feature, a new feature
     is computed, based on the combined evidence
     of a cell and its six neighbors. This is
     done for 1/4 of all cells, as shown in
     figure 7. This is the "ordinary mode" of
     processing.

A message propagating algorithm has been
designed to propagate messages in 12 "dodecants"
$D_1,....,D_{12}$ corresponding to the 12 segments of
a clock. This algorithm will not be described
in detail here, but figure 6 shows the division
of a hexagonal array in the 12 dodecants.

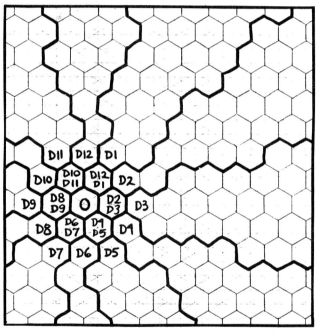

Figure 6. The twelve dodecants $\{D_1, D_2, ...D_{12}\}$
           message propagate in hexagonal wave-
           fronts. D is the origin of a message.

While all my work to date has been on static
pictures, there are two interesting variations
for propagation if we consider a sequence of
pictures (e.g. a movie).

(1) "Snapshot mode".

In snapshot mode, all information propagates
outward synchronously from cells of origin until
all activity ceases, then a new snapshot is taken

4. By "continuous" I mean that (potentially) several messages may leave one cell before the next "snap-
    shot" arrives; greater message strength could be represented by the propagation of more messages,
    much like a neuron firing.

David L. Waltz

Figure 7.

At each cell marked
"x", the six
neighbors are
used to com-
pute a new
feature for
x for the next
layer of pro-
cessing. Cells
marked x form
the hexagonal
array for the
next layer.

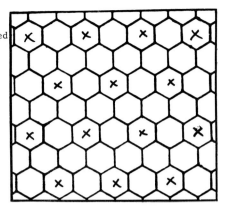

(2) Rather than moving on to the next layer,
features at a given layer can be used to
selectively focus attention and adjust
thresholds. As an example, if a feature
point may lie on a line completion, the
original scene can be examined to see if
there is any evidence, perhaps much weaker
than would ordinarily be considered, to
support this interpretation.

(3) Since direction and distance of the original
feature points from the intersecting cell
sites are available, "interesting" portions
of the original scene can be grouped, enhanced or selected (e.g. one could generate or enhance feature points which had
a symmetry relation with other feature
points). These points can be found by
simply "running the process backward,"
an operation I will call retransforming.
This processing should become clearer once
the examples are presented.

4. Examples of processing using the model

Once we have defined the overall model, it
is quite simple to generate algorithms for recognizing various scene patterns. For purposes
of exposition, I will only show single layer
algorithms for computing patterns; in a full
vision system one would use layered processes,
e.g. once symmetry axis candidate features were
isolated, a line completion algorithm would be
applied to the features, etc. Assume that all
retinal features are edges (not lines or gradients); this makes all example expressions much
simpler. It should be clear by the end of
this section how lines could be similarly dealt
with.

4.1 Example 1 - Axes of Reflectional Symmetry

Some problems with the use of prairie fire
methods to find symmetry axes were mentioned
earlier. These included (1) knowing where to
start fires, (2) dissimilar skeletons for
similar figures, and (3) skeletons which do not
correspond to what we would judge as symmetry
axes.

As a first example of the use of this
model, consider the points of a scene for
which $F_{rs} > 0$, where

$$F_{rs} = f(t)m_1 m_2 \delta(D_1, D_2 + \pi) [\delta(D_1, d_1) \delta(D_2, d_2)$$
$$+ \delta(D_1, d_1 + \pi) \ \delta(D_2, d_2 + \pi)]$$

In this expression, $f(t)$ is a global distance
decay function (described above) each m_i is
a local feature magnitude; and D_i is the
message propagation direction; each d_i is
a local feature brightness gradient direction;

and $\delta(x,y) = \begin{cases} 1 & \text{if } x=y \\ 0 & \text{otherwise} \end{cases}$.

The following expansion should help understand
the components of this expression F_{rs}:

$\delta(D_1, D_2 + \pi)$ ensures parallel edges (within
about 30°)

$\delta(D_1, d_1)$ ensures that the direction of
$\delta(D_2, d_2)$ message propagation is the same
                      as the direction of the gradient
or

$\delta(D_1, d_1 + \pi)$ message propagation is 180° from
$\delta(D_2, d_2 + \pi)$ the direction of the gradient.

The situation which leads to a maximum F_{rs}
value for the intersection of two cells is
shown in figure 8. Figure 9 illustrates the fact
that variations of rectangles lead to similar
axes, a desirable property not shared by prairie
fire schemes.

Note that: (1) the axes (and retransformed
figures) are longer than the original figure;
this is because messages are propagated in a
sector, so that messages from two points meet
along a line. (2) Since all axes are similar,
retransformed figures are also similar (recall
that axis points contain information about the
local feature magnitude and direction as well
as the message directions). The use of a
retransforming process suggests a way of finding
"shape envelopes" of objects, even if the
objects may be locally incomplete or varied, or
if noise is present. (3) Because directions are
quantized within 30° sectors, edges need not be
exactly parallel in order to yield a symmetry
axis with F_{rs}; some interaction of edges which
are even less parallel could easily be added by
redefining F_{rs} to be less restrictive. This
may be desirable to avoid problems with edges
lying on the boundary of angle sectors.
(4) Strength of interaction varies along the
axes; this is not represented in figure 9, or
other figures in this section.

4.2 Example 2 - Corner Finder

Finding corners has long been a problem for
line-finders. Ofter line finders (e.g. Hueckl [7],
Horn-Binford [6]) produce line drawings like the
one in figure 10; the reason is that line/edge
finders use "templates" which are maximally
sensitive to edges and thus relatively insensitive
to corners.

Figure 8.

Schematic representation of maximum strength intersection of F_{rs}. Rotating d_1 and d_2 180° gives same intersection strength.

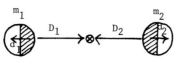

Figure 9.

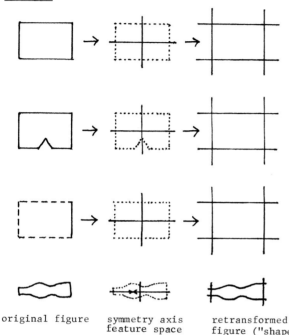

| original figure | symmetry axis feature space (solid lines) | retransformed figure ("shape envelope") |

Figure 10.

Line finders often miss corners.

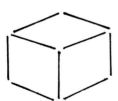

Often corners must be hypothesized and filled in by higher levels of processing. In constrast, people seem to be more sensitive to corners than to lines, rather than less sensitive; as an example, figure 11 shows "Attneave's cat" [1], which was formed by joining points with highest curvature by straight lines.

Corners may be found by marking points where $F_{cf} > 0$, where

Figure 11.

Attneave's cat

$$F_{cf} = f(t)m_1 m_2 [\delta(D_1, d_1 + \frac{\pi}{2}) \ \delta(D_2, d_2 + \frac{\pi}{2})$$
$$+ \delta(D_1, d_1 - \frac{\pi}{2}) \ \delta(D_2, d_2 - \frac{\pi}{2})] |\sin(D_1 - D_2)|$$

In this expression

$\delta(D_1, d_1 + \pi/2)$ — ensures that messages propagate along edges (90° away from the edge gradient)
$\delta(D_2, d_2 + \pi/2)$
$\delta(D_1, d_1 - \pi/2)$
$\delta(D_2, d_2 - \pi/2)$

$|\sin(D_1 - D_2)|$ — gives a maximum interaction for 90° corners.

By using variations (e.g. replacing $|\sin(D_1 - D_2)|$ with some other function of D_1 and D_2) F_{cf} could be made most sensitive to a broad range of angles.

Note that F_{cf} gives similar markings whether a corner is "sharp" or "rounded", as shown in figure 12b.

Figure 12.

(a) Schematic diagram for maximum corner finding interaction.

(b) Results of "corner finder", F_{cf}. Darkened areas are marked most heavily by F_{cf}.

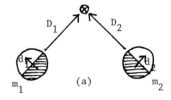

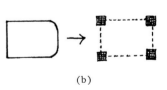

4.3 Example 3 - Edge Completion

To find plausible edge completions, $F_{ec} > 0$ can be used, where

$$F_{ec} = f(t)m_1 m_2 [\delta(D_1, d_1 + \pi/2) \ \delta(D_2, d_2 - \pi/2)$$
$$+ \delta(D_1, d_1 - \pi/2)\delta(D_2, d_2 + \pi/2)] \ \delta(D_1, D_2 + \pi)$$

David L. Waltz

In this expression:

$\delta(D_1, d_1 + \pi/2)$ ensure message propagation along
$\delta(D_2, d_2 - \pi/2)$ edges (90° away from edge gradient);
$\delta(D_1, d_1 - \pi/2)$
$\delta(D_2, d_2 + \pi/2)$

$\delta(D_1, D_2 + \pi)$ ensures that contributing elements are approximately aligned; along with products of terms above, ensures that proper relation of edge fragments exists (see figure 13a).

Figure 13.

(a) Maximum edge completion inter-action.

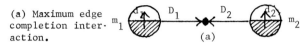

(b) Results of line completion using $F_{\ell c}$

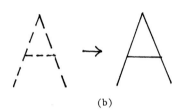

Using similar ideas, we can also define function $F_{\ell c}$ which can find <u>line</u> completion evidence. Lines are assumed to have a "pseudo-gradient," d_i, which is perpendicular to the line fragment direction at i, and which takes its values from the set $\{D_1, D_2, \ldots, D_6\}$. Let us also define ℓ_i, the line predicate, to be 1 if there is a line gragment at i and 0 otherwise. (Similarly e_i, the edge predicate, should be added to functions defined earlier if we assume that both lines and edges can occur.) Using these definitions we can define a line completion function $F_{\ell c}$ to be:

$$F_{\ell c} = f(t) m_1 m_2 \ell_1 \ell_2 [\delta(D_1, d_1 + \pi/2) \delta(D_2, d_2 - \pi/2)$$
$$+ \delta(D_1, d_1 - \pi/2) \delta(D_2, d_2 + \pi/2)] \delta(D_1, D_2 + \pi)$$

Inspection shows that $F_{\ell c}$ is the same as F_{ec} except for the inclusion of ℓ_1 and ℓ_2. The results of applying $F_{\ell c}$ are shown in figure 13b.

Note here that in order to completely fill in a dashed line, either (a) the dashes must be longer than the spaces between dashes, or (b) we must overlay the dashed figure and line completion, and repeat the process (recursively, or with more than one processing layer), or (c) we could assume continuous transmission of messages from each "feature point." One of these methods is clearly necessary to solve the "constellation problem" (see figure 14), since

Figure 14.

The "constellation problem;" line completion only finds points marked "x"

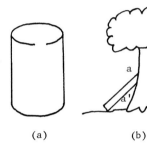

in snapshot mode, only points halfway between "stars" will be marked by $F_{\ell c}$. In contrast, in continuous transmission mode messages would constantly be propagated from each star, and would thus meet other oncoming messages head on at all points along the line between two adjacent stars.

Continuous transmission mode may also be more plausible as a model of human vision if we identify cells with neurons, and assume that neurons can fire more or less continuously.[5]

This method of line completion can take care of some classic problems of imperfect or occluded line drawings (see figure 15). It also

Figure 15.

Imperfect and occluded line drawings which can be completed by $F_{\ell c}$

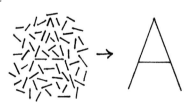

(a)   (b)

is subject to something like the same illusion of a bent stick seen by people, given in figure 15b, since the distance a-b' is shorter than a-b or a'-b, and with the $\pm 30°$ tolerance on directions, a-b' is as "straight" as a-b or a'-b. Thus the "phantom line" a-b' will be given heavier weight (due to the fact that message weights have decayed less) than a-b or a'b'.

This method is also able to find coherent figures in noise, as shown in figure 16.

Figure 16.

Figure can be found in noise by $F_{\ell c}$

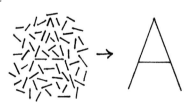

---

5. The author has attempted to provide here a model which has neurophysiological plausibility.

4.4   Example 4 - Binocular Range-Finding

To find the range of points in a scene, correlation of edges can be easily formalized in the model, by the following steps:

1. Assume that we have a left and a right view of some scene (L and R) plus points at infinity P_L and P_R, shared by both.[6] Overlay the two views, using the P_L and P_R to align them such that points in the left view <u>all</u> lie to the right of their corresponding points in the right view.

2. Propagate messages $\{m_L, d_L, D_9\}$ and $\{m_R, d_R, D_3\}$ from points in the left view and right view respectively (see figure 17).

Figure 17.

Finding depth
from binocular
images

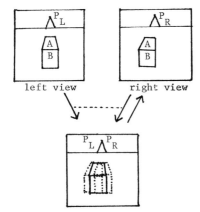

3. Use F_{br}, where $F_{br} = f(t) \delta(d_L, d_R) \delta(D_L, D_R)^7$ <u>Messages</u> <u>die</u> <u>when</u> <u>they</u> <u>intersect</u>. Save values of t for intersections. (Note that gradient values corresponding to approximately horizontal edges give very little depth information, since a message from <u>any</u> point on a horizontal edge in one view will match a message from <u>any</u> point on a horizontal edge in the other view.)

4. The points of message intersections, marked with distance values, may now (a) be used to judge distance - larger distances for intersecting messages correspond to points closer to the "eye"; (b) by retransforming back to one or the other view, a depth map can be overlayed on the scene. (Most people seem to map depth information back onto the view of the right eye; when the right eye blinks, the view seems to "jump", but it does not jump when the left eye blinks.)

Problems: Many remain. Most seriously, if a number of edges can correspond in the two views, it may be difficult to judge which constitutes the "true" correspondence.

4.5   Example 5 - Subjective Contours

It is also possible by slight extension of edge completion ideas to deal with "subjective contours" (see example in figure 18a).

Figure 18.

Subjective
contours with
straight edges;
these also suffer
from the
"constellation
problem"

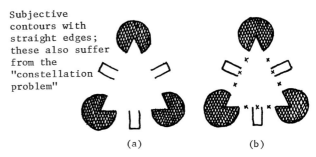

(a)   (b)

In the simplest model, messages are transmitted from "sources" as shown in figure 19.

Figure 19.

Subjective
contour
"message
sources"

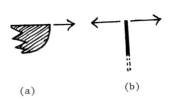

(a)   (b)

Note that the message source in figure 19a is already effectively generated by allowing only intersections of edge messages with property

$$[\delta(d_i, D_i + \pi/2) + \delta(d_i, D_i - \pi/2)] = 1.$$

These messages must be allowed to match messages from a truncated line as in figure 19b. (These truncated lines are suggestive of edges being occluded by a surface, and apparently this cue is a very strong one for people in the detection of the presence of surfaces.)

This process is subject to the same difficulties as the "constellation problem": unless sources transmit continuously, or unless the processing is applied recursively only points marked "x" in figure 18b will be found as intersections.

---

6.   This is not essential, but makes the process easier to state and understand.

7.   This equation assumes that viewing angles are close enough that corresponding edges have exactly the same d value in each view. This condition could be made less restrictive by replacing $\delta(d_L, d_R)$ with $(\delta(d_L, d_R) + \delta(d_L, d_R + \pi/2) + \delta(d_L, d_R - \pi/2))$, i.e. by allowing matches between local feature directions which differ by small angles.

Messages here are $\{t,d,D\}$ where d is the ordinary gradient (perpendicular to the straight edge) in figure 19a, and collinear with the terminated line in figure 19b. Intersections are marked in F_{sc} >, where

$$F_{sc} = f(t)m_1m_2[\delta(d_1,D_1+\pi/2)\ ^\delta(d_2,D_2-\pi/2)$$

$$+\ \delta(d_1,D_1-\pi/2)\ ^\delta(d_2,D_2+\pi/2)]$$

$$^\delta(D_1,D_2+\pi).$$

Here we are basically assuming that truncated lines generate messages that look like edges from points perpendicular to the line's end. F_{sc} is the same as F_{ec}, which I believe is as it should be.

This process works well for subjective contours like those in figure 18 (made up of nearly straight edges), but it has problems with examples like the one in figure 20, which can be

Figure 20.

Ambiguous subjective contour; may be seen as a square or a circle. (Hold at a distance)

seen as either square or circle. This example suggests that (a) more global processing is going on than we have postulated in this example; the contour in figure 20 is not seen as a part circle-part square, and (b) curved subjective surfaces are not well handled, except for ones with very slight curvature (note that the model does not transmit only in straight lines). See Ullman [13] for a treatment of these problems from a different point of view. While I have not worked out all details, I believe that Ullman's methods could be transferred to and represented fairly easily in this model.

4.6 Textures

First a caveat; I have only begun to work out details of handling textures, although I am encouraged by my progress to date.

Textures can only be handled in the model by using layered processors. By "handling textures", I mean grouping together regions of the same or similar texture characteristics; I do not mean identifying the texture. In fact I believe that grouping regions of similar texture is done by the human visual system prior to (and without necessarily ever)

identifying the texture by name, and that this grouping is "non-purposive" to use Rosenfeld's phrase, i.e. done automatically independent of the current top-level task.

Why must processing be layered? Because textures can occur at different levels of resolution. Consider Figure 21. At the finest

Figure 21.

Hierarchical texture; texture varies with "resolution", i.e. size of message propagation area

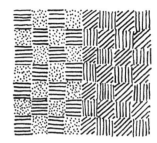

level of resolution, there are four textures: (a) dots, (b) horizontal lines, (c) diagonal lines, and (d) vertical lines. At a lower resolution there are two textures (a) and (b) together, and (c) and (d) together. At a still lower resolution, the entire figure could constitute a texture element, and so on.

How should texture be characterized? First, texture description should be independent of directionality of the texture. We characterize wood grain or corduroy or cloth without necessarily specifying vertical wood grain, etc. Second, relative local directions are important; while the overall "direction" of a texture (e.g. wood grain) is unimportant, local directions must have particular relations with each other. Third, texture should be describable independent of scale; the texture of a field is judged to be similar, but to become "finer" at greater distances. This suggests that all layers of a texture-recognizing model should be similar in operation, differing only in resolution, and that boundaries between regions with different textures should be described at all levels with a vocabulary of symbols similar to those which describe boundaries at the lowest levels. Thus at higher levels of processing regions with similar texture should be treated as homogeneous, analogous to retinal regions with uniform illumination. Features at higher levels can thus be texture discontinuities.

The problem then boils down to this: we need to have a process which begins with a plane of cells marked with features and homogeneous regions, and ends with adjacent groups of cells marked with the same values if the cells belong to a region having similar feature distributions. This output can then be used to find a new set of features; features arise in regions which contain "edges" separating regions with different feature distributions.

One simple type of characterization of a region around a cell is a histogram of the features occurring within the region. Such a histogram has certain problems: it requires

many bits per cell to store, it would thus be
expensive to compare the histograms of adjacent
cells, and most seriously, a histogram alone
clearly cannot account for texture differences
people perceive. (E.g. a black and white
checkerboard is perceived as a very different
texture from a random distribution of equal
numbers of black and white squares.)

I am currently working on schemes for
representing feature distributions in local
regions which (1) are compact, (2) are easy to
compute by the model, and (3) display a plausible
similarity metric with that judged by humans.
Some work involves using features from other
transform spaces (e.g. line completion) as
possible texture features. Critical to the
process of making the descriptions compact are
a measure of (1) orderliness, (what proportion
of features have matching features within a
region surrounding each feature?); (2) frequency
(are these matching features located at similar
distances?); and (3) directionality (are
matching features related by similar angles?).
These measures are all intuitively important
in describing textures, and relatively easy to
compute using the suggested model. Future papers
will describe this texture processing in greater
detail.

5. Preliminary Results

Figure 22 shows the spread of a signal from a
point of origin. Note that the wavefront is
always shaped like a hexagon. 0,1,...,9 stand for
$D_{12}, D_1, ..., D_9$ respectively, t stands for D_{10} (ten)
and e for D_{11} (eleven); these show the direction
each message is travelling.

Figure 23(a) shows a rectangle made up of
continuous lines on the top and right side, and
dashed lines on the bottom and left side. Each
"O" is a feature point origin of messages.
Figure 23(b) shows the equivalent line drawing.
This rectangle would have an area of about 1% of
a digitized TV image.

Figure 23(c) shows the result of the operator
F_{ec} for finding edges and edge completions. On
this and succeeding figures, the numbers represent
the value of

$$\left\lfloor \log_2 \left[40 \sum_{t=1}^{\infty} \frac{\langle \text{number of messages matched at time t} \rangle}{t^2} \right] \right\rfloor$$

for each cell. The number 40 was chosen arbitrarily
to make the numbers shown come out in a reasonable
range for printing.

(This scoring system is not satisfactory, and
will soon be replaced with one which divides by t^2
instead of $t+3$, and which takes the log of the
overall result.)

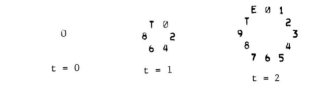
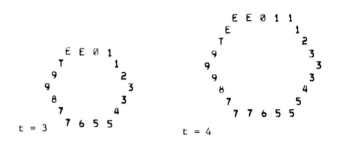
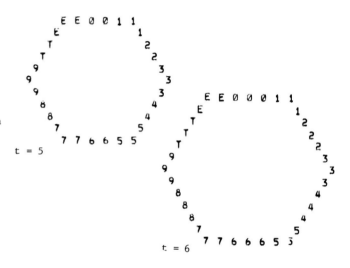
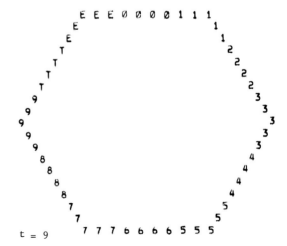

<u>Figure 22</u>

Spread of messages from a single point.

184   David L. Waltz

Figure 23(d) shows a similar result for the reflectional symmetry function F_{rs}, and Figure 23(e) shows the results of the corner finding function F_{cf}. Actual corners of Figure 23(a) are marked with boxes in Figure 23(e).

The program to implement the processing is being written by George Hadden; we hope to have many more results, including ones for real scenes, to report soon.

Figure 23

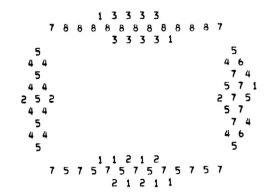

```
          1 3 3 3 3
    7 8 8 8 8 8 8 8 8 8 8 8 8 8 7
          3 3 3 3 1
    5                           5
    4 4                         4 6
    5                           7 4
    4 4                         5 7 1
  2 5 2                       2 7 5
    4 4                         5 7
    5                           7 4
    4 4                         4 6
    5                           5
          1 1 2 1 2
    7 5 7 5 7 5 7 5 7 5 7 5 7
          2 1 2 1 1
```

(c) Results of "edge completion" function F_{ec} after propagation and matching on (a).

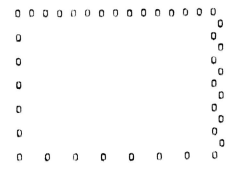

```
0 0 0 0 0 0 0 0 0 0 0 0 0 0 0 0
                               0
0                            0
                               0
0                            0
                               0
0                            0
                               0
0                            0
                               0
0                            0
                               0
0    0    0    0    0    0    0    0
```

(a) A rectangle made up of solid lines (top and right) and dashed lines (bottom and left).

```
                0 1
                  2 0
                  3 3
                    3 1
                  3 3
                    3 1
                  3 3
2 3 4 3 4 3 4 3 5 3 4 3 4 3 4 3 2
                  3 3
                    3 1
                  3 3
                    3 1
                  3 3
                    3 0
                0 0
```

(d) Results of "reflectional symmetry axis" function F_{rs} on (a).

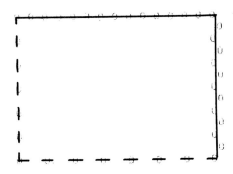

(b) Lines superimposed to represent real figure which would give rise to rectangle in (a).

```
1 2 2 2 2                0 2 2 2 2 2 0
0 3 3 3 3 1              1 4 6 6 4 3
1 5 [7] 3 2              0 2 6 [7] 6 4 1
0 4 4 4 3 1             0 3 4 4 4 3
1 1 1 1 1               1 3 3 3 3 1
```

```
0 1 0 1 0               0 0 0 0 0
0 1 1 2 1 0             0 2 4 4 4 0
1 2 [5] 4 0 0           2 3 [6] 5 3 0
0 1 3 4 3 0            0 2 3 3 3 0
0 0 0 0 0 0            1 2 1 2 1 0
0 0 0 0 0 0 0
```

(e) Results of "corner finding" function F_{cf} on (a). Actual positions of corners are marked with boxes.

References

1. Arnheim, R., _Art and Visual Perception_, University of California Press, Berkeley, 1954.

2. Bajcsy, R., Computer Description of Textured Surfaces, _3IJCAI_, Stanford Univ., 1973.

3. Blum, H., A Transformation for Extracting New Descriptors of Shape, Symposium on Models for the Perception of Speech and Visual Form, Boston, Mass., Nov. 1964. (I have never seen this, but it is acknowledged generally as the original idea source.)

4. Calabi, L., and Hartnett, W. E., Shape Recognition, Prairie Fires, Convex Deficiencies and Skeletons, Scientific Report No. 1, Parke Mathematical Laboratories, Carlisle, Mass., Feb. 1966.

5. Freuder, E. C., Synthesizing Constraint Expressions, Memo No. 370, MIT AI Lab., July 1976.

6. Horn, B. K. P., The Binford-Horn LINE-FINDER, Memo No. 285, MIT AI Lab., July 1971.

7. Hueckl, M., An Operator Which Locates Edges in Digitized Pictures, _JACM_, October 1973.

8. Marr, D., Early Processing of Visual Information, Memo No. 340, MIT AI Lab., 1975

9. Marr, D., A Note on the Computation of Binocular Disparity in a Symbolic, Low-Level Vision Processor, Memo. No. 327, MIT AI Lab., Dec. 1974.

10. Marr, D. and Nishihara, H. K., Spacial Disposition of Axes in a Generalized Cylinder Representation of Objects that Do Not Encompass the Viewer, Memo. No. 341, MIT AI Lab., Dec. 1975.

11. Marr, D., Analysis of Occluding Contour, Memo. No. 372, MIT AI Lab., Oct. 1976.

12. Riseman, E. M. and Hanson, A. R., Preprocessing Cones: A Computational Structure for Scene Analysis. COINS Technical Report 74C-7, Univ. of Mass., Sept. 1974.

13. Rosenfeld, A., Hummel, R. A., and Zucker, S. W., Scene Labelling by Relaxation Operations, Tech. Rpt. TR-379, Computer Science Center, Univ. of Maryland, May 1975.

14. Uhr, L., "Recognition Cones," and Some Test Results; The Imminent Arrival of Well-Structured Parallel-Serial Computers; Positions, and Positions on Positions. _Adv. Papers of the Workshop on Computer Vision_, Univ. of Mass., Amberst, June 1977.

15. Ullman, S., Filling-in the Gaps: The Shape of Subjective Contours and a Model for their Generation, Memo No. 367, MIT AI Lab., Oct. 1976.

16. Waltz, D. L., Generating Semantic Descriptions from Drawings of Scenes with Shadows, Tech. Rpt., AI-TR-271, MIT AI Lab., Nov. 1972.

17. Waltz, D. L., Understanding Scenes with Shadows, in Winston (ed.), _The Psychology of Computer Vision_, McGraw-Hill, N.Y., 1975.

18. Waltz, D. L., Automata Theoretic Approach to Visual Processing, in Yeh (ed.), _Applied Computation Theory_, Prentice-Hall, Englewood Cliffs, N.J., 1976.

David L. Waltz

VERTICAL AND HORIZONTAL PROCESSES IN LOW LEVEL VISION

Steven W. Zucker
Department of Electrical Engineering
McGill University
3480 University Street
Montreal, Canada

ABSTRACT

Low-level vision is plagued with many sources of ambiguity and noise. To counteract these disturbances, partial results from many different cooperating and competing processes can be used. This paper exemplifies the possibilities for process interaction in terms of two parallel relaxation labelling processes: one for labelling the functional roles that dots can play in clusters and one for computing similarity groupings. Both of these processes are horizontal in the sense that they attempt to achieve consistent labellings across all positions but at a single level of abstraction. Vertical relaxation labelling processes, which provide the structures for interprocess communication, are also described. These attempt to achieve consistent labellings across several levels of abstraction but over a single projected spatial position. Such use of mathematically identical vertical and horizontal processes creates a structure for complex understanding systems that is uniform enough to permit the theoretical study of other components also present in these systems. In particular, it is shown that the choice of a scheduling algorithm can effect the system's terminal state.

1. INTRODUCTION

The complexity of vision systems has given rise to sundry points of view about how the world is seen. One of these, that vision is a process in which a descriptive structure is abstracted from a given intensity array, is especially appropriate for computer vision systems. We attempt to use it to study several aspects of the organization of vision. One of the first barriers that we must overcome is that there are an enormous number of possible descriptions that can be abstracted from one particular intensity array. One time-honored organizational solution for coping with the complexity that this creates is to partition the processing into levels, each of which defines a stable, intermediate data description. Then processing proceeds by computing and using these successively more abstract descriptions of the data.

There is a second argument for the need to conceptualize distinct levels of processing within vision systems. It involves the specific data structures on which algorithms operate, and it centers around what psychologists refer to as constructive perception. If certain structures or properties are prerequisite for algorithms at a given level of processing, then their computation must precede this level. Presumably, such are the roles that explicit line end points and local orientation axes play for grouping algorithms, and that subjective contours and pseudo-edges play for shape and figure analyses. Other examples include more abstract constructs such as are necessary for forming relational patterns.

Although the distinct levels of processing may differ drastically in terms of specific computations, purposes, and types of knowledge employed, there is one problem common to all of them: the presence of ambiguity and noise. Ambiguity derives from the non-unique character of visual symbols and noise derives from physical sensors, quantization errors, and the like. Both can be treated analogously because both derive from one-to-many or from many-to-one relationships. For example, a particular line symbol may be part of many figural patterns while many continuous orientations may be indicated by a single quantized variable.

For systems to operate in the presence of ambiguity and noise, it is manditory that they be structured in a closed-loop, feedback configuration (Zucker, 1977). When the goal state is known explicitly, then feedback from the current state of the system can repeatedly be compared with the final goal state to determine the next step of activity. Or, when the goal state is only defined implicitly through criteria such as consistency relations, then techniques such as iterative constraint satisfaction can be used. For both of these cases, the important point is that without this iterative comparison, the corrupting influence of noise might not be detected until many incorrect (or unnecessary) computations have been performed. Furthermore, to reduce such incorrect computation to a minimal level, feedback should be as local as possible. Otherwise, when many computations take place before erronous activity is detected, extensive backtracking and, possibly, thrashing result.

Thus, two reasonable guidelines for developing a conceptual architecture of vision systems would seem to be that (1) it should be organizable into levels and that (2) it should contain closed-loop, feedback mechanisms. It can further be argued that the processing at each of these levels should be knowledge-based. In the light of the feedback requirement, this observation implies that the knowledge employed will, in part, enter into the feedback mechanisms. For example, knowledge about the semantic (or physical world) compatibilities between objects can be used to determine symbolic constraints between abstract labels for those objects. These can then be used within constraint-satisfaction algorithms.

The kind of knowledge employed can be structured to vary with level. At the lower levels the knowledge should be more general purpose while, as the level of abstraction increases, it can become more domain specific. Two different kinds of arguments can be advanced to support this claim for systems that are even weakly general purpose (i.e., designed to deal with a number of different classes of inputs) or with a capability for extension (Zucker, Rosenfeld, and Davis, 1975). First, while specific expectations can be used to facilitate image understanding, it is questionable how early they should (or need to) be used. People are certainly capable of seeing unexpected and un-familiar scenes and of describing their line, edge, and region content. Furthermore, certain depth relationships and surface impressions are strikingly apparent even in totally foreign classes of imagery such as electron photomicrographs. These observations suggest that processing can be largely data-directed at the lower levels and that it should be aimed at computing descriptions that make the above kinds of features explicit. E.g., knowledge about good continuation can be used to obtain descriptions of the lines in many kinds of images (Zucker, 1976b). It is not necessary to know the precise type of scene underlying the image.

The second argument for using more general purpose processes at the lower levels concerns computational efficiency. While it is in prin-ciple possible to hypothesize that a given image depicts a specific arrangement of finitely many objects, in practice it is impossible to enumerate and then to consider all of these possibilities. If, however, descriptions are computed at various levels of abstraction, then the elimination of a possibility at a lower level in effect eliminates all of the higher-level possibilities that derive from it. This notion of data reduction is directly analogous to implicit enumeration in mathematical programming.

In our paper, we emphasize the low-level end of vision processing, with its respective use of general purpose knowledge. One of the reasons that we chose to do this is that it is a fairly autonomous component of vision systems that is rich enough to exemplify many of the problems, yet restricted enough to be approachable.

2. EDGE-BASED AND REGION-BASED APPROACHES TO LOW-LEVEL VISION

One purpose of low-level vision is to build a description of the intensity patterns in an image. Since these patterns can be described in two com-plimentary ways, i.e., as similarity patterns and as difference patterns, two different classes of approaches have evolved to compute the low-level

descriptions. The first-class, region growing, has been developed to take advantage of the similarity relationships over patterns (see Zucker, 1976a, for a recent survey). The second class, which attempts to delimit the edge and line content in images, is based on local difference patterns (e.g., Riseman and Arbib, 1977).

Since these two classes of algorithms operate on data models which are strongly complimentary, many systems attempt to use one technique to improve upon the results of the other. For example, edge-based heuristic rules can be used to enhance an ambiguous response from a region-growing algorithm (Brice & Fennema, 1970), while region-based grouping rules can be used to improve the interpretation of responses from edge detection operators (Marr, 1976). While such sequential control strategies can function well in clear-cut situations, their per-formance in noisy or ambiguous situations may not be as good. Implicit constraints, imposed by the strict ordering of the edge and region based pro-cesses, can block intermediate or partial responses from influencing each other properly. In order to allow these two different classes of processes to interact uniformly, they need to be run simultan-eously in an environment which facilitates the nec-essary interprocess communication. A parallel coop-erative/competitive computational framework can provide this environment, so that edge processes operating at a given pictorial position can cooperate with other edge processes operating at neighboring pictorial positions while they are competing with the progress of a region growing process. Similarly, region-growing processes can cooperate with neigh-boring region-growing processes while competing with an edge process. Note that both cooperation and com-petition are necessary to provide the proper balance and control for reaching equilibrium solutions, or, in other words, for implementing implicit feedback between possibilities. This iterative cooperative/ competitive computation is described in terms of both a dot process, which attempts to describe the functional roles that dots appear to be playing as part of clusters, and a Gestalt-like similarity grouping process. This second process, which acts at a slightly more abstract level than the dot process, attempts to describe the inter-dot links that actually define the clusters. Both of these computations, i.e. the labelling or naming of primitive objects (e.g., dots) and the labelling or naming of abstract relations over these objects (i.e. the links) appear to be fundamental kinds of computations present at many different levels of early visual processing.

3. LABELLING DOT CLUSTERS

Dot patterns provide a simplified domain in which experiments with computational techniques for low-level vision can be conducted. The spatial density of dots is analogous to the distribution of gray levels in an an image. For example, a dense cluster of dots would correspond to a dark region in an image. Or, a thin light region (in the limit, a line) between two dark regions would be analogous to a sparse valley between two clusters. A low-level representation for an image requires at least a description of the edge, line, and region content in that image. For dot clusters such a description would require identifying and then labelling dots which are interior to clusters, dots which are functioning as part of the border around

Steven W. Zucker

clusters, and isolated dots which are lying outside or between clusters. Furthermore, a description of the shapes of the regions in an image would be analogous to a description of the shapes of the dot clusters, although the uses to which these descriptions would be put probably differ.

In order to identify the functional roles that dots are playing in a particular pattern, a model for the structure of dot patterns is needed. Since every dot pattern is equally likely a priori, this model should be general purpose in the sense discussed in Sec. 1. Or, more specifically, it should not contain any a priori biases for specific dot configurations. Beginning with the presupposition that dot clusters have some spatial extent, such a model can be stated implicitly in terms of relationships between pairs of dots. It should embody the observations that, for a rich set of dot patterns, (1) interior points will be located close (with respect to the average spacing) to neighboring interior points. This condition amounts to an assumption that most neighboring interior points will belong to the same cluster. (2) Interior points will be on the inside of edges and noise points will be on the exterior side. (3) Noise points, because they are lying outside of clusters, will be relatively far away from interior points.

This kind of model can be used by a relaxation labelling process to disambiguate the assignment of functional labels to dots in a pattern (Zucker and Hummel, 1977). Relaxation labelling processes (RLP) are computational schemes for updating the set of possible interpretive labels for an object on the basis of the current sets of interpretive labels for neighboring objects (Rosenfeld, Hummel, and Zucker, 1976). They allow the various possibilities to cooperate and compete with one another in parallel until a mutual equilibrium is achieved. This final equilibrium is based on a notion of data base consistency (Zucker, 1976b). For dot patterns, the labels indicate assertions about whether the dots are INTERIOR* to a cluster, are EDGE points bordering a cluster, or are isolated NOISE points lying outside of a cluster. The EDGE assertions carry, in addition, a local orientation quantized into 45° steps over the entire 360° range. This is necessary since EDGE assertions must indicate which side of the EDGE points toward the interior of the cluster. Thus there are ten possible labels: eight oriented EDGE labels, an INTERIOR label, and a NOISE label.

Since it is possible for any of these labels to describe the role a dot is playing in a given pattern, all of these labels are initially attached to each dot. They are ordered by an index in the range [0,1] which is an estimate of the probability $p_i(\lambda)$ that label λ is correct for dot i. A neighbor relation over the dots is introduced so that each dot is connected to its K-nearest neighbors, and the distance relationships between these neighboring dots are used to compute the initial probabilities for each label. If a dot is very close to the center of gravity of its K neighbors, then it is biased toward being an INTERIOR. If it is a median distance from its

*The actual label assertions are indicated by capital letters.

neighbors and they are predominantly to one side, then it is biased toward being an oriented EDGE point. Finally, if it is far from its neighbors, then it is biased toward being a NOISE point.

These initial probabilities are updated on the basis of the probabilities distributed over neighboring label sets and the current label probabilities. (For a specific discussion of the updating rule, see sec. 6.) The model for dot clusters is used at this point so that INTERIOR points are supported by (i.e., cooperate with) (i) nearby neighboring INTERIOR points, (ii) EDGE points with the proper orientation, and (iii) NOISE points which are far away. EDGE points are oriented properly if the indicated INTERIOR point is on the cluster side of the EDGE. EDGE points are supported by (i) INTERIOR and (ii) NOISE points on the proper sides and (iii) nearby EDGE points with proper orientations. That is, EDGE points support each other if they form a locally continuous curve. On the other hand, INTERIOR points which destroy the good continuation of EDGES detract support, as do INTERIOR and NOISE points on the incorrect sides of an EDGE. The model is specifically embedded into the RLP through compatibility functions such as:

$$r_{ij}(\text{INTERIOR, INTERIOR}) = W_{II}(e^{-\alpha_{II}d} - C_{II}).$$

This compatibility indicates that an INTERIOR label on dot i is supported by an INTERIOR label on dot j by a function of the distance d separating them: for small distances the support is positive and for large distances it is negative. An exponential function was chosen because, if support is considered to travel in straight lines through a viscous medium, it would follow such a law. The constant W_{II} indicates the maximum support at $d \approx 0$, α_{II} the rate at which support decreases with distance, and C_{II} the negative support at large distances.(For the following experiments, the values $W_{II} = 1.0$, $\alpha_{II} = 0.5$, and $C_{II} = 0.1$ were selected.) Compatibility functions involving EDGEs further require an angular component, e.g.,

$$r_{ij}(\text{INTERIOR,EDGE}) = \cos\theta \, e^{-\alpha_{IE}d}.$$

θ is the angle between the vector joining points i and j and the orientation of the EDGE label. It guarantees that INTERIOR points are only strengthened by EDGEs if they are on the cluster side of the EDGE. (For a detailed discussion of the remaining compatibilities, see Zucker and Hummel, 1977.)

An example of this process operating on a figure-eight shaped cluster (after Zahn, 1971) is shown in Fig. 1. If the termination (or fixed) point for the RLP is defined as that iteration in which all the label probabilities remain unchanged (i.e., within an ε-bound), it is clear that all the points in this example become uniquely labelled except for those few in the center of the figure. That is, the probability attached to most of the displayed labels has attained the value one, while the probabilities for the other labels on those dots have gone to zero. For the uncertain points, the accumulated local evidence is insufficient for determining whether this example consists of two circular clusters which are just touching or one figure-eight shaped cluster. That is, the final probability measure is distributed over the INTERIOR and EDGE labels. (Note: only the maximum probability labels are displayed in the figure and, because of the coarse quantization of the EDGE orientations, the final EDGE probability was spread over two adjacent orientations. Thus, although the distribution was approximately 50% EDGE and 50% INTERIOR, the INTERIOR was displayed). The distribution of final probabilities makes the particular ambiguity in this figure explicit, and suggests that a more informed process is necessary to resolve it. However, the process was powerful enough to remove all of the other ambiguities in the initial detectors' responses. Additional examples and further discussion of this RLP are in Zucker (1976b) and Zucker and Hummel (1977).

4. THE SEQUENTIAL APPEARANCE OF PARALLEL RLP

The RLP for labelling dot clusters provides a framework in which various processes can co-operate and compete with one another until a mutual equilibrium is obtained. The label sets can be organized into two separate types: the INTERIOR and NOISE labels and the EDGE labels. These label types, together with the appropriate compatibilities, define the region-based and the edge-based subprocesses. Cooperation within a subprocess is determined by mutual compatibility functions, e.g., EDGE-EDGE compatibilities, while competition between processes is determined by the cross compatibilities, e.g., EDGE-INTERIOR.

Although these processes are operating simultaneously, there is a strong sequential appearance to their output. This takes the form of local centers where activity appears to be taking place, such as is illustrated by the example in Fig. 1. The initialization operator only returns strong responses for a few of the most interior points, and labels many of the edge points incorrectly as INTERIOR or NOISE. However, after 5 iterations, many of the INTERIOR labels became highly certain of their interpretation as if a grouping operation had been taking place over the most certain points first. Thus, where appropriate, a kind of "best-first" strategy for focusing the attention of the process appears to emerge from the parallel simultaneous operation. This certainty then propagates outward to establish EDGE labels, finally disambiguating the highly uncertain lower-right-hand corner. A second example is provided in Fig. 2, in which the corners converge before the sides.

This apparent behaviour for the process can be understood by recalling that all of the compatibilities are applied to the labels associated with each dot at every iteration. However, certain of these form contradictory pairs that cancel each other's individual effects, leaving perhaps only one process which has the observable overall effect. Thus the effective control problem of selecting the proper process for execution at each

dot is accomplished automatically on the basis of accumulated partial evidence (Zucker, 1977). As long as the local structure remains ambiguous, partial evidence is gathered to move incrementally toward a less ambiguous description. No definitive changes appear to occur. Thus the places where activity appears to be taking place are directed by relative interpretations for all of the data, rather than by a given attention focussing heuristic (cf. Hayes-Roth and Lesser, 1976). No "best" decision-making mechanism is explicitly necessary nor is it necessary to determine an explicit order in which grouping operations are to be applied (Marr, 1976). Furthermore, such parallel, iterative schemes also elminiate the control problems inherent in histogram-based techniques, in which both the feature to be histogrammed and the size of the region over which the feature is to be evaluated need to be determined (e.g., Ohlander, 1975).

5. AN RLP FOR SIMILARITY GROUPING

With the functional roles for the dots labelled, it still remains for them to be linked into groupings corresponding to the individual clusters. One possibility that immediately suggests itself is to construct a tracking algorithm that links the EDGE points together while keeping INTERIOR and NOISE points on proper sides of the border. However, such tracking algorithms are highly sequential (e.g. Horn, 1973), causing an extra order dependence to be imposed on the final result, or requiring substantial back tracking and heuristic control to handle the multiple possibilities.

A more uniform solution, which takes advantage of the context around each primitive construct (e.g., the dots in the previous example), would be to implement a similarity grouping algorithm. Similarity grouping is a concept which derives from early experiments by the Gestalt psychologists and which has more recently been studied by Beck (1967, 1972) and Olson and Attneave (1970). It is a process that occurs very early in visual processing and that groups local primitive objects according to features such as brightness, orientation, color, and size. Although Beck (1972) suggested that similarity grouping was a parallel process, he did not suggest any specific algorithms for similarity grouping.

The computational purpose behind similarity grouping algorithms seems to be related to obtaining initial hypotheses about the surfaces present in a visual scene. These hypotheses are based on monocularly derived data and can be made to work with a few basic (yet realistic) assumptions. Namely, at some level of description the surfaces are characterized, almost everywhere, by smooth functions of reflectance, of illumination, and of orientation. For example, metallic surfaces will appear smooth in their gray-level distribution, while tree bark will only appear smooth in terms of certain textured properties. Abrupt changes in these properties should correspond to edges between surfaces. Empirically situations will arise in which some of these assumptions are violated. Therefore an algorithm which simultaneously takes advantage both

Steven W. Zucker

of similarity properties within surfaces and of
edge properties between surfaces would seem to be
most viable. This once again implies the use of
cooperative/competitive computational techniques.

The cooperative/competitive algorithm for
computing similarity groupings can be described
as an RLP. The purpose of this process is to
label each of the links between spatially neighboring primitives with one of two possibilities:
CONNECTED and NOT-CONNECTED. With respect to
the surface interpretations, the CONNECTED
label suggests that the primitives belong to the
same surface, while the NOT-CONNECTED label
suggests that they span an edge. It is important
to keep in mind that this new kind of RLP will be
operating at a more abstract level than the dot
process already described, and that, as will be
shown shortly, the two can be designed to run concurrently.

A simple version of the pure link RLP can be
demonstrated on the Beck-like visual field shown
in Fig. 3. This field contains only uniquely described line segments (primitives), such as could
be obtained from a line-labelling process analogous
to the dot-labelling process just described. The
primitive line segments are each connected to
their K-nearest neighbors (with, e.g., K=8) to
generate the links. Each of these links is
initially labelled with both CONNECTED and NOT-
CONNECTED, and the initial probabilities on these
labels are set to 0.5 to introduce no _a priori_
bias.

With the links considered as objects in an
RLP, neighboring links are defined as those
emanating from a common primitive line segment.
In other words, if i and j are two line segments
connected by the link l_{ij}, then the neighbor set
of l_{ij} is the union of link sets
$\{l_{ki}, k=1,2,\ldots,n_k\}$ and $\{l_{jm}, m=1,2,\ldots n_m\}$.

The initial probabilities are updated by the
standard relaxation algorithm (see the next
section) by using the model for surfaces embedded
into the compatibility functions. For this
example it is sufficient only to describe the
compatibility function for the CONNECTED label
between two neighboring line segments i and j
as a function of the underlying line segment
orientations:

$$R\{OR(i), OR(j)\}= \begin{cases} 1 \text{ if } OR(i) = OR(j) \\ -1 \text{ if } OR(i) = OR(j) \pm 90° \end{cases}$$

In other words, if i and j have similar orientations, then they support the CONNECTED label on
the link between them. If they have perpendicular
orientations, then they detract support. By the
renormalization process within the updating rule
this detracted support effectively strengthens the
NOT-CONNECTED label. The process clearly terminates with CONNECTED links only between similarly oriented line segments. The edge separating
the two orientation fields can be inferred readily
from the NOT-CONNECTED links.

The extension of this RLP to more realistic
similarity grouping provlems will certainly involve
objects more complex than Beck's line segments, as
well as compatibilities based on the brightness,
size, color, texture and shape of these objects. It
could also be extended to group the dot patterns into clusters by labelling links between the dots.
Two classes of compatibility functions for this new
process are useful. The first class makes use of
information present only in the link-labelling process. These compatibility functions are of the
standard form:

$$r_{l_i l_j}(\Lambda,\Lambda')$$

$$=f\{\text{label } \Lambda \text{ on link } l_i \text{ and } \Lambda' \text{ on } l_j\}.$$

For example, if all the links to a given point are
strongly labelled NOT-CONNECTED but one, then the
point is most likely a NOISE point and the CON-
NECTED link should be weakened by interaction
through a negative compatibility.

The second class of compatibility functions
allows interaction between the link process and
the dot process. These compatibility functions
resemble those just described for the similarity-
grouping process and are of the form:

$$r_{il}(\lambda,\Lambda)$$

$$=F\{\text{label } \Lambda \text{ on link } l \text{ and label } \lambda \text{ on dot } i\}$$

where Λ is a variable used to denote link labels
(such as CONNECTED) while λ denotes dot labels
(such as INTERIOR). In general, the compatibility
between links labelled CONNECTED and underlying
dots labelled INTERIOR or EDGE (with proper orientation) should be positive, while the compatibility
between CONNECTED links and improperly oriented
EDGEs should be negative. Similarly, NOT-CONNECTED
links should be strengthened by certain EDGE and all
NOISE points, while they are weakened by neighboring
INTERIORs.

Compatibility functions that describe the consistency relationships between labels at different
levels of abstraction define a new application of
RLPs. Traditional RLPs attempt to disambiguate
label sets on the basis of label sets attached to
spatially neighboring objects. They iterate toward
a labelling that is consistent across the image
(dot pattern) but at a single level of abstraction.
Examples of this kind of process, which will be
referred to as _horizontal_ process, include the pure
dot-labelling and link-labelling processes. The
other kind of RLP, which will be referred to as a
vertical process, is defined by mixed compatibilities
such as $r_{il}(\lambda,\Lambda)$. These processes iterate toward a
labelling that is consistent across adjacent levels
of abstraction. However, the associated object nodes
all project onto the same spatial positions. (See
Fig. 4).

6.   INTERPROCESS COORDINATION AND COMMUNICATION

The next step in studying horizontal and
vertical RLPs is to examine their interaction. Two

issues are paramount: the creation of processes at different levels and then their concurrent operation. To facilitate our discussion of interprocess organization, we shall consider the link process to be more abstract than the dot process, because each link encompasses (i.e., projects onto) two dots. However, this difference is only slight, and most conceptual levels are probably more distinct than these.

The first issue is how to establish potential data structures and processes at one level using the data obtained from the preceeding level. Since the rationale for having levels is that the elimination of possibilities at one level implicitly removes possibilities from subsequent levels, it seems sensible to allow each horizontal process to run before its labels (states) are used to construct possibilities at the next level (Zucker, 1977). For example, production rules could be defined to build a link-labelling RLP out of the results of a dot-labelling RLP. In this case, the link process built out of initial dot label sets would be more complex (i.e., larger) than a link process built out of disambiguated dot labels. The pure horizontal disambiguation must necessarily be very conservative to guarantee that no possibly appropriate labels are discarded.

Such unidirectional information propagation only need occur once to establish processes at different levels. Once this has taken place a second kind of information flow - disambiguating feedback - can be established. It is at this point that vertical processes are introduced to transfer information back and forth between levels and constraints on the existing horizontal processes can be tightened. Now both vertical and horizontal processes will be active simultaneously, which makes interprocess regulation a more sensitive problem; namely, the danger exists that oscillations may arise. As a simple example of such interaction, consider a configuration consisting of two dots (d_1 and d_2) for the dot process and a single connecting link (1) for the link process. The dots have only two possible labels, INTERIOR and EDGE, and these EDGE labels are oriented so that they are back-to-back (i.e., indicating that they are each part of the border around a different cluster). The link can be labelled either CONNECTED or NOT-CONNECTED. Thus, for this example, there are two final label assignments which are <u>mutually consistent</u> between the process:

(i) both dots are labelled INTERIOR and the link is labelled CONNECTED

(ii) both dots are labelled EDGE and the link is labelled NOT-CONNECTED

To update the initial probabilities, the standard rule is used (Rosenfeld, Hummel and Zucker, 1976):

$$p_n^{k+1}(\lambda) = \frac{p_n^k(\lambda)\,[1 + q_n^k(\lambda)]}{\sum\limits_{\lambda} p_n^k(\lambda)\,[1 + q_n^k(\lambda)]}$$

$$q_n^k(\lambda) = \{ \sum_{\substack{m=neighbor \\ of\ n}} c_{nm} \cdot$$

$$\cdot [\sum r_{nm}(\lambda,\lambda')\,p_m^k(\lambda')]\}$$

where $p_n^{k+1}(\lambda)$ indicates the probability that label λ is correct for object n on the iteration k+1. For this example, m=1 and the only compatibility functions which we shall define initially are for the vertical process. This will allow information to flow vertically between levels, but not horizontally across levels. In particular, let the compatibility between the events "link 1 is labelled CONNECTED" and "dot d_i is labelled INTERIOR" be:

$$r_{i1}(I,C) = +1$$

That is, INTERIOR labels are compatible with CONNECTED links. On the other hand, INTERIOR labels are not compatible with NOT-CONNECTED links:

$$r_{i1}(I,NC) = -1$$

The remaining compatibilities are:

$$r_{i1}(E,C) = -1$$

$$r_{i1}(E,NC) = +1$$

$$r_{1i}(C,I) = +1$$

$$r_{1i}(C,E) = -1$$

$$r_{1i}(NC,I) = -1$$

$$r_{1i}(NC,E) = +1$$

All other compatibilities are zero.

We can evaluate the performance of this process by first letting the initial probabilities be such that one process is highly certain and one process is ambiguous, i.e., let

$$p_{d_1}^0(I) = p_{d_2}^0(I) = 0.9;$$

$$p_{d_1}^0(E) = p_{d_2}^0(E) = 0.1$$

$$p_1^0(C) = p_1^0(NC) = .5$$

This link process is immediately disambiguated by the dot process:

$$p_1^1(C) = 0.9;\ p_1^1(NC) = 0.1.$$

These results can be used to update the dot process:

$$p_{d_1}^1(I) = p_{d_2}^1(I) \approx 1.0$$

and then the link process:

$$p_1^2(C) \approx 1.0$$

Steven W. Zucker

For information travelling in the other direction, i.e., from the ambiguous process to the highly certain process, there is no effect until the ambiguous process acquires some structure:

$$p^1_{d_1}(I) = p^1_{d_2}(I) = 0.9$$

$$p^1_{d_1}(E) = p^1_{d_2}(E) = 0.1$$

$$p^1_1(C) = 0.9; \quad p^1_1(NC) = 0.1$$

$$p^2_{d_1}(I) = p^2_{d_2}(I) \approx 1.0$$

$$p^2_1(C) \approx 1.0$$

This difference in direction produced a (phase) delay of one iteration between the two sequences. However, in both cases, mutually consistent probability assignments accelerated convergence to the mutually consistent labelling.

As a second example, consider initial probabilities which are mutually inconsistent:

$$p_{d_1}(I) = p_{d_2}(I) = 0.6$$

$$p_1(NC) = 0.4$$

After one iteration, both processes are totally ambiguous:

$$p^1_{d_1}(I) = p^1_{d_2}(I) = 0.5$$

$$p^1_1(C) = 0.5$$

This is exactly what should happen for conflicting evidence: the process should converge to an ambiguous state. To resolve this ambiguity an additional information source is necessary. Since in actual situations there are both vertical and horizontal processes, with the vertical process providing interlevel feedback between horizontal processes, the horizontal processes would be the additional source. In the event that these indicated mutually consistent labellings, then, as we have seen, convergence to this labelling would be rapid. However, if they indicated inconsistent labellings then oscillations could be introduced. To demonstrate this, suppose that the vertical process is obtaining its probabilities from two horizontal processes, and suppose further that these horizontal processes have reached the approximate equilibrium values:

$$p = \begin{bmatrix} p_{d_1}(I) & p_{d_1}(E) \\ p_1(C) & p_1(NC) \end{bmatrix} = \begin{bmatrix} .6 & .4 \\ .4 & .6 \end{bmatrix}$$

(with $p_{d_2}(\lambda) = p_{d_1}(\lambda)$).

Then one iteration of the vertical process would yield:

$$p^1 = \begin{bmatrix} .5 & .5 \\ .5 & .5 \end{bmatrix}$$

Since, as we have shown, these values have no effect, and since the horizontal processes are assumed to be approximately constant, we would again obtain:

$$p^2 = \begin{bmatrix} .6 & .4 \\ .4 & .6 \end{bmatrix}$$

$$p^3 = \begin{bmatrix} .5 & .5 \\ .5 & .5 \end{bmatrix}$$

$$\vdots$$

This oscillation was created by alternating iterations between balanced, but opposite horizontal processes and a uniform vertical process. It could have been avoided had the three processes been run simultaneously, with convergence toward the maximally ambiguous state maintained.

The potential for oscillatory configurations is not necessarily bad. They are apparently present in human perception (Attneave, 1971), and they can be detected in RLPs either by a formal stability analysis (LaSalle and Lefschetz, 1961) or, more practically, by dynamic bounds on the entropy of processes. However, the point of the above example was a more general one. Most implementations of complex systems (e.g. Hearsay-II) involve a sequential algorithm for scheduling different knowledge sources. While the need for such schedulers derives from computational resource limitations, their effects on total system performance have never before been studied theoretically. What we have just shown is that, under certain circumstances, the choice of a scheduling strategy will effect the system's state. Although this is only a first step toward the analysis necessary for more complex systems, it does allow the important conclusion that scheduling algorithms, like all of the components in strongly inconnected, cooperating systems, contribute to the total performance.

7. CONCLUSIONS

The usefulness of a formalism for studying complex systems is directly proportional to the clarifying structure it imposes onto those systems. Visual systems are certainly complex and, while organizing them into levels has been a first step, precise mechanisms for structuring these levels and their intercommunication have been elusive. With the additional observation that both noise and ambiguity are present at all levels, the requirement that the mechanisms include some sort of feedback can also be imposed.

Relaxation labelling processes are general mechanisms for reducing such ambiguity and noise through local feedback. They iterate toward globally consistent interpretative states. Because this consistency can be both horizontal (i.e., across all positions) and vertical (i.e., across all levels of abstraction), their usefulness as a model for the mechanisms within vision systems increases. They can be used not only as enhancement processes at single levels of abstraction, but also to implement the necessary feedback between levels.

There are many other algorithms that could have been designed to implement the specific applications described in this paper. The advantage of using RLPs everywhere was in part a theoretical one, in that the resulting complex system of cooperating and competing vertical and horizontal processes was a structure uniform enough to permit some degree of analysis. This led, for example, to the demonstration that two reasonable, but different, classes of scheduling algorithms can lead to widely different final results. It also indicated that there are two essentially different kinds of information flow in complex understanding systems. The first flow, which propagates in only one direction, builds the descriptive structures at each level of abstraction. These descriptions are then operated on by processes implementing the second kind of information flow. This takes place in all directions and uses a form of feedback to disambiguate the now explicit descriptions.

The notion of consistency in our paper was specified in terms of binary compatibility relations over pairs of labels on communicating nodes. This is the most local specification possible. While there are some situations in which higher-order relations are necessary, (e.g., line labelling), the study of the power of binary compatibilities suggests how locally determined many aspects of vision could be. The extension of the compatibilities to higher-order relations is straightforward.

The study of algorithms and their interactions within vision systems must be complimented by the study of representations for visual information. To simplify these representations as much as possible, the examples in this paper were derived from the domain of dot clustering. While some of the extensions of this work to more complex, gray-level domains are reasonably clear cut,such as allowing each dot to represent the spatial location of a more arbitrary visual construct, the absolute limitations of such an approach are much more obscure. Ultimately this limitation will be bounded by the conceptualization of vision systems in terms of interacting processes that lies at the foundation of our work. However, since the visual system presumably evolved in response to the physical world, and since this also can be conceptualized in terms of interacting local pieces, such structural dualities between the two are very encouraging.

ACKNOWLEDGEMENTS

This research was supported in part by the National Research Council under Grant A4470. The algorithm for labelling dot clusters was developed with R. Hummel, and conversations with J. M. Tenenbaum and H. Barrow had an early influence on the link-labelling process. Finally, I would like to thank Y. Leclerc for his help in producing the photographs and B. Rose for her help in preparing this paper.

REFERENCES

[1]   Attneave, F., 1971, Multistability in perception, Scientific American, 225, 62-71.

[2]   Beck, J., 1967, Perceptual grouping produced by line figures, Perception and Psychophysics, 2, 491-495.

[3]   Beck, J., 1972, Similarity grouping and peripheral discriminability under uncertainty, Am. J. Psych., 85, 1-9.

[4]   Brice, C. and Fennema, C., 1970, Scene analysis using regions, Artificial Intelligence, 1. 205-226.

[5]   Hayes-Roth, F. and Lesser, V., 1976, Focus of attention in a distributed-logic speech understanding system, Technical Report, Computer Science Dept., Carnegie-Mellon Univ., Pittsburgh.

[6]   Horn, B.K.P., 1973, The Binford-Horn line finder, AI Memo 285, Artificial Intelligence Laboratory, M.I.T.,Cambridge.

[7]   LaSalle, J., and Lefschetz, S., 1961, Stability by Liapunov's Direct Method with Applications, Academic Press, New York.

[8]   Marr, D., 1976, Early processing of visual information, AI Memo-340, Artificial Intelligence Laboratory, M.I.T., Cambridge.

[9]   Ohlander, R., 1975, Analysis of natural scenes, Ph.D. Thesis, Carnegie-Mellon Univ., Pittsburgh.

[10] Olson, R. and Attneave, F., 1970, What variables produce similarity grouping?, Am. J. Psych., 83, 1-21.

[11] Riseman, E. and Arbib, M., Computational techniques in vision systems, II: Segmenting static scenes, Computer Graphics and Image Processing, 1977, in press.

[12] Rosenfeld, A., Hummel, R.A., and Zucker, S.W., 1976, Scene labelling by relaxation operations, IEEE Trans. Systems, Man, Cybernetics, SMC-6, 420-433.

[13] Zahn, C.T., 1971, Graph-theoretical methods for detecting and describing Gestalt clusters, IEEE Trans. Computers, C-20, 68-86.

[14] Zucker, S.W., 1976a, Region growing: Childhood and adolescence, Computer Graphics and Image Processing, 5, 382-399.

[15] Zucker, S.W., 1976b, Relaxation labelling and the reduction of local ambiguities, Proc. Third Int. Joint Conference on Pattern

Steven W. Zucker

Recognition, San Diego, 1976. Also, Pattern Recognition and Artificial Intelligence, C.H. Chen (ed.), Academic Press, New York.

[16] Zucker, S.W., 1977, Production systems with feedback, in F. Hayes-Roth and D. Waterman (eds.), Pattern-Directed Inference Systems, Academic Press, New York.

[17] Zucker, S.W., and Hummel, R.A., 1977, Computing the shape of dot clusters, I: Labelling edge, interior, and noise points, Technical Report TR-543, Computer Science Center, University of Maryland, College Park.

[18] Zucker, S.W., Rosenfeld, A., and Davis, L.S., General purpose models: Expectations about the unexpected, Adv. Papers Fourth Int. Joint Conference on Artificial Intelligence, Tbilisi, USSR, 1975.

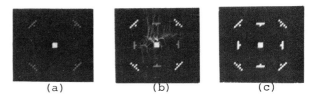

(a)   (b)   (c)

Fig. 2.   Relaxation labelling of a square-shaped cluster from uniform initial probabilities. (a) 15 iterations; (b) 25 iterations; (c) 40 iterations.

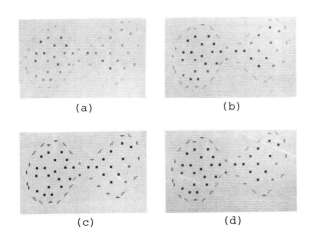

(a)   (b)

(c)   (d)

Fig. 3.   A Beck-like display of two oriented fields for similarity grouping.

Fig. 1.   Relaxation labelling of a figure-eight shaped cluster. The label with the highest probability for each dot is displayed at an intensity proportional to that probability. Solid squares indicate INTERIOR, empty squares NOISE, and EDGES are indicated by oriented line segments. (a) 0 iterations (initialization); (b) 5 iterations; (c) 10 iterations; (d) 20 iterations.

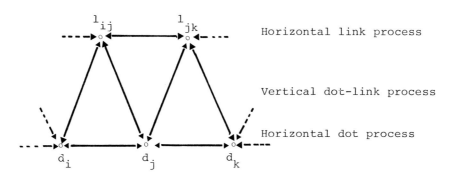

Fig. 4.   Horizontal and vertical processes.

Theory and Psychology

While the primary focus of this book is directed at efforts towards the construction of (practical) computer vision systems, theoretical and psychological approaches to problems in vision should not be ignored. A mathematical understanding of aspects of our physical world or the computational paradigms employed in various approaches to vision should lead, in the long run, to a theory of vision that is not based on empirical results from a particular system, or collection of systems. Given the state of development of computer vision systems, there are significant benefits to be derived from even a limited understanding of biological vision. Studies of living systems have been carried out by neurophysiologists, physiological psychologists, and cognitive psychologists for some time and the available literature is quite vast. Theoretical and psychological studies can provide guidance in selecting among the myriad of alternative approaches that stand before us, and in concert with computer-based systems may begin to unravel the fantastic machinery of human vision.

Haralick explores a theoretical paradigm for unifying our view of the very different kinds of processing which take place in the interpretation of an image. He shows that the integration of world knowledge at any level of processing can be viewed as the establishment of a homomorphism between the world knowledge and the relevant information in the image. Huffman provides a mathematical analysis of surface curvature and the ways in which it can be distributed over surfaces, particularly at edges and vertices. A related dual-picture representation captures complex relationships of surfaces in a way that allows simple solutions to apparently difficult problems. In addition Huffman provides a discussion of the theory of paper-folding: the flexing properties of zero-curvature surfaces. Kosslyn and Shwartz explore human visual imagery by means of a computer simulation which treats images as spatial representations in a short term memory. The model, based on extensive testing of human subjects, incorporates stored representations of objects, classification procedures, and spatial transformation processes for expansion, contraction, rotation, and scanning of pictorial images. Weisstein and Maguire also provide a view of human vision, one based on visual psychophysics. Normally such studies are confined to low-level mechanisms involved in topographic mapping of the retinal image, but they have extended the experimental framework to study how humans represent and interpret images. The investigation of contour illusions, perceived occlusion, and the apparent three-dimensionality of line drawings suggest that low-level visual mechanisms are influenced by feedback from high-level interpretations.

Although only Haralick's paper is directly concerned with computer vision, all provide a different perspective on aspects of vision.

Organization of processes, constraints on surface orientations, representations of spatial information in memory, and the manner in which
higher interpretation processes filter, enhance, and even override the
actual image data are questions common to both human and computer vision.

COMPUTER VISION SYSTEMS

SCENE ANALYSIS, ARRANGEMENTS, AND HOMOMORPHISMS

Robert M. Haralick

Electrical Engineering and Computer Science Departments
University of Kansas
Lawrence, Kansas

ABSTRACT

A number of scene analysis tasks can be
understood and solved from a point of view
which we call the theory of arrangements. An
arrangement is a set of one or more labeled
N-ary relations. The theory of arrangements
suggests that the solution to some seemingly
different high and low level scene analysis
tasks can be found by the construction of a
homomorphism from one arrangement to another,
if such a homomorphism exists. In this paper
we discuss the arrangement concept and its
application to scene analysis. Then we illustrate how a general discrete constraint
relaxation method can be used to construct
homomorphisms from one arrangement to another.

I. Introduction

Scene analysis and image understanding tasks
encompass everything from low level preprocessing
and image enhancement operations through boundary
delineation, feature extraction for color, texture
and shape, to labeling objects in an image and
interpreting their relationships. It is often the
case that each kind of scene analysis task is
explored independently from the tasks which pre-
ceed it and the tasks which follow it. In part,
this is due to the enormous complexity of the
problem and the lack of any unified conceptual
view by which the whole problem can be understood.

Since the technical language of analysis is
the language of mathematics, the conceptual problem is really a mathematical one. If there were a
consistent way of expressing the high-level and
low-level operations and their compositions, we
could begin to ask what we are really doing in
scene analysis, what we are trying to optimize,
and why it is that a particular sequence of compositions of image operations produces a best
result. Without a conceptual view and a corresponding notational system, scene analysis and
image understanding will be forever a piecemeal
problem.

It is the purpose of this paper to explore in
a unified approach (1) the way in which the different levels of scene analysis depend on one
another and (2) the way in which world model
information can be integrated into the processing
on any given level. We will show that a data
structure, which we call an arrangement, is often
a suitable data structure for representing information about a scene at any given level of
processing, as well as representing world model
information. Furthermore, we suggest that the
way in which world model information can be
integrated into any level of processing requires
the establishment of a homomorphism between the
world model information and the image information.

II. Scene Analysis

Scene analysis consists of a sequence of
information extraction tasks. The initial tasks
work on the raw image which can be considered as
a low-level, noisy data source. The later tasks
work on successively higher level data sources,
finally producing a concise description of the
scene. At each level of processing, information
from a world model may be available to help guide
the interpretations being produced.

The basic units being processed at each level
are different. In the early stages the units
might be groups of pixels with their associated
gray tones or colors. Early processing can consist of textural feature extraction, edge
detection, or small homogeneous region delineation.
The basic characteristic of the early processing
is its almost exclusive reliance on local
properties to perform detection or produce descriptions. This is illustrated in Figure 1 which
shows a local property extractor moving across
the image examining a row of 4 pixels at a time.

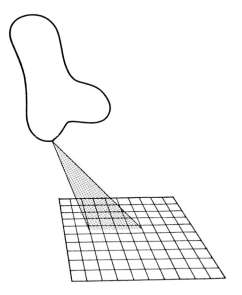

Figure 1 illustrates a local property extractor
moving across the image and generating a property
value for each row of 4 pixels.

The basic characteristics of the later stages
of processing are their use of larger units; their
emphasis on integrating, in some consistent
fashion, the piecemeal information produced by the
earlier processing; and their greater reliance on
world model information to help guide the interpretation of the global scene. If, for example,
an early stage of processing detects and labels
edges according to type, a later stage of processing might use the labeled edges as the basic
units and employ a world model to help make the
edge labeling more complete and consistent.

Often, a stage of local processing will be
followed by a stage of global processing guided
by world model information. It is this pair of
processing steps which we want to discuss in
greater detail in order to characterize its
general form.

To do this, we first illustrate a low-level
processing example: boundary delineation. The
first step in boundary delineation is micro-edge
property extraction. Any pixel can be labeled as
a micro-edge if it has on either side of it
parallel, elongated, homogeneous areas of significantly different average gray tones. The label

Robert M. Haralick

micro-edge consists of a quadruple whose components are the angular orientation, the elongation, and the average gray tones of each of the two homogeneous areas. Figure 2 illustrates a simple set of micro-edge property masks. Each micro-edge can be in one of eight orientations and have one of two possible elongations: straight and corner. Each homogeneous region consists of a connected set of pixels with a corresponding average gray tone. Its homogeneity can be measured by some criterion such as the variance of its gray tones. Since it is not guaranteed that each pixel will be associated with any micro-edges, a pixel may have associated with it none, one, or more than one micro-edge label. We consider that the local processing stage assigns each pixel the label "no edge" plus some possible micro-edge labels.

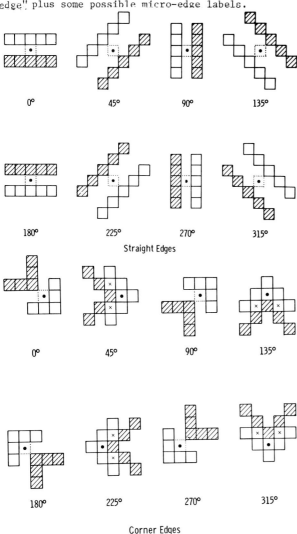

Straight Edges

Corner Edges

Figure 2 illustrates a simple set of masks which a local processing operation might use to detect straight or corner edges oriented at 8 possible angular directions. The striped resolution cells indicate that it is on the darker side of the edge.

The problem with the local labeling process is that the labels may not be unique and there may be incompatibilities of labels from one group of units to another. The world model information helps guide the next stage of processing by constraining labels of related groups of units to be compatible. By eliminating the incompatibilities, the ambiguity of the labeling can be reduced.

Hence, the next level of processing uses world model information. It groups neighboring pixels if they are labeled with micro-edge shapes and orientations which make smooth transitions from one to the other. For example, the world model may permit a straight micro-edge oriented horizontally to be connected to other neighboring straight micro-edges when such edges are oriented no further than 45° from the horizontal. Also it may be connected to a corner micro-edge, if the corner micro-edge is to its left and oriented at 180°. A world model for this level can be a list showing the pairs of micro-edges which join to form a smooth transition. Such a list is given in Table 1. Robinson (1977) uses a similar constraint. More complex world models could have a greater variety of elongations, orientations, and include probabilities or conditional probabilities for each allowed pair of micro-edge connections.

Type of Spatial Relationships

	horizontal	left diagonal	right diagonal	vertical
unordered pairs	(s0,s0)	(s135,s135)	(s90,s90)	(s45,s45)
	(s0,s45)	(s135,s180)	(s90,s135)	(s45,s0)
	(s0,s315)	(s135,s90)	(s90,s45)	(s45,s90)
	(s180,s180)	(s315,s315)	(s270,s270)	(s225,s225)
	(s180,s225)	(s315,s0)	(s270,s315)	(s225,s180)
	(s180,s135)	(s315,s270)	(s270,s315)	(s225,s180)
ordered pairs	(s0,c90)	(s135,c315)	(s90,c270)	(s45,c225)
	(s180,c0)	(s315,c45)	(s270,c0)	(s225,c315)
	(c180,s0)	(c135,s315)	(c90,s270)	(c45,s225)
	(c270,s180)	(c225,s135)	(c180,s90)	(c135,s45)

Table 1 lists the allowable connections between micro-edges as specified in an example world model. There are four relationship types: vertical, horizontal, left diagonal, and right diagonal. Under each relationship type is a list of the micro-edge pairs which can be smoothly connected when they are in the given relationship. The pair (s0,c90) under ⊡⊡ specifies that straight micro-edge oriented at 0° to the left of corner micro-edge oriented at 90° is allowable. Under any of the four types of spatial relationships, any micro-edge can be next to a pixel labeled no edge.

The grouping at this level of processing has the following effect: those micro-eges which cannot be grouped with some other micro-edges lose their status as micro-edges and become pixels labeled no edge. Each micro-edge which can be grouped with some other micro-edge is allowed to retain its label. In this manner micro-edges are allowed to reinforce one another. If the reinforcement is done iteratively until there are no more changes, and all effects have had a chance to propagate from each part of the image across the entire image, then the resulting micro-edge image is fully consistent with the world model information and the number of pixels falsely labeled as micro-edges is reduced.

Thus the first two processing levels in boundary delineation consist of a local property extraction stage followed by a processing stage that uses world model information. The local property extraction processing at each pixel of the image does not influence the property extraction at any other pixel of the image. The world model processing locates those pixels labeled as micro-edges that are not compatible with anything around them and changes their labels. This status change can affect the pixel's neighbors, its neighbors neighbors, and so on until the whole image has been affected. Because such processing propagates changes throughout the image, each pixel change can affect every other pixel, and we say the processing is global.

III. Scene Analysis and Homomorphisms

In the last section we described how the local property extraction step which groups units together, defining larger units, and giving each of the larger units one or more labels is followed by a global processing step which determines the relationships among the larger units. The global processing step specifies these relationships in a structure which we will define to be a arrangement (a labeled N-ary relation). Then the world model constraints are imposed to force the labels assigned to the larger units by the previous process to be mutually compatible. The world model constraint itself is an arrangement and in this section we will show that the imposing of its constraints amounts to determining a homomorphism from the first arrangement to the world model constraint arrangement which is consistent with the labels assigned by the lower processing level.

We illustrate this idea with the help of a simple abstract example. Let us suppose that our initial units are pixels and that some of the pixels in an image are named p_1 to p_{12} and q_1 to q_9. To do local processing, each group of related pixels must be examined. To keep our example simple, we will only concern ourselves with the related groups of pixels in the set p_1 to p_{12} and q_1 to q_9. As Figure 3 illustrates, there are four groups of related pixels:

$\{p_n \mid n = 1,\ldots,7\}$, $\{p_n \mid n = 5,\ldots,12\}$,

$\{q_n \mid n = 1,\ldots,5\}$, and $\{q_n \mid n = 6,\ldots,9\}$

Each of these four groups are given names indicated by the shapes associated with these groups in Figure 3. The values the local property extractor associates with each unit group comes from the label set $\{a,b,c,d,e\}$. The labels for each unit group appear inside the shape which names the groups. Thus, the labels a and b are associated with the unit group $\{p_n \mid n = 1,\ldots,7\}$.

Relative to our earlier boundary delineation example, a group of related units is any set of pixels in one of the spatial configurations of the

micro-edges masks shown in Figure 2. The label set consists of the label no edge and the various different kinds of micro-edges distinguished by their type and angular orientation. Note that in the boundary delineation example, the name of each group of related units is the pixel in the output image into which the property extractor places the labels associated with the unit groups. Hence, different unit groups may have the same name.

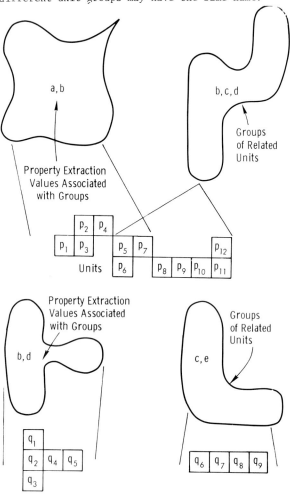

Figure 3 shows related units being grouped together and a local property extraction operation associating labels from the set $\{a,b,c,d,e\}$ with each of the unit groups.

The world model in the global processing step names the relationships among sets of unit groups. For a two-dimensional world model, relationships between pairs of unit groups are named. For the boundary delineation example, there are four spatial relationships which are named in the top of Table 1. In general, the specifying of relationships between unit groups can be illustrated as in Figure 4. Then such a world model specifies the allowable or meaningful property extraction label pairs that can exist for each kind of unit group relationship pair. For the boundary delineation example, these are the constraints listed in Table 1. The specifying of the kind of constraint a two dimensional world model can impose on the labels associated with unit groups is illustrated in

Robert M. Haralick

Figure 5. The arrow from label a to label c for
relationship x means that if a pair (G,H) of unit
groups is related by relationship x, then it is
allowable or meaningful for group G to have label
a and group H to have label c. However, since
there are no arrows from label a to labels b, d,
or e, if the unit group G only has label a, the
unit group H cannot have the labels b, d,
or e.

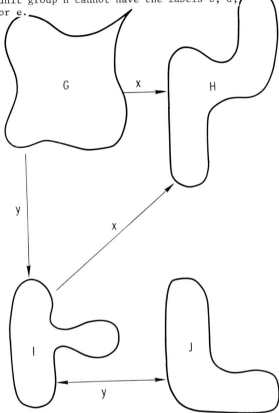

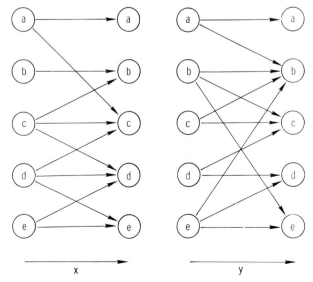

Figure 4 shows the names x or y a two-dimensional
world model may give to pairs of unit groups. We
call this relation the unit constraint relation.

Figure 5 shows for each different unit pair relationship the constraints a world model can impose
on the labels of unit groups. An arrow from label

a to label c under relationship type x means that
if a pair (G,H) of unit groups is related by relationship x, then it is allowable or meaningful for
group G to have label a and group H to have label
c. We will call this relation the label constraint
relation.

To make our data structures take a uniform
appearance, we show in Figure 6 the binary relation
produced by the property extraction step illustrated in Figure 3. The constraint imposed by the
world model can readily be understood by first
examining Figures 4 and 6. Figure 4 indicates that
a pair of unit groups, say (G,H), has the relationship x. Figure 6 indicates that unit group G can
have label a and unit group H can have label d.
Therefore, there is an induced relationship x on
the label pair (a,d). The induced relationship is
obtained as the composition of the relations in
Figures 4 and 6.

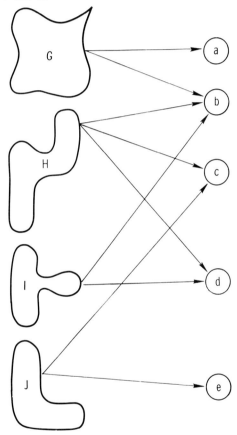

Figure 6 shows the binary relation produced by the
property extraction step which assigns labels to
units. This binary relation carries the same information as that shown in Figure 3.

The composition is done in the following way.
If one group has labels a and b and is related by
relationship type x to another unit having labels
b and d, then links (a,b), (a,d), (b,b), and (b,d)
are added to a graph for relationship x. The results of such a composition are shown in Figure 7.

Notice that there are links which are not in the
world model constraint relation of Figure 5. Such
links, e.g., (a,b), for relationship type x,

indicate that there is some group having label a which is related by relationship x to a group having label b and that this pair of labels is not compatible with the world model. Upon eliminating all incompatible pairs of labels, the labeling of Figure 8a results.

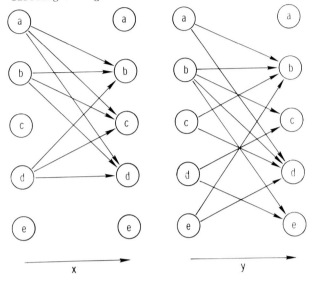

Figure 7 shows the composition of the relation of Figure 4 with the labeling relation of Figure 6. Notice that there are links shown here which are not shown in the relation of Figure 5, the world model constraints. Such links, like (a,b) for relationships type x, indicate that there is some group having label a which is related by relationship x to a group having label b and that this pair of labels is not compatible with the world model.

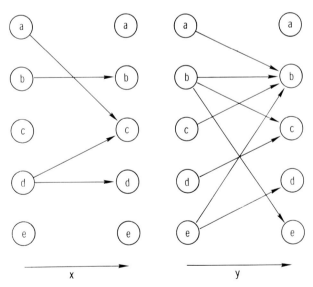

Figure 8 shows the compatible pairs of lables of Figure 7 after removing those not in Figure 5.

Certainly those pairs of labels in Figure 7 which are not in Figure 5 are not compatible and we may eliminate them. The resulting relation of compatible labels is shown in Figure 8. This

relation may be used to help disambiguate labels assigned by the local processor to unit groups G, H, I, and J.

Suppose group G can keep label a. Since H is related to G by relationship x, then H can only keep label c because the only label that can relate to label a by relationship x is c (See Figure 8). Now if H keeps the label c, since I relates to H by relationship x, then I can only have labels a or d. But the local processor assigned labels b or d to I. Hence I must take the label d.

Now consider the fact that G relates to I by relationship y. G has the label a and I has the label d. Figure 8 indicates that label a does not relate to label d by relationship y. Hence, unit group G cannot take the label a.

Suppose that unit group G keeps the label b. Then since H is related to G by relationship x and the only label that can relate to label b by relationship x is label b (see Figure 8), H must take label b. Also, unit group I must take label b. Now I is related to G by relationship y. Since the label b can relate to itself by relationship y, everything is still all right. Unit groups I and J are related by relationship y. Since label b can relate to labels c or e by relationship y, unit group J can keep both its labels c and e.

By this process of tracing compatible labels around, it is possible to reduce the ambiguity of the initial labeling done by the local processing stage. For our example, the resulting labeling is shown in Figure 9a. In general, the result is not single-valued as can be seen from this example.

Figure 9b shows the relation which is the composition of the unit constraint relation (Figure 4) with the labeling of Figure 9a. Notice that all links in Figure 9b are links in the label constraint relation of Figure 5. Whenever the composition of one relation with a second results in a relation which is contained in a third relation, we call the second relation a homomorphism from the first relation to the third relation. Thus the labeling of Figure 9a is a homomorphism from the unit constraint relation to the label constraint relation.

In the next sections we will develop the precise mathematical idea of arrangement homomorphism, describe how a variety of scene analysis tasks can be posed as problems in finding arrangement homomorphisms, and describe a general method for tracing compatible labels around in order to eliminate the incompatible labels.

Robert M. Haralick

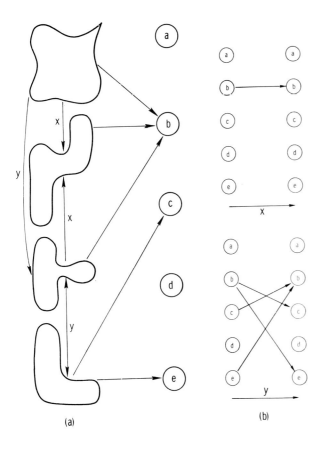

(a)

(b)

In this section we give the definition for arrangements and arrangement homomorphisms. The definitions here are a generalization of that given by Haralick and Kartus (1976).

Let A be the set of elements whose arrangement is being described. Each group of related elements from A is given a label from the label set L. Let R be the labeled N-ary relation which consists of labeled N-tuples of elements from A. Then a <u>simple order-N arrangement</u> is a triple (R,A,L) where $R \subseteq A^N \times L$. When the sets A and L are understood, the relation R is called an arrangement for short.

A <u>general arrangement</u> is a set of simple arrangements, each simple arrangement being of different order, being defined on the same set, and having the same label set. If there are K simple arrangements in the arrangement A, then we write

$$A = \{R_1, R_2, \ldots, R_K; A, L\} \text{ where}$$
$$R_k \subseteq A^{N_k} \times L, \quad k = 1, \ldots, K.$$

Let $A = \{R_1, \ldots, R_K; A, L\}$ be a general arrangement and $H \subseteq A \times B$.

The <u>composition</u> of arrangement A with H results in an arrangement B which we define as

$$A \circ H = B = \{S_1, S_2, \ldots, S_K; B, L\}, \text{ where}$$
$$S_k = \{(b_1, b_2, \ldots, b_{N_k}, \ell) \in B^{N_k} \times L \mid \text{for some}$$
$$(a_1, a_2, \ldots, a_{N_k}, \ell) \in R_k, \ (a_n, b_n) \in H,$$
$$n = 1, \ldots, N_k\} = R_k \circ H, \quad k = 1, \ldots, K.$$

An arrangement $A = \{R_1, \ldots, R_K; A, L\}$ is <u>contained</u> in an arrangement $D = \{T_1, \ldots, T_K; A, L\}$ if and only if

$$R_k \subseteq T_k, \quad k = 1, \ldots, K.$$

In this case we write $A \subseteq D$.

Two arrangements $A = \{R_1, \ldots, R_K; A, L\}$ and $B = \{S_1, \ldots, S_N; B, M\}$ are <u>comparable</u> if the number of relations in each arrangement is the same (K=N), the label sets are the same (M=L), and the relation R_k has the same order as the relation S_k ($R_k \subseteq A^{N_k} \times L$ and $S_k \subseteq B^{N_k} \times L$).

Figure 9a shows the unit labeling compatible with the world model constraints and unit group relationships. This labeling contains two homomorphisms from the unit constraint relation of Figure 4 to the label constraint relation of Figure 5.

Figure 9b shows the composition of the relation of Figure 4 with the label assignment of Figure 9a. Notice that all links in Figure 9b are also in Figure 5. This indicates that the labeling of Figure 9a contains homomorphisms.

Let $A = \{R_1,\ldots,R_K; A,L\}$ and $B = \{S_1,\ldots,S_K; B,L\}$ be two comparable arrangements.

Let $H: A \to B$. The function H is a homomorphism from arrangement A to arrangement B if and only if $A \circ H \subseteq B$.

V. Examples

In this section we show how some boundary delineation tasks, scene labeling tasks, and image understanding tasks can be described within the mathematical framework of simple arrangements.

V.1 Boundary Delineation

The local processing operation for boundary delineation is usually some kind of gradient operator. We will assume that the gradient operator associates with each neighborhood of resolution cells a set of possible edge labels. Each such a set of labels includes the label no edge. The first part of the boundary delineation problem is to use some higher level world model information to retain in each neighborhood as many of the labels assigned by the local processing operation as possible and at the same time make sure that incompatible labeling situations are removed. The second part of the boundary delineation problem is to use the micro-edges retained by first part and fill in all likely gaps in the borders. Both parts have a similar mathematical description.

Let R be the set of resolution cells of the image and let $S \subseteq R^N$ be the group of spatially related resolution cells. We call S the set of neighborhoods of the image. In a simple case, N could equal 9 and S could be the set of all 3 x 3 neighborhoods. In our example in Section II, N is 49 and S is the set of all 7 x 7 neighborhoods. Let L be the set of the names for some of the possible relationships which groups of neighborhoods can be in. In our example in Section II, K is 2 and L has the names horizontal, vertical, left diagonal, and right diagonal. Let E be the set of possible micro-edge labels. In our example in Section II, E contains the labels no edge, straight edge at angular orientation θ, and corner edge at orientation θ where θ can be a multiple of 45°.

The local processing step associates edge labels with neighborhoods. For the first part of boundary delineation, the association is determined by some sort of a compass gradient operator on the original image. When a gradient at a particular orientation is high enough, the label micro-edge at the particular angular orientation is instantiated. For the second part of boundary delineation, the association is determined by some kind of neighborhood operator in the class of region growing operators operating on the edge image created in the first part of the boundary delineation operation. In either case, the local processing operation determines a binary relation $G \subseteq S \times E$ which pairs neighborhoods to edges.

The world model consists of a pair of arrangements (T,C) where $T \subseteq S^K \times L$ is the unit constraint arrangement and $C \subseteq E^K \times L$ is the label constraint arrangement. These relations are the general form for the unit constraint and label constraint relation used in our abstract example in Section III (Figure 4 and Figure 5). T indicates for each relationship type in L the ordered group of neighborhoods which have the relation. C indicates for each relationship type in L the ordered groups of micro-edge labels which are compatible when situated in neighborhoods of the given relationship type.

Each step in boundary delineation then corresponds to finding a mapping $H: S \to E$, $H \subseteq G$, satisfying the homomorphism condition $T \circ H \subseteq C$. Hence the problems of boundary delineation can be posed as a problem of finding a homomorphism H, contained in G, from the arrangement (T,S,L) to the arrangement (C,E,L).

V.2 Scene Labeling

Suppose a scene has been divided into segments $S = \{s_1,\ldots,s_K\}$. A low level feature extractor with decision rule using gray tone, color, shape, and texture of each segment assigns some possible description from a set D of descriptions to each segment. This operation defines a relation $G \subseteq S \times D$. The problem with this low-level assignment is that each segment may be associated with multiple descriptions. The desired labeling of the scene would have each segment described unambiguously.

A similar situation arises in the line labeling problem of Waltz (1972). Here, S is the set of line segments found in a scene and D is a set containing labels that can be associated with any line. The labels in D could be, for example, convex, concave, occluding left, occluding right. The relation F, determined from low level processes, associates with each line in S one or more labels from D. The desired line labeling would be some subset of F that associates each line with only one label.

One way of reducing the possibly ambiguous description a line or segment initially has is to use constraints from a higher level world model. Such a model specifies the relevant relationships between groups of related segments of lines and specifies the associated labeling constraints. To employ such a model, related (ordered) sets of N segments or lines must be determined. Segments can be related on the basis of their relative spatial positions. Lines can be related on the basis of the junctions they form. Then for each kind of relationship the model can specify a constraint which the labels of each kind of related segments or lines must satisfy.

For instance, pairs of segments in S could be related if they mutually touch each other. There could be different kinds of touching such as to the left, to the right, above, below, in front of, in back of, supported by, and contained in. Suppose L is the set of such relationship labels. Then the set of spatially related segments or lines could be specified by the relation $A \subseteq S \times S \times L$, where $(s,t,i) \in A$ if and only if label i describes the way segment s relates to segment t. In the general case, the relationships in L can describe

Robert M. Haralick

the way N segments or lines are related so that the relation A is a labeled N-ary relation: $A \subseteq S^N \times L$ and is, therefore, a simple arrangement.

The world model also contains labeling constraints. For example, pairs of segments whose relationship label is i can be constrained by the world model to have associated with them only certain allowable description pairs. In this case the world model label constraint is an arrangement $C \subseteq D \times D \times L$, where $(d_1, d_2, i) \; \varepsilon \; C$ if and only if it is legal for a pair of segments s_1 and s_2 having relation i to have respective descriptions d_1 and d_2. In general, the relation C is a labeled N-ary relation, $C \subseteq D^N \times L$ which includes in it all labeled N-tuples of compatible descriptions for an ordered set of N related segments.

To summarize the information we have available:

(1) $G \subseteq S \times D$, the assignments of descriptions given by a low level operation;

(2) The world model (A,C) where
$A \subseteq S^N \times L$ is the labeled sets of related N-tuples of segments and $C \subseteq D^N \times L$ is the N-ary relational labeling constraints.

The scene labeling problem is to use F,A, and C to determine a new labeling relation H which contains fewer ambiguous descriptions than G and which is consistent with the constraints specified by the world model. In essence we want

(1) H: $S \to D$, $H \subseteq G$

(2) $A \circ H \subseteq C$

Notice that (A,S,L) is a simple arrangement, (C,D,L) is a simple arrangement, and H is a binary relation which successfully translates the structure of arrangement (A,S,L) into the structure of arrangement (C,D,L). The binary relation H is the homomorphism from arrangement (A,S,L) into arrangement (C,D,L) which is contained in G.

Our discussion of scene labeling is more general than that of Rosenfeld, Hummel, and Zucker (1976) who consider only binary relational labeling constraints. We consider N-ary relational labeling constraints; any ordered set of N segments can have a N-ary relation labeling constraint. For the particular binary case (N=2), if we define a unique label for each pair of segments, then the treatment given here exactly corresponds to that in Rosenfeld, Hummel, and Zucker.

V.3 Image Understanding

We will illustrate the arrangement concept in image understanding by considering a few highly stylized problems. This example is taken from Haralick and Kartus (1976). Suppose we have a segment in terms of certain basic attributes, for example, shape discriminators. Using these attributes, we could assign a shape label to each of the segments. To define an arrangement from these labels, we can group related segments together, N

at a time, and form the corresponding set of N-tuples of their labels.

Depending on the particular segmentation task, the order of the segments in the groups may or may not be important. For example, it may be reasonable in some kind of image understanding problems to order the segments in a left-right top-bottom manner. On the other hand, if the order of the segments in the group is not important, an arbitrary fixed order based on the segments shape can be used.

The label given to each N-tuple can be the name we might give to a group of related segments whose shapes are the components of the given N-tuple. Another possibility is to use the interpretation label as a counter. We can assign the integer label "1" to all N-tuples arising from a group of segments the first time the N-tuple is encountered. The label "k" can be assigned the kth time the same kind of N-tuple is encountered.

One criterion by which segments can be considered related is spatial connectivity or nearness. Two segments are eligible to be included in the same related group when their interaction lengths overlap. To make things simple in our examples we will use interaction lengths of zero. Thus, two segments are related only when they are touching. In the stylized examples we give, segments are represented by circles, squares, triangles, etc.

Arrangements can be used to establish the likeness of two images when one image is essentially the same as the other, but the order or placement of the image parts is different. In this case template matching the images will not work. Often geometric transformations of rotation, magnification, translation, skew will also not work. The example shown in Figure 10 illustrates one way of handling this problem using the notion of connectedness and simple order-3 arrangements. Suppose the image has five basic kinds of figures: squares, triangles, circles, arrows, and hexagons. A quadruple whose first three components are these shapes taken in the order square, triangle, circles, hexagons, and arrows will be considered to belong to the arrangement of the image if all three shapes touch each other in a pairwise manner. In general, we may use the criterion consider any N-tuple if enough of its components interact in a pairwise or K-wise manner. A label of 1 or 2 will also be associated with each triple of shapes to make the quadruple; in this example such a label will just count the number of times that the triplet it is associated with occurs. In Figure 10, there are four drawings. Each drawing has two triangles, one circle, one square, and one arrow. Using the order-3 arrangement concept, there are two pairs of drawings whose arrangements are isomorphic by the identity function. The drawings themselves, however, have their parts placed differently in absolute position and orientation. This isomorphism becomes clear upon examination of Figure 11 which shows the arrangements for the drawings. The drawings on the left are isomorphic to the arrangement labeled A. The drawings on the right are isomorphic to the arrangement labeled B.

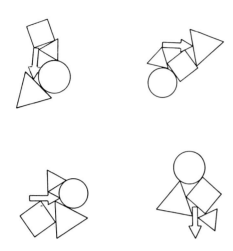

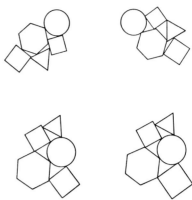

Figure 10 illustrates four drawings, each of which has two triangles, one square, one circle, and one arrow. Using the order-3 arrangements concept, there are 2 pairs of drawings whose arrangements are isomorphic.

Figure 12 illustrates four drawings each of which has two squares, one circle, one hexagon, and one triangle. Using the order-3 arrangement concept, there are 2 pairs of drawings whose arrangements are isomorphic. The arrangement for each drawing is isomorphic to the arrangement for one of the drawings in Figure 10.

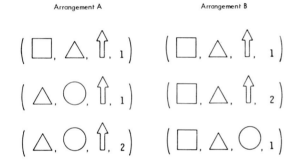

Arrangement A   Arrangement B

Figure 11 illustrates the quadruples in the order-3 arrangements for the drawings of Figure 10. The two drawings on the left in Figure 10 are isomorphic to Arrangement A and the two drawings on the right in Figure 7 are isomorphic to Arrangement B. The quadruple ($\square,\triangle,\uparrow,2$) means that the drawing has a piece that consists of a square, triangle, and arrow pairwise touching each other and the label two designates that this is the second such piece in the drawing.

The situation becomes slightly more complicated when the function that establishes the isomorphism is not the identity function. This is illustrated in Figure 12 which also has four drawings. Each drawing has two squares, one circle, one hexagon, and one triangle. Taking the order as square, hexagon, triangle, and circle, and using the order-3 arrangement concept, there are two pairs of drawings in Figure 12 whose arrangements are isomorphic. Also the arrangement for each drawing in Figure 12 is isomorphic to the arrangement for one of the drawings in Figure 10. The isomorphism, however, is not the identity function: a square stays square, a hexagon becomes a triangle, a triangle becomes an arrow, and a circle remains a circle.

More complicated still is the case where the correspondence between one drawing and another is by an arrangement homomorphism which does not establish a one-one correspondence. Such a case is illustrated in Figure 10 which depicts two drawings. Taking the order as hexagon, circle, triangle, arrow, and square and using the name or label 1 for all triplets except the triplet (arrow, triangle, square) which gets the name 2, we may use the arrangement concept to establish the correspondence between one of the drawings (the one on the right) in Figure 13 and two of the drawings in Figure 10 (the ones on the left). The correspondence is a homomorphism and finding it, although easy, should begin to give the reader some idea of the combinatorial problems involved. The drawing on the left of Figure 13 is homomorphic to neither of the drawings in Figure 10.

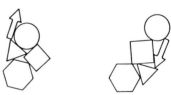

Figure 13 illustrates two drawings. Using the arrangement concept, labels of 1 or 2 can be assigned to each triplet to make one of the drawings in Figure 10 a homomorphic image of one of these drawings.

The problem of finding homomorphisms is truly one of establishing the correspondence using relationships. Figure 14 shows the quadruples in the arrangement for the right-hand drawing of Figure 13 and the arrangement for the left-hand drawing of Figure 10. The homomorphism which establishes the relationship between the arrangements appears in the central bottom part of Figure 14.

Robert M. Haralick

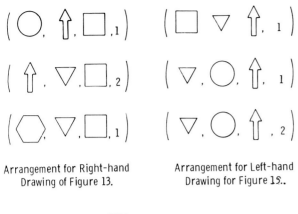

Arrangement for Right-hand   Arrangement for Left-hand
Drawing of Figure 13.   Drawing for Figure 15..

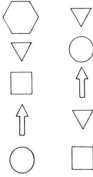

Homomorphism

Figure 14 illustrates the arrangement for one of
the drawings in Figure 13 and the arrangement for
one of the drawings in Figure 10. Below the
arrangement is the homomorphism.

VI. Discrete Relaxation

In the last few sections we have illustrated
how a variety of scene analysis problems can be
posed as problems of finding homomorphisms from
one arrangement to another. In this section we
describe a discrete relaxation algorithm which can
be used to help determine all the homomorphisms
from one arrangement to another. The form of the
discrete relaxation algorithm given here is a
generalization to N dimensions of Waltz filtering
(Waltz, 1972) and the discrete scene labeling
relaxation (Rosenfeld, Hummel, and Zucker, 1976)
and network consistency relation (Mackworth, 1977).
Let (R,A,L) and (S,B,L) be two order-N simple
arrangements. Let $T_0 \subsetneq A \times B$ be a given constraint
which must contain any homomorphisms we are interested in finding. By definition a function
$H: A \to B$ is a homomorphism from arrangement
(R,A,L) to arrangement (S,A,L) if and only if
$R \circ H \subseteq S$. We would like to find all such functions
H satisfying the constraint $H \subseteq T_0$.

To motivate the algorithm, consider that each
labeled N-tuple of R must be translated through H
to some labeled N-tuple in N. Since H is contained in T_0 we might begin by pairing each
labeled N-tuple in R to those labeled N-tuples in
S it can be translated to through any pairs in T_0.

So, for example, if R has the labeled triple
(a,b,c,ℓ) and $T_0 = \{(a,\alpha), (a,\beta), (b,\beta), (c,\beta),$
$(c,\alpha)\}$ then the list of triples $(\alpha,\beta,\beta,\ell)$,
$(\alpha,\beta,\alpha,\ell)$, (β,β,β,ℓ), and $(\beta,\beta,\alpha,\ell)$ are all the
possible labeled triplets to which T_0 can trans-
late the labeled triplet (a,b,c,ℓ). Suppose of
these four labeled triplets only $(\alpha,\beta,\beta,\ell)$ and
$(\beta,\beta,\alpha,\ell)$ are in S. Then the pairing establishes
the correspondence of (a,b,c,ℓ) to $(\alpha,\beta,\beta,\ell)$ and
$(\beta,\beta,\alpha,\ell)$.

This correspondence of labeled N-tuples in R
to labeled N-tuples in S carries information which
can eliminate pairs in T_0 which cannot possibly
contribute to any homomorphism. It can do so in
the following way. If the pair (a,b) is to be in
some homomorphism, then each labeled N-tuple in R
which has a component with the value a must be able
to be associated with some labeled N-tuple of S
having the corresponding component with value b.
The association of labeled N-tuples of S with
labeled N-tuples of R is carried by the composition through T_0 as described in the previous
paragraph.

The discrete relaxation process iterates first
using a T to establish a labeled N-tuple to labeled N-tuple correspondence and then using this correspondence to determine a smaller T which can be
used to establish the labeled N-tuple correspondence for the next iteration. At each iteration
T, which is assumed finite, becomes smaller. The
iterations finally reach a fixed point since T is
bounded below by the empty set. If a homomorphism
H satisfying the constraint $H \subseteq T_0$ exists and is
unique, then H will be the fixed point of the
iterations. If more than one homomorphism exists,
then the fixed point will not be single-valued and
will contain all homomorphisms satisfying the constraint $H \subseteq T_0$. In the next section we will discuss a combination of a tree search and discrete
relaxation process to divide a multi-valued relation into its component homomorphisms. In the
remainder of this section we give a precise mathematical description of the discrete relaxation and
illustrate its use on the abstract simple example
we worked in an intrutive manner in Section III.

To begin we will need some notational conven-
tions. Let $R \subseteq A^N \times L$, $S \subseteq B^N \times L$, and $T_0 \subseteq A \times B$.
The iterations define $T_1, T_2, \ldots, T_K$ each relation
being a restriction of the previous one. We will
suppose that T_k is defined. The first part of the
iteration goes through each labeled N-tuple of R
and associates it with each labeled N-tuple of S it
can by composition through T_k. We will want to
have a way of describing such an association. So
let $(a_1, \ldots, a_N, \ell)$ be a labeled N-tuple of R and
let $G(a_1, \ldots, a_N, \ell; S, T_k)$ be the set of all labeled
N-tuples in S which can be reached by the composition of $(a_1, \ldots, a_N, \ell)$ through the relation T_k.
$$G(a_1, \ldots, a_N, \ell; S, T_k) = \{(b_1, \ldots, b_N, \ell) \in S \mid$$
$$(a_n, b_n) \in T_k, n = 1, \ldots, N\}.$$

We know that a pair $(a,b) \in T_k$ is not a contributor in any homomorphism if for some labeled N-tuple $(a_1,\ldots,a_N,\ell)$ in R having a component with value a and label ℓ, we cannot find in $G(a_1,\ldots,a_N,\ell; S,T_k)$ a labeled N-tuple having a corresponding component with value b. To write this easily we need a notation which lets us select from any set of labeled N-tuples all those N-tuples with a given label and which for a specified component have a particular value. So if we desire to select from R those N-tuples having label ℓ and value a for component n we need only write $R_n(a,\ell)$ which we define by

$$R_n(a,\ell) = \{(a_1,a_2,\ldots,a_N,\ell) \in R \mid a = a_n\}$$

The next step in the iteration process is to select a value a for component n and select a label ℓ. Then go through each labeled N-tuple in $R_n(a,\ell)$. Suppose $(a_1,\ldots,a_N,\ell) \in R_n(a,\ell)$. The labeled N-tuples of S which correspond to $(a_1,\ldots,a_N,\ell)$ can be found in $G(a_1,\ldots,a_N,\ell; S,T_k)$. The pair $(a,b) \in T_k$ can be a pair which participates in some homomorphism only if there is some labeled N-tuple in $G(a_1,\ldots,a_N,\ell; S,T_k)$ having its nth component with value b. There is some labeled N-tuple in $G(a_1,\ldots,a_N,\ell; S,T_k)$ havings its nth component with value b if and only if the projection of $G(a_1,\ldots,a_N,\ell; S,T_k)$ onto its nth coordinate contains the element b.

We clearly need a notation for projection. For any $Q \subseteq C^N \times L$ we define the projection to the nth coordinate by

$$\pi_n Q = \{c \in C \mid \text{for some } (c_1,\ldots,c_N,\ell) \in Q,$$
$$c_n = c\}$$

Hence the set of values which exist in the nth component for the labeled N-tuples in $G(a_1,\ldots,a_N,\ell; S,T_k)$ can be written as $\pi_n G(a_1,\ldots,a_N,\ell; S,T_k)$.

If the pair (a,b) has a possibility in participating in some homomorphism, then for each label ℓ, for each component n, and for each labeled N-tuple $(a_1,\ldots,a_N,\ell)$ in $R_n(a,\ell)$, there must exist some labeled N-tuple in $G(a_1,\ldots,a_N,\ell; S,T_k)$ whose n^{th} component has value b. Hence,

$$b \in \bigcap_{\ell \in L} \bigcap_{n=1}^{N} \bigcap_{(a_1,\ldots,a_N,\ell) \in R_n(a,\ell)} \pi_n G(a_1,\ldots,a_N,\ell; S,T_k)$$

The discrete relaxation defines the restriction T_{k+1} by

$$T_{k+1} = \{(a,b) \in T_k \mid$$
$$b \in \bigcap_{\ell \in L} \bigcap_{n=1}^{N} \bigcap_{(a_1,\ldots,a_N,\ell) \in R_n(a,\ell)} \pi_n G(a_1,\ldots,a_N,\ell; S,T_k)\}$$

The following theorem proves that if $H \subseteq T_k$ and H is a homomorphism from R to S, then $H \subseteq T_{k+1}$. Hence, those pairs which were in T_k but not in T_{k+1} do not participate in any homomorphism.

Theorem: Let $R \subseteq A^N \times L$, $S \subseteq B^N \times L$, and $H \subseteq T \subseteq A \times B$. If $H: A \to B$ satisfies $R \circ H \subseteq S$, then $H \subseteq \phi(T)$ where

$$\phi(T) = \{(a,b) \in T \mid$$
$$b \in \bigcap_{\ell \in L} \bigcap_{n=1}^{N} \bigcap_{(a_1,\ldots,a_N,\ell) \in R_n(a,\ell)} \pi_n G(a_1,\ldots,a_N,\ell; S,T_k)\}$$

Proof: Suppose $(a,b) \in H$. Since $H \subseteq T$ is given we need only show that

$$b \in \bigcap_{\ell \in L} \bigcap_{n=1}^{N} \bigcap_{(a_1,\ldots,a_N,\ell) \in R_n(a,\ell)} \pi_n G(a_1,\ldots,a_N,\ell; S,T).$$

So let $\ell \in L$ and $n \in \{1,\ldots,N\}$ be given. There are two cases: either $R_n(a,\ell) = \phi$ or $R_n(a,\ell) \neq \phi$. If $R_n(a,\ell) = \phi$, then the result is immediate since intersections over empty collections are always full. If $R_n(a,\ell) \neq \phi$, let $(a_1,\ldots,a_N,\ell) \in R_n(a,\ell)$. By definition of $R_n(a,\ell)$, we must have $a_n = a$.

Since H is a function, it is defined everywhere and there exists $b_1,\ldots,b_N \in B$ such that $(a_n,b_n) \in H$, $n = 1,\ldots,N$. Since $a_n = a$ and $(a,b) \in H$, we may take $b_n = b$.

By definition of $G(a_1,\ldots,a_N,\ell; S,T)$, $G(a_1,\ldots,a_N,\ell; S,T) = \{(b_1^*,\ldots,b_N^*,\ell) \in S \mid (a_n,b_n^*) \in H, n = 1,\ldots,N\}$. Now $(a_1,\ldots,a_N,\ell) \in R$ and $(a_n,b_n) \in H$, $n = 1,\ldots,N$ imply $(b_1,\ldots,b_N,\ell) \in R \circ H$. By assumption, $R \circ H \subseteq S$. Hence, $(b_1,\ldots,b_N,\ell) \in S$ and we must have $(b_1,\ldots,b_N,\ell) \in G(a_1,\ldots,a_N,\ell; S,T)$. Then $b = b_n \in \pi_n G(a_1,\ldots,a_N,\ell; S,T)$. Therefore,

$$b \in \bigcap_{\ell \in L} \bigcap_{n=1}^{N} \bigcap_{(a_1,\ldots,a_N,\ell) \in R_n(a,\ell)} \pi_n G(a_1,\ldots,a_N,\ell; S,T)$$

The next proposition proves that if H is a fixed point of the iteration process, then H single-valued implies that $R \circ H \subseteq S$. This means that if a function H is a fixed point of the iteration process, then H is a homomorphism.

Proposition: Let $R \subseteq A^N \times L$, $S \subseteq B^N \times L$, and $H \subseteq A \times B$. If

Robert M. Haralick

$$H = \{(a,b) \; \varepsilon \; H \;|\;$$

$$b \; \varepsilon \bigcap_{\ell \varepsilon L} \bigcap_{n=1}^{N} \bigcap_{(a_1,\ldots,a_N,\ell)\varepsilon R_n(a,\ell)} \pi_n G(a_1,\ldots,a_N,\ell; S,T)\},$$

then H single-valued implies $R \circ H \subseteq S$.

Proof: Let $(b_1,\ldots,b_N,) \; \varepsilon \; R \circ H$. Then for some $(a_1,\ldots,a_N,\ell) \; \varepsilon \; R$, $(a_n,b_n) \; \varepsilon \; H$, $n = 1,\ldots,N$. By definition of H,

$$b_k \; \varepsilon \bigcap_{\ell \varepsilon L} \bigcap_{n=1}^{N} \bigcap_{(a'_1,\ldots,a'_N,\ell)\varepsilon R_n(a_k,\ell)} \pi_n G(a'_1,\ldots,a'_N,\ell; S,H), \quad k=1,\ldots,N.$$

Now for each $\ell \varepsilon L$ and $n \varepsilon N$ $b_k \; \varepsilon \; \pi_n G(a_1,\ldots,a_N,\ell; S,H)$ $k = 1,\ldots,N$. In particular,
$b_k \; \varepsilon \; \pi_k G(a_1,\ldots,a_N,\ell; S,H)$, $k = 1,\ldots,N$. But H single-valued implies that for each $(a'_1,\ldots,a'_N,\ell)$ there exists a unique
$(b'_1,\ldots,b'_N,\ell) \; \varepsilon \; G(a'_1,\ldots,a'_N,\ell; S,H)$. Hence,
$(b_1,\ldots,b_N,\ell) \; \varepsilon \; G(a_1,\ldots,a_N,\ell; S,H)$ and by definition of $G(a_1,\ldots,a_N,\ell; S,H)$ this implies that
$(b_1,\ldots,b_N,\ell) \; \varepsilon \; S$.

To provide an example of the relaxation process, Figure 15 puts in list form the unit constraint arrangement and label constraint arrangement of the world model for the abstract example in Section II. The initial T_0 is shown in Figure 16 where the reader can follow the steps of the iterations. The fixed point is reached in 3 iterations.

R	S	
GHx	aax	aay
GIy	acx	aby
IHx	bbx	bby
IJy	cbx	bcy
	ccx	bey
	cdx	cby
	dcx	ccy
	ddx	dcy
	dex	ddy
	edx	eby
	eex	edy
		eey

UNIT CONSTRAINT ARRANGEMENT	LABELING CONSTRAINT ARRANGEMENT

Figure 15 lists the triples in the unit constraint relation and the labeling constraint relation for the abstract example of Section II.

T_0	
G	ab
H	bcd
I	bd
J	ce

N-Tuple	Association
GHx	acx bbx
GIy	aby bby
IHx	bbx
IJy	bcy bey
JIy	cby eby

T_1	
G	ab
H	b
I	b
J	ce

N-Tuple	Association
GHx	bbx
GIy	aby bby
IHx	bbx
IJy	bcy bey
JIy	cby eby

T_2	
G	b
H	b
I	b
J	ce

N-Tuple	Association
GHx	bbx
GIy	bby
IHx	bbx
IJy	bcy bey
JIy	cby eby

T_3		H_1	H_2
G	b	b	b
H	b	b	b
I	b	b	b
J	ce	c	e

Figure 16 shows how in three iterations the initial labeling T_0 can be reduced. The two homomorphisms H_1 and H_2, which T_3 contains, are shown to the right of T_3.

The application of the discrete relaxation to general arrangements is simple. Let $\{R_1,R_2,\ldots,R_K; A,L\}$ and $\{S_1,S_2,\ldots,S_K; B,L\}$ be two comparable arrangements. Let $T_0 \subseteq A \times B$ be given. Let the discrete relaxation operate beginning with T_0 and using relations R_1 and S_1. Call the resulting relation T_1 and let the discrete relaxation operate with T_1 using relations R_2 and S_2. After the Kth relation has finished, use the resulting relation T in a discrete relaxation for relation R_1 and S_1 and continue cycling through in this manner until relation T does not change for a whole cycle. The limiting relation T will then contain all homomorphisms from the first arrangement to the second that T_0 does.

VII. Tree Search

Should the discrete relaxation not reduce the initial relation T far enough and it is desired to obtain a unique assignment of labels to units, a tree search must be done to determine all the homomorphisms T has. The tree search can proceed as follows. Find the first unit which has more than one label. Successively instantiate each of these possible labels to the unit, thereby branching the tree out. Each instantiation produces a T relation which is a restricted version of the previous level's relation.

Each restricted relation can be put through the discrete relaxation procedure yielding two possible outcomes. Either the fixed point relation is not defined everywhere, in which case that branch of the tree search terminates, or the fixed point relation is defined everywhere, in which case the branch may continue. If the fixed point relation is defined everywhere, then either the relation is single-valued or multi-valued. If the relation is single-valued, it is a homomorphism. If it is multi-valued, then we can again find a unit which has more than one label and successively instantiate these possible labels to the unit and continue to branch the tree out.

VIII. Generalizations: Probabilistic Models

The world model discussed in this paper has been the discrete model. Those labeled N-tuples in the unit constraint relation or label constraint relation had no weights or probabilities associated with them. One natural generalization of this model is to have a weight function defined on each of the constraint relations. The discrete relaxation, then becomes a probabilistic relaxation, which could be similar to that defined by Rosenfeld et al (1976), Davis and Rosenfeld (1976), or Hanson and Riseman (1977). Each of these researchers have reported some success with such procedures.

The problem with the probabilistic relaxation is that it is not yet known if, in fact, the normalized weights used have probability interpretations. Unlike the discrete relaxation which has been shown to preserve homomorphisms, it is not known what the various forms of probabilistic relaxation preserve or optimize. It appears to be a difficult theoretical problem on which more work needs to be done.

IX. Conclusion

In this paper we have introduced the concept of an arrangement as a set of labeled N-ary relations of different orders. We discussed some general scene analysis processes and have illustrated how some of these processes can be viewed as determining or identifying homomorphisms which are constrained by local processing results on the scene data. The homomorphisms are between the unit constraint arrangement and the label constraint arrangement defined by world model. Finally, we have discussed how discrete relaxation,

followed by a tree search, can determine homomorphisms from one arrangement to another.

It is our hope that by illustrating the underlying mathematical unity of a diverse set of scene analysis processes, some generality and power can be gained in formulating the total scene analysis problem.

References

1. Haralick, Robert M. and Jess Kartus, "Theory of Arrangements," University of Kansas, Department of Electrical Engineering and Computer Science, June 1976 (to be published in IEEE SMC).

2. Rosenfeld, Azriel, Robert A. Hummel, and Steven W. Zucker, "Scene Labeling by Relaxation Operations," IEEE Trans. on Systems, Man, and Cybernetics, Vol. SMC-6, No. 6, June 1976, pp. 420-433.

3. Waltz, David L., "Generating Semantic Descriptions from Drawings of Scenes with Shadows," MIT Technical Report AI271, November 1972. For briefer versions see D. Waltz, "Understanding Line Drawings of Scenes with Shadows," in P.H. Winston, ed., The Psychology of Computer Vision, McGraw-Hill, New York, 1975, pp. 19-91; and D. Waltz, "Automata Theoretic Approach to Visual Processing," in R.T. Yeh, ed., Applied Computation Theory, Englewood Cliffs, New Jersey, Prentice-Hall, 1975.

4. Hanson, Allen R. and Edward M. Riseman, "Pattern-Directed Boundary Formation Via Relaxation," Machine Vision Workshop, University of Massachusetts, Amherst, Massachusetts, June 1-3, 1977.

5. Mackworth, Alan K., "Consistency in Networks of Relations," Artificial Intelligence, Vol. 8, 1977, pp. 99-118.

6. Robinson, Güner, "Edge Detection by Compose Gradient Masks," Computer Graphics and Image Processing, Vol. 6, No. 5, 1977, pp. 492-501.

7. Davis, L.S. and Azriel Rosenfeld, "An Application of Relaxation Labeling to Spring-Loaded Template Matching," Proceedings of the Third International Joint Conference on Pattern Recognition, San Diego, California, November 1976, pp. 591-597.

Robert M. Haralick

SURFACE CURVATURE AND APPLICATIONS OF THE DUAL REPRESENTATION

David A. Huffman
University of California at Santa Cruz

Abstract:

The concepts of Gaussian curvature and total curvature are defined and examples are given of the ways in which these curvatures can be distributed over the surfaces and along the edges or con- centrated at the vertices of objects. Behavior of normals near special kinds of surface points are considered with use made of mappings onto the Gaussian sphere. Properties of a closely related "dual-picture" representation are then summarized. An example is given of how this representation can be exploited to facilitate the analysis of a picture to determine the location of features hid- den from the camera. Finally, the dual-picture is used in another example to reveal the unusual flexing properties of a certain kind of configuration of lines ruled on a zero-curvature, or "paper", surface. The inherently sim- ple and elegant behavior of this apparently haphazardly constructed configuration is easily predictable from its dual-picture.

Introduction:

Often solutions of individual problems or new insights into entire problem areas come about when they are viewed in novel ways. Problems that initially seem im- possibly complex can yield quickly to analysis once an especially appropriate representation is found. For instance, the game of Nim (in which two players alternately take one or more tokens from one of several piles having initially arbitrary numbers of tokens, with the object of taking the last tokens and thereby leaving one's opponent with no possible move) seems to be a quite complex one. However, the analysis of the game is straightforward once the sizes of the various piles are written in the base-2 number system.

Another of the many possible exam- ples of more practical consequence is of the analysis of continuous waveforms in the frequency domain rather than as the time series we more directly experience. In this case maximum insight is gained from the interplay of these dual view- points, each one complementing the other.

Similarly, for certain scene analysis problems it is productive to think of the object and surfaces not only as existing in the scene itself but also as entities in a "dual" space [1]. In the first part of this paper I will review some of the properties of a certain mapping and of the concepts of Gaussian and total curva- ture to which it is closely related. In the second part of the paper I will give two representative examples that demon- strate the power of the dual-picture viewpoint. The second of these examples also illustrates some of the essential properties of zero-curvature ("paper") surfaces [2]. I believe that a deep understanding of these surfaces will play an important role in understanding more general surfaces.

Spherical representations and curvature definitions

A productive method of recording evidence about the surface orientation at a given point on an object is to map the surface normal at that point onto a corresponding image point on the surface of a unit-radius sphere (the Gaussian sphere). This image point can be deter- mined by envisioning the Gaussian sphere in the same three-dimensional space as the object itself and then moving the surface normal parallel to itself so that it begins at the center of the sphere in- stead of on the object. The point at which the vector intersects the sphere is the desired image point. If at two or more different points on the object the surface orientations are the same they will have a common image point on the Gaussian sphere.

Consider a simple closed contour on a surface to be analyzed. Each point of that contour has a corresponding image on

Supported by NSF grant MCS-75-12814-A02.

the Gaussian sphere. Therefore the contour itself maps onto a corresponding closed contour on the sphere. That image contour (which the author refers to as the "trace" of the surface contour) encloses some region of the sphere just as the surface contour encloses some region on the object itself. The total curvature of the surface region bounded by the surface contour is defined to be the area on the Gaussian sphere that is enclosed by the corresponding trace. This curvature is, by definition, positive if when the surface contour is traversed in one direction (say, clockwise) the image of that contour is traversed in the same direction, and is taken to be negative when the image contour is traversed in the opposite direction. Imagine a surface point enclosed by a small contour. The Gaussian curvature at that point is defined to be the limit of the ratio of the area enclosed by the image contour on the sphere to the area enclosed by the surface contour as that contour is shrunk to the given point. It is apparent from the definitions that Gaussian curvature is dimensionless and that total curvature has the dimensions of area.

I shall now consider specific examples, first of regular surface points (see below), second of points on edges, and finally of points at vertices. We shall see that the Gaussian curvature at singular points on edges and at vertices is generally infinite while the total curvature at both regular surface points and points on edges is zero.

A regular surface point is a point at which the tangent plane is uniquely defined. It follows that the normal and the spherical image are also uniquely defined. For a point on a plane surface we can quickly conclude that the Gaussian and total curvatures are both zero. Consider more generally a contour enclosing only regular points on a surface. As the contour is shrunk to a given point the trace will also shrink to the corresponding image point. Thus we can conclude that the total curvature at the regular surface point is zero, but that the Gaussian curvature may be non-zero.

Curvature at edge-points

Now consider a typical point on an edge or crease of a surface. On either side of such a line the surface is regular but at the edge itself the direction of the normal changes abruptly. If we enclose the typical edge-point by a contour that passes arbitrarily close to the edge on either side the corresponding spherical image of the contour consists of four distinct arcs: two that correspond to the portions of the contour that lie in the regular regions on either side of the edge and two that are associated

with the two points at which the contour crosses the edge. In Figure 1, for instance, I portray a situation in which two cylindrical surfaces intersect. The part of the edge inside the contour shown is presumed to be convex (+). The two solid lines (a,b and c,d) of the image are arcs of great circles because the associated surfaces are both cylindrical.

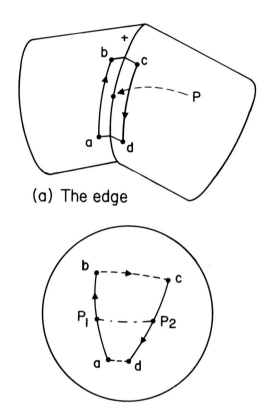

(a) The edge

(b) The spherical image

Fig. 1. An edge and its image

Consider now the situation in the vicinity of the edge between points "b" and "c". There the edge is approximated by a straight line segment and the tangent planes on either side of the edge contain that segment. The normals to these two tangent planes are represented by points "b" and "c" in the image. Visualization of the orientations of the infinite set of normals to the surface between "b" and "c" will be facilitated if the reader will imagine that the edge is slightly rounded off so that the edge segment is replaced by a cylindrical surface of small radius that is tangent to the two surface tangent planes mentioned above. If the radius of that imagined

David A. Huffman

cylinder is reduced to zero the original edge is approached as a limit. Throughout the limiting process, however, the orientations of the associated normal vectors remain essentially the same. They have directions that are orthogonal to the edge-segment and therefore their images determine the arc of a great circle on the Gaussian sphere, as is represented by the upper dotted line in Figure 1-b. A similar argument holds for the dotted line associated with points "a" and "d"

For the contour shown the total curvature is non-zero even when the two finite-length portions of the contour are only infinitesmally far away from the edge and the area within the contour is arbitrarily close to zero. Thus the total curvature along the non-zero length of edge shown is non-zero. When the contour is shrunk to the point P by letting its length also approach zero the image shrinks to the pair of points P_1 and P_2.

(The angular distance between P_1 and P_2 is the dihedral angle between the pair of planes associated with the edge at point P.) The total curvature associated with point P is therefore zero. On the other hand as the contour was shrunk to the point the ratio of image area to surface area was infinite. It is thus appropriate to conclude that for a point on a general edge the Gaussian curvature is infinite.

We may conclude that the non-zero total curvature that is generally to be associated with a finite length of an edge is distributed along that edge. Even though the total curvature at regular surface points and at edge-points are both zero they are zero in essentially different ways. The difference is revealed when we determine the corresponding Gaussian curvatures.

As an example for which computations are easy to make consider the edge of the right circular cylinder of radius R in Figure 2. The image of the contour is a spherical triangle with interior angle Θ at one vertex and angles measuring $\pi/2$ at the other two vertices. The lengths of the great circular arcs b,c and a,d of the image are 90° (because the angle associated with the edge is 90°). That is, we can picture "c" and "d" at the north pole of the sphere and "a" and "b" on its equator. Since the total area of the sphere is 4π it becomes an easy matter to determine that the area enclosed by the triangular image is Θ even when the contour is shrunk until it lies arbitrarily close to the edge itself. That is, the total curvature along the portion of edge inside the contour is Θ. Because the length of that portion of edge is R Θ we can conclude that the total curvature

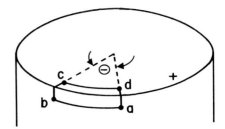

(a) The edge

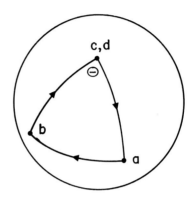

(b) The spherical image

Fig. 2 An edge of a cylinder

is distributed along the edge with a density of 1/R units per unit length. The total curvature for the entire edge that is shown is 2π.

Curvature at vertices

At a point on an edge there are two associated tangent planes. There is also a <u>one</u>-parameter family of planes that contain the edge at that point. In our example of Figure 1-b the normals to that family of planes were represented on the arc between P_1 and P_2.

At a <u>vertex</u> of a surface we can think of an associated <u>two</u>-parameter family of planes that contain that vertex. The normals to this family of planes are represented on the Gaussian sphere by the region enclosed by the image of a surface contour that encircles the vertex. This region will in general have a non-zero area even as the contour is shrunk to the point. Thus a vertex is usually associated with a non-zero total curvature and an infinite Gaussian curvature. Vertices of polyhedra and apices of cones are examples of this kind of singular point.

Consider as an example the cube corner shown in Figure 3-a. Its image is a spherical triangle with interior angles that are all $\pi/2$. The area within the triangle is $\pi/2$ and is enclosed clockwise

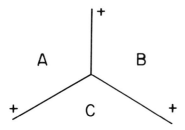

(a) A convex vertex

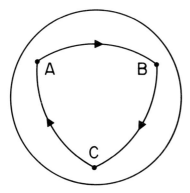

(b) The spherical image

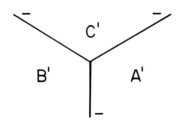

(c) A concave vertex

Fig. 3 Two vertices with
positive curvature

(when the corresponding contour enclosing the cube corner is oriented clockwise). Therefore the total curvature at the cube corner is $+ \pi/2$.

Imagine now that the concave cubical indentation depicted in Figure 3-c is placed so that its three faces A', B', and C' are parallel, respectively, to the faces A, B, and C of the cube corner of Figure 3-a. A contour that encloses the concave vertex clockwise traverses its three faces in an order that corresponds to the order in which the faces of the convex vertex were traversed. Therefore the spherical image of a contour around the concave vertex is exactly the same as the spherical image of a contour around the convex vertex. We may therefore conclude that a total curvature of $+ \pi/2$ is associated with the concave vertex of our example.

In Figure 4 we portray a junction of two walls. The image of the vertex shown is a triangle in which the orientation of the boundary is opposite to that of a contour enclosing the vertex. Therefore the total curvature at the vertex is $- \pi/2$.

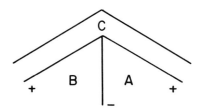

(a) The top of a wall

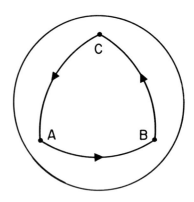

(b) The spherical image

Fig. 4 A vertex with negative
curvature

In general the total curvature at a polyhedral vertex is equal to 2π minus the sum of the sector angles of the planes that contain that vertex. (For example, in Figure 4-a the planes A, B, and C have sector angles of $\pi/2$, $\pi/2$, and $3\pi/2$, respectively at the vertex they share. Therefore the total curvature at that vertex is $2\pi - 5\pi/2 = - \pi/2$.). This conclusion is valid whatever the number of planes associated with the vertex may be and it can be derived from

i) the fact that the area of a spherical triangle on a unit-radius sphere is equal to the sum of its interior angle minus π (this difference is referred to as the "excess angle") and

ii) the fact that the sector angles associated with a polyhedral vertex determine (are equal to) the amount of (clockwise) turning at the corresponding vertices of the polygonal trace on the Gaussian sphere.

David A. Huffman

For a general vertex (for instance, at the apex of an arbitrary cone) the total curvature is again 2π minus the sum of the "sector angles" even when each sector angle is infinitesmal.

I wish to give special attention to the special case of vertices on "paper" surfaces. For them both the total curvature and the Gaussian curvature are zero. It is easily shown that a polyhedral vertex on a paper surface must have at least four edges if the configuration is to be flexible (assuming that the regions between those edges are to remain planes and that the only flexing is at the edges). In the case of a degree-4 vertex the boundary of the image is, in general, that of an asymmetric butterfly, as is shown in Figure 5. The net area enclosed is zero; the positive area of the left wing is exactly cancelled by the negative area of the right wing.

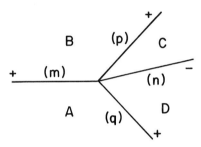

(a) The vertex

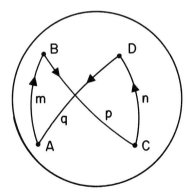

(b) The spherical image

Fig. 5 A vertex on paper

Before proceeding further I note that the net total curvature over a surface that is topologically equivalent to that of a sphere is 4π. As an example the total curvature of a cube is concentrated at its eight vertices, at each of which the total curvature is $\pi/2$. As another example I note that the total curvature for the completed cylinder of Figure 2 is concentrated along the two

circular edges; 2π for each edge.

Any surface topologically equivalent to that of a torus has a net total curvature that is zero. For instance, imagine punching a square hole through a cube. In addition to the eight original vertices there are now eight more (all like that in Figure 4) at each of which the total curvature is $-\pi/2$. Each new hole adds an increment of -4π to the net total curvature. Thus an object with n holes has a surface total curvature of $4(1-n)\pi$.

Spherical images of special types of regular surface points

I now return to consider in somewhat more detail the spherical images of certain special types of regular points on surfaces. First consider a point on a sphere of radius R. It is easy to show that the Gaussian curvature of all points of the sphere is $+1/R^2$. That is, the total curvature (4π) associated with the entire surface is distributed uniformly over the surface.

In a region containing only regular points on a paper surface I make use of the fact that a one-parameter family of straight lines may be embedded in that surface [2]. Furthermore there exists a single common plane tangent to the surface at all points of such a line. As a consequence the image of a closed contour enclosing only regular points is a single line on the Gaussian sphere. The area associated with this line is, of course, zero.

Certain important features of the saddle surface z = xy are depicted in Figure 6-a. The value of z is assumed to increase in the direction away from the viewer. Therefore a line on that surface going from "a" to "c" (for which y = x) is a parabola that is convex toward the viewer; a line going from "b" to "d" (for which y = -x) is a parabola that is concave with respect to the viewer. Consequently a normal to the surface at "a" would point to the lower left, at "b" to the lower right, at point "c" to the upper right, and at "d" to the upper left. In addition it is possible to show that the four segments of the surface contour (for which either x or y is constant) map onto arcs of great circles on the Gaussian sphere, as is shown in Figure 6-b. Note especially that a clockwise orientation of the surface contour leads to a counterclockwise orientation of its image on the sphere.

It is easily proved that the Gaussian curvature is -1 at the point x = y = 0 on the saddle surface. The Gaussian curvature is also negative elsewhere on the saddle although its magnitude decreases as

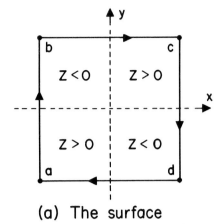

(a) The surface

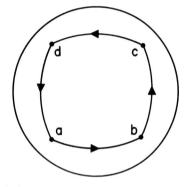

(b) The spherical image

Fig. 6 A saddle surface

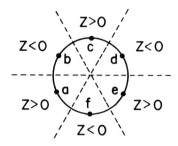

(a) The surface

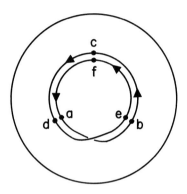

(b) The spherical image

Fig. 7 A monkey saddle

we travel away from the origin. In the case of a saddle surface of higher order (for example, the 3-legged "monkey saddle" of Figure 7) the spherical image of a contour that encloses the center of the saddle will enclose a corresponding region on the sphere two or more times. In general the image of such a contour on a saddle with n legs will proceed around the region on a sphere n-1 times. In computing the Gaussian and total curvature in such cases we must take into account how many times a region is enclosed.

It is possible to analyze the behavior of surface normals near a regular point on an arbitrary surface by thinking of the surface as the sum of a spherical component, a plane component, and components that are saddle surfaces of various orders. This decomposition is somewhat like the decomposition of a periodic waveform into its Fourier components. It will be reported on in more detail in a future paper.

Some properties of a dual-picture

In reference [1] I defined the properties of three-dimensional "dual-scenes". Planes that are tangent to surfaces in the original scene (in the (x,y,z) space) are mapped onto points in the dual-scene (in the (u,v,w) space), and points in the scene are mapped onto tangent planes in the dual-scene, and vice-versa. The transformation is unusual in that it treats the third dimensions (z and w) quite differently from the others. However, for the two problems treated in the next sections of this paper it is unnecessary to have the full dual-scene representation available to us and I shall ignore the third dimensions, working only with the projected picture of the scene (in the (x,y) space) and the projected dual-picture of the dual-scene (in the (u,v) space).

We can alternatively obtain the dual-picture by mapping the images on the Gaussian sphere onto the dual-picture plane by a central projection. For this projection we let the sphere be tangent

David A. Huffman

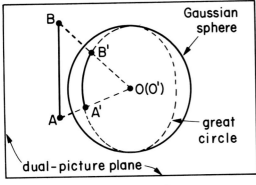

(a) front elevation

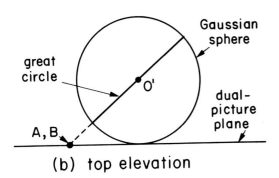

(b) top elevation

Fig. 8. Two views of a mapping from
the Gaussian sphere to the
dual-picture plane

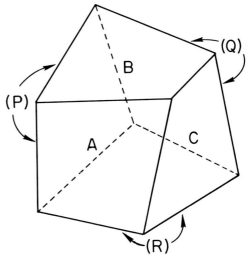

(a) The skew cube

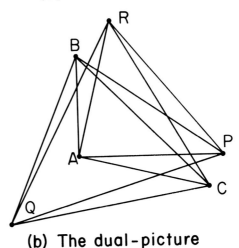

(b) The dual-picture

Fig. 9 A hidden vertex problem

to the dual-picture plane at its origin
(see Figure 8). Imagine, for example,
that the image points A' and B' on the
surface of the Gaussian sphere shown are
associated with two planes on some object (for instance, the two correspondingly labelled planes on the example of
Figure 9 that will be discussed below).
We have already observed that the segment
of the great circular arc between two
image points such as A' and B' represents the one-parameter family of
planes that are tangent to the object
along the edge common to the two planes.
This great circular arc maps onto a
straight line in the dual-picture
plane. Perhaps the most important
property of the dual-picture image is
that the image line in the dual-picture
is perpendicular to the corresponding
line in the picture itself. Note, for
example, in Figure 9 the horizontal
picture line and the vertical dual-picture
line associated with the planes A and B.
The reader who is interested in other
properties of the dual-picture and the
dual-scene will find them discussed at
length in reference [1].

A hidden vertex problem

The picture of an object somewhat
like a cube, except that no two faces need
be parallel, is given in Figure 9-a.
Assume that we have knowledge that each of
the vertices is associated with just
three planes; that is, that the object
is a trihedral object. Our problem is to
determine the exact location in the picture of the hidden vertex. We are
initially given only the positions of the
six peripheral lines and of the three
lines incident at the fully visible vertex in the center of the picture.

I begin by noting that there must be three hidden planes. In each of these planes (P, Q, and R) we can see a pair of lines that are the intersections of the hidden plane with two of the visible planes. These are indicated by arrows.

The drawing of the dual-picture proceeds as follows. Construct the triangle ABC with sides at right angles to the corresponding lines of the picture. The size of the triangle is unimportant for our purposes. Next draw pairs of construction lines from points A and B that are at right angles to the lines PA and PB in the picture. The intersection of these two lines determines point P. In a similar fashion determine the point Q (from lines QB and QC) and point R (from lines RA and RC). Since the planes P, Q, and R all have normals that point away from the viewer it is actually the negatives of the normal vectors that are displayed. We can now draw the sides of the triangle PQR. Its three sides determine the directions taken by the hidden lines PQ, QR, and PR in the picture. Their intersection is at the location of the hidden vertex.

What may be surprising to the reader is that the position of the hidden vertex in the picture can be determined independent of any information other than what is given in the picture itself. It is not likely that the reader will be able to find a construction leading to the determination of the hidden lines and vertex that is nearly as easy as the one given here. It is clear that the interplay between the picture and the dual-picture representations of the object has made the solving of the problem quite straightforward.

A simplifying constraint for polyhedral paperfoldings

My second analysis problem requires a small amount of background information, some of which is to be found in reference [2] and some of which has not been reported until now. I first note that in general the relationships among the magnitudes m, n, p, and q of the dihedral angles at the edges of a degree-4 polyhedral vertex on a paper surface (see Figure 5) are quite complex. However there is a constraint that we can impose among the four sector angles that leads to an enormous simplification in these relationships. For example (see Figure 5-a) if the sector angles for the planes A and C sum to π the sector angles for the planes B and D will also sum to π. This condition (called the "π-condition") results in $m = n$ and $p = q$.

When the π-condition holds the dual-picture becomes that of a symmetric butterfly rather than the more general asymmetric one. The point at which the

two wings join is a point that represents the normal to the plane that contains the line common to B and C and the line common to A and D. Moreover when the π-condition holds $\tan(p/2)$ is proportional to $\tan(m/2)$; their ratio is a constant that depends only upon the four sector angles at the vertex.

For infinitesmal dihedral angles we can also conclude that the angles $p(=q)$ and $m(=n)$ themselves are proportional to each other in that same ratio.

A paperfold analysis example

In Figure 10-a is a picture of a network of lines on a flat sheet of paper, each line intended to be made an edge that is either concave (-) or convex (+) when the paperfold is flexed. Because essentially the same picture is valid when the various dihedral angles are not zero but still infinitesmal the directions of the corresponding lines in the dual-picture shown in Figure 10-b are immediately determinable. Note especially however that the lengths of lines in the dual-picture are proportional to the various dihedral angles only when the dihedral angles are small.

We can see from the dual-picture that the π-condition is met at each vertex. Note, for instance, the sequence of the four planes A, B, S, R associated with the lowest vertex and the corresponding butterfly-shaped trace in the dual-picture. Such butterfly shapes are characteristic of vertices at which the π-condition is satisfied. When the π-condition is satisfied at a degree-4 vertex it can be proved that the four associated dihedral angles are equal in pairs. At the lowest vertex, for example, the dihedral angles between the pair of planes A, B and the pair of planes R, S are equal, and the dihedral angles between the pair of planes A, R and the pair of planes B, S are also equal. Thus the line segments in the dual-picture that are representative of these two angles are also equal in pairs (see Figure 10-b). That the butterflies are all symmetric in our example follows from the fact that a single point Q is used for the junction of all wing pairs and that the tips of the wings lie on the two concentric circles shown. The appropriate interpretation of Q is that it represents a single plane which contains all of the convex (+) lines of the "spine" of the paperfolding (at least when all of the dihedral angles are small).

For the small angle situation the constants of proportionality among the various angles can be read directly from our dual-picture. But since the π-condition holds these same constants of proportionality are valid for the tangents of the corresponding half-angles even when these angles are not small! The dual-

David A. Huffman

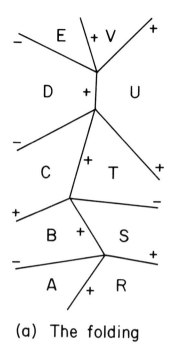

(a) The folding

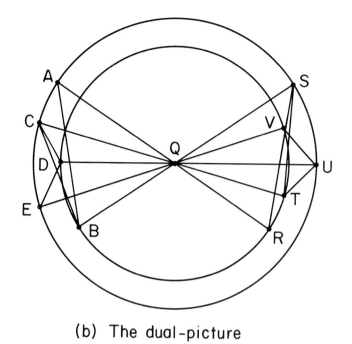

(b) The dual-picture

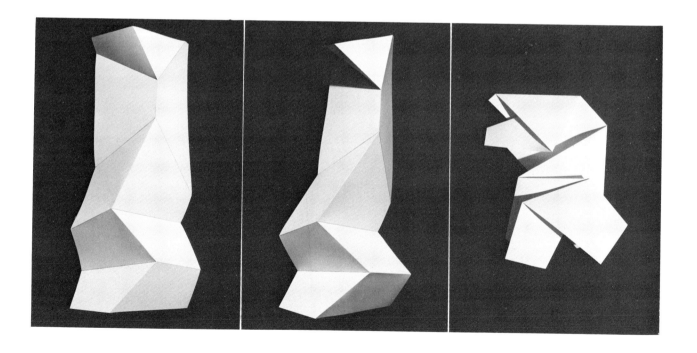

(c) Three views of the paperfold

Fig. 10. A paper fold with remarkable properties

picture in this situation therefore
serves the same purpose as would the
portrayal of images on the Gaussian
sphere. It is also much easier to work
with.

We can also conclude that however our
paperfolding is flexed the lines of its
spine will move in such a way that they
always lie in a single plane. This
remarkable result is certainly not apparent from the placement of the lines in
the paperfolding itself. These, even
when studied closely, have no easily
discernable pattern. Only when we view
the dual-picture does the underlying
structural order become obvious and allow
us to predict the true and unusual
behavior of the folding.

It is now time to reveal what the
reader has probably already suspected:
The dual-picture was constructed first,
and the paperfolding was derived from it
later. Thus this example was actually
a synthesis example rather than an
analysis example.

The pictures in Figure 10-c show a
paperfolding that was constructed to
the specifications of the dual-picture
and photographed as it was flexed. In
the final photograph the dihedral angles
are all nearly 180°; that is, the
object is nearly "folded flat".

Summary

I hope that the reader as a result
of my efforts here will have a better
intuitive understanding of concepts of
curvature. I also hope that the two
brief examples of the application of the
dual-picture representation will have
been so provocative that the reader
might be encouraged to find others.

References

[1] Huffman, D. A. A duality concept
     for the analysis of polyhedral
     scenes. in "Machine Representations
     of Knowledge" published as Machine
     Intelligence 8, Elcock, E. W. and
     Michie, D. (Eds.), Ellis Horwood
     Ltd. and John Wiley, 1975.

[2] Huffman, D. A. Curvature and
     creases; a primer on paper. IEEE
     Transactions on Computers, Volume
     C-25, No. 10, pp. 1010-1019, Oct.
     1976.

David A. Huffman

Visual Images as Spatial Representations in Active Memory

Stephen M. Kosslyn
Harvard University

Steven P. Shwartz
The Johns Hopkins University

ABSTRACT

Research on human visual imagery suggests that images are spatial representations that occur in active (short-term) memory. This chapter describes some of this research and how it motivated a running computer simulation of human imagery. The simulation involves a "pictorial" image represented by selectively filling in cells of a matrix; this representation is generated from stored "perceptual" and "conceptual" representations. Interpretative procedures act as a "mind's eye" that classifies images and parts thereof in terms of semantic categories; transformational procedures operate to expand, shrink, rotate and/or scan pictorial images. Two alternative ways of implementing the image representation are discussed. In addition, possible uses of imagery representations for visual processing during pattern recognition are considered. The chapter includes tracings of actual runs of the simulation, flowcharts, and examples of output from the program.

1.0   Introduction

Visual imagery stands at the intersection of memory and perception, and understanding imagery may provide a gateway into understanding these more general topics and how they interrelate. The most important issue in the current study of imagery probably is whether or not the experienced, quasi-pictorial mental image is functional. The traditional point of view assumes that images are not only functional, but play a key role in mental life. Periodically, however, it has been argued that images are not functional, but rather are meaningless concommitants of more abstract underlying processing. The last generation of proponents of this view were the Behaviorists, such as John B. Watson; in the present generation, this idea is espoused most often by those involved in computer simulation of mental processes [e.g., see 1, 22]. According to the recent view, all internal representation is accomplished by abstract propositional (also called "symbolic") data structures; propositions are language-like entities that specify how some arguments are related [see 1, 22] and usually are hypothesized to be organized into some sort of network structure. These representations resemble descriptions; mental images, in contrast,

purportedly depict or portray information, as opposed to stating it (see 14 for a detailed discussion of this issue).

Because encoded perceptual information presumably is used to construct mental images, the issue of whether images are epiphenomenal is important for our understanding of how perceptual processing takes place in humans. Thus, if images preserve the metric, spatial properties evident in our experiences of them, then perceptual processing also must preserve such information. That is, one must account for how the information underlying images is encoded, if it is in fact present in memory; a perceptual system that loses this sort of information in the course of higher-order processing will not correctly model human perception.

The view that images are functional has long been popular in psychology and philosophy [see 2, 21], but has often been attacked because this idea is rarely developed or formalized [e.g., 22]. The present chapter describes a computer simulation of human visual imagery that treats images as functional, nondiscursive spatial representations that occur in active memory. Before turning to the model proper, let us briefly consider why we felt impelled to adopt the second position noted above, and treated images as functional representations.

The present work was funded by NSF Grant BNS 76-16987 awarded to the first author. We wish to thank Susan Williams and Terry Coyle for invaluable assistance in preparing the manuscript.

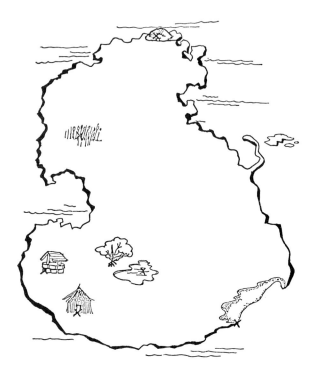

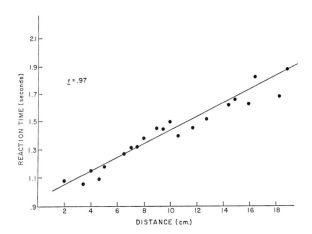

Figure 1. The map scanned and time to scan different distances across an image of it.

2.0 Data about human visual imagery

2.1 Images are functional spatial representations: four basic findings

Our model was motivated by results of experiments on how people process visual images. The obtained data seemed most consistent with the notion that visual images are functional spatial representations much like those that underly our experience of seeing during perception. As such, images seem to represent distance by embodying spatial extent, not describing it. This inference is grounded pri-

marily on the sorts of findings described below. The present paper is concerned primarily with the implementation of an imagery simulation, and not with the data that motivated it; thus, the interested reader is directed to 13, 14, and 20 for a more detailed treatment of relevant data.

2.1.1 Distance affects time to scan images

In one series of experiments [12, 18], we showed that more time was required to scan further distances across images. In one study, people imaged a map containing seven locations and scanned between all possible pairs. Time to scan increased linearly with increasing distance between the 21 possible pairs of locations (each separated by a unique distance). The map and these results are illustrated in Figure 1. In other experiments, people imaged schematic faces wherein the eyes were either dark or light and located either 2, 3, 4, or 5 inches above the mouth; in all other respects the faces were identical. Upon imaging a given face, the subject mentally focused on the mouth and waited until he heard the word "light" or "dark." As soon as either word was presented, the subject "glanced up" to the eyes of his imaged face and saw whether or not they were appropriately described by the word. Time to judge whether the eyes were light or dark increased linearly with distance from the mouth. Further, in another experiment, overall scanning times were reduced when people were asked to "shrink" an imaged face mentally prior to scanning it, and times were increased when subjects "expanded" a face before scanning. These results are difficult to explain if images are simple "abstract propositional" list structures, but follow naturally if images are spatial representations that preserve metric distance information [see 14, 20].

2.1.2 Images overflow if expanded too large

The notion that images represent spatial extent suggests that they may have spatial boundaries (after all, they do not extend on indefinitely). If images occur in a spatial representational medium [e.g., within something like an array representing a matrix; see 14, 20], then their maximum spatial extent may be constrained by the extent of the medium. We used the following paradigm in an attempt to test this idea: People were asked to image an object as if it were being seen from very far away. They then were to imagine that they were walking towards the object and asked if it appeared to loom larger; all subjects reported that it did. We asked if there was a point where the image loomed so large as to seem to "overflow." At this point, the subject was to "stop" in his mental walk and to estimate how far away the object seemed in the image. That is, the subject was asked to estimate how far away the object would be if s/he were actually seeing it at that subjective size. We did this basic experiment in a variety of ways, having subjects image various sorts of pictures or image animals when just given their names and sizes; in addition, subjects estimated distance by verbally assessing feet and inches or by moving a tripod apparatus the appropriate distance from a blank wall.

If images occur in a spatially constrained medium, then the larger the imaged object, the

Stephen M. Kosslyn and Steven P. Shwartz

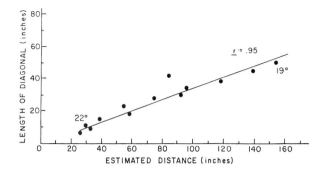

Figure 2. Judged distance at the point of overflow for different sized images.

further away it should seem at the point of overflow. In addition, a constant angle should be subtended by the imaged objects at the point of overflow. Using simple trigonometry, we were able to compute the "visual angle of the mind's eye" from the estimated distances and longest axis of each imaged object. In all of our experiments, the basic results were the same: First, people claimed that smaller objects seemed to overflow at nearer apparent distances than did larger apparent distances (the correlation between object size and distance was always very high), and distance usually increased linearly with size of the imaged object. Second, the calculated "visual angle" at the point of overflow remained constant for different sized objects when non-verbal assessment techniques were used. The actual size of the angle varied depending upon instructions: more stringent definitions of "overflow" resulted in smaller angles. These last findings imply that images do not overflow at a distinct point, but seem to fade off gradually towards the periphery. The best estimate of the maximal angle subtended by an image while still remaining entirely "visible" seemed to be around 20 degrees. The results of one of these experiments are illustrated in Figure 2. In this experiment, people were shown different sized line drawings of animals, imaged them, and then estimated the apparent distance at the point of overflow; distance estimates were indicated non-verbally by positioning a tripod relative to a blank wall.

These results, then, support the claim that the images we experience are spatial entities, and their spatial characteristics do in fact have real consequences for some forms of information processing [see 17].

2.1.3 Subjectively smaller images are more difficult to scrutinize

If asked which is higher off the ground, a horse's knees or the tip of its tail, many people claim to image the beast and to "inspect" the image, evaluating the queried relation. It makes sense to suspect, then, that images might be appropriately processed by the same sorts of classificatory procedures brought to bear in classifying perceptual representations [see 10,14]. If so, then we might expect constraints that affect ease of classifying parts perceptually also to affect ease of imagery classification. Parts of smaller

objects are "harder to see" in perception, for example, and also may be harder to "see" in imagery. This result was in fact obtained [10]; parts of subjectively smaller images of objects required more time to classify mentally than did parts of subjectively larger objects. In addition, simply varying the size of the part per se also affected time to examine an image. In this case, smaller parts--like a cat's claws--required more time to see on an image than did larger parts--like its head. This last result was obtained [11] even though the smaller parts were more strongly associated with the animal in question, and were more quickly verified as being appropriate when imagery was not used (more highly associated properties are typically affirmed as appropriate more quickly than less associated ones in studies of "semantic memory"--see 26). These findings are illustrated in Figure 3. These results, then, not only are consistent with the notion that images are functional spatial representations that may be interpreted by other processes, but also serve to distinguish between processing imaginal and non-imaginal representations.

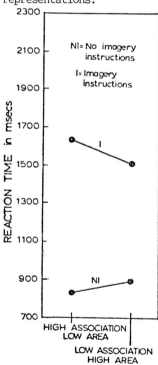

Figure 3. Time to judge two sorts of properties using imagery or not using imagery.

2.1.4 Images are transformed gradually

Cooper & Shepard [see 5,6] and others have demonstrated that more time is required if images must be "rotated" through greater arcs. Similarly, we have found that more time is required to expand or contract images to greater degrees. These findings seem to indicate that images pass through intermediate positions in the process of being transformed. A propositional model of the sort offered by Gips [7] does not lead us to expect this. A spatial model, wherein a pictorial image is transformed, seems to imply in a straightforward manner that images will pass through intermediate positions as they are transformed, given that the same image is being retained and processed [see 20].

2.2 The origins of images

Some information must exist in memory prior to our experiencing a seemingly spatial image in consciousness. The present claim is that the image we experience is not simply "retrieved" but is generated from more abstract representations in long-term memory. If images are generated, more effort should be required to generate more complex images [10, 13, 20, for an expanded rationale]. Weber & Harnish [27] found that longer words required more time to image, supporting this claim. Kosslyn, Reiser & Greenbarg [19] asked people to remember pictures of animals and objects that were drawn either with minimal detail or with many details. More time was required to form a visual image of a picture when it was drawn with many details. In addition, we also asked people to remember letters of the alphabet arranged to form patterns which contained different numbers of perceptual groups (as determined by the Gestalt Laws of organization). People then imaged these patterns at one of two sizes. Interestingly, more time was required to image patterns with more groups, and larger patterns required more time to image than smaller ones. Kosslyn [10] also found that subjectively larger images (of animals, in this case) required more time to generate than smaller ones. If more "detail" is inserted into larger images, these effects of subjective size also indicate that images are in fact constructed and that construction takes time.

The results described above seem to indicate that images are not simply retrieved in toto or projected wholistically into consciousness. Given that images are constructed, the main question now concerns the sorts of representations used in this construction process. On one hand, images could be the result of assembling separate perceptual memories, like one assembles a jigsaw puzzle. On the other hand, images could be constructed using both perceptual and conceptual information, like arranging a set of photographs on a table in accordance with a description of the total configuration. It seemed to us that the latter alternative almost had to be true: after all, people apparently can construct images of novel scenes upon being given a description of them. For example, nobody we've talked to seems to have trouble imaging "Jimmy Carter standing on a surfboard riding a gigantic wave," although no one claimed to have ever witnessed such an event. In this case, people seem to be able to use the conceptual information underlying their understanding of the words to amalgamate various perceptual memories into a common scene. We performed a very simple experiment in order to demonstrate that conceptual information can in fact be used in image construction: People saw a 6 x 3 matrix of letters, which was then removed and named either the matrix of "3 rows of 6" or the matrix of "6 columns of 3." When later asked to image this matrix, more time was required if it had been conceptualized in terms of 6 columns instead of 3 rows. Thus, the conceptual information inherent in the name clearly influenced time to reconstruct the

appearance.

3.0 The Simulation

As psychologists, we have two reasons for thinking about our work in terms of a computer simulation: 1) this forces us to be explicit, and 2) this insures that we will be self-consistent in our explanations for a diverse set of results. In addition, we have three reasons for actually constructing a running program: 1) to discover whether our theoretical ideas are in fact sufficient to account for the data; 2) to derive new predictions and hence to be led to collect interesting data; and, 3) to bring new issues and questions to our attention. This last goal is not a common motivation for implementing programs, so let us say a word or two more about it: We were determined to use actual data to motivate the construction of our simulation, as opposed to simply making "sensible" or "intuitively sound" decisions when implementing. That is, we use the implementation procedure as a crutch, as a way of forcing us to perform experiments on interesting and valuable questions. We use the simulation to help us to form explicit hypotheses about human processing. In keeping with this aim, after presenting an overview of our current model, the present paper presents two alternate ways in which a functional "image" could be implemented, the first of which is part of a currently running program (described in detail in 20) and the second of which is currently being implemented. Following description of the representations, we will compare and contrast the two along several criteria.

It may be convenient to treat the simulation as if it were comprised of two main components, a structural one and a processing one. Let us consider these components in turn.

3.1 The image representation

Images (i.e. , the quasi-pictorial entities we experience) are treated as "surface" representations generated from more abstract "deep" level representations.

1) An image is represented in short-term (active) memory as a configuration of points in a matrix. A "picture" is depicted by selectively filling in cells of the matrix. This representational medium is not equally activated throughout; instead, the central region is most sharply in focus and activation tapers off until no cells are activated (and material in this region of the matrix has "overflowed"). This representation is spatial in the sense required to account for the data on scanning and overflowing. The details of implementing the surface display will be discussed below.

2) An image is represented in long-term memory in terms of files addressed by the name of the imaged object. There are two types of image deep representations: First, the perceptual memory of the appearance (which is not semantically interpreted but corresponds to the products of "seeing that," not the products of "seeing as") is stored in a file containing R, Theta coordinates. These polar coordinates specify locations where points

Stephen M. Kosslyn and Steven P. Shwartz

should be placed in the surface matrix. A polar coordinate representation was chosen because a) it allows easy placement of images at different locations in the surface matrix, b) it allows images to be easily generated at different subjective sizes (i.e., different sizes in the display). It also allows images to be generated at different angular orientations. The perceptual memories that underlie the actual surface display may be stored in several files; one file corresponds to the "global" or "central" shape and serves as a skeleton upon which "details" may be placed.

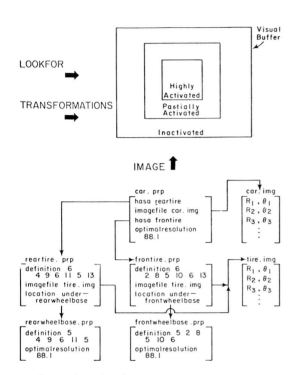

Figure 4. The data structures of the simulation. The ".prp" files contain propositional information whereas the ".img" files contain literal perceptual information.

The second type of image deep representation consists of stored facts about the image; these facts are represented in a "propositional" format. Facts include information about a) how and where a part (represented as a file containing locations of points) is attached to the global or central image (e.g., a cushion is "flush on" a seat), b) how to find a given part (i.e., a procedural definition of a part, like a seat of a chair), c) the name of the file that contains the "perceptual memory," d) an index of the resolution necessary to see the object or part, and e) the name of the superordinate category.

Figure 4 schematizes the data structures underlying an image of a car (the actual implementation of the pictorial image, schematized at the top right, will be taken up in some detail shortly). The numbers following the designations of "definition" in the files with .PRP (propositional) extensions index procedures in a library; when these procedures are executed in the specified ord-

er, the pictorial image is searched and the sought part—if present—is found. Also of interest is the fact that only a single image of a tire is used for both the front and rear; we hypothesize that most people assume that all tires look the same, and do not bother to encode multiple representations. The words in block letters symbolize processes that operate upon these representations. The data structures are best understood in the context of how they are used, so let us now turn to the processes that utilize them and describe the actual operation of the simulation.

3.2 Image processes

There are two sorts of image processes: There are routines for generating and inspecting the image, and there are routines for transforming the image. In addition, we have also begun to hypothesize how imagery representations and propositional representations of general world knowledge are accessed in the course of question-answering.

3.2.1 Image Generation

The IMAGE procedures are schematized in Figure 5, that depicts the sequence of events underlying the construction of an image. In generating an image of an object, the program first looks for the file which contains the propositional information about the object (i.e., the file whose name is the concatenation of the object's name plus the extension .PRP). If this file is then successfully located,[1] it is searched for the name of the file that contains information about the literal appearance of the object (i.e., a list of R, Theta coordinates that specifies where points should be placed in the surface matrix). This image file is then accessed and the specified points are turned on in the surface matrix. Before each point is turned on, the R and Theta values are adjusted appropriately if a non-default size, orientation, or origin is specified by the user.

The program tracings for the generation of a skeletal image of a car can be found in Table 1 in the appendix, and the skeletal image of the car that was generated by this run is illustrated in Figure 6. The skeletal image is meant to contain "first glance" information. Whether this is some sort of global shape information, or simply information about the most centrally structured part, is a question for future research.

Once the skeletal image is printed out in the surface matrix, the program will stop unless the user has requested that a detailed image be generated (some data suggest that people do not add detail unless it is needed--see [20]). If detail is requested, the program goes back to the propositional file of the object and checks for an

1. In a detailed flow chart there would be a test for the presence of a sought representation after every attempt to search; if a sought representation is not found, the program returns an error message. We have deleted most of these tests for clarity as they are not important in the interesting behavior of the simulation.

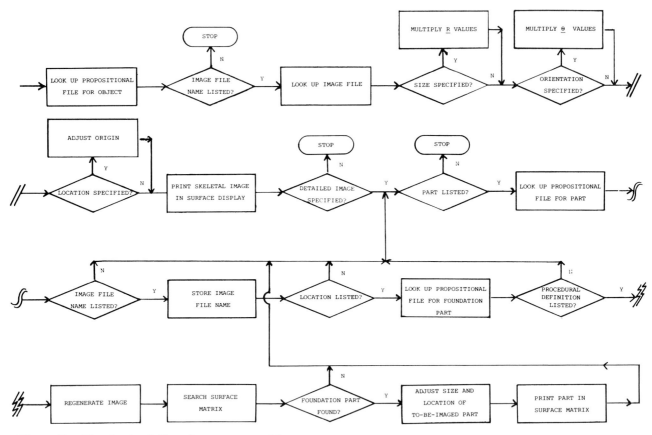

Figure 5. Flowchart of the imagery generation process.

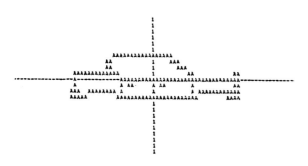

Figure 6. A skeletal image generated by the simulation.

assertion that a particular part belongs on the object (e.g., HASA REARTIRE). If such an assertion is found, the propositional file for the part is located and searched for the name of the image file (i.e., the file containing information about the literal appearance of the part). If this information is found, the name of the image file is stored (rather than looked up later when needed, because if it is not there, the program need not continue). Following this, the location of where the part should be placed in the image is looked up. This information consists of a relation and a foundation part (e.g., UNDER REARWHEELBASE—as evident in Fig-

ure 5). Next, the propositional file for the foundation part (rearwheelbase, in this case) is located and searched for the procedural definition of the part. The procedural definition is a subset of a collection of library procedures that test for various spatial configurations in the surface matrix. The procedures that make up a particular procedural definition are listed by number in the propositional file. We do not claim that these are the procedures actually used by people (to solve this problem would be to solve much of the problem of how people recognize patterns), but only that people use something like our procedures in similar ways. The procedures in this definition are then executed one at a time, and, if successful, delineate the boundaries of the foundation part. The coordinates of the foundation part are then passed to another procedure which prints out the part at the correct size and location in the surface matrix. After the part is successfully integrated into the image, or, if any of the above procedures failed, the program returns to the propositional file of the object and checks for further parts, and attempts to integrate these parts into the image.

Table 2 in the appendix traces the progress of the program as it generated a detailed image, illustrated in Figure 7.

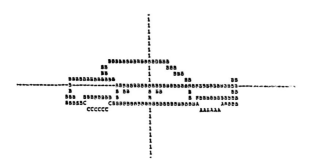

Figure 7. A detailed image generated by the simulation.

Here, the skeletal image is constructed first, as in the previous example. This time, however, two parts (i.e., the front and rear tires) are also integrated into the image. The different letters used in delineating the parts indicate recency of being "refreshed": Once an image is constructed, we hypothesize that it begins to fade and that effort is required to maintain it. This hypothesis is supported by experiments which show that complex images are more difficult to maintain than simple ones [10]. We simulated this image "degeneration" by simply re-cycling (regenerating) parts of the surface image before inspecting or transforming the image, and by printing out each part with a different letter. The most recent part is printed with A, and the remaining letters re-assigned so that the more recently printed parts have lower letters (see Figure 7).

Table 3 of the appendix traces the program's execution when asked to generate a small, detailed image. As can be seen in Table 3, the skeletal image is successfully generated, but the image inspection procedures fail because the resolution is too poor for the wheelbases to be clearly delineated. The resulting image is illustrated in Figure 8.

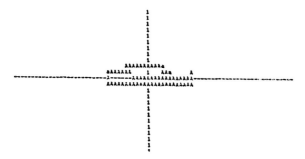

Figure 8. A subjectively small image generated by the simulation.

This is consistent with experimental findings that people are faster to generate subjectively smaller images than larger ones, but smaller images take longer to inspect [10]. We assume that this is in part because fewer details are placed on smaller images: People, like our program, may have difficulty in locating the foundation parts on subjectively smaller images, and thus may integrate fewer

details into them.

Images may also be constructed so large that they overflow the activated partition of the surface matrix, as is illustrated in Figure 9.

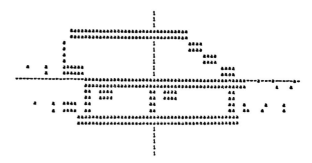

Figure 9. A subjectively large image generated by the simulation.

As is evident, overflow at the periphery is not all-or-none, but occurs gradually, as mandated by the data described earlier. Interestingly, the program will also fail to locate the foundation parts (wheelbases) here, and fail to place the tires; the program trace for this run was identical to that of Table 3 except for the size factor indicated. Thus, we would predict that this size image may be constructed faster than a medium size one if enough foundation parts overflow; this prediction has not yet been tested.

3.2.2 Inspecting images

The LOOKFOR procedures allow one to search an image for a given property or part. The operation of these procedures is schematized in Figure 10. Let us consider an example: An image of a car, like that depicted in Figure 7, is present in active memory and the program is asked whether it can find the rear tire. When asked to find a given part (or object) in an image, the program first looks for the propositional file for the specified part. If this file is found, the program looks within it for a notation indicating the optimal resolution (indexed by dot density) necessary to see the part. If this information is not stored with the propositional file for the part, the program looks in the propositional file associated with the foundation part for the optimal resolution. The program will not bother to search an image until the image is of the correct resolution. Thus, the program then checks to see if the resolution (dot density) of the image in active memory is within the range of the optimal resolution. If not, the image is expanded or shrunken, as appropriate. Following this, the procedural definition of the part is looked up and the image searched as described above for image generation. If the procedures comprising the procedural definition of the part are successfully executed, the program responds that the part is present. If one of the procedures fails, the procedures used in the procedural definition of the part are examined, and the direction of search at the time when the procedure failed is noted. The program then scans in that direction by moving the image such that the material previously at the appropriate edge of the

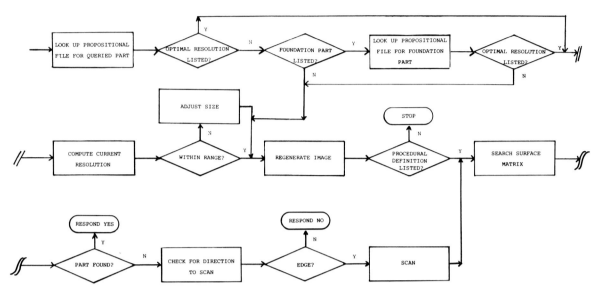

Figure 10. Flowchart of the imagery inspection process.

activated partition is shifted into the center, moving previously inactivated material into the activated region. The program then repeats the search procedure and responds positively if the search procedures are successfully executed. If any of the procedures fails, the program checks to make sure that it has not already scanned past the edge of the image. If it hasn't, the scanning and inspecting cycle is repeated until either the part is found or the edge is scanned past. The process of scanning and inspecting probably should be continuous, but we perform the scans in leaps in order to save time. Once the part is found, the program scans to the part so that it is in the center of the most highly activated region.

Table 4 of the appendix traces the execution of the program as it successfully finds the rear tire on an image of a car. The resulting image is illustrated in Figure 11. Note that since the rear tire is now in the center of the activated region, the front tire is now in the overflowed region and is not clearly visible. Table 5 of the appendix traces the execution of the program as it attempted to locate the front tire on this image. As can be seen, the program failed to locate the front tire when it is in the overflowed region, but after executing a scan in the appropriate direction, the front tire was successfully located.

Finally, we wish to illustrate what happens when the initial image is too large or small to "see" a sought part. Table 6 of the appendix is a trace documenting what occurred when the program tried to find a rear tire on an image that was so large it overflowed (i.e., see Figure 9). In this case, we constructed only a skeletal image, so that the program could not in fact locate the tire. Before concluding that no tire was present, however, the program reduced the size of the image after discovering that the resolution was too high

(higher resolution is indicated by lower case letters, indicating that dots are more separated and contours more distinct; capital letters indicate overprinting when contours have blurred into one another, as in evident in Figure 8).

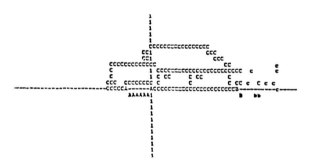

Figure 11. The program after the rear tire has been located and focused upon.

3.2.3 Image transformations

Images are altered in two ways: A "shift tranformation" shifts the points defining a surface representation in some specified fashion. "Scanning" an image consists of moving the points across the surface matrix such that different portions of the depicted object seem to move under the center (which is most highly activated and most sharply in focus). "Moving" points often corresponds to cell-to-adjacent cell translation; the actual distance of the shift is determined by a number of factors (e.g., size), however. "Rotating" an image consists of moving the points "around" a specified pivot. "Expanding" or "contracting" an image consists of migrating the points away from or towards a specified pivot (usually the geometrical center

Stephen M. Kosslyn and Steven P. Shwartz

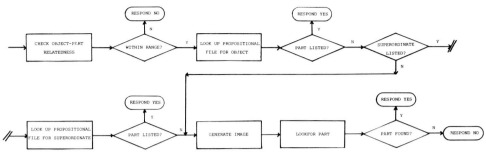

Figure 12. Flowchart of the question-answering process.

of the image). A "shift" transformation moves only a part of an image at a time, and the rate of transformation is limited by how far portions may be shifted before the image seems to fragment. The advantage of this type of transformation is that no information need be stored in a buffer, as would be necessary if the locations of all points composing the image were transformed before any were printed out. The disadvantage of this sort of transformation is that the procedure is iterative: Larger transformations require more operations. (And thus larger distances to be scanned, rotated or expanded/contracted will require more time than when smaller distances are involved.)

The other sort of image transformation, a "blink" transformation, is not iterative. In this transformation, an initial image is "erased" and a new one--exhibiting the required alterations--is generated. In general, this sort of transformation requires more effort than a shift, and hence most transformations should be accomplished by shifting portions gradually. Although this erase-and-regenerate process does require considerable effort, the amount of effort does not depend upon the size of the transformation to be performed as it does with iterative shift transformations. Thus, for very large transformations a "blink" transform may be more economical than a shift. (There are special problems with blink rotations, however, due to the fact that the procedures for integrating parts into an image are not orientation-invariant. Thus, it is difficult to add details when the image is constructed at a specified angular orientation--see [13, 20].

3.3 Imagery and question-answering

We also have developed the beginnings of a model of how the imagery system interfaces with a question-answering system using propositional representations of general world knowledge. We felt this was important to do for two reasons: First, just as we claim that the nature of memorial representations places constraints on the nature of the perceptual encoding devices, so do the various aspects of the total cognitive system mutually constrain each other. If our system were incompatible with a question-answering system, it obviously would be awry. Second, within our particular problem domain, it seems clear that imagery is used in conjunction with other sorts of information, and we felt it necessary to explore how such interaction occurs. This seemed especially important if imagery representations are in fact used in pattern recognition, as we shall suggest shortly; in this case, world knowledge obviously is used, and we

must specify how imagery and such knowledge interact if we have even a hope of discovering how imagery representations per se are used in perception.

Figure 12 depicts the sequence of events involved when the program is given an ANSWERIF command. The ANSWERIF procedures answer questions which ask if an object has a particular part. The first step the program takes when given an ANSWERIF command is to determine if the query is a reasonable one. For example, if one were asked "Does Jimmy Carter have horns?," one could respond with a very fast "no." Our model handles this phenomenon by providing an interface to a semantic memory system which we envision to be somewhat similar to that of Smith, Shoben & Rips [see 26]. In order to make a fast "no" response, we hypothesize that the semantic memory system makes a global feature comparison resulting in a measure of how related are the object and part. If this value is lower than a set criterion value, a fast "no" response is made. The actual program simulates this global comparison process by calling up a "dummy" subroutine that simply looks up the "relatedness value" of the object and part in a table. (We leave actual simulation of this comparison process itself to someone studying semantic memory per se.) Table 7 of the appendix traces the program's execution when asked if a car has a brain - a clearly unlikely question. If the question is reasonable (i.e., the object-part relatedness value is above the criterion), the program first looks up the propositional file for the object in question and checks the file for an assertion that the object has the part. If so, a positive response is made. Table 7 of the appendix contains a trace for the question of whether a car has a rear tire.

If the queried part is not listed directly in the propositional file of the object (unlike the example in Table 8), the propositional file is checked for the name of the object's superordinate, and if found, the program checks the superordinate's propositional file for an assertion that the superordinate object has the specified part. Table 9 of the appendix traced program execution for the case where the part is not explicitly noted in the object's propositional file, but is explicitly noted in the propositional file of the object's superordinate.

If the part is not listed explicitly in the object's file nor in its superordinate's file (or if the superordinate's propositional file was not found), the program uses the GENERATE procedures to create a detailed image of the object and uses the

LOOKFOR procedures to search the image for the part. Tables 10 and 11 trace program execution for the case where the program must generate and search an image in order to determine if an object has a part. In Table 10, the sought part is in fact present in the image, whereas in Table 11 the sought part—a cushion—is not in fact evident in the image. In this latter case, it is of interest to note that the program scans the trunk, roof, and hood looking for a cushion (!).

The present implementation, crude as it is, seems able to provide qualitative accounts for the basic findings in the area of semantic memory [26]: First, it has been shown repeatedly that more highly associated "true" properties are affirmed for an object more quickly than less associated ones. In our model, highly associated properties would be listed directly in an object's propositional file (and the most highly associated ones would be entered nearest to the top of the list), and thus would be retrieved most quickly, less highly associated properties would be stored not in the object's file, but in the superordinate's (requiring a deduction stage like that suggested by Collins & Quillian [4]); and the least highly associated concrete properties would not be listed explicitly in either sort of file, but would be accessible only via image generation and inspection. Second, the findings for "false" properties are the reverse of those with "true" ones: more related false properties take more time to reject (e.g., a bat has feathers vs. a bat has wheels). In our model, very unrelated false properties would be rejected at the initial relatedness check (why should search proceed if the property obviously is foreign for an object?), whereas more related (i.e., sharing more features) properties would be searched for as in Table 11. The reader is reminded of the purpose of the present implementation of the semantic memory interface: we wanted to make sure that there was some sensible way of interfacing our imagery system with a more general semantic memory. We do not claim that the current notations are any more than general hypotheses.

In closing this section, it seems worth noting two details of our current simulation that are probably incorrect. First, Kosslyn, Murphy, Bemesderfer, & Feinstein [16] present data suggesting that images are not constructed only after propositional search and deduction have failed, but instead are generated and inspected at the same time such search is under way. This makes little difference in terms of the actual implementation, of course, given the inherently serial nature of the computer. But this operating characteristic does have consequences on real-time performance [see 16], and thus will have to be dealt with by our model eventually. The second problem is more of a detail: it seems likely that people do not always search through all relevant portions of memory before making a judgment of a related false property. Sometimes a contradictory piece of information is probably located and used in decision making [see 8, 26]. We have not implemented this as it seems irrelevant to our basic concerns.

3.4 Status of the program

The program currently operates as described for two images, that of a schematic chair and a car. Further development has been impeded, however, by the high cost of running the program. The second proposal outlined in the next section promises to ameliorate this problem, however, so let us now consider alternative ways of implementing the surface display.

4.0 Two ways of implementing spatial representations

4.1 A spatial display with properties of lateral inhibition and fading activation from the center

In our model, images are constructed by selectively filling in cells of a matrix, delineating a "picture".[2] Interpretive procedures operate upon this internal display, and classify objects and parts in accordance with membership in given semantic categories. In actuality, the image is now being represented by two matrices, in order to simulate properties of lateral inhibition and fading activation towards the periphery. That is, we assumed that when images are generated at very small sizes one cannot discern parts because contours are obscured by lateral inhibition. When images are expanded, however, hidden contours become evident. In order to mimic this, we have one matrix—the "visual buffer"—which is very fine-grained; each square of four adjacent cells in this matrix maps into one cell of another matrix—the "activated partition buffer." If at least one of the four cells in the visual buffer is filled, a point will be placed in the appropriate cell in the activated partition; although we do indicate when more than one point in the visual buffer has been mapped into a single point in the activated partition (by capital vs. lower case letters), information about the pattern of points in the visual buffer is lost in this mapping process. That is to simulate the notion that when points are too close together, they mutually interfere with each other and subtle contours are lost.

The activated partition matrix is the one actually "inspected" by the mind's eye interpretive procedures that attempt to classify spatial patterns. The visual buffer is filled in from long-term memory, but material in this buffer is automatically mapped into the activated partition. The mapping function results in a loss of resolution when images are constructed at a subjectively small size, as is evident in Figure 8, but allows contours to become distinct when expansion occurs, as is evident in Figures 7 and 9.

---

2. We have represented pictorial images in a two dimensional matrix for convenience and economy. Obviously, this may be inadequate if people do in fact construct images that embody information about three-dimensionality. Perhaps it is best to think of our representational medium as a three dimensional space wherein all values on the z dimension are zero.

Stephen M. Kosslyn and Steven P. Shwartz

Not only is there a many-to-one mapping function between the two matrices, but only the central portions of the visual buffer are fully mapped into the activated partition buffer. The amount of material mapped into the activated partition decreases with distance from the center of the visual buffer, in order to simulate fading activation. This property was motivated by results of experiments that indicated that people's images gradually faded at the periphery.

4.2 A spatial display with limited resolution and fading activation from the center

In this model we have only one matrix, which supports the spatial image as did the "activated partition buffer." The number of cells which are "on" (i.e., available to the interpretive mechanisms) decreases with distance from the center. In contrast to the previous model, this one does not have any provisions for "lateral inhibition." Instead, we assume that the spatial display has a "grain" that limits the resolution of the image. Unlike the previous model, in this one images are not generated directly from the underlying long-term memory (disk) representation. Instead, the polar coordinates of the cells which are to be filled in are first copied from the long-term memory representation onto a linked list which resides in short-term memory. This linked list—a "token" of the long-term memory representation—is then manipulated. This seems sensible, since altering a given image (e.g., mentally placing two horns on a unicorn) does not preclude later imaging of the unaltered original, which would occur if the original representations were modified directly. The files are adjusted as they are copied (e.g., size and location parameters set) in order to print out the correct configuration of points in the spatial display. Unlike the first implementation, we do not assume that all points are uniquely located in an underlying spatial buffer, even if all are not distinct in the available activated partition. Instead, each cell in the activated partition is (essentially) broken into two parts; one part contains brightness information, and the other part contains a pointer back to a linked list in the visual buffer. This linked list consists of all the R, Theta specifications that have been mapped into that cell in the activated partition. This inverse mapping function undergoes a continuous updating process whenever images are transformed (e.g., shifted in some way). In the process of transforming the R, Theta values, sometimes a list is broken into two or more lists when a new cell or cells are able to be filled in the activated partition (as occurs when images are expanded). The linked list structure is simply an easy way of keeping track of which R, Theta pairs are mapped into which cells of the display.

4.3 A comparison-contrast

In many respects the two implementations of the surface display are indistinguishable. Both posit that a spatial display is derived from more abstract representations and then may be processed by interpretive and/or transformational procedures. In the first case, however, we assume that all information is in fact in an image, even if it is too small to "see." The problem with this model is

that we claim only information in the activated partition is available to be operated upon ("seen"). If so, then shifting points around will result in some of the points in the "visual buffer" not being shifted, which could result in "ghost" images when the size of the image is changed by moving the points. In order to solve this problem, we had the transformations work directly upon the visual buffer, but allowed interpretive procedures to "look" only at the pattern in the "mind's eye" buffer. This seems lamentably ad hoc. In addition, although we assume that the visual buffer is infinitely fine, it in fact is not; thus, we still have to contend with the situation where multiple points are mapped into a single cell (in the visual buffer itself). Finally, transformations which require repeated iteration through the matrix become exceedingly expensive in the first model.

The second model eliminates all of the problems with the first. The inverse-mapping function from the surface matrix to the activated partition allows us to have a model wherein all operations occur in the "visible" matrix, and there are no problems due to "forgotten points" which were lost due to overprinting in the matrix. In this system, it is easy to make sense out of a conglomerate of separate files containing unordered R, Theta (by inspecting the single display produced in the matrix), and portions of the list in the activated partition (corresponding to parts of the image)—or coordinated portions of several lists—can be manipulated from the surface. That is, the points specifying the tire of an imaged car, for example, might be printed out from several files (one representing a "global shape" obtained at first glance, and others representing information encoded upon more careful "second looks"). Modifying the image by imagining a flat tire will automatically adjust all relevant R, Theta points in the appropriate files. Thus, all modifications of an image are automatically translated into a form that is easily re-encodable into memory. In addition, the second model allows transformations to be performed very efficiently; instead of having to iterate through all cells of a large array, only points on a list need be manipulated.

From the point of view of a working program, our proposed second method of implementing the model is clearly to be preferred. At present, however, we have been able to discover only one contrasting prediction that may allow us to empirically distinguish between the implementations: If erasing images is an active process (as pilot data suggests), then we might expect that the more material to be erased the longer it should take. If so, then we are led to the following expectation: In the first implementation, the subjective size of the image should not dictate erasure time—since the same amount of material is in the image (albeit not necessarily detectable); the number of points in the visual buffer does not change, theoretically, with different sized images. In contrast, in the second model only the points in the activated partition would need to be "turned off" (and the pointers severed). Since there are fewer points with smaller images, subjectively smaller images should require less time to erase. If this result is in fact obtained, we will have to eliminate other explanations (e.g., people scan the image when erasing, and smaller images are more quickly scanned). If we can show that less material really is in the image when it is smaller, we will have at least one hint that the second implementation is a better reflection of human processing.

5.0 Spatial representations and pattern recognition

Images are constructed in part from information encoded during previous perceptual processing. It would be very elegant if the same information used to generate images were also used in recognizing visual input. How such information would be used depends in large part upon how it is represented in memory. It is not clear whether perceptual information itself is encoded into an abstract propositional form or is stored in a form that mirrors the structural isomorphism that seems to exist between real-world objects and mental images. Clearly, the most general type of machine representation of real-world objects is a propositional structure (for a digital computer; cf. Ruzene Bajcsy's paper). However, as M. A. Fischler (in this volume) states, there are two major problems of translation of a real-world scene, with its inherent spatial properties, into a non-isomorphic propositional format. First of all, the primitives of the scene must be specified. However, in order to broaden the generality of any given system and/or to allow processing of reasonably complex scenes, the number of primitives needed seems to be astronomical. The second problem lies in describing the many potential relationships between primitives in a scene. Again, as generality and ability to recognize complex scenes increases, the number of necessary types of relationships soars drastically.

An "analogue" representation [see 16] that preserves a structural isomorphism with the percept could overcome both of these problems. The experiments reported in this paper indicate that such a functional, isomorphic representation does exist in the human information processing system, at least in active memory (i.e., mental images). Certainly, such an isomorphic structure in long-term memory is also within the bounds of possibility. We found such a structure (i.e., the polar coordinate representation) to be adequate for generating mental images. Furthermore, this type of representation seems to be most efficient both in terms of capacity demands and computational requirements for constructing mental images. Only one set of coordinates per point must be stored, the coding of the real-world information requires only a simple many-to-one mapping, and the decoding (i.e., generation of images) requires only a direct isomorphic mapping.

Many theories of human information processing of the last decade have argued that activation of long-term memory structures by perceptual input occurs automatically and does not require search [cf. 23], which may suggest that long-term memory is content addressable. If so, a "global" representation in short-term memory (the surface matrix of our model) could be encoded (e.g., converted from Cartesian to polar coordinates) and used to look up the concept associated with the most similar spatial representation already stored in long-term memory. The spatial information accessed in long-term memory could be the very same information used in generating images, stored in terms of R, Theta coordinates in our model. Since it is unlikely that there will be an exact match between an encoded representation and one already in memory, the most similar representation would be accessed; to prevent "false alarms," mistaken recognitions, a further procedure may be necessary: After the most similar image deep representation is accessed, the propositional list associated with it could be looked up, and information about the object (or scene, or part) could be used to initiate "secondary checks" for particular properties of the object (e.g., for a car, a hood, tires, etc.). If these procedures are satisfied, the input would be "recognized." This sort of notion, then, entails a purely "bottom-up" initial stage, wherein input is placed in the matrix, encoded and used to look up already-encoded material. Following this would be a top-down operation, of checking to see whether characteristics of the hypothesized (best-matched) object are in fact present in the display. The very same information already utilized by the program to find a wheelbase prior to integrating a tire into an image of a car, for example, or finding the seat of an imaged chair before placing the cushion, could be used in this secondary check operation. After all, an elegant model would make use of as much material in as many different circumstances as possible. And a model that processes images and percepts in similar ways would not only be elegant, but consistent with data demonstrating modality-specific interference between imagery and concurrent perception [e.g., 3, 24]. There is no guarantee that the mind is an elegant entity, of course, but it seems most useful to assume so until convinced otherwise.

6.0 Conclusions

This chapter has presented a description of a computer simulation of visual imagery in humans, and attempted to illustrate how this simulation was motivated by data. We feel that the basic premise of our model--that spatial, pictorial images are in fact functional--is an important clue as to what sorts of information ought to be preserved in the course of perceptual processing.

In addition to this particular point, we also wish to make a broader one, concerning the basic approach used here: Human cognition offers a proof that the problems of AI in general, and of computer vision in particular, are solvable. As in the case of imagery, it seems reasonable to suppose that programs can be written to follow the blueprint of human processing. The main problem with this idea, of course, is in revealing said blueprint. With the advent of the field of "cognitive psychology," a technology has been developing that allows one to externalize mental structures and processes. This technology offers an alternative to using simple introspection as a guide--as usually seems to occur in AI. Many of these techniques make use of reaction-time paradigms, wherein one measures the amount of time necessary to perform some operation(s). In much of the research discussed above, we often assessed how long it takes people to perform certain tasks introspectively (e.g., to "see" some part of an imaged object) By systematically varying instructions, which presumably varies internal events, the operating characteristics of imagery processing were explored. So, instead of simply relying upon an introspection, the introspection is used to design an experiment and to predict the outcome. If it seems more difficult to "see" smaller parts of images, for example, then this ought to be reflected by the time people will take when asked whether or not they can "find" smaller parts of an image. If one's introspection is not spurious, one ought to be able to demonstrate real consequences of the supposed process of structure. In so doing, one has firm grounds for one's direction in implementing a simulation or a "performance mode" program.

In addition to the flimsiness of using raw introspections as data, there is another problem with this approach: After a few basic intuitions about the process or structure are gleaned, one's introspections may lose force, may be too gross to provide additional guidance. Not so with the present technique: experiments may be designed to distinguish between relatively subtle alternatives in a non-abritrary way. Thus, one may be able to take advantage of the "human proof" further along the path with our approach, and presumably thereby increase the probability of ultimate success.

Clearly, the computer simulation approach is a slow process. However, given the enormous problems that researchers in the machine vision field are currently encountering and the limitations of generality in most of the current approaches, we argue that is a reasonable approach to try to understand human pattern recognition and to mimic the processes involved.

REFERENCES

1 Anderson, J. R. & Bower, G. H. Human Associative Memory. V. H. Winston & Sons, New York, 1973.

2 Bower, G. H. Mental imagery and associative learning. In L. Gregg (Ed.), Cognition in Learning and Memory. New York: Wiley, 1972.

3 Brooks, L. The suppression of visualization by reading. Quarterly Journal of Experimental Psychology, 19, 1967, 289-299.

4 Collins, A. M. & Quillian, M. R. Retrieval time from semantic memory. Journal of Verbal Learning and Verbal Behavior, 1969, 8, 240-248.

5 Cooper, L. A. Mental rotation of random two-dimensional shapes. Cognitive Psychology, 7, 1975, 20-43.

6 Cooper, L. A. & Shepard, R. N. Chronometric studies of the rotation of mental images. In Chase, W. G. (Ed.) Visual Information Processing, Academic Press, New York, 1973.

7 Gips, J. A syntax-directed program that performs a three-dimensional perceptual task. Pattern Recognition, 6, 1974, 189-199.

8 Holyoak, K. J. & Glass, A. L. The role of contradictions and counterexamples in the rejection of false sentences. Journal of Verbal Learning and Verbal Behavior, 1975, 14, 215-239.

9 Kosslyn, S. M. Constructing visual images. Ph.D. Dissertation, Stanford University, 1974.

10 Kosslyn, S. M. Information representation in visual images. Cognitive Psychology, 7, 1975.

11 Kosslyn, S. M. Can imagery be distinguished from other forms of internal representation? Evidence from studies of information retrieved time. Memory and Cognition, 4, 1976, 291-297.

12 Kosslyn, S. M. Visual images preserve metric spatial information. Paper presented at the Psychonomic Society meetings, St. Louis, 1976.

13 Kosslyn, S. M. Imagery and internal representation. In Rosch, E. & Lloyd, B. (Eds.). Categories and Cognition, Lawrence Erlbaum Associates, New Jersey, 1977, in press.

14 Kosslyn, S. M. & Pomerantz, J. R. Imagery, propositions, and the form of internal representations. Cognitive Psychology, 9, 1977, 52-76.

15 Kosslyn, S. M. & Alper, S. N. On the pictorial properties of visual images: Effects of image size on memory for words. Canadian Journal of Psychology, 1977, 31, 32-40.

16 Kosslyn, S. M., Murphy, G. L., Bemesderfer, M. E., & Feinstein, K. J. Category and continuum in mental comparisons. Journal of Experimental Psychology: General. In press.

17 Kosslyn, S. M. Measuring the visual angle of the mind's eye. Manuscript submitted for publication.

18 Kosslyn, S. M., Ball, T. M., & Reiser, B. J. Visual images preserve metric spatial information. Journal of Experimental Psychology: Human Perception and Performance, in press.

19 Kosslyn, S. M., Reiser, B. J., & Greenbarg, P. E. Generating visual images. Manuscript submitted for publication.

20 Kosslyn, S. M., & Shwartz, S. P. A simulation of visual imagery. Cognitive Science, in press.

21 Paivio, A. Imagery and Verbal Processes. New York: Holt, Rinehart and Winston, 1971.

22 Pylyshyn, Z. W. What the mind's eye tells the mind's brain: A critique of mental imagery. Psychological Bulletin, 80, 1973, 1-24.

23 Schneider, W. & Shiffrin, R. M. Controlled and automatic human information processing: I. Detection, search, and attention. Psychological Review, 84, 1977, 1-66.

24 Segal, S. J. & Fusella, V. Influence of im-
    aged pictures and sounds on detection of visu-
    al and auditory signals. Journal of Experi-
    mental Psychology, 83, 1970, 458-464.

25 Simon, H. A. What is visual imagery? An in-
    formation processing interpretation. In L. W.
    Gregg (Ed.). Cognition in Learning and
    Memory. John Wiley, New York, 1972.

26 Smith, E. E. Theories of semantic memory.
    In W. K. Estes (Ed.), Handbook of Learning and
    Cognitive Processes: Vol. 5. Hillsdale, New
    Jersey: Erlbaum Press, 1976.

27 Weber, R. J. & Harnish, R. Visual imagery for
    words: the Hebb test. Journal of Experimen-
    tal Psychology, 102, 1974, 409-414.

APPENDIX

Tracings of the Simulation

Table 1. Constructing a skeletal image at default
size and location.

*IMAGE CAR

LOOKING FOR PROPOSITIONAL FILE FOR CAR
CAR.PRP OPENED

CHECKING PROPOSITIONAL FILE FOR NAME OF IMAGE FILE
NAME OF IMAGE FILE FOUND: CAR.IMG

LOOKING FOR IMAGE FILE CAR.IMG
CAR.IMG OPENED

TURNING ON POINTS IN SURFACE DISPLAY WITH SIZE FAC-
TOR = 1.0

IMAGE COMPLETED

Table 2. Constructing a fully-detailed image at
default size and location.

*IMAGE FULL CAR

LOOKING FOR PROPOSITIONAL FILE FOR CAR
CAR.PRP OPENED

CHECKING PROPOSITIONAL FILE FOR NAME OF IMAGE FILE
NAME OF IMAGE FILE FOUND: CAR.IMG

LOOKING FOR IMAGE FILE CAR.IMG
CAR.IMG OPENED

TURNING ON POINTS IN SURFACE DISPLAY WITH SIZE FAC-
TOR = 1.0

CHECKING PROPOSITIONAL FILE FOR NAMES OF PARTS
PART FOUND: HASA REARTIRE

LOOKING FOR PROPOSITIONAL FILE FOR REARTIRE
REARTIRE.PRP OPENED

CHECKING PROPOSITIONAL FILE FOR NAME OF IMAGE FILE
NAME OF IMAGE FILE STORED: TIRE.IMG

CHECKING PROPOSITIONAL FILE FOR LOCATION OF REAR-
TIRE
LOCATION FOUND: UNDER REARWHEELBASE

CHECKING PROPOSITIONAL FILE FOR PROCEDURAL DEFINI-
TION OF REARWHEELBASE
PROCEDURAL DEFINITION FOUND

REGENERATING IMAGE

BEGIN SEARCHING ACTIVATED PARTITION FOR REARWHEEL-
BASE

SEARCHING FOR LOWEST POINT LEFT
FOUND AT   -23   -3

FOLLOWING HORIZONTAL RIGHT TO END
FOUND AT   -19   -3

STORE COORDINATES OF LEFT ANCHOR POINT

SEARCHING FOR NEXT HORIZONTAL POINT RIGHT
FOUND AT   -10   -3

STORE COORDINATES OF RIGHT ANCHOR POINT

BEGIN TO PUT ON PART: REARTIRE

LOOKING FOR IMAGE FILE: TIRE.IMG
TIRE.IMG OPENED

TURNING ON POINTS IN SURFACE DISPLAY WITH SIZE FAC-
TOR = 0.9

CHECKING PROPOSITIONAL FILE FOR NAMES OF PARTS
PART FOUND: HASA FRONTIRE

LOOKING FOR PROPOSITIONAL FILE FOR FRONTIRE
FRONTIRE.PRP OPENED

CHECKING PROPOSITIONAL FILE FOR NAME OF IMAGE   FILE
NAME OF IMAGE FILE STORED: TIRE.IMG

CHECKING PROPOSITIONAL FILE FOR LOCATION   OF   FRON-
TIRE

LOCATION FOUND: UNDER FRONTWHEELBASE

CHECKING PROPOSITIONAL FILE FOR PROCEDURAL   DEFINI-
TION OF FRONTWHEELBASE
PROCEDURAL DEFINITION FOUND

Stephen M. Kosslyn and Steven P. Shwartz

REGENERATING IMAGE

BEGIN SEARCHING ACTIVATED PARTITION FOR FRONTWHEEL-
BASE

SEARCHING FOR LOWEST POINT RIGHT
FOUND AT   24   -3

FOLLOWING HORIZONTAL LEFT TO END
FOUND AT   21   -3

STORE COORDINATES OF RIGHT ANCHOR POINT

SEARCHING FOR NEXT HORIZONTAL POINT LEFT
FOUND AT   12   -3

STORE COORDINATES OF LEFT ANCHOR POINT

BEGIN TO PUT ON PART: FRONTIRE

LOOKING FOR IMAGE FILE: TIRE.IMG
TIRE.IMG OPENED

TURNING ON POINTS IN SURFACE DISPLAY WITH SIZE FAC-
TOR = 0.9

CHECKING PROPOSITIONAL FILE FOR NAMES OF PARTS
CAN'T FIND ANY MORE PARTS

IMAGE COMPLETED

Table 3.   Constructing a fully-detailed image at a
subjectively small size and default location (centered).

*IMAGE FULL CAR SMALL

LOOKING FOR PROPOSITIONAL FILE FOR CAR
CAR.PRP OPENED

CHECKING PROPOSITIONAL FILE FOR NAME OF IMAGE FILE
NAME OF IMAGE FILE FOUND: CAR.IMG

LOOKING FOR IMAGE FILE CAR.IMG
CAR.IMG OPENED

TURNING ON POINTS IN SURFACE DISPLAY WITH SIZE FAC-
TOR = 0.5

CHECKING PROPOSITIONAL FILE FOR NAMES OF PARTS
PART FOUND: HASA REARTIRE

LOOKING FOR PROPOSITIONAL FILE FOR REARTIRE
REARTIRE.PRP OPENED

CHECKING PROPOSITIONAL FILE FOR NAME OF IMAGE FILE
NAME OF IMAGE FILE STORED: TIRE.IMG

CHECKING PROPOSITIONAL FILE FOR LOCATION OF REAR-
TIRE
LOCATION FOUND: UNDER REARWHEELBASE

CHECKING PROPOSITIONAL FILE FOR PROCEDURAL DEFINI-
TION OF REARWHEELBASE
PROCEDURAL DEFINITION FOUND

REGENERATING IMAGE

BEGIN SEARCHING ACTIVATED PARTITION FOR REARWHEEL-
BASE

SEARCHING FOR LOWEST POINT LEFT
FOUND AT   -11   -1

FOLLOWING HORIZONTAL RIGHT TO END
FOUND AT   12   -1

STORE COORDINATES OF LEFT ANCHOR POINT

SEARCHING FOR NEXT HORIZONTAL POINT RIGHT
PROCEDURE FAILED

CHECKING PROPOSITIONAL FILE FOR NAMES OF PARTS
PART FOUND: HASA FRONTIRE

LOOKING FOR PROPOSITIONAL FILE FOR FRONTIRE
FRONTIRE.PRP OPENED

CHECKING PROPOSITIONAL FILE FOR NAME OF IMAGE FILE
NAME OF IMAGE FILE STORED: TIRE.IMG

CHECKING PROPOSITIONAL FILE FOR LOCATION OF   FRON-
TIRE
LOCATION FOUND: UNDER FRONTWHEELBASE

CHECKING PROPOSITIONAL FILE FOR PROCEDURAL DEFINI-
TION OF FRONTWHEELBASE
PROCEDURAL DEFINITION FOUND

REGENERATING IMAGE

BEGIN SEARCHING ACTIVATED PARTITION FOR FRONTWHEEL-
BASE

SEARCHING FOR LOWEST POINT RIGHT
FOUND AT   12   -1

FOLLOWING HORIZONTAL LEFT TO END
FOUND AT   -11   -1

STORE COORDINATES OF RIGHT ANCHOR POINT

SEARCHING FOR NEXT HORIZONTAL POINT LEFT
PROCEDURE FAILED

CHECKING PROPOSITIONAL FILE FOR NAMES OF PARTS
CAN'T FIND ANY MORE PARTS

IMAGE COMPLETED

Table 4.   Attempting to find a reartire on a
fully-detailed, medium-sized, central image of a
car.

*LOOKFOR REARTIRE

LOOKING FOR PROPOSITIONAL FILE FOR REARTIRE
REARTIRE.PRP OPENED

CHECKING PROPOSITIONAL FILE FOR OPTIMAL RESOLUTION
OPTIMALRESOLUTION NOT FOUND

CHECKING PROPOSITIONAL FILE FOR FOUNDATION PART
FOUNDATION PART FOUND: REARWHEELBASE

LOOKING FOR PROPOSITIONAL FILE FOR REARWHEELBASE
REARWHEELBASE.PRP OPENED

CHECKING PROPOSITIONAL FILE FOR OPTIMAL RESOLUTION
OPTIMAL RESOLUTION FOUND: 85.0

CHECKING SIZE OF IMAGE CURRENT RESOLUTION = 81.6

CHECKING PROPOSITIONAL FILE FOR PROCEDURAL DEFINI-
TION OF REARTIRE
PROCEDURAL DEFINITION FOUND

REGENERATING IMAGE

BEGIN SEARCHING ACTIVATED PARTITION FOR REARTIRE

SEARCHING FOR LOWEST POINT LEFT
FOUND AT   -23   -3

FOLLOWING HORIZONTAL RIGHT TO END
FOUND AT   -18   -3

STORE COORDINATES OF LEFT ANCHOR POINT

SEARCHING FOR NEXT HORIZONTAL POINT RIGHT
FOUND AT   -11   -3

STORE COORDINATES OF RIGHT ANCHOR POINT

CHECKING FOR PART BELOW
REARTIRE FOUND

SCANNING TO   -11   -3

Table 5.   Attempting to find a front tire on a
fully-detailed, medium-sized, off-centered image of
a car.

*LOOKFOR FRONTIRE

LOOKING FOR PROPOSITIONAL FILE FOR FRONTIRE
FRONTIRE.PRP OPENED

CHECKING PROPOSITIONAL FILE FOR OPTIMAL RESOLUTION
OPTIMALRESOLUTION NOT FOUND

CHECKING PROPOSITIONAL FILE FOR FOUNDATION PART
FOUNDATION PART FOUND: FRONTWHEELBASE

LOOKING FOR PROPOSITIONAL FILE FOR FRONTWHEELBASE
FRONTWHEELBASE.PRP OPENED

CHECKING PROPOSITIONAL FILE FOR OPTIMAL RESOLUTION
OPTIMAL RESOLUTION FOUND: 85.0

CHECKING SIZE OF IMAGE CURRENT RESOLUTION = 78.4

CHECKING PROPOSITIONAL FILE FOR PROCEDURAL DEFINI-
TION OF FRONTIRE

PROCEDURAL DEFINITION FOUND

REGENERATING IMAGE

BEGIN SEARCHING ACTIVATED PARTITION FOR FRONTIRE

SEARCHING FOR LOWEST POINT RIGHT
FOUND AT   34   0

FOLLOWING HORIZONTAL LEFT TO END
PROCEDURE FAILED

CAN'T FIND FRONTIRE

LOOKING FOR PROPOSITIONAL FILE FOR FRONTIRE
FRONTIRE.PRP OPENED

CHECKING PROPOSITIONAL FILE FOR DIRECTION TO SCAN
DIRECTION FOUND: SCAN RIGHT

SCANNING TO   25   0

CHECKING PROPOSITIONAL FILE FOR PROCEDURAL DEFINI-
TION OF FRONTIRE
PROCEDURAL DEFINITION FOUND

REGENERATING IMAGE

BEGIN SEARCHING ACTIVATED PARTITION FOR FRONTIRE

SEARCHING FOR LOWEST POINT RIGHT
FOUND AT   10   0

FOLLOWING HORIZONTAL LEFT TO END
FOUND AT   6   0

STORE COORDINATES OF RIGHT ANCHOR POINT

SEARCHING FOR NEXT HORIZONTAL POINT LEFT
FOUND AT   -1   0

STORE COORDINATES OF LEFT ANCHOR POINT

CHECKING FOR PART BELOW
FRONTIRE FOUND

SCANNING TO   31   0

Table 6.   Evaluating an obviously absurd query.

*ANSWERIF CAR HASA BRAIN

CHECKING QUESTION FEASIBILITY

LOOKING FOR LIST OF OBJECT-PART RELATEDNESS VALUES
RELATEDNESS INDEX = 0.001

ANSWER: CAR DOES NOT HAVE A BRAIN

Stephen M. Kosslyn and Steven P. Shwartz

Table 7. Evaluating a very easy query.

*ANSWERIF CAR HASA REARTIRE

CHECKING QUESTION FEASIBILITY

LOOKING FOR LIST OF OBJECT-PART RELATEDNESS VALUES
RELATEDNESS INDEX = 0.900

LOOKING FOR PROPOSITIONAL FILE FOR CAR
CAR.PRP OPENED

CHECKING TO SEE IF PROPOSITIONAL FILE HAS PART
LISTED
PART LISTED FOR CAR

ANSWER: CAR HAS A REARTIRE

Table 8. Evaluating a query via making an inference.

*ANSWERIF CAR HASA SEAT

CHECKING QUESTION FEASIBILITY

LOOKING FOR LIST OF OBJECT-PART RELATEDNESS VALUES
RELATEDNESS INDEX = 0.800

LOOKING FOR PROPOSITIONAL FILE FOR CAR
CAR.PRP OPENED

CHECKING TO SEE IF PROPOSITIONAL FILE HAS PART
LISTED
PART NOT LISTED

CHECKING PROPOSITIONAL FILE FOR NAME OF SUPERORDI-
NATE
SUPERORDINATE FOUND: VEHICLE

LOOKING FOR PROPOSITIONAL FILE FOR VEHICLE
VEHICLE.PRP OPENED

CHECKING TO SEE IF PROPOSITIONAL FILE HAS PART
LISTED
PART LISTED FOR VEHICLE

ANSWER: CAR HAS A SEAT

Table 9. Evaluating a query requiring generation
and inspection of an image.

*ANSWERIF CAR HASA HOODORNAMENT

CHECKING QUESTION FEASIBILITY

LOOKING FOR LIST OF OBJECT-PART RELATEDNESS VALUES
RELATEDNESS INDEX = 0.700

LOOKING FOR PROPOSITIONAL FILE FOR CAR
CAR.PRP OPENED

CHECKING TO SEE IF PROPOSITIONAL FILE HAS PART
LISTED
PART NOT LISTED

CHECKING PROPOSITIONAL FILE FOR NAME OF SUPERORDI-
NATE
SUPERORDINATE FOUND: VEHICLE

LOOKING FOR PROPOSITIONAL FILE FOR VEHICLE
VEHICLE.PRP OPENED

CHECKING TO SEE IF PROPOSITIONAL FILE HAS PART
LISTED
PART NOT LISTED

CHECKING PROPOSITIONAL FILE FOR NAME OF SUPERORDI-
NATE
SUPERORDINATE NOT FOUND

GENERATING IMAGE OF CAR

LOOKING FOR PROPOSITIONAL FILE FOR CAR
CAR.PRP OPENED

CHECKING PROPOSITIONAL FILE FOR NAME OF IMAGE FILE
NAME OF IMAGE FILE FOUND: CAR.IMG

LOOKING FOR IMAGE FILE CAR.IMG
CAR.IMG OPENED

TURNING ON POINTS IN SURFACE DISPLAY WITH SIZE FAC-
TOR = 1.0

LOOKING FOR PROPOSITIONAL FILE FOR HOODORNAMENT
HOODORNAMENT.PRP OPENED

CHECKING PROPOSITIONAL FILE FOR OPTIMAL RESOLUTION
OPTIMAL RESOLUTION FOUND: 90.0

CHECKING SIZE OF IMAGE
CURRENT RESOLUTION = 86.0

CHECKING PROPOSITIONAL FILE FOR PROCEDURAL DEFINI-
TION OF HOODORNAMENT
PROCEDURAL DEFINITION FOUND

REGENERATING IMAGE

BEGIN SEARCHING ACTIVATED PARTITION FOR HOODORNA-
MENT

SEARCHING FOR HIGHEST POINT RIGHT
FOUND AT   24   1

STORE COORDINATES OF LEFT ANCHOR POINT

SEARCHING FOR FIRST DOWNWARD HORIZONTAL
FOUND AT   25   0

STORE COORDINATES OF RIGHT ANCHOR POINT

CHECKING FOR PART ABOVE
HOODORNAMENT FOUND

SCANNING TO   24   0

ANSWER: CAR HAS A HOODORNAMENT

Table 10. Evaluating a difficult query requiring a "false" response.

*ANSWERIF CAR HASA CUSHION

CHECKING QUESTION FEASIBILITY

LOOKING FOR LIST OF OBJECT-PART RELATEDNESS VALUES
RELATEDNESS INDEX = 0.600

LOOKING FOR PROPOSITIONAL FILE FOR CAR
CAR.PRP OPENED

CHECKING TO SEE IF PROPOSITIONAL FILE HAS PART
LISTED
PART NOT LISTED

CHECKING PROPOSITIONAL FILE FOR NAME OF SUPERORDI-
NATE
SUPERORDINATE FOUND: VEHICLE

LOOKING FOR PROPOSITIONAL FILE FOR VEHICLE
VEHICLE.PRP OPENED

CHECKING TO SEE IF PROPOSITIONAL FILE HAS PART
LISTED
PART NOT LISTED

CHECKING PROPOSITIONAL FILE FOR NAME OF SUPERORDI-
NATE
SUPERORDINATE NOT FOUND

GENERATING IMAGE OF CAR

LOOKING FOR PROPOSITIONAL FILE FOR CAR
CAR.PRP OPENED

CHECKING PROPOSITIONAL FILE FOR NAME OF IMAGE FILE
NAME OF IMAGE FILE FOUND: CAR.IMG

LOOKING FOR IMAGE FILE CAR.IMG
CAR.IMG OPENED

TURNING ON POINTS IN SURFACE DISPLAY WITH SIZE FAC-
TOR = 1.0

LOOKING FOR PROPOSITIONAL FILE FOR CUSHION
CUSHION.PRP OPENED

CHECKING PROPOSITIONAL FILE FOR OPTIMAL RESOLUTION
OPTIMALRESOLUTION NOT FOUND

CHECKING PROPOSITIONAL FILE FOR FOUNDATION PART
FOUNDATION PART FOUND: SEAT

LOOKING FOR PROPOSITIONAL FILE FOR SEAT
SEAT.PRP OPENED

CHECKING PROPOSITIONAL FILE FOR OPTIMAL RESOLUTION
OPTIMAL RESOLUTION FOUND: 26.6

CHECKING SIZE OF IMAGE
CURRENT RESOLUTION = 84.2

EXPANDING IMAGE

CHECKING SIZE OF IMAGE
CURRENT RESOLUTION = 60.9

CHECKING SIZE OF IMAGE
CURRENT RESOLUTION = 37.5

CHECKING SIZE OF IMAGE
CURRENT RESOLUTION = 20.2

CHECKING PROPOSITIONAL FILE FOR PROCEDURAL DEFINI-
TION OF CUSHION
PROCEDURAL DEFINITION FOUND

REGENERATING IMAGE

BEGIN SEARCHING ACTIVATED PARTITION FOR CUSHION

SEARCHING FOR HIGHEST POINT LEFT
FOUND AT   -40   2

SEARCHING FOR FIRST DOWNWARD HORIZONTAL
PROCEDURE FAILED

CAN'T FIND CUSHION

LOOKING FOR PROPOSITIONAL FILE FOR CUSHION
CUSHION.PRP OPENED

CHECKING PROPOSITIONAL FILE FOR DIRECTION TO SCAN
DIRECTION FOUND: SCAN LEFT

SCANNING TO   -25   0

CHECKING PROPOSITIONAL FILE FOR PROCEDURAL DEFINI-
TION OF CUSHION
PROCEDURAL DEFINITION FOUND

REGENERATING IMAGE

BEGIN SEARCHING ACTIVATED PARTITION FOR CUSHION

SEARCHING FOR HIGHEST POINT LEFT
FOUND AT   -35   3

SEARCHING FOR FIRST DOWNWARD HORIZONTAL
PROCEDURE FAILED

CAN'T FIND CUSHION

LOOKING FOR PROPOSITIONAL FILE FOR CUSHION
CUSHION.PRP OPENED

CHECKING PROPOSITIONAL FILE FOR DIRECTION TO SCAN
DIRECTION FOUND: SCAN LEFT

SCANNING TO   -25   0

CHECKING PROPOSITIONAL FILE FOR PROCEDURAL DEFINI-
TION OF CUSHION
PROCEDURAL DEFINITION FOUND

REGENERATING IMAGE

BEGIN SEARCHING ACTIVATED PARTITION FOR CUSHION

SEARCHING FOR HIGHEST POINT LEFT
FOUND AT   -11   3

SEARCHING FOR FIRST DOWNWARD HORIZONTAL
PROCEDURE FAILED

CAN'T FIND CUSHION

```
LOOKING FOR PROPOSITIONAL FILE FOR CUSHION
CUSHION.PRP OPENED

CHECKING PROPOSITIONAL FILE FOR DIRECTION TO SCAN
DIRECTION FOUND: SCAN LEFT

CAN'T SCAN PAST EDGE OF IMAGE

ANSWER:  CAR DOES NOT HAVE A CUSHION
```

Computing the next step: Psychophysical measures
of representation and interpretation[1]

Naomi Weisstein and William Maguire

Department of Psychology
State University of New York at Buffalo
Buffalo, New York 14226

Abstract

A strategy for investigating how humans
represent and interpret images is described. The
strategy assumes that higher-level activity is
accessible to the same kind of psychophysical
measurement as are lower-level processes.

Contour illusions, perceived occlusion,
connectedness and apparent three-dimensionality
are investigated in a series of experiments,
using psychophysical techniques similar to those
already developed for exploring the characteristics of lower-level visual effects.

Among our experimental findings are the
following. a) A "grating" constructed from subjective contours produces psychophysical effects
similar to those found for a physically present
grating. b) Partially occluded contours produce
psychophysical effects similar to those found
for unobstructed contours. c) "Phantom"
contours (an illusion of moving contours) produce a motion after-effect in a retinal region
where no retinal image motion is present. d)
Certain apparently three-dimensional
line drawings of objects improve detection
accuracy for component lines, even though these
drawings provide no information useful in
detecting the lines. e) Temporal functions of
accuracy for the lines when they are presented
before the drawings differ from those obtained
with flatter designs.

These findings indicate that higher-level
processing filters, overrides, or enhances the
perception of the details in an image. By
studying what happens to these details as a
result of various global factors in a pattern,
we may be able to obtain considerable insight
into the structure of higher-level representation and interpretation.

[1]This work was supported in part by National Eye
Institute grant NIH 5 R01 EY01330 and National
Science Foundation grant BNS76-02059 to Naomi
Weisstein. Some parts of this paper are based on
Weisstein(in press).We thank Fanya Montalvo for her
extensive and insightful comments; we also thank
Charles S. Harris, James Sawusch, Howard Nusbaum,
Patrick Cavanagh, John Tangney, and Michael
Jackson for their useful comments and assistance.

1: Introduction

Researchers in computer vision have been
struggling with the puzzle of how best to represent an image for use in further pattern
analysis. Significant insight into the necessary
mechanisms might be provided if the human visual
system could tell us how it represents and interprets images. However, up until now, visual
psychophysics has mostly been concerned with low-
level mechanisms involved in topographic mappings
of the retinal image, and has had little to say
about higher-order representation and interpretation.

This silence about higher-level processes
may be due to an erroneous assumption about what
visual psychophysics can tell us. It is assumed
that psychophysical techniques and phenomena can
only give information about local, low-level
processes, and cannot tell us about those which
are higher-level and more global. Implicit in
this assumption is the idea that higher-level
processes involve completely different kinds of
mechanisms and thus cannot be measured in the
same way. But this may not be true. Our work has
explored the possibility that by using stimulus
configurations that go beyond those currently
popular, some of the same well-developed psychophysical techniques and phenomena that are
providing detailed information about elementary
mechanisms can give us comparable information
about higher-level ones.

1.1: Elementary Processes

Let's begin by looking at some of the techniques and phenomena that appear to give us
information about the elementary mechanisms.

1.1.1: Receptive Fields

Consider first the neurophysiological data
which have figured prominently in notions about
the elementary mechanisms in pattern analysis.

An enormous amount of neurophysiological
work has shown that single cells in the mammalian
visual pathway fire selectively to specific
simple, local properties of a pattern. For
instance, in the cat cortical "simple cells"
(Hubel & Wiesel, 1962) respond optimally to a

light-dark edge, or to a light or dark bar with a certain width and orientation. A common variety of simple cells respond more strongly when more light falls on a certain narrow strip of the retina and more weakly when more light falls on two adjacent inhibitory areas that flank the excitatory strip. (Other simple cells do the opposite, responding more to light in the flanking areas). Different cells have receptive fields with different widths and orientations of the center and flanking regions and, in addition, different sensitivities to velocity and direction of motion. Each retinal point feeds into a variety of cells, meaning that by looking at which cells are firing most rapidly, one can deduce the orientation and separation of contours within each small region of the retinal image.

1.1.2: Psychophysical data

The neurophysiological findings provide a starting point for what one might look for in early stages of pattern analysis: retinotopic mechanisms selectively sensitive to variations in simple geometric properties of patterns over small regions of the image.

Detection of Compound Gratings. For instance, one currently popular technique investigates whether, as might be suggested by the different sizes of receptive fields, separate mechanisms can be shown psychophysically to respond to different sizes.

In particular, the technique tests whether different sizes are detected independently of each other. A good example of the technique is an experiment by Graham & Nachmias (1971). Their stimuli were sine-wave gratings, consisting of light and dark stripes whose luminance varies sinusoidally across the grating. The gratings can differ in orientation, spatial frequency (stripe width), amplitude (contrast), and phase (relative position of the stripes). Graham and Nachmias superimposed two vertical sine wave gratings, differing in spatial frequency by a factor of three. They found that each grating was detected only when its contrast was high enough for it to be detected when presented alone. The second grating neither helped nor hindered detection of the first. Moreover, the composite stimulus was equally detectable whether the peak of the lower frequency stimulus was lined up with the trough of the higher frequency stimulus, or when the phase was adjusted so that the peak luminances added. Thus, peak-to-trough luminance differences did not appear to determine detection; rather, the contrast of each sine wave component determined its own detection.

Subsequent psychophysical studies have tried to estimate the weighting functions (the physiological analog would be a quantitative description of a receptive field) of each separate mechanism (Macleod & Rosenfeld, 1974). These estimates have agreed in general with neurophysiological findings for cortical simple units. Recent studies have also indicated that there are at least several of

these mechanisms for each position in the visual field (Wilson & Bergen, 1977; Graham, Robson & Nachmias, 1977).

Adaptation and Masking. Two other techniques widely used to find out whether certain aspects of a pattern stimulate separate mechanisms are adaptation and masking.

In these procedures a pattern, typically (but not exclusively) a grating of a particular stripe width and orientation, is presented for some duration and then immediately or a short time later, another pattern is briefly flashed. (In adaptation studies, the first pattern is viewed for several seconds or minutes; in masking, the pattern is viewed for a relatively short duration.) Measures are obtained of how exposure to the first stimulus (the "mask") interferes with perception of the second stimulus (the "target"). It is assumed that to the extent that a common mechanism responds to both patterns, the perception of the target will be affected--its visibility threshold will increase, or its apparent light-dark contrast will be lowered.

Adaptation procedures have shown that patterns having sufficiently different sizes (Pantle & Sekuler, 1968; Harris, 1970), orientations (Blakemore & Nachmias; 1971, Fidell, 1970), lengths (Nakayama & Roberts, 1972) and directions of motion (Sekuler & Ganz, 1963; Pantle & Sekuler, 1969) will not affect each other, indicating that there are separate mechanisms responding to different values of these stimulus properties. Adaptation depends on retinal, not perceived size (Blakemore, Muncey & Ridley, 1973; Harris, 1970), occurs before binocular rivalry (Lehmkuhle & Fox, 1975), follows approximately the same time course as cortical simple units (Maffei, Fiorentini & Bisti, 1973), yields estimates of weighting functions which more or less agree with receptive field response profiles of cortical simple units (Macleod & Rosenfeld, 1974) and results in a reduced visual evoked potential for patterns identical or very similar to the adapting pattern (Maffei & Campbell, 1970; Blakemore & Campbell, 1969). With the exception of some of the work to be discussed below, adaptation effects have been found to be localized, that is, restricted to those retinal areas where the adapting stimulus fell.

The motion after-effect. After-effects of adaptation have also been found to be localized, and are also often considered to reflect the activity of local mechanisms selectively sensitive to different aspects of a pattern (for example, the McCollough effect, McCollough, 1965; the spatial frequency shift, Blakemore, Nachmias & Sutton, 1970).

The motion after-effect is a good example. After a pattern of light and dark stripes moves steadily across a region of the visual field (e.g., left to right) for a prolonged duration, a similar pattern that is actually stationary will nevertheless appear to an observer to be moving in the opposite direction (e.g., right to left). The motion after-effect is strongest when the orientation of the adapting and test

Naomi Weisstein and William Maguire

grating match (Over, Broerse, Crassini & Lovegrove, 1973), and when the temporal frequency (rate of alternation of dark and light stripes at a given point) of the adapting grating is close to that for which the visual system is maximally sensitive (Pantle, 1974). Depending on their contrast, gratings moving at various speeds in the direction opposite to the adapting grating cancel the effect, and the cancellation function appears strikingly similar to simple visual threshold functions for flicker (Pantle, 1976).

Numerous experiments on motion after-effects indicate that they are confined to retinal regions that have actually been stimulated by moving contours (Wohlgemuth, 1911; Sekuler & Pantle, 1967; Masland, 1965). Perceived motion without retinal displacement (as when following a moving stimulus with the eyes) has been shown to be insufficient for producing a motion after-effect (Anstis & Gregory, 1965). This dependence on local retinal stimulation (as well as the other properties mentioned above) have made local mechanisms sensitive to opposite directions of motion the logical candidates for explaining the effect (Barlow & Hill, 1963).

1.2: Higher-level processes

The phenomena discussed so far appear to reflect a low-level analysis of the retinal image, implicating mechanisms which respond in a template-like manner to such properties of a pattern as size, orientation, and direction of motion. That is, the phenomena seem to be telling us about local, retinotopic mechanisms which, like cortical simple cells, respond only to simple geometric properties of the image pattern within a particular small region of the visual field.

Let us now summarize some of our own experiments. These experiments start out looking very similar to those above, and produce data very similar in most ways to those above, except that our data cannot be understood in terms of the elementary processes described so far. Instead it appears that higher-level interpretative processes are also involved. The mechanisms responsible for our effects cannot be responding only point-by-point or small-region-by-small-region and cannot be sensitive only to geometric properties of a pattern. Rather they respond differently depending on global configuration. In some cases, they supply missing information; in some cases, they enhance detection accuracy for components of patterns; in general, they read into the stimulus certain properties that aren't there, such as depth and connectedness.

We measured these higher-level processes with the same psychophysical techniques as used with lower-level sensory processes. In most respects, the measurements produce comparable results. The main difference is that we have found configurations in which local retinal stimulation is either not necessary for producing the results or does not exclusively decide the results.

2: What we have found

The results of a number of our experiments

have confirmed the fruitfulness of approaching higher-level activity by assuming that it may be accessible to the same kind of psychophysical measurement as lower-level processes. These experiments have used a number of different psychophysical techniques to study a variety of different perceptual phenomena, some of them summarized below.

2.1: Illusory Contours

How might psychophysical measures be coaxed into tapping into higher-level activity? We might begin by looking at the same kinds of properties of a pattern to which the elementary mechanisms are sensitive--width, orientation, direction of motion. In certain circumstances such properties are perceptually present, even though they're not actually present in the retinal image (Figure 1). Will the same kind of psycho-physical effects be obtained with illusory contours as are obtained with real ones?

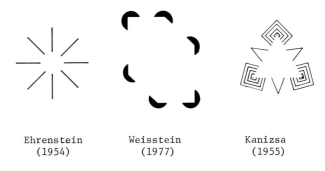

Ehrenstein   Weisstein   Kanizsa
(1954)   (1977)   (1955)

Figure 1. Some examples of illusory contours.

Illusory gratings. One way to test this is by using masking and adaptation. Suppose we construct a grating out of illusory contours, as in Figure 2a. If an illusory grating affects the same mechanisms as a real grating, then we might expect adaptation and masking between the two gratings.

That is what we found (Weisstein, Matthews & Berbaum, 1974). An illusory grating like the one in Figure 2a can mask, and be masked by, a real grating with the same orientation (Figure 2b). Control experiments indicate that it is the illusory contours, not the tiny black figures that produce them, that are responsible for the masking. (Recently, using figures somewhat similar to ours, Smith and Over (1977) also found masking by illusory contours.)

An intriguing aspect of our findings is that maximal masking of illusory contours by real contours occurs when the real contours have a much closer spacing than the illusory ones. Masking is greater when the masking spatial frequency is three times the illusory target frequency than when the frequencies are matched.

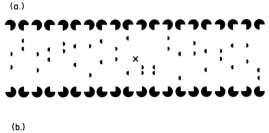

(a.)

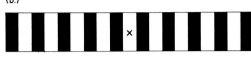

(b.)

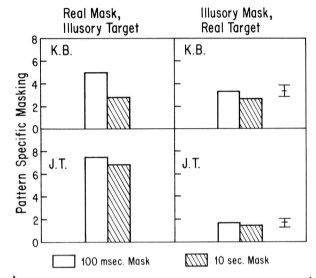

Real Mask, Illusory Target   Illusory Mask, Real Target

100 msec. Mask   10 sec. Mask

Figure 2. (a) An illusory grating. (b) A real grating. (c) Masking of illusory grating by real grating and vice versa.

For the illusory target, amount of masking with the physically present mask is subtracted from the amount of masking with a blank field of the same mean luminance. For the physically present target, amount of masking with the illusory mask is subtracted from the amount of masking with a pattern containing just the smaller half-discs. These blank field and half-disc controls allow us to subtract the components of masking which are not of interest here. The remainder is pattern-specific masking: the amount of masking of the illusory target due just to the presence of real contours, and the amount of masking of the physically present target due just to the presence of illusory contours. Error bars indicate ± one standard error; measurements are magnitude estimations of apparent contrast. The top and bottom panels show data for subjects K. B. and J. T. respectively. (Weisstein, Matthews & Berbaum, 1974)

this cannot be explained by the small half-discs in the center of the pattern since, even though they provide a third harmonic component, we obtained comparable results when they were absent. This finding suggests that the mechanism responsible for illusory contours may be particularly concerned with sharp contours, normally specified by high spatial-frequency

components, rather than differences in luminance over wider areas, as given by low spatial frequencies.

2.2: Occlusion

In many patterns, even though some contours are not perceptually visible, we know they're there. Figures 3(a), (b), and (i) obviously portray a cube in front of a grating. The grating stripes appear to extend continuously behind the cube. Indeed, one would be taken aback if removing the cube revealed a hexagonal hole in the grating! The perception of Figure 3(g) is more variable: sometimes to some subjects it looks like an opaque white hexagon resting against the grating; occasionally like a cube with some of the edges hard to see; and most often like a hole in the grating. In any case, the perception of an object standing out in depth in front of the grating is much less compelling in Figure 3(g) than in Figure 3(a), (b) or (i).

Cube in front of grating. Perhaps psycho-physical techniques can tap into our perception of occlusion. It's possible that just as we react to the cube as if the grating is continuous behind it, so do neural mechanisms which are capable of producing masking. Given the proper stimulus with suitable depth cues, such a mechanism could be adapted by a grating that is subjectively present but retinally absent at the place where a small patch of target is viewed.

Suppose we present as an adaptation stimulus the patterns shown in Figure 3(a) and (b) and ask subjects to judge the apparent contrast of a subsequently presented target patch like that in Figure 3(d) and (e). The masking stimulus is subjectively present but retinally absent--it does not impinge on the same retinal area as the target patch. Yet we find significant adaptation when the orientations of the mask and target match (Weisstein, 1970; Weisstein, 1973). This is shown in Figure 4.

What is especially interesting is that the mask in Figure 3(i) is more effective than the mask in Figure 3(g) (Weisstein, Montalvo & Ozog, 1972). This is shown in Figure 5. That is, adaptation is reliably obtained when the empty region appears clearly in front of the grating, but not when its depth is more ambiguous. It may be, then, that these kinds of masking effects are present because of mechanisms involved in the perception of objects, separation in depth, occlusion, and the ubiquitous "filling-in" processes in perception.

2.3: Phantom motion and filling in

Even more vivid perceptions of apparent depth and of contours that are not actually present in the retinal image occur when patterns are made to move.

Phantom Contours. A procedure for producing perception of moving contours where none are present retinally was recently described by Tynan and Sekuler (1975). If a horizontal strip of opaque black tape is used to cover up part of

Naomi Weisstein and William Maguire

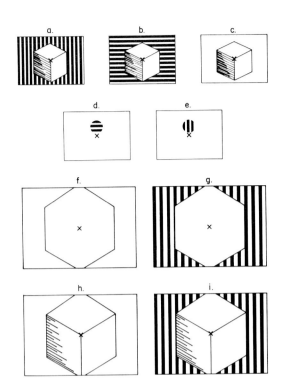

Figure 3. The patterns used to test occlusion--
cube or hexagon in front of grating.

Patterns (c), (f) and (h) are controls which
allow assessment of the components of masking
which are not of interest here. Masking of the
target patches (d) and (e) obtained with these
controls is subtracted from the amount of masking
obtained when a grating is added to that figure's
background. Amount of masking with pattern (c)
is subtracted from that with (a) and with (b);
masking with (f) is subtracted from that with
(g); and masking with (h) is subtracted from
that with (i) to yield estimates of grating-
specific masking. The top plane of the cube
and the target patch share the same retinal
location; X indicates the fixation point.
(Weisstein, 1970; Weisstein, 1973; Weisstein,
Montalvo & Ozog, 1972)

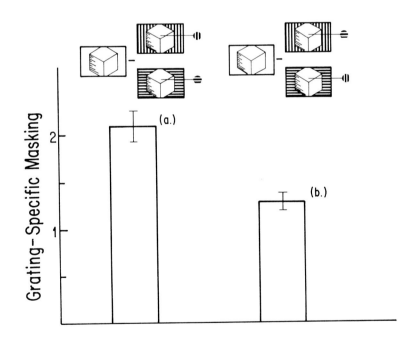

Figure 4. Cube in front of grating: orientation-selective masking.

Amount of grating-specific masking obtained is greater when
(a) the adaptation and test orientations match than (b) when they're
orthogonal. Error bars indicate ± one standard error; measurements
are magnitude estimations. (Weisstein, 1973).

Computing the Next Step

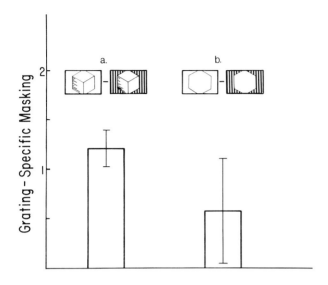

Figure 5. <u>Cube</u> and <u>hexagon</u> <u>in</u> <u>front</u> <u>of</u> <u>grating</u>: <u>masking</u> <u>dependent</u> <u>on</u> <u>apparent</u> <u>depth</u>.

Grating-specific masking is reliably obtained when (a) the occluding figure appears to be unambiguously in front of the grating but not when (b) the appearance of depth is more ambiguous. Shown are means for grating-specific masking with 20-40 sec masks and inter-stimulus intervals of 20-50 msec. Error bars indicate ± one standard error; measurements are magnitude estimations. (Weisstein, Montalvo, & Ozog, 1972).

to combine with the columns of X's above and below the taped-over region to give the impression of a continuous grating moving in a plane in front of the taped-over region. When this happens, the details of structure in the phantom X's almost match those in the physically present columns.

Other depth effects. Even if the grating is moving, phantoms are not seen if the opaque tape is oriented vertically instead of horizontally, as in Figure 6(c) and (f). We don't yet know why the orientation of the blank region matters, but here again there seems to be a connection with perceived depth: While the horizontal blank strip appears to lie either in the same plane as the phantoms, or behind them, the vertical blank strip typically appears to be standing out an inch or more in front of the grating and to be opaque. Similarly, we have found that if the blank region is trapezoidal (Figure 7) phantoms are seen whenever the trapezoid appears to be in the same plane as or in back of the stripes, but not when it appears to stand out in front of the stripes.

of a moving vertical grating, the contours are perceived to continue--clearly, but with lower contrast--in the taped-over region. With this configuration, unlike those illustrated in Figure 1, no subjective contours are seen if the grating is stationary. For that reason, Tynan and Sekuler applied a new term, "phantoms", to distinguish these movement-dependent contours from the illusory contours that occur in stationary displays.

Filling in the structure. We have found that the moving contours that produce the phantom conotours need not be physically present-- moving illusory contours will do just as well (Figure 6d.) In fact, this leads to a surprising observation: one sees not only phantom contours crossing the blank region, but also--dimly but unmistakably--columns of X's! As with other illusory contours, the vividness of the phantom X's appears to be connected with perceived depth. Generally, the phantoms seem to lie practically in the same plane as the taped-over region. However, at times they can be seen

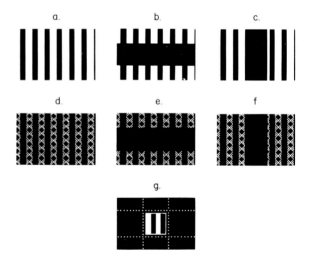

Figure 6. <u>Phantom</u> <u>motion</u> <u>and</u> <u>filling-in</u>.

When the grating is moving, phantom contours are seen in the blank region of (b) and (e) but not in the blank region of (c) and (f). The phantom contours crossing the blank region in (e) appear to consist of columns of X's.

After viewing the moving phantom contours (or the moving real contours in (a) and (b)), a subsequently presented stationary patch (g) will appear to move. It will not appear to move after viewing the blank regions in (c) or (f). For clarity, the width of the bars in (a-g) is half the width used in the experiment. The dotted lines (g) indicate the location of the horizontal and vertical empty regions. (Weisstein, Maguire & Berbaum, 1976, 1977).

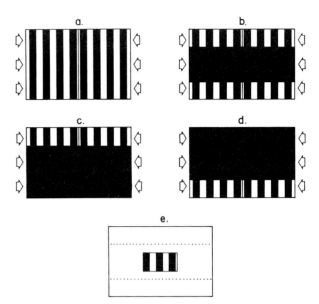

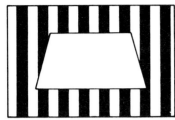

Figure 7. <u>Ambiguous depth and phantom motion</u>.

When the grating is moving, phantoms are seen whenever the trapezoid appears to be in the same plane as, or in back of the stripes, but not when it appears to stand out in front of the stripes. (Maguire & Weisstein, 1977b).

Figure 8: <u>Interruption versus partial presence</u>.

When the grating is moving, phantom contours are seen in the blank region of (b) but not in (c) or (d). In this experiment the field was split, and the left and right halves of the grating moved toward each other, as indicated by the arrows.

After viewing the moving phantom contours in (b) (or the moving real contours in (a)), a subsequently presented stationary patch (e) will appear to expand. It will not appear to move after similar viewing of (c) and (d). The moving gratings in (c) and (d) were alternated in a condition which has twice the duration of (a) or (b). (Maguire & Weisstein, 1977a).

<u>Completion</u>. Finally, if the moving grating is present only above or only below an empty region, phantoms are not seen (Figure 8 (c) and (d)). Apparently, half or a third of a grating does not convey the same message that an interrupted grating does. Where interruption does not seem to be a likely interpretation, filling-in by phantoms does not occur.

<u>Phantom-Motion After-Effect</u>. We found that moving phantom contours produce a strong motion after-effect (Weisstein, Maguire & Berbaum, 1976, 1977; Maguire & Weisstein, 1977a, b). After observing the moving phantoms for two minutes, fixating on a luminous point within the blank region, a small stationary patch of grating that falls entirely within that region appears to move in the opposite direction (Figures 6 (g) and 8 (e)). The after-effect depends on the perceived phantom contours rather than on the physically present moving contours: with the blank strip vertical (Figure 6(b) and (e)), or with the grating only above or only below the blank region (Figure 8 (c) and (d)), phantoms are not seen and there is little after-effect (Figure 9).

<u>Implications for Local Motion-Detecting Mechanisms</u>. The phantom-motion after-effect was our most unexpected finding. As mentioned above, virtually all of the literature on motion after-effects has indicated that such after-effects are confined to retinal regions that have actually been stimulated by moving contours. So compelling was the evidence that even when an exception was found (a motion after-effect produced by a

stationary region that only appeared to move because of motion in the surrounding area) local relative-motion detectors were invoked as explanation (Anstis & Rinehardt-Rutland, 1976). Our after-effect, though, is different from this one: in addition to going in the opposite direction, ours cannot be explained by detectors that straddle moving and stationary regions.

2.4: <u>Context effects on detection</u>

<u>Drawings of objects</u>. So far we've been describing situations in which perceptual effects occur within retinal regions that have not been subjected to the presumably pertinent stimulation. Now let's consider a case in which there is pertinent stimulation, and all the information needed for performing the designated perceptual task is confined to a small retinal region; will the configuration of stimuli in a much more extensive region nevertheless influence performance?

<u>Object-superiority</u>. In our basic experiment (Weisstein & Harris, 1974),

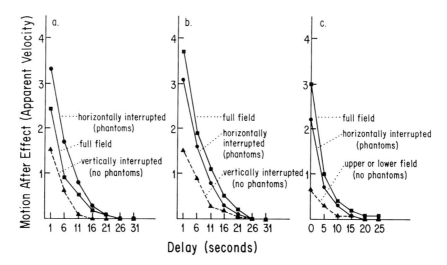

Figure 9. The phantom-motion after-effect. Strength of the motion after-effect for physically present moving contours (full-field, squares), moving phantom contours (horizontally interrupted, circles) and no perceived contour movement (vertically interrupted, or upper or lower field, dashed lines, triangles). In (a) the basic stimulus was a square wave grating (Figure 6 (a), (b), and (c)); in (b) the basic stimulus was an illusory grating (columns of X's, Figure 6 (d), (e) and (f)); and in (c) the basic stimulus was a square wave grating again, but the no-phantom condition was produced by having only the top or only the bottom of this grating visible at any moment (Figure 8 (c) and (d)). Apparent velocity is plotted as a function of the delay in seconds after termination of the adapting condition.

the task seems ideally suited to elementary retinotopic mechanisms that specialize in signalling the presence of contours with a certain orientation at a certain retinal location. The subject simply has to report on each trial which one of four (or two) diagonal line segments, differing in orientation and location, has been briefly flashed (Figure 10, (a) - (d)).

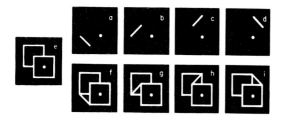

Figure 10. Object-superiority. The basic task is to detect briefly-flashed target lines (a) - (d). These are combined with context (e)--overlapping squares--to yield perceptions of unitary, apparently three-dimensional figures (f) - (i). The fixation point is continuously visible. (Weisstein & Harris, 1974.)

Object-superiority. What we found is that other lines, vertical and horizontal, can greatly affect accuracy in identifying the diagonal lines, depending on their total configuration. This is true even though the extra lines are irrelevant to the required judgment: they are identical regardless of which diagonal line is flashed, and

hence convey no information about the correct choice.

Certain configurations of these context lines, such as the overlapping squares in Figure 10 (e), combine with each diagonal line to yield a very distinctive perception of a unified, three-dimensional object (Figure 10, f - i) whereas other arrangements of the same lines don't (e.g., Figure 11, c - f).

Accuracy in identifying the diagonal lines proved to be greater with the overlapping squares than with any other arrangement that has been tried (Figures 11 and 12), even when the extra lines in the immediate neighborhood of the diagonal line are arranged identically (Figure 13). This basic finding has now been replicated in a number of laboratories (Womersley, 1977; Klein, 1976; Spoehr, 1975; McClelland, 1976.)[2]

Object-line-superiority. Accuracy on the diagonal lines is also greater when the lines are part of the connected three-dimensional pictures than when presented alone (Williams & Weisstein, 1976, a, b, 1977; McClelland, 1976.)[2] It is especially interesting that adding a context to the diagonal lines can increase accuracy: adding extra lines normally decreases accuracy in detecting a target (through simultaneous masking,

[2]There are certain experimental conditions that do not produce this result, but this doesn't change the interpretation of the basic finding.

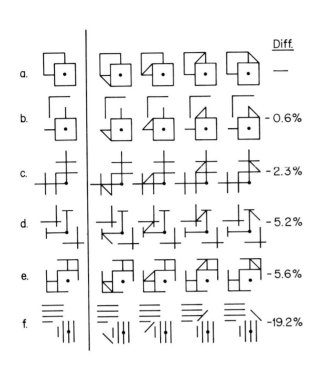

Figure 11. Relative accuracy in identifying line segments (Figure 10 a - d) when presented in the contexts used by Weisstein and Harris (1974). Each context configuration is shown in the first column; the patterns these make when combined with the line segments are shown in the next four columns. Diff is the mean deficit in accuracy with each context as compared to the overlapping squares (a).

reduced signal-to-noise ratio, and so on).

These "object-superiority" and "object-line" effects are closely analogous to the much-studied "word-superiority" and "word-letter" effects: a letter is typically detected better when flashed as part of a pronounceable word than in an unpronounceable string of letters or alone (for a review, see Baron, in press). In both cases, a constituent element (letter or line segment) is perceived better when the context creates a well-formed unit, even if the context provides no clues about the correct choice on a given trial (as in Figures 10-13). Since the identity of the whole unit depends on the identity of the critical constituent, it seems paradoxical that the overall configuration can aid perception of the constituent.

In particular, such findings create difficulties for theories of pattern analysis which assume that elementary features must reach some perceptually available threshold value before overall structure can be ascertained from the identified features. In fact, we have found that, using masks that reduce identification to chance

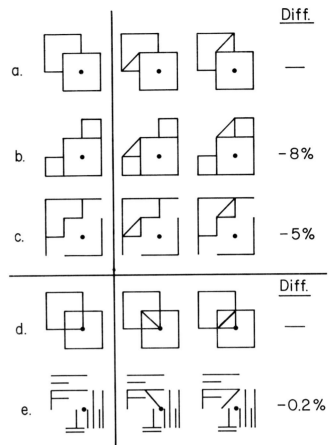

Figure 12. Additional contexts. Patterns b and c were used by Williams & Weisstein, (1976 a, b; 1977) and d and e by Womersley, (1977). Diff for the top three rows is again the mean deficit in accuracy with each context as compared to the connected, three-dimensional context (a); with this context modified to produce a flatter appearance (d), accuracy differences between it and a flat, unconnected pattern (e) vanish.[3]

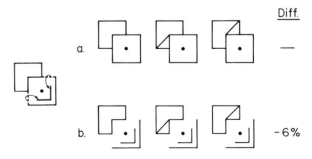

Figure 13. The two line segments indicated by the arrows are shifted from (a) to (b), leaving the local neighborhood of the target line segments identical; nevertheless, accuracy is significantly better by 6% for the more connected, apparently three-dimensional drawing. (Williams & Weisstein, 1977).

[3]We thank Marcus Womersley for permission to use his figures 12 (d) and (e) and for providing the raw data with which to compute the percentage deficit in accuracy.

for a single letter in isolation, or for a letter in a non-word, the same letter can be identified quite reliably when part of a word. (Matthews, Weisstein, & Williams, 1974).

The factors accounting for word-superiority have been studied much more extensively (Baron, in press) than those for object-superiority. Initial evidence however suggests that both connectedness and perceived depth contribute to the object-superiority effect. The rank ordering of accuracies with our patterns and with a different set used by Greg Ozog in an unpublished experiment seem to fit well with this analysis, as do the data of Womersley (1977) showing that the accuracy advantage obtained with the overlapping squares disappeared when they were modified slightly so that, together with a different placement of the diagonal line segments, they yielded much flatter, less three-dimensional perceptions (Figure 12d).

Additional evidence comes from a pilot study in which Harris and Weisstein asked subjects not only to identify the diagonal line but also to indicate on each trial, whether the figure appeared unitary and three-dimensional. Subjects were more accurate in identifying the diagonal line on trials when they incorrectly perceived Figure 11b as a unitary object.

We've also looked for these effects with single vertices, reasoning that perception of three-dimensionality may not be essential for these effects if the configuration is one that normally plays an important role in object perception. There's some evidence for vertex effects: with the same task, but with the diagonal target lines forming one or another single vertex—contexts that are too incomplete to reliably lead to perceived depth—Berbaum, Weisstein and Harris (1975) found that accuracy corresponds to the reliability with which each vertex would indicate a single solid object according to Guzman's (1968) program.

However, these vertex effects do not appear to account for "object superiority", at least not in any simple, linear way (Berbaum, 1977). When pairs of vertices are tested, accuracy differences disappear, even though one might expect certain combinations of vertices to convey more reliable information about a single solid object than each does alone. When a number of vertices are present, such as in the patterns we used (Figs. 11 and 12), performance is not predicted from the differences in accuracy established previously for separate vertices. In addition, when local environments are exactly equated (using the same task, but having only two diagonal line segments—Fig. 13), accuracy is still better for the coherent three-dimensional context, even though now the vertices formed by the diagonal line segments (as well as everything else in their immediate neighborhood) are identical.

3: Implications of these results for representation and interpretation

The results we've just described seem to confirm our working hypothesis that higher-level processes are accessible to psychophysical measurement. What are the implications of these results?

3.1: The conditions necessary for producing these effects

In most respects, the effects we have found are very similar to those obtained when measuring elementary mechanisms. They differ because local retinal stimulation is not necessary for producing these effects or does not exclusively determine these effects, if the overall configuration is suitable.

We should emphasize that most overall configurations are not suitable. For instance, although we have shown that a motion after-effect occurs when a particular kind of illusory motion—phantoms—is perceived, most other circumstances of perceived motion without corresponding retinal displacement will not produce a motion after-effect.

So one can't just substitute a perceptual variable for a stimulus variable and automatically produce a cognitive or perceptual counterpart for each phenomenon that normally seems to measure elementary processes. Rather, our results indicate that a class of effects commonly believed to measure elementary processes aren't found exclusively under the simple local stimulating conditions that were previously thought essential for their occurrence: there are certain significant exceptions.

3.2: The mechanisms responsible for these effects

The conditions under which these significant excpetions are found might lead us to speculate that the higher-order processes we are measuring involve some of the same kinds of representational structures that are involved in the more elementary processes.

Indeed, it's possible that our effects are tapping into top-down influences on exactly the same structures that, with simpler stimuli, respond to restricted patches of the retinal image: higher-level processes may be feeding back to lower-level mechanisms, and our results may reflect the outcome of successive computations by these mechanisms.

3.3: What these effects can tell us about higher-level processes

Feedback is just one of many possibilities however, and it is not directly established by our results. What does seem to be established is that the perception of low-level details in an image is filtered, enhanced, or overriden by higher-level processes. This suggests that the representation of an image might be similar at successive levels of processing; and it leads to a number of paradigms for studying the structure of higher-level processes.

Filling-in. Our results with the phantom-motion after-effect and with cubes in front of gratings suggest that certain kinds of higher-

Naomi Weisstein and William Maguire

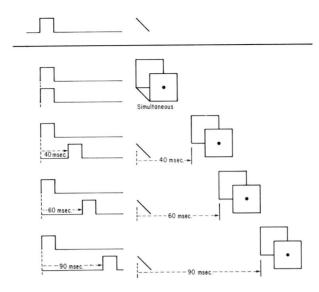

Figure 14. Procedure for testing time course.

The delay between briefly flashed target line and context is varied. This is illustrated on the left which shows the duration of the two flashes. On the right (with an expanded time scale) how the patterns appear in time is shown.

level processes involve pictorial representation. Neural mechanisms appear to be responding as if to continue a pattern which has been occluded. Measurement of the details of this response might indicate how certain kinds of relations involving depth are computed--behind, in, on, in front of.

Recently, Burt (1974) has utilized some of these same ideas in a network simulation of motion, occlusion and depth. His network represents motion in an analog fashion on a neural layer. Particularly interesting from our point of view is his assumption of a mechanism whereby the representation of an object as it passes behind another is maintained as a form of truncated activity.

Object-superiority. Global aspects of a pattern influence representation in symbolic, non-linear ways. Our object-and word-superiority effects show that such global factors as apparent depth and connectedness improve accuracy for detecting individual line segments. This provides a way to assess how specific line and vertex configurations enter into object and depth perception. (Previously, machine vision has had to rely on good guesses about such structural cues.)

Time course. In addition, combined with other techniques, object-superiority might be able to tell us something about the stages at which various global factors enter into processing, and perhaps even something about the speed with which they do so. This is described in detail in the next section.

4: How global factors enter in: The time course of object superiority

This section differs from previous ones in a number of ways: The work described here is currently in progress; there are many experiments that we'd like to run, but haven't gotten to yet; the chain of speculation is more extensive than in previous sections. We build on the idea that differences in accuracy for detecting a line segment reflect differences in grouping, and we go on to use this accuracy measure to get clues to some of the different structural factors involved, and the stages in processing where they may enter in.

4.1: When do coherence and three-dimensionality enter in?

Our object-superiority results showed that a connected, apparently three-dimensional pattern improves accuracy for detecting individual line segments. We don't know when in pattern analysis this happens--whether it occurs at a fairly early stage, or whether it occurs rather late in the process. And we don't know whether connectedness and three-dimensionality influence accuracy at the same time or at different times. How would we go about measuring when such factors enter in?

4.1.1: Procedure: Varying the delay of the context

Suppose we flash a context pattern at various delays after we've flashed a line segment. We could find out how much later the pattern can be flashed and still have some influence on detection of the line segment. We could then make the delays shorter and shorter, and see how influence from the pattern develops as it gets closer and closer in time to the line segment. If different context patterns produce different

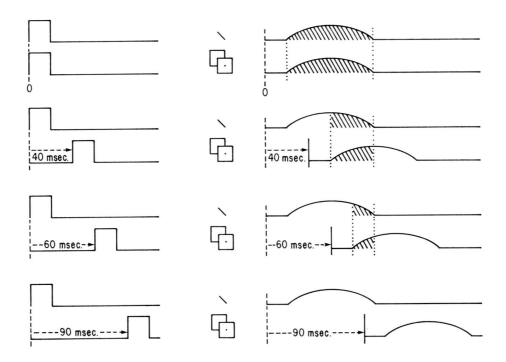

Figure 15. Neural response to target and context.

   Various delays between target (upper flash) and context (lower flash) are illustrated on the left; for each delay, schematic neural responses to the target and to the context are shown on the right. The shaded area indicates where the responses overlap.

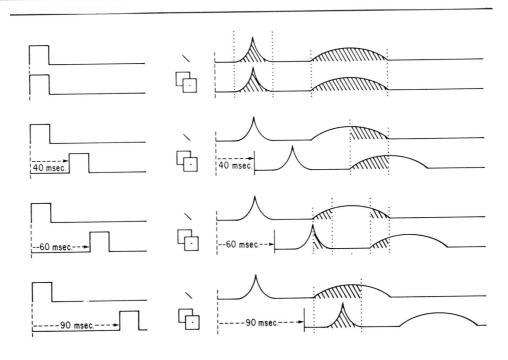

Figure 16. Two-component neural response.

Naomi Weisstein and William Maguire

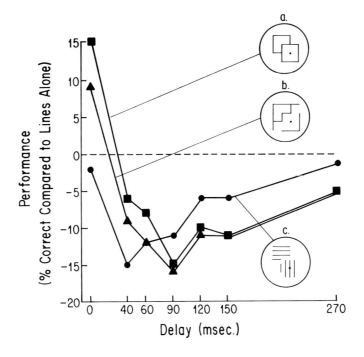

Figure 17. Accuracy for a briefly flashed line segment as a function of delay between line segment and various contexts, plotted in terms of difference from accuracy for a line segment alone (dashed line at zero). Each pairing of line segment and context produces a different temporal function. These are indicated by a dashed line (circles) for the unconnected-lines context; by a solid, light line (triangles) for the partial square context; and by a solid heavy line (squares) for the overlapping squares context.

temporal functions, the temporal differences might suggest _when_ such factors as connectedness or perceived depth have their influence.

This is shown in Figure 15 (Williams & Weisstein, 1976a, 1977; also see Weisstein, 1971, for a like design to separate the effects of brightness and contour). One of four diagonal line segments (target line) is briefly flashed, followed by the context. Sometimes the context appears right after the target line; sometimes it appears well after the target line has been flashed and sometimes the target and context lines are flashed simultaneously, as in the original experiment.

The subject's task, as before, is simply to report on each trial which one of the four diagonal line segments has been flashed. Also as before the extra vertical and horizontal lines which make up the contexts are irrelevant to the required judgment: they are identical, regardless of which diagonal line is flashed, and hence convey no information about the correct choice. Different contexts are constructed by arranging the same vertical and horizontal lines in different ways.

Visual system response. How long a delay

would we need to prevent the context lines from influencing detection of the target line? This would depend on how long information about the target line remains at a place in the visual system where it can be influenced by the context and on how fast information from the context can get to the information about the target line. The longer information from the target line stays in a vulnerable place and the faster the context travels to that place, the greater the delay at which the context lines would have an influence. This is illustrated in Figure 15, which shows schematically a possible neural response to the target line, and to the context. As the delay between context and target line gets longer, the responses overlap less. Assuming some rough linearity, the less they overlap, the less the context lines should be able to influence performance on the target line.

Elaborating the diagram. Figure 16 shows another, more elaborate diagram which is closer to what our results seem to require.[4] Here each

[4]Actually, to obtain good fits to empirical meta-contrast functions, a diagram with more realistic neural response components would be needed (see Weisstein, 1968, 1972; Weisstein et al., 1975).

neural response has two components to the target and to the context rather than just one: a fast component (Figure 16, a) and a slower component (Figure 16, b). The details of these assumed components have been worked out elsewhere (Weisstein, 1968, 1972; Weisstein, Ozog & Szoc, 1975; Breitmeyer & Ganz, 1976; Matin, 1976): for now, it's worth noting that the fast component seems to respond to luminance over wide spatial areas (low spatial frequencies) and the slow component seems to respond to fine detail and sharp edges (high spatial frequencies).

4.1.2. What the temporal functions look like.

Figure 17 shows how accuracy changed in our experiment as a function of increasing delay between the line segment and three of our contexts (Williams & Weisstein, 1977). The plotted points represent the difference from accuracy for the target line alone--indicated by the dashed line at zero--that is, the context-dependent accuracy.

Consider first the solid, heavy line (squares). This is the function for the overlapping squares-- the context which, when combined with each of our diagonal target lines yields the perception of a connected, three-dimensional object.

When the target line and the overlapping squares are flashed simultaneously (0 msec. delay), accuracy is considerably higher than when the target line is flashed alone. However, when the overlapping squares are flashed after the target line, accuracy is less than for the target line alone. As the delay between target line and overlapping squares increases, accuracy first decreases and then increases, finally approaching the level for the target line alone.

Why the function looks like this. Why don't the overlapping squares always help accuracy? A detailed answer would take us too far afield; let us simply note that a good deal of previous work with procedures like these ("metacontrast" experiments--for a presentation which includes a review see Weisstein, 1972 and Weisstein, Ozog & Szoc, 1975), implies that accuracy should be impaired for most delays. Referring to the schematic diagram (Figure 16), we can say more specifically that over the range where the fast portion of the response to the context overlaps the slow portion of the response to the target, we would expect decreases in accuracy. However, to find out about the time course of grouping and aggregation processes, it is not crucial whether accuracy is impaired or helped by the overlapping squares. What is important is the differences between the temporal functions for different contexts.

Comparing different contexts. Overlapping squares vs. unconnected lines. Let's now compare the function for the overlapping squares (which yielded the highest accuracy in our original experiment) with the function for the pattern of unconnected vertical and horizontal lines (which yielded the lowest accuracy in our original experiment). The function for the unconnected lines is indicated by a dashed line (circles); we've already looked at the

function for the overlapping squares, which is indicated by the heavy line (squares).

The difference between these two functions is striking. The delay where accuracy is lowest with the overlapping squares is some fifty milliseconds greater than the delay where accuracy is lowest with the unconnected lines. And at the longest delay, where the unconnected lines have no influence at all, the overlapping squares still have some effect.

The fact that these two functions are parallel to the right of their minima suggests that one might be a horizontal translation of the other over this range. (A variety of simple stimulus variations have been found to produce horizontal shifts like these (Weisstein, 1972; Rogowitz, 1977)).

A horizontal shift might indicate that the two contexts have similar influences, but that the overlapping squares context influences accuracy some fifty milliseconds before the unconnected lines can. This might mean that the overlapping squares context was processed faster. (If the overlapping squares have to be delayed by 50 msec. in order to have the same effect as the unconnected lines, the squares must be traveling 50 msec. faster.)

There's an alternative interpretation of the similarity and differences between the two functions. If we assume that the overall function for the overlapping squares is the sum of two functions, one of them U-shaped (due to a process which impairs accuracy), and one of them monotonically and steeply decreasing with increasing delay (due to a second process which enhances accuracy), then the actual minimum of the U might occur at the same delay as the minimum for the unconnected lines but be hidden by the rapid fall-off of the other function. In that case, the U-shaped functions for the two contexts might be identical except for a vertical translation. Such a vertical shift would indicate that the two contexts have similar influences at similar times, but that the over- lapping squares have a magnified influence.

We can't yet say whether the difference in the two functions are a result of the overlapping squares having a magnified influence or a faster one. Either way, there's a difference throughout the entire temporal range, even at delays as great as 270 msec. This might suggest that the contexts are grouped differently quite early in processing.

It's worth noting that neither differences[5] in the frequency spectra of the two functions, nor local factors, such as the proximity of the vertical and horizontal lines to the diagonal target lines account for the differences between these two functions. That is, the differences in local environment are small enough so that the

[5] We thank Patrick Cavanagh, Université de Montreal, for computing the two-dimensional Fourier trans- forms of our stimuli.

Naomi Weisstein and William Maguire

large difference in the functions obtained would not have been predicted on the basis of previous metacontrast data (Alpern, 1953; Growney, Weisstein, & Cox, 1975). Nor can a difference in size account for the differences obtained, because the overall extent of each pattern is almost the same.

Overlapping squares versus partial square. We can also compare our overlapping squares to a context in which the local environment for the target lines is more nearly identical. Figure 18 shows how this context differs from the overlapping squares: we've moved one line segment horizontally, one vertically, so now we have a small hollow, block "L" inside a large incomplete or partial square. The functions for the overlapping squares and for the partial square (heavy and light unbroken lines) coincide at long delays and differ only at the shorter delays. This would be consistent with the idea that a fast component of the response to these two contexts (Figure 16) is the same, and it's only the slower component that's sensitive to the differences in overall configuration or perceived depth.

4.1.3: Summary of the differences.

Comparing all three functions leads to some speculations about when and how various aspects of patterns exert their influence. It's possible that the distinction between something that might be a connected figure (overlapping or partial square) and something that probably isn't (unconnected lines) occurs quite early in processing: At long delays, the overlapping and partial squares give identical curves, different from that for the unconnected lines (Figure 17).

Once the separation on the basis of connectedness is made (if it is made on this basis), it would appear that the specific interpretation that one pattern represents a distinctive three-dimensional object, and the other doesn't, affects accuracy well after visual processing has begun.

This interpretation of our results would seem to make a certain amount of sense for image analysis. One might expect that three-dimensionality would not be computed until an initial segmentation into regions had occurred; and one might expect the initial segmentation to occur quite early in processing.

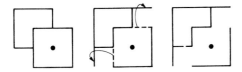

Figure 18. The two line segments indicated by the arrows are shifted as indicated to produce the partial square context.

5: Conclusion

A number of experiments measuring higher-order representation and interpretation have been described. These have touched on a variety of different perceptual phenomena, and have used a number of different psychophysical techniques, all of which had been developed to explore the characteristics of much lower-level processes.

Our results indicate that these higher-order processes can override, filter, or enhance input, even to the point of filling in for something that's not actually there, or improving accuracy for something that might be there. Our experiments lead us to speculate that information from high-level interpretations is fed back to influence low-level mechanisms. The experiments on the time course of object-superiority might even suggest that the global configuration of a pattern influences speed of processing with certain coherent configurations, resulting in very rapid processing, with the results of this processing feeding back to lower-level mechanisms.

Rather than emphasizing the specific conclusions or suggestions about interpretation and representation that we can make at this time, however, we would like to stress the usefulness of the strategy that we are using for exploring these questions. The strategy approaches the investigation of higher-level activity by assuming that it is accessible to the same kind of psychophysical measurement as lower-level process.

The strategy appears to be working. Our experiments have shown that sensory psychophysical techniques can measure higher-level processes. The results of these measurements provide important clues about interpretation and representation. The techniques reveal how the perception of local details of an image depend on higher-level processes; by further studying what happens to these details, we can obtain insights into the structure of representation and interpretation in the human visual system.

6: References

Alpern, M. Metacontrast. Journal of the Optical Society of America, 43, 1953, 648-657.

Anstis, S. M., & Reinhardt-Rutland, A. H. Interactions between motion aftereffects and induced movement. Vision Research, 16, No. 12, 1976, 1391-1394.

Anstis, S. M., & Gregory, R. L. The aftereffect of seen motion; the role of retinal stimulation and of eye movements. Quarterly Journal of Experimental Psychology, 17, 1965, 173-174.

Barlow, H. B., & Hill, R. M. Evidence for a physiological explanation of the waterfall illusion and figural aftereffects. Nature, 200, 1963, 1434-1435.

Baron, J. The word superiority effect. In W. K. Estes (Ed.) Handbook of learning and cognitive processes, 5, New Jersey: Erlbaum (In Press)

Berbaum, K. The psychological reality of certain computer models for scene parsing. (Manuscript), 1977.

Berbaum, K., Weisstein, N., & Harris, C. A vertex-superiority effect. Bulletin of the Psychononomic Society, 6, 1975, 418.

Blakemore, C., & Campbell, F. W. On the existence of neurones in the human visual system selectively sensitive to the orientation and size of retinal images. Journal of Physiology, 203, 1969, 237-260.

Blakemore, C., & Nachmias, J. The orientation specificity of two visual aftereffects. Journal of Physiology, 213, 1971, 237-260.

Blakemore, C., & Sutton, P. Size adaptation: A new aftereffect. Science, 166, 1969, 245-247.

Blakemore, C., Nachmias, J., & Sutton, P. The perceived spatial frequency shift: Evidence for frequency-selective neurones in the human brain. Journal of Physiology, 210, 1970, 727-750.

Blakemore, C., Muncey, J. P. J., & Ridley, R. M. Stimulus specificity in the human visual system. Vision Research, 13, 1973, 1915-1931.

Breitmeyer, B., & Ganz, L. Implications of sustained and transient channels for theories of visual pattern masking, saccadic suppression, and information processing. Psychological Review, 83, 1976, 1-36.

Burt, P. An examination of possible low level spatial processing in the visual system. Masters Thesis, University of Massachusetts. Amherst, Mass. 1974.

Ehrenstein, W. Probleme der ganzheitspsychologischen Wahrnehmungslehre. Leipzig: J. A. Barth, 1954.

Fidell, L. S. Orientation specificity in chromatic adaptation of human "edge detectors". Perception & Psychophysics, 8, 1970, 231-234.

Graham, N., Robson, J. G., & Nachmias, J. Grating summation in fovea and periphery. Investigative Ophthalmology and Visual Science, 16, April, 1977, (ARVO Meeting Supplement) (Abstract).

Graham, N., & Nachmias, J. Detection of grating patterns containing two spatial frequencies: A comparison of single-channel and multiple-channel models. Vision Research, 11, 1971, 251-259.

Growney, R., Weisstein, N., & Cox, S. I. Measurement of metacontrast. Journal of the Optical Society of America, 65, 1975, 1379-1381.

Guzman, A. Computer recognition of three-dimensional objects in a visual scene. Project MAC Technical Report 59, MIT Artificial Intelligence Laboratory, Cambridge, Mass. 1968.

Harris, C. S. Effect of viewing distance on a color aftereffect specific to spatial frequency. Psychonomic Science, 21, 1970, 350 (Abstract).

Hubel, D. H., & Wiesel, T. N. Receptive fields, binocular interaction, and functional architecture in the cat's visual cortex. Journal of Physiology, 160, 1962, 106-154.

Kanizsa, G. Marzini quazi-percettive in campi con stimolazione omogenea. Rivista di Psicologia, 1955, 49, 7-30.

Klein, R. Visual detection of line segments: When the object is not superior. 47th Annual Meeting of the Eastern Psychological Association (Abstract) 1976.

Lehmkuhle, S., & Fox, R. Effect of binocular rivlry suppression on the motion aftereffect. Vision Research, 15, 1975, 855-859.

McClelland, J. Perception and masking of wholes and parts (Manuscript) 1976.

McCollough, C. Color adaptation at edge detectors in the human visual system. Science, 149, 1965, 1115-1116.

Macleod, I. D. G., & Rosenfeld, A. The visibility of gratings: Spatial frequency channels or bar-detecting units? Vision Research, 14, 1974, 909-915.

Maffei, L., & Campbell, F. Neurophysiological localization of the vertical and horizontal visual coordinates in man. Science, 167, 1970, 386-387.

Maffei, L., Fiorentini, A., & Bisti, S. Neural correlate of perceptual adaptation of gratings. Science, 182, 1973, 1036-1038.

Maguire, W., & Weisstein, N. Temporal factors in nonretinolocal motion aftereffect (Manuscript) 1977a.

Maguire, W., & Weisstein, N. The effect of apparent depth upon the phantom motion aftereffect (Manuscript) 1977b.

Masland, R. H. Visual motion perception: Experimental modification. Science, 165, 1969, 819-821.

Matthews, M., Weisstein, N., & Williams, A. Masking of letter features does not remove the word-superiority effect. Bulletin of the Psychonomic Society, 4, 1974, 262. (Abstract)

Matin, E. The two transient (masking) paradigm. Psychological Review, 82, No. 6, 1975, 451-461.

Naomi Weisstein and William Maguire

Nakayama, K., & Roberts, D. J. Line length detectors in the human visual system: Evidence from selective adaptation. Vision Research, 12, 1972, 1709-1713.

Over, R., Broerse, J., Crassini, B., & Lovegrove, W. Spatial determinants of the aftereffect of seen motion. Vision Research, 13, 1973, 1681-1690.

Pantle, A. Motion aftereffect magnitude as a measure of the spatiotemporal response properties of direction-sensitive analyzers. Vision Research, 14, 1974, 1229 - 1236.

Pantle, A. A null technique for measuring the temporal contrast sensitivity of human direction-sensitive mechanisms. Paper presented at meeting of Association for Research in Vision and Ophthalmology, Sarasota, Florida, April, 1976.

Pantle, A., & Sekuler, R. W. Size-detecting mechanisms in human vision. Science, 162, 1968, 1146-1148.

Pantle, A., & Sekuler, R. W. Contrast response of human visual mechanisms sensitive to orientation and direction of motion. Vision Research, 9, 1969, 397-406.

Rogowitz, B. E. Backward masking with sinusoidal gratings: A look at spatial frequency and temporal response. Investigative Ophthalmology and Visual Science. April 1977, 16, ARVO Meeting Supplement) (Abstract) p. 122.

Sekuler, R., & Ganz, L. A new aftereffect of seen movement with a stabilized retinal image. Science, 139, 1963, 419-420.

Sekuler, R., & Pantle, A. A model for aftereffects of seen motion. Vision Research, 7, 1967, 427-439.

Smith, A. T., & Over, R. Orientation, masking and the tilt illusion with subjective contours. Perception (In Press).

Spoehr, K. Personal Communication, 1975.

Tynan, P., & Sekuler, R. Moving visual phantoms: A new contour completion effect. Science, 188, 1975, 951-952.

Weisstein, N. A Rashevsky-Landahl neural net: Simulation of metacontrast. Psychological Review, 75, 1968, 494-521.

Weisstein, N. Neural symbolic activity: A psychophysical measure. Science, 168, 1970, 1489-1491.

Weisstein, N. U-shaped and W-shaped masking functions obtained for monoptic and dichoptic disc-disc masking. Perception & Psychophysics, 9, 1971, (3A), 275-278.

Weisstein, N. Metacontrast. In D. Jameson & L. Hurvich, (Eds.) Handbook of sensory physiology, Springer-Verlag: Berlin, 1972.

Weisstein, N. Beyond the yellow Volkswagen detector and the grandmother cell: A general strategy for the exploration of operations in human pattern recognition. In Solso, R. (Ed.) Contemporary issues in cognitive psychology: The Loyola Symposium. W. H. Winston & Sons, Washington, D. C., 1973.

Weisstein, N. Masking and unmasking of distributed representations in the visual system. In Harris, C. S. (ed.) Visual coding and adaptability. Hillsdale, N. J.: Lawrence Erlbaum Associates. In press.

Weisstein, N., & Harris, C. S. Visual detection of line segments: An object-superiority effect. Science, 186, 1974, 752-755.

Weisstein, N., Maguire, W., & Berbaum, K. A phantom motion aftereffect. Bulletin of the Psychonomic Society, 8, 1976, 240 (Abstract).

Weisstein, N., Maguire, W., & Berbaum, K. Motion aftereffects in retinal regions that have not been stimulated by moving contours. Investigative Ophthalmology and Visual Science, 16, April, 1977, (ARVO Meeting Supplement) (Abstract).

Weisstein, N., Matthews, M., & Berbaum, K. Illusory contours can mask real contours. Bulletin of the Psychonomic Society, 4, 1974, p. 266 (Abstract).

Weisstein, N., Montalvo, F. S., & Ozog, G. Differential adaptation to gratings blocked by cubes and gratings blocked by hexagons: A test of the neural symbolic acitivty hypothesis. Psychonomic Science, 27, 1972, 89-91.

Weisstein, N., Ozog, G., & Szoc, R. A comparison and elaboration of two models of metacontrast. Psychological Review, 82, 1975, 325-343.

Williams, A., & Weisstein, N. The time course of object superiority. Bulletin of the Psychonomic Society, 8, 260, 1976a (Abstract).

Williams, A., & Weisstein, N. Line segments are perceived better in a coherent context than alone: An object-line effect in visual perception. Manuscript, 1976b.

Williams, A., & Weisstein, N. Effects of overall structure on the temporal course of masking in a simple detection task. Investigative Ophthalmology and Visual Science, 16 April, 1977 (ARVO Meeting Supplement) p. 123 (Abstract).

Wilson, H. R., & Bergen, J. A four mechanism
    model for spatial vision. Investigative
    Ophthalmology and Visual Science. April,
    1977, 16, (ARVO Meeting Supplement)
    p. 46. (Abstract)

Wohlgemuth, A. On the aftereffect of seen
    movement. British Journal of Psychology.
    Monograph Supplements, 1, 1911, 1-117.

Womersley, M. A contextual effect in feature
    detection with application of signal
    detection methodology. Perception &
    Psychophysics, 21, 1977, 81-92.

A PARTIALLY ORDERED WORLD MODEL
AND NATURAL OUTDOOR SCENES*

Ruzena Bajcsy[+] and Aravind K. Joshi[+]
Department of Computer and Information Science
The Moore School
University of Pennsylvania, Philadelphia, PA 19104

ABSTRACT

A partially ordered world model useful for recognition of natural outdoor scenes is presented here. The methodology used is that of an inference system based on production rules, which allows inferencing on partial information. We have chosen to put the domain dependency into the representation of the world and have a domain independent control structure rather than the other way around. We hope thereby to learn more about the nature and principles which govern our domain. We have also discussed some design issues in constructing an interactive query system with a natural language interface.

1. INTRODUCTION

Traditionally, in the computer vision literature (and in artificial intelligence, in general) general graphs have been used as the representation for the concepts, commonly called world model (see for example, Winston (1970), Barrow and Popplestone (1971), Fischler and Elschlager (1973), Yakimovsky and Feldman (1973), Bajcsy and Lieberman (1974), and others).

Although general graphs constitute a very general structure available for representing knowledge, they are not always the most preferable ones for the search techniques used to traverse them. Thus, we are motivated to look for a representation which will be general enough for fully modelling the concepts involved in our particular domain, natural outdoor scenes, yet restricted enough to yield efficient search techniques.

Again, in the A.I. spirit, in order to cut down the exponential search problem, we have used various heuristics. Often, the heuristics showed

up explicitly in the design of the control structure of the search process or, in vision, of the recognition process; for example, decisions about the order in which low-level operators are applied to the scene (color, texture, shape, etc.) or about the order of interpretation of objects (the largest region, the brightest region, the topmost one, etc). One clearly has a choice in putting the domain dependencies (the specific knowledge) either into the world model (structure), or in the recognizer. In this paper, we shall present a system where specific knowledge is embedded in the world model and thereby the control structure is made more systematic and general than otherwise. The pictorial data is from static scenes as viewed by a static observer (one view); we have not considered motion in this paper. As the title suggests, we have chosen a partially ordered structure for modelling the concepts of outdoor scenes. Some of the reasons for this choice are as follows.

(1) It is a more restricted structure than a general graph. That is, the arcs have uniform labels and they represent only the partial ordering relationships and no others. All other relationships are implicit in the labels of the nodes; the interpretation is therefore more uniform.

(2) A tree structure is a more desirable structure (as far as search is concerned) than a general graph; however, it is too restricted.

Many concepts belong to more than one higher order category or are parts of several different objects; take for example, a leg which could be a part of a chair, an animal, or a human.

(3) A partial ordering which is more general than a tree structure is possibly a desired compromise. We could consider a lattice structure which will allow only a unique least upper and greatest lower bound. But, sometimes it is desirable to allow several least upper and greatest lower bounds. For example, during the recognition process we may wish to keep several possible interpretations which are valid at a given time (local ambiguity).

---

* March 1977, Revised, September 1977

* This work was partially supported by NSF Grant MCS76-19465 and NSF Grant MCS76-19466.

We shall also dicuss two different modes of processing: 'batch' and interactive? During the batch processing the observer (the artificial eye) processes the pictorial data from the beginning till the end of recognition without any outside intervention (either from the user or from the observer such as getting new pictorial data). In the interactive mode, this is not so; the user by his interogations influences the observer's focus on the scene and his consequent actions.

2. BACKGROUND

In the past, there have been efforts to use a more structured approach towards world model, for example, Fu and Bhargav (1973), Shaw (1969), and others, who modelled the world as a tree structure. The tree structure is very convenient for modelling hierarchies in general.

As a matter of fact, hierarchies are the first thing that people recognize when one attempts to find a structure on a set of concepts. The obvious weekness of such a representation is that concepts of the real world do not form a strict hierarchy, but more often a partially ordered structure.

In the domain of computer vision, this fact was recognized for the first time by Tidhar (1975) and a lattice-like structure was used for describing 2-D patterns by him. In parallel, similar ideas, though not implemented, were presented by Fahlamn (1975). Tidhar's world model was composed of two separate structures both formed as lattices; one structure represented the 'KIND-OF' or the 'INSTANCE' relationship and the other represented the 'PHYSICAL PART-WHOLE' relationship.

This model allowed one to design a recognizer for the concepts by simple computation of the greatest lower bound or the least upper bound. Recognition was possible by checking for only partial features. The idea of recognition by matching partial information was first mentioned by Uhr (1970), though in a different context.

Tidhar's idea about partial matching was generalized and applied by Rosenschein (1975) in the natural language domain for representing lexicon in terms of primitives and intermediate level concepts. In particular, Rosenschein replaced the two types of arcs ('KIND-OF' and 'PHYSICAL PART-WHOLE') by one uniform arc and also introduced N-ARY predicates (as opposed to binary), variables

(as opposed to only constants), and explicit negation into the structure, both at the primitive level[2] and intermediate levels. Later an inference system, using these ideas, was designed and implemented using the production system methodology, (Newell (1973)), (Rosenschein and Joshi (1976) and Joshi (1977). (See Appendix A for s short description of the system.)

Using these ideas, Sloan (1977) (Sloan and Bajcsy (1977)) has implemented a more systematic recognizer for real outdoor scenes. Sloan's system has the following components:

1. Data Base
2. Interpreter
3. Rules

The data base contains information about the state of the world. As it stands now, the data base is partitioned into two parts: the long term facts (LFACTS) and the short term facts (FACTS). The information in LFACTS is a set of assertions which are known to be potentially interesting but not of immediate importance. FACTS contains the immediate relevant information. Similar memory organization to this has been also described by (Hanson et all (1976). The rules represent relationships among different concepts. The interpreter carries out the matching process between the data bsse, as well as it executes actions which arise as consequences of the applied rules (See Appendix A).

Joshi (1977) has described a substantial extension of the current system. In particular, he hss introduced the particular, he has introduced the partitioning of the rules also into long term rules (LRULES) and short term rules (RULES). In addition, he discusses several possibilities for going beyond simple tagging of rules (which is somewhat contrary to the philosophy of production rules) by considering schemes for context dependent and dymanic clustering; that is, techniques for clustering different rules and facts with respect to the current demands or needs. Several strategies for resolving ambiguities (conflict resolution) are also considered, including a scheme for describing intermediate concepts.

---

1. We distinguish the observer, the artificial eye, from the user who may or may not interrogate the observer via query. Only the observer has direct access to the visual data.

2. Explicit negation at the primitive level is necessary in the linguistic domain but does not seem to be relevant in the visual domain, perhaps in the perceptual domain, in general.

Ruzena Bajcsy and Aravind K. Joshi

3. PARTIAL ORDERING AND NATURAL OUTDOOR SCENES

We are interested in finding relationships in the real world, which impose a partial ordering on a set of objects (or their associated concepts). Examples of such relationships are:

(1) 'KIND-OF' relationship (or the instance, or the category relationship)

(2) 'PHYSICAL PART-OF' relationship

(3) Ordering with respect to the size of objects, for example, larger, smaller, etc.

(4) Ordering with respect to the distance between the object and the observer, for example, closer, farther, etc.

(5) Ordering with respect to the number of elements in a group, for example, one tree, two trees, a row of trees, and a forest.

Having singled out these relationships, how are we going to build our world model which will use them? Following the scheme designed by Rosenschein, Sloan, and Joshi, we will describe each component separately.

Facts - Data Base:

Facts are classified into the long term facts (LFACTS) and short term facts (FACTS). The distinction is based purely on the immediate usage as opposed to the long term usage. This distinction as well as that for rules (described earlier) also help to control the combinatorial growth in the matching problem.

In general, FACTS are visual properties, either directly measurable or are derived from properties of the category that the concept belongs to, and from some distinguished property within the category, which is directly measurable. This representation of FACTS is similar to that of Moran (1973).

Facts are represented as a list structure in LISP. The first element in the list is the name of the concept and the rest of the elements are descriptions (properties) of the concept.

Examples:

    (ABOVE <r1> <r2> Region <r1> is higher than region <r2>

    (BOTTOM <r> <y> The lowest part of region <r> is at y i.e., coordinate <y>

    (COLOR <r> <y>) Region <r> is a piece of a cloud

    (SKY <r>) Region <r> is a piece of sky

    (SUBR <r1> <r2>) Region <r2> is a subregion of region <r1>

The low-level operators that make measurements on regions are FORTRAN routines. The information about a region is translated from FORTRAN data structure to assertions about the region by an appropriate LISP function which creates assertions such as

    (SIZE (REGION 5) 1200)

    (TOP (REGION 5) 38)

    (LEFT (REGION 5) 20)

Rules:

The general form of rules is an ordered pair (LHS, RHS) where the interpretation is that the left hand side (LHS) is a condition which has to be satisfied (partially, if necessary (See Appendix A)) in order for the right hand side (RHS) i.e., the action to take place. The action may consist of either instantiating new facts or invoking certain procedures, or both.

In addition to the usual forms, there are two special forms which have particular meaning to the system. The form (MUST <x>) which may appear in the LHS means that it is absolutely essential to the success of the matching of the LHS with FACT. Another special form (EXEC <x>) may appear in the RHS.

The EXEC is used for invoking certain procedures for communicating with the visual data base at some appropriate level (in our case, regions) and communicating with the user. It can also be used for communicating with LFACTS and LRULES (See Appendix A).

We will now present some rules for outdoor scenes grouped with respect to different criteria. Variables are prefixed by ?.

Rules which indicate the 'PHYSICAL PART WHOLE'
relationships:

((TREE ?REGION1) ((TREE-TRUNK ?REGION1 ?REGION2)

(TREE-CROWN ?REGION1 ?REGION2)

(SUBREGION ?REGION1 ?REGION2)

(SUBREGION ?REGION1 ?REGION3)))

((TREE-CROWN ?REGION1)

((TREE-BRANCH ?REGION1 ?REGION2)

(TREE-LEAVES ?REGION1 ?REGION3)

(SUBREGION ?REGION1 ?REGION2)

(SUBREGION ?REGION1 ?REGION3)))

((FLOWER ?REGION1) ((FLOWER-HEAD ?REGION1 ?REGION2)

(FLOWER-STEM ?REGION1 ?REGION3)

(FLOWER-LEAVES ?REGION1 ?REGION4)

(SUBREGION ?REGION1 ?REGION2)

(SUBREGION ?REGION1 ?REGION3)

(SUBREGION ?REGION1 ?REGION4)))

Rules which correspond to the 'KIND OF' relations:

(((GROUND ?REGION)

(GRASSY-GROUND ?REGION) or

(SANDY-GROUND ?REGION) or

(WATERY-GROUND ?REGION)))

((SKY ?REGION)

((CLOUDY-SKY ?REGION)

(CLEAR-SKY ?REGION)

(FOGY-SKY ?REGION)))

Rules which represent the group membership relationships:

((TREE ?REGION1) ((FOREST ?REGION1 ?REGION2)

(SUBREGION ?REGION2 ?REGION1)))

((GRASS-BLADE ?REGION1)

((GRASSY-FIELD ?REGION1 ?REGION2)

(SUBREGION ?REGION2 ?REGION1)))

4. THE CONTROL STRUCTURE

The ground and the sky are the fundamental
concepts in an outdoor scene. The reason for this
is that in order to determine them, the only thing
one has to know is the observer's position and the
fact that the observer is outdoors.

We start the recognition process with the
recognition of the ground and sky. These rules,
called orientation rules, have the highest priority. Their application (or call) follows from:

(A) The initial assumption about the observer.

(B) The least number of necessary identifiable
features.

After this rule what do we do next? Should
we continue to identify the instances of the
ground and/or sky or should we identify the objects
on the ground and in the sky? How should we organize the rules (or order them)? We view this
system in two basic modes: 'Batch' and Interactive.

4.1 The 'Batch' Mode

The 'batch' mode corresponds to a mode where
a user asks the system: 'TELL ME WHAT YOU SEE'.
After this question, the user just waits for a
complete description of the scene. This situation
may occur for instance, when the user is remote
with respect to the artificial eye, and wants to
orient himself towards where the eye is, with as
much detail as possible.

In this case, the control structure follows
completely from the structure of rules and built-
in strategies. Thus, the question of how to
structure knowledge (the rules and the facts)
arises. Several researchers recognized this
problem and grouped the rules into chunks using
tags (Davis and King (1975)). We allow two types
of tags: Implicit tags and Explicit tags. An
explicit tag is a name of a concept which is
common to every assertion in the cluster. For
example, we might have a cluster with the tag
'BLUE'. Each assertion in this cluster could
be about some thing which is asserted to be
BLUE. (e.g., (COLOR SKY BLUE), (COLOR (REGION5)
BLUE), etc.) The implicit tags on the other
hand represent natural groupings with respect
to those relationships which render the partially
ordered structures; these tags are of particular
interest to us.

It is clear that while the 'KIND OF',
'PHYSICAL PART OF' 'GROUP MEMBERSHIP' relationships cluster the rules implicitly, the
comparison relationship between sizes and distance will cluster the facts. This is so
because the size of objects and the distance
vary from scene to scene. What are the possibilities, depending on the different orderings.

(1) Use the ordering of regions with respect to
their size, that is, larger the object-region is,
one can recognize it faster (this method is implemented by Sloan (1977)).

Ruzena Bajcsy and Aravind K. Joshi

(2) Use the ordering with respect to the distance from the observer. That is, objects closer to the observer (the artificial eye) get more of its attention.

(3) Use the ordering with respect to the visibility of objects. This problem was already discussed by Bajcsy and Tavakoli (1975). The visibility of an object is a combined property of the size, distance and contrast.

In the context of outdoor scenes, it is useful to group the rules with respect to spatial and conceptual proximities. Thus we have ground rules which interpret different instances of ground as well as any object on the ground. Similarily we have sky rules, mountain rules, etc., see Sloan (1977).

We will now give a very brief description of the system. We start with a set of regions obtained by color separation. Then we apply the orientation rules.

```
(((COLOR ?REGION BLACK)

((SHADOW ?REGION) (GROUND ?REGION)) )


((GROUND ?REGION)

((EXEC (FOUND-GROUND ?REGION))) )


((MUST (TOP ?REGION))

 (MUST (BRIGHTNESS ?REGION PLUS)) )

 (SKY ?REGION) )


((BOTTOM ?REGION)

 (GROUND ?REGION))


((SKY ?REGION))

((EXEC (FOUND-SKY ?REGION))) )
```

The orientation rules interpret the first black region as shadows and ground. Also the bottommost region gets interpreted as ground. Similarly, the topmost region and the brightest one is interpreted as the sky.

The next step is to grow the ground and/or sky respectively, using ground rules or the sky rules.

The ground rules, for example, include rules for interpreting foliage as an instance of a ground as well as rules for finding tree-trunks as an object on the ground. The skyline and the horizon is a result of growing the sky and the ground and the associated objects on the ground. An actual example is shown in Figures 2,3, and 4. Figure 2 represents the scene. Figure 3 shows the ground (black points) the sky (the gray points), and the horizon (the crossing line). The white

are uninterpreted points on that scene. Finally, Figure 4 displays the skyline which is different from the horizon.

It is important to emphasize that the whole recognition strategy is encoded in the rules. In this mode, the 'batch' mode, the decisions are more of an a priori nature than data driven.

4.2 The Interactive Mode

This mode is useful when we would like to provide interaction with the type of processing described in Section 4.1. The interaction can be of two types:

1. <u>visual interaction</u>: This can happen, for example, when the observer's position is changed or the nature of the scene has changed as in change of visibility.

2. <u>user interaction</u>: This happens when the processing is affected by some user input, mostly in the form of a query.

The overall processing is thus controlled by initial visual data, possible changes in the data due to visual interactions as in 1. above, and user's interaction with the system.

Production system methodology is primarily suitable for data driven processing and is thus appropriate for handling the interactions mentioned above.

Suppose the system has produced some intermediate description in terms of the GROUND and SKY. The user may now request identification of specific objects with specific properties (e.g., near the horizon). Further processing will be controlled by this query (Rosenthal (1977).

Such interaction is necessary because the user would like much of the processing, except some gross descriptions obtained by the 'batch' processing, to be carried out on demand only. The system cannot be expected to compute in advance all the answers to all potential questions. It has to have the 'capability' of answering all these questions, but the computation is to be carried out on demand only.

Simple a-priori tagging of rules is not adequate for this purpose. The facts and rules have to be dynamically clustered depending on the context (current state of the system) and the demand (determined by the visual interaction or the user interaction). Mechanisms for such clustering allow dynamic modification of FACTS and RULES (see Figure 1).

User interaction need not be always in the form of a query. The user may provide visual information indirectly. Suppose the user were to tell the system that the time is 6 p.m., this symbolic input can be used by the system to modify appropriately its object recognition process, for example, by adjusting for visibility and the colors associated with objects).

5. CONCLUSIONS

In this paper, we have presented a world model for natural outdoor scenes in the framework of production systems. The scenes that we consider are medium to long range views of the outdoors, without any man-made objects. Visually it is quite a rich domain, yet in terms of the number of recognized objects, one can restrict it, so that it is computationally manageable.

Our primary goal is to design such a system where the control structure is as systematic as possible. Thus, the specific knowledge pertinent to the outdoor scenes is embedded into the representation of concepts, that is, into the world model.

Production systems offer several important advantages for implementation of perceptual processes. Each production system rule is an intelligible piece of operational knowledge (see Farley (1974)). The control structure is determined by the content of the memory (FACTS), which are inspected by the condition halves of the production rules. This leads to the data driven recognition, which has been emphasized among others by Barrow and Tenebaum (1975). The data driven recognition is especially pertinent to the interactive mode. In order to cope with the combinatorial growth during the matching process, the rules and the facts are partitioned into groups with respect to some relationships. This allows us to operate with only that knowledge which is currently needed.

We have partially implemented a system as described above and the results indeed show that, without any tuning, the system finds ground, sky and the horizon skylines in scenes which are visually very different.

We have also discussed some design issues in constructing an interactive query system with a natural language interface.

REFERENCE

1. Bajcsy, R. and Lieberman, L., "Computer Description of Real Outdoor Scenes", Proceedings of the 2nd International Joint Conference on Pattern Recognition, pp. 174-179, Copenhagen, August 1974.

2. Bajcsy, R. and Tavakoli, M., "Image Filtering - A Context Dependent Process", IEEE Trans. on Circuits and Systems, Vol. CAS-22, No. 5, May 1975.

3. Barrow, H.G. and Popplestone, R.J., "Relational Description in Picture Processing" Machine Intelligence 6, pp. 337-396, 1971.

4. Barrow, H.G. and Tenebaum, J.M., "Representation and Use of Knowledge in Vision", SRI Memo 108, July 1975.

5. Davis, R. and King, J., "An Overview of Production Systems", Stanford AI Laboratory, AIM-271, Computer Science Department, Stanford University, Stanford, California, October 1975.

6. Fahlman, S.E., "Thesis Progress Report: A System for Representing and Using Real World Knowledge", AI Lab., MIT, Memo 331, May 1975.

7. Farley, A.M., "VIPS: A Visual Imagery and Perception System; The Result of a Protocol Analysis", Ph.D. thesis, Computer Science Department, Carnegie-Mellon University, 1974.

8. Fischler, M.A. and Elschlager, R.A., "The Representation and Matching of Pictorial Structures", IEEE Trans. on Computers, Vol. C-22, No. 1, pp. 67-92, January 1973.

9. Fu, K.S. and Bhargav, B.K., "Tree Systems for Syntactic Pattern Recognition", IEEE Trans. on Computers, Vol. C-22, pp. 1087-1099, December 1973.

10. Hansen, A., Riseman, E. snd Williams, T., "Constructive Semantic Models in the Visual Analysis on Scenes", Proc. of IEEE MSAC, April 1976, pp. 97-102.

11. Joshi, A.K., "Some Extensions of a System for Inferencing on Partial Information", To appear in the Proceedings of the Workshops on Pattern Directed Inference Systems, Honolulu, May 1977, To be published by the Academic Press (ed. F. Hays-Roth and D. Waterman), 1978.

12. Joshi, A.K. and Rosenschein, S., "Some Problems of Inferencing: Relation of Inferencing to Decomposition of Predicates", Proceedings of the Int. Conf. on Computational Linguistics, Ottawa, 1976.

13. Newell, A., "Production Systems: Models of Control Structures", in Visual Information Processing, William G. Chase (Ed.) pp. 463-526, Academic Press.

14. Moran, T.P., "The Symbolic Nature of Visual Imagery", The Proceedings of 3rd Int. Joint Conference on AI, Stanford University, Stanford, California, pp. 472-477, August 1973.

15. Rosenschein, S., "Structuring a Pattern Space with Applications to Information and Event Interpretation", Ph.D. Dissertation, University of Pennsylvania, Philadelphia, 1975.

16. Rosenthal, D., "Inquiry Driven Computer Vision System Designed for Use of Multi-spectral and Multi-resolution Image Data", Forthcoming CIS Report, Univ. of Pennsylvania, Philadelphia, PA.

17. Quillian, M.R., "Word Concepts: A Theory and Simulation of Some Basic Semantic Capabilities", Behavioral Science, Vol. 12, 1967.

Ruzena Bajcsy and Aravind K. Joshi

18. Shaw, A., "A Formal Picture Description Scheme as a Basis for Picture Processing Systems", Information and Control, 14 pp. 9-52, 1969.

19. Sloan, K.R., Ph.D. thesis in preparation, University of Pennsylvania, Philadelphia, 1977.

20. Sloan, K.R. and Bajcsy, R., "World Model Driven Recognition of Natural Scenes", Proceedings of the 1977 IEEE Workshop on Picture Data Description and Management, Chicago, Ill., April 1977.

21. Tidhar, A., "Using a Structured World Model in Flexible Recognition of 2-D Patterns", Ph.D. Dissertation, University of Pennsylvania, Philadelphia, 1974.

22. Winston, P.H., "Learning Structural Descriptions from Examples", AI Technical Report 231, AI Lab., MIT, September 1970.

23. Yakimovsky, Y. and Feldman, J.A., "A Semantic Based Decision Theory Region Analyser", Proceedings of the 3-D Int. Conference on AI, Stanford University, Stanford, California, August 1973.

Figure 2

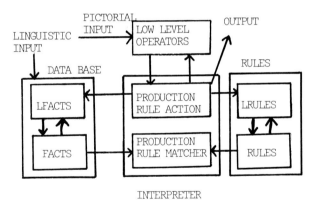

Figure 1.

Figure 3

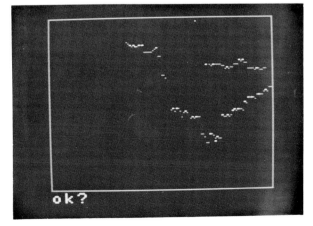

Figure 4

A Partially Ordered World Model

APPENDIX A

A Short Description of the Inference System

Except for some well-structured domains and aside from the most logical systems, inferencing is never in the context of total information. In general, in the context of dynamic and interactive situations, at each stage of interaction, interpretations have to be made, accounting for all of the input. Hence, a flexible system for inferencing is essential. The problems of partial match and best match are central to such flexible inference systems. The inference system described here structures the pattern space in a specific way, enabling us to set up internal (structural) criteria for best match. We will briefly describe the system and illustrate it by several examples. For further details see (Joshi (1978)).

First we need some definitions.

LRULES: User defined, potentially large set of productions (rewrites).
RULES: A small subset of LRULES, which is active at any given time. The rewrite rules in RULES are partially ordered by specificity. RULES is the current focus of LRULES.
LFACTS: A potentially large data base of facts.
FACTS: A small subset of LFACTS, which is active at any given time. FACTS is the current focus of LFACTS.

Let CONS and VARS be set of constants and variables (including predicate variables), respectively. The set of forms (FORMS) is defined as follows:

1) $A \in$ CONS $\Rightarrow A \in$ FORMS; ( ) ϵ FORMS
2) $?X \in$ VARS $\Rightarrow ?X \in$ FORMS
3) $A \in$ CONS & F1, F2, ... Fn ϵ FORMS $\Rightarrow$ (A F1 F2 ... Fn) ϵ FORMS
4) Nothing else.

Examples A.1

1. (P A B) ;P,A,B are constants, P is a predicate constant.
2. (HIT JOHN BILL)
3. (P ?X ?Y)
4. (P A/?X ?Y) ; ?X has been bound to A.
5. (WANT ?X (DO ?X ?P)) ;WANT has DO as an argument, ?P is a predicate variable.

LFACTS and FACTS are sets of forms. The productions or rewrite rules are defined as follows. Each rule is of the form

<antecedent> $\Rightarrow$ <consequent>

where <antecedent> and <consequent> are lists (representing sets) of forms. Rules in RULES are partially ordered by specificity. The antecedent may contain an item of the form (MUST <x>; in this case, <x>'s absence on occasion may be overlooked by the inferencer, when the whole rule is a good approximation for FACTS, according to the inference rule described later.

For our present purpose we can briefly describe the partial ordering on RULES as follows. Rule Ri is equal to or less than rule Rj if and only if the antecedent of Ri (represented as a set of forms) is a subset of the antecedent of Rj (represented as a set of forms). Thus R1: (P Q R) → E1 is less than R2: (P Q R S) → E2, (R1 is the minimal of the two), but it is not comparable to R3: (P Q U V) → E3, since the antecedent of R1 is not a subset of the antecedent of R3 and vice versa. Further if Ri = (P ?X ?Y) and Ri' = (P ?X B/?Y) then Ri' is less than Ri.

The consequent of the rule may contain items of the form (EXEC <x>). In this case, <x> is evaluated for effect in LISP when the rule is invoked. EXEC is used for calling INPUT and producing OUTPUT; it is also used for communicating with the usual data base.

Example A.2: 1. ((P ?X ?Y) (Q ?Y ?Z)) $\Rightarrow$ ((P ?X ?Y) (Q ?Y ?Z) (R ?Z))

The operation (REWRITE) transforms FACTS with respect to RULES in the following manner. A subset S ⊆ FACTS is maximal if S identifies one or more rules in RULES and for all S' ⊆ FACTS and S' ⊃ S, S' does not identify any rule in RULES. If FACTS is the only maximal subset then we choose the minimal rule that covers FACTS. Otherwise, for each maximal subset we find the minimal rule that covers the subset, i.e., no single rule was able to cover FACTS; we needed more than one rule to cover FACTS, one for each maximal subset. We will call this multiple response (see Examples A.3). The result of the application of a rule (or rules) is (the union of) the instantiated consequents(s) of the rule(s) corresponding to the maximal subset(s). The set of these instantiated consequents become the new FACTS.

Let us assume for simplicity that the forms have constants only.
Example A.3.1 Let RULES be R1: (P Q R S M) $\Rightarrow$ (P Q R S M U); R2: (P Q R S T) $\Rightarrow$ (P Q R S T G V) R3: (P Q R) $\Rightarrow$ (P Q R W)
If FACTS = (P Q) then antecedents of R1, R2, and R3 all cover FACTS. (P Q) is the only maximal set. R3 is minimal because it has the fewest unmatched items as compared to the other covers which are comparable to it, in terms of the partial order on RULES; this is so because (P Q R) is a subset of both (P Q R S M) and (P Q R S T G). Hence, we choose R3 and instantiate the consequent, so now FACTS = (P Q R W). Note that R was not matched, but since R3 has been selected, R has been instantiated also i.e., it has been inferred. W has been inferred also.

Example A.3.2 Let RULES be the same as before. If FACTS = (P Q M G) then there are two maximal sets, (P Q M) and (P Q G). R1 covers (P Q M) and R2 covers (P Q G). Hence, the result is the union of the instantiated consequents of R1 and R2, i.e., (P Q R S T G V M U). Again, R,S,T, have been instantiated, although not matched in the antecedent of R1 or R2. (P Q R S T G V M U) is the new FACTS. One rule was unable to cover FACTS; we needed more than one. See (Joshi (1978)) for further details about conflict resolution and dynamic clustering of FACTS and RULES.

AN APPROACH TO KNOWLEDGE-DIRECTED IMAGE ANALYSIS

D.H. Ballard, C.M. Brown, J.A. Feldman
Computer Science Department
The University of Rochester
Rochester, NY, 14627, U.S.A.

Abstract

A vision system is described which uses a semantic network model and a distributed control structure to accomplish the image analysis process.

The process of "understanding an image" leads to the instantiation of a subset of the model, and the identification of nodes in the instance of the model with image features. The instantiated nodes and the relations between them form another data structure called the sketchmap. The sketchmap explicates the relation of the model to the image; this model-image mapping is accomplished by mapping procedures which are part of the procedural knowledge in the model.

The procedures are accompanied by descriptions which contain at least pre- and post-conditions for the procedure and performance measures for it. Nodes which have attached procedures may also have an executive procedure attached. This executive is responsible for deciding which of several possibly effective procedures to run. Thus through the executive the system does a very general kind of procedure invocation based not only on what the executive knows about global state, but on a rich description of the procedure's capabilities.

The user's program is generally responsible for allocating effort at a level above that of the individual executive procedure. Thus no single domain-independent formulation or methodology is imposed on all vision tasks. One facility provided by the system is the use of geometric constraints between model objects to guide search for the objects in the image.

The system is an attempt to bring together many current ideas in artificial intelligence and vision programming and thereby to cast some light on fundamental problems of computer perception. The semantic network facilitates the interplay between geometric and other relational constraints which are used to direct and limit search. The use of attached procedures in the network gives a mix of declarative and procedural knowledge, and the executive provides an unusually powerful procedure invocation scheme. The multiplicity of procedures allows modelling objects under radically different conditions and levels of detail. This tends to make the system robust in that an object which could not be located initially may be found later when knowledge about the image has increased.

The system is illustrated throughout the chapter with illustrations from two particular applications: the finding of ships in a dock scene and the finding of ribs in a chest X-ray film.

1. Knowledge-Directed Image Analysis

Image analysis is the process of attaching meaning to an image. One way to do this is to use an explicit model of what the image can contain, and then construct a mapping between the model and the image. Since a particular image is only an instance of the class of images that the model was intended for, the model must be in some sense "larger" than the image. That is, a useful model of the domain of an image will typically contain a large amount of information on possible image content. However, the mapping generated by the analysis process (if we have a good model), will typically use only a small portion of this model.

An even smaller portion of the model is used in specialized analyses, for example, analysis performed to look for particular objects in the image. These processes typically require that only a small portion of the image be mapped onto a small relevant part of the model that explains that image. For example, in analyzing a radiograph for pneumoconiosis, we might use only a small portion of a radiograph model. We term a task which instantiates a subset of the model a query, to emphasize that only a portion of a large possible mapping is generated, and that we expect the working environment to be one consisting of a sequence of such tasks. Examples of a sequence of queries would be:

- returning to an aerial photo on different days to perform different tasks;
- different physicians requesting different differential diagnoses of a radiograph;
- generating different land use maps for agricultural and social scientists from ERTS data.

The preparation of this paper was supported by the Alfred P. Sloan Foundation under Grant No. 74-12-5 and by the Defense Advanced Research Projects Agency under Grant No. F30602-77-C-0050.

Given this approach to image analysis, we have defined a representation that allows for extensions of partial mappings which may be known a priori or acquired sequentially. Additionally, we have a way of defining quantitatively when the query has been satisfied so that we do not perform unnecessary mappings (e.g., the system may or may not need to know where all parts of an object are if it has "found" the object at some coarse level of detail). Thus the concept of a query is central to our approach to image analysis. Given a richly descriptive image model, our objective is to code a query to require mapping a minimum of model structure onto the image.

One of the problems in generating the mapping to satisfy a query is that the mapping is between very different structures. The natural elements of the model are objects which are represented symbolically, whereas the natural elements of the image are "picture elements," or pixels. To bridge this gap, we have structured our vision system in layers as shown in Figure 1. At the most abstract end of the structure is a semantic network representing our model. The model contains generic information encoded as idealized prototypes of structures from low level (such as edges) to high level (such as complex assemblages of objects in the world).

In the middle we have a sketchmap. This is a data structure that is synthesized during image analysis and provides associations between the model and the image, that is, the synthesized sketchmap is a network of nodes which turn out to be instantiations of a subset of model nodes. The need to differentiate between generic objects and instantiations of generic objects has been recognized in natural language understanding work, e.g. [Hayes, 1977]. We believe that it is also necessary for image analysis. Besides associations with the model, sketchmap nodes contain associations with image structures, such as edges and regions, specific to the particular image being analyzed.

At the other end of the vision system is a third structure termed the image data structure. This consists of the original image at different magnifications, spectra, resolutions, etc., together with various filtered versions of the image, texture images, edge images, etc. The parameters for generating all the image data structures are typically specialized to a particular model-image mapping context.

This multi-layered structure is reminiscent of the VISIONS System [Hanson and Riseman, 1977]. Both systems are designed to take advantage of variable resolution, both have a knowledge base or model of the world, a subset of which is mapped into the image. Perhaps the main difference is that in VISIONS, segmentation of the image into edges, regions, etc., is made to a level determined by the model so that the image will be understood to the fullest possible extent, given the knowledge in the model. In the system described here, the user's query is responsible for the level of detail the system pursues.

A successful analysis of an image contains

two parts: the generation of the proper links between sketchmap nodes and image data structures and the generation of the proper links between sketchmap nodes and model nodes. We describe a procedure that generates the image-sketchmap link as a mapping procedure. A mapping procedure is a low-level procedure which is attached to a particular node in the sense of [Bobrow, 1977] and whose function is to refine the description of that node. The need for these kinds of procedures in image analysis has also been recognized by [Sloman, 1977]. The construction of links between the relational world model and the sketchmap is one of the functions of the executive procedure. The executive procedure embodies the overall strategy for achieving the goal(s) and is programmed in a high-level language (currently SAIL).

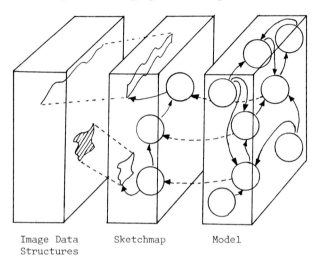

Image Data   Sketchmap   Model
Structures

Figure 1. Basic Layer Structure

Since the best procedures for finding structures in real-world images are special-purpose, we have avoided imposing a uniform problem-solving regime on the mapping procedures; instead they must be coded especially to take advantage of the user's specialized knowledge of the domain. However, some program autonomy is allowed in the choice of mapping procedures. Where different mapping procedures can generate the same links between sketchmap nodes and image data structures, the executive procedure can select the most appropriate based on a description attached to each mapping procedure. Also, the executive procedure can use general geometric relational constraints to pin down the location of objects.

2. The Structure of the Model

2.1 The Concept of Template Nodes

The model holds different kinds of knowledge about the image domain. It includes a relational network of nodes which are identifiable with (primitive and complex) objects and concepts in the domain from which the scene is taken. The answer to a query is a synthesized sketchmap or description; this is an instantiation of a subset

D. H. Ballard *et al.*

of the model. The model, therefore, contains knowledge in the form of all potential instantiable
descriptions. An example of this kind of knowledge
is the assertion:

"the sternum is above the heart."

This can be readily included in the model network.
It is potentially part of the model-image mapping
("the sternum" and "the heart" could be instantiated with pointers to regions of the picture). The
model also contains knowledge which is not in the
form of a synthesized description but which, for
instance, could be used in generating a description. An example of this kind of knowledge is:

"ships are about 6 times as long
as they are wide."

This knowledge can be included in the model network and may help a program that is searching for
a ship, but will not become part of the model-
image mapping. When it is meaningful to differentiate between these two kinds of knowledge, we will
refer to the parts of the network that represent
the former kind as template nodes. Synthesized
descriptions will be directly related to these
nodes and their arcs.

Each template node has a substructure which
represents the sense in which that node is to be
"understood." Prior to a query, the meaning of a
node is defined in terms of a substructure of
mapping procedures and constraint relations. After
a query has been satisfied, the template node is
represented by instantiated nodes with attached
specialized location descriptions, as shown in
Figure 2.1. Four basic types of links provide a
simple syntax to the network structure. A powerful advantage to this syntax is that the executive
procedure can direct the analysis in a more
general way, by using programs that function on
classes of links representing different kinds of
concepts, rather than on some set of specific
links. The need for this organization in natural
language understanding has been recognized by
Brachman [1976].

2.2 Constraints

Links to other model nodes encode (perhaps
parametrized) constraint relations between model
nodes. Links can encode:
- the probability that the relationship
  holds;
- a quantifier representing the expected
  value of the relationship.

For example, the relationship SHIP ADJACENT DOCK
might have a certain probability of being true, and
and an expected distance that the ship is from the
dock. We refer to the template nodes and geometric
relations between them as the constraint network.
This network may be interpreted from two viewpoints.
First, the existence of crucial constraint relations may be checked. This may be done through the
matching features of the associative structures in
SAIL. Secondly, if particular parameters arising
from a constraint are needed, the network may be
evaluated like a program to find subsets of the
model or the image that satisfy the constraints.
Its results take account of partial or unspecified
information, and it may be updated upon receipt of
better data with a minimal amount of work. It is
much like the graph of variable dependencies in AL
[Feldman et al., 1975]. In brief, each node has a
"Constraint Operation," such as Intersection,
Translation, Union, or indeed any function of up to
two arguments; it has two operand nodes; a father
node; a status that may be "Up-To-Date" or "Out-Of-
Date"; and a value that is some data structure such
as a number, a list of linear objects, a region,
etc. Additionally, it may have information on how
difficult the node is to evaluate, as a function
of the contents of its operand nodes. This last
feature allows some cost/benefit analysis of
evaluation of sections of constraint networks.

The constraint network for the prose:

"The centroids of docked ships are on
lines parallel to the intersection of
coastlines with dock areas at a distance
of one-half a ship width"

is shown in Figure 2.2.

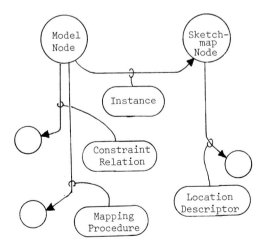

Figure 2.1 The Next Level of Detail in Model-
Sketchmap Nodes

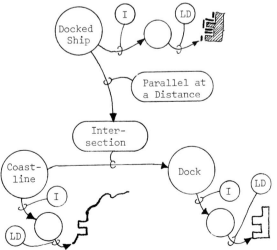

Figure 2.2 A Portion of a Constraint Network
(I = Instance, LD = Location Descriptor)

The network starts out with data (from the model or from previous scene analysis) as the values of the tip nodes, but no values at non-terminal nodes and all nonterminals marked Out-Of-Date. Data at a tip node can have one of three statuses: it can be known that the object does not exist in the scene (so the value of the node is the null set), it can be known to some degree of accuracy where objects are in the scene (so the value of the node is a subset of image or world points), or perhaps nothing is known (in which case the object could be anywhere, and the value is implicitly the universe of image or world points).

When the constraint network is evaluated to determine what is known about the location of its object, each node recursively evaluates its Out-Of-Date operand nodes, performs its operation, and stores the result in its value. It marks its status Up-To-Date. Intersection and Union work properly with the definitions of partial information of the last paragraph. When new (or better) information about an object at a tip of the network comes in, all nodes on a path from the tip to the root are marked Out-Of-Date. Then when the network is next evaluated, (only) the necessary partial results are re-computed. In keeping with our philosophy, the network is not self-activating, but is run on explicit user command.

2.3 Location Descriptors

A location descriptor provides information about where to find an entity. The part of the location descriptor which specifies a point set enclosing the region has been referred to as a tolerance region [Bolles, 1975]. A shape location descriptor might have the structure shown in Figure 2.3.

```
[ ShapeLocationDescriptor
    nodetype:     specialization prototype
    instance-of: a LocationDescriptor
    locates:      OneOf {(a ShapeObject),
                         (a ShapeFeature)}
    coordsystem: a CoordinateSystem
    centroid:     a PointSet
    //allows for "fuzziness"
    orientation: an AngleRange
    //...ditto
    tol. region: a PointSet ]

    ...similarly for Point, Linear, and
    AreaLocationDescriptors

[ CoordinateSystem
    nodetype:     abstract prototype
    units:        a LengthUnitSpecification
    scale:        a NumberRange
    //length units / system unit
    transforms:  SetOf {((a Coordinate  Transform)
                         (a Coordinate System)),
                         ...} ]
```

Figure 2.3 Example of a Shape Location Descriptor

This organization is suggestive of a frame-like structure [Minsky, 1975]. However, not all the entries need exist; just the syntax is necessary to allow the entries to be found. In practice only the properties relevant to a particular query will be generated. Such partial instantiations are easy in the SAIL associative structures [Feldman and Rovner, 1969].

Our examples of geometrical constraints, locations, etc., are two-dimensional. There is a large class of interesting images that are inherently two-dimensional (ERTS images, light or transmission electron microphotographs, CAT scanner images, bio-ultrasound images) as well as some that for some purposes may be treated as two-dimensional (aerial reconnaisance imagery, medical X-ray imagery, natural scenes, etc.). Of course it is often helpful to know about 3-D when processing natural scenes [Garvey, 1976], and it has been demonstrated that a 3-D model of the world is necessary to accomplish some tasks with aerial mapping photographs taken from 35,000 feet [Barrow, 1977]. Within the framework of the system described here, 3-D world coordinate systems would be linked through camera-transformation coordinate transforms to image coordinate systems. The location descriptors would be in terms of the relevant co-ordinate systems.

There are many advantages to having a standard representation for object locations:

a. If such descriptions are data types, their computations can be separated from the procedures that use them. If they can be passed as arguments, they provide a certain "common currency" between procedures, thus simplifying and modularizing the procedures that use them.

b. Location descriptors can represent approximate locations, which is useful for queries unconcerned with exact answers.

c. Constraints between locations can propagate knowledge throughout the model. Location descriptors can be computed from other location descriptors via relations, or by union and intersection of the described point sets. A system which applied linear programming techniques to the problem of locating regions through constraints placed on their boundaries was developed in [Taylor, 1976].

d. Use of location descriptors is geared to an abandonment of the exhaustive segmentation paradigm wherein every region must correspond to some object. Different location descriptors may refer to disjoint point sets or may overlap on the image.

3. Control

3.1 General Philosophy

Generally a query results in the synthesis of a sketchmap with instance nodes whose location descriptors are accurate enough for the purposes

D. H. Ballard *et al.*

of the query. A query might also result in further refinement of location descriptors of the extension of an existing sketchmap to account for more image structure. A query-directed vision system should thus be able to use relevant information (i.e., the state of the analysis) generated in successive queries. Most queries will take the form of user-written executive programs, since nontrivial tasks usually require fairly rigid recommendations about how the system should go about solving them. Initially the system will not attack the problem of automatically translating queries in some command language into executive programs.

Figure 3.1 shows the SAIL code used in a very simple executive procedure for selecting mapping procedures which identify instances of rib nodes in chest radiograph images. Each mapping procedure has pre-conditions, including an associated accuracy measure, which can depend on its neighbors, as well as a cost measure. The cheapest rib procedure which satisfies the pre-conditions is selected. Each rib node is searched for once and there is no facility for dealing with failures or mistakes. But the important point here is that the executive can have a relatively simple structure. This facilitates experimentation with various control strategies other than the depth-first strategy shown in the example.

3.2 Characterizations of Mapping Procedures

Mapping procedures have associated descriptions which are used by executive procedures. The descriptions contain the following:
- the slots in the data object which must be filled for the procedure to run;
- the slots the procedure can fill in;
- the cost and accuracy of the procedure in some meaningful units;
- the a priori reliability of the procedure.

Some rib mapping procedure descriptions are shown in Table 4.1, but these do not tax our representation scheme. More difficult examples of the kinds of facts we expect to be able to encode in this structure are (for a straight-line structure) that a Hough transform [Duda and Hart, 1972] cannot find the endpoints of a line but is more reliable than the cheaper Shirai tracker [Shirai, 1975], which itself needs to know the direction of a line before it can track it, and that a Heuckel operator [Heuckel, 1971] is more expensive, but can furnish many facts about the line with little known a priori, and can rate itself on reliability of its result.

There are several advantages to separating the executive procedure from the mapping procedures and their descriptions:

a. The executive procedure can be written more easily without considering the implementation details of mapping procedures in great depth.

b. Mapping procedures are similarly simplified without the burden of determining an appropriate context for their application [Sloman, 1977].

c. The executive procedure can automatically select alternative procedures in the event of mapping procedure failures.

d. Descriptions allow a choice between methods (if several are available) based on capability, resource requirements, and a priori reliability. (Also, recovery from failure of individual routines can be automated through planning [Feldman and Sproull, 1975].)

e. If the mapping procedures can produce reliable a priori estimates of their success the analytical results of [Bolles, 1975] and [Taylor, 1976] could be extended to select the procedure which produces sufficiently exact data objects.

```
Recursive Procedure MatchRib(itemvar Node);

begin
   itemvar x, v; integer Var;
   if INSTANCE of Node is ANY
   then

   begin
     Print("rib ", Node, " already matched");
     return;
   end

   else
   ! find and run procedure to do job at min cost;

   begin
     itemvar TempProc; integer MinCost, TempCost;
     MinCost := VeryLarge;
     foreach x such that
       RIB!PROCEDURE of Node is x do

       begin
         Var := GetConstraintsAndVariance(Node, x);
         if Var < Tolerance
         then

         begin
           TempCost := FindCost(Node, x);
           if TempCost < MinCost
           then

           begin
             TempProc := x;
             MinCost := TempCost;
           end;

         end;

       end;

     if MinCost = VeryLarge
     then
       Print("No proc. can do job for rib ", Node)
     else ApplyProc(TempProc, Node);
     foreach v such that NEIGHBOR of Node is v
                 and TYPE of v is RIB
                 do MatchRib(v);

   end;

end;
```

Figure 3.1 Executive Procedure for Ribs

4. Applications

4.1 Finding Docked Ships

Finding ships in a dock scene illustrates how high-level metrical knowledge about the image (such as provided by a topographic map) can make certain scene analysis problems easy.

The model contains, in a Constraint Graph form (see Section 2.2), the knowledge that docked ships are in the ocean adjacent to dock areas, parallel to the dock and with a centroid a distance away related to the width of the ship. In a Shape Object Descriptor, some facts about the sorts of ships we are trying to find are stored, viz., a template for matching them (in our case, a rectangle of 1's in an array for template-matching), their width, length, average brightness, etc. Template-matching is among the simplest vision primitives. Only in a context having a great deal of structure could it be expected to work in scenes as complex as Figure 4.1a.

Figure 4.1a is from a USGS mapping photograph. It roughly corresponds to the topographic map of Figure 4.1b. Included in the map are such linear features as coastlines and dock areas. From the digitized photo, a small (196 x 164) window is extracted and stored on disk. A half-toned version of this window is shown in Figure 4.1c. From the map, the coastline and a dock area are extracted and stored on disk; this information is shown in Figure 4.1d. Map information may be automatically registered with photographic images to high accuracies by techniques developed at SRI [Barrow et al., 1977]. For our study the registration was performed manually.

The system, under direction of the user-written query, begins by deciding where to look by satisfying a constraint network; the more information provided, the narrower the focus of attention. In the case illustrated in this section, the constraint network looks as it does in Section 2.2. Presupposition of "perfect" registration leads to sharp lines of search specifying loci of ship centers. Imperfect registration would give fuzzier loci.

The linear loci and the orientational constraint on the ships means a simple template-matching technique will suffice to do the ship-finding job efficiently. (In this exercise it was the only technique, but an executive procedure might well have chosen it as applicable.) The ship template is rotated to be parallel to the midline as given by the constraint graph, and template-matching is done along the line; note is taken of where the score for the match goes over threshold, and when it comes back down under threshold. The average of these two positions is taken as the location of a ship. The black squares in Figure 4.1d show the results.

Our USGS mapping photograph is digitized to 256 grey levels on a .007" grid. The image is stored on disk with comprehensive and expandable header information. The image may be windowed and sampled at integral size reductions into an integer array in core for processing.

The system has representations for linear objects and regions. Linear objects are SAIL records making linked lists of (x,y) points. They can have three types at present: a list of points to be connected in order; a list of segments, i.e., pairs of endpoints to be connected pairwise; and logically circular lists of points representing boundaries. A robust and general routine based on merging was written to compute the intersection of such linear features. Other useful geometric routines find the distance of a point from a segment (not a line), and compute a segment parallel to and some distance from another segment.

Regions (except for templates, which are arrays) are SAIL list items. A region is a list of y-lists; a y-list has a y-value followed by an even number of x-values. The first x-value is an "entering region" boundary point, the second is a "leaving region" boundary point, and so on alternately. The region:

```
001
101
011
```

would be represented as

$$((1\ 2\ 3)(2\ 1\ 1\ 3\ 3)(3\ 3\ 3)).$$

Routines were written, again based on merging, to create the union and intersection of such regions, and to convert (via an asymmetric DDA algorithm [Newman and Sproull, 1973]) linear objects to regions. We find multiple representations of objects simplifies the work of routines such as the constraint primitives.

Template-matching utilities can produce an array containing a rotated and scaled version of a template and can compute the correlation of a template (at some rotation and translation) with the image array.

4.2 Finding Ribs in Chest Radiographs

The problem of finding ribs in chest radiographs illustrates the use of multiple procedures attached to the same template node (cf. Section 3.1). It uses the less precise geometric constraints arising from anatomy rather than cartography.

The model contains nine right and left ribs (the maximum amount normally visible on a chest film). Presently only the lower edge of each rib is detected. Each rib is modelled as a template node with offset parameters from itself to each immediate neighbor (above, below, opposite). Additionally, three different mapping procedures are attached to each rib node as shown in Table 4.1.

276

LookForARib uses the Wechsler parabolic model [Wechsler and Sklansky, 1975] to find a rib segment. AffirmARib translates that segment using the offset parameters and attempts to verify the presence of a rib by a correlation technique. HallucinateARib instantiates a rib by translating a neighbor with no verification.

Table 4.1   RibFinding Mapping Procedures

Procedure	Preconditions	Cost	Var.	Postconditions
LookForARib	none	20	0	instance of rib
AffirmARib	instance of neighbor in sketchmap	4	1	instance of rib
HallucinateARib	instance of neighbor in sketchmap	1	5	instance of rib

Figure 4.2 shows a trace of the display during the rib-finding process. For this trace a slightly more complex executive than the one shown in Figure 3.1 was used. If a mapping procedure failed, another was chosen from the remaining applicable set. In Figure 4.2a large rectangles enclosing the lung fields have been found (by a lung query executive) and the smaller rectangles are plans for LookForARib, which is the only mapping procedure that can be applied. The horizontally-oriented rectangle defines an area to look for rib edges for the model node RIGHTRIB4 and the vertically-oriented rectangle defines an area for foci of a parabola representing the rib border. Figure 4.2b shows the resultant rib found. Figure 4.2c shows the plan derived from the constraints for the opposite rib, LEFTRIB4. Note that the plan now has the shape of RIGHTRIB4. Figure 4.2d shows the instantiation of LEFTRIB4 found by AffirmARib. Figure 4.2e shows the next two ribs found and Figure 4.2f shows the entire set of ribs. The ribs marked with the box (□) are found by HallucinateARib, due to the failure of AffirmARib. AffirmARib fails when the edge data is extremely poor.

To appreciate that the ribs found by the rib executive actually match the edge data, compare Figure 4.3a with 4.3b, which shows the results from another chest radiograph. Figure 4.3a shows the principal edges in the image and the latter has the ribs overlaid on top of those edges.

5.   Summary

The semantic network is a kind of lumped parameter model in the spirit of [Fischler and Eschlager, 1973]. The geometric constraints in the network relate template nodes whose descriptions (the "lumped parameters") are generated by attached mapping procedures. The key difference is that information found during the analysis can change the way template nodes are located.

In analyzing an image it is crucial that the generating of abstract descriptions of parts of the image (i.e., segmentation) be intimately connected with the interpretation of those parts. In our system the former operation corresponds to generating sketchmap-image links whereas the latter corresponds to generating model-sketchmap links. Interpretation and segmentation are united through multiple mapping procedures and the executive, which can efficiently change the way a part of the image is analyzed as new information about the rest of the image develops.

Finally, we want the image analysis process to do as little work as possible to satisfy a given task or query. This is attempted through the specialization of all parameters to the given task, the inclusion of performance and accuracy measures in the mapping procedure descriptions, and the use of the constraint network. All of this is just the beginning of a long-term effort to study what can be done in a general way for goal-directed image understanding tasks.

References

Barrow, H.G. Interactive Aids for Cartography and Photo Interpretation SRI, Semi-Annual Technical Report, November 1976 - May 1977.

Barrow, H.G., Tenenbaum, J.M., Bolles, R.C., and Wolf, H.C. Parametric Correspondence and Chamfer Matching; Two New Techniques for Image Matching, DARPA Conference, Minneapolis, MN, April 1977.

Bobrow, D.G. and Winograd, T. Experience with KRL-0: One Cycle of a Knowledge Representation Language, Proc. IJCAI5, M.I.T., August 1977.

Bolles, R. Verification Vision Within a Programmable Assembly System, Stanford AI Memo, AIM-275, December 1975.

Brachman, R.J. What's in a Concept: Structural Foundations for Semantic Networks, BBN REP #3343, October 1976.

Duda, R.O. and Hart, P.E. The Use of the Hough Transformation to Detect Lines and Curves in Pictures, Comm. ACM, Vol. 15, January 1972.

Feldman, J.A., Finkel, R., Taylor, R., Bolles, R., and Paul, R. An Overview of AL, A Programming System for Automation, Proc. IJCAI4, Tbilisi, U.S.S.R., 1975.

Feldman, J.A. and Rovner, P.D. An Algol-Based Associative Language, Comm. ACM, Vol. 12, No. 8, August 1969, pp. 439-449.

Feldman, J.A. and Sproull, R.F. Decision Theory and Artificial Intelligence II: The Hungry Monkey, TR2, U. of Rochester, Computer Science Dept., Rochester, NY, November 1975.

Fischler, M.A. and Eschlager, R.A. The Representation and Matching of Pictoral Patterns, IEEE Trans. on Computers, C-22, January 1973.

Garvey, T.D. Perceptual Strategies for Purposive Vision, SRI AI Center, Tech. Note 117, September 1976.

Hanson, A.R. and Riseman, E.M. A Progress Report on VISIONS: Representation and Control in the Construction of Visual Models, COINS Tech. Report 76-9, July 1976.

Hayes, P.J. On Semantic Nets, Frames and Associations, TR19, U. of Rochester, Computer Science Dept., Rochester, NY, August 1977; also Proc. IJCAI5, M.I.T., August 1977.

Heuckel, M.H. An Operator which Locates Edges in Digitized Pictures, J. ACM, Vol. 18, No. 1, January 1971.

Minsky, M. A Framework for Representing Knowledge in Winston (Ed.), The Psychology of Computer Vision, New York, McGraw-Hill, 1975.

Newman, W.M. and Sproull, R.F. Principles of Interactive Computer Graphics, McGraw-Hill, 1973.

Shirai, Y. Analyzing Intensity Arrays using Knowledge about Scenes, in Winston (Ed.), The Psychology of Computer Vision, McGraw-Hill, 1975.

Sloman, A., et al. Popeye's Progress Through a Picture, Cognitive Studies Programme, School of Social Sciences, U. of Sussex, March 1977.

Taylor, R.H. Generating AI Programs from High-Level Task Descriptions, Ph.D. thesis, Stanford AI Lab, 1976.

Wechsler, H. and Sklansky, J. Automatic Detection of Rib Contours in Chest Radiographs, Proc. IJCAI4, Tbilisi, U.S.S.R., 1975.

Figure 4.1a Aerial Mapping Photograph

Figure 4.1b Topographic Map of Area in 4.1a.

Figure 4.1c Halftoned Representation of Window
from Digitized Version of 4.1a.

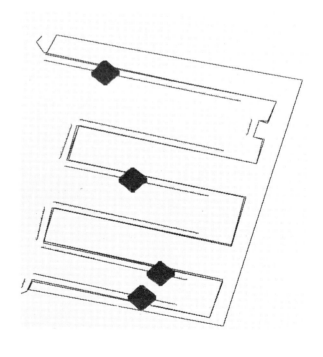

Figure 4.1d Coastline, Dock Area, Loci of Possible
Ship Centers, Points of Application of
Ship Template and Location of Ships.

Knowledge-Directed Image Analysis

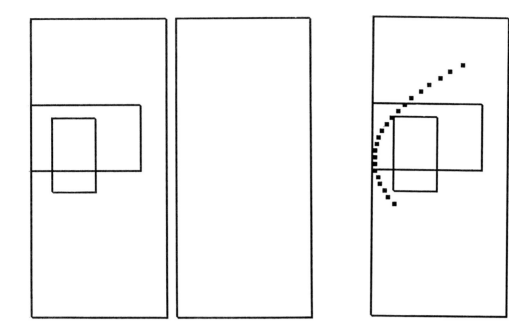

Figure 4.2a Lung Boundaries and Plan for
RIGHTRIB4

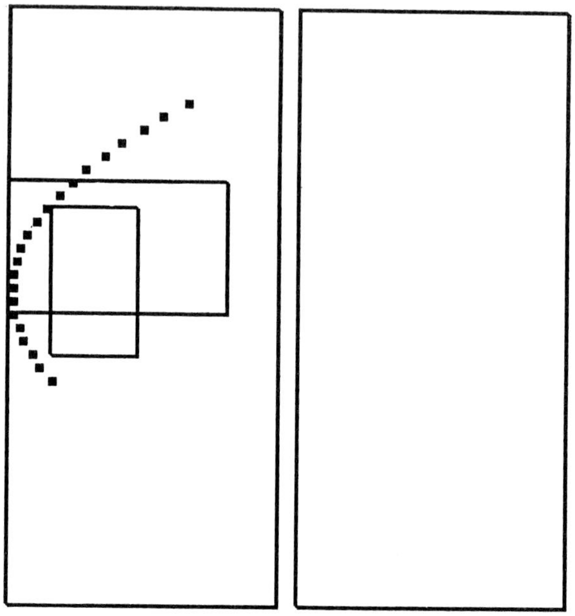

Figure 4.2b RIGHTRIB4 Found

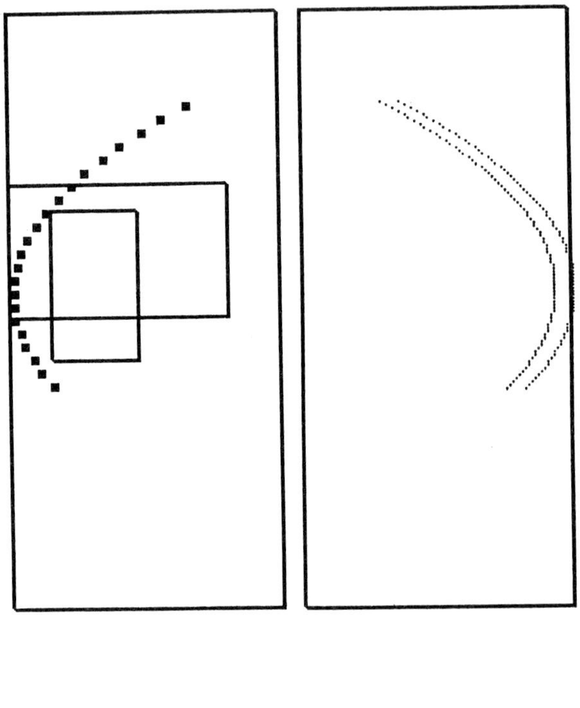

Figure 4.2c Plan for LEFTRIB4

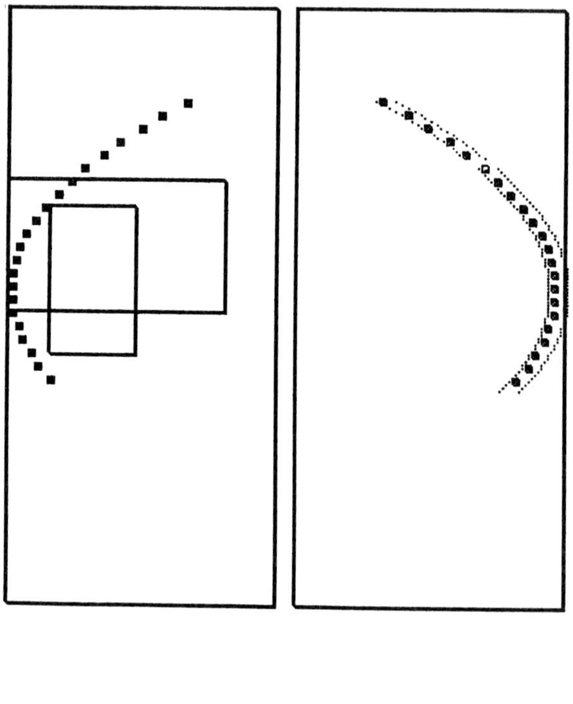

Figure 4.2d LEFTRIB4 Found

D. H. Ballard *et al.*

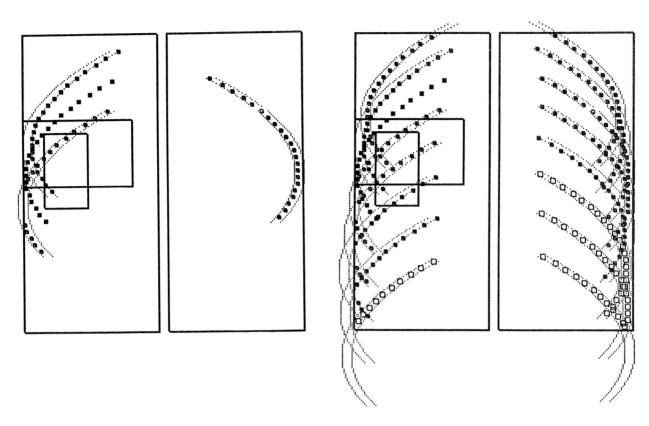

Figure 4.2e RIGHTRIB3 and RIGHTRIB5 Found   Figure 4.2f Final Result

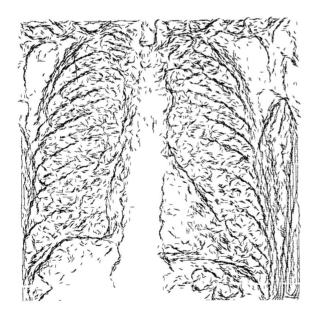

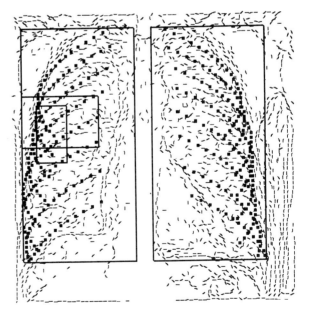

Figure 4.3a Edges Detected by the Heuckel   Figure 4.3b The Overlay of Rib Borders
             Operator

Knowledge-Directed Image Analysis

READING THE WRITING
ON THE WALL

J. M. Brady
and
B. J. Wielinga

University of Essex, U. K.

Abstract

The image processing aspects of a program to read Fortran coding sheets are described. Character descriptions based on strokes, junctions and relations are outlined and the use of histogram techniques and a (primal) stroke sketch are discussed. Problems encountered with an early Conniver-like program are related and the general uncertainty problem for vision is formulated. It is argued that vision programs must face up to the consequences of explicitly representing a large number of intermediate levels of description, corresponding to partially-formed percepts. A region occupancy description of characters is sketched, and its relation to space occupancy and generalised cylinder models discussed.

1. *Introduction*

1.1 *Overview of the Fortran coding sheets project*

This paper is founded in our experience with the image processing aspects of a project to develop a program capable of reading hand-printed Fortran coding sheets like that in figure 1 [8]. As such it is an updated, greatly expanded version of [11]. However, sensing the spirit of the Workshop to be an appraisal of the current state of computer vision, we shall look critically at our current program, and attemt to relate our ideas and experiences to our previously stated position on computer vision [10] and to the work of several other participants. In particular, we shall describe the problems we encountered with a stroke-based representation of characters and show how they are largely avoided by a representation based on region occupancy. This is essentially a two dimensional analogue of Binford's (1971) generalised cylinder representation, although as we shall discuss further in section 7, there are a number of differences.

The overall emphasis of the Fortran coding sheets project is on the kinds of knowledge and its representation, and the organisation of processes which effectively use that knowledge, which appear to be necessary to facilitate the interpretation as a Fortran program of the massive amount of data culled from a coding sheet. By "massive" we mean 1400 by 1000 pixels, each pixel representing one of the 256 grey levels [9].

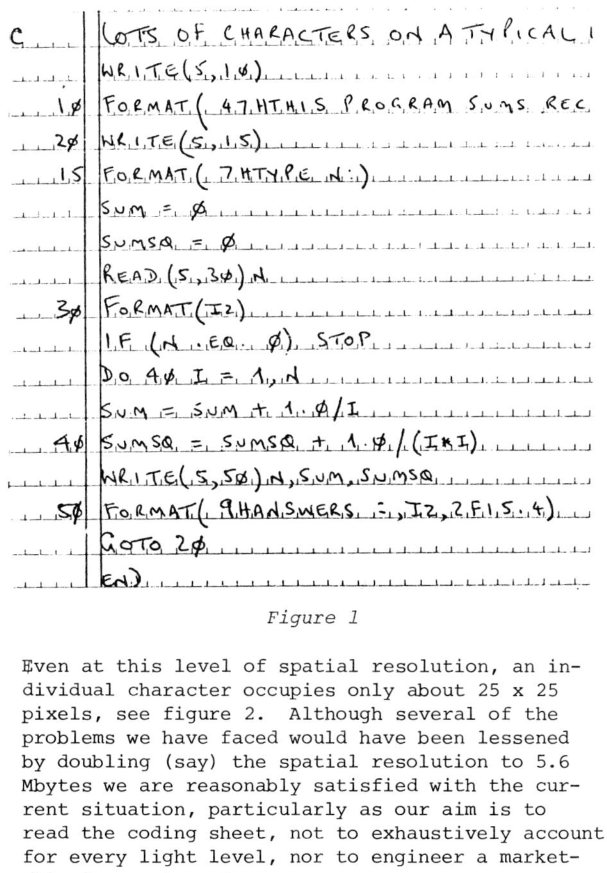

Figure 1

Even at this level of spatial resolution, an individual character occupies only about 25 x 25 pixels, see figure 2. Although several of the problems we have faced would have been lessened by doubling (say) the spatial resolution to 5.6 Mbytes we are reasonably satisfied with the current situation, particularly as our aim is to read the coding sheet, not to exhaustively account for every light level, nor to engineer a marketable document reader.

Intensity data clipped to 26 levels for display.

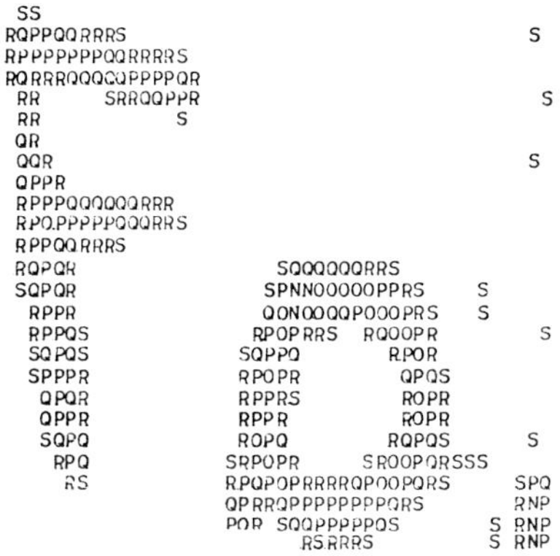

Figure 2

There is a great deal of knowledge which can be deployed in the microworld of Fortran coding sheets and it seems to fall naturally into two sections. Knowledge about the coding sheet grid, about individual characters, and about segmentation, is clearly useful for addressing the intensity array. On the other hand, knowledge about Fortran programming seems *a priori* to be essentially non-visual, and would probably be generally reckoned to be the "high level" knowledge component of the project. Given this division of knowledge we divided our process into two groups, which interact in a coroutining fashion.

A prototype program Mark 1 [7] was constructed by Richard Bornat to deploy knowledge of Fortran programming on "blob" data which can be delivered by our segmentation routines. Blobs are classified as either "alphanumeric-or-bracket" sequences or "operator-or-punctuation". Mark 1 operates rather like a top-down parser, and attempts to assign roles to the blobs on each line, merely by working through the possible statement types in a pre-determined sequence. Its main virtue is that it vividly illustrates the enormous reduncancy present in the intensity array. It is surely surprising that such a simple algorithm, using such simple knowledge and data, cah achieve the performance it does. It often guesses the identity of a statement correctly, and always includes the correct guess among the few proferred.

Of course, Mark 1 makes a number of unwarranted assumptions about the data (such as that spaces do not appear in keywords), and its behavior is unsatisfactory in several ways; consequently we are currently designing Mark 2. In particular, it is now clear that knowledge about Fortran is *not* entirely non-visual, and this calls into question the overall division and coroutining organisation outlined above. Firstly, each Fortran line has an expected visual appearance, and this can be used to reduce the search space on the much richer though uncertain information which can in fact bedelivered by the character experts and seg-menter. Conversely, certain (visual) patterns of blobs are compelling evidence for certain statement types, and they seem to correspond to entire syntactic units. Fortran is distinguished from Algol 60 (and natural language) by the shallowness of its parse trees. Thus if a pattern of blobs is interpreted as a particular syntactic unit, it strongly constrains the possible interpretation of a whole line.

Although Mark 1's performance is surprisingly good, it is still necessary to do a great deal of low level image processing, including the analysis of characters. The remainder of the paper describes our experience in constructing the low level and character reading processes, which were designed to interact with a Fortran reasoner.

1.2 *Reading as a perceptual process*

Unlike most previous work in optical character recognition, and in pattern recognition, we do not consider the task of our program to be solely to classify an input. We view character

reading as a process not essentially different from other picture perception tasks. Indeed, the positions on computer vision adopted in [10] apply in microcosm to the character reading and low level processing parts of the project. Perception is not a naming process; rather it is a process of constructing the most plausible interpretation of an image not only on the basis of cues which can be extracted from the image but also on the basis of prior expectations of what it is that the image depicts. The effect of working within the context of Fortran is in the extra knowledge which can be brought to bear in trying to see a pattern as a character. Waltz's [47] work suggested that extra knowledge, if used appropriately, can make interpretation more straightforward since there are more consistencies to exploit.

It may be objected that although the coding sheets project raises interesting A.I. issues about co-operating knowledge sources, the image processing problems which arise are fundamentally different and simpler from those occasioned by "real" vision, presumably natural scenes. To be sure, our images are essentially two dimensional, and thus avoid the fundamental ambiguity of depth. Furthermore, we avoid problems of texture, colour, lightness, specularities, transparency and a number of other difficult issues. It may also be objected that images of text are distinguished in computer vision by the fact that people obviously and consciously have to learn to interpret them, usually around the age of five. Although these objections may well be straw men, it seems reasonable to counter them by concluding this introduction with a list of some of the general vision issues which have confronted us in our work. Other issues, such as the amount of computation involved in vision, and the use of thresholds and histograms, are discussed in the body of the paper.

First, however, a general caveat must be issued regarding the fact that our project aims for detailed and interesting behaviours in a surprisingly rich but nontheless small microworld. What we sacrifice in general applicability of our methods, and the vision issues we inevitably avoid, are more than counterbalanced by the considerable attention we have to pay to the representation of character models, segmentation of units, organisation of processes and so on. Our system has to interface to Fortran experts, and has to interpret the characters in figure 3 "correctly". The enormous detail of our character models may be

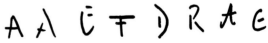

Figure 3

contrasted with those used in the majority of vision programs. To caricature the point: many a vision program (indeed A.I. program generally) is made to generate impressive sounding descriptions of a scene such as "dog trotting beside his faithful master". When one examines the program closely however, it turns out that "dog" is equivalent to "brown rectangle, 8 pixels by 5". Ultimately, the question concerns the number of intermediate levels of representation which a program uses. A microworld program can afford to represent more intermediate levels because of its relatively narrow semantic base. A program with a broader semantic base typically represents considerably fewer intermediate levels.

The objection that we have to learn to read is easy to counter. It is also obviously true of ERTS, spectogram, encephalogram, and bubble chamber images. But the issue is clearly only one of extent. Babies may well have a number of innate visual capabilities, such as the ability to see faces, but most of our visual ability develops, albeit unconsciously, as we progress in the world.

To counter the objection that our problems are simpler than those which occur in "real" vision, we outline some of the difficulties we have faced, under the headings of control, cue extraction and their elaboration to address stored models, and the representations of models.

Control

One of the main reasons for working in a microworld is the fact that it is possible to generate detailed hypotheses or predictions about the intensity array, which can then be checked out. A number of authors, notably Shirai [43] , have described how knowledge can be used effectively to address the intensity array, to guide or to choose thresholds. On the other hand, it is also necessary to account for all the evidence which is present (as Shirai [43] was very much aware), and this inevitable commits one to a certain amount of knowledge-free computation. This in turn raises the problem of the extent to which knowledge actively intervenes in perception, and at what stage. It also raised the spectre of Marr's primal sketch [27]. As we shall discuss in section 2 below, we employ a kind of primal stroke sketch, although the implications of our use of the word "primal" may be different from Marr's.

A related issue concerns the combination of different kinds of evidence. This is relatively straightforward so long as everything is in agreement. Conflicting evidence is much more difficult to deal with since the piece of evidence which is being assimilated when the conflict is first noted may not be the one which one eventually rejects and tries to explain away. We shall argue in section 3 that this has a number of far-reaching consequences for representation.

Extraction of cues and their elaboration

We describe how we extract strokes (section 2.2), and curves (section 5), and we relate our experiences of using a histogram to cut down search for cues by providing global information about the ones likely to be present. The models we use are structured by relation such a "left", "above" and by various sorts of junction. We describe (section 4) the difficulties we faced in computing relations and junctions, and the way in which we were led to a better representation which is at once more robust and yet obviates the need for a lot of computation used previously. The discussion of relations and junctions in section 4 enables us to draw attention to what we feel is a vital problem for vision (indeed A.I.) research,

namely the way in which seemingly solid precepts are grounded in uncertainty.

Representation of models

At the outset of the project we adopted a (Conniver-like) procedural approach to representing characters since we intended to model the co-operation of distinct knowledge sources by process interaction. As we shall describe in section 3, a number of problems led us to abandon the approach and to implement a version of frames [30].

2. *Components of character descriptions*

2.1 *Preliminary remarks*

Any character system embodies, albeit usually in a highly inflexible form, at least one description of each character model in the alphabet. The elements from which those descriptions are constructed must be computationally discoverable. Practical pattern recognition systems generally make such stringent demands on performance, such as 99% recognition rate, 0.1% error rate, at 1000 characters per second, that the description elements also have to be discovered extremely cheaply. Inevitably this leads in practice to restrictions on the input, special inking, high contrast paper and local feature extraction [3]. This tends to be based on topological features such as the number of line endings, junctions, cusps, crossovers, and concavities in the image. Thus, if the features extracted are the number of line endings, T-junctions and L-junctions, F and A would be described as subspaces of 3-space centred on <3, 1, 1 and 2, 2, 1> respectively.

Unfortunately, on the basis of that description, figure 4 would be classified as F, to which it is topologically equivalent. In the late sixties, a number of authors [31], [13] inspired by phrase

Figure 4

structure grammars for natural language, argued that such problems would be solved by working with explicit structural descriptions, which computed properties of the parts and described the ways in which the parts were related and/or connected. Given such a richer description, figure 4 matches A much better than F. However, the relatively rich description is correspondingly more expensive to compute and therefore leads to poorer performance, at least according to the yardstick of performance outlined above.

Even if one forgets cheap processing in an attempt to understand observed human competence, there is still a problem. Simple graph traversal algorithms, walking over the structural descriptions in predetermined manners, confront the considerable problem of contradictory or missing evidence, such as strokes having the wrong slope (fig. 5a), being in the wrong position (5b), or junctions having the

wrong type (5c), or not being present at all (5d).
Figure 5e disobeys just about every assertion one
would expect *a priori* to make about F, and yet it
is clearly an F (in the context of 5a - 5d).

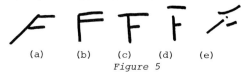

(a)   (b)   (c)   (d)   (e)

Figure 5

We started out with the idea that it was indeed necessary to use structural descriptions, but,
in line with the dictates of the bandwaggon of
heterarchy, felt that it was also necessary to add
the missing ingredient of computational flexibility to bring the idea to fruition.
Following [15] and [37], we decided that characters
should be described in terms of strokes and curves
of the restricted number of types displayed in
figure 6. Our descriptions also involved
relations such as 'right' and 'above', assertions
about the positions of strokes, such as 'top' and
'left' and junctions such as L-junction, V-junction

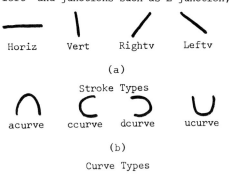

Horiz   Vert   Rightv   Leftv

(a)

Stroke Types

acurve   ccurve   dcurve   ucurve

(b)

Curve Types

Figure 6

and T-junction. Thus the model for F might be
expected to be something like:

```
STROKES       3 [HT HB V]   // Horizontal Top and
                            // Vertical
DIRECTIONS    horizontal [HT HB]
              vertical [V]

RELATIONS     [ (ABOVE HT HB)
                (ABOVE HT V)
                (RIGHT HT V)
                (RIGHT HB V)]

POSITIONS     [ (H-TOP HT)
                (H-MIDDLE HB)
                (V-LEFT V)]

JUNCTIONS     [ (L-JN V HT)
                (T-JN V HB)]
```

Postponing for a while the considerable
problem of how to integrate computational
flexibility into such a description, we now
describe how we compute strokes.

2.2 *Strokes*
The extraction of strokes is essentially the
problem of edge finding, and we approached it in
the conventional way of applying a gradient operator and noting responses above a present threshold.
The relatively low spatial resolution (25 x 25 pixels) of characters has two consequences for the

choice of operator. Firstly, strokes are only
about two pixels wide in intensity space, while
perceptually separate strokes, and the inside
radii of curves, are only around six. Even a 3 x 3
operator such as Pingle's [38] smeared characters
hopelessly, so we resorted to a 2 x 2 operator
similar to Roberts [40]. This has proved satisfactory in practice, although Brooks [12] has
pointed to the error in the estimates of gradient
direction of several famous operators, including
ours. Given the restricted set of roles to which
we intended to assign strokes (figure 6a), we
worked with quantised gradient directions at those
points where the gradient size exceeded a thresh-
hold. We quantised the gradient direction to six-
teen equally spaced values which we label A to P to
allow for a margin of error in the eight ideally
expected values (four each in both black-to-white
and white-to-black intensity step). Examples of
gradient space data are shown in figure 7.

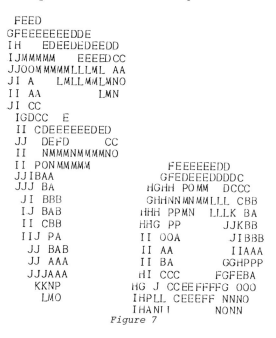

Figure 7

Letter F

Letter O

Figure 8

J. M. Brady and B. J. Wielinga

The example F in figure 7 suggests extracting straight strokes as regions of sets of quantised directions, such as [H I J] or [P A B]. This idea was developed independently of[44] to which it is rather similar. Originally, we had the idea of choosing the stroke sets by analysing a histogram of occurrences of quantised directions such as figure 8. This works fine for characters composed of straight strokes, such as F, although the usual problems arise of deciding upon a suitable threshold which corresponds to the existence of significant strokes.

When we compromised our intellectual integrity yet again with another *ad hoc* empirically-determined threshold, the technique collapsed in the face of curves and characters, such as X, composed entirely of short strokes. Intuitively, a (circular) curve gives rise to a slowly and evenly changing gradient direction, and thus to an even "plateau" in the histogram spreading over "several" directions. A character such as X gives rise to a jagged profile with no one direction value being particularly large. In reality, curves aren't circular, and the plateau/ jagged distinction is impossible to make. A major problem with the histogram analysis can be illustrated with reference to a D. There will almost certainly be a strong peak corresponding to the vertical stroke; but extracting all vertical strokes also destroys the curve. Moreover, quickly-written junctions between straight strokes tend to be curved, and so "misleading" evidence for curves is generated in the histogram. Finally a character such as A in figure 9(a) tends to suggest two parsings of the

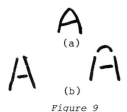

Figure 9

histogram, corresponding to the alternatives in figure 9(b).

These problems seem typical of the use of histograms. The advantage of a histogram is that it gives some relatively cheap global indication of what is present, and thus raises one's hopes of a narrowed search space. The fact that histogram analysis is cheap derives directly from forgetting the spatial distribution of the points whose properties are recorded in the histogram. In particular, many very different spatial distributions can give rise to the same histogram, and this can lead to totally unwarranted or misleading inferences being drawn. However, it may quite properly be objected that a histogram-based analysis is not designed to operate on *all* images, but only a restricted class. Thus the histogram technique works fine on characters wholly composed of horizontal and vertical straight strokes, as Ohlander's [36] program works fine on scenes with large areas which are uniform with respect to one of his nine measures.

To a first approximation, the retinal impression of a natural scene is a patchwork quilt, and much of psychophysics has been concerned with developing precise measurements for intuitive concepts such as hue and brightness, which express ways in which the regions in the patchwork are apparently, or ideally, uniform. A peak in a histogram of such measures implies a great many instances of pixels with the same property value, and although the spatial distribution is omitted from the histogram, it is a reasonable heuristic to suppose that the pixels corresponding to peaks do in fact correspond to uniform regions. In like manner, a character usually contains few strokes, and so a peak in a particular gradient direction may reasonably be expected to correspond to significant strokes (i.e., substantial regions of gradient direction values). This is what is meant by the remark in [10] that a histogram analysis embodies knowledge, albeit in a highly inflexible and brittle form.

Like all heuristics, the two referred to above aren't always justified, and in such cases the histogram analysis goes badly wrong. In our case, curves of lots of short strokes caused problems, while Ohlander's analysis is exposed by regular textures such as a leopard or by images where pictorial similarity does not correspond closely to object region segmentation [46].

2.3 *The primal stroke sketch*

About this time, we were influenced by Marr's [27] argument for a primal edge sketch which results from extracting knowledge-free all the edges in each of a small number of directions. Mindful of figure 6(a), and allowing for variation, we extracted all the strokes defined by the stroke sets [H I J], [P A B] (vertical), [D E F], [L M N] (horizontal), [B C D] [J K L] (leftv) and [F A H], [N O P] (rightv). The "primal sketch" versions of the F and O in figure 7 are shown in figure 10. It is clear that the problems referred to above, which inevitably arise with histogram analyses, have been completely finessed, and that all the significant straight strokes actually present have been extracted. Moreover, figure 10 suggests extracting curves as sequences of appropriately overlapping short strokes. We shall show in section 5 that although the idea leads to a lot of computation, it generally works well.

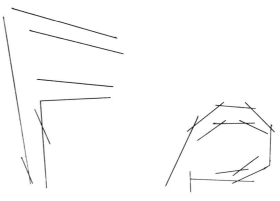

Figure 10

When we consider the strokes which were extracted as regions derived from the standard three element sets of gradient directions, we find that the direction descriptions P A B or "vertical" are not fine enough to support the operations of merging, joining and collinearity (qv). The sets each give rise to strokes with a wide variety of perceptual slopes, and so, reluctantly, we "hallucinate" a best fit line onto a stroke by computing a least squares estimate of its angle θ. This leads naturally to the representation of the line formed by a stroke as a (ρ, θ) pair [14], [35]. We also compute the end points of the line. Figure 11 gives the lines corresponding to the strokes extracted from the F in figure 10. (Figure 11 is at the end of paper)

Once we have this representation of strokes it is possible to combine collinear strokes or to merge what appear to be the black-to-white (BW) and white-to-black (WB) intensity steps of the same stroke in intensity space. The raster scan of the gradient operator constrains the strokes which can be merged in this way. The outstanding experience we have from this part of the project is the sheer amount of computation which is necessitated. Consider joining two strokes to form a larger one. They need to be "close", "reasonably parallel" and to "overlap sufficiently" (figure 12 (a)).

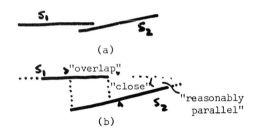

(a)

(b)

Figure 12

Given our essentially Cartesian representation of stroke-lines, it is easy to formulate precise notions of "parallel", "close", and "overlap" (figure 12(b)), although they inevitably involve setting even more thresholds and carrying out an enormous amount of expensive trigonometic hacking. Although we agree with Marr's argument [28] that the computational cost of vision is inevitably enormous, even unacceptably so on current machines, we nevertheless have the feeling that the Cartesian representation of space is fundamentally inadequate for our purposes (see also section 7).

At this point, we detour slightly to justify our use of the phrase "primal sketch", which was introduced by Marr in his essays on the early processing of visual information. Marr [26], [27] introduces the primal sketch as a data base of

atomic assertions which result from parsing the responses of a number of operators, applied across the intensity array in a small number of pre-determined directions. The assertions are claimed to be closely related to those delivered by the retinal "hardware", and, as such, cannot be challenged, in the sense that a program cannot directly investigate the intensity data which originally gave rise to them. The crucial claims seem to be that they are produced knowledge-free, and are the lowest level raw data which a vision program should use. Presumably, the argument is only intended to apply to a single sensing of a scene. Visual accomodation[38], as well as control over pan, tilt and focusing could, for example, correspond to lowering thresholds on the response of the bar and edge masks or on the parsing process the *next* time the scene is sensed. Once thresholds have been set, however, processing proceeds as before.

If a primal sketch is *produced* knowledge-free, it is far from obvious that it is likewise *consumed*. It is hard to make sense of demonstrations such as those of Johanneson [23], Heider-Simmel [20], Bartlett [4] and Harmon's [19] "Mona Lisa" without emphasising the active role of the perceiver, who, at the least suggestion, constantly tries to impose important, often animistic, knowledge schemes to direct the construction of precepts out of the mass of data which constitutes the primal sketch.

This is not to deny the importance of data-driven, (relatively) knowledge-free, grouping processes which can extract contours or uniform textures. Rather it suggests that the interactions between model driven and data driven processes, and indeed between different data driven or different model driven processes, are as yet poorly understood.

A large number of vision programs are (almost) wholly based on data-driven processing. Such programs essentially work as recognisers, and while they might well perform satisfactorily on a restricted class of images, they cannot account for the way in which expectations or prejudices influence perception. On the other hand, as we discuss more fully in the next section, wholly model-driven programs usually fail to account for all the evidence which can be extracted relatively cheaply from a scene, and cannot account for the fact that we are eminently capable of making sense of a totally unexpected image.

In order to account for all the cheaply available evidence, one must first extract it. Since cheaply available can be considered synonymous to knowledge-free, this implies that any vision program (indeed any A.I. program according to [48] must decide on an atomic level of information, which is provided knowledge free, and on which all later processing is based. It is in this sense, rather than on the grounds of neurophysiological or psychological reasonableness, that we call our stroke data a "primal sketch".

3. *Stroke relations, stroke junctions and the uncertainty issue*

In the previous section we noted that character instances frequently do not match models precisely. We now discuss some of the problems involved in computing a typical stroke relation, namely above (s_1, s_2), and a typical junction between strokes s_1 and s_2, together with its use in seeing a character as F. We use the discussion to highlight what seems to us to be a crucial problem in computer vision, although as we shall show in section 6 the specific problems we refer to here can be somewhat alleviated by a better representation.

The simplest computational definition of above (s_1, s_2) is that stroke s_1 should be wholly above s_2. This is satisfied by the instances of T is figure 13(a),(b); but not that in figure 13(c). An obvious refinement is to insist merely that the centre of s_1 should be above s_2. This is

(a)   (b)   (c)   (d)   (e)

Figure 13

satisfied by figure 13(c), but not by figure 13(d). An alternative refinement is to insist that the point of intersection of s_1 and s_2 should be above s_2. This is in fact rather more useful, as it implicitly relies on the usual process for constructing a T. However, figure 13(e) shows that it is not foolproof. In fact, the uncertainty which surrounds segmentation may even lead to part of the coding sheet line above being taken as a horizontal stroke, in which case the separation between s_1 and the top of s_2 will be "too large". In this way, a computational definition of a predicate such as "above" develops in response to counter examples, eventually reaching some fairly *ad hoc* rendering, whose application is always fraught with uncertainty.

The computation of junctions is even less certain, and for a good reason. The gradient operator, even though it is only 2x2, produces edge effects at a sharp junction like figure 14(a), yielding a response something like figure 14(b). When straight strokes are extracted, figure 14(c) results. It follows that *most* straight strokes do

(a)   (b)   (c)

Figure 14

not in fact directly intersect in the gradient data. There are two obvious ways to establish a junction's presence, both of which we have tried. The first is to predict the set of intermediate gradient directions [D E F] and attempt to connect the two straight strokes with pixels whose gradient directions are in the set. An alternative approach is to compute the intersection point of the lines hallucinated onto the strokes and check how close

the intersection point is to each line. The latter formulation has to be used in cases where the junction is not even present in the intensity data.

If the computation of a junction is uncertain, its realisation in a character model is doubly so. The structural descriptions outlined above call for a "roughly" horizontal stroke s_1, a "roughly" vertical stroke s_2, and a junction between s_1 and s_2 which "roughly" encloses a right angle. Unfortunately examples like those shown in figure 15 are all too common, and very complex programs are needed if all eventualities are to be catered for (see section 4.3).

(a)   (b)
                    wrong type

Figure 15

Every A.I. vision project we've ever heard of encounters model instances which depart from the model. Thus, every project faces the question of the *extent* to which variations are allowed, and the issue is nearly always settled by thresholds which are determined experimentally on a few cases. It is at precisely these points that so much of the brittleness of A.I. programs is concentrated.

We discuss an alternative representation of junctions in section 6, which alleviates (but does not entirely remove) some of the problems referred to above. The point we wish to make here is this: how are we (introspectively) so certain of what we perceive when there is so much uncertainty surrounding every factor contributing to that percept. Practical systems usually entirely avoid this problem by forcing unique interpretations everywhere. The class of images which are processed correctly is correspondingly reduced. Other systems have modelled "uncertainty" by assigning stochastic or fuzzy values but this seems to be a retrograde step in the light of the discussion of structural descriptions given in section 2.1.

Given the general direction of our project, we approach the problem by relying on "context", in the guise of Fortran knowledge, and by coroutine control structures (see section 4.3). Thus, we might be unable to establish the intersection point in figure 15, and suspend our attempt to interpret the character as F. On being restarted, we might increase the threshold or grow the strokes towards each other and try again. This helps, but of course it merely pushes the problem back one level. The question then arises of how often one repeats the process until one gives up or decides that the junction is "really" not there at all.

4. *Character models*

4.1 *Partial percepts*

The previous sections described the way in which we compute the basic elements of our character models. We now turn to the question of an overall representation for characters, in order to implement the considerations outlined in section 2.1. Recall that the major emphasis of the project is on the way in which the perception of a huge intensity array as a Fortran coding sheet emerges as a result of a series of interactions between knowledge about Fortran and knowledge about hand-printed characters. An important paradigmatical aspect of the computational theory of vision is that interactions between different kinds (and levels) of knowledge can be precisely modelled by process interactions. A number of Artificial Intelligence experiments have suggested that such process interactions cannot be restricted to recursive subprogram activation, and there have been several successful experiments with more flexible, well-understood, control structures such as coroutines, software interrupts and backtracking [16], [18], [49], [25]. This explains the overall structure of our program, and the main requirement it imposes on the character models is that they should be capable of adapting to take advantage of what is known and what is required.

The Fortran reasoner may advise our program that "this character is probably C" (e.g., a comment line is hypothesised), "this character is probably the same as the third one on the previous line", or "I expect an arithmetical operator". The latter advice may bias our program's inter-pretation of the examples in figure 16 (after Bartlett).

Figure 16

On the other hand, the character experts may advise "I think this character is F", "I can confirm A but prefer H", "I deny that it is +, and suggest T", "the character descends below the cod-ing sheet line", or "it is curvy". The latter may well lead the Fortran reasoner to hypothesise an eight character blob as CONTINUE rather than as FUNCTION or EXTERNAL.

The crucial point is that the two co-operating programs almost always work in a state of partial knowledge. This leads us to the position that a vision program should explicitly represent partially-formed percepts, and should operate by incrementally refining such partial percepts by looking at each stage for what seems to be the information which can be computed most cheaply. Initially, we suppose that all cheaply available information (our primal stroke sketch) has been computed, while the Fortran reasoner starts out merely knowing that the image to be read depicts a Fortran program. Studies of reading emphasize that reading does not involve exhaustively accounting for every individual pixel; rather, processing is terminated as soon as hypotheses become "suffici-ently strong".

In fact, our arguments about perception apply equally well to looking at characters in isolation (see figure 3). We showed in the previous section that the computation of relations and junctions is considerably more uncertain than the computation of strokes and curves. Thus while finding a

particular junction strongly constrains the probable character interpretations, it is also true that partly hypothesising a character's identity (e.g., M or N) can enable the deployment of a great deal of detailed effort to verify the appropriate junction. The idea of partial per-cepts led us to extend our character-building kit from individual strokes to include parts such as those shown in figure 17 (b).

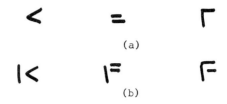

Figure 17

Suppose that at a particular stage of in-terpretation the information available to the program is represented by I. I, being partial, could be accomodated within several higher level structures. On the basis of that information, the program decides to compute what is expected to be the most cheaply available information. Notice that our discussion does not prejudice the use of parallelism. We are concerned here with inter-actions, although we do accept that our ideas about the kinds of interaction involved will even-tually be influenced by parallel activations. It is, however, no panacea. Suppose that our program returns information h as a result of looking for the cheapest information; h now has to be com-bined with I. If, as is most often the case, I and h seems to refine the current partial percept then the process can be repeated. This guarantees that in cases where everything is easily available the perception process rapidly converges. Intro-spectively, it should be "easier" to interpret figure 18(a) than figure 18(b).

Figure 18

Unfortunately, as figure 5 shows, it is not always the case that I + h is consistent; junctions may not appear to be present, expected relations may not be satisfied, and unexpected evidence may be found. Clearly something has to be done to resolve the inconsistency and there are two basic ways to proceed (cf. [30]).

(i) Deem h to be an "acceptable" variant to what was required. Thus the downstroke of figure 5(a) can be accepted despite its slope, as can the bottom stroke of figure 5(b), despite its position. This leaves the thorny problems of the extent to which something can vary while still being "acceptable" (see section 3), and the amount of effort which should be expended to determine "acceptability". For example, the L-junction of an F is expected to enclose a right angle. Allow-ing variations in the slopes of the stroke form-

J. M. Brady and B. J. Wielinga

ing the junction leads to an enormous range of acceptable enclosed angle (figure 18(b)).

(ii) Contemplate I + h, and regroup it into I' + h', which although it is still inconsistent (necessarily so, given our definition of partiality), seems to be the best partial interpretation of what is available. Eventually h' may have to be explained away as a ligature, segmentation problem or whatever, but only if the overall percept is in reasonable doubt. Notice that h may well be in I', since the order in which evidence becomes available is no guarantee of reliability.

If the perception of figure 18(a) is 'easy' and converges directly, (i) and (ii) constitute approaches to dealing with "difficulties". We believe that it is possible to generate useful descriptions directly from a trace of the difficulties encountered in the perception process. Thus difficulties resolved by accepting variants generate descriptions of the form: "I accepted ... even though it was ...". Applied to figure 5 this generates intuitively satisfying descriptions. On the other hand, the type (ii) approach leads to a description of the form "I thought it was ... until I saw ... and then I realized ...". For example stroke s_2 in figure 19 is a stronger candidate for the role of topstroke of the F than s_1, until it is discovered that there is then no bottom stroke.

Figure 19

We have genuinely been surprised at the sheer number of intermediate levels that we have been forced to represent explicitly in our program. If this is true for handprinted characters, then the number needed to perceive natural scenes must be quite staggering. This observation gives force the objection we made in section 1 about "faithful dog trotting beside master" level skipping, done in the name of impressive "performance". It necessary (though not sufficient) to maintain a massive number of intermediate levels, with small intermediate computational steps to avoid what Riseman (personal communication) calls the "combinatorics of the huge implicit search space". Newell and Moore [33] seem to focus on a similar idea with their notion of "grain".

Our approach of incrementally developing an explicitly represented partial percept by looking for what seems to be the cheapest information to compute is in marked contrast to the behaviors of a number of A.I. programs, which generate high level hypotheses on the slenderest of evidence, and are then forced to back up. Marr and Nishihara [29, page 28] refer to a "principle of least commitment" which seems closely related to our approach, although we haven't seen a detailed statement of the principle. Thus, from our point of view, it is not the hypothesize-and-test paradigm which is at fault *per se* but the number of intervening levels of partial knowledge which are skipped in a single hypothesis.

4.2 *Obituary for a Conniver-based program*

In an early stage of the project we built an (unpublished) program in POP-2, using the POPCORN system developed by Steven Hardy [18] for his thesis. POPCORN essentially provides the same primitives as CONNIVER [45], and it seemed to be the best system available to us for experimenting with reasonable flexible control structures. We exploited a variant to Conniver's HABG primitive to enable us to simultaneously gather all cheaply available evidence while setting traps after noting strong constraints such as three horizontal strokes. When all cheap cues had been discovered, the traps were sprung, so that the downstroke for an E might be hypothesized and searched for even when it is not cheaply available. It can be seen that the program alternately works in recognition mode, in which it assumes nothing is known, and verification mode, in which it thinks it knows everything. This early disloyalty to the idea of partial knowledge proclaimed in the previous sub-section was just one of a number of problems we encountered in the course of developing the POPCORN program, and which we believe are intrinsic in Conniver-like programs.

Firstly, the primitives IFADDED and IFNEEDED 'naturally' suggest data driven and goal driven control structures. We found it difficult to express with the Conniver primitives a control structure which was sufficiently flexible to make efficient use of partial evidence available. Of course it is possible in theory to circumvent this problem, but we agree with Sussman and McDermott [45] that the primitive control structures provided in a programming language are closely inter-related with the problem solutions which a programmer effectively considers.

The second problem concerns the (lack of) structure of CONNIVER's data base of assertions, which makes it extremely difficult (even using contexts) to impose structure on the available information. This is however a vital prerequisite if programs are to operate at varying levels of abstraction (cf. [29, page 9]). In particular, it is difficult to organize the program's knowledge to distinguish CALL and READ say.

In addition, it is difficult to make the program 'aware' of its own behavior. For example, if knowledge is represented procedurally, it is usually nontrivial to discover what evidence is available in support of a particular character, what contrary evidence has been found, and what has not yet been confirmed. Typically, demons are triggered as evidence is added to the data base, but they leave only indirect evidence of their effect in the form of new assertions. However, the implications of a piece of evidence can usually only be assessed in the light of what has already been discovered. An example of this is provided by the F in figure 16. This kind of behavior is difficult to achieve in CONNIVER, where character models are not very explicit and the program is relatively unaware of the reasons supporting a particular interpretation.

4.3 An implementation of frames

To overcome the problems discussed in the previous section, we have based our current program on an implementation of Minsky's [30] frames. In a wide-ranging discussion of various aspects of intelligence Minsky reminded A.I. workers that knowledge, as well as control, needs to be carefully, and richly, structured, and he proposed structures called frames, consisting of related facts and procedures, as a representation of knowledge. If Minsky's discussion was intuitive, it was also sufficiently attractive to inspire a number of groups to implement their understanding of the suggestion, thereby making the ideas more precise. Our implementation is based on the discussions of the Xerox PARC group tuned to the needs of the character program.

Frames are characterised by a name, type, slot-descriptions and actions. The purpose of type is to link the frame in an ISA-hierarchy, i.e., to make certain properties of a class of frames generally available for each instance of the TYPE. For instance, when we are considering a frame of type STROKE we may directly access general properties of STROKE-type frames, such as: how we can find strokes, what are the general attributes of strokes.

Slots basically provide a means to describe a frame or its applicability. Slots are filled either with an invariant description of an important feature of the frame, or contain a template description of the entity which can fill the slot when the frame is instantiated (see below). For example, a frame for the letter A may contain three slots providing descriptions of three strokes and several slots to describe the relations between the strokes.

Actions form the procedural part of frames. They typically consist of a precondition and an action specifier. The action specifier describes the action to be performed when the precondition becomes true. Preconditions generally become satisfied when certain operations on the frame get performed, e.g., instantiation, filling a slot, confirmation.

The central operation in the system is frame instantiation. Instantiation of a frame occurs in a context. A context contains frames which have been instantiated in earlier stages of the computation either by hypothesizing them or by being created by low-level operations such as finding strokes. When a frame is instantiated, it can be mapped onto the evidence that is already present in the current context. This means that frames in the context are matched against the slot-descriptions of the frame that is being instantiated. During the process of instantiation a frame might 'grab control' in a demon-like way, when the preconditions for an action get fulfilled. An instantiated frame remains in a context until it is explicitly removed. When a frame is only partially instantiated, any new evidence will be matched against the slots which have not yet been filled. This technique provides a means to create demons which will only trigger on a combination of several preconditions.

These ideas are now illustrated with reference to a frame for a character junction, which was discussed in section 3 (figure 20). The frame has two slots, corresponding to the strokes forming the junction, and three actions, with preconditions TOACHIEVE, WHENFILLED and WHENCONFIRMED. The TOACHIEVE action is of use when the hypothesized junction is being verified, and consists of ACHIEVING the horizontal and vertical strokes in turn. This will then enable the WHENFILLED action, although it could have been enabled in the absence of the junction hypothesis, by finding two appropriate strokes. The WHENFILLED action tries to establish that stroke 1 and stroke 2 do indeed form a junction (see section 3 for details).

If they do, the junction is confirmed, and this in turn enables the WHENCONFIRMED action. Note that this is not the only way the junction may be confirmed. We may confirm the presence of a character mainly on the grounds of Fortran reasoning, and this will confirm a constituent junction. In addition, the WHENCONFIRMED action sees if all troublesome evidence can be explained away, perhaps as segmentation problems, and then tries to assimilate it into the current context, by matching the instantiated it frame against hypothesized slots in the context. Besides the instantiation operation there are operations on frames like store, retrieve and matching operations. Frames are indexed in a multi-level associative memory, i.e., they can be retrieved by name, type and by any part of a slot description. Thus we can retrieve for example all character frames with, say, a big vertical and an L-type junction as components.

If the WHENFILLED action fails to find the junction between stroke 1 and stroke 2, the frame suspends itself by executing the routine leave ( ). This means that the frame has difficulty, but could be restarted to try harder, by growing the strokes and trying again. (Recall the discussion of this point in the previous section.)

```
Junction isa strokerelation
    with.slots ( stroke1 - [? isa stroke
                                with.slots slope - horizontal]
                 stroke2 - [? isa stroke
                                with.slots slope - vertical]
    with.actions ( [TOACHIEVE]
                       achieve(stroke1); achieve(stroke2)
                   [WHENFILLED <allof stroke1 stroke 2>]
                       test findjunction(stroke1, stroke2)
                       then confirm(junction)<>return
                       or$(leave( )
                           growstroke(stroke1); growstroke(stroke2)
                           test findjunction(stroke1, stroke2)
                           then confirm(junction)<>return
                           or deny(junction)<>return
                       $)
                   [WHENCONFIRMED]
                       test present([character is +ch] )
                       then assimilate(junction)
                       or fetchframewithslots(+junction, +type)
```

Figure 20

292   J. M. Brady and B. J. Wielinga

4.4 *Some residual difficulties*

We do not wish to pretend that the frame structures outlined in the previous subsection solve all problems. Far from it, in fact. Marr and Nishihara [29] discuss four particularly thorny problems which relate to computing referents of names in such systems. Yet another problem stems from the difficulties of controlling the interactions between the data and control structures we have described.

In section 4.1, we stressed that any vision program has to be flexible enough to adapt its behavior to exploit the information it currently has and the goals it is currently working on. This raises the question of where control should reside in the system. It is very tempting to concentrate a great deal of control in a particular frame, such as the junction frame outlined in the previous section. This enables it to deploy considerable effort to establish the presence or absence of a junction. Indeed, if a program is to have such highly specific knowledge, it is hard to see how else it could be represented other than as local control. The problem is that it may well be inappropriate from a global, strategic point of view to give control to a local structure if it can lead to a potentially enormous amount of misguided computation.

The only idea we know of that seems relevant to handling this local/global problem is the "research director" [18], which amounts to attaching a bureaucratic control interface process A to a group of local processes P_1, ... P_k.. Each P_i is so organized that when it is started (by A), it quickly announces its preliminary assessment, and then suspends itself. The routine A monitors the early responses, and, if they show a consensus, the P_i's are restarted to release any secondary analyses. These are also monitored by A.

Although Hardy only used one such grouping, there seems to be no reason why the <A, P_1, ..., P_k> groups cannot serve as units at the next higher level of clustering (cf. [30]), while the metaphor of administration is itself rich in suggestion.

5. *Curves*

In section 2, we observed that an examination of instances of several curves in gradient space suggested that they corresponded to a sequence S of up to eight consecutive gradient directions, and further suggested that they might be extracted by progressing a three element subsequence through S as the direction of the tangent to the curve changed. This is essentially related to chain coding and we spent some time devising measures for the curvature and descriptions for an entire curve. Quite straightforward things such as the end points of the curve, it's radius, and the angle it subtended, were difficult to compute. These problems were compounded by the fact that the expectation that a curve would give rise to a plateau in a histogram did not materialise.

After we abandoned the histogram analysis for a primal stroke sketch, the idea of a curve as a sequence of appropriately intersecting straight strokes immediately suggested itself. By "intersect", we mean eight-point connecting [41]. Since quickly written L-junctions often appear curved we only admit 'short' strokes as parts of curves, where 'short' means at most half the length of the diagonal of the character's minimal enclosing rectangle. This seems to work in practice, except on curves (figure 21) which have small curvature. Our current idea for handling this problem is sketched below.

Figure 21

Following [47] we use a filtering technique to assign curve roles (such as top.of.dcurve) to strokes, after first assigning labels to individual short strokes. The choice of the initial label set is extremely important. If the "right" label is not included in the initial set, the filtering algorithm goes badly astray. This is guaranteed by including (nearly) all labels in the initial label sets, but then the filtering algorithm doesn't converge to unique labelings. Our approach has been to be as restrictive as possible whenever it seemed safe to do so, as generous as possible otherwise. This is now illustrated with respect to stroke position, which, together with the stroke angle, forms the only basis for generating the initial label sets.

The restrictive-when-safe part of the label set generation is implemented by dividing the minimal enclosing rectangle (MER) into a 3 x 3 grid (figure 22). The set of labels for a leftv

TL	TM	TR
ML	MM	MR
BL	BM	BR

Figure 22

stroke (i.e., a short stroke whose slope is in the in the range 25 to 65) is defined initially for the grid corners TL, TR, BL, BR by considering curves in characters. Thus the TR set for a leftv sloping curve is [[Dcurve Topright] [Acurve Topright]

[Curve Toprightextension]

[Ucurve Toprightextension]]

The generous-as-possible-otherwise part of the label generation is implemented as follows:

$$TM = TL \cup TR$$
$$BM = TL \cup BR$$
$$ML = TL \cup BL$$
$$MR = TR \cup BR$$
$$MM = TL \cup TR \cup BL \cup BR.$$

The filtering algorithm is notable only for its treatment of what [21] calls the "gangrene"

problem. Consider the character zero shown in
figure 23. The intersecting strokes s_1, s_2, s_3 and

Figure 23

s_4 form a Dcurve (figure 6(b)), and at a particular stage in the filtering process are reduced to
single labels such as [s_1[Dcurve topright]]. The
problem is that the diagonal stroke s intersects
s_1 but they have no label in common. The basic
filtering algorithm would reduce the label sets
of each to NIL. We merely reduce a label set to
NIL. Although this is a potentially unreliable
part of the program, it has never caused problems,
possibly because of the way the label sets were
generated.

Following filtration, a curve has some or all
of its slots filled by several strokes. Some of
these strokes may be collinear and mergable
(section 2.3), although there may be two or more
genuinely different strokes in a single slot.
Figure 24 shows an example of how this can arise;
both s_1 and s_2 can be assigned to the topstroke

Figure 24

of the lower loop of a B. Each of these problems
is handled by computing (using Warshall's algorithm [24] the transitive closure of a particular
relation. In the first case the relation is
collinearity or mergability, in the latter case,
the relation is junctions acceptability.

Consider figure 25, which is the primal
sketch of two strokes. s_1 and s_2 intersect,

Figure 25

have the right relative slops, and are in the
right positions, and so s_2 is assigned the role of
bottomstroke of the Dcurve formed by the others.
In order to reject s_2, we note that it is on the
'outside of the curve formed by t_1, t_2, t_3, and
s_1.

By way of contrast to the earlier representation, it is already possible to generate useful
descriptions of curves by noting which slots are
not filled. Thus the curve in figure 26(a) might
be described as "squarish", while that in figure
26(b) is "sharp".

(a)   (b)

Figure 26

Having extracted overlapping sets of strokes,
and assigned them to roles in curves, we least
squares fit a circle for much the same reason that
we fit a line to a stroke. It is quite straightforward to compute the centre, radius, end points,
and angle subtended by the curve. This yields a
surprisingly rich description, for example, the
difference in radius enables us to discriminate
between the left bracket, C, and top loop of 8
shown in figure 27.

Figure 27

We still have the problem shown in figure 21,
where the left bracket is parsed as a curve and a
tangential (long) stroke as shown in figure 28.

Figure 28

Our first thought was to restart the label
generator, but it is in fact considerably easier to
try to extend the already existing curve by looking
for tangential strokes which merge with a stroke
component of the curve.

6. *Curve junctions, and an alternative
    representation*

In section 3, we drew attention to the problem of certainty arising from uncertainty with a
discussion of some of the difficulties which are
posed by stroke relations and stroke junctions.
The variations which arise from pairs of straight
strokes are trivial compared with those which are
finds between a stroke and a curve. Consider the
letter D. Knowing that the curve is composed of
straight strokes, one may forget its description
as a circle and attempt to establish an L junction
between the down stroke and the top of the Dcurve.
Figure 29 illustrates the difficulties.

(a)   (b)   (c)

Figure 29

Our approach has been to virtually abandon
the stroke based description described so far for
one based on the region of space occupied by a
character. Thus a curve defines a sector of a
circle by giving its centre, radius and angle
subtended. A straight stroke cuts the Mer into
two subregions. Consideration of the intersections
between such subregions yields a rather robust
description of characters.

In these terms, the letter D is formed by a roughly vertical stroke acting as a chord of the circle defined by the curved part. Figure 30 shows the results of considering the region occupied by the example Ds in figure 29. Observe that the descriptions "shallow" and "roundish" correspond to the chord being on opposite sides of the centre of the circle. The description for figure 30(c) might additionally be "forward sloping".

(a)　　　(b)　　　(c)

Figure 30

The letter P may be subjected to a similar analysis; but unlike the D, the stroke chord if not wholly inside the circle. To be sure, the representation doesn't entirely remove uncertainty, and there are genuine ambiguities such as figure 31 (taken from [6]). The P/D distinction is

Figure 31

naturally made in terms of the amount of chord outside the circle as a proportion of the diameter of the circle.

From our point of view, the main attraction of the idea is its insensitivity to the presence or absence of junctions. This is demonstrated in figure 32, where the variations in (a) and (b) are completely equivalent to the region occupancy model in (c).

It is also easier to generalize one part of the definition of above given in section 3 as follows. Consider figure 13 again. We see that

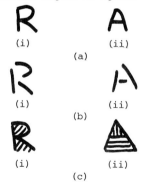
(i)　　　(ii)
(a)

(i)　　　(ii)
(b)

(i)　　　(ii)
(c)

Figure 32

stroke s_1 divides the mer into two parts, and that s_2 is almost wholly contained in the lower part. This still applies if s_1 is curved (figure 33).

Figure 33

Our concluding remark on the region occupancy

representation of characters is more speculative. Consider the expected A in figure 34(a), and a common variant in figure 34(b). The region occupancy representation of A expects a triangular region at the top, and while this is satisfied by figure 34(a), figure 34(b) has a sector of a circle at the top. It would be possible to cater for

(a)　　　　　(b)

Figure 34

this problem by having two or more models for A; but this seems to miss the point that figure 34(b) results directly from the dynamics of handwriting. Notwithstanding the claims of (psycho-) graphology a person's handwriting style involves a number of labour-saving (and therefore time-saving) techniques, which are used for example when writing quickly. It is a common observation that a person's handwriting or hand-printing changes when it is done especially quickly or especially slowly (e.g., deliberately painting a slogan on a poster).

In these terms, we can see figure 34(b) as the result of a modification to the process of drawing the triangular contour of figure 34(a). This corresponds to defining an acceptable transformation on the triangular part of the region occupancy representation (recall section 3.3). This is shown in figure 35(a), while the only other such transformations we know of are shown in figure 35(b).

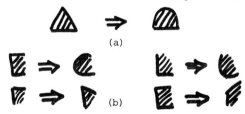
(a)

(b)

Figure 35

Some common applications of figure 35(a) are shown in figure 36. In fact, not every instance of

Figure 36

a triangular section can be subjected to these transformations; for example, the characters in figure 37 seem weird. The crucial point seems to

Figure 37

be that the distortions are only applicable in cases where the contour is drawn as a whole without the pen leaving the paper, that is, in a single stroke. This observation applies in particular to cursive handwriting, and it seems that our approach meshes well with James' [22] ideas about the linking problem faced by a writer of cursive script.

The ideas in this section are obviously applicable to studies of the reading of lower case printing, where it has long been known that the shape of words is a powerful cue. The major stumbling block is describing the region occupied by a complex shape like a word in terms of the simple building blocks we are currently using. This is being investigated by one of our students [42], in connection with generating descriptions of cartoon drawings of faces. []7], [1].

7.   *Region-occupancy and generalised cylinders*

In this section, we discuss the relationship between our region occupancy representation of characters, Binford's pioneering work on generalised cylinder representations, and Marr and Nishihara's Image-space processor [29]. We shall argue that there is more to our problem than the mere application of the general idea to the two-dimensional case, and point to certain issues that have to be faced in the three-dimensional case. Many of the ideas outlined in this section have developed in conversations with Richard Bornat, and in part from a lecture by Max Clowes. We apologize for the discursive, speculative nature of this section, which we include in the hope that it will stimulate discussion.

Binford's basic insight has two distinct parts:

(i) to represent objects by the volume of space which they occupy, rather than in terms of surface attributes.

(ii) to describe those volumes mathematically by generalised cylinders, which consist of a space axis and a function describing the changes in the planar cross sections along the curve.

In fact, Agin and Binford [2] simplify (ii) to circular cylinders, while Nevatia and Binford [32] distinguish circular cones and circular cylinders. These simplifications are quite reasonable given the class of objects which they describe: horse, doll, hammer, etc. We believe that it is in fact inevitable that the general case outlined by Binford will always be replaced in practice by specific computationally-tractable mathematical functions for the space axis and cross sections. We wish to draw attention here to a problem which [32] discuss briefly. Almost spherical objects, such as heads, and rectangular objects, such as bricks, have no obvious axes when viewed as general cylinders. [32] by-passes the problem by choosing the longest putative axis in such cases.

Essentially, the problem is that no *single* volume prototype, based on specific computationally tractable functions, is sufficient by itself to cater for objects as diverse as bricks, wedges, spheres, cylinders and two-dimensional sheets such as leaves or pieces of paper. The same consideration applies to our representation of characters, and we use triangles, rectangles and sectors of

circles as the building blocks for our region descriptions.

The obvious solution to the problem is to have several "primitive" prototypes, and to describe complex objects as being composed of them in suitable ways (such as junctions in [32], and our intersections and amalgamations). Neglecting the issue of the choice of a set of primitives, two substantial problems are raised by multiple building blocks.

(a)   The fact that objects have alternative representations. We have nothing further to say about this beyond our idea of acceptable transformations discussed in the previous section.

(b)   The problem of indexing for recognition [29, page 19], which refers to the way in which an appropriate (class of) model is accessed from low level information.

The crucial point is that the indexing problem is made considerably more difficult since one has to reason from visual appearance to spatial occupancy. Consider figure 38(a), which is supposed to be a mallet, and figure 38(b) which is a (very bad) drawing of a leg of a table. In both cases, sharp edges, meeting at a junction,

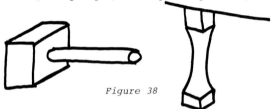

Figure 38

suggest a boxlike prototype part, while the absence of such visual features in the mallet handle and parts of the table leg *suggest* a circular cross section. (Of course this naive inference is invalidated by longitudinal wood grain but the point still holds). [32] largely avoids this problem by working with accurate depth information, and by equating the axis centre with the midpoint of a line drawn on the visible surface. Marr and Nishihara assume throughout that they are working with a general animal model. We have to face this problem in a much much simpler setting by reasoning from part of an outer contour shape to a particular region.

Of course, for complex objects, such as animals, faces, trees and motor cars, the space occupancy description will be an enormous structure with many intermediate levels between the top level name and the primitive prototypes. This very complexity may well account for the observed human inability to articulate such shapes. Furthermore, and this is consistent with Marr and Nishihara's theory, *shape* descriptions closely relate to known structural decompositions, such as anatomical structure in the case of animals.

We suggest that one of the main attractions of a spatial occupancy representation is the relative ease with which it can support inferences about movement. The belief that I can walk through a doorway, crawl under a fence, climb over a stile or jump through a hoop can be based on my

belief that I can transform my body into a particular volume. This presupposes that I maintain
a model of the space which my body currently occupies, and of the transformations which I can
effect upon it to place it in the desired volume
of space. These ideas seem to be closely related
to Marr and Nishihara's space frame representation, and indeed their image-space processor seems
to provide some of the inferencing capability
that we are conjecturing here. However, the
image-space processor works exclusively with a
stick figure representation, much like Nevatia
and Binford's symbolic description of a Barbie
doll, and from our point of view this means that
they by-pass some of the difficult issues raised
by relating surface attributes to volume description. Similarly, the image-space processor is incapable of representing activities such as pulling
on a glove.

A further aspect of reasoning about movement
is that a path from here to there corresponds to a
snake-like volume carved out by my body over time.
It seems from studies of mental maps that we are
particularly adept at solving problems such as
figuring out how to cross a crowded room. We
agree with [29, page 3] that it is vital to be
able to reason at many levels of abstraction.

If we do indeed have so much understanding
of our body space, and the way it moves, Johanneson's compelling demonstrations begin to seem more
amenable to explanation, particularly when the
above observations are coupled to our obvious determination to impose animistic perceptions at the
least suggestion.

Acknowledgements

This paper owes a great deal to discussions
we have had with the entire Essex A.I. community,
especially Richard Bornat and Pat Hayes. We have
also discussed it at length with the Sussex and
Edinburgh groups. Harry Barrow, Marty Tenenbaum,
Dave Waltz and David Marr and the MIT vision group
have commented on earlier parts of the work.

References

[1] Adler, M.R. Recognition of Peanuts Cartoons. *Proc. 2nd AISB Conf.*, Edinburgh, 1976, 1-13.

[2] Agin, G.A., and Binford, T.O. Computer description of curved objects. *Proc. 3rd IJCAI*, Stanford, 1973, 629-635.

[3] Balm, G.J. An introduction to optical character reader considerations. *Pattern Recognition,* 1970, 151.

[4] Bartlett, F.C. *Remembering: a Study in Experimental and Social Psychology,* Cambridge University Press, Cambridge, U.K. 1932.

[5] Binford, T.O. Visual perception by Computer. *IEEE Conf. on systems and controls,* Miami, 1971.

[6] Blesser, B., Shillman, R., Kublinski, T., Cox,C., Eden, M. and Ventura, J. A theoretical approach for character recognition based on phenomological attributes. *Int. J. Man-Machine Studies, 6,* 1974, 701-714.

[7] Bornat, R. Reasoning about handprinted Fortran programs. *Proc. 2nd AISB Conf.,* Edinburgh, 1976, 38-46.

[8] Bornat, R. and Brady, J.M. Using knowledge in the computer interpretation of handwritten Fortran coding sheets. *Int. J. Man-machine Studies,* 8, 1976, 13-27.

[9] Bornat, R. and Brady, J.M. Finding blobs of writing in the Fortran coding sheets project. *Proc. 2nd AISB Conf.,* Edinburgh, 1976, 47-55.

[10] Brady, J.M. Position paper on computer vision. *First round papers, Mass. Conference,* Amherst, 1976, 17-22. (available from author)

[11] Brady, J. M. and Wielinga, B.J. Seeing a pattern as a character. *Proc. 2nd AISB Conf.,* Edinburgh, 1976, 63-73.

[12] Brooks, M.J. Locating intensity changes in digitised visual scenes. *CSM-15,* University of Essex, 1976.

[13] Clowes, M.B. Scene analysis and picture grammars. *Graphic Languages,* Nake and Rosenfeld (Eds.), North-Holland, Amsterdam, 1972, 144-159.

[14] Duda, R.O. and Hart, P. Use of the Hough transformation to detect lines and curves in pictures. *Comm. ACM,* 15, 1, 1972, 11-15.

[15] Eden, M. Handwriting generation and recognition. *Recognising Patterns,* Kolers and Eden (eds).

[16] Fahlman, S.E. A planning system for robot construction tasks. *Artif. Intelligence,* 5, 1973, 1-48.

[17] Guzman, A. Analysis of curved line drawings using context and global information. *Machine Intelligence 6,* Meltzer and Michie (eds.) Edinburgh University Press, Edinburgh, 1971, 325-375.

[18] Hardy, S. Synthesis of LISP junctions from example computations. *Ph.D thesis,* University of Essex, U.K., 1976.

[19] Harmon, L.D. The recognition of faces. *Perception,* Held and Richards (Eds.), Freeman, San Francisco, 1975, 183-195.

[20] Heider, F. and Simmel, M. An experimental study of apparent behaviour. *Amer. J. Psychol.* 57, 1944, 243-259.

[21] Hinton, G. Using relaxation to find a puppet. *Proc. 2nd AISB Conf.,* Edinburgh, 1976, 148-157.

[22] James, P.L. The structure of cursive handwriting. *Tech. report,* University of Sussex, U.K., 1974.

[23] Johanneson, G. Visual motion perception: a model for visual motion and space perception from changing proximal stimuli. *Report 98,* Department of Psychology, University of Uppsala, Sweden, 1971.

[24] Mackworth, A.K. Consistency in networks of relations. *TR 75-3,* University of British Columbia, Canada, 1975.

[25] McDermott, D.V. Assimilation of new information by a natural language understanding system, *M.S. thesis,* AIM 291, MIT, 1974.

[26] Marr, D. The low-level symbolic representation of intensity changes in an image. *AIM 325,* MIT, 1975.

[27] Marr, D. Analysing natural images. *AIM 334,* MIT, 1975.

[28] Marr, D., and Forbus, K. Vision machine-preliminary assessment. *WP 94,* MIT, 1975.

[29] Marr, D., and Nishihara, H.K. Spatial disposition of axes in a generalised cylinder representation of objects that do not encompass the viewer. *AIM 341,* MIT, 1975.

[30] Minsky, M. A framework for representing knowledge. *The Psychology of Computer Vision,* Winston, (Ed.), McGraw-Hill, New York, 1975.

[31] Narasimhan, R. On the description, generation and recognition of classes of pictures. *Automatic Interpretation and Classification of Images,* Grasselli (Ed.), Academic, New York, 1969.

[32] Nevatia, R. and Binford, T.O. Description and recognition of curved objects. *AIM 250* Stanford, 1974.

[33] Newell, A., and Moore, J. How can Merlin understand? *Knowledge and Cognition,* Gregg (Ed.), Erlbaum, Baltimore, 1973.

[34] O'Gorman, F. Edge detection using Walsh functions. *Proc. 2nd AISB Conf.,* Edinburgh, 1976, 195-206.

[35] O'Gorman, F., and Clowes, M. B. Finding picture edges through collinearity of feature points. *Proc. 3rd IJCAI,* Stanford, 1973, 543-555.

[36] Ohlander, R. Analysis of natural images. *Ph.D. thesis,* CMU, 1975.

[37] Parks, J. R. A multi-level system for mixed font and hand-blocked printed character recognition. *Automatic Interpretation and Classification of Images,* Grasselli (Ed.), Academic, New York, 1969.

[38] Pingle, K.K. Visual perception by computer. *Automatic Interpretation and Classification of Images,* Grasselli (Ed.) Academic, New York, 1969.

[39] Pingle, K.K. and Tenenbaum, J.M. An accommodating edge follower. *Proc. 2nd IJCAI,* 1971, 1-7.

[40] Roberts, L.G. Machine perception of three-dimensional solids. *Optical and Electro-Optical processing of Information,* Tipet, (Ed.), MIT, 1965, 159-197.

[41] Rosenfeld, A. *Picture Processing by Computer,* Academic, New York, 1969.

[42] Rowbury, C.R. A frame system approach to the computer interpretation of hand-drawn cartoon faces. *CSM 16,* University of Essex, U.K., 1976.

[43] Shirai, Y. A context-sensitive line finder for recognition of polyhedra. *Artif. Intelligence,* 4, 1973, 95-119.

[44] Shirai, Y., and Tsuju, S. Extraction of the line drawings of 3-dimensional objects by sequential illumination from several directions. *Proc. 2nd IJCAI,* 1971, 71-79.

[45] Sussman, G.J., and McDermott, D.V. The Conniver reference manual. *AIM 259/259A,* MIT, 1972/4.

[46] Tenenbaum, J.M., and Barrow, H.G. Experiments in interpretation-guided segmentation. *TR 123,* SRI, 1976.

Reading the Writing on the Wall

[47] Waltz, D. Generating semantic descriptions
      from drawings of scenes with shadows. *The
      Psychology of Computer Vision,* Winston (Ed.),
      McGraw-Hill, New York, 1975.

[*48*] Waldinger, R.J. Achieving several goals
        simultaneously. *Machine Representation of
        Knowledge,* Elcock and Michie, (Eds.), Wylie,
        1976.

[49] Winograd, T. *Understanding Natural Language.*
      Edinburgh.U.P., Edinburgh, 1972.

```
DEBUG STREAM
1-MAR-1977 8:52:12
*TRUE
-pslist (infstream, strokelist)
<STROKE: 2Ø9,X: 2Ø5,2Ø7 Y: 777,782 SIZE: 11,DIR:
   J,SLOPE: VERT,SET: [12 11 1Ø]>
<LINE S2Ø9 IS THETA:  72, RHO: 42, X1,Y1: 2Ø5, 777
   X2,Y2: 2Ø7,782,L: 5>

<STROKE: 57X: 2Ø2,2Ø7 Y: 761,78Ø SIZE: 43,DIR:
   J,SLOPE: VERT,SET: [1Ø 9 8 ]>
<LINE S57 IS THETA: 79m RHO: -55, X1,Y1: 2Ø2,761
   X2,Y2: 2Ø6,78Ø,L: 19>

<STROKE: 253,X: 2Ø3,217 Y: 759,762 SIZE: 31,DIR:
   E,SLOPE: HORIZ,SET: [4 5 6]>
<LINE S253 IS THETA: 9, RHO: 716,X1,Y1: 2Ø3,760
   X2,Y2: 217,762,L: 14>

<STROKE: 315,X: 2Ø4,217 Y: 762,765 SIZE: 27,DIR:
   M,SLOPE: HORIZ,SET: [14 13 12]>
<LINE S315 IS THETA: 11, RHO: 711, X1,Y1: 2Ø4,762
   X2,Y2: 217,764,L: 13>

<STROKE: 261,X: 2Ø7,216 Y: 767,769 SIZE: 15,DIR:
   E,SLOPE:  HORIZ,SET: [4 5 6]>
<LINE S261 IS THETA: 176,RHO: 781, X1,Y1: 2Ø7,768
   X2,Y2: 216,768,L: 9>

<STROKE: 319,X: 2Ø7,216 Y: 77Ø,771 SIZE: 16,DIR:
   M,SLOPE: HORIZ,SET: [14 13 12]>
<LINE S319 IS THETA: 178, RHO: 778, X1,Y1: 2Ø7,771
   X2,Y2: 216,770,L: 9>

<STROKE: 15,X: 2Ø6, 21Ø Y: 771, 781 SIZE: 26,DIR:
   A,SLOPE: VERT,SET: [16 1 2]>
<LINE S15 IS THETA: 74, RHO: 9,X1,Y1: 2Ø7,771
   X2,Y2: 21Ø,281,L: 1Ø>

<STROKE: ]25,X: 2Ø6, 2Ø9 Y: 772,776 SIZE: 1Ø,DIR:
   B,SLOPE: VERT,SET: [2 3 4]>
<LINE S125 IS THETA: 58, RHO: 233, X1,Y1: 2Ø6,772
   X2,Y2: 2Ø9,776,L: 5>
```

Figure 11

VISIONS: A Computer System for Interpreting Scenes[1]

Allen R. Hanson
School of Language and Communication
Hampshire College
Amherst, Massachusetts 01002

Edward M. Riseman
Computer and Information Science
University of Massachusetts
Amherst, Massachusetts 01003

Abstract

The design of a general system for interpreting static, monocular, color images of natural scenes is described. Interpretation of an image involves the construction of an internal model which is a description of the major semantic elements in the scene, as well as their three-dimensional relationships in the physical world. This paper examines the structure of the interpretation system including the representation of knowledge, the processes which form the model, control of these processes, and search through the space of possible models. All components have been designed modularly to provide a tool which will facilitate the local exploration and evolution of a very complex system. Initial results demonstrate selected aspects of the combined segmentation and interpretation processes.

Table of Contents

I.   Introduction

This paper discusses the design and initial performance of the semantic processes of a computer vision system, called VISIONS (Visual Integration by Semantic Interpretation Of Natural Scenes), for interpreting static monocular scenes [RIS74,HAN75, HAN76a,b,WIL77].[2] This work represents an empirical approach to the design and implementation of an extremely complex system. We have decomposed the system into "low-level" segmentation processes which operate on numeric arrays of visual data, and "high-level" interpretation processes for constructing a description of the world portrayed in the scene. The global structure of the VISIONS system is outlined in Figure 1. The companion paper in this volume [HAN78] describes the segmentation system of VISIONS. In the present paper, we assume that the low-level segmentation and feature extraction processes have provided adequate information and describe how this can be used to interpret the image.   Initial results demonstrate

---

[1]This research has been supported by the National Science Foundation under Grant DCR75-16098.

[2]Many of the ideas in this paper are under continuing development by members of our research group. We will reference those papers that already document these efforts, and mention in footnotes the individuals responsible where documentation is not yet available.

selected aspects of the combined segmentation and semantic processes.

For alternative views on complex interpretation processes, in this volume refer to [BAJ78, BAL78, BAR78, BRA78, LEV78, MAC78, MAR78, RED78, SHI78, UHR78, WOO78]; as a sample of previous efforts towards general vision systems refer to [BAR72, FIS73, YAK73, LIE74, TUR74, MIN75, BAR76, TEN76, KAN77, RUB77] and for related work in speech recognition systems refer to [ERM75, LOW76, LES77, WAL77, WOO77].

I.1 A Strategy for the Evolution of a Very Complex System

The goal of VISIONS is the transformation of patterns of sensory visual input from a two-dimensional (2D) image of a scene into a description which captures the meaning of the scene. Interpretation of an image, then, involves the construction of a model which includes a description of the major conceptual entities present and a volume-surface occupancy description of the three-dimensional (3D) space of the world in the scene. The process by which this description is constructed is called model-building.

Our approach to model-building consists of four major components, as shown on the right-hand side of Figure 1:

1) representation - multiple levels of representation for both the image-specific model and long-term general knowledge,

2) processes - a set of modular knowledge sources for the transformation of data (patterns) between particular levels of representation,

3) control - a hierarchical modular strategy to control the application of the knowledge sources, and

4) search - a tree representing the history of search through the space of possible models.

One of our design goals is to provide maximum flexibility during the evolution of a system which may need to be modified along lines which cannot be anticipated in advance -- for example, representations may have to be added or modified, processes may not prove to be sufficiently reliable, etc. It is naive to believe that all of the complexities in controlling such a wide range of processes can be predicted without empirical investigations. Therefore, the initial design of VISIONS has been modular -- geared towards the development of a tool which allows local investigations of a range of issues and which permits modifications to the system without major disruptions in its functioning as a system. This work was primarily influenced by some of the system design criteria of the HEARSAY-II speech understanding system [ERM75, LES77], and we have further extended the general design philosophy to other aspects of system development, in particular the strategies for controlling the processes.

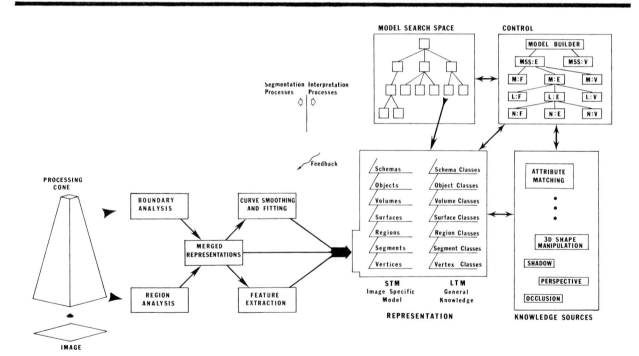

Figure 1. Overview of the VISIONS system. The left hand side represents the segmentation processes which are described in the companion paper in this volume. The right hand side represents the mechanisms for the formation of a descriptive model of a scene. The interpretation components are structurally divided into a representation of knowledge, modular knowledge sources (processes) for the formation of hypotheses, a hierarchical modular strategy to control the application of the knowledge sources, and a tree for representing the history of search through the space of models.

Allen R. Hanson and Edward M. Riseman

I.2 An Overview

Figure 2 portrays the layered graph which is the underlying representation of stored general knowledge about the world; in this representation, an interpretation of a specific image becomes an inter-linked collection of instantiations of the stored concepts. General a priori knowledge can be viewed as long-term memory (LTM). The set of instantiations, viewed as short-term memory (STM), constitutes the system's internal model, or description, of the world in that particular image.

Declarative knowledge about the world has many forms. The system must have access to knowledge of objects, including attributes of color, texture, size, shape, etc., including the functional and spatial relationships between (parts of) objects, as well as information about the way simple 3D volumes and surfaces project as regions, boundaries, and vertices in a 2D image [MIN75]. The SCHEMA level of the knowledge base will be used to describe the prototypical structure of common scenes (road scene, house scene) and objects (house, person, car) in terms of their parts; the importance of each part to the schema and the spatial relationships between the parts will be stored with each schema. This will provide a hierarchical description of the world down to finer levels of detail, but instantiation from the image can take place at any level of detail (e.g., instantiation of the house as a whole or instantiation of the parts of house).

For other kinds of visual knowledge, a procedural form is more natural; for example, the laws of perspective which govern the mapping between the 3D world and its projection onto a 2D image. Thus, we have implemented a procedure to compute the expected image size of an object of known dimensions at a given distance viewed through a lens with a given focal length. Each such process is called a "knowledge source" [ERM75] and will be used to form instantiations, also referred to as hypotheses, in the process of building a model of the scene in the image.

There are a number of knowledge sources (KSs) potentially relevant to vision. Many of these are sketched in Figure 3 across the levels of representation at which they operate. Although several KSs have already been implemented or are nearing completion, some of them are not as sophisticated as one might desire. Here our strategy is to incrementally improve a particular KS after a simpler working process has been made available to the system.

The construction of an interpretation is guided by a strategy which we refer to as a control strategy. When the knowledge that is being manipulated is procedural, it is necessary to determine which processes are to be activated, in what order, and how new information is to be integrated with existing information. When the knowledge is declarative, as in our long-term memory, an active mechanism is needed to employ this information. For example, the predictive power of a schema rests in the stored relationships of the schema to its parts. The way in which it is used still remains to be specified since the information itself does not lead to the generation of hypotheses; in this case a useful strategy might involve the examination of the most likely unexplored schema part suggested by an instantiated schema.

The interpretation of an image is achieved by constructing a description in short-term memory and it requires the generation of many hypotheses. As we have just shown, the paths available for hypothesis formation (Figure 3) involve both procedural and declarative knowledge. These paths are often divided [ERM75] into those which are bottom-up (or generative) and those which are top-down (or predictive):

(a) bottom-up: hypotheses are formulated on the basis of characteristics and features stored in STM which were derived from the specific image being analyzed; examples include the analysis of spectral properties (color and texture) of regions for hypothesizing objects; and the fitted shapes of boundaries and regions for hypothesizing surfaces, volumes, and objects;

(b) top-down: hypotheses are formulated by analysis of predictions from stored knowledge in LTM; examples include object prediction from instantiated schemas, or the manipulation of stored 3D shape representations for matching regions.

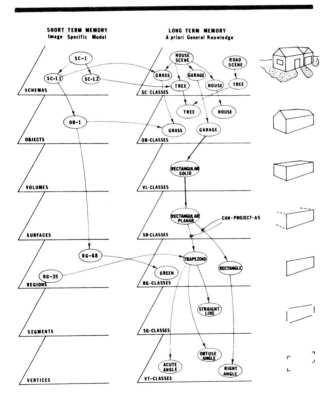

Figure 2. An example sketch of a partial model and the decomposition of declarative knowledge. The knowledge is divided into: 1) a hierarchy of levels of representation defining the key levels of abstraction which are necessary for a general system of visual perception; and 2) short-term memory (STM) representing an interpretation of the specific image and long-term memory (LTM) representing general visual knowledge of the world.

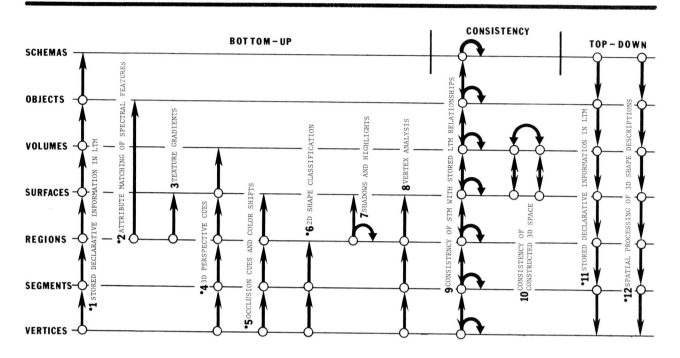

Figure 3. Bottom-Up and Top-Down Paths for Hypotheses. Knowledge sources, using both declarative and procedural forms of knowledge, can generate and verify hypotheses along many paths through the multi-level representation. These are some of the prime cues in static, monocular, 2D color images of 3D scenes. Additional paths are available from motion and stereo data. Those mechanisms for hypothesis formation which are in a more advanced state of development in the system are marked with a ● in the diagram. (1) Hypothesis generation via symbolic labels and relationships stored in LTM, including primitive types at each level, subclass/superclass and part/whole relationships, shape, spatial relationships, etc. (Figures 2 and 10). (2) Object identity hypotheses via attribute matching of spectral features of regions in STM with stored objects in LTM (Figure 4). (3) Surface hypotheses via texture gradients. (4) Volume and surface hypotheses via 3D perspective cues and projective geometry; this analysis includes vanishing points and lines, type of polyhedral vertices, comparison of region size in STM with stored object size in LTM, etc. (Figure 6). (5) Hypotheses of relative distances via occlusion cues (Figure 6) and color shifts. (6) Hypotheses from analysis and classification of 2D shapes (Figures 27-29 in companion paper). (7) Shadows and highlights provide cues to surface orientation and can direct merging of regions for truer projection of surfaces (Figure 27 in companion paper). (8) Analysis of polyhedral vertex types for surface and volume hypotheses; extensions to smoothly varying surfaces (Figure 6). (9) Verification of the consistency between STM and stored relationships in LTM. (10) Verification of the consistency of volume/surface occupancy in constructed 3D space. (11) Predictions via symbolic labels and relationships stored in LTM (inversion on arcs in Figures 2 and 10). (12) Predictions via rotation and projection of 3D shape descriptions stored in schemas (Figure 5).

Some type of control is required for manipulating both procedural and declarative information. In order to generate hypotheses, knowledge sources must be activated, and/or information in LTM must be examined. The hierarchical modular control structure (Figure 8) is intended to provide the flexibility necessary to explore a range of strategies for the construction of an interpretation. This structure is decomposed horizontally according to the classic hypothesize-test paradigm (here, focus-expand-verify). The vertical decomposition captures the sequence of events which must occur in order to expand a partially constructed interpretation: selection of one of a collection of competing interpretations, selection of a level in the multi-level structure, and finally selection of a node (or set of nodes) upon which to focus.

Let us illustrate one of very many strategies for applying these KSs in the construction of the model of a rural road scene. For sake of discussion, assume the road has grass and trees to either side, a dotted yellow line down the center, and that there is a red car coming towards the camera. Initially, the regions which are largest, brightest, and most highly color saturated can be examined first. Stored attributes of object classes (which have been extracted from a training set in our data base of images) are compared to the features of each region. The sky region should be easily recognized, but there may be some uncertainty between the grass and tree regions. If a dark (possibly brown) region with parallel vertical sides is found below a green textured region with an irregular boundary below the sky region, this will imply that a tree is present. Note that here the tree schema would be used to recognize the parts of tree.

Projective geometry can be used to determine
that the width of the trunk region and the height
to the top of the crown region imply a physical
object in the world whose dimensions lie within the
stored size range of the parts of tree. In order
to perform this analysis, hypotheses would be made
concerning the levelness of the ground, the
vertical orientation of the tree to the ground, and
the lowest point in the image where the trunk
region touches the ground. Occlusion analysis
would be invoked to determine whether the bottom
of the trunk appears to be obscured. The hypothesis of grass would be increased when the trunk is
instantiated. The converging sides of the road
region, the gray color of that region, and the
presence of small elongated yellow regions contained in the road region are cues for road; perspective analysis would verify consistency between
the sizes of image region and the stored size range
of road in a fashion similar to the tree; here the
road is assumed (via stored information) to be in
the horizontal ground plane. If the road-scene
schema is instantiated, the identity and locations
of the regions already examined fit the schema.
Now the road-scene schema predicts the possibility
of car, and the saturated red region (man-made
objects are often highly saturated) matches the
shape and expected location of car; of course the
car might be recognizable without the road-scene
schema. The analysis can proceed in this fashion
using the stored knowledge and any of the KSs at
various places in the image. There are usually
many redundant visual cues present and obviously
many control strategies for employing these cues.

I.3 Goal Orientation

The successful construction of the model description is the goal of our current research in
this first phase of system development. In most
practical applications, however, the goals of a
vision system would guide this model-building
process. Manipulation of the 3D volume-surface
levels in the model would allow a mobile robot
to form plans for movement in the environment;
here, the goal-orientation of the robot (e.g.,
to move to a particular place) would require the
system to selectively construct a detailed model
only in the relevant areas of the environment,
that is, in areas which have semantic importance
in relation to the current goal(s). In some cases
the description being formed will by its very nature
attain the desired goals; e.g., if we consider the
automatic scanning of tissue samples for malignan-
cies, the naming of the regions at the object level
(or the formation of the attributes of these
regions/objects) could actually be the results
desired by the pathologist.

The current design has not been directed
towards any particular goal, but rather is an
attempt to design a general system in which a
variety of goals can be incorporated. Therefore,
in this paper we will usually refer to an interpretation
without reference to the particular goal at hand.
We expect that the presence of more constrained
goals would allow greater efficiency in model
construction.

I.4 Schemas: A Bridge Between General-Purpose and Special-Purpose Vision Systems

Schemas[1] are the highest level knowledge
structures currently in our system. They describe
objects and scenes in terms of a related set of
parts; spatial relationships between parts and the
importance of a part to the schema as control for
model building are included (refer to Section VI).
The house scene schema would encode expected information about the relationships of house, lawn,
driveway, garage, etc. The house schema would
describe the relationships of windows, doors,
walls, roof, etc. These structures are related to
Minsky's frames [MIN75], Schank's scripts [SCH77],
Piaget's schemas [PIA71], Neisser's schemas
[NEI76], and Arbib's slides [ARB72] and schemas
[ARB77]. Note that interpretation should not
require the use of scene schemas -- there cannot be
a schema for every situation encountered, and objects
ought to be recognized in unexpected contexts.

Let us consider the relationship between a
schema and a system tuned to a particular application. A special purpose system (e.g., a system to
analyze a chest x-ray image [WEC75,BAL78]) incorporates many constraints from the domain being
viewed. It can take advantage of a fixed context,
use features that are particularly useful in
achieving the specific goal, and choose a strategy
which may be very bad in general but which is
effective in the given application. To some degree
the use of schemas reduces the complexity of
general vision systems towards that of special
purpose systems.

Consider the problem of intermediate difficulty -- a general system which is being used to
recognize known objects and scenes [BUL78,NEV78].
Once the correct schema is selected, the system
could use recognition strategies which vary the
visual features used in segmentation, the order
in which parts are searched for, the location in
which matching processes are attempted, the type
of matching, the confidence which is acceptable

----

[1]In our earlier work the term "frame" [MIN75] was
used for the representation of these stereotyped
situations. We have chosen to change our
terminology in order to avoid confusion with the
common usage in TV and motion pictures. There is
also confusion with the "frame problem" in AI
literature [McC69] which concerns the determination of what remains constant as the environment
changes. The term "schema" has a history of usage
with a general sense that fits our purpose. From
this point on we will use "schema" in place of
frame, while acknowledging the general influence
of frame theory. With respect to the choice of
"schemata" or "schemas" as the correct English
plural of "schema," we quote Arbib [ARB77]

"Most English dictionaries offer the Greek plural schemata for the
word schema, but we prefer the English plural schemas. Fowler's 'Modern
English Usage' states: 'Of most words in fairly common use that have a
Latin as well as or instead of an English plural the correct Latin form
is given in the word's alphabetical place. ... There is a tendency to
abandon the Latin plurals, and when one is really in doubt which to
use the English form should be given the preference.' (The cited
comments refer to Latinized-Greek as well.) This tendency to abandon
classical plurals is part of the pattern of historical change of
English. For example, the 19th century had already seen dogmas
achieve parity with dogmata, and in current usage only the English
form appears unaffected. Amongst authors who share our preference for
schemas, we may cite P.H. Lindsay and D.A. Norman: 'Human Information
Processing', 2nd Edition, Academic Press (1977)."

for a match, etc. The front view of a specific known house should be no more difficult (and probably far easier) than an unknown chest x-ray image. Now the problem is that for a general vision system to be functional, it will often not have schemas for particular objects/scenes, but a more general description of a class of objects/ scenes. In addition, at many stages of the processing one cannot be sure whether the correct schema is being used or which one to use next.

Our approach is to separate the problem of recognizing a house when a house is assumed to be present and actually is present, from the problem of first hypothesizing that a house is present or recovering from the erroneous hypothesis that it is a different object. Consequently the development must proceed along two lines, one dealing with the specific, and the other with general levels of processing. The development of an individual schema and the verification that it is applicable may be as tractable as the development of a particular strategy in a special purpose system. The general strategy by which schemas are instantiated, verified, and rejected is a separate research question whose answer will bring us a long way towards the development of more general vision systems. Our argument is that there are many steps by which the advantages of a special purpose system can be extracted so that there is a continuum in the development of general vision systems from special purpose systems [NEV78]. We believe this formulation of the problem will allow the incremental development of a general system, which can take advantage of constrained contexts. This is a major characteristic of the design in [BAL78].

II.   Representation of Declarative Knowledge and Models

II.1 Multiple Levels of Representation

From our point of view the process of image understanding is a series of transformations from numeric entities representing the sensory information to a symbolic structure capturing those concepts relevant to the goals of the system. The input is a very large array of integer values representing brightness and color at local points of the image, while the information that we expect our system to derive involves the names of classes of objects and the important relationships between these classes. In order to manipulate data across such a range of representations, we have found it necessary to form a hierarchy of representations (or abstractions) [ERM73] which capture many of the natural characteristics of our visual and physical world. These levels of abstraction divide into two types of representation: a) 3D concepts concerned with the physical world; and b) 2D concepts associated with projections of the physical world onto an image plane.

Figure 2 depicts the levels that currently are being employed in our system. The primary levels of representation include schemas of stereotypical situations, the objects taking part in those situations, the volumes and surfaces which delimit those objects, and the regions, boundary segments and vertices defining the visible portions of those surfaces from particular points of view [WIL77]. The lower region, segment, and vertex (RSV) levels

provide the means for describing information in a photograph; RSV is the data structure which receives segmentation output in symbolic form and is a major interface between the low-level and high-level systems (see companion paper [HAN78], this volume). It also is the representation for describing the way physical objects appear from particular views. The surface, volume, object, and schema levels permit description of the physical world. The 3D world and the 2D projections interface at the surface and region levels [MAR76b], where the laws of projective geometry govern the relationships between them.

We believe that if any of these levels are removed, the system will be deficient in its ability to interpret images in a general manner. For example, removal of surface descriptions will leave the system deficient in its understanding of three-dimensional space, while removal of schemas will leave the system ignorant of situations such as road scenes in which there are many constraints on the relationships between members of a particular set of objects. Neither of these deficiencies can be easily overcome in a vision system which is to exhibit some of the characteristics of general visual perception.

Of course all of these levels of representation are not necessary if the environment or goals are restricted to some special-purpose application. Analysis of blood cells [BRE74] would not require a general representation of surfaces, while an assembly line system designed to inspect a single industrial part [BAI75] would not need a general schema level since the system has a fixed context in which it operates.

II.2 A Visual Model in Terms of Stored General Classes: STM and LTM

The hierarchical set of representations provides rich descriptive capabilities, but we must also distinguish between the representation of a specific instance of a visual entity and the general class to which it belongs. For example a particular object labelled TREE appearing in the image is a member of the general TREE-CLASS at the object level, and it will inherit the basic properties of TREE from its class association. However, the instance of TREE in the image will have specific values for these properties and will in general differ from its prototype. These values should be stored with each particular instance of tree, since there may be several in the image.

This suggests that, in addition to dividing visual knowledge into hierarchically related levels of abstraction, each level should also be subdivided into short-term memory (STM) and long-term memory (LTM); these are also depicted in Figure 2. Consequently, a model of a specific image can be viewed as a set of instantiations of stored general concepts which are relevant to understanding the image. The information that is specific to a particular image will be stored as a set of instantiations in STM, while the general knowledge about the world (which the system has been given prior to interpreting a given image) will be stored as classes in LTM.

Allen R. Hanson and Edward M. Riseman

It is important to distinguish between what is known about cars -- the fact that they have four wheels, for example -- and the appearance of a particular car in which only two of these wheels are visible in the image. Each of the two regions would be instantiated as a member of the class of wheels and general knowledge from the car class in LTM would indicate that two more wheels are probably present. There is further information in the image (occlusion cues) and in LTM (the 3D spatial relations between the parts of car) which can be used to verify that the absence of two wheels in the image is consistent with our stored knowledge of cars.

One point of potential confusion in the discussion to follow is the distinction between a physical object (surface, volume,...) in the world and the representation of that object (surface, volume,...) in short- and long-term memory. In most cases, the context of the discussion should make the intended meaning clear. Wherever necessary, we will distinguish between the physical object (or scene, volume, surface), the representation of that particular object, and the representation of that object class.

Finally, it should be understood that both the range of knowledge in LTM and the low-level system's ability to extract from an image the attributes stored in LTM will delimit the range of the interpretation process. If color attributes do not appear in LTM or if they cannot be extracted from the sensory data, then color cannot be used in the interpretation process. If LTM does not contain the decomposition of car into its parts, then the interpretation process will only be able to use the attributes of car as a whole.

II.3 The Implementation of Declarative Knowledge

We represent declarative knowledge as a directed graph in the classic style of semantic networks [QUI68,SIM73,FAH75,HEN75,RUM75,WOO75]. Nodes represent primitive entities (objects, concepts, situations, etc.) and labelled arcs represent relationships between them. Although each arc is directed, this does not imply that it can only be traversed in a single direction. The directionality of edges is for increased semantic power and is not meant to imply a strict one-way access in the pointer structure. This directed graph is partitioned into the different levels of abstraction, so that it is actually a collection of directed graphs, each residing on a distinct labelled plane, with labelled directed arcs between planes. Each level of abstraction is further subdivided into two planes, one for image-specific entities in STM and the other for general class knowledge in LTM. This structure has been implemented in GRASPER [LOW78], a graph processing language (implemented in LISP), and is an extension of the work of [FRI69,PRA71].

Arcs between levels relate concepts at a given level to the concepts on planes in neighboring higher and lower levels; they are organized in terms of AND/OR relationships. Thus, arcs leading up from an object node can be followed to nodes at the schema level, representing those schemas in which the object participates, and arcs leading down can be followed to volume and surface nodes indicating

the spatial occupancy or 3D shape of the object; the same is true for nodes on the object class plane where prototypical information about a class of objects is stored.

Arcs between the STM and LTM planes at the same level are instantiations of general classes for image-specific elements. For example, an instantiation of a green car could be represented by an image-specific node, say OB-38, with arcs to the car class node and to the green class node in LTM. In addition, each node at any level can have a list of properties and values associated with it. These will be very useful for matching image features to class descriptions, as in the case of matching region attributes with object class attributes. Further discussion of this representation appears in [WIL77].[1]

Finally arcs and nodes in long-term memory carry information about the coarse likelihoods of concepts and relationships [YAK73,DUD76]. Each node will have an a priori estimate of its likelihood and each arc will have a conditional probability attached to it.[2] This will provide useful control information for ordering alternative hypotheses, and allows belief in hypotheses to be represented. For example a cylinder CAN-PROJECT-AS a rectangle with a very low probability because there is a very restricted set of views from which this can take place; a rectangular solid will have rectangular planar surfaces which CAN-PROJECT-AS regions whose 2D shape is rectangular with some probability, or trapezoidal with higher probability. It is obvious that these estimates will be quite heuristic, but they do provide relative weights on paths upward and downward where we feel there is justification to prefer some paths.

II.4 An Example of a Partial Model

Figure 2 is an example of a partially developed model. Region RG-68 has been recognized as having the color GREEN, while region RG-35 has been recognized as an instance of the shape TRAPEZOID. On the STM side RG-68 has been identified as an object OB-1 which is an instance of the object class GRASS, and plays the role of a schema part in schema SC-1 which is an instance of the class of schemas called HOUSE-SCENE. The remainder of this example should be obvious.

Note that Figure 2 is just a rough sketch of the network. The actual representation is developed more carefully, since there would be an exclusive-OR on the CAN-PROJECT-AS relationship in this example. Also there are various part-whole and subclass-superclass relationships on the arcs [WIL77]; for example a rectangular planar surface is just one part bounding the rectangular solid and 5 other surfaces must be defined. And finally the system must know that GREEN is a type of COLOR;

_____

[1]The development of the knowledge structure is part of the ongoing work of John Lowrance of the COINS Department, University of Massachusetts

[2]Note that if necessary a procedure for analyzing a given situation could be associated with an arc or node if a number is not sufficient to represent the likelihoods of the alternatives.

this can be represented either with an intra-planar LTM arc between COLOR and GREEN, or else it could be attached implicitly as (COLOR GREEN) on the property-value list associated with GRASS. However, there are still serious difficulties in recognizing a distribution of the input data as the color "green", which is a rather fuzzily defined term. We bypass the symbolic naming of color and texture by storing distributions of spectral features for objects and comparing them with the distributions of regions in the image. There is not room to discuss further the details of all these problems. However, the part-whole relationships at the schema and object levels will be expanded on in Section VI.

This highly structured form of declarative knowledge forces the incomplete development of a specific model to be readily apparent. A node which does not have expected arcs to levels above and below may be a portion of the model which is not fully developed. Examples of incomplete portions of a model include a region not explained as a surface (i.e., a region node of STM without at least one arc from a surface node in STM), a surface not explained as (part of) an object, and a surface not explained as a region. Of course, most human perception seems to be similarly incomplete in the sense that not all areas of an image can be, or need be, interpreted; only those that are necessary to achieve the current goals of the perceptual system need be interpreted.

III. Knowledge as Processes

Model-building is viewed as the process by which image specific entities in STM, at all levels of abstraction, are constructed and related to general entities on the LTM side of the hierarchy. At any instant during model-building, the current set of hypotheses about the image is represented in STM as a collection of nodes and arcs dispersed through the different levels of abstraction. This set of hypotheses is a partial model and includes not only inter-planar and intra-planar arcs in STM, but intra-level arcs from STM to LTM as well. Partial models are expanded incrementally by adding hypotheses (nodes and arcs) to the current set. These hypotheses result in the creation of arcs between two or more levels of STM, and/or between the STM and LTM planes at the same level. This section discusses some of the processes which form these hypotheses, while the next section discusses ways in which they can be applied as part of a comprehensive model-building process.

III.1 Independence and Interaction of Modular Knowledge Sources

The levels of abstraction and the decision to construct models incrementally (see next section) provides a structure which leads directly to the decomposition of the active processes. To the degree that processes -- knowledge sources -- can be defined to operate upon information at one level and produce hypotheses at another level, the levels of representation selected provide the input-output relationships required of potential model-building processes.

If no process can be defined to transform data from the representation at one level to the representation at the next level, there are several possible implications. One possibility is that an intermediate level of data description is absent; if it were present, several different processes could cooperate in performing the task, some forming hypotheses at the new level while others operate on that new level to form hypotheses at other levels. A second possibility is that there is not sufficient information for any process to be constructed which operates on a given level alone and that it must be a function of several levels simultaneously; this can be handled in our structure and some KSs will use input from several levels. A third possibility is that the levels of representation are organized along insufficient or incorrect dimensions.

During our initial definition of the model-construction processes in VISIONS, the sufficiency of our levels of pattern description for processing by independent knowledge sources is being tested. In most cases it appears that the patterns of information at one level do bear clear relationships to the patterns at other levels. Often a KS can be defined to operate independently, using its own set of cues and analyses of the available data in order to focus upon, generate, and/or verify hypotheses. A region may represent (a part of) a surface and cues derived from shading or from 2D shape, when they are present, provide important clues about the type and orientation of the surface. The boundary between a pair of regions can provide spatial information about the occlusion of surfaces and can be used to determine which surface is nearer the viewer. The size of a volume can provide hypotheses about the identity of an object. The identities of objects and the relationships between them, such as a car on a horizontal surface with two parallel bars down the middle of the surface, provide hypotheses about the type of scene present, in this case a road scene.

Before more complex approaches to KS development will be attempted, the efficacy of the modular decomposition of processes operating on a small subset of levels will be explored. In order to achieve the desired reduction in complexity, it is quite important that the choice of levels decompose the model-building processes into subprocesses. To the degree that each KS can be implemented more or less independently, they can be developed and evaluated separately. If the assumptions made concerning the structure of the problem space are correct, the approach will help to clarify the component parts of the model-building process. The implementation of a KS will be unrestricted except that it should execute independently of all other KSs, although it certainly will operate upon the output of some KSs and provide the source of input to other KSs.

III.2 Bottom-Up and Top-Down Formation of Hypotheses

The overview in Section I.2 described bottom-up and top-down processing, but this dichotomy is not quite as clear as one might expect. Bottom-up processing is data-directed based upon the analysis of the particular image, while top-down processing is considered to be knowledge-directed (or goal-directed) based upon prior knowledge stored in LTM. It is clear that the fitting of shapes to regions, or the examination of region adjacency for occlusion cues, are both bottom-up (see Figure 3). The prediction of a garage on the basis of an instantiation of the house-scene schema is an example of top-down analysis. However, the distinction blurs to some extent when region attributes extracted from the image are compared to stored attributes of object classes in LTM, since both types of information are involved; nevertheless, attribute matching of regions and object classes is usually thought of as a bottom-up process.

The confusion is most evident when the declarative knowledge paths of symbolic labels in LTM are considered. Figure 2 showed examples of relationships between levels via symbolically labelled nodes. Each node at one level has an arc from (to) a node at a higher level if the nodes have a part/whole relationship (e.g., straight line and rectangle, or rectangular solid and house), subclass/superclass relationship (e.g., house and building), or special relationships such as shape relationships (e.g., rectangular surface CAN-PROJECT-AS trapezoid). Once a region node in STM is instantiated, say with a symbolic label to the class of shapes, then a set of surfaces/volumes/objects are accessible via these paths of declarative information. In order to avoid this confusion, paths will be considered to be bottom-up or top-down depending on whether the hypothesis is formed from information stored at lower or higher levels relative to the hypothesis, recognizing that hybrid processes are also possible.

It is also worth emphasizing that some of the knowledge source mechanisms of Figure 3 are based on active processes which perform non-trivial computation while forming hypotheses. However, paths based on symbolic labels are basically declarative in nature and a relatively simple process is required to access alternative hypotheses and order them for consideration. A node instantiated in STM by whatever means is then available to be operated on by any of the defined mechanisms.

Clearly, the range of processing described in Figure 3 can be quite complex. We are not in a position to discuss results obtained by bringing all of these KSs together. They are in various stages of implementation at various levels of sophistication. If they were not being developed independently, the problems would appear insurmountable. However, each KS is being developed separately, tested in the system, and then refined. As it is added into the system, the clearly defined discrete levels of representation will allow the full system to come into being incrementally. The quality of the KSs and the degree to which the KSs are redundant will determine the effectiveness of the system.

Space does not permit a complete discussion of each of the KSs. Therefore, in some of the following sections of the paper, we will provide only a brief description of several, and then sketch a simple example of the type of cooperation between processes that is being incorporated.

III.3 Matching of Attributes: Object Hypothesis and Verification

The variability in the spectral features of color and texture is too great to provide a high degree of reliability in the labelling of objects. The lighting, distance, perspective viewpoint, distortions in the photographic and digitization processes, and the inherent variability in the physical characteristics of a class of objects affect our ability to form prototypes for each object in some feature space. Given that such problems are unavoidable, an approach that has computational advantages for directing analysis in productive directions is to divide the problem into two stages: object hypothesization and object verification. The goal of forming object hypotheses is to determine plausible alternative object identities for a given region such that the probability that the correct identity is included in the set is high. The goal of object verification is to examine a small set of alternative hypotheses, while weighting more heavily those features which provide the best discrimination between the hypotheses [TEN73,HAN76c]. It should also be possible for the verification process to be invoked with hypotheses formed from other stages of the model-building system.

The comparison of color and texture features requires knowledge of the typical patterns exhibited by objects. In order to form an initial knowledge base that is representative of some of the general classes of objects that the system must recognize, we have formed a data base of approximately 25 outdoor scenes.[1] Approximately 60 features have been extracted for 77 samples of trees, shrubs, sky, grass, roads, etc., across the images; the number of samples must be greatly expanded in the future. These features are identical to the features which are extracted from the segmented regions of an unknown image under analysis. This is a rather massive amount of information which must be analyzed in many different ways. It has turned out to be extremely useful to use the relational data base facility [KON77] implemented in ALISP [KON75], the UMass version of LISP. This is an effective tool for adding, deleting, and restructuring the different features which are labelled with image name and the region from which they were extracted. Information can be indexed by image, region, object class, and/or feature subset to facilitate testing of the utility of the features.

The feature set includes raw RGB (red, green, and blue) data, YIQ (color TV standard) [KEN77], intensity, edge/unit area [ROS71], number of extremum/unit area [CAR77], moments around orientation-dependent adjacency matrices [HAR73], spatial

---

[1]This data base consists of about 8 outdoor scenes kindly supplied by R. Reddy at Carnegie-Mellon University, while the remainder are new images selected by our group and digitized at the University of Southern California.

A Computer System for Interpreting Scenes   311

features such as centroid and the coordinates of
the enclosing rectangle in X and Y dimensions, etc.
Many of these features are initially extracted as a
histogram of feature values, but typically we are
using scalar values of the mean (μ) and the variance
(σ^2) as representative parameters of these distributions. Thus, a scalar feature f_i may be a μ_i or a
σ_i, but to avoid confusion in what follows it will
be referred to as f_i. The problem, now, is that
not only is there variation, for example, between
samples of tree within one image, but even greater
variation across different images. These variations are rather unpredictable and we do not believe
it is reasonable to utilize a theoretical statistical model of this information which requires any
assumptions about the data until a very large image
data base is formed.

In light of these problems, a strategy which
is flexible with respect to the expected variability
has been adopted [WIL78]. For <u>each feature f_i of
each object O_j</u>, there is a range of possible feature
values X_{ij}. We have formed a template which summarizes the information in the distribution of the
means of the training set of samples of O_j. Note
that <u>each</u> sample that is used has a μ which has been
computed across the set of pixels from the image
sample of an object. The template shown in Figure
4 has the minimum and maximum μ among the samples
for an object, and then a μ_μ and a σ_μ across the
samples; i.e., the mean of the means and the
variance of the means. This template will serve in
place of the likelihood $P(f_i|O_j)P(O_j)$ derived
from Bayesian decision theory, and will not be as
prone to error when the number of samples in the
training set for O_j is small. Our motivation is to
move to the most global level of feature information while retaining information on the image-to-
image variation.

The heuristic process of matching unknown
region R_k with known object O_j will use the template of each feature f_i to determine the contribution C_{ij} of that feature to a linear decision
function $\sum_i C_{ij}$. The contribution of a feature will
be largest (a value of 1) if the mean of R_k is
within distance σ_μ of μ_μ of O_j; otherwise the
response is scaled down linearly out to zero at
MIN_μ and MAX_μ; there is a negative contribution
of -1 for the feature if it falls outside the min-
max range because no sample of O_j has been observed
outside that range. It is not difficult to extend
the template and matching process to particular
pairs of good features by capturing information
about the way they covary, but we have not yet
needed to do so.

The next important aspect in developing this
approach is to weight the contribution of each
feature in matching object O_j on the basis of its
effectiveness in discriminating O_j from the rest
of the object classes. This will give a weighted
linear discriminant function $\sum_i W_{ij}C_{ij}$ for each O_j.
If a particular feature returns a similar value for
many object classes, it is not useful for object
hypothesis. For some feature if the distribution
of the means of the samples for O_j and O_k overlap,
then this feature will not be useful in discriminating between O_j and O_k; e.g., the color of a region
will not be effective in separating trees from

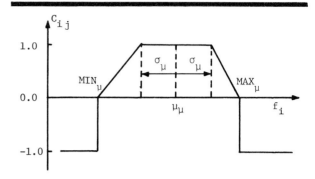

Figure 4. Matching of region attributes with feature templates stored with each object. The value
X_i of feature f_i will be used to compute the contribution $C_{ij}(X_i)$ to the discriminant function for
the hypothesis of object O_j. For each object O_j
the information stored about f_i will be extracted
from the distribution of the means μ from the
various samples in the training set of O_j. This
includes the mean of the sample means (μ_μ), the
variance of the sample means (σ^2_μ), and the minimum
and maximum of the sample means. C_{ij} will be the
contribution of feature f_i in matching μ of the
region under consideration. A set of W_{ij} will be
computed as a measure of the ability of f_i to
discriminate O_j from other objects, forming a
linear decision function $\sum_j W_{ij}C_{ij}$ for each O_j.

shrubs (although it could be effective for discriminating the foliage superclass, if present,
from other classes). This means that the importance of features will change in ways that cannot
be predicted as the system moves from hypothesis
to verification. The weights for hypotheses among
the whole set of objects can be precomputed. However, the proper weight for a feature will change
when the set of hypotheses under consideration
changes; the system must have the ability to change
the weighting of features dynamically, particularly
in the object verification stage when a small
number of hypotheses is present. Thus, the amount
of computation involved must not be exorbitant.

Our first attempt at forming a weight W_{ij} for
each f_i of O_j involves the ratio of the number of
other object samples ($O_t \neq O_j$) which fall inside to
the number that fall outside the range $[\mu_\mu-\sigma_\mu,$
$\mu_\mu+\sigma_\mu]$. Another choice is to intersect the interval at one standard deviation around the means of
object classes. Those features of O_j whose range
overlaps other classes little will be weighted more
for discrimination.

A final point that is noteworthy (and somewhat
distressing) concerns the limitations of spectral
data. While we have good information for identifying sky, trees, shrubs, grass, roads, sidewalks,
telephone poles, and people's skin, we cannot rely
on color and texture for shirts, cars, houses,
windows, doors, and in general most man-made
objects. Some of these objects have distinctive
shapes while others really are identifiable only in
context. The full impact of these problems and the
addition of heuristic knowledge to handle particular cases is a subject currently under examination.

III.4 Representation of 3D Surfaces and Volumes

In order to understand the three-dimensional world we will need to store information about the 3D space filled by objects and the 3D relationships between (parts of) objects in scenes. All such information will be stored in LTM at the schema level for reasons discussed in Section VI. We will briefly describe several representations, and refer the reader to [YOR78a] for more detail.

Most objects in the world are not symmetric in all physical dimensions, and consequently there are definable axes by which they can be oriented. The lack of unique natural axes for objects such as a sphere or cube are unusual in this respect. Therefore, we will choose an axis-based description of objects, which thereby allows the relative orientation of parts to be compactly specified and manipulated [MAR76a]. Given an axis, simple volumes can be described by sweeping a cross-section down an axis to form a "generalized cylinder" [BIN71,

AGI72,NEV74,MAR76a]. The axis can be specified to be any curve in 3D space, the planar cross section can be of any shape, and the cross section can be defined to vary down the length of the axis. However, the representation is often restricted to an unvarying (often circular) cross section with a straight line for an axis as shown in Figure 5(a).

One of the problems with this representation is that it does not permit surface descriptions to be accessed with the flexibility available for accessing volume descriptions. Note that surfaces and volumes have a dual relationship analogous to regions and boundaries. The orientation, shape, and spatial relationships of surfaces play a key role in recognizing the projection of volumes and objects as regions. Another problem with this representation is that it is difficult to describe local variations (distortions) of a surface because a description of the variations must be represented as a function across the length of the axis.

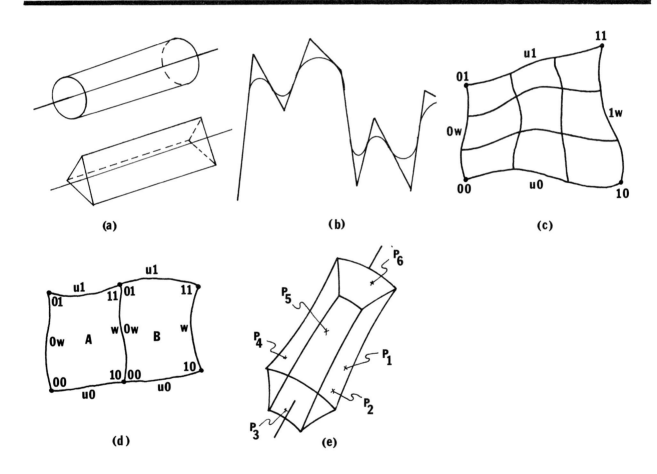

(a)   (b)   (c)

(d)   (e)

Figure 5. The Three-Dimensional Representation of Shape. (a) The generalized cylinder representation. (b) Cubic B-splines can smoothly fit a polynomial through a set of points in 2-space or 3-space. (c) A Coons' surface patch P(u,w), where u and w are parameterized on the interval [0,1], employs four B-splines P(0,w), P(1,w), P(u,0), P(u,1) to delimit the surface patch boundary; blending functions which are also B-splines interpolate between opposite sides of the surface patch. (d) Two adjacent surface patches A and B can be smoothly joined at a common boundary if the blending functions are constrained properly. (e) Six surface patches can define the shape of a volume around an axis which is used to relate the spatial orientations of such volumes.

Consequently, we are employing techniques from functional approximation and computer-aided design called B-splines [COO74,GOR74] and Coons' surface patches [COO67,74] to form compact descriptions of the surfaces and volumes of irregular objects. Briefly, cubic splines allow a set of points (in 3-space) to be smoothly fitted with a unique curve which is a cubic polynomial on each interval (Figure 5(b)). Proper use of a special type of spline, namely B-splines, allows changes in any interval between a pair of these points to be isolated to that interval and not affect the neighboring intervals. As shown in Figure 5(c), we will define a surface patch $P(u,w)$, where u and w are parameters on the interval $[0,1]$, by using four B-splines $P(0,w)$, $P(1,w)$, $P(u,0)$, $P(u,1)$ to delimit the surface patch boundary. Blending functions (which can also be B-splines) can be used to interpolate between opposite sides of the surface patch. Two adjacent surface patches A and B can then be defined with a common boundary as in Figure 5(d). These surface patches can then be smoothly joined if the first and second derivatives of the blending function at the common boundary are constrained to be equal. Each surface patch can be locally deformed by appropriate choice of the blending functions without distortion of the adjacent patch, and without disturbing the smooth join of the patches.

Let us summarize the surface and volume representations that are now available:
1) an axis with simple pre-defined shapes as cross-sections sweep out volumes;
2) an axis with closed B-splines defining the cross-sections sweep out volumes; and
3) six surface patches spatially related to an axis define volumes as in Figure 5(e); each patch can be described in its own local coordinate system (a point chosen as an origin) and cubic B-splines can be used as the surface boundary and blending functions.

All of these representations are axis-based descriptions where each primitive component is stored in a local coordinate frame of reference. In general these representations require a relatively small number of points and therefore allow compact storage; for example the description in Figure 5(e) would only require about 64 points, if the blending functions are assumed to be stored in a common library which is used by a spatial processor. Thus, rotation of these figures via standard computer graphics techniques is relatively inexpensive.

The third representation allows access to both surface and volume representations. We have not yet had sufficient experience in using the different representations, and therefore will not comment on details for matching of regions to particular views. However, the goals of such processing are to use 2D region shapes as shown in Figure 2 (or some of the other KSs) to access possible object identities for a region. This would be facilitated by storage of standard 2D views corresponding to projections of the 3D representation. The mechanisms for manipulating the 3D description of an object to match 2D projections against 2D regions is the subject of ongoing research.[1]

III.5 An Example of KS Interaction

In addition to the spectral attribute matching process, we are implementing three major types of processing which lead to hypothesis formation at the region, surface, volume, object, and schema levels. These are hypotheses based on: (i) curve fitting of region boundaries and contours [HAN78 in this volume,YOR78b]; (ii) surface and volume constructions using 2D shape descriptions, results of perspective, shadow, and occlusion analyses, and additional semantic information; and (iii) manipulation of stored 3D descriptions of objects.[1] Several of these processes, or portions of them, are discussed in other sections of this paper or in the companion paper. It is our contention that although much of the interpretive power of a system is embodied in the active model construction processes, there is an important component captured in the redundancy of information obtainable from disparate sources. The highly idealized example which follows illustrates the kinds of hypotheses which are possible and exemplifies typical KS interactions that are expected.

Consider the 2D image of a scene shown in Figure 6. Even with all color, texture, and lighting information removed from the image, one still is able to identify several objects. However, what is of primary importance to the discussion at hand is the rich set of cues that allow a volume-surface plan of three-dimensional space to be constructed without access to the identity of objects. The key point is that three-dimensional space can be constrained prior to object recognition. Of course much additional information will be made available by accessing stored descriptions of objects and by further constraining 3D space via top-down processing and checks for consistency of the resulting hypotheses. However, for the moment we will just examine a few of the hypotheses which can be formed at the surface and volume levels by analyzing data at the RSV levels.

The vertex cues for polyhedral objects have been studied extensively [GUZ68,CLO71,HUF71,DUD73, WAL75,SHA77]. Of the five building vertices where the visible portions of planar surfaces meet in the 2D image, in Figure 6 we have distinguished only E_1, E_2, and E_5. There are four more vertices, where the right tree occludes the building, that provide further cues of occlusion. Boundary dominance seems to be a striking visual cue. At the points E_3 and E_4, for example, the heuristic associated with boundary dominance at polyhedral T-junctions can be generalized to deal with nonplanar surfaces. Consider the segments S_1, S_2, and S_3 which meet at E_3. The similarity of the shape properties of segments S_2 and S_3 provide a hypothesis that R_1 occludes R_2.

A rather different cue is available from a perspective analysis of the segments bounding regions R_3 and R_4, which represent two of the surfaces of the building. The nearly parallel sides of the segment pairs S_4-S_5 and S_6-S_7 provide an interesting cue for focussing attention on this area. A supporting cue is that there are a pair of vertical parallel boundaries in this area. If the

---

[1]This research, currently in progress, is being performed by B. York, COINS Department, University of Massachusetts.

Allen R. Hanson and Edward M. Riseman

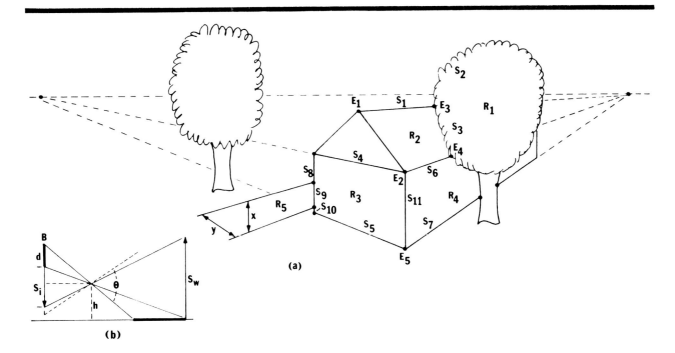

(a)

(b)

Figure 6. Bottom-Up Cues from Shape, Perspective, and Occlusion Interaction. (a) By occlusion analysis the vertices E_3 and E_4 provide information about the depth of the surface associated with R_1 relative to the surfaces associated with R_2 and R_4. Shape analysis allows R_3 and R_4 to be hypothesized as rectangular planar surfaces, which then allow perspective analysis to determine vanishing points and the horizon line. Perspective and shape analysis employ projective geometry to compute the following. With assumptions concerning the height, angle (relative to the ground plane), and focal length of the camera, as well as levelness of the ground plane, then the distance of E_5 from the bottom of the image (refer to 6b) allows its physical 3D distance to be computed. This allows the height of S_{11} in the physical world to be computed from its length in the image, under the assumption that S_{11} represents a line (surface boundary) perpendicular to the ground plane. The analysis proceeds without knowledge of the object identities of the regions. (b) Segment S_w in the physical world projects as segment S_i in the image. The distance from the camera of a point in the ground plane is determined by the distance d from the bottom of the image B.

system assumes that R_3 and R_4 are planar surfaces with parallel sides, the two vanishing points can fix the horizon line. Once the horizon is determined, additional cues are sometimes available (although not in this case) to provide hypotheses about whether the ground plane is level.

The near parallel lines to the left side of the image lead to two alternative hypotheses, although several assumptions are necessary to generate them. The first assumption is that the pair of line segments are parallel in the 3D world and that they bound a planar surface. Two further alternative assumptions are that this surface lies either: a) perpendicular to the ground plane (actually parallel to the gravitational vertical), or b) in the ground plane. In the first case region R_5 is "wall" and distance X represents the projection of its actual height onto the image; in the latter case R_5 is "road" and distance Y is the projection of its actual width onto the image. The objects do not have to be identified in order to determine the placement of this planar surface in the system's surface-volume model of 3D space.

Finally, an interesting interaction between the shape KS and the perspective KS is available at

region R_3. The 2D shape analysis determines that R_3 is trapezoidal. Information is available in LTM that rectangular planar surfaces often project as trapezoids. Thus, it can make available to the perspective KS the assumption that S_{12} (a new segment formed from S_8, S_9, and S_{10}) and S_{11} are parallel, have equal length, and lie in a planar surface. We utilize knowledge of the focal length, height, and orientation of the camera,[1] and the additional assumption that the ground is level; then the orientation of the surface relative to the camera can be computed using relatively simple principles of projective geometry [DUD73]. If the vertex E_5 is assumed to be the projection of a point in the ground plane (i.e., R_3 represents a surface rooted to the ground plane), then the height of vertex E_5 from the bottom of the image allows the distance of the house from the camera to be computed; the trigonometry is sketched in Figure 6(b). If a house is hypothesized, a verification of this analysis is available by checking that the

---

[1] As default values we assume that the height of the camera is 5'6" and the orientation is horizontal. These can be modified once a known physical size is detected in the image.

height of this surface (via S_{11}) is roughly within the range of the height of one story of a house. This semantic information about houses is available in LTM. This is just one example of KS interaction. Thus, occlusion, shape, perspective, and projective geometry can all be used to determine the position of the house in a surface-volume plan of 3D space.

IV. Search and the Model Search Space

The organization of our system leads quite naturally to the notion of model formation as the sequential incremental expansion of a partial model. Given a partial model and a strategy for expanding it (see Section V), there will be many places where the model could be expanded. At each of these points a subset of the available KSs will undoubtedly be applicable and each KS might produce several competing hypotheses which are promising and worth following. Thus, there is a large implicit search space of partial models which can be generated, only a small subset of which will be consistent with each other and adequately "explain" the image. From this point of view, the process of model construction decomposes into two highly related subproblems -- control strategy and representation of a search space of competing partial models.

Since the size of the model search space is enormous, one cannot expect to explore even a small fraction of possible interpretations. On one hand biological systems seem to plunge effortlessly and quickly down correct paths, probably due to a combination of factors which include the use of constraints available from the many sources of cues which somehow operate in parallel.[1] On the other hand we are quite sure (unfortunately) that alternative hypotheses have to be considered because KSs will be unreliable, and at other times the best local hypothesis does not fit the global set of hypotheses.

In response to this problem, several speech recognition systems [ERM75,LOW76,WOO77] tried to explore as many paths as computational costs permitted using various strategies to explore promising paths, while leaving unpromising paths unexplored. The number of paths that must be examined is certainly a function of the quality and reliability of the KSs that are employed, just as the amount of search necessary in game playing programs is a function of the quality of the heuristic evaluation function [NIL71]. However, we do not have a single evaluation function, but rather a number of KSs, and the manner in which the hypotheses from various sources is brought together is a crucial factor in selecting and constraining the search paths.

Rather than seek to explore many paths, our initial research methodology has been to develop a tool whose use will allow insights into the ways of bringing the diverse sources of knowledge together. While some form of parallel interaction of various constraints ultimately appears to be desirable, we have committed ourselves to the sequential

---

[1]Note that even biological systems admit ambiguous and sometimes incorrect interpretations in cases where competition between alternative explanations of data cannot be resolved [ESC71,GRE66].

development of partial models. The goal will be the examination and an understanding of a few paths in the search space in an attempt to plunge down a correct interpretation path. Examination of the history of search and the history of applied processes should provide valuable insights into where and why incorrect decisions were made. Consequently, we are interested in developing a general representation for storing alternative search paths in a tree of partial models even though our strategies will seek to move down few paths.

VI.1 Approaches to Search

Let us discuss some alternative ways in which related partial models can be represented for some type of search process. At one extreme a complete, separate structure could be built for each partial model generated during the search. This leads to gross space inefficiency when one considers that each partial model varies from its parent only by some small amount, and to gross time inefficiency when attempting to determine similarities or differences among alternative models. This approach is totally unacceptable.

At the other extreme only the current partial model is saved, and updates are made to this partial model. Note that this could involve destroying old data, e.g., if later in the search one hypothesis is replaced by an alternative hypothesis. This can be implemented as a single directed graph which contains all alternative partial models; Figure 7(a) portrays a simple example. Essentially this is the "blackboard" approach of the HEARSAY-II speech understanding system [ERM75]. In some respects this is a very useful representation because it allows all competing or consistent submodels to be directly available. If a better alternative to a hypothesis is developed later, it can just be added. This is equivalent to having, at any moment in time, a network containing the relationships between the entities in the tip nodes of a partial model search tree. Its primary disadvantage is that the history of the model development is not available.

An alternative technique for managing the history of search is provided in the "contexts" of the CONNIVER programming language [McD74]. Here, a tree of contexts is formed during the search. This design was in response to the problems encountered using automatic backtracking as the control mechanism in PLANNER [HEW68]. At any moment during processing, a context can be "pushed" so that any further changes in the stored environment could be undone at the user's discretion by a "pop" context command. In addition, other contexts can be examined while the system is bound to a given context. This allows earlier contexts to be examined while deciding what to do in the current context. This approach provides the flexibility necessary to reconsider previous decisions, to determine why they were made, as well as examining the implications resulting from a change to an earlier hypothesis or set of hypotheses. In particular, hypotheses subsequent to the change(s) which do not depend on them may be retained without contradiction; this point is elaborated on in the next section. Figure 7(b) sketches this approach

Allen R. Hanson and Edward M. Riseman

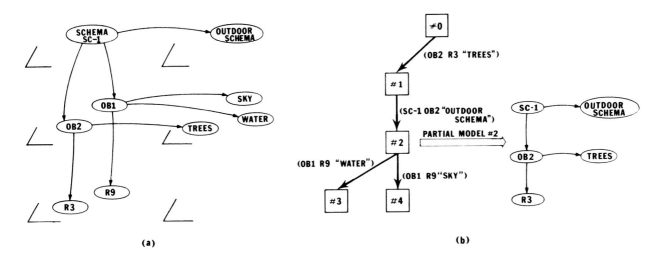

Figure 7. Alternative Representations of Models during Search. For simplicity note that Schema-Parts have not been specified. (a) In the blackboard approach of HEARSAY-II [ERM75], all partial models are stored in a single network, e.g., two partial models involving different hypotheses for OB1 are simultaneously represented. This provides the advantage of easy access to competing partial models, but has the disadvantage of not maintaining the history of the development of each partial model. (b) In the VISIONS approach, contexts [McD74] are used to store each partial model in the sequential model-building process. This tree of partial models has the advantage of maintaining the search space history as both an interactive debugging tool and for control decisions, but it has the disadvantage of making access to competing models more difficult.

to search. Any node in the search tree (other than the root node which contains the initial state -- RSV and all of LTM) explicitly contains only those items which differ between it and its parent. Each node implicitly contains the initial state as well as all changes along the path leading to that node from the root.

These two representations have different advantages. While history is maintained by using context packets, linkages between "brother" paths emanating from some higher level node are not provided without additional modifications. Thus, the system does not have easy access between competing models, nor does it have easy access to compatible submodels in different parts of the search tree. In addition, user control of backtracking has turned out to be a non-trivial task [FAH74].

For the initial design of VISIONS we have chosen the context representation of the search space because of the availability of the history of decisions. This allows interactive examination of search paths by the human user during system development. However, as the problems of model-building are explored further, we may provide some form of scratch space for collapsing the tree (as in HEARSAY) into a network of parallel competing models, or incorporate pointers between relevant contexts that are not in the same partial model path.

IV.2 History of Search and Error Recovery

Error recovery and backtracking are important aspects of search, particularly when the hypothesis generators are potentially unreliable. They have serious implications relating to the feasibility of systems

which have large computational overhead [WIL77].

The first problem has to do with error detection: how does the system know an error (or errors) has occurred and how does the system begin to isolate candidates for those hypotheses which might be in error? A partial solution to this problem is to maintain a model confidence measure based on confidences of individual hypotheses and their semantic relationships to each other. Presumably, as a model is developed, the confidence of the model should increase (if it is a correct model) as more and more hypotheses are developed and expected semantic relationships between them are satisfied. A decrease in the confidence of the model signals the possibility of an erroneous hypothesis. However, it is important to realize that there is no guarantee that it was the last hypothesis which was in error. It could just as easily have been an earlier hypothesis which was erroneous and which only now is causing the contradiction. The problem of reliable error detection has not been adequately explored in the context of image understanding systems and deserves much more attention.

Assuming errors are detectable and their cause determinable, then the second problem relates to the correction of the error (or errors). Is the error correctable without backtracking? If provision is made to store in the search space the interdependencies of sequential decisions, then it would be possible to tell by inspection if a previous erroneous instantiation could have propagated other instantiations. If it did not, then such an error could be corrected by "un-doing" the error rather than backtracking and regenerating the search tree from the point of error down. Even if it did propagate errors, those instantiations which were not directly or indirectly dependent upon the error are acceptable without redoing the computation.

The final problem has to do with the efficiency of error correction if backtracking is necessary. Is the process of backtracking easy and efficient? When returning to the state where an error occurred, how much computation is going to be redundant? During the generation of alternative hypotheses, the KSs applied may have required a large amount of computation. If this computation is not to be repeated, then the alternatives must be saved for later use. This is not too difficult -- the system must know which processes produced the results so that they will not be reapplied, while at the same time others which have not yet contributed to the analysis can be invoked. More generally, is directed backtracking possible where the analysis of the error provides information about what to work on next? This is a difficult question to answer and will be the subject of future research.

In order to deal with the problems raised, the information which must be collected and stored during sequential model building includes:
  a) the order in which the hypotheses were generated;
  b) the KS(s) responsible for generating each hypothesis;
  c) the alternative hypotheses that were sufficiently interesting to be saved, but were not followed; and
  d) the dependencies of each hypothesis; i.e., at the point of generating a hypothesis, the set of earlier hypotheses which contributed to the generation of the new one.

It may be worth a brief aside to compare the differences in our form of search with that of general problem solving. In the construction of a plan for a robot, for example, the order in which operations are carried out may be an integral part of the solution because of the problem of interdependent subgoals [SAC75]; certain operations necessary to achieve one subgoal may interfere with achieving another subgoal if the operators are applied in the wrong order. In our work, order is important only insofar as it is useful in arriving at a "solution." The solution is a set of hypotheses, with constraints between them, but there is no order inherent in the representation of a semantic interpretation of a scene.

In summary, the search space mechanisms we have described will serve two purposes. The first is that it will allow a user to interactively explore the model-building process so that we can understand the contexts in which the system makes errors. The second is that it opens the possibility that the model-builder could, ultimately, employ strategies to automatically recover from errors by examining these contexts.

V. Hierarchical Modular Control

As we have shown, the complexity of the virtually unconstrained image interpretation task necessitates the integrated application of many different processes. While the preceding sections have been concerned mainly with problem space representation and decomposition, this section focusses upon issues arising from the need for controlled application of the system resources (e.g., knowledge sources, utilization of semantic constraints, etc.) during the model-building process. It is often very difficult to anticipate some of the underlying issues prior to a system implementation and the familiarity with the problem space that the implementation provides. The penalty can be a complete redesign of the system in order to take into account unforseen problems which arise. Although major changes to a system may be unavoidable, it is possible to structure the system so that these changes are localized with minimal disturbance to the remainder of the system. This has been our approach to problems of representation and search and is also evident in the design and implementation of control strategy mechanisms. Again, we emphasize that our approach is designed to provide a tool which can be used to explore issues of control in the model construction aspect of the image understanding task.

V.1 Decomposition of Control

"Strategy" is our term for a set of mechanisms (or instructions) which examine the prevailing situation and then decide what to do next, eventually leading to some extension of the current partial model. Rather than attempt to define a single very large strategy, we have chosen to decompose it into a hierarchical set of smaller strategies. The purpose is to allow the researcher flexibility of expression and ease in making local changes, while at the same time maintaining a clear functional structure. We hope it will provide us with a better understanding of the tradeoffs between parallel/sequential, top-down/bottom-up, local/global, and distributed/centralized control mechanisms.

Our decomposition of control corresponds to the structure of the rest of the system. A strategy must determine which partial model in the model search space to expand, which level of representation (the submodel) within the model is to be selected, and which instantiated node (hypothesis) at the selected level will be expanded.

This allows the strategy at the model search space level to be decoupled from the strategy for node selection in that model. This seems to be quite reasonable since the two decisions are based on very different types of reasoning. One model search space strategy could be biased towards a depth-first strategy while another might lead to a more breadth-first search which attempts to explore a larger number of parallel paths. The strategy for focussing on a region node, on the other hand, might be based upon the size and color of the set of regions. This strategy ought to be independent of the strategy for focussing upon an object node based on an instantiated schema, etc. From the point of view of the KS processes, we are also suggesting that the strategy for applying the object-region attribute matching KS, let us say, be separated from the strategy for applying the more expensive spatial processor and occlusion analysis in the verification of the shape of an object volume.

V.2 Structure of the Control Hierarchy

Now let us describe our hierarchy of modular control (Figure 8) more carefully.[1] We have already provided arguments for the vertical decomposition according to the data acted upon: model search space, model, level, and node. In addition, we decompose control horizontally in the classic hypothesize-test paradigm into _types_ of control modules:

1) FOCUSing on an element of the task,
2) EXPANDing that element by generating new hypotheses, and
3) VERIFYing the new hypotheses.

Each control module makes strategic decisions at its level by determining which lower level control modules and/or KSs to apply. For example, the model search space expander calls: 1) a model focusser (strategy to select a partially developed model from the search space), 2) a model expander (strategy to hypothesize an incremental change to the partial model), and then 3) a model verifier (strategy to determine the correctness of the hypothesis based upon its relationship to the rest of the partial model). Figure 9 provides a dynamic view of the activity of four control units which

---

[1] These ideas were discussed in [WIL77] in a somewhat different form, but with the same general purpose in mind. Further research on these topics is currently in progress by J. Lowrance, COINS Department, University of Massachusetts.

would be executed during a typical model expansion task. The region-object attribute matcher is the KS invoked in node expansion in this example.

Notice that both Focussers and Verifiers at any level are atomic units of control because they do not call other units of control; rather they cause programs to be executed which operate on data (the model search space or the partial model) to make a decision. The program(s) which they execute, however, can be arbitrarily complex. Initially our Focus strategies are relatively simple, while Verification will vary from being absent (i.e., accept the highest ranked hypothesis) to calls to complex programs before accepting a hypothesis.

All Expanders are non-atomic units of control except at the bottom level. In order to expand the model search space (by generating a hypothesis), a model must be expanded, a level must be expanded, and finally a node must be expanded. Each action is sandwiched around the execution of a Focus program and a Verification program, but centrally involves a call to another Expander which must return some value from the bottom before it

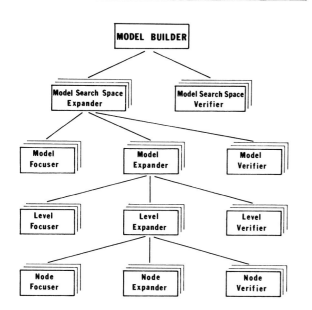

Figure 8. The Hierarchical Modular Structure of Control. The control modules are organized according to type (FOCUS, EXPAND, VERIFY) and the data acted upon (Model Search Space, Model, Level, Node). All Expanders, except the Node Expander, are non-atomic in that they call other control modules. The remainder are atomic because they call KSs to be applied in the model-building process. The functions for focussing, hypothesizing, and verifying are distinct so that commitments of resources can be specified in different model-building strategies.

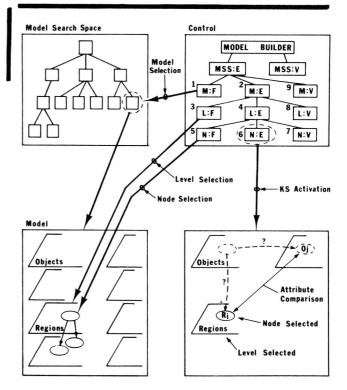

Figure 9. A Dynamic View of Control. A model Focusser is a sub-strategy to select a partial model in the search space. The level and node Focussers are distinct sub-strategies to pick a level and a node to work on. The node Expander calls in the KS which actually forms the hypotheses; the KS attribute matcher is shown in the example. The remaining control units are not shown in their execution. The selection of the level, node, and particular KS to be applied specify whether model development proceeds in a bottom-up or top-down fashion.

has completed execution. The key calls are made by the node expander and node verifier since these will involve the execution of the most reliable KS(s) that we have been able to construct.

This control structure decouples each local control module from the others except to the extent that Expanders will call a Focusser, Expander, and Verifier. We see the possibility of having libraries of control strategies and easily replacing individual modules during experimentation. This approach does impose constraints on the strategies that can be attempted and makes hybrid strategies more difficult. However, it also imposes a discipline concerning the function of control, and is an attempt to avoid entirely ad-hoc mixtures of a wide range of programs. Although we will step outside this paradigm as necessary, it appears to suit our needs in many ways. Default strategies at all control levels have been defined and are just beginning to be used, but we have not yet had sufficient experience to make substantive comments.

VI. Schemas and the Organization of Visual Information

There is a great deal of structure in our visual environment and it seems evident that such expectations are useful in processing visual information. Although our layered semantic network directly incorporates simple relationships between elements, there are larger complexes of related elements whose organization will be quite important to efficient analysis of scenes. Many of the higher order dependencies that we are interested in are a function of the three-dimensional spatial relationships between surfaces, volumes, and objects. It will be quite useful to have this information collected as a single packet of information in a standard data structure. This organized collection of information, built around a stereotyped scene, event, or object, is stored in our version of a visual schema.

Let us assume that we have stored a fairly extensive body of information about surburban house scenarios. In particular, information about a driveway to a house could include facts such as its functional purpose (to provide a path for autos), its shape and spatial extent (planar, approximately 12' wide, arbitrary length but usually less than 50' long), its spatial relationship to other entities (often leading to a garage, in the ground plane, often perpendicular to the road, etc.). The driveway information as part of the house context has a particular meaning and an expected visual appearance. It could be used to direct analysis (at the region, surface, and/or object level) of the area around a 2D region in order to verify that the region represents a roughly planar surface leading to a house. This analysis can be data-driven (bottom-up) because the hypothesis could have been formed on the basis of the visual attributes of the driveway region. On the other hand, the recognition (or hypothesis) of a house would allow a driveway to be predicted and searched for in a goal-oriented manner (top-down).

Local hypotheses emanating from attributes of individual regions or boundary segments are usually not sufficient in themselves for interpretation.

The reader can easily verify the importance of more global contextual information and semantic relationships by restricting the field of view of an image to a small local area, so that the surrounding context is not available. Only in restricted circumstances are the semantics of a scene available from local spectral and shape attributes. This implies that in many cases a representation which captures more global information is required to adequately disambiguate between locally competing hypotheses.

The full description of Minsky's frames [MIN75] involves many characteristics which appear useful, but which would be very difficult to implement. Rather we seek to define the minimal requirements of a visual frame (our schema) and gain some experience with simple structures before attempting to capture relatively esoteric information processing capabilities. It has been our recurring experience that many of the problems which appear when operating on the actual data of real scenes cannot be anticipated. When design considerations become rather elegant and yet fail to face the critical issues which appear, the effort is a pointless exercise. Our initial evaluation of the utility of simple types of schemas must necessarily involve complicated processes operating across many representations and data structures. Until we understand the reliability of the knowledge sources which are producing hypotheses, the redundancy of this information, and a range of top-down and bottom-up strategies for scene interpretation, we believe it prudent to be rather conservative in our design of schemas.

There are three types of information stored in our schemas[1] corresponding to the roles that schemas must play:
1) the parts named in a schema provide a hierarchical partitioning of the knowledge base;
2) the 3D spatial relationships of these parts provide an understanding of shape and space for object recognition and the construction of a surface/volume description; for each part there must be information about the size, the shape, number of parts contributing, etc.; and
3) rough estimates of the conditional probabilities between the presence of the schema and the presence of each part (i.e., part-whole relationships) provide control information for data-driven instantiation of a schema and top-down direction of hypothesis formation.

VI.1 An Object in a Schema -- An Object as a Schema

Schemas will be used to represent both physical objects and scenes when they are composed of a set of related parts. Our schema defines a stereotypic grouping of elements and focusses upon the relationships between elements. An object with a set of parts (e.g., a house composed of roof, wall,

---

[1]The ideas involved in the structure and control information in schemas is the work of J. Lowrance, while the use of shape in schemas is the research of B. York, both in the COINS Department at the University of Massachusetts.

window, door, etc.) requires a mode of representation similar to that of a scene with a set of objects (e.g., a road scene composed of road, car, guard rail, centerline, tree, etc.).

The naming of the schema-parts defines the semantic entities which are to be grouped under a label and also defines the predictive capabilities of the schema in top-down processing. All elements which either have a relatively high likelihood of being in the schema or are of strong semantic importance should be named. In effect, this serves to partition the major semantic level in the knowledge base -- the network of representations of objects in the world. Schemas provide the ability to hierarchically group subsets of items by defining their parts in a recursive fashion until each tip node is defined by an object class node which is not decomposed further. Thus, objects appearing in a schema may also have their own schema specifications.[1] For the tip nodes we are assuming that the primitive attributes of color, texture, and shape are a sufficient description of this object and more detailed information on its parts is unnecessary.

Let us examine more carefully the ways in which a concept can be a part of a context, and also be providing a context. Many concepts can be described at three different levels:

---

[1]The decomposition of scene-schemas into parts which are themselves scene-schemas (not objects) is currently under investigation.

a) as a symbolic entity with properties that are independent of both larger contexts and potential decompositions;
b) as a part of a schema where the associated information is relevant to the role that it plays within the schema context; and
c) as a schema itself with specification of its parts and their relationships.

As an illustration consider Figure 10, where the concept of a car is represented in three ways: as a schema, as a schema-part, and as an object. At the object level the CAR class node has properties that are independent of the contexts in which it may appear and its physical decomposition into parts. For CAR these attributes could include its overall physical size, color, price, etc. However, there will be contexts such as the Road-Scene Schema in which the concept of a car plays a role. Here, a node for CAR is created as a schema-part which can have information about cars in road scenes added to it; for example, the expected spatial relationships of cars to the scene, possible directions of movement, their relationship to stop signs, how likely their presence is in the scene, etc. Note that it is not necessary to repeat invariant properties of the CAR class node in the Road-Scene Schema class and that the same car node can be used for all the schemas in which it appears. Only additions and modifications in description that are relevant to the car in each different schema in which CAR appears will have its own schema-part node for CAR [MIN75], but all of these will point to the same CAR node at the object level. The third representation of the concept for

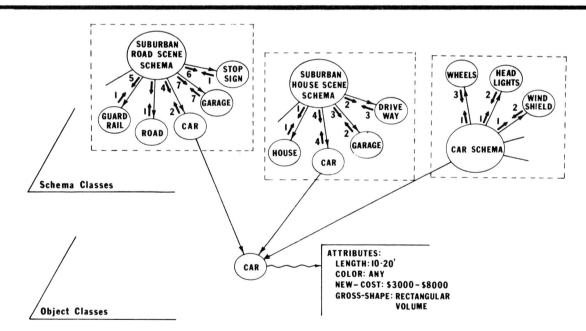

Figure 10. The Structure of Schemas. A physical object can appear as an Object, as a Schema-Part, and as a Schema. At the Object level CAR has attributes which are independent of its parts or the contexts in which cars may appear. As a Schema-Part CAR can be described as part of the Road-Scene Schema, e.g., where it will typically appear in the scene. At the Schema level the CAR-Schema describes the relationships of the parts of cars. Schemas provide control information in terms of rough conditional probabilities (as at all other levels of LTM) where ↑ ≡ P(Schema|Schema-Part) and ↓ ≡ P(Schema-Part|Schema). The probabilities are denoted on a scale of 1 to 7 where 1 denotes P(X|Y) = 1. and 7 denotes P(X|Y) = 0.

car is as a Car-Schema class, where the parts of CAR and relationships between parts of CAR are specified.

VI.2 Schemas Organize Space and Shape

The second role for schemas is to provide information for building a volume/surface description of the world depicted in the image. In order to do this it is essential to have a volume/surface representation of typical objects and scenes stored in long-term memory. For example, the features of a tree in the distance (even if the trunk and crown are visible) are not sufficient to infer the three-dimensional structure of the object. In a goal-oriented situation where this level of detail is of interest to a human, much of the spatial information must be made available from memory (stored experience) of closer views and prior interactions with trees.

In vision we face a world with dependencies between a large number of variables [FIS78], and often we attempt to approximate these dependencies with binary relationships between elements. To some extent this is compensated for in our system because n-ary relationships become available by attaching 3D representations of objects and scenes at the schema level. If a particular view of a prototypical house is assumed, then a stored 3D representation allows potentially complex relationships between a set of regions representing window, door, roof, etc. in the 2D image to be inferred. In general, a 3D shape representation of an object or scene can provide n-ary relationships between entities at all the lower levels of objects, volumes, surfaces, regions, segments, and vertices. In our first implementation of VISIONS the stored relationships at the lower levels of LTM will be restricted to either binary or AND/OR relationships. These stored static dependencies can be enriched dynamically during the processing of a schema where more complex relationships can be extracted as they are needed.

Minsky suggests that a frame system consisting of a set of 2D projections of a scene (representing typical viewpoints) might be sufficient for recognition of the scene from most viewpoints. We believe that standard 2D views will be quite useful because they provide patterns for direct matches at the region level with little computational overhead; rotations of stored 3D descriptions are avoided. Different views of a house would show a window as a rectangle or as a trapezoid. We have already described ways for accessing a 3D view via pointers in LTM given such 2D region shapes (Section II).

If a set of 2D views are to be sufficient, however, many views must be stored or else there must be means by which the system can interpolate between views. If a human has a slightly unusual perspective of a scene, it does not cause a great deal of difficulty. Looking down upon a road at a 30° angle, the volumes and surfaces of the road, cars, and telephone poles can be interpreted without ambiguity. However, the 2D regions of the projected image change shape. At a minimum these changes of shape would be necessary in order to interpolate between pairs of views. Although such

mechanisms can be quite useful, we believe this approach does not provide the desirable flexibility since the system will not really understand crucial aspects of our three-dimensional world. A human has a rough sense of the 3D form of an object; one can sketch the volume filled by an object if he has some artistic abilities and can imagine the 3D spatial extent of an object. These capabilities are not easily derived from a set of 2D views.

In addition to familiar 2D views of an object or scene, we will store 3D information about objects and scenes using the 3D shape representation described in Section III.4. This will open a range of matching strategies between the 3D representation and their expected 2D projections as regions in the image.

VI.3 Schemas Provide Control Information

The third role of a schema is to guide the instantiation of hypotheses during construction of a model. Here, the minimum information necessary involves implications between each part and the schema, i.e. the rough specification of the importance of the presence of each object to the presence of the schema, and vice versa. In addition a priori likelihoods of the schema and its parts will be useful. Some type of information of this sort appears necessary for ordering expectations based on partial models.

In Figure 10 upward and downward arrows between schemas and schema-parts have associated conditional probabilities, or weights, representing $P(\text{Schema}|\text{Schema-Part})$ and $P(\text{Schema-Part}|\text{Schema})$, respectively. Since we do not have reasonable means of statistically estimating these probabilities, we choose to form intuitive estimates on a coarse scale of values between 0 and 1. They capture to a first approximation the relative importance between particular objects and a schema. For example, the presence of a guard rail strongly implies the road scene schema (w = 1.), while the inverse implication is much weaker (w = .25), since the absence of a guard rail in a road scene is to be expected in many cases.

Of course this is a crude approximation to the dependencies between objects in a schema. However, the accurate estimations of the joint distribution of all the subsets of the objects in a road scene is not feasible. Even with this simplification, the tuning of the weights might cause difficulty, but since we only intend to use these values as rough estimates, we expect the problems to remain tractable.

VI.4 The Size and Overlap of Schemas

In our domain a driveway will not be of sufficient importance around which to organize its own context. It might be possible to store a model of the visual context around every object which is in the pool of identifiable objects. However, this could involve a great degree of redundant storage of information. Certainly a schema for the curb of a suburban street should not be necessary. Rather our schemas will initially be constructed around those entities which have significant semantic importance and will vary with

Allen R. Hanson and Edward M. Riseman

the goals of the vision system. For the moment, let us assume that the house scene and the road scene are situations which have schemas organized around them. In this case the driveway will play a secondary role in both the house-scene schema and the road-scene schema. At the object level, the node for driveway will have properties of a stereotypical driveway attached to it which are independent of the context of the driveway. This node can be used in the description of both the house-scene schema, the road-scene schema, and all larger contexts in which such a driveway may appear.

One should note the implications of developing a knowledge base in this fashion, particularly if each schema organizes a relatively small number of concept nodes. Essentially it divides our layered semantic network into overlapping partitions at the schema and object levels [HEN75]; each partition has a particular focus and with each there will be a packet of information useful for top-down and bottom-up processing, including 3D shape representations useful for matching.

One could put the road-scene and house-scene schemas together so that any investigation of a driveway would have a more complete context available in a single place. This decision appears to be poor in light of the purpose which schemas play in focussing attention upon objects which are likely to be present. The size and content of the schemas will directly affect the power and efficiency of knowledge-driven strategies. The presence of a subset of schema-parts (quite possibly a subset of one element) will predict as alternative hypotheses the remaining elements of the schema. If a schema is composed of a small number of very likely elements, then each of the few alternatives is a promising choice for further processing and this set is computationally manageable. If, on the other hand, the house scene and road scene schema are joined, gross inefficiency could result when only one of these contexts is actually present. By keeping them separate the instantiation of additional object nodes proceeds in two stages. First, the alternative schemas that are implied by the current partial model can be weighed. Then an ordering on the objects potentially present in each schema can be computed.

VII. Results

The experiments that are reported here are the very first with the system in its current form. At this point we have not yet attempted to build a model nor have we examined interesting control strategies or grappled with the difficulties of a large search space. Rather, the analysis has focussed on the quality of the information produced by individual KSs, the content and structure of long-term memory, and the combined effect of KSs in forming hypotheses at the object and schema levels. The results reported were obtained just prior to the writing of the final version of this paper. They are included to provide a sense of the status of the system and the quality of information available from preliminary versions of several of our KSs. We expect that as the result of a more complete analysis of the data, we will begin to refine the knowledge sources and the contents of LTM.

Although we attempted to avoid estimates of a priori and conditional probabilities in stages of earlier development of our system, it has proven very useful for integrating the output of the various KSs. Three KSs are reported here:
    a) region-object attribute matches,
    b) size estimates from perspective analysis,
and c) 2D shape fitting.
Each is being structured to output confidences of results in terms of a scale from -100 to +100, where a value of 0 implies no information. This allows normalization of the KSs by correlating the zero information point of each KS hypothesis (whether it be a hypothesis of a shape label or an object identity) with the a priori probability of that concept stored in LTM. Currently, our knowledge base includes 40 objects, 57 schema-parts, and 17 schemas. It is almost impossible to maintain consistency (according to Bayes rule) when the a priori and conditional probabilities in the network are subjectively estimated by a human. A method which reduces the severity of this problem and which includes some of the rigor of Bayesian decision theory is provided by the inference net approach of [DUD76]; this problem was also examined in the MYCIN system [SHO75].

(a)
                     (b)

Figure 11. House Scene. (a) Black and white intensity image of suburban house scene. (b) Segmentation produced by early histogram-based region analysis. Numbered regions are those used in the experiments described in the text.

Figure 11a is a black and white image of a suburban house, while Figure 11b is a segmentation produced by a histogram-guided region analysis [NAG77]. It should be pointed out that these segmentation results do not utilize our most recent algorithms that are described in [HAN78] in this volume.

Table I lists sample results obtained by matching attributes of objects and regions. Due to the limited statistics of the training set, and the lack of spectral invariance for many objects, the attribute matching experiments were aimed at classifying only five "target" objects: bush, grass, tree (crown), road and sky. We have listed examples of regions whose actual object identity is in the target set and several in the non-target set. Again remember that the scale is between +100 and -100 using the weighted linear sum of features as described in Section III.3.

Note that if an object, such as the house roof of region 20, does not have expected spectral attributes, it could match some other object in the target set reasonably well, in this case grass. In many cases the errors made are not unreasonable given the visual appearance of the scene; for example, the white house wall (region 21) is matched as sky due to the fact that it has virtually no discernable texture and is almost the same color as the sky. These types of errors ought to be correctable from additional sources of information, such as shape, position in the image, and relationships with surrounding regions.

Table II summarizes the results of applying the attribute matching KS on two images, the example image of Figure 11 and the image of Figure 21a in the companion paper. The results are presented in various ways. Based upon size, we have examined

a) all regions, b) those regions large enough to entirely contain at least one 5×4 window (i.e., those regions for which textural features are computable), and c) large regions which contain at least 65 pixels. In all three groups, the accuracy of recognition of regions whose identities were in the target set was fairly high -- greater than 75%. The majority of errors occurred between tree and bush which is not unexpected, since these objects have similar spectral characteristics and differ primarily in size. When these two object classes were collapsed into one, the recognition rate among the four target classes was greater than 90%.

In order to provide a sense of the confidence in erroneous hypotheses for non-target regions, Table II also summarizes the average values of the heuristic confidence measure for the best hypothesis for correctly identified targets, incorrectly identified targets, and non-targets. The associated distributions are also provided in Figure 12. These results are very promising in their overall accuracy and in the difference in confidences between target and non-target distributions. However, the distributions do overlap, and this single knowledge source cannot be expected to separate targets from non-targets without error. As part of the development of this knowledge source, we will be extending the set of features used and improving the prototype representations in LTM as a larger data base of images becomes available. Of course the single biggest problem with this KS will still remain -- many object classes in LTM are not characterized by features that tend to be invariant in color and texture.

Table III provides samples of the ranges of sizes (mainly heights, but all dimensions that can be simply stated will be specified) for object classes in LTM. Using this information, a computed

Region Identification (Figure 11b)	Actual Region Identity	Hypothesized Region Identity	Hypothesis Correct?	Confidence Region is:					Area of Region (pixels)	Number of 5×4 Windows in Region
				Bush	Grass	Road	Sky	Tree		
1	TREE	TREE	YES	31	-72	-92	-62	61	4300	2888
2	SKY	SKY	YES	16	1	-55	35	16	407	299
3	TREE	TREE	YES	33	-21	-89	-38	95	846	611
4	SKY	SKY	YES	-58	-44	0	68	-78	1763	1577
7	TREE	TREE	YES	-27	-18	-71	-65	80	97	33
13	TREE	TREE	YES	12	-17	-89	-74	84	195	74
20	ROOF	GRASS	NO	-43	35	32	-20	-54	854	609
21	WALL	SKY	NO	2	3	- 8	47	-16	2207	1347
35	TREE	TREE	YES	37	- 7	-85	-56	42	31	2
45	SHUTTER	TREE	NO	-48	-29	-67	-47	- 4	42	0
65	WALL	SKY	NO	-12	-43	-26	14	4	79	30
68	GRASS	GRASS	YES	0	69	-56	-50	31	2588	1904

Table I. Attribute Matching. Sample results obtained from the region-object attribute matching KS on the segmentation shown in Figure 11b. The last two columns show the area of the region in terms of the number of pixels it contains, and the number of 5×4 windows (used to compute the texture features) totally contained in the region.

Allen R. Hanson and Edward M. Riseman

	Summary of Identification Accuracy					
	All Regions		Regions in Which at Least One 5×4 Window Will Fit		Large Regions (area ≥ 65 pixels)	
	All 5 Objects	4 Objects After Collapsing Bush-Tree	All 5 Objects	4 Objects	5 Objects	4 Objects
Total Number of Regions	209		83		45	
Number of Target Regions	99		50		25	
Number of Non-Target Regions	110		33		20	
Number of Target Regions Correctly Identified	76	91	40	45	19	23
Number of Target Regions Incorrectly Identified	23	8	10	5	6	2
% Target Regions Correct	76.7	91.9	80.	90.	76.	92.
	Summary of Averages of Confidence Measures					
Correctly Identified Target Regions	31.8	29.9	49.5	49.1	63.2	59.8
Incorrectly Identified Target Regions (highest value)	21.4	23.8	36.9	28.2	37.6	25.
Non-Target Regions (highest value)	8.4		24.9		27.3	

Table II. Summary of Region Identification Results from Attribute Matcher Applied to Two Images.

physical size will be assumed to provide no information (0) if it is exactly at the limits of the range, linearly increasing positive support for a hypothesis as it approaches the limits of the expected range, maximum support (100) inside the expected range, and negative support (-100) if it is outside the range. This value is then scaled by a coefficient which represents an importance measure based on the discriminability of a particular size value in a manner similar to that described in Section III.3. The a posteriori probability estimate of an object is a function of the a priori probability, and the match of the attribute information (here size) provided by the KS with the stored object attribute in LTM, modified by the discriminability of the attribute computed on the basis of the overlap of the attribute values with other objects. Thus, a particular physical size value, even if it falls inside the expected size range for an object, will not significantly raise the a priori probability estimate, if that size falls inside the expected range of many other objects.

We have already described (in Section III.5) the range of assumptions that is necessary before the physical size of an object can be computed on the basis of image size. Determining this size requires computing the distance of the object from the camera lens. The computation is very sensitive to the height and inclination of the camera and to the elevation of the object above the ground plane (perhaps available from perspective cues). This sensitivity is most pronounced for distant objects.

Table IV shows the computed physical sizes of particular regions in the image (Figure 11), and the assumptions that were necessary in order to carry out their computation. We have not yet automated the strategies by which these assumptions can be generated, and consequently the results shown were based on interactive guidance by a user.[1] The reader should note, however, that there are various sources for suggesting and constraining these assumptions. For example, the attributes of region 68 imply grass (the ground plane) with high probability, and it is at the lower part of the image where the ground plane is expected. This allows

---

[1]This work is currently in progress. It is based on initial investigations by Kurt Konolige (now at SRI, International) and is being continued by Daniel Corkill of the COINS Department at UMass. The results of this work will be reported in the future.

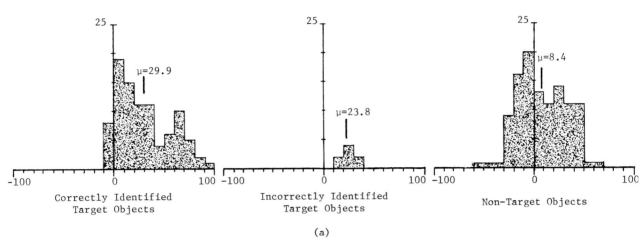

(a)

Distributions of confidence measure for all regions with 4 target objects (grass, road, sky, bush/tree).

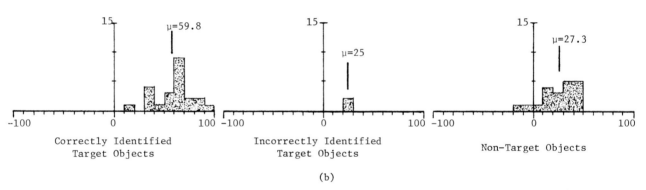

(b)

Distribution of confidence measure for large regions (area ≥ 65 pixels) with 4 target objects (grass, road, sky, bush/tree).

Figure 12. Distributions of values produced by heuristic confidence measure for attribute-matching. The horizontal axis is the value of the measure and the vertical axis is the number of regions with that value.

distances of surfaces to be computed relative to their image location in region 68. The attribute matching KS implies the strong, likelihood of tree for regions 1 and 3 and they can be located in relation to the grass surface of region 68. The shape of region 45 suggests that there is a reasonable possibility that it is a surface perpendicular to the ground plane. There is also top-down guidance from stored sizes of objects. Thus, occlusion of the tree, region 3, by region 20, and the knowledge that regions 20 and 21 are part of a house (by other analyses) would allow the lower bound on the size of the tree to be raised by increasing, by the stored prototypical width of the house class, the distance at which the tree is rooted to the ground.

Admittedly, there is a non-trivial sequence of assumptions that must be made in order to arrive at the results that are shown. However, if the assump-

tions can be generated, then in many cases there is a check on the validity of each hypothesis because size must be consistent with stored expectations (as with the trees, window, and house). In addition, the assumptions must be consistent with any contexts which were employed (e.g., the relative locations of tree rooted to grass, house, windows, shrubs, and sky). There appears to be a rich and interesting line of research that is available here. These results only outline our first attempts in this area.

In order to make use of the 2D shape analysis described in the companion paper, the confidence of primitive shape labels associated with a region must be determined from the RMS errors of the curve fits and the constraints on the way in which the individual segments fit together. For example, quadrilateral, trapezoid, rectangle, and square are

Allen R. Hanson and Edward M. Riseman

Object Class	Prototype Values (in meters)		
	Minimum Expected Size	Expected Range of Computed Sizes	Maximum Expected Size
Car (length)	2.2	3.7 – 5.0	6.7
Door	1.5	2.0 – 2.5	3.7
Garage	3.0	4.6 – 5.0	5.5
Garage-Body	2.2	3.0 – 4.4	4.9
Garage-Door	2.0	2.2 – 2.5	3.7
House	3.0	4.6 – 7.7	10.8
House-Body	2.2	3.0 – 5.5	7.7
Human	1.2	1.6 – 1.9	2.2
Roof-Projection	0.0	0.0 – 3.0	3.7
Telephone-Pole	3.0	5.0 – 8.0	11.0
Tree	2.5	4.3 – 9.2	15.4
Tree-Crown	1.3	2.5 – 5.5	9.7
Tree-Trunk	1.3	1.9 – 3.7	6.2
Window	.6	.9 – 1.5	2.5

Table III. Ranges of sizes.(height unless otherwise specified) associated with sample object classes as stored in LTM.

shapes which share a common property (all are composed of four straight lines which intersect at four corners) but with increasing constraints on the manner in which the lines are combined; a quadrilateral is a superclass of a trapezoid, which is a superclass of a rectangle, etc. The computation of the confidences, then, should reflect not only the RMS errors of the fits of the individual lines but also the effects of these constraints. In the case of geometrically regular regions for which these labels might apply, all might be present with varying degrees of confidence. A heuristic function, which produces confidence values between 0 and 1, has been developed as a function of the RMS error fits and the expected constraints. Note that we have not yet examined the discriminability of shape labels, nor the points of zero information as used in the other two KSs. Because of the very preliminary nature of this research, we will present limited results. Table V summarizes the average RMS errors for straight line fits of sets of segments bounding selected regions in Figure 11b, and confidences associated with these regions (see also Section V in the companion paper).

The next experiment involved exercising the long-term knowledge base by combining the results of various KSs in order to obtain an initial test of the propagation of information. That is, we wished to see the way in which LTM allows KSs, which make hypotheses at different levels, to bring their influence together at a common node. The importance of these results resides not as much in the final a posteriori values to be shown, but rather in the manner in which the evidence propagates and the direction of the change in the

a priori probabilities as more evidence is added. Again, we emphasize that the results are very preliminary, and do not adequately represent what we hope to achieve.

In order to combine the 2D shape KS and the size KS, the probability of the hypothesis of a 2D region shape label (e.g., region 47 as a rectangle) must be propagated upward to the object level via conditional probabilities on the arcs. This information may then be combined with the result of a size analysis and the results used as the new evidence of the object ("window"). The results of this experiment are tabulated in Table VI. Note that the size KS drives the a posteriori probability of the hypothesis that region 47 is a tree crown to 0, since the size of this region lies totally outside the minimum/maximum values of the expected size range for tree crown. This produces the proper results in this case, but for the case of region 3, it produces incorrect results. The maximum size of tree crowns was set at 9.7 meters (Table III) while the computed size of region 3 was 11.7 (Table IV). There are two ways to solve this problem: either an increase in the stored maximum value of tree crowns, or a weaker effect of sizes outside the range (proportional to the distance outside the extremes of the range). Several erroneous hypotheses have also been included in Table VI for comparative purposes.

The final experiment is tabulated in Table VII. Here several pieces of evidence from the various KSs are introduced and the cumulative effect of this evidence upon several schema is shown. Both the house-scene and lawn-scene schemas have significant increases in their a posteriori probabilities. It is worth noting that the influence of tree probably should not increase the probability of lawn-scene so sharply, nor should window increase drive-scene so dramatically (even though garages in drive-scenes have windows).

VIII.   Conclusion

VIII.1   Flexibility for System Evolution

Our design involved modularization of data into levels, modularization of processes which transform data from one representation to another, and modularization of the strategies which employ them. It should allow us the flexibility to explore local interactions between executing processes, and the control issues at a more global level.

With this approach to representation, processes, control, and search, we believe that the system can be reconfigured incrementally with modest (although sometimes not trivial) effort. For example, suppose one of the paths to surface hypotheses turns out to be ineffective without the addition of another process, say motion cues (provided by optic flows of motion currently under investigation by our colleagues); this might well require some intermediate level of representation in order to combine those results with our own surface cues based on shape. It would not be surprising for such a change to have so major an impact upon a system that it would need to be entirely recoded. Although it would still take some effort in our system, we expect that most of

A Computer System for Interpreting Scenes   327

Region(s)	Elevation	Distance	Height	Width	Actual Identity
71	0.0	18.3	.79	.24	Tree Trunk
1	.794	18.3	≥ 4.06	≥ 3.11	Tree Crown

Assumptions:
  RG-71 is perpendicular and attached to ground plane
  RG-71 is split into two sub-regions with only right part considered, and width measured on upper
      portion
  RG-1 is perpendicular to ground plane and elevated above volume for RG-71
  RG-1 is occluded by image boundary at top and left
  RG-1 is subdivided by partitioning the shrub area in front of house; it was <u>not</u> sub-divided in-
      to two separate regions corresponding to the two actual trees

Region(s)	Elevation	Distance	Height	Width	Actual Identity
3(a)	0.0	≥ 34.7	≥ 7.71	≥ 3.95	Tree (Crown)
(b)	0.0	≥ 57.9	≥ 11.7	≥ 6.57	Tree (Crown)
(c)					

Assumptions:
  RG-3 is occluded by RG-20 (from occlusion analysis)
  (a) RG-3 is perpendicular and attached to ground plane at a distance further than the top of
      RG-68, whose spectral attributes imply grass
  (b) house is identified; distance and size will be computed by adding the prototypical width of
      house stored in LTM to the physical distance of the top of RG-68 (grass)
  (c) RG-3 is perpendicular and attached to ground plane behind RG-1, RG-20, and RG-21.

Region(s)	Elevation	Distance	Height	Width	Actual Identity
21	0.0	34.7 – 43.4	5.19 – 6.08	4.44 – 5.55 (a)(b)	House Wall

Assumptions:
  RG-21 is perpendicular and attached to ground plane at a distance between the physical distance
      to the top of RG-68, and the distance to bottom of RG-21 based upon a slight occlusion
      cue from shrub area (RG-1).
  (a) RG-21 is perpendicular to the line-of-sight
  (b) RG-21 is subdivided into two house walls; refer to Figure 28b in the companion paper

Region(s)	Elevation	Distance	Height	Width	Actual Identity
20	2.77 – 3.13	34.7 – 43.4	2.35 – 3.13	5.52 – 6.90	House Roof

Assumptions:
  RG-20 is elevated above the volume for RG-21
  RG-20 is perpendicular to ground plane (an incorrect assumption)

Region(s)	Elevation	Distance	Height	Width	Actual Identity
47	1.05 – 1.20	34.7 – 43.4	1.04 – 1.36	.394 – .493	House Window

Assumptions:
  RG-47 lies in plane of RG-21, and therefore its distance is defined by the range of RG-21
  RG-47 is perpendicular to the line-of-sight

Region(s)	Elevation	Distance	Height	Width	Actual Identity
76	0.0	Not Applicable	Not Applicable	1.76	Road (Narrow Driveway)

Assumptions:
  RG-76 is in ground plane
  Two long segments forming RG-76 are actually parallel in the physical world

Table IV. Computed physical (real world) sizes of selected regions of Figure 11. The assumptions necessary to make the computation are summarized below the computed values.

Region	Average RMS Error of Straight Segment Fits	Shape Label	Confidence of Label	Actual Identity of Region
20	.98	Triangle	.971	House roof
45	0.0	Quadrilateral Trapezoid Rectangle Square	1.0 1.0 1.0 .33	Window shutter
47	2.01	Quadrilateral Trapezoid Rectangle	.92 .88 .45	Window
76	.41	Quadrilateral Trapezoid Rectangle Triangle	.98 .912 0. .96	Road

Table V. Preliminary results from 2D shape KS.

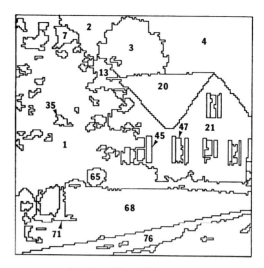

Region Identification
(same as Figure 11b)

Region	Hypothesized Identity	a priori probability of hypothesized identity (stored in LTM)	a posteriori probability given evidence from					Actual Identity of Region
			attribute KS	size KS	shape KS	attributes and size	size and shape	
1	Tree-Crown	.1211	.657	.237	———	.812	———	Tree-Crown
3	Tree-Crown	.1211	.956	0.	———	0.	———	Tree-Crown
21	Tree-Crown	.1211	.101	.268	———	.229	———	House-Wall
47	Tree-Crown	.1211	.490	0.	———	0.	———	Window
47	Window	.0049	———	.326	.018	———	.639	Window

Table VI. Combination of evidence from various KSs at the object level.

Hypotheses at Object-Class Level	KS(s) Used to Form Hypotheses at Object-Class Level	Effect of Combined Hypotheses on a priori Probability of Schema Classes									
		House-SC		Drive-SC		Lawn-SC		Road-SC		Walk-SC	
		a priori	a posteriori	a priori	a posteriori	a priori	a posteriori	a priori	a posteriori	a priori	a posteriori
R47-Building-Window	Size	.2344	.907	.11	.643	.24	.2354	.13	.1311	.03	.0304
R1-Tree-Crown	Spectral Attribute and Size	.2344	.738	.11	.1065	.24	.997	.13	.1311	.03	.0304
R47-Building-Window and R1-Tree-Crown	Size Spectral Attribute and Size	.2344	.988	.11	.643	.24	.997	.13	.1311	.03	.0304
R21-House-Body	Size	.2344	.363	.11	.1065	.24	.2354	.13	.1311	.03	.0304
R47-Building-Window and R1-House-Body	Size Size	.2344	.948	.11	.643	.24	.2354	.13	.1311	.03	.0304
R47, R21, (hypotheses and R1 as above)	Size Size Spectral Attribute and Size	.2344	.994	.11	.643	.24	.997	.13	.1311	.03	.0304
R47-Human (incorrect hypothesis)	Size	.2344	.236	.11	.110	.24	.240	.13	.136	.03	.038
R1-Tree C R21-House-Body R47-Human (incorrect)	———	.2344	.845	.11	.1068	.24	.997	.13	.136	.03	.038

Table VII. Results from combining hypotheses at the object-class level and the effect on the schema-class level.

the energy expended in order to add these capabilities would require specification of the local relationships of these additional processes with various aspects of the system. The required intermediate representation would be added as a distinct level of representation without directly affecting the other levels. Next, processes would have to be defined to transform patterns from lower levels to this level and from the new level to higher levels. These should not affect the functioning of other modular processes except to the extent that the internal steps of the analysis are dependent upon internal steps of existing processes -- in such a case reorganization of the dependent existing processes would be inevitable. After adding the necessary knowledge sources for transformation of the patterns, strategies for deciding how to employ these new processes locally can be added without causing changes throughout the system. Finally, during the development of these changes, the careful examination of the history of selected local paths in the search space provides a dynamic trace of the processing and should aid in analyzing the effectiveness of these changes.

VIII.2 Feedback to the Low-Level System

Once semantic hypotheses are formed, there is a rich source of information to direct segmentation processes which initially have no semantic guidance [HAN78, this volume]. The hypotheses of object identities allows selection of more effective features for segmentation, as well as extraction of more descriptive features for hypothesis verification. The fitting of shape descriptors to regions and segments also provides more global information for the refinement of boundaries which were initially based upon very local views of the sensory data. Investigation of these interesting problems is planned for the future.

VIII.3 Results

The results shown in Section VII are our first attempts at exercising initial versions of several of the knowledge sources and long-term memory on actual data. Although they were obtained just prior to the writing of the final draft of this paper and should not be taken as conclusive, they are demonstrative of the kinds of experiments we are now beginning to run. Each of the KSs employed must be improved, and there are several others being implemented, such as 3D shape matching, whose influences have not yet been incorporated.

As we have repeatedly stressed, one of the motivations behind VISIONS has been the construction of a tool with which we can begin to explore the complexity of the problem domain of unconstrained complex images. Even this limited set of experiments has begun to show areas where modifications are necessary. Once the reliability of the KSs is understood, we can begin to explore interesting control strategies in the development of interpretations, including top-down schema-driven control.

VIII.4 System Evaluation

It is impossible to predict the power and effectiveness of our approach to computer vision.

Ultimately the power of the system is limited by the quality of the knowledge sources which are forming and evaluating hypotheses. We will consider the high level design of VISIONS successful if it permits the system to evolve with relative ease while exploring those limits. The success of a general vision system is another matter and awaits further stages of experimentation, redesign, and improvement of knowledge sources. This long range task, although rather formidable, appears feasible.

As of this writing, the core of the VISIONS system has been implemented; default strategies are available, the knowledge base has been filled out, initial versions of several of the knowledge sources are complete and being refined, 2D shape processing is being completed, and segmentation data is being passed from the low-level system. We are currently designing and carrying out a series of experiments to begin the assessment of the system. These results, as they become available, will be reported in the literature.

Acknowledgements

This research was supported in part by the National Science Foundation under Grant DCR75-16098. We would like to express our gratitude to the Computer and Information Science Department at the University of Massachusetts for providing a congenial atmosphere in which to conduct this research. The support, constructive criticism, and advice offered by many of our colleagues, particularly Michael Arbib and Victor Lesser, is gratefully acknowledged. The research reported here is based primarily upon the untiring efforts of John Lowrance, Thomas Williams, and Bryant York, with contributions from Daniel Corkill and Kurt Konolige. These individuals and those who have contributed to the segmentation system of VISIONS have formed a rare cooperative research group whose dedication, and sometimes personal sacrifice, will always be appreciated. Finally, we wish to thank Ms. Janet Turnbull for her help and patience in producing the various drafts of this manuscript and many others during the last three years.

References

[AGI72] G.J. Agin, "Representation and Description of Curved Objects," Stanford AI Memo 73, 1972.

[ARB72] M.A. Arbib, The Metaphorical Brain: An Introduction to Cybernetics as Artificial Intelligence and Brain Theory, Wiley-Interscience, 1972.

[ARB75] M.A. Arbib, "Artificial Intelligence and Brain Theory: Unities and Diversities," Annals of Biomedical Engineering, 3, 238-274, 1975.

[ARB77] M.A. Arbib, "Parallelism, Slides, Schemas, and Frames," in Systems: Approaches, Theories, Applications (W.E. Hartnett, Ed.), D. Reidel Publishing Co., 27-43, 1977.

[ARB77] M.A. Arbib, Personal communication.

[BAI75] M.L. Baird, J.J. Olsztyn, W.A. Perkins and L. Rossol, "The GM Research Laboratories' Machine Perception Project," Technical

Report, General Motors Research Laboratories, Warren, Michigan, October 1975.

[BAJ78] R. Bajcsy and A. Joshi, "A Partially Ordered World Model and Natural Outdoor Scenes," in Computer Vision Systems (A. Hanson and E. Riseman, Eds.), Academic Press, New York, 1978.

[BAL78] D.H. Ballard, C.M. Brown, and J.A. Feldman, "An Approach to Knowledge Directed Image Analysis," in Computer Vision Systems (A. Hanson and E. Riseman, Eds.), Academic Press, New York, 1978.

[BAR72] H.G. Barrow, A.P. Ambler, and R.M. Burstall, "Some Techniques for Recognizing Structure in Pictures," Frontiers in Pattern Recognition (S. Watanabe, Ed.), Academic Press, New York, 1972.

[BAR76] H.G. Barrow and J.M. Tenenbaum, "MYSYS: A System for Reasoning About Scenes," Technical Note 121, AI Center, Stanford Research Institute, April 1976.

[BAR78] H.G. Barrow and J.M. Tenenbaum, "Recovering Intrinsic Scene Characteristics from Images," in Computer Vision Systems (A. Hanson and E. Riseman, Eds.), Academic Press, New York, 1978.

[BIN71] T.O. Binford, "Visual Perception by Computer," presented to the IEEE Conference on Systems and Control, Miami, December 1971.

[BRA78] J.M. Brady and B.J. Wielinga, "Reading the Writing on the Wall," in Computer Vision Systems (A. Hanson and E. Riseman, Eds.), Academic Press, New York, 1978.

[BRE74] J. Brenner, E. Gelsema, T. Necheles, P. Neurath, W. Selles, and E. Vastola, "Automated Leukocytes," The Journal of Histochemistry and Cytochemistry, 22, 697-706, 1974.

[BUL78] B.L. Bullock, "The Necessity for a Theory of Specialized Vision," in Computer Vision Systems (A. Hanson and E. Riseman, Eds.), Academic Press, New York, 1978.

[CAR77] S.G. Carlton and O.R. Mitchell, "Image Segmentation Using Texture and Gray Level," Proc. Pattern Recognition and Image Processing, Troy, NY, June 6-8, 1977, 387-391.

[CLO71] M.B. Clowes, "On Seeing Things," Artificial Intelligence, 2, 79-116, 1971.

[COO67] S.A. Coons, "Surfaces for Computer-Aided Design of Space Forms," MIT Project MAC TR-41, June 1967.

[COO74] S.A. Coons, "Surface Patches and B-Spline Curves," in Computer Aided Geometric Design (R.E. Barnhill and R.F. Riesenfeld, Eds.), Academic Press, New York, 1974.

[DUD73] R.O. Duda and P.E. Hart, Pattern Classification and Scene Analysis, John Wiley and Sons, 1973.

[DUD76] R.O. Duda, P.E. Hart, and N.J. Nilsson, "Subjective Bayesian Methods for Rule-Based Inference Systems," Proc. of the National Computer Conference, 1976.

[ERM75] L. Erman and V. Lesser, "A Multi-Level Organization for Problem-Solving Using Many, Diverse, Cooperating Sources of Knowledges," Proc. IJCAI-4, Tbilisi, USSR, September 1975, 483-490.

[ESC71] The World of M.C. Escher, (J.L. Locher, Ed.), Harry N. Abrams, Inc., New York, 1971.

[FAH74] S.E. Fahlman, "A Planning System for Robot Construction Tasks," Artificial Intelligence, 5, 1-49, 1974.

[FIS73] M.A. Fischler and R.A. Eschlager, "The Representation and Matching of Pictorial Structures," IEEE Trans. on Computers, January 1973.

[FRI69] D.P. Friedman, D.C. Dickson, J.J. Fraser, and T.W. Pratt, "GRASPE 1.5 - A Graph Processor and Its Application," Tech. Report, University of Houston, 1969.

[GOR74] W.J. Gordon and R.F. Riesenfeld, "B-Spline Curves and Surfaces," in Computer Aided Geometric Design (R.E. Barnhill and R.F. Riesenfeld, Eds.), Academic Press, New York, 1974.

[GRE66] R.L. Gregory, Eye and Brain: The Psychology of Seeing, McGraw-Hill, New York, 1966.

[GUZ68] A. Guzman, "Decomposition of a Visual Scene into Three-Dimensional Bodies," Proc. of Fall Joint Computer Conference, 33, 291-304, 1968.

[HAN75] A. Hanson and E. Riseman, "The Design of a Semantically Directed Vision Processor (Revised and Updated)," COINS Technical Report 75C-1, University of Massachusetts, February 1975.

[HAN76a] A. Hanson, E. Riseman, and T. Williams, "Constructing Semantic Models in the Visual Analysis of Scenes," Proc. of IEEE Milwaukee Symposium on Automatic Computation and Control, April 1976, 97-102.

[HAN76b] A. Hanson and E. Riseman, "A Progress Report on VISIONS: Representation and Control in the Construction of Visual Models," COINS Technical Report 76-9, University of Massachusetts, July 1976.

[HAN76c] A. Hanson, E. Riseman, and E. Fisher, "Context in Word Recognition," Pattern Recognition, 8, 35-45, 1976.

[HAN78] A.R. Hanson and E.M. Riseman, "Segmentation of Natural Scenes," in Computer Vision Systems (A. Hanson and E. Riseman, Eds.), Academic Press, New York, 1978.

[HAR73] R. Haralick, K. Shanmugan, and I. Dinstein, "Textured Features for Image Classification," IEEE Trans. on Systems, Man and Cybernetics, SMC-3, 610-621, Sept. 1974.

[HEN75] G.G. Hendrix, "Expanding the Utility of Semantic Networks Through Partitioning," Proc. IJCAI-4, 115-121, August 1975.

[HEW68] D. Hewitt, "PLANNER: A Language for Manipulating Models and Proving Theorems in a Robot," MIT Project MAC, AI Memo 168, 1968.

[HUF71] D.A. Huffman, "Impossible Objects as Nonsense Sentences," in Machine Intelligence 6 (B. Meltzer and D. Michie, Eds.), Elsevier, 295-323, 1971.

[KAN77] T. Kanade, "Model Representation and Control Structures in Image Understanding," Proc. IJCAI-5, Cambridge, MA, August 1977.

[KEN77] J. Kender, "Instabilities in Color Transformations," Proc. of Conf. on Pattern Recognition and Image Processing, Troy, NY, 266-274, June 1977.

[KON75] K. Konolige, "The ALISP Manual," Univ. Computing Center, University of Mass., August 1975.

[KON77] "The ALISP Relational Database, COINS Technical Report 77-9, University of Mass., November 1977.

[LES77] V.R. Lesser and L.D. Erman, "A Retrospective View of Hearsay-II Architecture," Proc. IJCAI-5, Cambridge, MA, August 1977.

[LEV78] M.D. Levine, "A Knowledge-Based Computer Vision System," in Computer Vision Systems (A. Hanson and E. Riseman, Eds.), Academic Press, New York, 1978.

[LIE74] L. Liebermann, "Computer Recognition and Description of Natural Scenes," Ph.D. Thesis, University of Pennsylvania, Philadelphia, June 1974.

[LOW76] B.T. Lowerre, "The Harpy Speech Recognition System," Tech. Report (Ph.D. Thesis), Carnegie-Mellon University, 1976.

[LOW78] J. Lowrance, "GRASPER Reference Manual," COINS Tech. Report, University of Mass., in preparation.

[MAC76] A.K. Mackworth, "Model-Driven Interpretation in Intelligent Vision Systems," Tech. Report 76-2, Dept. of Computer Science, University of British Columbia, June 1976.

[MAC78] A.K. Mackworth, "Vision Research Strategy: Black Magic, Metaphors, Mechanisms, Miniworlds, and Maps," in Computer Vision Systems (A. Hanson and E. Riseman, Eds.), Academic Press, New York, 1978.

[MAR76a] D. Marr and H.K. Nishihara, "Representation and Recognition of the Spatial Organization of Three-Dimensional Shapes," MIT AI Memo 377, August 1976.

[MAR76b] D. Marr, "Analysis of Occluding Contour," MIT AI Memo 372, October 1976.

[MAR78] D. Marr, "Representing Visual Information," in Computer Vision Systems (A. Hanson and E. Riseman, Eds.), Academic Press, New York, 1978.

[McC69] J. McCarthy and P.J. Hayes, "Some Philosophical Problems From the Standpoint of Artificial Intelligence, in Machine Intelligence 4 (B. Meltzer and D. Michie, Eds.), University of Edinburgh Press, 463-503, 1969.

[McD74] D. McDermott and C. Sussman, "The CONNIVER Reference Manual," MIT Memo 259a, January 1974.

[MIN75] M. Minsky, "A Framework for Representing Knowledge," The Psychology of Computer Vision (P. Winston, Ed.), McGraw-Hill, 211-277, 1975.

[NEI76] U. Neisser, Cognition and Reality: Principles and Implications of Cognitive Psychology, W.H. Freeman and Company, 1976.

[NEV74] R. Nevatia, "Structured Descriptions of Complex Curved Objects for Recognition and Visual Memory," Stanford AI Lab Memo AIM-250, October 1974.

[NEV78] R. Nevatia, "Characterization and Requirements of Computer Vision Systems," in Computer Vision Systems (A. Hanson and E. Riseman, Eds.), Academic Press, New York, 1978.

[NIL71] N.J. Nilsson, Problem Solving Methods in Artificial Intelligence, McGraw-Hill, New York, 1971.

[PIA71] J. Piaget, Biology and Knowledge: An Essay on the Relations Between Organic Regulations and Cognitive Processes, Edinburgh University Press, 1971.

[PRA71] T. Pratt and D. Friedman, "A Language Extension for Graph Processing and Its Formal Semantics," Communications of the ACM, 4, 1971.

[QUI68] R. Quillian, "Semantic Memory," Semantic Information Processing (M. Minsky, Ed.), MIT Press, 1968.

[RED78] D.R. Reddy, "Pragmatic Aspects of Machine Vision," in Computer Vision Systems (A. Hanson and E. Riseman, Eds.), Academic Press, New York, 1978.

[RIS74] E. Riseman and A. Hanson, "The Design of a Semantically Directed Vision Processor," COINS Technical Report 74C-1, University of Massachusetts, January 1974.

[ROS71] A. Rosenfeld and M. Thurston, "Edge and Curve Detection for Visual Scene Analysis," IEEE Trans. Computers, 562-569, 1971.

[RUB77] S.M. Rubin and D.R. Reddy, "The LOCUS Model of Search and Its Use in Image Interpretation," Proc. IJCAI-5, Cambridge, MA, August 1977.

[SAC75] E.D. Sacerdoti, "The Non-Linear Nature of Plans," IJCAI-4, Tbilisi, USSR, September 1975, 206-214.

[SCH77] R.C. Schank and R.P. Abelson, Goals, Plans, Scripts and Understanding: An Enquiry into Human Knowledge Structures, Erlbaum Press, NJ, 1977.

[SHA77] R. Shapira and H. Freeman, "Reconstruction of Curved-Surface Bodies From a Set of Imperfect Projections," Proc. IJCAI-5, Cambridge, MA, August 1977, 628-634.

[SHI78] Y. Shirai, "Recognition of Real-World Objects Using Edge Cues," in Computer Vision Systems (A. Hanson and E. Riseman, Eds.), Academic Press, New York, 1978.

[SHO75] E.H. Shortliffe and B.G. Buchanan, "A Model of Inexact Reasoning in Medicine,"

Mathematical Biosciences, 23, 351-379, 1975.

[SIM73] R.F. Simmons, "Semantic Networks: Their Computation and Use for Understanding English Sentences," in Computer Models of Thought and Language (R.C. Schank and K.M. Colby, Eds.), H. Freeman and Co., 1973.

[TEN73] J. Tenenbaum, "On Locating Objects by Their Distinguishing Features in Multi-sensory Images," SRI Technical Note 84, AI Center, Stanford Research Institute, September 1973.

[TEN76] J.M. Tenenbaum and H.G. Barrow, "Experiments in Interpretation-Guided Segmentation," Technical Note 123, AI Center, Stanford Research Institute, 1976.

[TUR74] K.J. Turner, "Computer Perception of Curved Objects Using a Television Camera," Ph.D. Thesis, Dept. of Machine Intelligence, School of Artificial Intelligence, University of Edinburgh, 1974.

[UHR78] L. Uhr, "Recognition Cones and Some Test Results," in Computer Vision Systems (A. Hanson and E. Riseman, Eds.), Academic Press, New York, 1978.

[WAL77] D.E. Walker, W.H. Paxton, et al., "Procedures for Integrating Knowledge in a Speech Understanding System," Proc. IJCAI-5, Cambridge, MA, August 1977.

[WAL75] D. Waltz, "Understanding Line Drawings of Scenes with Shadows," in The Psychology of Computer Vision (P.H. Winston, Ed.), McGraw-Hill, 19-91, 1975.

[WEC75] H. Wechsler and J. Sklansky, "Automatic Detection of Contours of Ribs in Chest Radiographs," Univ. of California at Irvine, TR-75-2, 1975.

[WIL77] T. Williams and J. Lowrance, "Model-Building in the VISIONS High Level System," COINS Technical Report 77-1, University of Mass., January 1977.

[WIL78] T. Williams, forthcoming COINS technical report, University of Massachusetts, 1978.

[WIN75] P.H. Winston, The Psychology of Computer Vision, McGraw-Hill, 1975.

[WOO77] W.A. Woods, "Final Report on Speech Understanding Systems," Bolt, Beranek and Newman, Inc., Cambridge, MA, 1977.

[WOO78] W.A. Woods, "Theory Formation and Control in a Speech Understanding System with Extrapolation Towards Vision," in Computer Vision Systems (A. Hanson and E. Riseman, Eds.), Academic Press, New York, 1978.

[YAK73] Y. Yakimovsky and J.A. Feldman, "A Semantics-Based Decision Theory Region Analyzer," Proc. IJCAI-3, 580-588, August 1973.

[YOR78a] B. York, "Shape Representation in the VISIONS System," COINS Technical Report, University of Massachusetts, in preparation.

[YOR78b] B. York, "Symbolic Classification of Primitive Two-Dimensional Shapes," COINS Technical Report, University of Massachusetts, in preparation.

A KNOWLEDGE-BASED COMPUTER VISION SYSTEM

Martin D. Levine
Department of Electrical Engineering
McGill University
3480 University Street
Montreal, Canada

ABSTRACT

A three-level hierarchical computer vision
system which is knowledge driven is described. The
objective is to develop an interactive system which
will allow for experimentation, with particular
stress on data and procedure modularity and independence. At the lowest level pictures are segmented
into regions possessing similar primary features and
no scene context is employed. The next intermediate
level of processing is applicable to the resulting
regions in the picture or portions of the picture,
where complete knowledge regarding model features
and topological structure are available. A local
graph search and global optimization using dynamic
programming are employed to merge regions and to
assign label sets to them. The highest level of
processing uses a relational data base to store
knowledge, and a vision strategy akin to production
systems. The system is being developed hierarchically so that the highest level is in the earliest
stage of development.

1. INTRODUCTION

1.1 A Methodology for Research in Computer Vision

The goal of computer vision can be stated
simply as that of developing a machine which can
correctly interpret real pictures. Two aspects
come to the fore immediately: first, real pictures
imply sensory data represented digitally by an array
of numbers, and second, interpretations involve a
delineation of objects and thence a symbolic description of the scene. Probably the most difficult and
frustrating aspect of this problem is how to meld
these numbers and symbols at suitably chosen interfaces. Suggested paradigms for accomplishing this
have not been adequately verified and comparatively
little guidance related to human vision is available
from the fields of psychology and physiology. After
approximately twenty years of research in picture
processing there is not even agreement on the terminology and how best to decompose the analysis. We
may conclude therefore that while the problem is
admittedly difficult, it is also very interesting
and challenging. Indeed, although we may hold out
the hope of eventually achieving a satisfactory
solution of suitable generality, this should not
restrain us from carrying out research on significant subproblems whose solution will ultimately
lead to the desired goal. The only major proviso,

in light of past experience, is to recognize that
such research must be concerned with real data
emanating from several problem domains. In this
way, the danger of neglecting significant and basic
difficulties is minimized.

This paper deals with a particular approach
to the problem of computer vision and introduces
the basic structure. The work of Hanson and
Riseman [10] is most closely related to it in
philosophy. The described system consists of a
hierarchy of three interconnected stages: low,
intermediate, and high level processing. Each
stage will be discussed in detail and the argument
is made that the research study and the implementation of the stages should occur in the order of
their appearance in the sequence. As indicated by
Rubin [25]:

"The notion of processing phases, so popular
in compiler design, has been largely neglected
in AI paradigms, often because the different
stages were so interdependent. Perhaps, however, a more valuable approach is to start out
with distinct processing stages, making the
assumption that they don't interact – and then
adding inter-stage communication as it becomes
necessary."

A prime concern in the design is that both the control structure and the knowledge representation
have the property of modularity. It is highly
desirable to be able to "plug in" and "pull out"
items of information and parts of analysis strategies in order to experimentally observe the resulting system behavior. In our case, this research is
being facilitated by means of the software system
MIPS [19], an interactive image processing and
experimentation system.

We have adopted a methodology that stresses
the development of modular subprocesses, each of
which is meant to deal with a major vision subtask.
From the outset it was expected that each of these
subprocesses would have to communicate with the
others in some significant manner in order to implement feedback, top-down, and bottom-up analysis
strategies [33]. Because each subprocess is the
responsibility of a different individual, often
working within different time-frames, a uniform
method of communication is imperative. The lingua
franca in our case is a common data structure within
MIPS: to date the two basic data types are image

arrays and feature vectors. Consequently, all modules in MIPS will input and output in one of these two formats.

In many respects the development of our computer vision system can be compared to perceptual development in children [5]. According to the theory of Piaget, visual perception is not exclusively either genetically preformed or acquired by learning and interaction with the environment, but rather a combination of the two. More important, during the early stages of childhood development, the nonpurposive visual processes dominate and the operational characteristics, Gestalt in nature, can be described as similarity, proximity, good continuation, and closure. These are the very properties which are descriptive of low level region analysis where the input image array is segmented into a restricted number of regions consisting of pixels largely exhibiting the same primary features. As the child grows older, he develops so-called perceptual regulations which are the logical constructions which allow him to mentally organize, analyze, and interpret a picture. Elkind [5] has isolated such regulations as perceptual exploration ("systematic exploration of the visual field"), perceptual transport ("making perceptual comparisons across a distance"), and expectation. He notes that:

> "It is important to emphasize, however, that the development of regulations and the resulting ... schematization ... are constructed by most children on their own and without specific tutelage. This happens because such constructions are necessary to survival; the child is forced to construct them as he interacts with the physical world."

Further, in reply to the question:

> "What is the extent to which performance can be accelerated by training? Piaget's answer (to what he terms the "American question") is that there is an optimal time for the development of operations and regulations that cannot be hurried."

With regard to the development of a computer vision system, we propose an analogous research paradigm where the early stages must be well developed and understood before the higher levels can be perfected. Implementation of these stages must be initiated in an orderly, hierarchical fashion which imbues the system with the ability to analyze and to cope with progressively more difficult problems. One of our goals is to be able to delineate the capabilities of the system as a function of the number of stages existing in the hierarchy, that is, the system complexity.

1.2   Image Segmentation

A schematic of the knowledge-based computer vision system is shown in Figure 1. At the bottom of the hierarchy, low level processing is concerned with the segmentation problem and is discussed in detail in Section 2. At this stage, the input image is divided into regions containing pixels whose primary features such as intensity, hue, saturation, and texture are similar. This procedure is general purpose in nature in that every picture is treated in exactly the same fashion.

We may distinguish two types of segmentation. The first, which has been termed complete segmentation, achieves a final result consisting of the outlined regions which correspond exactly to the objects in the picture. Obviously this is the ideal outcome, and therefore the ultimate goal for the overall computer vision system, not just for the low level processing stage. We observe that in general it will be necessary to invoke the high level processor and a knowledge representation to achieve such a complete segmentation. Not only is this not an insignificant problem as is sometimes intimated, it is necessarily at the heart of the vision problem. However there does exist a class of problems where low level processing is indeed completely effective. This is the case where the picture can be modeled by objects superimposed on a uniform background, such as for example, nonoverlapping chromosomes or blood cells [32]. Histogram thresholding applied independently to each pixel neighborhood will generally result in a complete segmentation of objects and background. This is a context independent segmentation process as no descriptive information is utilized to perform the region analysis.

The second type of segmentation has been called partial segmentation; in this case the region outlines do not necessarily correspond to the objects in the picture. When applied to a normally complex image, such as for example a typical suburban scene, the result is a list of regions which are uniform in the sense of their primary features. Further processing of a different nature is required. The segmented regions are stored in a short term memory (see Figure 1) where subsequent stages in the hierarchy will use them as input data. Under these circumstances the advantage of having such a partial segmentation is primarily one of data compression, in the sense that fewer entities need be considered. For example, the input to the low level processing stage might be an array of dimension 256 by 256, the output some two hundred regions, yielding a compression ratio of about 300:1. In the system under discussion partial segmentation is used and this compression is significant in that it allows for a more sophisticated subsequent analysis of this limited data set.

Kasvand [16] has commented on a significant paradox regarding partial and complete segmentation. In order to determine the correspondence between a group of regions with a specific object model, the latter must correspond to this group of regions so that their properties can be compared with a previously stored description in the knowledge representation database. However, until we know what the object is, how do we extract the pertinent information from the database in order to make the original comparisons? This requires at least an intermediate level of processing as described subsequently.

1.3   Interpretation Using Complete Models

The main characteristic of intermediate level processing, which is described in Section 3, is its dependence on a detailed two dimensional model of

Martin D. Levine

the picture class under analysis. The input data are the segmented regions obtained from the low level processing stage and also the information stored in the knowledge representation; the output is an ordered list of possible symbolic interpretations for these regions. It is at this level that the sensory data/symbolic description interface is first met and dealt with. As such it is concerned with matching properties in both domains. In a sense, the intermediate level deals with pictures containing "standard" views and "standard" objects. Just as with humans, interpretation and recognition should therefore be less complex and require less time.

Under certain circumstances it would seem that intermediate level processing is an adequate upper level in the hierarchy to perform the analysis. An insufficient amount of experimentation has been done to date to confirm this premise and it may have to be revised in light of new evidence. We postulate that the pictures for which intermediate level processing is deemed sufficient are more complex than those which can be completely segmented by low level processing. For example, this class of pictures includes those where there is no clear demarcation between what constitutes the objects and what the background.

Four attributes characterize this class of pictures. First, although the background is not uniform, a model is available which completely describes its properties. It is also essentially "flat" in that the third dimension of depth is not necessary for its recognition and description. The second attribute is similar except that it pertains to the objects in the scene which are superimposed on the background. Again a good model must be available and no specific reference is made to the projective aspects of the three dimensional nature of the objects. Thirdly it is assumed that spatial relations for the objects are known, both for those that constitute the background as well as the foreground. Lastly we make the major assumption of completeness: that is, the objects in the picture are the only ones in the knowledge representation. This restriction severely limits the search process and may probably be relaxed to a certain extent. Insufficient experimentation with actual images at this point relegates any elaboration of these four attributes to mere hypotheses, although most research in picture processing to date has dealt with problem domains restricted as described. What these four points really amount to is that we have very specific expectations about the picture content. Examples of this are face recognition, landscapes with perhaps some man-made objects such as houses, and automatic visual inspection problems as might arise in industrial automation. A subclass of this category of picture analysis problems is object recognition, where the background is generally assumed to be uniform as in the case of complete segmentation. However, the introduction of the third dimension tends to complicate this scene.

Intermediate level analysis takes as its input the regions produced by the low level processing stage which yields a partial segmentation. Although we shall describe a specific approach to segmentation in Section 2, it seems probable that many different methods of partial segmentation based on

plausible similarity criteria would suffice. The degree to which this holds probably depends on the power of the higher levels of processing, and what is more important, the feedback (or top-down) processes that are brought to bear on the problem. The output from the intermediate level is an ordered list of interpretations for each region in the scene, where the latter may consist of a group of regions previously obtained by partial segmentation which have been suitably merged.

Two basic processes constitute intermediate level processing, one local, the other global. The local process is concerned with matching object descriptions. This is a form of template matching where for _each_ region suitable candidates for merger with it are examined. The search is model driven and is based on a comparison of two dimensional shape and primary features such as color and texture. Heuristic graph search is employed to determine a list of plausible region fusions and thus local interpretations. The second process, more global in nature, is also model driven and incorporates knowledge relevant to the spatial relations which are pertinent to the specific local interpretations. As we are seeking the best global interpretation, this task may be framed as a classical optimization problem whose solution lends itself to the method of dynamic programming. The optimum regions merges and their best interpretations constitute the result.

Specific knowledge about the two dimensional picture of interest is obviously the kernel of this approach. This knowledge must be provided to the system in as natural a manner as possible, and in our case this is done interactively using a database embedded in the MIPS system. Two modes of input to this database are desirable. In the first mode, which used a light pen, the user may either sketch a line drawing on a display or he may outline a picture, such as a chest radiograph, currently being displayed. By interactively designating the subobjects, computing their features, and then updating the parameters of the model in the database, classical pattern recognition techniques could be used to achieve a learning process. However, at this point we are using prototype pictures to simulate the learning. In the second mode, descriptive prototypical symbolic information could be entered directly. While these are rather basic forms of knowledge acquisition, they do provide a foundation upon which more advanced learning strategies could be implemented [30,31].

Whereas the intermediate level processor expects that the semantic information in the database will match the required data needed for the analysis of the picture, no such assumption is made at the highest level. This necessitates more complex search and decision processes.

1.4 Complex Scene Analysis

At the top of the analysis hierarchy, a vision production system [4] in conjunction with a relational database [3] are used to complete the analysis. Section 4 will deal with this stage of high level processing which was motivated by the HEARSAY system described by Erman and Lesser [6] and the writing of Arbib [1].

What are the characteristics of scene understanding problems which require the complete power of the structure shown in Figure 1? There are three important ones. First, the number of objects that appear in a given picture may constitute only a small fraction of those that possibly could be seen and are modelled in the knowledge representation. This, of course, is a situation much closer to human vision which is capable of recognizing any number of objects even out of context. For the moment it is expected that computer vision systems will need to be primed by the input of contextual clues, but nevertheless will be required to search a database to infer a suitable picture description. We may refer to this process as semantic guided segmentation. The second characteristic is concerned with the recognition and interpretation of scenes by taking into account depth (the third dimension), occlusion, shadows, and highlights [22]. The latter two can generally be avoided by careful photography and therefore are not as significant as the perception of depth and occlusion. Finally, the third aspect relates to the fact that the regions used as input to the intermediate and high levels of processing are the result of a <u>partial</u> <u>segmentation</u>. It may therefore be necessary to reconsider the low level segmentation in certain neighborhoods of the picture. Boundaries might have to be readjusted or regions split in light of higher level information and analysis. This can only be achieved by feedback from the higher levels down to the lower levels in the hierarchy (see Section 2.2).

In general we would expect that local feedback which has been designed to optimize each particular stage would be superior to a system which relied totally on global top-down control to correct interpretation errors. Because of this, the system to be described in the following sections has been optimized at each stage as much as possible. Local feedback abounds although the connections are not exhibited in Figure 1. However, they will become evident during the more detailed descriptions provided in the following sections.

In a sense the above three characteristics constitute a compendium of all of the difficult and unsolved problems in computer vision today. To arrive at a satisfactory solution to these problems will require approaches with a large degree of flexibility. We have been greatly influenced by this requirement and have therefore proposed that the high level processing stage be simple in structure, and what is more important, modular in function. This has also been imposed on the knowledge description configured as a standard management-type, relational database [3] which represents information in a tabular format, thereby providing associative storage and retrieval. An interesting aspect of systems which contain explicit databases which are used for analysis, is their potential use for picture synthesis, the complimentary problem to vision. Surely if there is enough information for interpreting pictures, the same database (with certain additions) could be employed to provide a picture generation capability with a rather high level input description language [1].

The computations outlined in Figure 1 and discussed above would seem to require large amounts of

computer time, and this is indeed so. No claim is made to the practicality of such an implementation. However the advent of distributed computation based on microcomputer nets at least holds out the hope that a speed-up could be obtained. Considerations of process parallelism to take advantage of such developments are therefore of great interest.

In this section we have discussed three stages in a hierarchy of computational processes. All three deal with the problem of image segmentation, but with increasing degrees of complexity. At the lowest level a partial segmentation is obtained and no problem-dependent knowledge is used. At the intermediate level it is assumed that an adequate model exists so that a form of template matching becomes feasible. Under these assumptions, the results of the partial segmentation obtained by low level segmentation can be converted to a complete segmentation. The input to the highest level is also this same set of regions obtained by the low level processing stage. However in this instance, the scene semantics found in the database are employed to achieve a complete segmentation. In some cases, because of a priori information, certain portions of the picture under examination may be analyzed using intermediate level processing. In any event, at this highest level, we make no assumptions that the regions in the picture can be identically matched to surfaces or objects in the scene as described in the database.

2. LOW LEVEL PROCESSING

2.1 An Algorithm for Partial Segmentation

Low level processing is at the bottom of the analysis hierarchy outlined in the previous section. Considered from a bottom-up point of view, the objective of this level is to segment or break-up the image into regions consisting of pixels possessing similar primary features. Viewed from the top of the hierarchy, that is, the high level processor, this stage can be invoked in order to implement top-down feedback. Thus, guided by the evidence obtained at the highest level and upon command from above, the low level segmentation process could be called upon to re-examine and re-analyze certain parts of the picture. Both of these aspects will be discussed in this section, with feedback considered in Section 2.2.

Region based approaches to picture segmentation could be considered to be a process of grouping pixels in two spaces simultaneously. Similarity in feature space based on such features as intensity, hue, saturation [27], and texture [11] is a primary prerequisite. However the additional condition of pixel connectivity which defines the concept of a region must also be imposed in the so-called measurement (picture) space. We use a shared nearest neighbor clustering method [15] modified by the connectivity requirement to achieve these goals. The method is relatively insensitive to absolute thresholds, and all pixels are examined in parallel and not in any prespecified order. The starting point for region growing is automatically selected by the program and chosen to be the largest most uniform area in the picture. In fact the sequence of initiation of new regions is approximately in

Martin D. Levine

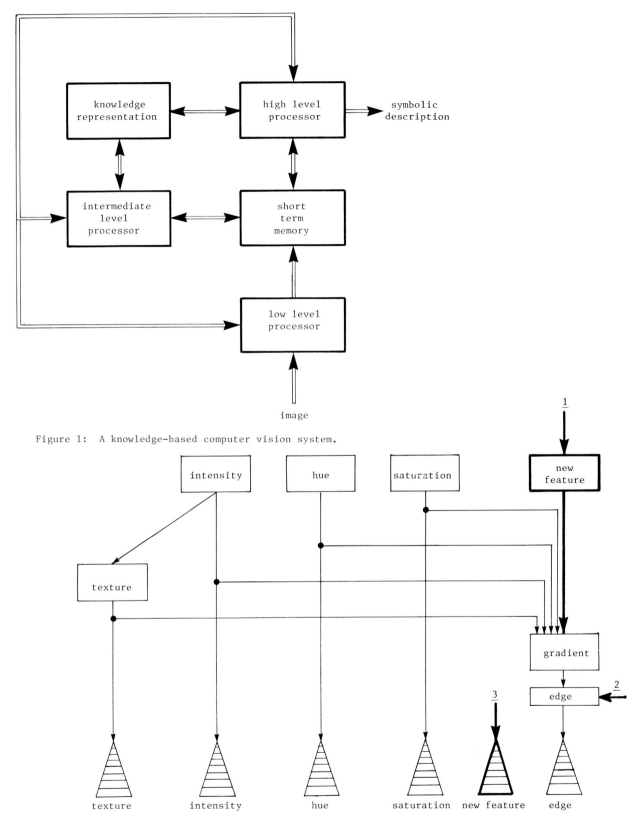

Figure 1: A knowledge-based computer vision system.

Figure 2: The initialization of the low level processing requires the
creation of pyramids as shown above. The texture, intensity,
hue, and saturation pyramids are computed using the AVERAGE
operation while the edge pyramid is obtained using the logical
OR. Points 1, 2, and 3 are possible entries of feedback from
the high level processing.

descending order of size.

The method depends on the use of a pyramidal data structure [26] which is created by dividing the image into four pixel square neighborhoods and mapping each neighborhood into one pixel at the next highest level in the pyramid. The mapping functions used were AVERAGE and logical OR, the latter for binary edge pictures. The mapping process is recursively applied at each level until the top of the pyramid is reached. Once the pyramids are created, the segmentation analysis proceeds to work down to the bottom level as described below. New regions are initiated and old ones are re-adjusted during this descent.

Figure 2 is a representation of the initialization stage where the four feature pyramids are computed. Darkened arrows deal with the top-down feedback and can be ignored for the moment. Another important pyramid, since it is used to guide the analysis, is the edge pyramid. It is determined by first computing the gradient of the image in multidimensional space using a Roberts operator [24]. Edges are then found by a locally adaptive procedure due to Haralick and Dinstein [11]. With this binary image as the base, an edge pyramid is built using the logical OR operation. The effect as one proceeds up the pyramid is to thicken the edges at each successive level. These edges act like expanding wavefronts until at some level in the pyramid the complete array is labelled as being edge and all regions have therefore been extinguished. Areas of the picture which are farthest away from edges and therefore the most unifrom tend to be labelled as edges higher up in the pyramid. Consequently, the starting regions are defined by the level just below the extinction point and are the only pixels not labelled as edges. An example of such a pyramid is shown in Figure 3.

The process of segmentation beginning with the starting region is outlined in Figure 4. A region map in the form of a pyramid is used to maintain a historical record of the pixel labels. Initially all pixels at all levels in this pyramid assume the null label. Projection from one level to the next one below involves expanding a pixel into the associated four pixels at this next level. Three kinds of pixel labels may ensue. First, comparison with the edge pyramid will reveal which of these pixels at this higher resolution are labelled as edges. Those that are edges are not considered any further at this particular level (Figure 5a). Second, those that are not labelled as edges are marked for clustering at this level using the shared nearest neighbor algorithm. Finally, any pixel that has been labelled by this algorithm transfers the identical label to all four pixels at the next low-est level (Figure 5b). There is an exception to this rule: when two adjoining pixels are labelled differently as shown in Figure 5c, the possibility of the existence of a more precise edge between them is postulated, even though there is obviously no evidence of an edge in the corresponding edge pyramid. As shown, the adjoining pixels are marked for reclustering and in this way the boundary be-tween these two regions is refined sequentially as the analysis proceeds down the pyramid. At the lowest level, that of the original image, all edge points are merged with the existing regions, using

a nearest neighbor classification process (Figure 4).

Typically, this analysis may result in a compression of the data from a 128 x 128 image to about one or two hundred regions for a sample scene as shown in Figure 6. The labelled regions are then used as input to the intermediate level analysis.

2.2 Top-down Feedback

Feedback points from the higher levels in the analysis to this partial segmentation level are labelled as 1, 2, 3, 4, and 5 in Figures 2 and 4. It is not intended that only one of these be opera-tive at any one time, and indeed it would be expec-ted that most often a combination of inputs would be involved. For example, input 4, which is con-cerned with the selection and initialization of a sub-area of the picture prior to reclustering, would usually be invoked in conjunction with others. It is generally not necessary to re-examine the complete picture and selected areas could be marked as unassigned and then clustered. At input 1 an additional feature is introduced for recalculating the gradient prior to its subsequent thresholding to create a new edge pyramid. This feedback might be employed to verify the existence of a particular region boundary. An alternate approach to the creation of a new edge pyramid is via input 2 whence an edge picture could be postulated directly. Input 3 in Figures 2 and 4 is a means for adding new features for partial or complete reclustering. We note that as a result of the high level process-ing, certain interpretations for a region or group of regions could be hypothesized and ordered accord-ing to their credibility. Each of these inter-pretations might then be used as an additional feature. The clustering in the now expanded multi-dimensional feature space would include these features in the similarity computation. It would most likely take place at only one level (resolution) in the pyramid, thus not imposing a heavy computa-tional load. A weighted distance function where each interpretation was ranked according to high level confidence could provide a new region seg-mentation for the chosen area of the picture. Finally input 5 could be used to mark certain areas of the picture for re-assignment using the nearest neighbor classification rule. This would generally be invoked to perfect a boundary between two regions and would be most powerful when paired with input 3 in the form of hypothesized interpretations.

Although this lowest level of processing has been designed to accept such feedback commands from above, no experimentation has as yet been carried out.

3. INTERMEDIATE LEVEL PROCESSING

3.1 Template Matching

In computer vision problems where an accurate two dimensional picture model describing the objects and their spatial structure is available, the optimal search provided by the intermediate level of processing described in this section becomes feasible. When such a relational model [2] is not

Martin D. Levine

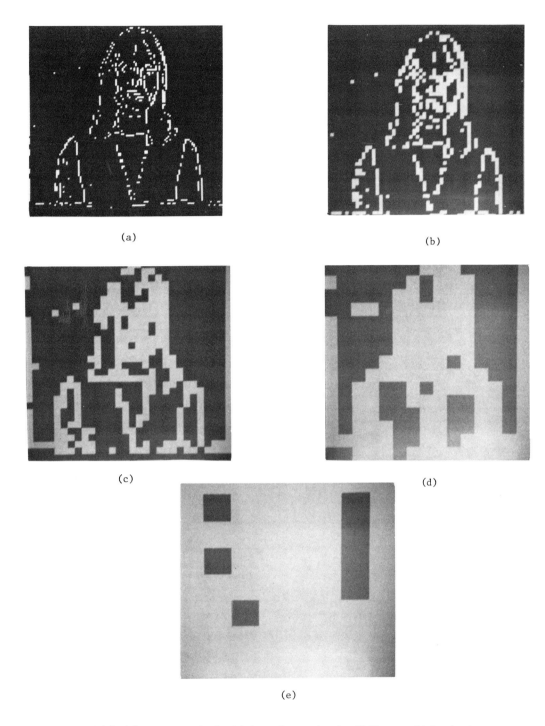

Figure 3(a)-(e): Successively higher planes in the EDGE pyramid beginning at 128 x 128 and automatically terminating at 8 x 8. Figure 3(e) shows the four starting regions.

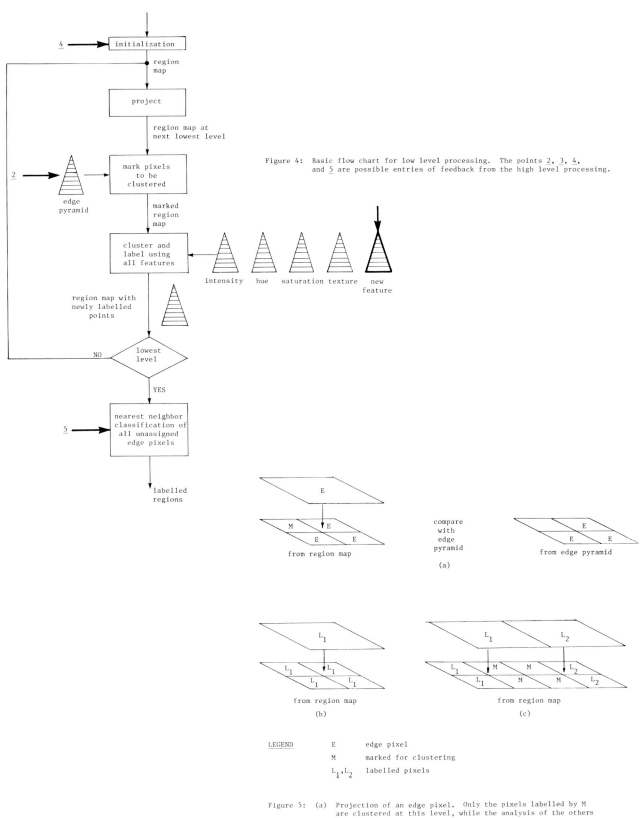

Figure 4: Basic flow chart for low level processing. The points 2, 3, 4, and 5 are possible entries of feedback from the high level processing.

LEGEND

E   edge pixel

M   marked for clustering

L_1, L_2 labelled pixels

Figure 5:   (a)   Projection of an edge pixel. Only the pixels labelled by M are clustered at this level, while the analysis of the others is postponed to lower levels in the pyramid.

           (b)   Projection of a pixel labelled as region L_1 by the shared nearest neighbour clustering process.

           (c)   The case of two adjacent labelled pixels.

Martin D. Levine

given, optimization becomes impractical, and a sub-optimal higher level of processing is demanded. At times this level may call upon the intermediate level for a selective analysis and this aspect will be discussed in the next section.

A partial segmentation of the image is the input to the intermediate level processing. The latter consists of two stages, one local and the other global. Local template matching is used to match collections of adjacent regions against all stored object prototypes. This is followed by an optimal search (in the form of dynamic programming) which incorporates a knowledge of the topological constraints to eliminate incorrect interpretations. This search resolves the competition between the possible local object matches and the permissible global structure.

The local template matching is based on the object feature model. The features $\Phi(1)$ describing the object are ordered into three categories according to decreasing relative importance in reducing the search time. The first category contains two particularly powerful features: $\Phi(1)$ the approximate location as defined by the minimum containing rectangle, and $\Phi(2)$ the approximate size as defined by the area. They have the effect of absolutely specifying which regions could be considered for merging, given an hypothesized object. The intrinsic features make up the second category; the four features of intensity $\Phi(3)$, hue $\Phi(4)$, saturation $\Phi(5)$, and texture $\Phi(6)$ are more relative in nature in that many objects may provide partial matches based on them. In the third category, the system uses two types of geometrical descriptions. The first, rough shape $\Phi(7)$, is measured in terms of the first six moment invariants [14] of the boundary of a particular region. These moment functions are invariant under linear operations such as translation, rotation, and dilation. The detailed shape $\Phi(8)$ is represented by a set of Fourier coefficients derived from a Fourier series approximation to a boundary function which defines the outline of the object. The Fourier descriptors as defined by Granlund [9] and Persoon [23] are used for the final template evaluation only because of time constraints and the fact that rough shape is adequate in the early stages of the matching process. Note that not all features can always be employed or need be available in the picture model. For example, if the same object is to be viewed at different magnifications, feature $\Phi(2)$ cannot be used.

We assume that the relational model for the picture class under consideration has been stored in the long term memory (described in the next section) in terms of the above features. Also, the same features are computed for each region segmented by the low level processing stage and presented as input to the intermediate level. A search is carried out for each region in the picture to determine the best neighborhood merge of the smallest number of regions, and is based on the optimization of an appropriate matching criterion. The A* graph search algorithm [21] is used: this ordered-search algorithm is based on the evaluation function $\hat{f}(n)$:

$$\hat{f}(n) = \hat{g}(n) + \hat{h}(n)$$

where $\hat{g}(n)$ is an estimate of g, the cost of an optimal path from a given start node s to node n

and $\hat{h}$, the heuristic power, is an estimate of h, the cost of an optimal path from n to the goal node.

Each node in the graph represents a region, while the arcs represent region adjacency in the sense of sharing a common boundary. Let $\hat{g}$ equal the number of nodes expanded since the start node s. Also $\hat{h}$ is a metric defining how close a particular region and a selected number of neighboring regions are to the stored model, given a particular interpretation:

$$\hat{h} = \sum_{i} \omega(i) \mid \Phi(i) - \Phi_{model}(i) \mid$$
all features

where $\omega(i)$ is a weighting factor which can be adjusted according to feature importance (often $\omega(1)$ is set to zero). Each path in the graph represents a specific collection of regions centred at the region under study. At any node n, all features are recomputed for the cluster of regions which is then treated as a single region as a result of the possible merge represented by the path. Because many of the features are additive, the computation is not as onerous as might seem.

All regions adjacent to the current region n are candidates for successors. Expansion of a node n is accomplished in two stages. First the features $\Phi(1)$ and $\Phi(2)$ are used to limit the number of successors on the basis of approximate location and size. A tolerance level related to the confidence that the user has in each of the features is initially input by him and associated with the model, making it highly unlikely that the global nature of the search will be effected. Then $\hat{h}$ is computed for each of the remaining candidates for each of the stored prototype models and hence interpretations. The best value of $\hat{h}$ is retained for each candidate and the minimum of these is then expanded. This process is continued until the goal node is reached, as defined by one of the following conditions:

(i) $\hat{h}$ is less than a threshold.
(ii) If all nodes are CLOSED (that is, all regions within the confines specified by $\Phi(1)$ and $\Phi(2)$ have been expanded).
(iii) If the number of expanded nodes exceeds a certain threshold.

The resulting path yields the best interpretation and grouping of regions for all possible clusters centred at the region of interest. Confidence in this interpretation is given by $(1-\hat{h})$.

We note that since a given region may form part of many optimal clusters, it is possible for more than one interpretation to be assigned to it. These are ranked in order of decreasing confidence $C_k(j)$, where the latter is the confidence that a given region k has an interpretation j. Figure 7 shows a simple test example with the regions obtained from the low level segmentation. Plausible interpretations for a particular region (no. 17) based on the graph search are shown in Figure 8. The shaded region is the one under consideration as the nucleus of the region cluster.

3.2 Optimal Search Based on Structural Descriptions

The above classification process can be seen as multiple template matching for various combinations of regions based on a composite feature analysis of each object. The relational model stored in the long term memory also contains structural information about the objects in the picture. This information is employed in the next stage, the optimal search. Spatial relations can be calculated between every pair of regions and assigned a value between 0 (false) and 1 (true) according to the strength of the relationship [8]. The relations used are: LEFT-OF, RIGHT-OF, ABOVE, BELOW, ADJACENT-TO, CONTAINS, and CONTAINED-BY [28]. The method of forward discrete dynamic programming is used to search for an optimal path where each stage represents a regions input from the low level processor. The states are the possible interpretations for the region as determined by the local template matching. State transitions are defined by the structural relationships.

Figure 9 depicts the forward dynamic programming problem. Note that the regions k obtained from the low level processing stage may be ordered either according to decreasing region area or decreasing Max $C_k(j)$ for a given k. Let $P_k(j)$ represent the path value for some accumulated path terminating at $j = J$ where $P_1(j)$ is initialized by letting $P_1(j) = C_1(j)$. For two regions at stages $k = K-1$ and $k = K$ we wish to estimate the consequence of assigning interpretation J to region $K-1$ and interpretation J' to region K. This is accomplished by comparing the actual structural relations existing between the two regions and the relations defined by the stored model given the postulated interpretations $j = J$ and $j = J'$. Let $\bar{S}(J,J')$ be the vector defining the structural relations between interpretations J and J', as stored in the long term memory and $\bar{R}(J,J')$ be the vector of actual relations as they exist in the scene between regions $k = K-1$ and $k = K$. A measure of the proximity of the two structual descriptions is computed as follows:

$$E_{k-1,k}(J,J') = 1 - \sum_{i=1}^{n_r} \frac{\omega_i |S_i(J,J') - R_i(J,J')|}{n_r}$$

where S_i and R_i denote the individual components of the vectors $\bar{S}(J,J')$ and $\bar{R}(J,J')$, respectively, and are scaled to lie between 0(false) and 1(true), and n_r equals the number of structural relations. The path cost for all permissible transitions from stage $k = K-1$ to $j = J'$ at stage $k = K$ can be computed as

$$P_k(J') = P_{k-1}(J) + E_{k-1,k}(J,J')$$

The optimal transition from stage K-1 to K is computed as follows. Find the state $j = J$ in stage K-1 such that $P_k(J')$ is optimized. This is equivalent to finding $j = J$ such that

$$P_k(J') = \max_{\text{all } J}[P_{k-1}(j) + E_{k-1,k}(j,J')] + C_{k-1}(j)$$

is maximized. The first term can be associated with the structural relations, while the second measures local similarity. This process is then repeated for all $j = J'$ so that at stage $k = K$, we are left with the maximal path cost $P(j=J')$. The latter value is then representative of the match between the regions on the path and similar interpretations of the stored model. This process is then repeated over the remaining stages. At the last stage the state with the maximum value of $P_k(j)$ represents the optimal path and the best global scene interpretation can be obtained by simple backtracking. Figure 10 shows the result of the optimal search for the test picture.

Note that because of the properties of dynamic programming, the above process could be cut off at any stage k, yielding the best interpretation for this subset of regions in the picture. By the same token, we can obviously initially choose to analyze only certain regions that appear in the original partial segmentation.

4. HIGH LEVEL PROCESSING

4.1 Introduction

Recently there has been some interest in the application of management-type relational databases for both picture analysis [18] and synthesis [29]. The basic property of these structures is that the data is stored in an associative format by means of tables. This provides for the important qualities in a knowledge database of modularity and data independence. In addition, the accessing mechanisms, which constitute a relational algebra, are independent of the data. Such operations as JOIN, PROJECT, INTERSECT, UNION, and RESTRICT are available to be used by the system for complex interrogation. A detailed introduction to relational databases can be found in [3].

The knowledge database or long term memory (LTM) shown in Figure 1 is a relational database and the high level processor presently being designed can best be characterized as a production system [4]. The latter is data driven and results in certain actions being carried out following data matching and the satisfaction of certain data preconditions. General information regarding the world models and their constituents are entered into the LTM as described in Section 1.3. To date we have restricted ourselves to pictures where recognition can be achieved on the basis of models of two dimensional projections of three dimensional scenes. The LTM therefore contains only two dimensional information, although in future we plan to expand the database to include the third dimension.

A temporary buffer or short term memory (STM) acts as a depository of data from various sources. In its role as a communication channel between these sources it is dynamically changing and being updated to represent the best current explanations of each region in the input picture data. This process is controlled by the actions which are stored in the LTM and constitutes the picture

Martin D. Levine

Figure 6: The result of the low level processing of a typical scene.

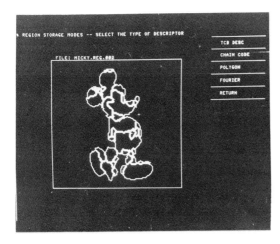

Figure 7: A simple test example with the regions obtained by low level processing. The MIPS menu is shown at the right.

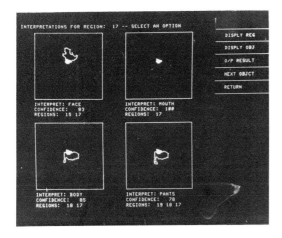

Figure 8: Plausible interpretations for region 17 (shaded area) associated with adjacent regions and based on the local search process.

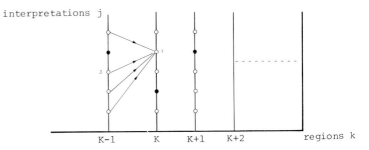

Figure 9: The search for the best global interpretation defined as a dynamic programming problem. The interpretations (states) represented by dots are those for which $C(j,k) = 0$ and are therefore ignored. The allowable state transitions to J in stage k = K from stage K-1 are shown by the directed arrows.

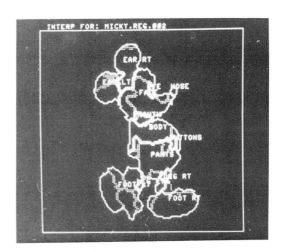

Figure 10: The result of the grouping and interpretation process using dynamic programming.

interpretation strategy (see Section 4.4).

The work described in Section 4 is in its early experimental stages and therefore alterations are expected in the future.

4.2 Long Term Memory

The LTM is a relational model which stores relevant information about the visual world. Many subworlds may form significant portions of this memory; for example, outdoor natural scenes, office scenes, kitchen objects, and so on. Awareness by the user of the particular pictorial context (subworld) can be conveyed to the LTM via computer interaction. Employing the relational algebra sublanguage, we may PROJECT the database over this particular subworld to extract all information relevant to it. This might in many cases require a complex search on its own. To circumvent this problem at this point in our research, a different subworld is used for each picture class.

Each object in the LTM has associated with it an action or set of actions which is called into play under conditions to be described below. These conditions are predicated on the state of the STM at any instant in time. We note that the relations in the LTM are stored in the so-called Third Normal Form, thereby providing an adequate level of data integrity [3].

The particular subworld sketched in Figure 11 is represented by the OBJECT relation in Figure 12. General knowledge about objects are contained in system relations, such as for example, those containing data on the mapping of color names and the definition of common shapes such as rectangles and triangles. The latter are defined in terms of moment invariants [14] and several definitions may exist for each 2D object. It follows that the objects in the subworld will be described by means of these data and definitions; this is accomplished by the relations OBJECT ATTRIBUTES and OBJECT SHAPE. We note that the latter relation pertains to the "Attributive" conceptual class as presented in Table 3 of Firschein [7]. These classes were used by humans to describe complex pictures and serve as a good basis for the definition of the database. Topological information is provided by the type of relations shown in Figure 13. We observe that objects need not necessarily appear only once in the first domain. More complex relations such as "perpendicular to" and "stretches across" could also be included. Conceptual classes "qualifying", "locational", "joining", intrusion, division", and "containment" as defined in Firschein [7] may be addressed by these relations.

The "localizing" conceptual class [7] or the complexity predicate is shown in Figure 14(a). This relation can be extremely powerful in limiting subsequent search after a particular object has been recognized with some confidence. Knowing what parts constitute the object, actions may be invoked in an attempt to create a match between the items in the STM and this subset of object-parts. Other important relations in the database may deal with the display of pictorial

information [29] for objects and "Comparison" [7] as embodied by an IS-A relation [30] (Figure 14(b)). Subsequent experimentation with the system will force the introduction of additional relations.

4.3 Short Term Memory

The STM as alluded to above, contains a list of the regions and their interpretations, both ordered to reflect the current state of knowledge. The regions are matched sequentially unless an action is involved which alters the sequence. The matching process may result in STM actions which will reorder the data in the STM (region or interpretation order); otherwise it may trigger a complex test procedure or a feedback signal to the low and intermediate level processing stages.

Information regarding these actions is stored in the LTM which contains an EXPLICIT ACTIONS relation as shown in Figure 15. The domain A is a pointer to a list of actions for each object, where each action may be an operation on the STM, a pointer to a test procedure, or feedback to a lower level. In this way it is possible to implement plans [11, 13, 17, 20, 31] whenever such information is available. It seems reasonable to assume that plans are employed by humans in the recognition process and this concept has proved to be useful in some rather complex automatic inspection applications [12]. Figure 16 is an example of a PLAN relation where the entries might actually be pointers to procedures. The tuples are ordered and implemented sequentually unless an action is invoked which alters the sequence.

Obviously a plan represents a considerable amount of information about a particular image and how it should be analyzed. Often this is readily available, such as in the case of face recognition, but consideration should be given to the inclusion of a learning mechanism so that the system could be taught to construct its own plans based on experience.

The short term memory (STM) contains pixel data, regions and their attributes, topological information, and current interpretations. Figure 17 shows the STM which obviously can be considered to be a workspace accessible by all levels of the analysis (see Figure 1) and is similar to the HEARSAY "blackboard" [6]. It is an _ordered_ list of regions obtained by the general purpose segmentation process. Note that via these regions, the original detailed image and associated pyramids are available. On the other hand, the link to the higher level information in the LTM is achieved by the interpretations. For each region, the latter are ordered in a list according to decreasing confidence. Since these interpretations are a direct result of references to the relational model (LTM), the STM has access to general knowledge, plans, contextual clues provided by user interaction, and so on. We see therefore that it plays the role of a depository of the best current image interpretation and accomplishes this by being a communications channel among various data sources.

Allusion was made above to the fact that actions specified in the LTM could result in

Martin D. Levine

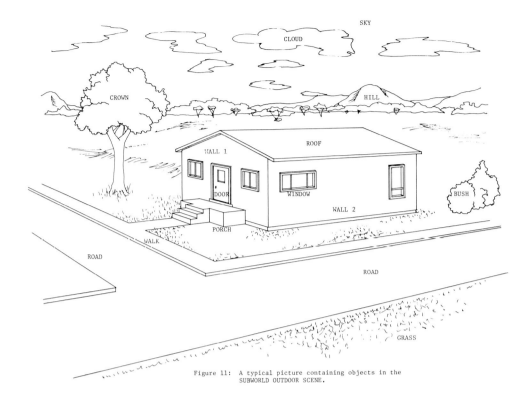

Figure 11: A typical picture containing objects in the
SUBWORLD OUTDOOR SCENE.

SUBWORLD OUTDOOR SCENE

OBJECTS	MINIMUM NUMBER
SKY	1
CLOUD	ANY
TREE	ANY
HOUSE	ANY
GROUND	1
LAKE	ANY
.	.
.	.
.	.

Figure 12: The relation SUBWORLD OUTDOOR SCENE.

ADJACENT

OBJECT	OBJECT	ADJACENCY
WALL 1	WALL 2	1.0
WALL 1	ROOF	1.0
WALL 2	ROOF	1.0
WALL 1	GROUND	1.0
WALL 2	GROUND	1.0
ROOF	SKY	0.5
BUSH	GRASS	0.7
ROAD	GRASS	1.0
TRUNK	GRASS	1.0
TRUNK	SKY	0.5
.	.	.
.	.	.
.	.	.

CONTAINMENT

OBJECT	OBJECT
WALL	DOOR
DOOR	DOORKNOB
WALL	WINDOW
GRASS	ROAD
SKY	CLOUD
.	.
.	.
.	.

ABOVE

OBJECT	OBJECT
SKY	GRASS
SKY	CROWN
ROOF	WALL 1
WALL 2	WINDOW
CROWN	TRUNK
.	.
.	.
.	.

Figure 13: Some relations describing topological information.

PART-OF

PART	OBJECT	MINIMUM NO. IN VIEW	MAXIMUM NO. IN VIEW
WALL	HOUSE	2	2
DOOR	HOUSE	1	ANY
WINDOW	HOUSE	1	ANY
ROOF	HOUSE	1	1
FRAME	WINDOW	1	1
PORCH	HOUSE	1	2
DOORKNOB	DOOR	1	1
CROWN	TREE	1	1
TRUNK	TREE	1	1
.	.	.	.
.	.	.	.
.	.	.	.

(a)

IS-A

OBJECT	OBJECT
GRASS	GROUND
SAND	GROUND
ROAD	GROUND
WALL 1	WALL
WALL 2	WALL
.	.
.	.
.	.

(b)

Figure 14(a): The complexity predicate.

(b): The IS-A relation.

Martin D. Levine

EXPLICIT ACTIONS

objects	A action pointers
O_1 O_2 . . . . . O_j	

Figure 15: EXPLICIT ACTIONS relation which provides pointers
for each object to pertinent actions and plans.

PLAN

number	name	search location	search neighbor-hood	test	test fail action	test succeed action	STM action	feedback to lower level

Figure 16: A PLAN relation.

STM

region #	pixel data	attributes	spatial relations	interpretations

Figure 17: The Short Term Memory (STM)

operations on the STM. These may either be applicable to a single region or a group of regions. The former includes insertion and deletion of region interpretations, as well as a complete reordering of the list for a particular region. The latter consists of a reordering of the list of regions itself. Since the high level processor analyzes (as described below) the regions in the STM in the order they appear, this reordering will have a major influence on the analysis process.

4.4 Interpretation Strategy

The high level processor involves two stages, initialization and search. One aspect of the initialization is the use of contextual clues provided by the user to limit the subworld under consideration. Obviously the more context that is provided, the more efficient the ensuing search stage. The flexibility of the associative relational database should allow for some interesting experiments to investigate the influence of such contextual clues on the interpretation process. We note that if part of the selected subworld is known to correspond exactly in number and kind of objects to those appearing in a certain area of the picture under study, then the system could employ intermediate level processing for this part of the analysis.

The input from the low level processing is a list of regions with no associated interpretations. In the initialization stage, each region is considered independently as a candidate for matching with the objects in the selected subworld and this is only done once in order to generate a set of feasible hypotheses. Possible interpretations are entered into the STM in order of decreasing confidence in the match. If the user sufficiently specified any part of the picture and if a PLAN for this part existed in the LTM, the system would temporarily feedback (see Figure 1) to the intermediate level. Here a local template matching process would attempt to group the regions in the neighborhood as described in Section 3. Interpretations from this analysis would be entered into the STM. Initialization is complete when all regions in the STM possess an ordered list of interpretations and the list of regions is itself ordered according to the degree of confidence in the most confident interpretation in each region's list.

The second stage of processing involves a search which uses the information in the LTM and is guided by two kinds of actions: implicit and explicit. This search is a complex matching process between data in the STM and LTM where the attributes of the regions as well as their relationships based on the stored interpretations are used to evaluate the region being considered. Details of this process are presently under study.

The implicit actions are invoked by the system when a given region X matches an object Y in the LTM with a degree of confidence above a certain threshold. The following occurs:

(i) The list of interpretations for the region is updated by reordering and Y is put on top of the list.

(ii) Region interpretations may be deleted when found to be incompatible with neighboring regions.

(iii) The regions in the STM are reordered to reflect the desire to examine neighbors of X.

Explicit actions are invoked if the list of interpretations for a region contains only one item. This may occur either as a result of the matching process or by enforcement in the initialization stage. The system executes the actions associated with the object in the LTM (see Figure 15). Such actions might include:

(i) The implementation of a PLAN (see Figure 16).

(ii) The merging of regions by the execution of the safest merge.

(iii) The re-ordering of the regions in the STM to reflect the present confidence based on this new discovery.

(iv) Feedback to the low and intermediate levels (as discussed in Sections 2 and 3).

The analysis terminates when each region in the STM is labelled with one interpretation.

5. CONCLUSIONS

The primary objective of the research described in the previous sections is to develop a computer vision system to experiment with different picture analysis strategies. Two important characteristics are representative of our approach. First, the system is being developed by taking full advantage of the power and convenience of interactive computation and man/machine communication using computer graphics. Second, a great deal of emphasis is being placed on the creation of a modular database, and what is more important, a modular decision strategy. By doing this, we hope to greatly facilitate the experimentation process.

The reader may have noted a certain degree of ambivalence regarding the intermediate level of processing. As the situation stands presently, we are developing the three stages described in the previous sections in a relatively independent fashion, subject to the relationships already described. Experimentation with low and intermediate level processing are well advanced and detailed results will be reported on in the near future. Implementation of the high level processing level is in its earliest stages. Therefore studies of its behaviour and integration with the other two levels have not yet commenced. Quite possibly the intermediate level of processing will be simply integrated within the structure of the high level processor. Only extensive experimentation and study will eventually lead to a resolution of this problem.

The vision problem is extremely complex and difficult. Therefore the approach we have taken is to construct a modular and extensible experimentation system which will permit the examination of alternate hypotheses about various aspects of this

Martin D. Levine

problem. In light of our initial research, this paper has discussed the structure of such an experimental knowledge-based computer vision system.

REFERENCES

[1] Aoki, M., Levine, M.D., Computer generation of realistic pictures, Report No. R-77-8, Dept. of Electrical Eng., McGill University, Montréal, Québec, October 1977.

[2] Arbib, M.A., Two papers on schemes and frames, COINS Tech. Report 75C-9, Computer and Information Science, Univ. of Massachusetts at Amherst, October 1975.

[3] Baird, M.L., An application of computer vision to automated IC chip manufacture, Proc. of the Third International Joint Conference on Pattern Recognition, Coronado, California, November 8-11, 1976, pp. 3-7.

[4] Date, C.J., An Introduction to Database Systems, Addison-Wesley Publishing Co. Inc., Reading, Massachusetts, 1975.

[5] David, R., King, J., An overview of production systems, Memo AIM-271, Artificial Intelligence Laboratory, Stanford University, Palo Alto, California, 1975.

[6] Elkind, D., Perceptual development in children, American Scientist, vol. 63, no. 5, Sept.-Oct., 1975, pp. 533-541.

[7] Erman, L.D., Lesser, V.R., A multi-level organization for problem solving using many diverse, cooperating sources of knowledge, Proc. $IJCAI, Tbilisi, Georgia, September 1975, pp. 483-490.

[8] Firschein, O., Fischler, M.A., A study in descriptive representation of pictorial data, Second International Joint Conference on Artificial Intelligence, London, England, Sept. 1-3, 1971, pp. 258-269.

[9] Freeman, J., The modelling of spatial relations, Computer Graphics and Image Processing, vol. 4, 1975, pp. 156-171.

[10] Granlund, G.H., Fourier preprocessing for hand character recognition, IEEE Trans. on Computers, Feb. 1972, pp. 195-201.

[11] Hanson, A., Riseman, E., The design of a semantically directed vision processor: revised and updated, COINS Technical Report 75C-1, Computer and Information Science, University of Massachusetts, Amherst, MA, February 1975.

[12] Haralick, R.M., Dinstein, I., A spatial clustering procedure for multi-image data, IEEE Trans. Circuits and Systems, vol. CAS-22, no. 5, May 1975, pp. 440-450.

[13] Harlow, C.A., Image analysis and graphs. TR IAL-TR 17-72, Image Analysis Laboratory, University of Missouri-Columbia, Columbia, Missouri, September 1972.

[14] Holland, S.W., A programmable computer vision system based on spatial relationships, Research Publication GMR-2078, Research Laboratories, General Motors Corporation, Warren, Michigan, February 1976.

[15] Hu, M.-K., Pattern recognition by moment invariants, Proc. IRE, vol. 49, September 1961, p. 1428.

[16] Jarvis, R.A., Patrick, E.A., Clustering using a similarity measure based on shared near neighbors, IEEE Trans. on Computers, vol. C-22, no. 11, November 1973, pp. 1025-1034.

[17] Kasvand, T., Some observations on linguistics for scene analysis, Proc. Conf. on Computer Graphics, Pattern Recognition, and Data Structure, UCLA, May 14-16, 1975, pp. 118-124.

[18] Kelly, N.D., Edge detection in pictures by computer using planning, Machine Intelligence, vol. 6, 1971, pp. 397-409.

[19] Kunii, T.L., Weyl, S., Tenenbaum, J.M., A relational database schema for describing complex pictures with color and texture, Proc. Second International Joint Conference on Pattern Recognition, Lyngby-Copenhagen, Denmark, August 1974, pp. 310-316.

[20] Levine, M.D., Malowany, A.S., Leemet, J., Luk, S.F., An interactive image processing, display, and programming system, Fourth Man-Computer Communications Conference, Ottawa, Canada, May 26-27, 1975.

[21] Levine, M.D., Leemet, J., Computer recognition of the human spinal outline using radiographic image processing, Pattern Recognition, vol. 7, no. 4, December 1975, pp. 177-185.

[22] Nilsson, N.J., Problem-solving methods in artificial intelligence, McGraw-Hill Book Company, New York, 1971.

[23] Ohlander, R.B., Analysis of natural scenes, Ph.D. thesis, Dept. of Computer Science, Carnegie-Mellon University, Pittsburgh, Pennsylvania, April 1975.

[24] Persoon, E., Fu, K.S., Shape description using Fourier descriptors, Second International Joint Conference on Pattern Recognition, Lyngby-Copenhagen, Denmark, Aug. 13-15, 1974, pp. 126-130.

[25] Roberts, L.G., Machine perception of three-dimensional solids, Symposium on Optical and Electro-Optical Information Processing Technology, Boston, 1964, pp. 159-197.

[26] Rubin, A.D., Hypothesis formation and evaluation in medical diagnosis, Report no. AI-TR-316, Artificial Intelligence Laboratory, Massachusetts Institute of Technology, Jan., 1975.

[27] Tanimoto, S., Pavlidis, T., A hierarchical data structure for picture processing,

Computer Graphics and Image Processing, vol. 4, 1975, pp. 104–119.

[28] Tenenbaum, J.M., Accomodation in computer vision, Memo AIM-134, Artificial Intelligence Laboratory, Stanford University, Palo Alto, California, October 1970.

[29] Ting, D., Feature calculation and storage, MIPS MEMO 76-2, Dept. of Electrical Eng., McGill Univ., Montréal, Québec, May 20, 1976.

[30] Williams, R., On the application of relational data structures in computer graphics, Proc. IFIP Congress, 1974, pp. 722-726.

[31] Winston, P.H. (Ed.), The Psychology of Computer Vision, McGraw-Hill Book Company, New York, 1975, Chapter 5.

[32] Yakimovsky, Y., Scene analysis using a semantic base for region growing, Memo IAM-209, Artificial Intelligence Laboratory, Stanford University, Palo Alto, California, June 1973.

[33] Youssef, Y.M., An automatic picture processing method for tracking and quantifying the dynamics of blood cell movement, M.Eng. Thesis, Dept. of Electrical Eng., McGill University, Montréal, Québec, Canada, June 1977.

[34] Zucker, S.W., Production systems with feedback, Pattern-Directed Inference Systems, F. Hayes-Roth & D. Waterman, eds., Academic Press, N.Y., 1977.

ACKNOWLEDGEMENTS

The author would like to thank Juhan Leemet, Samir Shaheen, and David Ting for their contributions to the research described in this paper and Allen Hanson, Ed Riseman and Steve Zucker for their constructive comments. This work was partially supported by the National Research Council of Canada under grant no. A4156, the Medical Research Council under grant no. MA3236, and the Department of Education, Province of Québec.

Martin D. Levine

RECOGNITION OF REAL-WORLD OBJECTS USING EDGE CUE

Yoshiaki Shirai

Electrotechnical Laboratory
Nagatacho, Chiyodaku, Tokyo

Abstract

A computer system for recognition of everyday
objects such as a telephone or a desk lamp is described. The system is to locate and identify
various objects using an array of light intensities.
It consists of (1) an edge finding process which
extracts edges of curved objects, (2) a description of edges by straight lines or elliptic curves,
(3) recognition of objects using a hierarchy of
features, and (4) a monitor which controls the
three modules to perform reliable and efficient
tasks. Control decisions are guided by the partial
results obtained on the scene. Thus, only a proper
number of edges are extracted to analyze a given
scene. Locating several objects on a desk takes
about 3 minutes using a 6 bit 256×256 intensity
array stored on a disk.

1. Introduction

This paper describes an approach to the
recognition of real-world objects using light
intensity data obtained by a television camera.
In general, scene analysis could be divided into
two stages: (1) extraction of features and
(2) recognition of objects based on these features.
It is often pointed out that the two stages should
not simply be connected serially, but should interact with each other to achieve efficient and
reliable recognition [1].

The author made an attempt to recognize
polyhedra using two stages: a line finder and a
line proposer [2]. For a polyhedra scene, a
sharp light intensity change usually corresponds
to an edge. Thus, most edges are easily extracted
and vertices composed of edges are good cues for
predicting the positions of other edges. However,
it is not easy to design these two stages to be
capable of recognizing real-world objects. We
don't know exactly what a particular light intensity
change corresponds to. Even if we can extract
some features, there is no general rule to propose
other features.

There has been some work on description of
curved objects using range data [3,4,5]. Garvey
and Tenenbaum [6] examined methods for locating
objects in office scenes using range and color
data. Range data played an important role in
finding candidate regions for a table top, a seat
of a chair or a wall. Yakimovsky [7] interpreted

outdoor scenes by region analysis using color data.
The method incorporated semantics of scenes as a
priori probabilities of the interpretation of each
region and the relations between neighboring
regions.

On the other hand, recognition of everyday
objects on a desk using only light intensity data
requires more complex features. There are fewer
constraints on the possible configurations of
objects on a desk than in outdoor scenes. The
light intensity of a point alone can not suggest
any meaningful facts. It is necessary to look at
the change of light intensity and its relationship
with other parts of the scene. Early work on
recognition of curved objects employed bottom-up
methods. In the Edinburgh system [8], for example,
both a scene and a model are described by properties of its constituent regions and the relations
between adjacent regions. Recognition was accomplished by a graph matching process that compared
the descriptive networks of a scene with a model.
Later, Turner [9] recognized the same objects by
hierarchical synthesis based on edges. Usually, a
region analyzer or a line finder used in the
bottom-up method is too costly to be employed
everywhere in a scene. The top-down method, on the
other hand, is also inefficient for analysis of a
general scene, because a priori knowledge about a
scene alone is not powerful enough to guide feature
extraction. Thus we need a method in the middle,
i.e., first, find some features, and then use them
to guide the further processing. This method is
explicitly defined by Freuder [10] as "recognition
using active knowledge."

The work presented here is an extension of [1]
to a more general system that analyzes scenes which
include multiple objects against a natural background. As the complexity of a scene increases,
in terms of the objects involved and the relationships existing between them, the amount of processing required to "recognize" the constituents of
the scene increases. Therefore, efficiency of
processing becomes increasingly important. The
system consists of (1) edge finding, (2) description of the edges, (3) recognition of objects, and
(4) a monitor. A simplified behavior of the system
is as follows. First, obvious edges are found in
an entire scene, and they are described by lines or
elliptic curves. Then, the recognition module

tries to find objects using the description. If enough objects are not recognized, more edges (which are less reliable than those found in the previous stage) are searched for or some edges already found are extended. This process repeats until enough objects are found or a termination condition is satisfied. Each time, the search area for more edges is reduced based on the recognition. The monitor interacts with the other modules in a simple way: it monitors the results of each process, and determines when to stop processing or what to do next.

2. Edge Finding

Edges are used here as the primary basis of representation. The choice of regions or edges depends both on which is more appropriate to the problem domain and on which is more easily obtained. In this system where features are collected gradually as recognition proceeds, the choice should depend on which provides more useful information for recognition at the same computation cost. Recognition in this domain is mainly based on the shape of objects, not on the brightness or size of regions nor on their positions. Although both features provide the same information, edges were chosen because of the cheaper cost of extracting them.

2.1 Edge point detection

An edge of an object surface is defined here as a series of smoothly connected edge points. An edge point is classified into three types (B, R and L) as shown in Figure 1 according to the light intensity profile across the edge point. If the direction of an edge is known (the direction is decided such that the right side of the edge is brighter), an edge point is detected using one-dimensional operator as follows.

Imagine Cartesian coordinates U-V such that V is the direction of the edge. Let $I(u,v)$ denote the light intensity at a point (u,v). The gradient value at (u,v) is defined as

$$D(u,v) = \sum_{i=1}^{a_i} \sum_{j=-a_j}^{a_j} I(u+i,v+j) - I(u-i,v+j)$$

Usually the area over which the averaging is done is small ($a_i=1\sim3$, $a_j=3$). Point (u,v) is determined to be an edge point if it satisfies the following three conditions

$$D(u,v) \geq D_t \qquad\qquad (C1)$$

$$\exists_i \{D(u+i,v) < f(D(u,v)) \wedge -w \leq i \leq w\} \quad (C2)$$

$$\forall_i \{ 2D(u,v) < D(u-i,v) + D(u+i,v) \wedge 1 \leq |i| \leq w\} \ (C3)$$

where D_t is a threshold, w is usually less than 4 and $f(x) = c_o + c_1 x$ ($c_1 > o$).

(C1) means that the light intensity must change at an edge. (C2) means that at least one neighbor point must have a smaller gradient value. (C3) ensures concavity of the gradient profile and rejects the points near the true edge.

In (C2), if there exist both positive i and negative i, the point is classified to be type B in Figure 1; if there is no negative i, then it is classified as type L; and otherwise to type R. The parameters a_i, a_j and w depend on the resolution of a scene and on the noise. Edge point (u,v) has a measure of reliability defined here as $D(u,v)$.

If the direction of an edge is unknown, a conventional two-dimensional operator [14] is used to get the direction and value of the gradient. The

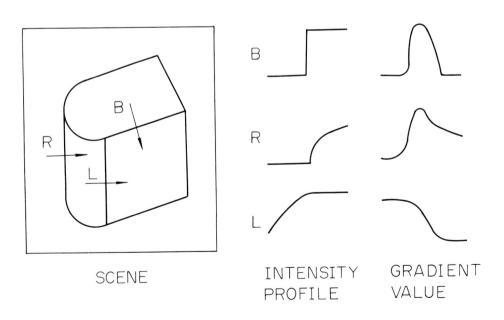

SCENE   INTENSITY   GRADIENT
             PROFILE   VALUE

Figure 1.   Intensity profiles of edges.

Yoshiaki Shirai

direction of an edge is determined as perpendicular to the gradient direction. Once the direction is determined, the edge point is detected in a manner similar to that described above [11].

2.2 Edge tracking

Figure 2 shows a simplified flow of the edge finding program. The program has two main tasks: (1) find an edge kernel whose reliability is above a given level, and (2) track along the edge starting from the kernel.

The edge kernel is a set of edge points of the same type which have similar gradient directions. Given D_t in (C1), a kernel finder first detects edge point E using the two-dimensional operator, and then detects other edge points in a rectangular region (3 × 5 picture elements) whose center is E and whose longitudinal axis is perpendicular to the gradient direction. If enough edge points with the same type and similar directions are found, the center and the direction of the kernel are computed based on the detected edge points. The edge kernel is also classified into the same type as that of the edge points.

The reference map in Figure 2 is used to form a "plan" in order to speed up the kernel finding and to mask some parts of the search area. The original picture is divided into rectangular regions (e.g., 4 × 4 picture elements) and initially, the map contains an approximate maximum gradient value in each region. This value at (i,j) is given by

$$D'(i,j) = \max_{\substack{-1 \le \Delta i \le 1 \\ -1 \le \Delta j \le 1}} |I(i + 2\Delta i, j + 2\Delta j)|$$

$D'(i,j)$ is computed at every four points in the original picture. The kernel finder searches for an edge point in the regions corresponding to the points in the map with values larger than a given reliability value. After an edge kernel is searched for in the candidate region, the corresponding $D'(i,j)$ in the map is updated in order to provide a more accurate value for the later processing.

When a kernel is found, it is extended in both directions by tracking the edge. The purpose is to find a smoothly curved edge which consists of proper edge points. The meaning of proper edge point depends on the case in which tracking is performed. In finding new edges, it means that the type of the point is the same as that of the kernel, and its reliability is above a given level and similar to that of the previous edge point. In extending an edge already obtained to find another edge connected to it, the type of the edge point does not matter.

In tracking curves, the parameters shown below are used to predict an edge point and are updated as the tracking proceeds. The type of the edge and the initial value of the parameters, such as the position X_c, direction β_c, and gradient D_c are given by the kernel finder. The main steps of the tracking at one cycle are:

1. Predict the position of the edge point using X_c and β_c.

2. Find a proper edge point.

3. Update X_c, β_c and D_c, and go to 1.

The prediction of the edge point P^n during the n-th cycle is based on the current edge position X_c^n and the direction β_c^n as shown in Figure 3. The distance between X_c^n and P^n is one of the parameters of the edge finder which determined the maximum curvature of the edge tracker. When a proper edge point E^{n+1} is found, X^{n+1} is advanced from X_c^n in β_c^n direction by one picture element and B_c^{n+1} is updated as shown in Figure 3. If the predicted

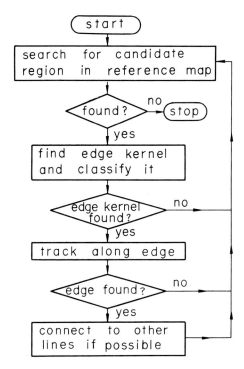

Figure 2. Flow chart of the edge finding process.

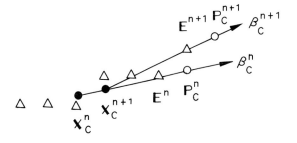

Figure 3. Prediction of edge point.

position of the edge is regarded as being on another edge already found, or on the other end of the same edge, the tracking terminates.

In step 2 of the tracking process, the one-dimensional operator is used to find an edge point of the same type near the predicted position. The direction of the gradient of the edge point is assumed here to be perpendicular to the current direction of the edge. If the gradient value of the detected edge point is close to D_c, it is assumed to be an extension of the edge. If no such points are found, a back up routine determines whether or not to stop tracking as follows.

a) If step 2 is the first attempt of the edge point finding, a different gradient direction is proposed to find a proper edge point again, and step 2 is repeated.

b) If an edge point is found in the previous cycle, then insert a simulated edge point at the predicted position and go to step 3.

c) Otherwise, stop tracking.

The purpose of the back up is to avoid the effects of a small amount of texture of an object, various kinds of noise, and digitization of directions.

When the tracking in both directions terminates, each end of the edge is checked to connect to another edge already found. If the tracking stops at an end of another edge of the same type and both edges can be connected smoothly, they are merged.

Figure 4 shows an example of the edge finding process. Usually, edge finding is repeated over the picture, each time changing the reliability to a lower level. The tracking of a less reliable edge can be blocked by more reliable edges which cross to it.

3. Description of Edges

Each edge obtained by the edge finder consists of a set of smoothly connected edge points. The description of the edges provides the recognition module with useful features of the edges.

There is a large body of literature on the mathematical approximation of curves by polygonal lines [e.g., 12] or piecewise polynomial functions [13]. These methods utilize a suitably defined error norm and attempt to find an optimal solution. However, they are not always suitable for recognition of complex scenes, because the representations are not easily handled by a human being in writing recognition programs.

In this paper, straight lines and elliptic curves are used to describe the edge curves. This description is sufficient for the edges of every-day objects, and they are simple enough to be intuitively understood by humans. The description process is divided into two parts: (1) segment an edge into lines or elliptic curves, and (2) approximate each segment by an equation. The former part is more difficult and has a great influence on the latter's performance.

The purpose of the first part is illustrated by Figure 5(a), i.e., to divide the edge AF into five segments (AB,BC,...,EF). The method is a heuristic one which makes use of the curvature of an edge as described in [2] (the curvature of an edge point P is defined as the angle δ between RP and PQ, where Q and R are on the edge and constant number (m_d) of points away from P). Thus, the curvature of AF is defined on the interval between A' and F' as in Figure 5(b) which is m_d points inside of AF. The main steps of the segmentation are as follows:

A. Find the candidates of the borders of segments (knots).

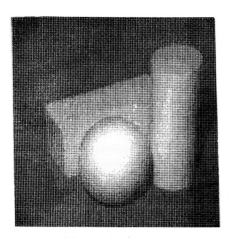

(a) Original scene
*: type B,   R: type R

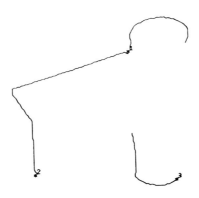

(b) Most reliable edges (pass 1)

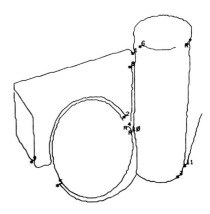

(c) Final result (pass 7)

Figure 4. An example of edge finding.

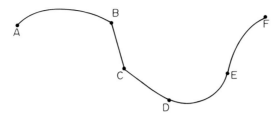

(a) edge to be segmented

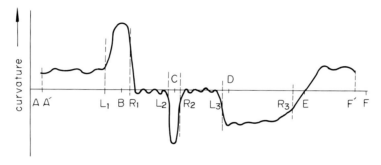

(b) curvature along the edge

Figure 5. Initial segmentation of an edge.

B. Classify temporary segments into straight lines, curves or unknown.

C. Merge segments if possible.

D. Determine the positions of knots.

First, to locate the knots where the direction of the edge changes abruptly, the regions are found which have large curvatures. The candidate regions of the knots are illustrated in Figure 5(b) as intervals $[L_i, R_i]$. The interval is defined with the curvature $\delta(P)$ as follows. Let δ_{max} denote the maximum of $|\delta(P)|$ in $[L_i, R_i]$, then the interval satisfies the following conditions.

$$\delta_{max} \geq \delta_t$$

$$|\delta(P)| \begin{cases} \geq h(\delta_{max}) & \text{for } P \in [L_i, R_i] \\ < h(\delta_{max}) & \text{for } P = L_i - 1 \text{ and } P = R_i + 1 \end{cases}$$

where $h(x) < x$ is a linear function of x.

The intervals may contain either real knots or curved segments. If the interval is short, it is regarded as a real knot region, otherwise a curved segment. New knots are inserted at the ends of curved segments. Now the temporary segments are defined as the intervals between the knot candidate regions (i.e., $[A', L_1]$, $[R_1, L_2]$, $[R_2, L_3]$, $[L_3, R_3]$ and $[R_3, F']$ in Figure 5(b)).

Step B classifies the temporary segments (excluding the curved intervals found in step A) into straight lines or curves using the constant (m_d) of the curvature, sum of δ's (S_δ) and the total number (N) of points in the segment. If the segment PQ is assumed to be an arc as in Figure 6,

the fan angle θ, and the maximum distance d between the line PQ and the arc are approximated as follows.

$$\theta = S_\delta (N-1)/m_d (N-2m_d)$$

$$d = (N/\theta)(1-\cos \theta/2)$$

Based on this arc assumption, the classification algorithm is given as follows. If $N \leq 2m_d$, then the segment is undefined; if $d > d_u$, then it is a curve; if $\theta < \theta_t$, then line; if $N < N_t$ and $d \leq d_\ell$ ($d_\ell < d_u$), then line; otherwise curve. A curved segment is further examined to determine if it includes a long straight line. If so, it is again segmented into a line and the rest, and step B is repeated.

Step C tries to merge adjacent undefined or curved segments. The criterion for a merge is based on the curvatures (θ/N) of the adjacent segments and the knot between them. If they are similar, the two segments are merged. This procedure is repeated until no more segments are

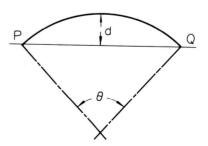

Figure 6. Arc approximation.

merged. Small segments of a smooth curve created in step A because of the effect of noise or digitization might be merged here. The unknown segments not merged here are regarded as lines.

The second part of the segmentation fits a straight line or curve to a set of edge points $(X_i, Y_i)(i=1,2,\dots,n)$ in each segment. Conventional least squares methods assume that only Y_i is accompanied with error. But the position of each edge point has error in both X_i and Y_i. Deming's method [14] is employed to find the parameters of the curve which minimizes the sum of the squares of the distance from the curve to each point.

Let the equation of the curve with m parameters be denoted by $f(x,y; a_1,a_2,\dots,a_m)=0$, then the method, starting from the approximated parameters, estimates better parameters iteratively until they converge to within a given error ratio. The initial parameters are obtained from an appropriate number of edge points which are sampled from the segment. If the segment is classified as a curved line, an attempt is made to fit it first by an elliptic curve. The parameters are the center position, major and minor axes and rotation. If the parameters do not converge in the iteration, the number of the parameters is decreased (i.e., the ellipse first degenerates into a circle, and then into a line). Figure 7 shows an example of the results of the segmentation and curve fitting.

4. Recognition

A strategy for recognizing an object in a scene depends on how much information is already known. The search can be constrained and directed by the presence of other objects. Assuming that several objects have been recognized, the search for a telephone ought to start within the desk region but outside the bookstand region; if the dial, a part of the telephone, has been found, regions adjacent to the dial should be examined for the remainder of the objects. The best way to analyze the whole scene is to start from the most obvious object first, and proceed to the next obvious object making use of the previous facts.

In this system, recognition procedures for an object depends on lines and objects already found. It involves the following three stages.

1. Find the main feature to get clues for the object.

2. Find a secondary feature to verify the main feature and to determine the range of the object.

3. Determine the range and find the other lines of the object.

The recognition procedure proceeds from stage one through three, but it may stop at any stage.

For recognition of a lamp, for example, the program locates a lamp shade in the first stage. If it succeeds, then it proceeds to the second stage and it searches for the lamp trunk supporting the lamp shade. If it succeeds, then it searches for a contour of the lamp base supporting the trunk. If it fails during the search for a certain part, it determines whether the features obtained so far seem to really belong to the lamp or not. Here, recognition of a lamp succeeds when the lamp shade and the trunk are found. If recognition succeeds, then it determines a region for the lamp. The region depends on the result of the previous stages. For example, if a lamp base occluded by some object is partly found, the region should not include that object. The lamp region is a good clue for finding the other lines of the lamp which have not yet been identified.

Table 1 illustrates a hierarchy of features used for recognition. The hierarchy of features for an object is based on two aspects of the features. One is the importance of the feature in implying the presence of the object, and the other is the ease with which it may be found in a scene. Most of the features consist of the edges represented by the equation and the terminal points. Care must be taken in finding a contour of a region because edges of a region do not always constitute a closed line. For recognition

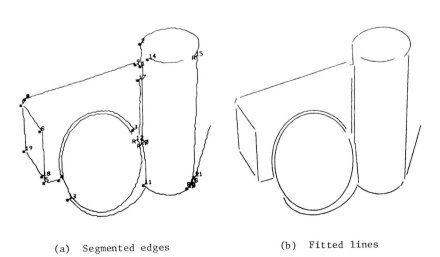

(a) Segmented edges   (b) Fitted lines

Figure 7. Representation of edges for Figure 5.

Yoshiaki Shirai

Object	Main feature	Secondary feature
Lamp	Contour of bright strip region corresponding to lamp shade.	Pair of vertical edges of opposite directions corresponding to trunk, and contour of base under trunk.
Book Stand	Long vertical lines clustered in a rectangular region.	Lines connected to main features.
Cup	Pair of vertical edges of opposite directions corresponding to side of cup.	Contour of cup connected to main features.
Telephone	Ellipse corresponding to contour of dial or outer circle surrounding number characters.	Contour of case surrounding main feature.
Small objects (pipe, pen, etc.)	Shape and size of contour.	Details of shape and light intensity changes.

Table 1. Example features used for recognition

of small objects, a fixed resolution is sometimes not enough to discriminate between similar objects such as a pen, a pencil or a ball-point pen. It is necessary to zoom in on an interesting part to examine the detail of an object.

5. Total System

This section describes how the system efficiently analyzes a scene to recognize various objects in it. Three modules described in the previous sections work under monitor control as shown in Figure 8. A priori knowledge consists of the orientation and direction of the camera as well as the parameters of the camera (zoom, iris, etc.).

First, some edges are necessary to get information about a scene. The problem is what and how many edges should be collected. The goal of edge finding in a scene is to provide initial information about the scene at as low a cost as possible. The monitor sets a reliability level for edge finding, and determines when edge finding should stop. The stopping condition is based on the number of edges, number of edge points and a reliability level. This initial setting of these conditions affects the efficiency. If it is too high, enough edges are not obtained; in this case the level must be lowered and another attempt made at finding edges. Many cycles of this process take much time. On the other hand, if the level is too low, too many edges are collected. The reference map described in section 2 is used to estimate the initial level. A histogram of D' provides a good approximation to the number of edge points to be found with a given reliability level. Thus enough edges are usually obtained in one cycle of edge finding.

An edge map in Figure 8 is a two-dimensional array (stored on the disk) corresponding to the scene containing edge numbers already found. It is used in both edge finding and recognition in order to find edges in a given area. Edge finding uses another map (called a bit map) whose one bit shows the existence of an edge element. The process for tracking an edge checks the bit map to see if there are other edges crossing the tracked edge. If other edges are detected, tracking terminates.

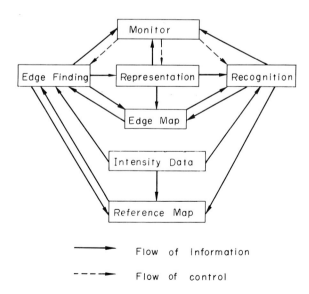

Figure 8. Information flow among the main components of the system.

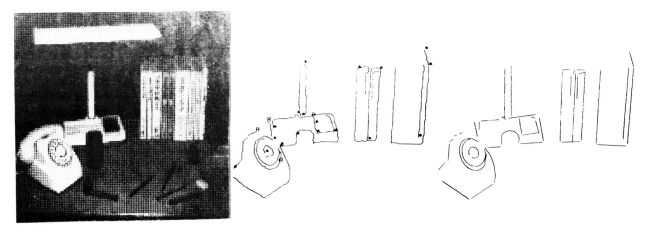

(a) Original scene (b) Edges found in cycle 1 (c) Description

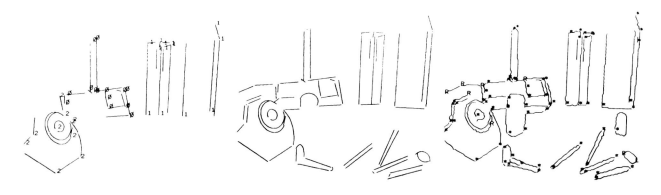

(d) Recognition (e) Description in cycle 2 (f) Edges found in cycle 4

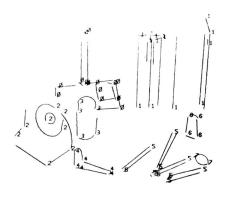

0: lamp
1: book stand
2: telephone
3: cup
4: pipe
5: pen, pencil, ball-
   pointpen or felt pen
6: ink pot
7: eraser

(g) Recognition

Figure 9. An example of the recognition process.

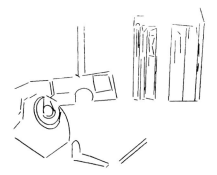

Figure 10. Description of edges
found without feedback
from the recognition
process.

Yoshiaki Shirai

Then the edge numbers are found using the edge map and relations of the edges with the tracked edge are determined.

When enough edges are found, before going to the fitted representation of objects, some edges are extended to fill small gaps between different edges. Because intensity profiles of edge points often change near vertices, tracking edge points of the same type may stop near the vertices. Such edges are extended disregarding the edge type.

After edge finding, control is transferred first to the description process and then to recognition. In recognition, an attempt is made to recognize big objects first, such as a lamp, a book stand or a telephone, because features for big objects are usually found easily and results from recognition may effectively reduce the search area for both recognition and edge finding. Small objects such as pens or an eraser are tried after many large objects are found or many edges are obtained. Otherwise, a small object might be confused with a part of a big one. When an object is recognized and the region is determined, the corresponding part in the reference map is changed so that no edge kernel may be found there in a later edge finding process.

If enough objects are not found, program control returns to edge finding, where by decreasing the reliability level more edges are collected. The monitor decides when to stop this process based on the number of edges and edge points obtained in the previous cycle, and those obtained in this cycle. The search area for edge kernels in this cycle is usually smaller and new edges are found efficiently.

Control is then transferred to the recognition process in a manner similar to the first cycle, where more objects or parts of objects are tried for recognition. This is the end of the second cycle. This cycle is repeated until enough objects are found or the reliability for edge finding reaches a certain level.

Finally, the system may take a new input image if the recognition module needs a close-up in order to discriminate between similar small objects. This feature is not described in this paper.

Figure 9 shows an example of locating various objects on a desk. All the objects are recognized in 4 cycles. Edge finding is performed 5 times with different reliability levels (twice in the second cycle). Figure 10 shows edges obtained without feedback from recognition. That is, starting from the same reliability level, edges are collected repeatedly decreasing the level until about the same number of edge points are obtained. Edge finding is performed 3 times in this case. We can observe many edges inside a telephone and a book stand which are not found in Figure 9. This means that more edges must be obtained before all the objects are recognized.

Computation time depends mostly on the complexity of a scene. For the above example about 3 minutes is required to recognize all the objects using intensity data (6 bit × 256 × 256 points) stored on a disk. Most of the time (80%) is spent for edge finding while recognition takes the least (5%). Without feedback from the recognition process, edge finding might take much more time for the collection of more edges. Experiments on recognition of various objects on a desk has been successful while varying both the distribution and orientation of objects and lighting conditions.

An approach to recognition of real-world objects using light intensity data has been described. Recognition proceeds gradually by applying edge finding, edge representation and recognition processes repeatedly. Each time new facts are found, they are used to make the following processing effective and efficient. Experiments on recognition of various objects have proved the validity of the method.

Future work is required to improve the total system. One is the use of various features such as color, range or texture to handle a variety of scenes. Another is a programming method. In this system, a recognition program for an object is constructed manually. We need an efficient technique to develop programs for many kinds of objects.

References

[1] Winston, P.H. The MIT robot. Machine Intelligence, 7, 1972, 431-463.

[2] Shirai, Y. A context sensitive line finder for recognition of polyhedra. Artificial Intelligence, 4, 2, 1973, 95-119.

[3] Agin, G.J., and Binford, T.O. Computer description of curved objects. Proc. 3rd Int. Joint Conf. Artificial Intelligence, 1973, 629-640.

[4] Oshima, M., and Shirai, Y. Representation of curved objects using three-dimensional information. 2nd USA-JAPAN Computer Conf., 1975, 108-112.

[5] Popplestone, R.J., et al. Forming models of plane-and-cylinder faceted bodies from light stripes. Proc. 4th Int. Joint Conf. Artificial Intelligence, 1975, 664-668.

[6] Garvey, T.D., and Tenenbaum, J.M. On the automatic generation of programs for locating objects in office scenes. Proc. 2nd Int. Joint Conf. Pattern Recognition, 1974, 162-168.

[7] Yakimovsky, Y. On the recognition of complex structures: computer software using artificial intelligence applied to pattern recognition. Proc. 2nd Int. Joint Conf. Pattern Recognition, 1974, 345-353.

[8] Barrow, H.G., and Popplestone, R.J. Relational description in picture processing. Machine Intelligence, 6, 1971, 337-396.

[9] Turner, K.J. Computer perception of curved objects using a television camera. Thesis, School of Artificial Intelligence, Edinburgh University, 1974.

[10] Freuder, E.C. A computer system for visual
      recognition using active knowledge. AI-TR-
      345, Artificial Intelligence Laboratory,
      Massachusetts Institute of Technology, 1976.

[11] Shirai, Y. A step toward context sensitive
      recognition of irregular objects. Computer
      Graphics and Image Processing, 2, No. 3/4,
      1973, 298-307.

[12] Pavlidis, T. and Horowitz, S.L. Segmentation
      of plane curves. IEEE Transactions, C-23, 8,
      1974, 860-870.

[13] Braess, D.D. Chebyshev approximation by
      spline fanctions with free knots. Numer.
      Math., 17, 1971, 357-366.

[14] Honma, H., and Kasuya, N. Dimensional analy-
      sis method of least squares and experimental
      formula. Course on Applied Mathematics, 5,
      Corona Publishing Co., Tokyo, 1969 (in
      Japanese).

Yoshiaki Shirai

"Recognition Cones," and Some Test Results;
The Imminent Arrival of Well-Structured Parallel-Serial Computers;
Positions, and Positions on Positions*

Leonard Uhr
Computer Sciences Department, University of Wisconsin

"Science must debate all admissible hypotheses in order to obtain a complete survey of all possible attempts at explanation....But it is unworthy of a thinker who claims to be scientific to forget the hypothetical origin of his propositions. The arrogance and vehemence with which such concealed hypotheses are defended are the usual result of the feeling of dissatisfaction which their champion harbors in the secret depths of his conscience about the justification of his cause." H. v. Helmholtz (the father of perception as a science).

Overview

1) This paper first presents a set of positions (on the issues posed for this volume) that argue for probabilistic parallel-serial variable resolution perceptual systems that can make use of large amounts of diverse contextually interrelated information, in a dynamic flow of mixed environment-driven (bottom-up) and internally driven (top-down) flow of processes. It further presents the position (on positions) that the open-minded application of scientific method by the whole community of scientists, attacking such a complex and difficult task as perception, is necessary, to insure as great as possible a diversity of considered approaches.

2) The imminent arrival of true hardware-embodied parallel-serial computers is briefly discussed, and the suggestion made that many of today's perceptual systems will gain orders of magnitude increases in speed and power when their highly iterated operations are coded for highly parallel computers built with arrays of 10^4 to 10^8 programmable processors.

3) Finally, the author's "recognition cone" systems are described, as an example of the parallel-serial probabilistic approach being suggested. A basic system for multi-layer recognition and description of a scene has been coded in EASEy (a variant of Snobol), Fortran, and Simula, and a few test results have recently been obtained. Extensions and variations have been coded in EASEy, to handle continuing scenes of objects that move about and change over time, binocular (and multimodal) perception, learning-by-discovery, and perception as embedded in a larger cognitive system (called "See-err").

* This research has been supported by NSF Grant MCS76-07333 and by the University of Wisconsin Graduate School.

Section 1. Positions, and Positions on Positions

This paper tries to do three different things: A) Positions are argued on some of the basic issues of perceptual models that have been posed this group. B) The final coming of very large arrays of (10^4 and, potentially, more) processors whose hardware is truely parallel, and the enormous potential power this promises for many perceptual processes, are discussed. C) The author's "recognition cones," for probabilistic parallel-serial perception, are described, as examples of the kind of architecture being proposed, and some test results are presented.

Introduction

All the participants in this volume were asked to state their positions on a number of key questions about how we should go about developing perceptual systems. It was suggested that I use my answers in this volume, I suspect partly because they express a rather extreme viewpoint, at least when compared with the mainstream approaches being taken today.

This field has seen several major swings, first to overly parallel systems (Rosenblatt's "perceptrons") and then to overly serial systems (Minsky and Papert's "serial algorithms"). I think the pendulum has begun to swing again. If I seem to be attacking a straw man, fine - that means things are becoming better faster than I had judged.

The Free Choice of Science

But far more important than any specific position that I (or anybody else) could possibly take is the following: All approaches that reasonable, thoughtful and knowledgeable people find promising should therefore be tried. No individual or grant-giving agency knows what the "truth" is, what the "correct" approach is - especially in such a complex and strange new field as this. People should listen to and try to build upon one another. But we should resist the impulse to propagandize and dogmatize mere opinions, or turn them into schools. We have already seen too many bandwagons, too many false hopes.

The scientific method means, above all, the free choice by each expert scientist of the problems, approaches and techniques that she or he has judged to hold the most promise. Thus individuals should spread themselves over the promising alternatives (those that one individual finds under-explored becoming for him especially promising in their likely pay-offs; those that many individuals find promising being more vigorously pursued).

This is the way for the whole community of science to advance as fast as possible. Each individual should realize the strong likelihood that he has chosen the wrong approach. Thus the failures as well as the successes play their vital role, and all participate in any success. And far more success can be achieved than if people expend effort trying to make everything look like success.

A Discussion of the Position Questions

I. The most important answer to the questions posed for this volume is the following simple and rather obvious set of observations:

A. Nobody knows today what the right approach will be. We are engaged in the empirical enterprise of designing by far the most complex and highly structured system man has ever attempted. All promising approaches should be pursued as vigorously as possible.

B. Worse, nobody even knows how to evaluate what is done. We still don't have a clear idea of our goals - e.g. what is a "description," or what would be a good "model for perception." We don't know how to compare the different dimensions of complexity - e.g. linear vs. non-linear transforms, depth, color, texture, motion, or the relative difficulties of straight vs. curved lines, or letters vs. chairs vs. faces vs. trees.

C. Ours is a most difficult problem. It has been a central preoccupation of psychologists and philosophers for thousands of years. For the first time we have a powerful enough tool in the large computer to grapple with it effectively. We are making much faster progress; but we should make clear and attack the difficulties, rather than evade them. There is little value in handling a particular suitably simple problem unless it can then be generalized (or is of real practical importance).

D. Learning is probably the key to the flexibility and general-purpose adaptability that is needed for a system that is able to recognize and describe changing scenes of unanticipated objects. Without learning, ad hoc programming can (cumbersomely) handle a few specific problems. But no system can be large enough to handle "all possible objects" (indeed this is a potentially infinite set, with new objects created all the time). Rather, a system must be able to learn about that subset of objects with which it must interact.

E. We have had arguments and proofs, that have often been falsely overgeneralized and misinterpreted, about the limitations of either of the extremes of, for example: strictly parallel vs. strictly serial; non-deterministic vs. deterministic; perceptual characterizing vs. heuristic problem-solving; pre-programming vs. learning; multivariate vs. syntactic vs. framed; bottom-up vs. top-down. Often a straw-man extreme is set up; often the supposedly opposing approaches boil down to much the same thing; often a judicious golden mean can combine the several approaches to exploit the strengths and eliminate the weaknesses of each.

II. To answer or respond to some of the questions posed:

1. There can be no "primary basis for segmentation" (unless we restrict the set of scenes the program is asked to handle to scenes that always contain the information (e.g. perfect contours) with which the program has been designed to segment). One object will have clean and sharp edges, but internal regions that vary in color, texture, intensity, etc. in wild and arbitrary ways (e.g. Hawaiian Mu-Mus). Another object will have homogeneous regions but no edges; or dotted, fragmented or foggy - essentially vague - edges (e.g. Chinese landscapes). Therefore perception systems must look for both regions and edges--and expect not to find them. They must be able to make do with fragmentary information, combined from diverse sources. And higher-level features are probably crucial: many objects can be segmented only after they have been perceived. Perception infers and constructs the object; segmentation can then be used to re-cover non-existent boundaries.

2. The more information the easier the segmentation process - if the system is capable of combining information from many diverse and unanticipated sources. Color can be especially helpful in giving qualitatively different regions between which edges can relatively easily be drawn. The motion of an object against a background is probably even more helpful, potentially (but this poses very difficult problems), since the perceiver now has a sequence of very slowly changing images from which to construct the object. Striking textures are helpful, like color; but many textures are quite subtle and variable. Perception of objects that move seems to me the most important problem still to be attacked. Once we achieve such systems we will be able to make powerful use of the additional information they can gather.

4. Parallel-serial systems are obviously needed, rather than either parallel or serial systems. Minsky and Papert devastated strictly parallel systems (1-layer "perceptrons"), showing their explosive inefficiency at handling global properties like parity or connectivity. Long before that Selfridge had pointed out that strictly serial systems are only as good as their weakest links. And attempts to use serial techniques for real-world patterns seem to develop intolerably long chains of tests. Parallel takes space; serial takes time.

But these are both straw-man extremes. By combining serial and parallel processes we can minimize time and space and gain the virtues of both. For example, to compute parity (that is, whether there is an odd or even number of 1s) over an array of 0s and 1s, a completely parallel "1-layer perceptron" takes only one moment of time, but needs 2^N elements, each with N connections (N = the Number of cells in the array) (Minsky and Papert, 1969). They propose instead a very simple serial algorithm, that looks at and counts (modulo 2) each cell in the array, and therefore takes N (times a small constant) moments of time. But a parallel-serial set of simple binary exclusive-or operators, where the first layer looked at the array, a second layer looked at the output array of the first layer, and so on, needs only N - 1 elements, each with only 2 connections, and takes only $\log_2 N$ moments of time! Thus both space and time requirements are brought down to acceptable

Leonard Uhr

small numbers. Input to a visual system, or to any sensor that is gathering information about an environment, is highly parallel, and it seems foolish to insist upon handling it in a serial manner. A serial approach usually has a problem-solving flavor; parallel-serial approaches force us to a more probabilistic combining of diverse sources of information - I think giving more the flavor of living perceptual systems and of semantic contextual interactions. They also give great efficiency, robustness over unanticipated distortions, and economies in speed.

5.-6. The human eye - like the computer - can get a global property only by successively compounding the local intensities and gradients sensed by its retinal receptors. It may well be useful to "glance" first at the higher-level things found, and then dip down to details, as needed. But if this "glance" entails computing lower-level partial functions in order to achieve these higher-level things it seems wasteful not to use them, to have them interact with "top-down" semantic guidance. Again, all levels are obviously needed. For example, grey-level gradients sometimes can be resolved into contours only after the highest semantic levels have resolved vague objects so that the level and type of fogginess can be assessed, and used to change the parameters for low-level edging and contour detection.

7. We can always construct counter-example-like problems that cannot be segmented at the retinal level. Therefore there must be an inner-directed top-down component to perception, one that allows higher-level characteristics, and "what the system expects and is looking for" to influence segmentation. This entails a judicious combining of both inner- and outer-directed processes. For example two eyes, one nostril and one lip can be enough to imply a face, which then segments cheeks, chin, etc.

We do not know what "primitive features" are necessary for vision. Attneave and Arnoult, Hubel and Wiesel, and others have suggested primitives that seem buildable into larger wholes. But the only way we can tell whether they work (and, more important, how efficiently, generally and powerfully) is to build a computer program around them, and test it.

Polyhedra recognition reduces the problem enormously, to straight-edge and regular-region detection. And many other scene-analysis systems similarly simplify to look for features that seem appropriate for recognition of a very small set of objects of special interest. This is fine if future expansion, to a wider variety of objects, is kept in mind, and effected. But too often ad hoc techniques are particularized to the simple problem, only to make it even more difficult to generalize.

For example, real-world objects can have almost any kind of complex (broken and fragmented) curve for their contours. They hardly ever have flat surfaces and straight edges.

11. Multiple sources of knowledge can be accessed and used when and if a serial program calls for them. Or they can be got by more or less independent processors or demons, and put in a common working memory for one another's use. But there are problems with such structures, and it seems best to impose a structure over the system that lets the flow of processes trigger needed processes, as appropriate. This needs techniques

to merge and combine, and to choose among, what is found. The parallel-serial pyramid/cone systems attempt to do this, and the living visual system does this with celebrated success.

13. Objects like furniture, faces, or letters have a 2- or 3-dimensional structure that is far more complex than is the "syntactic" structure of words in a sentence. The basic problem of perception is to characterize that structure. Almost any system for reasonably difficult real-world problems does just that, whether by compounding and interrelating primitive features, or by looking for features that are themselves structural.

14.-16. Much current work seems to attack a specific domain in order to chop the problem down to size, and develop ad hoc partial solutions, without any thought, or hope, of future relaxation and generalization. This is fine when there is an important practical problem to be solved, and enough general understanding of our techniques so that a particular solution can be achieved with a reasonable amount of effort. But too often we are jollied into thinking that a problem (e.g. polyhedra) is practical, or generalizable, and solvable. Then, when it proves to be more difficult than originally claimed, ad hoc devices are scotch-taped on to give a few striking demonstration results, but also eliminating any possibility of generalizing.

A "general vision system" must be our long-term goal, since it is simply a part of science's age-old goal of building a theory of the intelligent mind/brain. This is not a 5 or 10 year goal; it will probably only be set back by crash-project approaches. Applications can help move toward that goal, but only if they are chosen to give us a variety of experiences, so that we can examine, compare, generalize, and improve upon the specific systems we develop to handle each application. An application of overriding practical importance (that cannot be handled well enough, or cheaply enough, by humans) should certainly be attacked for its own sake. But progress will be faster, and results will be more informative, if we develop a general body of knowledge that can be applied to each application.

15. In my opinion, parallel-serial systems that integrate characterizing transforms for a variety of kinds of information in a combined outer- and inner-directed flow of processing are the most attractive. The transforms must be capable of assessing configurations of more or less loosely interrelated characteristics (which are themselves configurations of characteristics, etc.). Weights and thresholds should be used, to give efficiency, and to allow for the many non-linear variations and defective information that will always be present in any but artifical toy scenes.

More important, no system could handle "all possible objects." Rather, we must develop techniques for discovery-learning of sets of features and higher-level characteristics sufficient for the environmental scenes that confront such a learning system.

Most important, as wide as possible a variety of approaches should be explored, compared and evaluated.

17.-18. One of our biggest problems is just the development of criteria for evaluating and comparing systems. We don't even know what "description" means, or what are the basic dimensions of complexity. There are a potentially infinite number of possible objects, and of each object's parts, and momentary representations (think of all the faces, and noses, and expressions of Liv Ullman's face). How do we compare a system that can handle 26 printed vs. handwritten letters (by the same, vs. by different writer(s)) vs. 4 different polyhedra vs. chair-or-table, vs. chair-or-couch, vs. John-or-Teddy vs. John-or-Jackie? How compare scenes with only one object, vs. two or four, when they are separated, vs. touching or overlapping?

We have a rough idea of the dimensions, (e.g. 2-d, 3-d, time, intensity, color, texture, motion, linear transformation, noises, non-linear transformations). But it is too easy to find a problem that looks hard but turns out to be handleable - where we don't know whether that shows we have achieved an interesting system, or have shown the problem to be simpler than it appears.

But some steps can be taken immediately: Programs should be tested, and their performance compared to one another. Standard sets of test scene-instances would therefore be very helpful. They should fairly mirror the range of underlying problems, and should not be biased toward any particular approach. Tests should be made on scene-instances that the designer of the system has not seen himself, since that is the only way to guarantee that he has not built in overly specific ad hoc knowledge. (It is fine to build in knowledge. But the designer must be given an understanding of the whole set of scenes his system will be asked to handle, either by being given a good set of sample instances or, if possible, in some other way. But if somebody designs a program to handle one particular picture of a red house with evergreens, and tests his program on just that one picture, how can we judge the results?)

18. We don't know how "hard" vision is, or how long we must work. A good vision system must use contextual semantic knowledge of the most central sort, as and when it judges these appropriate. It must manipulate its world, construct its environment, and discover good concepts. So it needs a solution to the problems of "cognition" and "intelligence" as well. But we can certainly simplify. A full-blown vision system might need a $10,000^2$ retina, and the ability to describe scenes with hundreds of objects and thousands of qualities, features and peculiarities, from among millions of possible object-classes, each with billions of possible object instances (I have just been describing a human being). But we can develop our systems using a far smaller retina (500^2? 100^2?) and far simpler scenes (of 5 or 10 objects) and possible object classes (1000? 100?) each with far fewer possible instances (10^6? 10^4?). So today's (or next year's) computers should be sufficient. But we must try to develop systems that can handle more objects once given either more built-in knowledge or learning experiences.

III. To recapitulate some of the issues:

I think we need non-deterministic parallel-serial systems that intimately integrate large amounts of contextually relevant information in a mixed inner- and outer-directed way, combining weights and making choices, trying to do as well as possible and expecting very defective and unanticipated scenes. They must learn, and be as flexible, general and adaptive as possible.

I know we need to encourage all promising approaches, develop good criteria for evaluating and comparing systems, achieve a much better conception of our intermediate and longer-term goals, and be more realistic in our expectations and promises.

Several things seem compelling about perceptual systems. Their purpose is to gather useful information about the external environment. They must be efficient, robust over wildly fragmented and distorted scenes and fast enough to respond in time. The cognitive system lies within a two-dimensional "skin" that can most efficiently be used by a set of parallel input sensors, whose information can best be combined and analyzed by sets of relatively local parallel transforms. This means the overwhelmingly complex functions computed by perceptual systems are best decomposed into successively simpler sets of functions, and all applied in a parallel-serial flow of processes. Some of these functions should be built in, but some of them must be learned.

Such a picture fits well with the structure of living systems, with their highly parallel sensory organs, and successive layers of parallel and relatively local synapses/transformations in the retina, lateral geniculate and cortical projection areas. But nature is not peculiar; rather, such systems evolved because they are eminently sensible. I know of no good arguments why any unnatural "artificial" device gives advantages. We can exploit the computer's "brute force" only if we cut our problems down to toy size - just as a British Museum algorithm (randomly examine every move!) can win at tic-tac-toe but never at chess.

Could a nature capable of evolving protein molecules, DNA and neurons be unable to develop magnetic memories? Did nature build the awesome complexity of a cell just to slow neurons down to millisecond speeds, rather than the nanosecond speeds already available in inorganic metals? This is not to say that we shouldn't try to develop non-natural techniques, but to remind how intelligent nature is.

Section 2: Parallel-Serial Hardware Structured for Perception Systems

1976 saw the coming of two new computer systems that connect relatively large parallel arrays of programmable processors (100^2 in Duff's CLIP 4, 1976, and 512^2 in Kruse's PICAP, 1976) to a small serial computer system. Each processor would be cumbersome as a general-purpose CPU, but is quite appropriate for a wide variety of perceptual operations. Kruse's PICAP (which is serial at the hardware level, but fast enough because of its built-in array processor to handle TV images in real time) has already been used for very interesting fingerprint and microscope slide recognition. And Cordella, Duff and Levialdi, 1976, have shown that for thinning, contour extraction, and several other basic picture processes Duff's CLIP 4 is many orders of magnitude faster than a serial computer. And such arrays are now cheap. The parallel array increases the cost of Duff's total mini-computer-based system less than 20%.

But these systems are only the beginning. For the technologies are rapidly improving, so that more can be packed on a single chip, and the cost of chips continues to go down (and is even cheaper in larger quantities). Possibly even more important, there is a whole range of architectures for parallel-serial computers of this sort - ones with very large arrays, rather than the few dozens we see on systems like ILLIAC-4 - that are almost entirely unexplored.

Toward Parallel-Serial Architectures For Very Large Arrays

For example, a system with 5 or 10 arrays arranged in layers like the layers of pyramids and cones (see below) would literally be able to handle almost all of their processes in one fell sweep. New scenes could be input by a tv camera every 30 msec, or faster, so that real-time motions could be handled without any strain. Even better would be a large array (say 1200^2) that could be re-configured under program control, e.g. into one deep cone, or a binocular pair of slightly smaller cones.

A variety of configurations for networks of processors, and of arrays of processors, are now possible - if we knew what to do with them and how to program them. But for scene description we do know what to do with the large parallel arrays. And, as in this case, when parallel structures are appropriate, and are known, the savings can be enormously greater than what has become known as "Minsky's conjecture" - that concurrent processors speed things up only by $\log_2 N$ (N = Number of processors). On the contrary, for cone/pyramid structures they would speed things up by a factor of LN_r (where N_r = Number of processors in the largest (retinal) layer and L = the number of Layers). So a 10-Layer pyramid with a 1000^2 retina would be processed 10^7 times faster!

Systems that Would Benefit Greatly from Parallel-Serial Hardware

A number of researchers have been exploring layered parallel-serial variable-resolution structures for scene description, including Hanson and Riseman, 1974, 1976; Tanimoto, 1975, 1976; Levine, 1976; Douglass, 1977; Klinger and Dyer, 1974; Uhr, 1971, 1974; Uhr and Douglass, 1977. A variety of different strategies are being pursued, but all have in common a relatively well structured set of large numbers of parallel-serial operations and a regular flow of processes through this pyramid/cone structure. So these systems could literally gain 10^5 to 10^9 - fold in speed if they could be programmed for and run on a computer with hardware parallel arrays, one for each layer.

An increasing number of today's systems for scene description also seem to be moving in the direction of using successive stages of processes that are already conceived of as highly parallel, or would benefit greatly if re-structured into parallel form (as they almost certainly would be if the appropriate parallel-serial hardware were available). For example, the recent development of "spring-loaded" "relaxation" techniques, by Zucker, 1976; Davis and Rosenfeld, 1976; Tenenbaum and Barrow, 1976; and Fischler and Elschlager, 1973 use parallel and in some cases probabilistic operations that appear to speed-up and generalize earlier serial systems that resolve incompatibilities (e.g. Waltz, 1975; Guzman, 1968).

Still others are consciously exploring the values of parallel-serial processes (e.g. Waltz, 1977; Williams, 1976; Hannah, 1974; Zobrist, 1971; Zobrist and Thompson, 1975.)

Highly Parallel Aspects that are Present in Many Other Perceptual Systems

Finally, a number of systems that have not emphasized these aspects of their structure would appear to have important parallel and probabilistic components. These include, I think, some of the most interesting and powerful of today's perceptual systems, e.g. Ejiri, 1972; Sakai, Kanade and Ohta, 1976; Nagel, 1976; Mckee and Aggerwal, 1976; Moayer and Fu, 1976; Ohlander, 1975; Reddy, 1973; Lowerre, 1976. Such systems are usually described in terms of successive serial stages, or of a small set of demon-like processors that act concurrently. Superficially these may appear to demand a traditional serial computer, or, possibly, a multi-processor with 10 or 20 independent CPUs (and all the attendant headaches) interacting through one common working memory.

But usually when one looks at the details of the processes performed <u>within</u> each stage, or each demon, one finds very large amounts of parallel processing. For any scene description system must first process the very large array of parallel information input to the "retina." And almost always local averaging, differencing and edge detecting - all essentially parallel processes - go on at the early stages.

But even at the highest levels, the fact that the same objects might be found almost anywhere in the scene often entails large iterating loops that usually have an equivalent parallel algorithm. And the similarity-match of each of the alternative possible "models" or "descriptions" of the possible objects is often far more efficiently done by a parallel-serial sorting network of their partial features, much like a complex discrimination net, rather than by the serial matching of each possible model in turn (which becomes exponentially slow, and extremely complex e.g. in backtracking possibilities when "similarity" is assessed, as must be done for natural real-world objects) rather than the far simpler exact match that can be used for straight-edged polyhedra or similarly simplified sets of objects).

Section 3: "Recognition Cones" for Perception, and Some Results

The following describes the basic structure of the parallel-serial probabilistic "recognition cone" perceptual systems I have been developing. Extensions are briefly described that begin to handle motion and change, binocular and multimodal perception, learning-by-discovery, and perception as embedded in and aided by the larger set of processes of a wholistic cognitive system. A series of layers of transforms, applied in parallel at each layer, successively extracts, compounds, coalesces and abstracts information. Each transform acts much like a simplified synapse that fires when enough of its specified pattern of inputs is present to exceed its threshold. A large number of transforms must be programmed into or learned by the system. Only a few preliminary sets of transforms have been used so far.

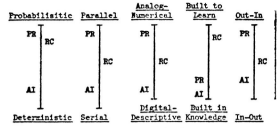

Figure 1. Recognition Cones (RC) compared with the (mythical) typical Artificial Intelligence (AI) systems for vision, and with typical Pattern Recognition (PR), on some of the basic dimensions and positions discussed above.

The Basic Perceptual System
for a Single Static Scene

The basic model (Uhr, 1971; 1974 see Figure 2) inputs a sensed scene onto its "Retina" (an array of any size specified). A first internal

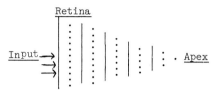

Figure 2. Recognition Cone Structure. Layers of transforms (dotted lines) look at and imply things into buffer stores, transforming from retina to apex.

layer of "transforms" looks at the cells of the retina. Each transform is located at a particular cell, and "looks at" any number of (usually neighboring) cells for specified information. When and if any transform succeeds (because the combined weights of the found parts exceeds its threshold) it merges those things that it implies into the corresponding cell of the internal buffer into which it fires. A single transform is thus roughly like a synapse, with a number of neurons firing into it from the cells it "looks at" and a number of neurons firing out of it, sending the messages as to what it implies (when it fires) into the next layer.

Layering

Thus the first layer of transforms looks at the retinal input and fires into the first internal buffer, an array that now stores information and is treated exactly like the retina.

A second layer of transforms looks at this first internal buffer and merges its successfully implied things into the next internal buffer. This process continues, with a third, a fourth, and whatever number of layers of transforms desired (that is, specified for a particular run).

Convergence

Convergence occurs at each layer, as desired, by having a Row and Column* STEP-size specified,

_____

*Caps are used to refer to actual names used in the computer program.

to indicate the amount of shrinkage from each layer to the next. E.g. the Retina might be set as a 16 by 36 array, and shrinkage factors used to divide this for convergence into the next layer occur as follows: 2 by 2 gives 8 by 18; 2 by 3 gives 4 by 6; 2 by 3 gives 2 by 2; 2 by 2 gives 1 by 1.

Cone Structure of Layers of Parallel-Serial Transforms

Thus the system forms a parallel-serial structure of many layers of transforms sandwiched between buffer arrays that store information. The overall structure is that of a cone whose base is the retinal input buffer and whose apex is the final buffer that contains a single cell. Each layer of transforms operates in parallel (that is, in simulated parallel time, as programmed on the serial digital computer).

The Structure of Transforms

Each transform has the following form: A DES-CRiption specifies the parts of the configuration that the transform is to look for. A "part" can be a specific thing, or a class, with an associated minimum acceptable value, a weight and relative location. (It can also be a procedure that computes any desired function that has been coded as a subroutine; but such procedures seem undesirable when modelling living visual systems, since they do not appear to be found in networks of neurons.) The transform looks for each part (as though neuronal processes were sending information about these parts to the transform-synapse) and combines the weights (which can be positive or negative) of those parts that are found (at the moment the combining function is simple addition or multiplication of weights, but any desired combining function can easily be inserted). If the combined weight exceeds the transform's THRESHold, the transform "fires," by MERGEing the things that it IMPLIES into the corresponding cell of the next layer internal buffer or one of the lists described below.

The Variety of Things, Names, and Structures that Transforms can Imply

This structure allows for a great enough variety of "things" that might be implied into the next layer so that the various processes that are usually handled by separate subroutines in most models of visual systems can be handled in a homogeneous way by this single general mechanism. Thus a transform can serve to "pre-process" in the sense of averaging out noise or differencing to enhance gradients and edges. Or it can imply internal things like "local horizontal edge" and then a next-layer transform can look for several of these things and build up bigger structures, like "long horizontal edge". Configurations can be got, like "horizontal connected to vertical" or "table-top." External names, like "A" or "FACE" or "TABLE" can also be implied. All this information is implied and merged back toward the apex of the cone.

A simple example of the structure we can give a cone follows: Transform layer 1 averages the intensity of light in each local region, or combines the primary colors. Layer 2 differences locally (e.g. looking at a 3 by 3 region, or if desired, a larger region), giving the center cell a high positive weight and the 8

Leonard Uhr

surrounding cells low negative weights). At layer 3 around 5 or 10 transforms reside at each cell, each transform looking for a relatively simple local feature (e.g. Hubel-Wiesel-like local oriented edges; or local sets of cell values that the system has generated through prior learning). At layer 4 transforms look for spatially related configurations of several of these local edges (e.g. to build up longer edges, contour segments, and angles). At layer 5 transforms look for higher-level configurations of these configurations.

In addition to implying transformed values and internal names, transforms at any layer can also imply external names, ones that will be chosen among when the output - the assigned names or description - is chosen. For example, a long vertical can imply the letter "I" with a high weight, and the letter "E" and "TABLE" each with a lower weight. Then a transform that compounds the long vertical with a horizontal at the bottom going to the right can imply "E" with a high weight and negatively imply, to inhibit, "I" and "TABLE". A more peripheral transform that implies a short local vertical edge or gradient (which will be one of the input parts that allow a higher-level transform to successfully imply a long vertical edge) can also imply "I" or "E" - albeit with only a low weight. Thus each transform can imply a variety of things, including internal names and external names, of parts, wholes, wholes made up of wholes, and also of qualities (e.g. "STRAIGHT" or "DARK") and internal transformations (e.g. the cleaned-up or enhanced gradient).

Dynamically Implied Transforms and Things to Look For

A successful transform can imply new transforms to apply, and/or new things to search for (which in turn point to transforms that imply them), along with relative projected positions. This means that not all transforms need to be assigned to cell locations within the recognition cone, and applied to all input scenes. Rather, particular transforms can be called and used only when information gathered so far suggests that they might be useful. It seems hard to give a physiological interpretation to such dynamically implied transforms. But to the extent that a very large number of transforms is needed to handle all the different things that a general-purpose eye must perceive they can effect an enormous saving, since only the small sub-set needed for each particular scene need be used, rather than using all transforms on every scene. (Note that it is not clear how many transforms will be needed. But the parallel-serial structure that allows transforms to build up larger wholes at successive layers is designed for economy.)

Such dynamic transforms serve three important purposes:

1) They allow the system to "glance about" (at least with the "mind's eye") to look for additional characteristics that would confirm or deny tentative hunches. E.g. a vertical edge might imply "look for a horizontal edge near the top" or "look for an 'F'" which further implies "look for the transforms that imply 'F'" which will include this particular transform. Or "D" might imply "look for 'DOG'" which implies "look for 'O' a bit to the right".

2) They serve to give feedback loops to earlier layers of processing. E.g. "D" implies "look for 'DOG'" which implies "look for 'G' to the right" which implies "look for 'Vertical-curve' and 'Horizontal-edge'" (which will be found at earlier, more peripheral, layers).

3) They allow for quick and convenient shifts of attention, for the system can imply and roll in the transforms related to the particular type of things the system now infers it is viewing. E.g. when "chair" is implied it can imply "furniture," which then implies characterizers that imply other kinds of furniture. Thus a bottom-up flow triggers a top-down flow that merges in with it.

Dynamically Implied Triggers to Decide

A transform can also imply a trigger that a decision be made. The trigger can specify the particular class of objects among which the single most highly weighted is to be chosen. The cell where the transform trigger fires is then looked at and the things stored in it chosen among, the choice being transferred to a FOUND list. The cell at which the choice is made serves as the apex of a sub-cone whose base is a sub-region of the retina. This helps the system handle scenes of several objects, by assigning descriptive names to sub-regions.

A Summary of the Overall Structure of "Recognition Cones"

The overall structure, then, is a parallel-serial "cone" that uses successive parallel layers of probabilistic configurational transforms to process information input to a sensory retina. Convergence and merging of information implied by successfully applied transforms from one layer to the next gives the cone structure, from retinal base to a final layer with only one cell, the apex.

Each transform looks at a whole set of inter-related parts (things or processes), combines the weights of those that it finds, and fires if this combined weight exceeds its threshold, by merging the things it implies into the corresponding cell of the next internal buffer (or into the list of dynamically implied transforms or things to look for, or triggering a choice in that cell, putting that choice into the FOUND list).

The number of layers, steps of convergence, and particular transforms must be specified for a particular run (or, if learning is being investigated, some or all may be the result of prior learning experiences).

Handling Continuing Scenes of Moving and Changing Objects

The program for single static input scenes re-initializes itself for each new scene by erasing all of its temporary lists, including the retina, the apex, and the other internal buffers of the cone. The program for scenes of moving and changing objects (Uhr, 1976b) simply "fades" rather than erasing these lists. Fading means lowering slightly the weights of the things stored in them, and erasing a thing whose weight has been lowered below a specified minimum.

Now an implied thing is merged into a cell that may already contain that thing, because it was merged into it at some recent prior moment in time (but not at the same moment of time, since there

has not yet been time to place it there). The
first time something is merged into a cell it is
given an initial high weight. This serves to make
new things salient, and also moving things, since
their motion means that they will be merged for the
first time into some local cell for which they are
new things. Thus salience - in the sense of the
size of the weight associated with a thing - is a
function of its newness (change) and motion. It is
also, of course, a function of the transforms that
imply it and, since transforms can imply other
transforms to apply, and also things to look for
which in turn imply transforms to apply that would
imply them, of a potentially very rich set of contextual information that implies it.

Depending upon the fade factor, the initial
and continuing merge weights, and the relative
weights associated with implied things, different
things will become salient, and different times
will be needed for them to fade out of memory.
Much playing around needs to be done to get good
weights (hopefully this will be done automatically,
by learning routines). But this appears to be a
simple and attractive way of giving continuity
over time, with a "short-term memory" that is dispersed throughout all the layers of the perceptual
system, from retina to apex.

Handling Two or More Eyes

Extending the recognition cone to handle two
eyes (Uhr, 1977b) turned out to be surprisingly
easy. Since this was basically a matter of putting the single-eye system into a higher-level
loop that iterates the same processes over the
second eye, it was just about as simple to have
the system handle any number of eyes, as designated to it at the start of a run.

The one-eye system must be given the specific layers at the start of a run. The multi-
input system must also be given, for each layer,
the "from-eye" and "to-eye" for each eye at that
layer. Two or more eyes therefore converge if
they all have the same "to-eye." This allows us
to specify a convergence layer wherever we wish.
We can even start with many eyes (and/or "ears,"
"fingers" or other input organs) and have several groups converge into several different eyes
at the same layer, and these, and others, converge at subsequent layers. That is, we can
set up a tree whose buds are the separate retinal
images of the several eyes, whose root is the
layer at which all inputs have been converged together, with any number of intermediate nodes
of convergence into which several converging
nodes link.

Learning by Discovery and Induction
of Transforms and Layers

Extensions were coded to the binocular vision
system that allow the program to generate and discover new transforms, both as a function of external feedback and of the internal feedback got from
the convergence of the transformed image from the
two eyes into a single internal array (Uhr, 1977b).
This was designed to explore issues of competition
between the two eyes, and the anomalies that occur
when one eye is sutured, so that its cone is not
given the experience needed to develop properly.
For the two eyes appear to be in a competitive-

cooperative situation, as determined by very interesting recent experiments by Guillery, 1974;
and others.

A second extension that learns much more extensively has been formulated, and is now being
coded (Uhr, 1977a). This system attempts to generate a new transform that is as different as possible from already-existing transforms (either
already-generated, or learned). It iterates the
transform out through the entire layer, collects
inductive evidence about this whole set of similar
transforms, feeding it back to each individual
transform in the set, and, after enough evidence
has been accumulated, tries to decide on the appropriate (sub-) array within which that transform
should reside, and be considered to have been "discovered as worth using." It also will generate a
whole tree of transforms, when needed, sprouting
back from the layer in which the root transform
has been indicated by feedback.

Perception Embedded in a Larger
Cognitive System

The perceptual recognition cone has been embedded in a larger "SEER"* system (Uhr, 1975a,
1975b, 1976a) that also begins to cycle through the
other major cognitive processes - remembering, simple problem-solving, language understanding, and
motor action. This gives a stronger inner-directed
component to the perceptual (sub-) system, and
allows perception to call on and interact with
memory searches, deductions, and external motor
actions (e.g moving the eye, searching for and
prodding the object).

It also raises a number of very interesting
problems that must be attacked if we want to put
the separate sub-systems that are typically embodied in separate programs back together into
well-integrated wholistic systems.

Tests of the Static One-Eye
Recognition Cone

The EASEy-Snobol programs are too slow and
take up too much core memory to be tested in any
reasonably economical way. So a Fortran and, more
recently, a Simula version of the basic recognition
cone have been coded, and a few tests have been
made (see Uhr and Douglass, 1977, for a first report). These include tests of:
a) one letter or symbol at a time, but varying
over many linear and non-linear distortions (e.g.
rubber-sheet stretchings, introduction of many gaps
and extraneous crossings, turning into dotted
lines);
b) "place-settings" that are scenes of knives,
forks, spoons and plates arranged in various traditional patterns;
c) natural "real-world" scenes, of houses,
trees, cars, sky, grass, etc.
Figure 3 shows approximate drawings of three
place-settings that the Simula program recognized
and described (the individual pieces, and also the
whole place-setting were correctly named). Table 1
summarizes the specifications of the actual layers
and sets of transforms used.

---

*Semantic Sensed Environment Encoder and Responder;
See-Errr).

Table 1. Specifications of the Cones Used for the Test Run

A) For simple letters
   and symbols:

Size of Array	Type of Transform Applied	Shrinkage
20 by 20	1. Local edge detectors	1/2
10 by 10	2. Feature detectors	1/2
5 by 5	3. Compound characterizers	1/5

B) For place-settings:

20 by 48	1. Local edge detectors	-
20 by 48	2. Feature detectors	1/2
10 by 24	3. Compound characterizers	1/2
5 by 12	4. Compound characterizers	1/5, 1/12

C) For outdoor scene:

	Size of Array	Type of Transform Applied	Shrinkage
Fortran	800 by 600	1. Average	1/4, 1/3
	200 by 200	2. Hue, saturation, intensity	cropped
Simula	120 by 120	3. Gradients	1/2
	60 by 60	4. Short edges, texture	1/2
	30 by 30	5. Long edges, compounds, textures of short edges	-
	30 by 30	6. Higher-level compounds	-
	30 by 30	7. Higher-level compounds	-
	15 by 15	8. Average	1/2
	8 by 8	9. Average	1/2
	4 by 4	10. average	1/2

Figure 3. Place-settings were input into a 20 by 48 array. About 30 transforms were used, in a 4-layer cone. It took roughly two hours for a human to formulate and code the transforms, and 8 seconds of 1110 CPU time to describe each scene.

Ohlander's (1975) color pictures were used for the natural "real-world" scenes. Figures 4-9 show how a 10-layer cone with approximately 70 transforms successively transformed a 600 by 800 array containing a house scene (also used by Hanson and Riseman, 1974, 1976), and, in the later layers, assigned names to regions of the scene. (It took roughly 120 hours to formulate and 40 hours to code the transforms, and 90 seconds of 1110 CPU time to process one scene.) The transforms were chosen to be useful and general over a wide variety of scenes. But additional tests will be needed to determine whether they are sufficient, or whether additional transforms are needed.

The following transforms were used, each transform iterated and applied everywhere to its input buffer (see Table 1c): (In general, weights of implications go up moving deeper into the cone.)

Layer 1: Averaging is effected by looking at each 4 by 3 local array of cells, and outputting the sum of the intensities for each of the 3 primary colors into the cell in the output buffer layer corresponding to the center of the 4 by 3, thus converging from an 800 by 600 to a 200 by 200 array.

This was done chiefly to reduce the very large amount of data in the 800 by 600 tv image. Averaging is probably usually a reasonable thing to do on most scenes. But if the scene might contain any tiny details of importance, then the system cannot take the chance of averaging such information out of existence. Rather, it should start with something like local differencing, to get gradients and edges.

Layer 2. The primary colors are combined, giving a) hue (the single combined color), b) saturation of that color, and c) intensity of that color. This combining is effected by a transform with 3 parts to its Conditions, where all 3 parts look at the same cell, giving a 200 by 200 output array.

The first two layers of transforms are effected by a Fortran program. The 200 by 200 image is now cropped to 120 by 120 and the Simula program takes over. (The Simula program is now being modified so that it will handle arrays larger than 120 by 120, so that the Fortran program will no longer be needed.)

Layer 3: Local gradients are computed, using a transform that looks at the 4 parts in a 2 by 2 array, and sums the absolute values of the difference between the Northwest and Southeast pair of cells, plus the difference between the Northeast and Southwest pair of cells.

Layer 4: Short local edges are searched for in a 4 by 4 array, using 4 edge detectors (one for each of the slopes 45°, 90°, 135°, 180°). A texture detector fires if more than 6 simple gradient points above a threshold of 16 (from layer 3) are found in a 4 by 4 local array.

Layer 5: Long edges, angles, curves and textures are compounded together, using transforms that typically fire if about 3 out of 5 parts are found.

Two additional textures are got, by counting the number of edges in a 4 by 4 window, and by getting the principal orientation of edges in a 4 by 4 window.

Layer 6: A number of different compounding transforms look for configurations of edges (e.g. vertical edge, slope) and region elements (e.g. wall, sky) and already-implied objects (e.g. roof, window, house). Three examples follow:
   a) Blue above a long horizontal edge above the previously implied object roof implies sky (above) and house (below):

$$\xrightarrow{\text{horizontal}} \frac{\text{Blue}}{\text{Roof}} \Rightarrow \frac{\text{Sky}}{\text{House}}$$

   b) A low saturation region, an angle of long edges, and brick color and brick texture on the

Recognition Cones and Some Test Results

371

other side of the edges implies house, with window
in the low saturation region and wall in the brick
region:

c) Blue above two long sloped edges giving an
upward pointing angle with green below implies
trees below:

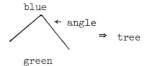

Layer 7: Still more higher-level compounds that
are combinations of previously-implied names are
looked for.

Layer 8: Each implied name is averaged over a 2 by
2 array.

Layer 9: Each implied name is averaged over a 2 by
2 array.

Layer 10: Each implied name is averaged over a 2
by 2 array.

This is but a first approximation to a good
set of transforms, and a good overall architecture.

Since the last three layers of the cone simply average and converge, they serve only to
merge implied names and labels into larger and
larger regions. They thus indicate what higher-
level identifications predominate; but they do
not actually add further information to the description process. Probably five or ten more layers
of transforms would be needed in a full-blown system.

Much more work is also needed in choosing the
individual transforms, and the weights of their
various implications. The present set of transforms was not chosen with the specific scene used
for this first test of the system in mind. So they
will probably work reasonably well on a variety of
outdoor scenes of this sort. But we can expect
that experience with new scenes will indicate difficulties, and that a good bit of work will be
needed to add, modify, and reweight transforms.

As the system is asked to describe a greater
variety of scenes and objects, it will need to be
given a larger set of transforms. There are good
reasons to think that this system's successive
compounding of the rather general probabilistic
configurational transforms that it uses means that
the total number of transforms needed will level
off at a manageable size. But only experimental
tests with a wide range of scenes will be able to
decide this issue.

The hope is to put as much as possible of the
burden of generating a good set of transforms onto
learning routines. The transform structure was designed with learning in mind, and first versions
of learning routines are being coded. But the
amount of computer time needed for the program to
generate and adjust the weights of a good set of
transforms may be quite large. It seems most
likely that a mixture of some learning by the program and a good bit of human effort spent in modifying and fine-tuning the set of transforms will
be needed to get as good performance as possible.
But learning becomes crucial when the system must
recognize and describe new and unanticipated objects.

The test results that follow should be examined
keeping in mind these possibilities for extending
and improving the system's overall architecture
and individual transforms.

Leonard Uhr

Figure 4 shows the results of three transformations layers
through the cone (only the results of local gradient detectors are indicated, by the asterisks; many other things
have been implied by this time).

Figure 5 shows the single most highly implied thing output
to each cell by Layer 6 (F = Window, G = Grass, H = House,
S = Sky, T = Tree, W = Wall).

```
S S S S S S S S S S S S S S S S S S S S S S S S S S S S S S
S S S S S S S S S S S S S S S S S S S S S S S S S S S S S S
S S S S S S S S S S S S S S S S S S S S S S S S S S S S S S
S S S S T T W T S S S S S S S S S S S S S S S S S S S S S S
S S S S T W W T S S S S S S S S S S S S S S S S S S S S S S
S S S S T W H H H H H S S S S S S S S S S S S S S S S S S S
S S S S H W H W H H T H H H H S S S S S S S S S S S S S S S
S S S S T W W T H H H G W G S H H S S S S S S S S S S S S S
S S S S T W W W W H H W W W T S G T T H H H S S S S S S S S
S S S H H W W W W W W H H H T H H T T G G T F H H H S S S
S S H H W W W W W W T T H H H H H T H H       S   T S H S S
S H H H W W W W H H R H H W W W H T H H H H H H H T S S T
S H W W W W W H W H H H H W W W G W W W W H H H H H H H T T
S T H W W W W W H H H W H W W W W W W W W W H H H H H H F F
S S H H W W W F H H H W H W W W W W W G H T R H H S H H G T
S S W H W W W W W H H W H H W W H H H R H H H W W H H H W W
S S T W W W W W W H W H W H W H W H H H H H H W H H H F W W
S S H W W W W W W W T H H H H R H H H W H W H H H F W
S S H W W W W W H W H H H T H H H H H H H H F F H H T F
F H W W W W W W H H W W W W H H H H H F F F F C H H W T
F H W W W W W W G W W W H H W H T T H H H H H H W T
T H W W W W W W W W W W H H W H T T T S H H S F H W
S H W W W W W W W W W W W H H H H T T T H S H S F H W T
S H W W W W W W W W W W W H T H T H T T H H S H S H H W T
S H W W W W W W W W W W W H H H T H T H H S H H H H T T
T T W W W W W W W W W W W W H T T G T H H H H H H H T T
W W W W W W W W W W W W W W W H T T W H H H H H H H H T G
W W W W W W W W W W W W W W W W H H H T T T T T H H T G G
W W W W W W W W W W W W W W T W H T T T T H T T T T T T
G T W W W W W W W W W W W W W W T W T T T T W T T T T T T T
```

Figure 6 shows only those cells in which House (H) was most
highly implied (this differs slightly from Figure 5, since
ties are shown here but may not appear there).

```
          H       H
          H     H H H H H
          H     H   H H     H H H
          H     H   H H H           H H H
          H     H                       H H H
        H H     H H     H H H H H H           H H H H
      H H               H           H H H H H H H H H H         H
    H H H           H H     H H           4     H H H H H H H H H
    H H H           H     H H H H                 H H H H H H H H
    H H H           H H H H     H                 H H H H H H H
      H H           H H H     H       H H H       H     H H     H H
      H H                 H H       H           H H H H H H H H H
      H               H H H H     H H H H H H H H     H H H H
      H                   H     H H H H     H H H H       H   H H H H
      H                 H     H H H     H H H H H H H H H H     H H
    H                   H H         H H H H H H H     H H H
    H                   H           H H H H       H       H H H H H H H
    H                   H           H H       H     H H     H
    H                   H           H H H H     H H   H       H
    H                   H     H   H H H       H H     H     H H
    H                               H H H H H     H H     H H H H
    H                               H         H H H H H H H H
                                    H           H H H H H H H H
                                H     H H           H H H
                                      H           H
```

374   Leonard Uhr
```
```

Figure 7 shows the most highly implied things in Layer 7,
the next layer.

```
S S S S S S S S S S S S S S S S S S S S S S S S S S S S
S S S S S S S S S S S S S S S S S S S S S S S S S S S S
  S S S S S S S S S S S S S S S S S S S S S S S S S S S
  S S S S T T H T S S S S S S S S S S S S S S S S S S S
  S S S S H H H H S S S S S S S S S S S S S S S S S S S
  S S S S H H H H H H S S S S S S S S S S S S S S S S S
  S S S S H H H H H T H H H S S S S S S S S S S S S S S
  S S S S H H H T H H H G H G H H H H S S S S S S S S S S
  S S S H H H H H H H H H T S G T T H H S S S S S S S S
  S S S H H H H H H H H H H H H T T G G T H H H H H H S S
  S S H H T H H H H H H T H H H H H H H H       S   T H H S S
  S H H H T H H H H H T H H T T T H T H H H H H H H H T S S T
  S H H H H H H H H H H H H H H G H H T H H H H H H H H T T
  S H H H H H H H H H H T H H H H H H H H G H H H H H H T T
  S S H H T H H T H H H H H H T H H H H G H T H H H S H H G T
  S S H H T H H T H H H H H H T H H H H H H H H H H H G H H
  S S H H H H H H H H H H H T H H H H H H H H H H H H H H T T
  S S H H H H H H H H H T H H H H H H H H H H H H H H H H T T
  S S H H H H H T H H H H H T H H H H H H H H H T T H H T T
  T H T H H H H H T H H T H H H H H H H H H H H H H H H T T
  T H T H H H H H H G H H H H H H H H T T H H H H H H H T T
  T H T H H H H H H H H H H H H H H H T T H S H H S H H H H
  S H T H H H H H H H H H H H H H H H T T H H S H S H H T T
  S H T H H H H H H H T T H H H H H H T H T T H H S H S H H T T
  S H T H H H T H H H H H H H H H H H H H T H H S H H H H T T
  T H T H H H H H H H H H H H H H H H T T G T H H H H H H T T
  T H H H H H H H H H H H H H H H H H T T T H H H H H H H T G
  T H H H H H H H H H H H H H H H T H H T T T T H H H T G G
  T T H H H H H H H T T H H H H H H T H H T T T T H T T T T T T
G T T H H H H H H T T H H T T H H T T T T T T T T T T T T T T T
```

Figure 8 shows only those cells into which House (H) is
most highly implied. Note how the higher-level compound
for house has turned many of the local "Wall" areas into
"House."

```
• • • • • • • • • • • • • • • • • • • • • • • • • • • • • • • • • • • • • • • • • •
•                                                                                 •
•                                                                                 •
•               H H                                                               •
•             H H H H                                                             •
•               H H H H H H                                                       •
•               H H H H H H     H H H                                             •
•               H H H     H H H     H     H H H H                                 •
•               H H H H H H H H H             H H H                               •
•             H H H H H H H H H H H H H H           H H H H H H                    •
•               H H H H H H H H H H H H H H H H H H H               H H            •
•     H H H     H H H H H H H H H H H H H         H H H H H H H H H                •
•     H H H H H H H H H H H H H H H H H       H H H H H H H H H H H                •
•     H H H H H H H H H H H H H H H H H H H         H H H H H H H H H H             •
•       H H H H H H H H H H H H H H H H         H H H H H H H H                    •
•       H H H H H H H H H H H H H H H H H H H H H H H H H H H H                    •
•       H H H H H H H H H H     H H H H H H H H H H H H H H H H                    •
•       H H H H H H H H H         H H H H H H H H H H H H H H H H H                •
•       H H H H H H H H H H         H H H H H H H H H H H H H H         H          •
•   H H H H H H H H     H H H H H H H H H H H H H H H H H H H H H                  •
•   H H H H H H H H H       H H H H H H H     H H H H H H H H                      •
•     H H H H H H H H H H H H H H H H H         H     H H     H H H H H            •
•     H H H H H H H H H H H H H H H H H H H H H         H H     H     H H H        •
•       H H H H H H H H H H H H H H H H H           H H     H     H H H H          •
•   H H H H H H H H H H H H H H H H H     H           H H H H H H H H H            •
•     H H H H H H H H H H H H H H H H H         H H H H H H H H H                  •
•     H H H H H H H H H H H H H H H H H H H     H           H H H                  •
•     H H H H H H H H H H H H H H H     H H         H H                            •
•         H H H H H H H H H H H H H H     H             H H H     H H H H          •
• • • • • • • • • • • • • • • • • • • • • • • • • • • • • • • • • • • • • • • • • •
```

Figures 9a, 9b, and 9c show the outputs from Layers 8, 9, and 10.

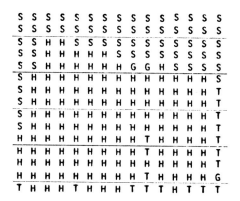

Figure 9a

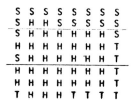

Figure 9b

```
S  S  S  S
H  H  H  H

H  H  H  H
H  H  H  H
```

Figure 9c

Conclusion

These are but first results, yet they seem quite comparable to those achieved to date by other perceptual systems on these very difficult scene description problems. The hope is that a wide variety of scenes of natural objects will be handled by this system, after it has been given, or has learned, a sufficient (yet economical, efficient and general) set of transforms. More transforms are needed to handle a wider range of scenes. But the present transforms were chosen to be general, not ad hoc to the particular test scenes. And when appropriately structured parallel-serial hardware becomes available this kind of system will certainly be extremely fast, and will hopefully be powerful.

References

1   Cordella, L., Duff, M.J.B. and Levialdi, S. Comparing sequential and parallel processing of pictures, Proc. IJCPR-3, 1976, 4, 703-707.

2   Davis, L. S. and Rosenfeld, A. Applications of relaxation labelling 2: spring-loaded template matching, Proc. IJCPR-3, 1976, 4, 591-597.

3   Douglass, R., Recognition and spatial organization of objects in natural scenss, submitted to IJCAI-5, Cambridge, 1977.

4   Duff, M.J.B., CLIP 4: a large scale integrated circuit array parallel processor, Proc. IJCPR-3, 1976, _, 728-733.

5   Ejiri, M., A prototype intelligent robot that assembles objects from plan drawings, IEEE Trans. Comp., 1972, 21, 161-170.

6   Guillery, R. W., Casagrande, V. A. and Oberdorfer, M.D., Congenitally abnormal vision in siamese cats, Nature, 1974, 252, 195-199.

7   Guzman, A., Decomposition of a visual scene into three-dimensional bodies, Proc. FJCC, 1968, 33, 291-304.

8   Hannah, M. J., Computer matching of areas in stereo vision, Unpubl. Ph.D. Diss., Stanford Univ., 1974.

9   Hanson, A. and Riseman, E., Pre-processing cones: a computational structure for scene analysis, Tech Rept. 74c-7, Univ. of Mass., 1974.

10 Hanson, A., Riseman, E., and Williams, T., Constructing semantic models in the visual analysis of scenes, Proc. Milw. Symp. Auto. Comp. & Contr., 1976, 4, 97-102.

11 Klinger, A. and Dyer, C., Experiments on picture representation using regular decomposition, TR Eng. 7497, UCLA, 1974.

12 Kruse, B., The PICAP picture processing laboratory, Proc. IJCPR-3, 1976, 4, 875-881.

13 Levine, M.D. and Leemet, J. A method for non-purposive picture segmentation, Proc. IJCPR-3, 1976, 4, 494-498.

14 Lowerre, B. T. The Harpy speech recognition system, Unpubl. Ph.D. Diss., Carnegie-Mellon Univ., 1976.

15 McKee, J. W. and Aggerwal, J. K. Computer recognition of partial views of three dimensional curved objects, Proc. IJCPR-3, 1976, 4, 499-503.

16 Minsky, M. and Papert, S. Perceptrons, Cambridge: MIT Press, 1969.

17 Moayer, B. and Fu, F. S., Application of stochastic languages to fingerprint pattern recognition, Pattern Recog., 1976, 8, 173-179.

18 Nagel, H., Experiences with Yakimovsky's algorithm for boundary and object detection in real world images, Proc. IJCPR-3, 1976, 4, 753-758.

19 Ohlander, R., Analysis of natural scenes, Unpubl. Ph.D. Diss., Carnegie-Mellon Univ., 1975.

20 Reddy, D. R., et al, The HEARSAY-1 speech understanding system, Proc. IJCAI-3, 1973, 185-193.

21 Rosenblatt, F. Principles of Neurodynamics, Washington, Spartan 1962.

22 Sakai, T., Kanade, T. and Ohta, Y., Model-based interpretation of ourdoor scenes, Proc. IJCPR-3, 1976, 4, 581-585.

23 Tanimoto, S. L., Pictorial feature distortion in a pyramid, Comp. Graphics Image Proc., 1976, 5, 333-352.

24 Tanimoto, S. L., and Pavlidis, T., A hierarchical data structure for picture processing, Comp. Graphics Image Proc., 1975, 4, 104-119.

25 Tenenbaum, J. M. and Barrow, H. G., IGS: a paradigm for integrating image segmentation and interpretation, Proc. IJCPR-3, 1976, 4, 504-513.

26 Uhr, L. Layered "recognition cone" networks that preprocess, classify and describe, Proc. Conf. on Two-Dimensional Image Processing, 1971. (reprinted in IEEE Trans. Comp., 1972, 758-768).

27 Uhr, L. A model of form perception and scene description. Computer Sciences Dept. Tech. Rept. 231, Univ. of Wisconsin, 1974.

28 Uhr, L. Toward integrated cognitive systems, which must make fuzzy decisions about fuzzy problems. (in L. Zadeh, et al., Eds. Fuzzy Sets, New York: Academic Press, 1975, pp. 353-393). (a)

29 Uhr, L. A wholistic cognitive system (SEER-2) for integrated perception, action and thought. MSACC-75 Proceedings, Milwaukee, 1975, pp. 25-52. (b)

30 Uhr, L. A wholistic integrated cognitive system (SEER-T1) that interacts with its environment over time, MSACC-76 Proceedings, Milwaukee, 1976, pp. 75-80. (a)

31 Uhr, L. "Recognition cones" that perceive and describe scenes that move and change over time, Proc. IJCPR-3, 1976, 4, 287-293. (b)

32 Uhr, L. Learning by discovery in parallel-serial "recognition cones," Computer Sciences Dept., Tech. Rept., Univ. of Wisconsin, 1977. (a)

33 Uhr, L. Toward a model of binocular vision, in preparation, 1977. (b)

34 Uhr, L. and Douglass, R. A parallel-serial "recognition cone" system for perception: some test results, Computer Sciences Dept. Tech.

Rept., Univ. of Wisconsin, 1977 (submitted for publication).

35 Waltz, D. Understanding line drawings of scenes with shadows, In P.H. Winston, Ed., The Psychology of Computer Vision, New York: McGraw-Hill, 1975.

36 Waltz, D. Position paper, Workshop on Computer Vision, Computer Sci. Dept. Univ. of Mass., Amherst, 1977.

37 Williams, H. A net-structure learning system for pattern recognition, Pattern Recog., 1976, 8, 261-271.

38 Zobrist, A. L., The organization of extracted features for pattern recognition, Pattern Recog., 1971, 3, 23-30.

39 Zobrist, A. L. and Thompson, W. B. Building a distance function for gestalt grouping, IEEE Trans. Comp., 1975, 24, 718-728.

40 Zucker, S. W. Relaxation labeling and the reduction of local ambiguities, Proc. IJCPR-3, 1976, 4, 852-861.

Theory Formation and Control in a Speech Understanding System
with Extrapolations towards Vision

W. A. Woods

Bolt Beranek and Newman Inc.
50 Moulton Street
Cambridge, Ma. 02138

1. Overview

High-level perceptual tasks such as reading, speech understanding, and visual scene interpretation are characterized by the need to discover a structured interpretation that accounts for the stimuli present. A naive view of speech understanding might consider it as a process of successively recognizing speech sounds (called phonemes), grouping phonemes into words, parsing word sequences into sentences, and finally interpreting the meanings of those sentences. However, considerable experience now indicates that the acoustic evidence present in the original speech signal is not sufficient to support such a process [Woods and Makhoul, 1974]. For sentences recorded from continuous speech, it is not generally possible to reliably determine the phonetic identity of the individual phonemes (or even to be sure how many phonemes are present) using the acoustic evidence alone.

Experiments in spectrogram reading [Klatt and Stevens, 1971] indicate that the reliability of such determinations can be increased by use of the redundancy provided by knowledge of the vocabulary, the syntax of the language, and semantic and pragmatic considerations. Moreover, tape splicing experiments [Wanner, 1973] seem to indicate that this low-level acoustic ambiguity is an inherent characteristic of human speech and not just a limitation of visual spectrogram-reading. Specifically, intelligibility of individual words excised from continuous speech is very low, but the intelligibility increases when sequences of two or three words are used. It appears that the additional constraint of having to make sense in a larger context begins to resolve the ambiguities that were present when only the acoustic evidence was considered.

Since vision shares many of these same characteristics, it may be useful for those concerned with visual scene interpretation to be aware of some of the difficulties that arise in continuous speech understanding and some of the techniques that have been developed to surmount them. In this paper I will attempt to give some of the results of my own experience in constructing a system to understand continuous speech.

2. Theories, Monitors, Notices, and Events - A Computational Framework for Perception

The BBN speech understanding system [Woods et al., 1976; Wolf and Woods, 1977] has evolved within a general framework for viewing perceptual processes. Central to this framework is an entity called a theory. A theory represents a particular hypothesis about some or all of the sensory stimuli that are present. Perception is viewed as the process of forming a believable coherent theory which can account for all the stimuli. This theory is arrived at by successive refinement and extension of partial theories until a best complete theory is found.

In general, a high-level perception process requires the ability to recognize any member of a potentially infinite class of perceptible objects that are constructed out of elementary constituents (or elements) according to known rules. That is, the object perceived is generally a compound object, constructed from members of a finite set of elementary constituents according to some kind of well-formedness rules. These elementary constituents, as well as the relationships among them that are invoked in the well-formedness rules, must be directly perceptible. Thus, a perceptual system must incorporate some basic epistemological assumptions about the kinds of things that it can perceive and the rules governing their assembly. The well-formedness rules can be used to reject impossible interpretations of the input stimuli, and may also be useable to predict other constituents that could be present if a given partial theory is correct.

This perception framework assumes mechanisms for using subsets of the input stimuli to form initial "seed" hypotheses for certain elementary constituents (stimulus-driven hypothesization) and mechanisms for deriving hypotheses for additional compatible elements from a previously derived partial theory (theory-driven, or predicted, hypothesization). It also assumes mechanisms for verifying hypotheses against the input stimuli and evaluating the well-formedness of compound hypotheses to assign them some measure of quality and/or likelihood. A theory may be thought of as a hypothesis that has been evaluated in this way and assigned a measure of confidence.

In the case of speech understanding, a theory can range from an elementary hypothesis that a particular word is present at a particular point in the input (a word match) to a complete hypothesis of a covering sequence of words with a complete syntactic and semantic interpretation. In general, a theory can be a set of compatible word hypotheses with gaps between them and with partial syntactic and semantic interpretations. A partial theory may be able to generate predictions for appropriate words or classes of words either adjacent to the words already hypothesized, or possibly elsewhere in the utterance.

Predictions are dealt with by two kinds of devices: monitors, which are waiting for expected constituents, and proposals, which are elementary hypotheses that are to be evaluated against the input. Proposals result in actively seeking stimuli that would verify them, while monitors passively wait for such hypotheses to be formed. The functioning of monitors assumes that there is an organizing structure against which all derived partial hypotheses are checked as they are discovered and that the monitors can essentially set "traps" for the kinds of events that they are watching for. This is to be contrasted with polling or continuous parallel evaluation of "demons" to watch for expected patterns in the input stream. Monitors perform no computation until and unless some other process makes an entry of the kind they are waiting for in some data structure.

The functioning of monitors is well illustrated in our first speech understanding system, SPEECHLIS [Woods, 1974], where for example, a word match for "concentration" would set monitors on the concept nodes for SAMPLE and CHEMICAL ELEMENT in a semantic network. If a word such as "Helium" was found anywhere else in the utterance, a check in the semantic network starting with "Helium" would lead to the superset category CHEMICAL ELEMENT where it would wake up the monitor from "concentration", thus discovering the

coincidence of a detected element and a predicted hypothesis [Nash-Webber, 1975].

When a monitor is triggered, an event is created (noticed) calling for the evaluation of a new hypothesis and the creation of a new theory if the hypothesis is not rejected. In general, a number of events are competing for service by the processor at any moment. In some aspects of human perception, there may be full parallel processing of such events, but in a serial machine, these events must be queued and given processing resources on the basis of some priority ordering. (Even in human perception, there is probably some sort of priority allocation of resources, since various kinds of interference can occur.) In our computational framework, events are maintained on a queue in order of priority, the top event being processed at each step. The processing of an event can result in new proposals being made, new monitors being set, and existing monitors being triggered to produce new events. Since what is perceived depends on the events chosen for processing, a major issue is that of assigning priorities to events in order to find the most likely interpretation of the input.

3. Control Issues

The above discussion leaves open issues such as when should seeds be formed, how many should be considered, should all seeds be worked on in parallel, etc. These issues we refer to as control issues. They have been critically important in speech understanding systems and I suspect are even more so in vision systems. In the BBN speech system, for example, there are a variety of different control strategies that all fit within the above paradigm. In one class of strategies, seeds are formed wherever sufficiently salient word matches are found. Another forms seeds only at the left end of the utterance. In the first case, subsequent theories are grown in both directions from the middle out, while in the latter theories are grown strictly left-to-right. In a class of hybrid strategies, seeds are started within a bounded distance from the left end of the utterance, and are grown right-to-left until they reach the left end, after which the remainder of the processing is left-to-right.

In the middle out strategies, a theory may be derived by adding successive words one at a time, or the strategy may permit the combination of two or more multiple-word theories which have been grown separately from different seeds (island collisions). Several strategies [Woods, 1977] have been developed for discovering the best scoring theory for a given utterance without exhaustively enumerating all of the different

W. A. Woods

possibilities (usually an infinite or impossibly large set).

Essential in all of these strategies is that at any given time there are a number of incomplete, competing possible interpretations, requiring a strategy to determine when a given theory is so remote that it can be pruned from further consideration, when a theory is sufficiently strong that further extensions should be performed only for it, and when attention should shift from one partial theory to another.

4. First Attempts at a Control Strategy

In our original speech understanding system, SPEECHLIS, [Woods, 1974; Rovner et al., 1974], the control strategy was a direct implementation of the general perceptual strategy described above. An initial scan of a phonetic segment lattice (produced by an Acoustic-Phonetic Recognition component) was performed by a Lexical Retrieval component looking for robust words to form initial one-word theories (stimulus-driven hypotheses). Each such theory forced a call on a Semantic component to set semantic monitors and detect events. The events and theories resulting from this semantic processing consisted of non-overlapping collections of semantically related words (generally separated by gaps). When the top-ranking theory became semantically "complete", at least with respect to the words found in the initial scan (i.e., no more words could be added), a Syntactic component was called upon to evaluate it and propose words to fill the gaps.

This system contained separate queues of events, notices, and proposals, and was used experimentally to explore such issues as: when should proposals be done as opposed to doing another event, when should syntax be called to evaluate a theory and make proposals, when should semantics be called, and how dense should the initial word lattice be. This system was the culmination of our incremental simulation approach to speech understanding [Woods & Makhoul, 1974], and we learned a lot from it. As a result of our experience with this system, we evolved a more specialized framework for our second-generation speech understanding system, HWIM [Woods et al, 1976].

5. Island-driven Strategies

The type of strategy that appeared most effective as a result of our experience with SPEECHLIS is one which we have termed island driven. These are strategies in which all theories consist of a contiguous sequence of words with no gaps between them (an island). In the SPEECHLIS strategy, a theory generally contained several semantically-related islands separated by gaps.

The reason for grouping semantically-related islands into a single theory in SPEECHLIS was the assumption that the semantic hypothesis which created such a theory could affect the syntactic processing of the individual islands. However, we failed to find useful ways to capitalize on this possibility, and in actuality, the syntactic processing of a given island was almost totally independent of other islands in the theory. (The only significant place where this was not true was when two islands grew close enough together that the gap between them could be filled by a single word. In this case, the Syntactic component took them both into account, making strong proposals in order to try to fill the gap.) On the other hand, the multiple island theories had an associated cost in processing due to the possibility of the same island occurring in several different theories (i.e., theories which differed in what words they hypothesized at other points of the utterance). Although care was taken that a given island need only be evaluated once syntactically, independent of how many theories it occurred in, a major portion of the syntactic component's overhead lay in attempting to keep track of islands that had previously been parsed and recognizing them when they appeared again in new theories. Thus, in handling multiple island theories, we were carrying a burden for which we were deriving at most a marginal theoretical advantage.

It should be noted here that a continuing goal in our search for effective speech understanding strategies was to find ways for having what is found at one point in the utterance effect the analysis of other portions of the utterance. In most cases, syntactic information can only affect word hypotheses immediately adjacent to an island. The semantic intersection techniques explored in SPEECHLIS were an attempt to discover effective ways to get more global effects to lend support. However, while the semantic intersection technique can detect coincidences of semantic relationship between widely separated words, the way that this information was coupled into the control and syntactic components in SPEECHLIS did not provide sufficient support. I believe that a more effective way to tap this semantic intersection information might be to use it in the priority scoring of theories, without explicitly forming combinations of separated islands.

6. Differences Between SPEECHLIS and HWIM Control Frameworks

In our second generation system, HWIM, various features of the general perceptual strategy described above have been particularized, thus surrendering some flexibility for decreased overhead. In both SPEECHLIS and HWIM, an initial scan of some portion of the utterance is used to form initial one-word seed events. Beyond this point, however, the two systems differ considerably. In HWIM, an event is processed by giving it to a combined syntactic/semantic/pragmatic linguistic consultant to (a) determine whether the resulting theory could be part of a complete sentence; (b) produce proposals for adjacent words and/or categories; and (c) possibly adjust its score as a result of syntactic, semantic, pragmatic, or prosodic information. Whereas in SPEECHLIS we had the option of doing several events before actively pursuing proposals, as well as that of monitoring all predictions while only actively proposing some of them, in HWIM we propose all predictions. Moreover, where SPEECHLIS gave syntax the option of doing only a partial evaluation of a theory, in HWIM the linguistic consultant does all its processing on a theory the first time it is called, making all possible compatible predictions at that time. This is because our experience with SPEECHLIS did not suggest any effective criteria for deciding when to call the Syntactic component back for additional processing and predictions. Nor did it suggest a good criterion for calling for further unconstrained word scans in a portion of an utterance, so that monitors set without explicit proposals were only triggered by words from the initial scan or words independently proposed and serendipitously found.

Besides this single linguistic consultant replacing SPEECHLIS's independently operating Syntactic and Semantic components, a major difference between the two systems is the short circuiting in HWIM of much of SPEECHLIS's monitor-propose-notice activity. Whereas SPEECHLIS permitted a number of events to be processed before any of their proposals, in HWIM proposals are done immediately as part of the processing of the event. Also, where SPEECHLIS used monitors in a word lattice to catch the words that came back from Lexical Retrieval and put them together with the theories that proposed them, in HWIM there is only one proposing theory for each batch of proposals, and it can be remembered until the results are returned by Lexical Retrieval. This means that appropriate notices can be constructed directly, eliminating the need for word lattice monitors (and also eliminating one of the ·reasons for having a word lattice around!). This saves both the memory which had been required for storing these monitors and also considerable processing time.

Monitors remain in the HWIM system only for a detecting island collisions to combine two islands that notice the same word from opposite directions. Whenever an event is created to add an additional word to a theory, an island table is consulted to see if the same word has been noticed from the other direction. If so, a collision event can be created that will combine the two theories and the noticed new word into a single new theory. Each entry in an island table is effectively a monitor that is watching for a theory to notice a particular word in a particular direction.

Other major ways in which HWIM differs from the original SPEECHLIS system include the development of a uniform scoring philosophy for combining information from different knowledge sources, and several strategies for assigning priorities to events to guarantee the discovery of the best scoring interpretation of the utterance.

7. Scoring Philosophy

A major concern in the BBN speech understanding research was the development of a uniform scoring philosophy for combining the scores from different knowledge sources. In SPEECHLIS we explored this issue by allowing the Control component to form a total score for a theory by an arbitrary combination of scores from several different knowledge sources. This permitted us full freedom to attempt to rationalize the scores assigned by the individual knowledge sources (e.g., lexical, syntactic, and semantic), each of which constructed scores in its own way. At that time, the syntactic component gave arbitrary score adjustments, such as +10 or -15 to particular theories which it considered to be using unlikely constructions, while the word matching component used a combination of individual phoneme scores plus extra points for successful consistency tests and demerits for inconsistencies.

It was clear that in order to avoid comparing apples with oranges, we needed a principle for deciding how many points of syntactic score were worth one point of lexical matching score, how may points of lexical matching score were worth one point of verification score, etc. One might assume that the overall theory score should be some weighted sum of the scores assigned by the different knowledge sources, but the issue of concern would still be choosing the correct weights.

In HWIM, we have adopted a uniform scoring philosophy in which the score of each different knowledge source is statistically calibrated to a uniform scoring dimension. Here they are appropriately weighted to make the total score of a theory the sum of the scores

W. A. Woods

assigned by the individual knowledge sources. The scoring dimension chosen is that of log likelihood ratios, and the interpretation of a theory's score is an estimate of the probability of it being correct given the information from the various knowledge sources. The computation of this score involves a straightforward application of Bayes theorem, deriving the probability of a theory T_i given evidence E_j by the formula:

$$Pr(T_i/E_j) = Pr(E_j/T_i) * Pr(T_i) / Pr(E_j).$$

That is, the probability of a theory given the evidence is equal to the probability of the evidence given the theory times the a priori probability of the theory (this product is the joint probability of the theory and the evidence), divided by the a priori probability of the evidence (i.e., the probability of this particular evidence occurring independent of T_i).

When there are several types of evidence, each deriving from a different knowledge source, or several components of evidence within a single knowledge source, this equation can be factored into components:

$$Pr(T_i/E_{j1} \& E_{j2} \& \ldots \& E_{jn}) = [Pr(E_{j1}/T_i)/Pr(E_{j1})]$$
$$[Pr(E_{j2}/T_i)/Pr(E_{j2})]$$
$$\ldots [Pr(E_{jn}/T_i)/Pr(E_{jn})] \, Pr(T_i)$$

under the assumption that the different pieces of evidence are independent. (A corresponding equation can be derived which accounts for any significant dependencies.) In HWIM, this equation is used in combining evidence both from different knowledge sources (e.g., acoustic-phonetic, verification, and prosodic), and also within any given knowledge source (e.g., each relevant phonetic segment in the input utterance contributing evidence for a particular word hypothesis).

We assume then that the score assigned to a theory by a given knowledge source k is an estimate of the ratio $Pr(E_{jk}/T_i)/Pr(E_{jk})$, where E_{jk} is the evidence that k consulted in assigning its score. A ratio of 1 corresponds to essentially no information. That is, the evidence is as likely to occur by chance in any theory as it is for the particular theory T_i. A ratio less than 1 indicates that it is more likely to occur for some random theory than it is for this particular T_i. For the sake of computational efficiency, each ratio is represented in HWIM as 100 times its log, so that scores can be combined by small integer addition rather than multiplication of floating point numbers. Positive logs thus represent theories which in some sense "account for" the evidence, while negative logs correspond

to theories which are to some extent contraindicated.

A potential problem with using an estimate of the theory's probability as the criterion for choosing the preferred interpretation of an utterance is that if the a priori probabilities of the different T_i's are significantly different, system performance will be too colored by an attempt to guess the most likely thing to be said, possibly overriding the acoustic evidence. In particular, if there are two interpretations A and B with the acoustic evidence favoring A by a factor of 50%, but the a priori favoring B by more than that, then B would be chosen rather than A. This would of course maximize the overall success rate of such a system if its a priori probabilities were correct. But such a system would run a major risk of picking likely utterances with poor acoustic evidence over unlikely utterances even with perfect acoustic evidence. To avoid the above problems and obtain a system whose performance is based on its ability to hear and understand rather than its ability to guess what will be said, we have eliminated the a priori term $Pr(T_i)$ from our scores, corresponding to an assumption that all utterances are equally likely to occur.

8. Calibrating a Knowledge Source

Using the above scoring philosophy, the score returned by a given knowledge source should be an estimate of the probability ratio $Pr(E_{jk}/T_i)/Pr(E_{jk})$ where E_{jk} is the evidence it examined. To estimate that ratio, we use a process called calibration. Suppose a given knowledge source can compute an arbitrary parameter $f(T_i)$ which we believe to be correlated with the likelihood that T_i is a correct interpretation. (Assume for the moment that $f(T_i)$ has a finite set of possible values or a range that can be divided into a finite set of regions.) Then we can calibrate that particular parameter by constructing a histogram of its values for correct theories and another histogram of its values for all theories on which it could be evaluated at all. For any particular value of $f(T_i)$ then, we can approximate $P(f(T_i)/T_i)/P(f(T_i))$ as the ratio of the number of times correct theories had that value over the number of times that arbitrary theories had it. This gives us an appropriately calibrated contribution of this particular parameter $f(T_i)$ to the likelihood of T_i being the correct interpretation. In the case of continuous valued f's, refining the mesh of the histogram and increasing the number of samples used for calibration can make this estimate arbitrarily precise. Alternatively, other techniques (such as those used for vector modification in HWIM [Woods et al., 1976] Vol. II) can be used to estimate the probability ratios without the noise introduced by the histogram technique, gaining more precise estimates with smaller number of samples as the cost of a more complex computation at run time.

If a given knowledge source has a set of independent parameters, such as the $f(T_i)$ discussed above, then a total score for a theory can be constructed as the product of their individual likelihood ratios (sum of the log likelihood ratios). If two such parameters are not independent, then their joint distributions can be measured by experiments and used for determining the appropriate likelihood ratio for the particular combination of values observed. In this way, any given knowledge source and any given measurement can be calibrated in such a way that its scores are compatible with the scores of all other knowledge sources.

This calibration process is applied, for example, in the word verification component of HWIM, a component which does a parametric match between a synthesized ideal pronunciation of a word and the parametric representation of the speech utterance. This component measures a parameter which is essentially the spectral difference between the acoustic waveform present and that of a synthesized waveform for a particular word (actually the distance is measured from a synthesized spectrum against a spectrum derived from the waveform). To calibrate this score into a log likelihood ratio that can be added to the scores of other components, we divide the range of possible spectral distances up into a finite number of intervals and construct a histogram of the possible scores both for word verification requests which are known to be correct hypotheses and for all word verification requests independent of whether they are correct or not. To obtain these statistics, we actually run the speech understanding system in a "goodonly" mode which follows only correct partial theories, but makes many incorrect word verification requests in the process. Using these two histograms, we can assign an appropriate log likelihood ratio for any given spectral distance. This procedure is described more fully in Woods et al. [1976] Vol. II.

9. Priority Scoring

The score assigned to a theory by the summation of lexical retrieval scores (essentially the log probability of its words being correct) we refer to as the quality score of the theory. We distinguish from this a possibly separate score called the priority score, which is used to rank order events on the event queue to determine the order in which they are to be done. In early versions of HWIM, we used the quality score itself as

the priority score. However, we have developed several algorithms with interesting theoretical properties using priority scores that are derived from, but not identical with, the quality score. The first measures the difference between the particular quality score for a theory and an upper bound on possible quality score for any theory covering the same portion of the utterance. We call this the shortfall score, and it can be shown that using the shortfall score as a priority score under appropriate conditions guarantees finding the best scoring interpretation of the input utterance [Woods et al., 1976, Woods, 1977]. Using the quality score itself as a priority score does not guarantee this. Other priority scores are obtained by dividing either the quality score or the shortfall score by the time duration of the island to give quality density and shortfall density scoring, respectively. Since a fairly complete derivation of the shortfall and shortfall density scoring strategies together with proofs of their theoretical properties is given in [Woods, 1977], we will present here only a brief recapitulation of the strategies, and discuss differences we have observed between them.

9 (a). Shortfall Scoring

The shortfall score measures the amount by which the quality score of a theory falls below an upper bound on the possible score that could be achieved on the same region. When shortfall scoring is being used, a MAXSEG profile is constructed having the property that the score of a word match between boundaries i and j will be less than or equal to the area under the MAXSEG profile from i to j (call this latter the MAXSCORE for the region from i to j). The shortfall score for a theory is then computed as the sum over all the word matches in the theory of the difference between the score of the word match and the MAXSCORE for the same region. The preferred theory is the one with the smallest magnitude of shortfall.

The MAXSEG profile can be constructed incrementally by adding to the profile whenever a word match is found whose score is not bounded by it. Whenever the score of a word match exceeds the MAXSCORE for its region, the excess score is distributed over the region to raise its MAXSCORE to that of the word match. In HWIM, an initial profile is constructed during the initial scan for seed words and this profile is substantially correct. Occasionally a word match is found later which raises the profile and in this case all events overlapping the changed region are rescored.

In order to satisfy the theoretical claims of the algorithm, the way in which the excess score of a word match is distributed to raise the MAXSEG profile does not matter. However, it is desirable to do it in such a way as to minimize the amount by which the shortfall of other words that overlap the region is raised. Our current algorithm is to distribute the excess score over the segments covered by the word match that are not already bounded by the profile and to divide it proportional to the durations of the segments. Other distribution algorithms are possible, some of which have been tried. This one is better than some, but there are probably better strategies to be found. Keeping the MAXSEG profile as low as possible while still satisfying the upper bound condition is important since excessively conservative upper bounds translate directly into an unnecessary increase in the breadth-first nature of the search, requiring more events to be processed before finding the chosen interpretation.

The theoretical characteristics of the shortfall scoring algorithm are that if the words are returned by the Lexical Retrieval component in decreasing order of quality and events are processed in order of increasing magnitude of shortfall (plus a few other assumptions, documented in Woods [1977]), then the first complete spanning interpretation found will be the best scoring interpretation that can be found by any strategy. We refer to this condition as "completeness" (a more traditional term is "admissibility"). For speech understanding applications, completeness is a desirable property, but not necessarily essential if the cost of its attainment is too great. Shortfall scoring has the property of being complete without searching the entire space. It's completeness proof depends only on the fact that when the first complete spanning theory is found, all other events on the queue will already have fallen below the ideal maximum score by a greater amount. Thus the result does not depend on the scores being likelihood ratios, nor does it make any assumption about the nature of the grammar (e.g., that it be a finite state markov process) provided a parser exists that can make the necessary judgments. The completeness also does not depend on the order of scanning the utterance -- it is satisfied both for middle-out and for left-to-right strategies.

9 (b). Density Scoring

Another type of priority scoring is density scoring. Here the score used to order the eventqueue is some basic score divided by the duration of the event. Conceptually, we can think of this priority scoring metric as predicting the potential score for the region not covered by a theory to be an extrapolation of the same score density already achieved. (In these terms, the shortfall strategy can be

thought of as predicting that the upper bound for the uncovered region will be achieved.) Unlike the shortfall scores, density scores can get bad and then get better again as new words are added to a theory. Hence, the density score is certainly not guaranteed to be an upper bound of the expected eventual score. However, it has another interesting property: in exactly those cases where it does not bound the eventual score, there is a word to be added somewhere else that has a better score density and whose score density does bound the eventual score. This arises from the property of densities that the density of two regions combined will lie between the densities that they each have. It turns out that this alone is not sufficient to guarantee completeness for a density scoring strategy since it is still possible for the density score starting from the best correct seed to fall below that of some other less-than-optimal spanning theory before it can be extended to a complete theory itself. However, with the addition of a facility for combining islands that start from separate seeds when they collide with each other, the density scoring strategy, working middle-out from multiple seeds can be shown to be complete. Again, density scoring does not depend on any assumptions about the basic scores to which it is being applied other than that they be additive (and capable of division). Hence the density method can be applied to either the original quality score or to a shortfall score. The combination of the two methods in a shortfall density strategy seems to be more effective than either shortfall or density scoring alone.

10. Other Heuristics

In addition to the basic choice of priority scoring metric used for ranking the event queue, there are several additional heuristics that can be used to improve the performance of the island-driven strategies without loss of admissibility guarantees. Two of these are the use of "ghost" words, and the selection of a preferred direction for events from a given theory.

10 (a). Ghost Words

The ghost words option is a feature that can be added to any island-driven strategy, and does not affect the admissibility of the strategy to which it is added. Every time a theory is given to the linguistic consultant for evaluation, proposals are made on both sides of the resulting island (unless the island is already against one end of the utterance). Although events can only add one word at a time to the island, and this must be at one end or the other, eventually a word will have to be added to the other end, and that word cannot score better than the best word that was found at that end the first time. The ghost words feature consists of remembering with each event the list of words found by the Lexical Retrieval component at the other end and scoring the event using the best of the ghost words as well as the words in the event proper. The result is that bad partial interpretations tend to get bad twice as fast, since they have essentially a one-word look ahead at the other end that comes free from the linguistic consultant each time an event is processed. On the other hand, an event that has a good word match at the other end gets credit for it early so that it gets processed sooner. The ghost words feature, thus, is an accelerator that causes extraneous events to fall faster down the event queue and allows the desired events to rise to the top faster. Experimental use of this feature has shown it to be very effective in reducing the number of events that must be processed to find the best spanning event.

10 (b). Choosing a Preferred Direction

When a theory is evaluated by the linguistic consultant, predictions are made at both ends of the island. When one of the events resulting from these predictions is later processed, adding a new word to one end of the island, the predictions at the other end of the new island will be a subset of the predictions previously made at that end of the old island. In general, words noticed by this new island at that end will also have been be noticed by the old island, and if the score of the new island is slightly worse than that of the old island (the normal situation), then the strategy will tend to revert to the old island to try picking up a word at the other end. This leads to a rather frustrating derivation of a given theory by first enumerating a large number of different subsequences of its final word sequence. For example, to derive a theory (abcd), one might first start with the seed (b), then add a to get (ab), then go back to (b) to get (bc) then go back to (ab) and add c to get (abc), then go back to (bc) and notice a, but also notice that (abc) has already been made and then go back to (abc) to pick up the d.

Since any eventual spanning theory derived from an island must eventually pick some word at each end of the island, one could arbitrarily pick either direction and decide to work only in that direction until the end of the utterance is encountered, and only then begin to consider events in the other direction. This would essentially eliminate the duplication described above, but could cause the algorithm to work into a region of the utterance where the correct word did not score very well without the benefit of additional syntactic support that could have been obtained by extending

the island further in the other direction for a while.

Without sufficient syntactic constraint at the chosen end, there may be too many acceptable words that score fairly well for the correct poorly scoring word to occur within a reasonable distance from the top of the queue. By working on the other end, one may tighten that constraint and enable the desired word to appear, although this can never cause a better scoring word to appear than those that appeared for the shorter island.

The CHOOSEDIR flag in the HWIM system causes the algorithm to pick a preferred or "chosen" direction for a given theory as the direction of the best scoring event that extends that theory, and to mark the events going in the other direction from that theory so that they can only be used for making tighter predictions for words at the chosen end. This is accomplished by blocking from consideration any notices for one of the ghost words at the inactive end of an event if that event is going counter to the chosen direction. This blocking, alone, eliminates a significant number of redundant generations of different ways to get to the same theory. An even greater improvement is obtained by rescoring the events that are going counter to the chosen direction by using the worst ghost at the other end rather than the best ghost. Since only word matches that score worse than any of the ghosts at that end will be permitted by these events, this is a much better estimate of the potential score of any spanning theories that might result from these events.

The effect of rescoring the events in the non-chosen direction using the worst ghost is that, in most cases, these events fall so low in the event queue as to be totally out of consideration. Only in those cases where there was little syntactic constraint in the chosen direction and the worst matching word at that point was still quite good, do these events stay in contention, and in those cases, the use of the worst ghost score provides the appropriate ranking of these events in the event queue.

11. Empirical Comparison of the Different Strategies

Details of the HWIM system and its general performance are found in [Woods et al., 1976]. Comparative performance results for the shortfall (S), shortfall density (SD), and quality density (QD) scoring strategies are shown in Table 1 below. The option of using the quality score (Q) alone as a priority score is given for comparison.

W. A. Woods

These experiments were run using the ghosts, island-collision, and preferred direction heuristics with a resource limit of 100 theories to process before the system would give up with no response. Notice that with the quality score alone used as a priority score, the average number of theories processed is quite small, but two of the ten utterances were incorrectly understood. Notice also that the shortfall scoring alone failed to find any interpretations before the resource limitation was exceeded. The shortfall density strategy ranked superior to the quality density strategy in terms of the number of events that needed to be processed to find the first spanning interpretation and consequently found more correct interpretations within the resource limitations. The ten sentences used for the test were chosen at random from a test set of 124 recorded sentences.

The effects of the island collision (C), ghosts (G), and preferred direction (D) heuristics are shown in Table 2. The inclusion of a heuristic does not always guarantee that the system will understand an utterance in fewer theories, but the pooled results shown (note especially the series SD+0, SD+G, SD+GD, SD+GDC) suggest that the successively added heuristics produce improvements in both accuracy and number of theories required. (Note that our admissibility results hold only for the SD+C and SD+GDC cases above.)

12. Discussion

The shortfall scoring method is similar in some respects to the well-known branch and bound technique, except for the characteristic in the middle-out version that the same partial interpretation may be reached by many different paths, and the fact that the space of possible solutions is determined by a grammar. It can also be modeled as an example of the A* algorithm of Hart, Nilsson and Raphael [1968] for finding the shortest path through a graph, where, in this case, the nodes in the graph are partial interpretations of the utterance, and the connections in the graph correspond to the seed and word events. Consequently, it shares with that algorithm a certain kind of optimality that Hart, Nilsson and Raphael prove. It is simpler than the general A* algorithm, however, in that we are looking for the best scoring node, and we are not interested in scores of paths leading to that node (in fact all such paths have the same score in our case). The simple argument given previously suffices to show the admissibility of the shortfall method, whereas the general A* algorithm is more complicated.

Measuring the shortfall from any profile that is a per word upper bound of quality score would be sufficient to assure the theoretical admissibility of the method. However, the tightness of the

	Q	QD	S	SD
Found correct interpretation	4	3	0	5
Found incorrect interpretation	2	0	0	0
No response	4	7	10	5
Average number of theories processed*	8	47	–	32

Table 1. Comparison of different priority scoring functions.

	SD+0	SD+C	SD+G	SD+GD	SD+GDC
Correct	3	3	3	4	5
Incorrect	0	0	0	0	0
No response	7	7	7	6	5
Average number of theories processed**	54	40	48	43	32

Table 2. The effects of island collisions, ghosts, and direction preference.

- - - - - - - - - - - -

*Average is for the three utterances for which complete spanning theories were found by all three methods Q, QD, and SD.
**Averages shown are for the three utterances completed by all five methods.

upper bound affects the number of events tried and partial theories created in the search for a successful interpretation (i.e., the "breadth" of the search). By assigning the upper bound as a segment-by-segment profile determined by allocated shares of actual word match scores, a fairly tight upper bound is achieved. A further effect of scoring the shortfall from such a maxscore profile is that in the middle-out version the score differences in different parts of the utterance are effectively leveled out so that events in a region of the utterance where there are not very good scoring words can hold their own against alternative interpretations in regions where there are high scoring words. This promotes the refocusing of attention from a region where there may happen to be high scoring accidental word matches to events whose word match quality may not be as great, but are the best matches in their regions. This ability to shift attention to an event that initially didn´t score as well as some other event, but which can be pushed farther with an aggregate better score, is automatically handled by the shortfall scoring method. Thus, an apparently satisfactory and intuitively reasonable strategy for focusing attention emerges from the same strategy that guarantees to get the best scoring theory first.

As indicated in the above comparisons, the density strategy appears to be superior to the shortfall strategy, but the combination of the two strategies is superior to either one alone. In the combined shortfall density strategy, admissibility is guaranteed because of the density method admissibility, while the shortfall effectively evens out the differences between different portions of the utterance and promotes the appropriate refocussing of attention.

When using the shortfall or shortfall density strategies, the general tendency is for an event adding a new word to an island to pick up additional shortfall and fall some distance down in the queue. The result is that other events are processed before any additional work is done on that island. (Occasionally, the new word is the best word in its region and buys no additional shortfall, but this is a rarity.) The distance that this new event falls down the queue is determined by the amount of additional shortfall that it has just picked up and the shortfalls of the events that are competing with it on the queue. This distance directly affects the degree of "depth-first" vs. "breadth-first" processing done by the algorithm. If the new word scores well, the event falls only slightly, and few, if any, alternate events are processed before it. In this case the algorithm is relatively depth first. If the new word scores badly, the event falls further down

the queue, many more alternative events have priority over it and the algorithm is more breadth first. Thus, the shortfall scoring method provides a dynamically varying combination of depth-first and breadth-first search which is determined by the relative qualities of the events that are in competition.

13. Behavior under Error Conditions

If there have been no serious errors in the analysis of the input signal done by the acoustic-phonetic component, then the major competition that the correct interpretation of the utterance has to contend with are matches of words at various positions in the utterance that happen to score well by accident. In such cases, we do not expect the predictions for such accidental theories to find high scoring word matches, and such theories will eventually fall out of consideration by virtue of picking up word matches that do not score well. The events leading to the correct interpretation will soon rise to the top of the event queue, leaving a variety of events below them on the queue that have effectively picked up one bad word match (after they picked up the first bad match they fell out of consideration and were not extended further). If however, the acoustic-phonetic component has made a serious mistake (or equivalently the utterance was pronounced with a significant mistake), then the correct interpretation when it encounters the word containing the mistake will pick up a bad word score and fall down among all of the accidental theories that have also approximately one bad word score. In this case, two things might happen. Most seriously, one of the accidental theories may now complete with a better score than the correct interpretation giving rise to a misunderstanding (there is nothing the control strategy can do about it if another interpretation really scores better than the correct one). If this is not the case, then the correct interpretation will still be found, but only after all of its competitors are extended until they pick up additional bad scoring words and the correct interpretation again rises to the top.

If there are two significant errors in the acoustic-phonetic analysis, or a single error is twice as severe, then the correct interpretation falls farther down the stack and has to compete with events with two bad word matches or single very bad word matches (this is all a rather qualitative argument, but essentially correct). In general there are many more of these than there were events with one bad word match (which in turn outnumber the initial one-word theories that matched accidentally with high scores). In fact, the number of events with which the correct interpretation has to compete appears to go up exponentially with the amount of shortfall that the correct interpretation has to accept. Our current implementation of HWIM seems to be able to cope with one fairly serious APR error before the combinatorics of this situation overwhelm it. For utterances in which the APR has made two serious errors, we usually exceed a resource limit (usually 100 or 150 theories processed) before finding any interpretation.

14. Extrapolation to Vision

Since vision shares many of the characteristics of the speech understanding problem, it is appropriate to ask whether similar techniques may be applicable in that domain. The major differences in developing such methods for vision are that islands will now be two-dimensional regions of the visual field rather than intervals on a single dimension, and hence the boundary of an island will be a closed curve in two-space instead of two single points. Thus, where we have only two possible ends of an island to work on in speech understanding (and any single choice of a word at one end will be incompatible with other choices at that end), in the vision domain we will have possible predictions for elements at all points around the region, and different such predictions may "consume" different portions of the boundary of the island (i.e., two predictions may be incompatible by virtue of overlapping without being coextensive in the amount of the boundary of the old island that they consume). The initial scan will have to be done in two dimensions, and the enumeration of possible predicted elements adjacent to an island will have to be done systematically around the periphery.

However, it is still possible to consider any theory as being composed of some constellation of basic elements satisfying some "grammar" of well-formedness conditions, and it is still possible to construct a score density by dividing the score for an island by the area covered by it. It will also be the case that for any given island there will be some minimal scoring element which when removed leaves the remaining elements in either one or two connected pieces. In the latter case, an analog of island collision will provide a density scoring strategy that guarantees the discovery of the best scoring interpretation.

It is also possible to construct an analog of the shortfall scoring strategy by constructing an upperbounding function which will again upperbound the score of any region, and a combined shortfall density strategy will also be possible.

Combinatorically, the vision problem is apparently much more difficult than the speech problem, since there are many more positions around the periphery of an island to pursue alternatives. On the other hand, the analog of the vocabulary size may not be as great. In the HWIM system, the vocabulary size was approximately 1000 words and the number of words that are possible at each edge of an island averages 196. Although the number of positions along the boundary of an island will certainly be increased in the vision domain, the number of possible elements at each position my not be so great, at least for restricted classes of scenes. Of course vision differs in a major dimension from speech understanding in that possible scenes are governed by possible occurrences in the world rather than by human formalisms such as language. Consequently, the task of writing a grammar for possible scenes is nowhere as straightforward in this case as it is for speech. Likewise, the corresponding "visual phonetics" is not as constrained as the rather small set of phonemes used in human speech. Nevertheless, the techniques described here may well have useful application in the understanding of visual scenes.

Acknowledgment

This research was supported in part by the Advanced Research Projects Agency of the Department of Defense and was monitored by ONR under Contract No. N00014-75-C-0533.

References

[1] Hart, P., N. Nilsson, and B. Raphael (1968) "A Formal Basis for the Heuristic Determination of Minimum Cost Paths," IEEE Trans. Sys. Sci. Cybernetics, July, Vol. SSC-4, No. 2, pp. 100-107.

[2] Klatt, D.H. and K.N. Stevens (1971) "Strategies for Recognition of Spoken Sentences from Visual Examination of Spectrograms," BBN Report No. 2154, Bolt Beranek and Newman Inc., Cambridge, Ma.

[3] Nash-Webber, B.L. (1975) "The Role of Semantics in Automatic Speech Understanding," in Representation and Understanding: Studies in Cognitive Science, D. Bobrow and A. Collins (eds.), New York: Academic Press.

[4] Wanner, E. (1973) "Do We Understand Sentences from the Outside-In or from the Inside-out?," Daedalus, pp. 163-183, Summer.

[5] Wolf, J.J. and W.A. Woods (1977) "The HWIM Speech Understanding System," Conference Record, IEEE International Conference on Acoustics, Speech and Signal Processing, Hartford, Conn., May.

[6] Woods, W.A. (1974)
"Motivation and Overview of BBN SPEECHLIS:
An Experimental Prototype for Speech
Understanding Research," Proceedings of
IEEE Symposium on Speech Recognition,
Carnegie-Mellon University, Pittsburgh,
April, pp. 2-10.

[7] Woods, W.A. (1977)
"Shortfall and Density Scoring Strategies
for Speech Understanding Control,"
submitted to 1977 International Joint
Conference on Artificial Intelligence.

[8] Woods, W.A., M. Bates, G. Brown,
B. Bruce, C Cook, J. Klovstad, J. Makhoul,
B. Nash-Webber, R. Schwartz, J. Wolf,
V. Zue (1976)
"Speech Understanding Systems, Final
Report," November 1974 - October 1976, BBN
Report No. 3438, Bolt Beranek and Newman
Inc., Cambridge, Ma.

[9] Woods, W.A. and J.I. Makhoul (1974)
"Mechanical Inference Problems in
Continuous Speech Understanding,"
Artificial Intelligence, Vol. 5, No. 1,
pp. 73-91.